22077x

glossalalia

[f. Gr γλωσσο- GLOSSO–
+λαλια – speaking, f.
λαεεω to speak.]

The faculty or practice of
speaking with 'tongues'.

1879 FARRAR *St. Paul* I. 52
Those soliloquies of ecstatic
spiritual emotion which were
known as Glossolalia, or, 'the
Gift of Tongues'. **1882** *Early
Chr.* II. 446 In Corinth the terrible
abuses of glossolaly had led to
outbreaks which entirely ruined
the order of worship.
1898 W. S. LILLY in *19th Cent.*
Sept. 503 Those of the disciples
who possessed that singular
gift of glossolaly, or speaking
with tongues.

OXFORD ENGLISH DICTIONARY

It is not always entirely obvious
what items are, and what items
are not, in need of glossing. It
does not take long for the initial
dilemma (what do words mean?)
to become the dilemma of surfeit
of information . . . The statements
already made by others . . . may
totally invalidate the things one
wishes to say.

*ROLAND McHUGH,
ANNOTATIONS TO
FINNEGANS WAKE*

glossalalia

– an alphabet of critical keywords

EDITED BY *JULIAN WOLFREYS*. EDITORIAL ASSISTANT *HARUN KARIM THOMAS*

Edinburgh University Press

Concept, selection
and arrangement
© Julian Wolfreys, 2003

Individual chapters
© the contributors, 2003

Edinburgh University Press Ltd
22 George Square, Edinburgh

A CIP record for this book is
available from the British Library

ISBN 0 7486 1434 6 (hardback)
ISBN 0 7486 1435 4 (paperback)

The right of the contributors
to be identified as authors of
this work has been asserted in
accordance with the Copyright,
Designs and Patents Act 1988.

Typeset in Univers 57
by Servis Filmsetting Ltd,
Manchester

Printed and bound in
Great Britain by
Biddles Ltd, King's Lynn

contents

preface and acknowledgements

This is a project for which there is no justifiable introduction, no excusable prefatory remarks, no reasonable location from which to begin, no appropriate summarization. In the words of Michael Faraday, 'all this is a dream. Still, examine it with a few experiments' (1849).

It seems perhaps needless to thank the contributors to a volume; they are here, after all, because they want to be. However, it is necessary to thank the present contributors, those who originally agreed to participate, those who agreed to take part at various points in the evolution of this project due to the withdrawal, for various reasons, of others, and those who produced work within impossibly tight deadlines.

I would like to extend a special acknowledgement of gratitude to Harun Karim Thomas, whose expert editorial assistance saved this volume from being later than it was.

Jackie Jones, of Edinburgh University Press, has been, as ever, the best of editors with whom to work, and it is, I believe, her faith in, vision of and respect for the singular extremities of the critical voice that keeps me saying yes to even the most seemingly impossible of editorial tasks, even when good sense tells me otherwise: thank you.

The editor and publishers would like to thank the following for permission to reproduce copyrighted material:

- Theodor Holm Nelson, illustration from Nelson's *Computer Lib/Dream Machines*. South Bend, IN: The Distributors, 1974, DM45.
- Alfred D. Crimi, *Atlantic Monthly*, and Richard Bush, MD, illustrations of Bush's Memex, *Life*, 19.11: 123.

foreword: the alphabetic body | *BRIAN ROTMAN*

Cultures restructure the mind, not only in terms of its specific contents, which are obviously culture bound, but also in terms of its fundamental neurological organization.

Merlin Donald

Introduction

The end of the book? Yes – storehouse, producer and disseminator of knowledge, instrument of western monotheism, begetter of civilization – the ancient, self-standing, alphabetic text which folded so much between its edges and covers, is being opened up, distributed and outsourced; its content and functions disseminated, hypertextualized, transformed and multimediated into an edgeless web of a billion lexias, mathematical ideograms, icons and image streams circulating on the net.

Of course there are still books (more than ever) and reading will continue, increasingly dominated, no doubt, by the digital technology that obsolesced the printing press: books will be available on a chip that can be inserted into a backlit, take-to-bed, easy-to-hold, eyesight-friendly reading screen, equipped with indexing and concordance facilities, variable size typeface and other goodies. Or, further down the road, there'll be eyeglasses projecting micro-reduced words onto the retina (further still, directly into the brain via an implant). But is this reading and how long will the retina/brain be willing to be so engaged? A few hundred years, according to André Leroi-Gourhan's estimate in *Speech and Gesture* from the 1960s: 'For centuries yet reading will go on being important . . . but *writing* is probably doomed to disappear rapidly to be replaced by dictaphonic equipment with automatic printing' (1993, 404); or, as we'd say now, replaced by voice-recognition software and a printer.

The end of the book? Why not the end of the alphabetic medium in which (here in the West) the book is written. For some, the end of the alphabet would be the end of everything: 'Human society, the world, the whole of mankind is in the alphabet'. True, Victor Hugo, the alphabet is wonderful, out of its rigorously ordered spacing came universal codification, the bible, technoscientific reasoning, abstract logic and philosophy, history, democratic literacy and conferences on the book and its ends; a great source; more, as we shall see, than one realizes.

The alphabet is an extraordinary, simple, robust technology with a powerful viral capacity to disseminate and consolidate itself; a medium able to interface across multiple linguistic platforms and inscribe the speech of a huge variety of languages. But it is only one mode of writing speech, an action it achieves by notating the smallest hearable sound bits – segments – of spoken language. Closely related are syllabaries, super-segmental systems that notate entire syllables and in the opposite direction, the sub-segmental or 'featural' systems (as linguist Geoffrey Sampson calls them) notating distinct sonic features, of which Korean Han'gul is the only known naturally

1

evolved example. Distinct from these phonographic systems and more suitable than any of them to inscribe a heavily homophonic language like Chinese is the logographic system which works by notating sounds of the smallest separate meaning bits – morphemes – of speech. The Japanese use a mixture of both logographic and phonographic systems.

In the form familiar to us, alphabetic writing is the result of a long evolution from its proto-sinaitic beginnings which emerged out of Egyptian hieroglyphics. The details of this history needn't concern us, but two large-scale features of 'writing', namely pictures and ideographs, are relevant. Firstly, it seems generally accepted that the alphabet resulted through the acrophonic principle whereby the consonants of a word to be inscribed are represented by pictures of objects whose names begin with those consonants; a system of acronyms that works smoothly for semitic languages such as proto-sinaitic whose words always begin with a consonant. Then, through scribal needs or otherwise, the visual, iconic element of the representations was eliminated to produce purely abstract graphs for consonants, which were later supplemented by graphs for vowels when the system was taken up by the Greeks. The alphabet, then, by use or design, eschews the pictorial. But not perfectly: the original sonic marks – letters – have always carried some visually informed meaning, first through handwriting and later through typefaces and graphic design. Secondly, not all elements of what constitutes alphabetic writing notate sounds: the blank space between words, punctuation and diacritical marks, question marks, quotation marks, hyphens, marks of exclamation, ellipses, parentheses, and so on, do not indicate sounds of speech but notate symbolic practices or operations that are performed on what is written purely through letters. Moreover, as we shall see,

the ideographic principle plays a vital role in the larger elaboration of alphabetic literacy.

The alphabet is not only a particular textual implementation of the vocal body, a way of in-scribing it, it also impinges on and constructs this body in relation to the construction of other bodies – the visual, symbolic, but also the gestural – which continue to haunt it. What I would like to do here is to offer a certain provocation, a hypothesis which elaborates one aspect of this construction.

The alphabetic principle

If, like any cognitive technology, the alphabet alters the brain of its user, the alteration brought about by alphabetic writing is, as we shall see, particularly dramatic. The alphabet, as is acknowledged, does not notate speech as such: it writes down what's said but not how what is said is said, the words spoken not the manner of their saying; it transcribes, in Rousseau's terms, the voice (*voix*) but is silent about the sound (*sons*), what he variously called the passion and spirit of speech, what is designated here as prosody – the affect, tone, rhythm, emphasis, pitch and the movements of spoken language which among other things make song possible. The action of the alphabet thus institutes, that is allows to come into being and then perpetuates, a horizontal and vertical separation. In place of a balanced bilaterality – the integration within speech of right-brain prosody and left-brain syntax – there is intensification of the left and marginalization of the right; and instead of a two-way limbic-cortical traffic there is a hierarchy: a foregrounded neocortex over a weakly active or absent midbrain.

Omitting prosody in favour of the words themselves is one of several, perhaps the least important, alphabet-driven sources of an intensified left brain. More forceful is alphabetic writing's defining anti-pictorialism (refusal of right-brained image processing) and the ordering, linearizing force of inscribing one letter after another. The effects of linearization has been much commented upon positively – 'Writing', Leroi-Gourhan observed, 'has by dint of its one-dimensionality provided the analytic instrument indispensable to our philosophical and scientific thinking' (1993, 404) and negatively by many, from Marshall McLuhan's complaints about the baleful consequences of printing to those who, like Derrida, describe linearity, and all the scribal hierarchies associated with it, as being a 'repression of pluri-dimensional thought' (1976, 86).

But it is the vertical dimension which seems not to have been elaborated in relation to phonetic writing, alphabetic or otherwise, that interests me here, though the *effects* of the hierarchy of cortex over midbrain – as consonant (culture) over vowels (nature), for example – have been discussed ever since Rousseau. The alphabet disrupts the integrated complimentarity of upper and lower, tongue and larynx, articulation and breath, consonant and vowel; it effects a pulling apart and deactivating of circuits between the neocortex and the midbrain. The consequences of this separation constitute alphabetic writing's greatest and most visible achievement and its undeclared and invisible legacy. The achievement was the virtualization of speech: cutting words loose from the voice, internal and external gestures, the here-and-now breathing presence and corporeality of the one who utters them, and thereby creating the West's spectacular three thousand year efflorescence of literate culture's so-called 'speech at a distance'. Less obviously, this same cutting loose, to be precise the absented prosody that is the condition for its possibility, occasions the alphabet's hidden legacy, namely the installation of a certain metaphysical opposition within its texts.

In relation to its absenting and re-presencing of prosody, the alphabet's mediation of written discourse and creation of prose has been twofold. One, the attempt at more or less immediate reconstitution of the voice and its affects in the form of poetry as that form of textuality most committed to prosody's mimetic recuperation at its original level of the word. Two, the alphabet's production of an entire technology of textuality and apparatus of inscribing affect that goes beyond recuperation and beyond the level of the word by distributing new forms of textualized prosody onto the lexicon and syntax through the creation of phrases, usages, figures, formulas, textual diagrammatics and styles that make up the array of effects designated as 'literary'. Alphabetic writing's equivalent of prosody, then, the gestures which accompany and determine the reception of its texts, are rhetorics, figurations and styles. Styles, however, shuttle back and forth, oscillating between the written and spoken, between the poetic voice and the styled narrative, as the literary apparatus goes beyond speech to create new textual forms of affect while simultaneously forming a feedback loop that constantly reconfigures the speakable. The latter in terms of practice but also theoretical, in the sense that 'we introspect language', as David Olson puts it, 'in terms laid down by our writing systems' (1994, 8). Such then is a schematic of the alphabet's visible achievement.

The invisible effect – what I'm calling the alphabet's hidden legacy – issues in a form of subordination, more radical than witnessed earlier of various forms of gesture to speech. Here, prosody is the gesture and the words spoken are the 'speech', and the hierarchy is the foregrounding of the latter over the former. Thus, to return to the vertical neurological separation, the alphabet can be seen to institute and perpetuate a primary dualism, the familiar metaphysical hierarchy of mind over body, whose ultimate expression will be that of pure, disembodied mind. By separating prosody from words, the alphabet allows to come into existence, encourages the reality of, a free-standing cortical entity, an autonomous mind-agency detached from the affectual apparatus of the limbic region. An absent or under-represented or disenfranchised and repressed midbrain and an always present, inevitably fore-grounded, totalizing neocortex represent the neurological correlate of the hierarchy of mind, soul and spirit over body whose outworks – replicated and fractally reproduced at every level of discourse – constitute Western metaphysics. At its limit, the alphabet makes available – determines, sup-ports, gives credence to, provides a matrix for, perpetuates – a being for whom the loss of prosody is no loss at all; a psychic entity who speaks in a voice without tone, empha-sis, irony, distance from itself, humour, doubleness, affect, pain or the possibility of such things; an absent, invisible, bodiless being who/which has presided over the writing of speech in the West since its inception.

In his book, *The Alphabetic Effect*, which argues that the tablets of the law given by God to Moses in Sinai were written in an alphabetic script, Robert Logan points out that 'The occurrence of monotheism, codified law, and the alphabet all at the same moment in history cannot have been accidental' (1986, 87). Indeed not. And while carefully avoiding making a causal link, he suggests that the abstractness of the three innovations must have been mutually reinforcing (which of course is a kind of circular causality). Similarly, Gerard Pommier talks in the same breath of the 'jump from the hieroglyphic to the consonant, from polytheism to monotheism' and observes – fusing gods and writing – that '[a]t the very time Akhnaton was inventing monotheism, hieroglyphics were in the process of being destroyed in writing, beginning with those which featured divinities in the Egyptian pantheon' (cit. Ouaknin,

1999, 46). Evidently, the coming into being of the alphabet – whether this is seen as a de-picturing move in relation to Egyptian hieroglyphics or, as indicated earlier, a withering of the motivational content of signs as part of the action of acrophony – and the advent of a single, abstract and invis-ible God in the West are unlikely to be historically separa-ble.

In any event, God, speech, writing (divine or otherwise) and human hearing are certainly folded into each other in their original biblical appearances in Exodus. From 'And Moses wrote all the words of the Lord' to 'And he gave unto Moses, when he had made an end communing with him upon Mount Sinai, two tablets of testimony, tables of stone written with the finger of God'. What, it is possible to ask, are the differences here? God communed with Moses; God wrote the words with his own hand; God spoke the words out loud; God dictated the words to Moses who wrote them down. Did God's speech display any affect? Was the tone the same when communing (delivering the pretext or pre-amble?) as it was when declaiming? When dictating? Did or could Moses observe the presence or absence of feeling? Emphasis? Was God angry? Mournful? Jealously self-proclamatory? Businesslike, impersonal and neutral? Of course, to the author(s) of the alphabetic text, Exodus, and to theists in the Judeo-Christian tradition, as well as (with certain differences) Islamic theists, such questions have no sense, at least in so far as these traditions have no resources for establishing differences that could be humanly registered between the ways God spoke and wrote words.

How are we to imagine Moses heard the voice of the God of Western monotheism, the voice of a being for whom *voix* and *sons* coincide, for whom the question of prosody cannot arise because speaking and alphabetically writing the words spoken are indistinguishable, identical? Such would be the case if this being were an artefact of alphabetic writing, the manifestation of a cortex detached from its all too embodied limbic body and externalized as a being, an autonomous entity, in transcendental space. On this understanding, the alphabet operates an abstract onto-theological machine for the production of an absent, invisible, unembodied God-being; and it does this not by merely representing/alluding to it as a topic (which it has done from the beginning), or by being an origin. 'In the beginning was the word', or by serving as the vehicle for union with such a being. 'The word was with God, the word was God', but by constantly performing and causing to come into a transcendentally absent presence the voice of a speaker with no tone, no body.

But phenomenologically it would be more accurate to say theoretically toneless since it is virtually impossible for humans to receive a voice and not to impute tonality to words apparently addressed to them, however machinically denuded of tone their source is known to be. This being so, maybe a more interesting description of God's voice is to understand it as evincing and being received as an aboriginal gesture, as the murmur of language itself, as alphabetic writing's white noise, an undifferentiated heteroglossia of all possible tones, voices and manners of utterance that the medium makes available and onto which any desired affect can be projected.

Philosophical alphabetics

Let's leave God where we found Him, as the limit of the alphabet's dualizing effect, and return to the principle of alphabetic writing as such. Of the discourses most purely alphabetic, most rigorously committed to excluding pictures and symbols, while at the same time most affected by the dualism the alphabet installs – because most involved in articulating, challenging, repressing, embracing or twisting free from it – philosophy stands out. Thus, as an exchange of alphabetic texts (which it has always been), philosophy, both in its analytic and so-called continental forms, resists the ideogram by insisting (implicitly through disciplinary and institutional means) on being speakable, on its texts being able to be read aloud in principle if not practice. The same insistence on speakability excludes the pictographic – how does one utter a picture? – though in truth philosophy's inability/refusal to countenance the presence of images in its texts, its unease in the face of the picture, is too thorough, unexamined, universal and deep-rooted not to suggest other – iconophobic or anti-visualist – forces at work.

Thus, to cite a particularly telling (but completely representative) example, consider Husserl's essay *The Origin of Geometry*. Geometry, as distinct from arithmetic and algebra, and regardless of formalizations it undergoes, is a 'pictorial' subject in that diagrams are a means by which it furthers and creates itself and the objects and/or icons of the spatial objects it studies. Not only do diagrams (as means, objects or icons) not figure in Husserl's essay but their ubiquitous presence in geometry – whether necessary of otherwise – and their absence from his text receive no comment from him. One should perhaps set Husserl's blindness to images and his silence about it in a certain context: when he wrote his essay, a group of French mathematicians operating under the name Nicholas Boubaki was implementing a project, conceptualized (and known to Husserl) earlier in the century, to rewrite the whole of mathematics in the formal language of first-order set theory. The result – thousands of pages of 'words' made from a mathematical alphabet of a dozen or so symbolic 'letters' and governed by a linear syntax, without a single diagram; an entire corpus, alphabetizing in the name of a Platonist inspired programme of rigour, the richest, most elaborated trans-alphabetic discourse yet invented. Further, not only is Husserl's essay on geometry without diagrams or reference to them and without comment on this absence, but Derrida's extended commentary (whose principal focus is the question of ideality, signs and writing in Husserl's essay) is in turn silent on these omissions and indeed on the entire topic.

Unlike Christianity which long ago abandoned the second commandment (reducing its scope to the interdiction of flagrant idolatry), philosophical alphabeticism is faithful, like Judaism and Islam, to the commandment's original interdiction of *all* picturing. Like imageless religious texts and diagram-free rewritings of mathematics, such philosophical texts shield themselves from any connection to the body – of the text, of its creator, of its readers – introduced by the presence of the explicitly visual. Of course, it needs to be elaborated, which I'll not do here, why visual images, with their need to be looked at (and not looked through as is the case for letters and symbols) and so cognized outside the routines and protocols of 'reading', insist on the body, how they de-occlude it, and how such insistence counters the transcendentalizing forces at work in such faithful texts.

This fidelity to austere, alphabetic purity coupled with an inescapable mission to engage with the question of metaphysical dualism, theologized or otherwise, places a peculiarly intense burden on philosophy's prose since, from what's been said, it's at the level of prose style, poetics, textual voice, figuration and internal conceptual personae, that philosophy is obliged to stage its encounter with the ontotheological consequences of the alphabet's omission of prosody. (An obligation unnecessary in other alphabetic discourses such as history, law, scientific treatises and so on – with no comparable mission.) In a general sense, all this foregrounding of style and claims for its importance vis-à-vis philosophy would be surprising or foreign even only to philosophers in the analytic tradition for whom the question of prose and poetics of their texts is never an issue; for those outside this tradition it is hardly surprising. The texts of many figures from Hegel and Nietzsche onward are valuable, distinguished and philosophically pregnant precisely through their styles, cognitive poetics and figures; but the reason for it offered here, its structural necessity within the metaphysics of alphabetic writing, is perhaps novel.

Finally, and independently of the ideographical nature of literariness discussed earlier, philosophy might subvert, attempt to weaken or jump out of pure alphabeticism. Thus Heidegger's augmenting the stock of diacritical marks through his tmetic (*gestell*) and anti-tmetic (being-in-the-world) use of hyphens and his introduction of an ideogram of crossing-out (X-ing out the alphabetic word with a letter!); Derrida's silent, written 'a' of *différance* and his unspeakable (at least by a single voice) text *Glas*; and, somewhat differently, the strategic introduction of pictures into *A Thousand Plateaus* by Deleuze and Guattari. On this last, one has the programme outlined by Mark Taylor and Esa Saarinen: 'While marking the closure of the Western metaphysical tradition, deconstruction also signals the opening of post-print culture. Deconstruction remains bound to and by the world of print it nonetheless calls into question. What comes after deconstruction? Imagology' (1994, 10). Yes, but it's the *alphabet* that philosophy remains bound to and by, and imagology, manifested by Taylor and Saarinen in a consciously imagized and graphically stylized text that escapes print's linearities, is only part of the story.

The alphabet allowed (insisted) that words become objects, discrete items of awareness that could be isolated, studied, compared, replicated and systematized, giving rise to grammar, written discourse and literature, and a science of linguistics. Likewise gestures with respect to their digitally captured forms; they too are now being identified, individualized, examined, replicated and synthesized as discrete objects of conscious attention. The opportunity is thus opened for such newly digitized and objectified gestures to emerge from the shadow of speech, to be 'grammaticalized' and give rise to a gesturology, which might serve as the medium for Sign to possess a 'literature' and might do for the principled silences and unwords of the gesturo-haptic body, not least their production of its presence to itself and others, what linguistics has done for spoken language. Or, as Artaud wanted for his theatre of cruelty, such a gesturology might displace or silence speech, subordinating it to the imperatives and possibilities of pure gesture, screams and other 'primitive' signals of the body.

If alphabetic writing's particular reconfiguration of bodies at the level of neurophysiology installs a transcendental fissure inside its texts, whose ultimate ontological form is the disembodied God of the West, then the end of the alphabet as we know it would herald a seismic shift in Western theism, a dissolution of the mono-deity that might match in its consequences that deity's inauguration. But is such a thing possible? Is the end of the alphabet thinkable from within alphabetic writing here in the West? And having become aware of the alphabet's effects, one can ask about those of contemporary cognitive technologies and wonder what manner of being or beings are we facilitating, what new forms of metaphysical or post-metaphysical modes of religion are we installing inside the participatory, gesturo-haptic and immersive forms of digital writing now under construction?

Works cited

Armstrong, David, et al. *Gesture and the Nature of Language*. Cambridge, 1995.

Deacon, Terrence. *The Symbolic Species: the Co-evolution of Language and the Brain*. New York, 1997.

Derrida, Jacques. *Of Grammatology*, trans. Gayatri Spivak. Baltimore, MD, 1976.

Donald, Merlin. *Origins of the Modern Mind: Three Stages in the Evolution of Culture*. Cambridge, MA, 1991.

Kittler, Friedrich. *Gramophone, Film, Typewriter*, trans. Geoffrey Winthrop-Young and Michael Wutz. Stanford, CA, 1999.

Lane, Harlan. *What the Mind Hears: A History of the Deaf*. New York, 1984.

Leroi-Gourhan, André. *Gesture and Speech*, trans. Anna Berger. Cambridge, MA, 1993.

Logan, Robert. *The Alphabetic Effect: the Impact of the Phonetic Alphabet on the Development of Western Civilization*. New York, 1986.

McNeill, David. *Hand and Mind: What Gestures Reveal about Thought*. Chicago, IL, 1992.

Maffesoli, Michel. *The Shadow of Dionysus: a Contribution to the Sociology of the Orgy*, trans. Cindy Linse and Mary Kristina Palmquist. Albany, NY, 1993.

Olson, David. *The World on Paper*. Cambridge, 1994.

Ouaknin, Marc-Alain. *Mysteries of the Alphabet*. New York, 1999.

Pommier, Gerard. *Naissance et renaissance de l'écriture*. Paris, 1993.

Sampson, Geoffrey. *Writing Systems*. Stanford, CA, 1985.

Taylor, Mark and Esa Saarinen. *Imagologies: Media Philosophy*. London, 1994.

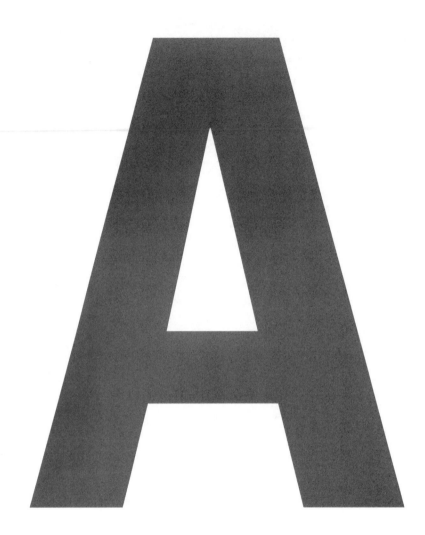

animality | NOTES TOWARDS A MANIFESTO | *FREDERICK YOUNG*

Let her dress up like a dog as the cynic does, put on the robes of a priest like the Alexandrine, or the fragrant spring garment of the Epicurean. It is essential for philosophy at this stage to put on the actors' masks.

Karl Marx

. . . by prowling around animal language, between an Aristotle who deprives the animal of language and word and mimesis, and a Nietzsche who, if it can be said, 'reanimalizes' the genealogy of the concept. The one who parodied Ecce Homo tries to teach us to laugh again by plotting, as it were, to let loose all the animals within philosophy.

Jacques Derrida

But this being-with is not an existing-with, because a dog does not exist but merely lives on.

Martin Heidegger

Empedocles' left and right hands: Che(z) Heidegger

Trotting animal where the word clicked shut.

Paul Celan

What is at stake, or, *who's* at the stake, with the question of the animal and animality? What could Martin Heidegger and Che Guevara possibly have in common in relation to animality? At stake is a problematics of politics, institution, mimesis and the human. Both were active to varying degrees in twentieth-century revolutions, Che, *on the left hand*, with the Marxist Cuban revolution, and, Heidegger, *on the right hand*, with the National Socialist Revolution.[1] Both Heidegger and Che passively inherit and assume a humanist and metaphysical project of what an animal is and determine or ontologize the animal in advance. A moment occurs within Heidegger's thinking and Che's actions in which the animal, specifically a dog,[2] is ontologized through the violent process of naming, by calling or determining the animal as such. As Jacques Derrida states in 'The Animal That Therefore I Am (More to Follow)', 'The animal, what a word! The animal is a word, it is an appellation that men have instituted, a name they have given themselves the right and the authority to give another living creature' (Derrida, 2002, 392). In *essence*, Heidegger and Che take on the humanist project and the left and right share the same economy, the mimetology of the same political and metaphysical logic.

Of course, for Heidegger, *being* ontologized would be scandalous, while Che probably could not have cared less. However, at stake is an economy in which an exchange between them takes place, an agreed upon currency (a coinage of truth-as-metaphysics) through the ontologizing of an event, both literal and figural, of a violence towards, and an arrest of, the animal that marks a moment of transcendence that ends in politics – a humanistic and traditional inheritance of the name and concept of 'animal'.

Lacking in both their *accounts* of the dog is the question, or rather, *performativity* of animality, which we'll get to in a moment. Stealing from *The Logic of Sense*, we have the tragic impulse of Empedocles in both Che and Heidegger, that which Deleuze describes as subversion,[3] perhaps a revolutionary process of sorts, caught within a contestation of a Platonic economy – subverting the converting in order to convert itself back to Conversion – the abstract Truth of metaphysics. Deleuze asserts that 'the Platonic conversion . . . corresponds [to] the pre-Socratic subversion' (Deleuze, 1990, 129). In the *Logic of Sense*, Deleuze speaks of a correspondence between Empedocles and Socrates, between the 'hammer blow' and the wings of Platonism. Empedocles stayed in the cave, 'smashing statues' and 'philosophized with a hammer' (Deleuze, 1990, 128) while Platonism had wings. Between the depths of the pre-Socratic cave and the heights of Platonism is a restricted economy – an exchange between the subversive depths and the Platonic heights – the verticality of manic depression. Crucially both share a logic, both subscribe to an economy of exchange, a fixed unventilated context, both share the same axiomatics. No height without depth, no depth without height: the nostalgia of Essence. Within this metaphysics, the surface is never thought, never taken seriously. In part, Deleuze turns to Diogenes and Nietzsche, to the animal, the Diogenic anecdotes, and the surface that

exceeds, confronts and ignores Platonism. 'This is a reorientation of all thought and of what it means to think: there is no longer any depth or height. The Cynic and the Stoic sneers against Plato are many. It is always a matter of unseating the Ideas, of showing that incorporeal is not high above (*en hauteur*), but is rather at the surface, that it is not the highest case but the superficial effect par excellence, and that it is not Essence but event' (Deleuze, 1990, 130).

A certain build-up of intensities, a dog *event and overdetermined*, 'the animals roaming let loose in philosophy', not the named essence, dog.[4] Heidegger and Che essentialized the dog, missing the animality, the performativity of surface. They arrest the 'becoming-animal' and essentialize it within humanist hierarchy – they missed the 'surface' and remain in the highs and lows of Platonism, the logical modes of what Deleuze calls the 'manic depressive' modalities of heights and depths of Platonic thought. However, Deleuze instead calls for a way out, of refiguring philosophy; instead of the conversive/subversive bind, we have the surface:

The autonomy of surface, independent of, and against the depth and height which are nonsense; the discovery of incorporeal events, meanings or effects, which are irreducible to 'deep' bodies and 'lofty' Ideas . . .

(Deleuze, 1990, 133)

For Deleuze, the other philosopher is not Platonic, but rather this

philosopher is no longer the being of the caves, nor Plato's soul or bird, but rather the animal which is on the level of the surface . . . [of becoming] What are we to call this new philosophical operation, in so far as it opposes at once Platonic conversion and pre-Socratic subversion? Perhaps we can call it 'perversion', which at least befits the system of provocations of this new type of philosopher – if it is true that perversion implies an extraordinary art of surfaces.

(Deleuze, 1990, 133)

This philosopher is the 'animal of the surface', velocities and speeds exceeding Platonic economies, the 'powers of the false' that 'rise to the surface' – we have, in effect, the 'non-classical' Diogenic and Nietzschean 'perversions', the art and becoming of surfaces – the irreducible singularities or becomings of animality.

As the Diogenic always already haunts and tracks down Platonism whether on the streets or at the Academy, so too Nietzsche haunts Heidegger and Che in relation to the animal and the violent politics of any logic of identity – perhaps the unforeseen Platonic dreams of conversion within the revolution. As Avital Ronell reminds us in 'Hitting the Streets', a 'dog's howl will return, or has already returned, to Nietzsche as the proper name of pain . . . and [the dog] follows him through the streets [of Turin] in the benevolent guise of a water glass' (Ronell, 1994, 67–8) about the time Nietzsche, on the verge of collapse, 'takes the horse in his hand' (Derrida, 2002, 403). Nietzsche's *hands*, not the 'hand' of Dasein, lend themselves to think the dog, to open up and 'let loose all of the animals within philosophy' (Derrida, 2002, 403). Perhaps we have the Diogenic dog haunting and following Nietzsche though the streets – not a mimetic relation between Diogenes and Nietzsche, but rather a strategic 'assemblage' of becoming, of the surface that is counter to the abstract negations and mediations of the history they are up against. In this manner, the dog who follows Nietzsche is Nietzschean and already Diogenic, the animals that the philosophers have always already 'let loose in philosophy' and out into the streets. Perhaps Nietzsche is unable to hold onto himself as he has opened himself through the strictures of metaphysics. Perhaps the 'pain' and 'howl' are too great for anything but collapse.

Following Nietzsche, if we can get his drift, perhaps there's a *non-dialectical dérive* of animality, of his dog's pain, that moves out into a becoming, offers 'lines of flight' on the restricted and regulating streets of 'man'. After all Guy Debord himself thought that the *dérive* was a mode of knowledge – perhaps, really, an epistemology of becoming, not being, in the street – a performative theatrics offering the possibility not determination of transformation. The dog is Nietzsche's pain, perverse and on the surface. Yet, for Heidegger, the domestic dog, 'lacking-in-world', is a '*not yet*'. But when? And if it could come, would it not already be invested in the structures of man, of humanism? This also brings up another problem of the humanist visions and productions of the pure breed dog, which, in a sense, is already inscribed and morphed by 'man'. By the classification and determination of the proper name 'animal' and 'dog', the fantasies and experiments of selective breeding of a humanist project are mobilized – within such a classical hierarchy of living creatures, such practices are normal.[5] But I'm getting ahead of myself. My interest in animality, following as much as possible Derrida, Deleuze, Diogenes and Nietzsche, is the 'non-classical' way (see Plotnitsky, 2001) in which the performativity of dog-as-animality has always already haunted Western metaphysics and the founding of its institutions, revolutions and violence that such things imply.

And what is Che's encounter with the dog? In his infamous *Episodes of the Cuban Revolutionary War*, he speaks, or rather makes a poignant confession, about the murder of a puppy in the jungles of the Sierra Maestra Mountains.

Haggard, travelling through the jungle, Che and his men must keep silent to avoid detection and yet they are followed by a puppy, their mascot, who will not keep quiet. Che instructs Felix, one of his men, to kill the dog:

> I remember my emphatic order: 'Felix, that dog must stop its howling once and for all. You're in charge; strangle it. There will be no more barking'. Felix looked at me with eyes that said nothing. He and the little dog were in the center of all the troops. Very slowly he took out a rope, wrapped it around the animal's neck, and began to tighten it . . . [Later that night] . . . Felix, while eating seated on the floor, dropped a bone, and a house dog came out meekly and grabbed it up. Felix patted its head, and the dog looked at him. Felix returned the glance, and then he and I exchanged a guilty look. Suddenly everyone fell silent. An imperceptible stirring came over us, as the dog's meek yet rougish gaze seemed to contain a hint of reproach. There in our presence, although observing us through the eyes of another dog, was the murdered puppy.
>
> (Guevara, 2001, 239–40; emphasis mine)

Guevara is clearly disturbed, in fact haunted, by the eyes of another dog (and we will later take this other dog quite seriously as to its haunting through the performativity of a Nietzschean and Diogenic strategy) by sacrificing the puppy for the sake of the revolution. In fact, 'the murdered puppy' was, for Che, actually 'present . . . observing [them] through the eyes of another dog'. But nevertheless, it is necessary to kill the dog (who follows and 'howls' at the revolutionaries that they are) for the greater sake of the people's revolution in Cuba in order for the eventual 'world' revolution to encompass all people, and the domination of humanism will occur – all human beings will be equal – the teleological triumph of a mimetic production.

Without reducing the complexity of Che to one specific instant, what is important, what I'm interested in, is this specific moment in the jungle, this arrest, and violent utilitarian decision to kill the dog – which involves, in advance, a specific understanding and determination of the dog in particular, and the animal in general – classical categories invested in the inheritance of philosophy. In other words, the dog is named; Che's dog is killed. And yet Che confesses to feeling a certain guilt at killing the puppy – an honesty quite remarkable in that it submits this 'murder' for the eyes of the world to see, examine and possibly judge. Che, unlike Heidegger who employs a philosophical distance in describing a dog, feels guilty. Heidegger states that the domestic dog 'eats with us – and yet, it does not really "eat"'. For Heidegger, only Dasein can 'eat'. At Che's table, everyone 'eating' feels guilty. Che confesses. Che is sad. The fact that this living creature was understood, determined and named through the traditional philosophical and humanistic concept of the 'animal' suggests a violent ontological moment in which the revolutionary reinscribes itself into an economics (and currency) of exchange that is conservative, preservative in advance: a humanist metaphysics – the subversive will attempt to convert to a new state of old philosophical affairs between 'man'.

At least two crucial operations are at stake here: Che *inherits*, does not *read* the philosophical assumptions of the animal, and, by this simple handiwork (*zuhandenheit*) of strangulation (*mea Felix culpa*), preserves the economy of a humanistic revolutionary, of 'man' – this time animality is in danger – caught in an endless exchange, a 'leveling process', between and within the metaphysical economy of the revolutionary, the tragic and the conversive promise of the state, the violent founding and inscription of an institutional and metaphysical logic. The manic-depressive oscillation Deleuze speaks of moving between the highs of Platonism and the lows of Empedocles – the pole of this metaphysical bipolarity, this axiomatic verticality rips through the animal. 'Arresting' the dog triggers a violent moment of institutionalization. The art of surfaces, the animal perversion, surfaces in excess of metaphysics is *out of the equation*. As a result, many hands are in danger: the hand that strangles (*zuhandenheit*) as well as Che's hands that will be cut off (*vorhandenheit*) by the CIA et al. as mimetic proof of his own murder by the US. 'The hand cannot be spoken about without speaking about technics' (Derrida, 1987, 169).

From Che to Heidegger: a few years after the publication of *Being and Time* (1927) and a few years before his famous *Rektoratsrede* (1933), Heidegger devotes, in part, his 1929–30 seminar to a discussion of the animal. Referring to this seminar, in '"Eating Well," or the Calculation of the Subject: An Interview with Jacques Derrida', Jean-Luc Nancy and Jacques Derrida speak of a certain violence that Heidegger has towards the animal. While Heidegger, still working in the problematics of Dasein at this point, 'arrests' the animal as being 'poor-in-world', of lacking in the 'world' that Dasein is always already in. As Derrida points out, the animal's *weltarm* ('lack of world') is neither within nor without world but rather holds an impossible liminal space – the animal is 'sad' – the animal contaminates the world, and in a sense, the possibility, or at least, stability, of Dasein.

Derrida:

The Heideggerian discourse on the animal is violent and awkward, at times contradictory . . .

[Heidegger] says the animal has a world in the mode of a not having. But this not having does not constitute in his view of indigence, the lack of a world that would be human . . . There is no category of original existence for the animal: it is evidently not Dasein, either as vorhandene or zuhandene (Being cannot appear, be, or be questioned as such [als] for the animal.) Its existence introduces a principle of disorder or of limitation into the conceptuality of Being and Time.

(Derrida, 1991, 111)

Through the arrest of the animal, of the animal not even having a 'category of original existence', Heidegger, in turn, reinscribes himself unwittingly back into a traditional notion of ontology that has been his task to 'destroy'. In a sense, Heidegger must turn his back on the 'principle of disorder' that his figuring of the animal produces. A Diogenic, or Nietzschean, dog haunts him . . . Heidegger describes the domestic dog in his 1929–30 seminar:

We keep domestic pets in the house with us, they 'live' with us. But we do not live with them if living means being in an animal kind of way. Yet we are with them nonetheless. But this being-with is not an existing-with, because a dog does not exist but merely lives on. Through this being with animals we enable them to move within our world. We say that the dog is lying underneath the table or is running up the stairs and so on. Yet when we consider the dog itself . . . It eats with us – and yet, it does not really 'eat'. Nevertheless, it is with us! A going along with . . . , a transposedness, and not yet.

(Heidegger, 1995, 210; emphasis mine)

'Not yet'. OK, when? How could the animal (animality) ever come to Heidegger? What is the relation between the 'not yet' of the domestic dog and the 'principle of disorder in the conceptuality of *Being and Time*?' As long as such violence, left, right or centre, involves an ontological determination of the dog, of the animal, then perversion, the performativity and art of the surface is missed – and the inscription of Platonism continues, though such 'disorder' might, in turn, produce a 'line of flight'. Heidegger's dog is 'sad'. Che is 'sad'. And the 'manic-depressive' highs and lows of philosophy continues . . . For both Che and Heidegger, the left hand shares the same axiomatic as the right – man's head is intact and attached – the encyclopedia and hierarchy are in order. Only metaphysics could make the exchange. Diogenes and Nietzsche are not read and the *coin*age of representation, truth and metaphysics remains.

'The Powers of the False': Diogenes and Nietzsche

Tricksters or fakes, assistants or toons, they are
all the examplars of the coming community.
Giorgio Agamben

As Nietzsche hugs the horse, all the while being followed through the streets of Turin by a dog disguised as a benevolent glass of water, what we have, in effect, is the impossibility of the *human* and the violence of making the *human* possible. The 'animal' is a signal or wager at the end of Platonism and yet began with it and exceeds or haunts it while already contained within it – a 'non-classical' (artistic, if it wills) denial of the occident, a mobilization against the currency of metaphysics and the restricted economy

of 'man'. At stake is a Nietzschean and Diogenic modality, performativity within performance, the 'rise of the pseudo', 'the powers of the false', and the 'anti-Platonism' that Deleuze argues for in *Logic of Sense*. The Diogenic dog returns to follow Nietzsche through the streets of Turin. Nietzsche's movements through the streets, like the *dérive* itself, are in themselves a 'mode of knowledge'. Within his performances exist a performativity, an interruptive epistemology irreducible to Form or concept, and the possibilities of the surface, the excessive Deleuzean perversion within and through the highs and lows of metaphysics – a modality of a surface ethics in excess of any classification or ontological determination of the animal. As Derrida states, it's 'a Nietzsche who . . . "reanimalizes" the genealogy of the concept. The one who parodied Ecce Homo tries to teach us to laugh again by plotting, as it were, to let loose all the animals in philosophy' (Derrida, 2002, 403).

What would it mean to prowl 'around animal language', and to read the rhetoric, textuality and physiognomics of Nietzsche's 'embrace', this performance? And, how do we unlock the performativity from within this singular performance? Here also lies the problematics of technics and technology, of what is produced, appears within and exceeds the confines of any state or revolution conceived by 'man'. What should we make of this dog figure in Nietzsche's thought that follows him through the streets of Turin before he collapses? How do we come to terms with such a dog, a dog that's always already 'let loose' 'within philosophy'? It would be too easy and unfair to say the dog is a figure of Nietzsche's madness (whatever that is). How do we read such a performative operation as Nietzsche's dog if it has already been 'let loose within philosophy'? Certainly, this dog doesn't have ears for, would it not pick up the call (*Ruf*) of metaphysics. Would not speak, or hang out with Aristotle, or any modality of classification, Kantian or otherwise. Would not easily offer itself to revolutionary's depressive strangulation or the calculated offer of *weltarm's* 'sadness'. If this dog is not simply arrested within the economy of philosophical thought, regulated within our cultural currency (studies?), then what could it mean to 'reanimalize the genealogy of the concept'? Perhaps a 'non-classical' performativity endlessly defaces the mimetic currency of the concept, of the coinage of 'man', that is neither Platonic, nor subversive.

What emerges from the problematic of animality is a Nietzschean problematic of thought, the problem of the surface, performativity and the inside out in philosophy – of what happens when philosophy is interrupted from the contained economics of its manic-depressive highs and lows, the shared coin of mimetic truth between Empedocles and Plato – their 'lead sandal' and the 'wing' – it's also a question of institutions, arrests and names. Deleuze's perversion, the power of the pseudo, the false, the question of truth not as resemblance but rather as surface will be on the side of animality. In the *Logic of Sense*, 'The Simulacrum and Ancient Philosophy', Deleuze asserts a Nietzschean (and I would argue Diogenic) modality that calls for a reversal of Platonism (Deleuze, 1990, 253). It refigures the notion of simulation and representation, of mimesis and metaphysics. For Deleuze, the 'simulacrum is a becoming-mad, or a becoming unlimited . . . a becoming always other . . . able to evade the equal, the limit, the Same, or the Similar: always more and less at once, but never equal' (Deleuze, 1990, 258). There is no Platonic economy, no essence or static being, no ontology that would name or freeze living creatures, no hierarchy that would put everything in its proper place. An interruption of economy, of the exchange that all institutions and communities need and the chance impossibility of their founding

violence – the question of animality also is the question of performativity, technics and economy.

Diogenes: destroying the cultural currency of institutional truth

Le chien de coeur n'avait pas geint.

René Char

The ancient Greek philosopher Diogenes usually gets a bad rap in the history of philosophy, although there has been a recent renewal of interest in him. He lived in a tub; didn't write anything down (as far as we know.); insulted his contemporaries; masturbated in public; walked through Athens backwards; and went through Athens in broad daylight with a lantern looking for an honest man (the irony of Plato's cave should not be over looked here). To say the least, Diogenes did not engage with philosophers through dialogue or dialectics. Peter Sloterdijk, in *The Critique of Cynical Reason*, expresses Plato and Socrates' absolute inability to understand, let alone figure out what Diogenes was up to:

> Socrates copes quite well with the Sophists . . . if he can entice them into a conversation in which he, as a master of refutation, is undefeatable. However, neither Socrates nor Plato can deal with Diogenes – for he talks to them in a language of flesh and blood. Thus, for Plato there remained no alternative but to slander his weird and unwieldy opponent. He called him a 'Socrates gone mad' (*Socrates* mainoumenos). This phrase is intended as an annihilation, but it is the highest recognition. Against his will, Plato places the rival on the same

level as Socrates, the greatest dialectician. It
makes clear that that with Diogenes something
unsettling but compelling had happened with phi-
losophy. In the dog philosophy of the kynic (kyon,
dog in Greek; – Trans.).

(Sloterdijk, 1987, 104)

Plato had no *idea* how to deal with Diogenes. For Diogenes refused to argue on Platonic grounds, refused dialectics and the rational 'voice' that goes with it by means of which 'man' speaks. With Diogenes, there's a different modality of argumentation, if we can even call it that, the performative and animality. The Diogenic is more than literal abject attack on Plato. More significantly, Diogenes' strategies are irreducible to any modality of dialectics or philosophy proper. Again, what we have is the problematics of the surface, of animality – a physiognomic performance that unleashes the performativity of animality into the Platonic landscape and architecture. Nietzsche is always already born in Diogenes – what Deleuze calls the 'animal' of the surface, the 'powers of the false'. In addition to his physiognomic attacks, to an irreducible performativity within Platonism, Diogenes literally defaces the coins of his town Sinope and accepts exile – all of these things signal something profound that philosophy can't handle.

Of further significance is Diogenes' exile from his city of Sinope (and, as we know, exile to any noble ancient philosopher would have meant death; no true philosopher worth his weight in gold would have accepted exile over death). Diogenes saw the same Oracle at Delphi, but was told not to 'know thy self', as his noble counterpart Socrates, but rather to 'Deface or adulterate the currency' (Navia, 1998, 17) – which meant not only a literal coin, but also 'customs', 'institutions'[6] and 'accepted values' – a war on philosophy, culture, mimesis and economics. A

Nietzschean surface, something in excess of mimetic truth and the 'auto-immunity' of communal and institutional violence. In 'Faith and Knowledge' Derrida speaks of the Kantian notion of the anthropo-theological pricelessness of all human life:

The price of human life, which is to say, of
anthropo-theological life, the price of what ought
to remain safe (helig, sacred, safe and sound,
unscathed, immune), as the absolute price, the
price of what ought to inspire respect, modesty,
reticence, this price is priceless. It corresponds to
what Kant calls the dignity (Wurdigkeit) of the end
itself, of the rational finite being, of absolute value
beyond all comparative market-price (Marktpreis).

(Derrida, 1998, 51)

And yet the coinage of metaphysics by means of the *human* community reduces, brings back all (human) life and the concept of human life back into the marketplace. Following the Diogenic and Nietzschean logic of the surface and animality, is there a way to refigure the problematics of institution and community, of a irreducible singularity of life that would not simply fall back and reinscribe itself into the human? Here again are the problematics of the animal or the excess of animality that interrupts the hierarchy and verticality of man. Instead of 'lead sandals' and 'big toes', let's keep it on the surface and open. The possibility of human community, as Derrida continues in 'Faith and Knowledge', always involves '*auto-immunity*'; community's homogenous identification always incorporates just enough of the 'other' to inoculate it from difference – a touch of difference in an attempt to arrest or suspend a radical difference. Derrida states, 'Community as *com-mon auto-immunity*: no community <is possible> that would not

16

cultivate its own auto-immunity' (Derrida, 1998, 51). And yet, contained within any community, or institution for that matter, is 'something other and more than itself: the other, the future, death, freedom, the coming or the love of the other, the space and time of a spectralizing messianicity beyond all messianism' (Derrida 1998, 51). Whatever that 'something and more and other than itself' to come might be, is also the question of the interruption of institutions, man's economy, the coinage of truth, hierarchy, man's *form* of revolution, and the violent humanist programme of the calculation of life. Diogenes and Nietzsche haunt metaphysics within its own logic and offer no promises, no proper names, 'a spectralizing messianicity beyond all messianism', the impossibility possible through the surface of animality.

Diogenes defaces the coinage of his age and the coinage to come . . . The Diogenic at one level literally defaces the coins of his town, of his cultural currency. At another level, when we begin to think about animality as a wild card that introduces undecidability into the conceptual framework of metaphysics, of a representational truth, then we can begin to figure how the Diogenic itself, this 'animal', this 'dog', has always already introduced a 'principle of disorder' into philosophy itself as well as perhaps the complex relations between institutions, technology and culture. As the Diogenic dog meets up with Nietzsche in Turin, so too the anthropomorphic coins of philosophy and the regulating truths of culture and economy are, at least, momentarily defaced:

> *What then is truth? A movable host of metaphors, metonymies, and anthropomorphisms: in short, a sum of human relations which have been poetically and rhetorically intensified, transferred, and embellished, and which, after long usage, seem to a people to be fixed, canonical, and binding. Truths are illusions which we have forgotten are illusions; they are metaphors that have become worn out and have been drained of sensuous force, coins which have lost their embossing and are now considered as metal and no longer as coins.*
>
> (Nietzsche, 1990, 84)

At stake especially for us is the Diogenic as a way of looking at animality – the way in which Diogenes haunts philosophy itself. The Diogenic is always already at work, unworking the event of philosophy, and the institutional violence of ontology. The Diogenic is a limit case – a wager of animality haunting the philosophical and its academies. Here, Diogenes, like Nietzsche, is 'prowling around animal language', defacing the coinage of metaphysics and the institutions in the service of philosophy that control as they inform humanist subjects.

When Diogenes takes the name dog, hears the dog's 'howl', this is the howl of *affirmation*, not the 'howl' that frightens Che, or perhaps Che, in the immediacy of his decision, didn't have ears for such things – missed the call of a Diogenic 'army of dogs', of the possibility of a 'non-classical' politics of perversion. Diogenes doesn't accept a classification and determination of the animal, but rather mobilizes a performativity that will haunt philosophy and its institutions throughout its career. I would argue that Diogenes' dog and the one that follows Nietzsche is, in a sense, the *same* dog not the Same dog. Diogenes took no part in Platonic dialogue and by means of performances conjured animality and insulted Socrates' seductions whenever he got the chance.

Diogenes always mistrusted the hermeneutic traps: the instituting and interpellating call from the 'piety' of the question, albeit Platonist or cop. What concerns us here are 'non-classical' registers of the dog-of-the-surface, these animality-performatives of truths, the modality of a relation of singularities, these pseudo-dogs that haunt philosophy, which are something that doesn't subscribe to or even subvert Plato – Diogenes is not tragic, depressed or sad. When Diogenes rushes into Plato's new institution, the Academy (a place where the Forms could 'come down' and hang out in the 'piety' of the question in relative safety) with a plucked chicken and exclaims 'behold Plato's man!' (which Plato defined as a featherless bipedal creature, or some such thing), it is more than a loon rushing the *stage* – *Socrates mainoumenos*.

At stake is a performativity in Diogenes' performance, a technics of animality always already 'before' any technology of man, as well as and his mobilization of an 'army of dogs' 'to-come' that haunt philosophy, and perhaps, at times, intervene, in order to transform, not abolish, its institutions – this 'dog' will not come to the call [*Ruf*] of 'Being' or 'man'. Perhaps they're hiding in Heidegger's house? 'Eating', 'living' and 'existing' in the performative excesses and lacks of ontology while the 'buildings think' and Heidegger's back is turned. The Diogenic performance (t)here attempts to interrupt the founding, both literal and figural, of the Platonic Academy, a determined technological *form*, the classification and dogma of what will become the History of Philosophy. As metaphysics begins Diogenes is defacing its curren(t)cy, warning of its flows, abstractions and restricted economy. However, this Diogenic is tied not only to the founding violence necessary for an institution, but also addresses the abstract ontological violence inherent in metaphysics itself and the economy of its exchange and the determination and understanding of Truth as representation, which, in turn, *informs* hierarchy, stability and classification. Such logic will ground, deter-

mine and delineate, among other things, the tripartite structure of human, animal and earth. The problematics of animality, which is a question of the animal per se, as always already understood by man is also a radical performativity that disrupts the restrictive classifications of man, of *his* institutions. A question of economics and mimesis and naming in general and the animal in particular: 'Yes, animal, what a word! Animal is word that men have given themselves the right to give. These humans are found giving it to themselves, this word, but as if they had received it as an inheritance. They have given themselves the word in order to coral a large number of living beings within a single concept: "the Animal," they say' (Derrida, 2002, 400).

The Diogenic is also a question of exile and defacing the cultural currency, the coin-age of truth-as-representation and the restricted economy of Platonism. Perhaps the modality the dog of Diogenes is not a literal dog but a performativity, an animality against the coinage and exchange of philosophy, of the 'levelling' which abstracts things to equivalencies and the endless exchange of subversions and conversions, revolutionaries and states. Kierkegaard reminds us, speaking of Hegelian Idealism, that the philosopher (of the book) never simply lives in the clouds of his system. Philosophy hangs out within and informs institutions – is it a technological overdetermination of technics? If so, what, then, is the relation between animality, performativity and technics? It is the Nietzschean truths, the masks, the powers of the false, the ethics-of-a-life, a 'face-to-face' without transcendence, without an appeal to God, an irreducible singularity that cannot be reduced to questions nor classification and perhaps could, for us, conjure a Diogenic 'army of dogs'. Perhaps the theatrical performances of Diogenes contain within them and inject a performativity which allows for a technics of sorts to weave into a determined technological or institutional space – a Diogenic and, I suppose, Nietzschean 'animal' of the surface could offer a politics without mimetology, without 'man'. I'm thinking in particular of the question of Heidegger and technology and of how to refigure the problems of technics in relation to those of animality. In *Of Spirit: Heidegger and the Question*, Derrida reminds us, as in *Geschlecht II*, of the importance of the 'hand' for Heidegger, and that 'this problem concerns, once more, the relationship between animals and technology' (Derrida, 1989, 11). For Derrida, Heidegger's hand signals 'the profoundest metaphysical humanism' (Derrida, 1989, 12). There's no room to fully unpack the implications of the question of animality and technology in relation to the constitution of an institution such as a university, either the National Socialist or the Kantian one. However, and crucially, the problems of animality and technics haunt any determined writing, methodology and technologically 'straited' space of any institution – of importance is how to open up this spectrality of haunting.

The powers of the false, of the pseudo, arise to the surface as Nietzsche is being followed through the streets of Turin by a dog, his pain, in the guise of a benevolent glass of water. The Diogenic will return as Nietzsche's dog in the sense in which the 'non-classical' always resists institutional violence. Can it do more, without risking and reinscribing metaphysics, teleology and the rest of philosophy? Is there a Deleuzean perversion possible? Something to make or write with that doesn't involve in advance humanism, Dasein's 'hand'. In other words, as we have Heidegger's pen and Nietzsche's typewriter, is there, with animality, another writing 'to come'? – a transformative way to write in, through and beyond the humanist institution and idea of a university without a programme in mind?

How would such a 'transformative critique' work, write? Problems of technics, technology and animality must all be brought into the fray to produce these 'inhuman' 'singularities' to come. At such moments, before Nietzsche is literally institutionalized, he conjures, perhaps, the possibility for thinking about the 'new humanities'. Both Diogenes and Nietzsche deface the coin-age of philosophy and its truth-as-representation, a mimetic exchange, which allows, calls for, the levelling of differences.

I would like to believe that it is no *coin*cidence that Nietzsche and Diogenes are called and surrounded by animals, that the dog plays such a vital role, and that the sheer performativity of their language and phsyiognomics mobilize metaphors of truths against the Truth of philosophy, and the violence that founds all institutions, which has always (tried) to name them. 'Hey you?' *Yes.* That they looked into the impossible eyes of those nameless irreducible singularities, creatures . . . exchanged the cop for becomings. With their animalities, the name 'animal' given to living creatures by man gives way to the surface, the pseudo and the powers of the false. Here, there is, I hope, the 'materiality' of singularities escaping the arrests of 'man' and the possibility of, beyond the subject of man, the refiguring of technics, writing and singularities.

Following thinkers such as Derrida, Nietzsche, Ronell, Deleuze and Diogenes, perhaps what calls now is a rethinking of animality, of its performative technics in relation to technology at the institutional site and to wager how the risk and danger of an overdetermination of techne can, in fact, perform at the site of the university – the possibility, not programme, of transformation, or 'transformative critique'. To then begin with Derrida, 'Nothing can ever take away from me the certainty that what we have here is an existence that refuses to be conceptualized' (Derrida, 2002, 379).

Notes

1. Of course, Heidegger's history and involvement with National Socialism is quite complicated – and I'm not, in the least, trying to reduce the thought of Heidegger to the major tenets of National Socialism. And simply to suggest that there is some chronological inevitability to Heidegger's thought is, of course, reductive in that it doesn't even begin to address or *read* Heidegger. My principal interest here is to explore Heidegger's relation to the animal.
2. In early 1980 the Shining Path (Sendero Luminoso) of Peru, headed by a former professor of philosophy, began their movement by hanging dead dogs from lampposts.
3. In the appendix of the *Logic of Sense*, Deleuze also speaks of Conversion, the Platonic, as well as of the Perversion, a Nietzschean project involving the 'power of the false'. Both the Subversive and Conversive are, in a sense, caught within an exchange, the same old philosophical Platonic economy.
4. One possible line of overdetermination concerning the dog is the death of the humanist utopian visionary Fleury Colon, who died when he was impaled on a doghouse shaped like a finial after falling off one of his buildings. Colon, a French avant-garde architect in self-imposed exile in Canada, was working on preliminary designs for an 'Animal Spaceship' before his tragic death. For a lucid introduction to the life and writings of Colon see Michael Peter's entry in the *Dictionary of the Avant-Gardes* (Kostelanetz, 2001).
5. As a ramdom example, let's look at the Golden Retriever, who was 'invented' by Lord Tweedmouth. By means of selective breeding, that visionary Tweedmouth created the first Golden Retriever by breeding Russian circus dogs with a hound. To what extent can we say that a Retriever is simply a dog and not also always already contaminated by man? To what extent, therefore, have these fantasies of selective breeding, the pure breed, always haunted a humanistic and scientific project? When I look at my Golden Retriever am I not already looking at a strange hybrid, an animal fully invested and haunted by man? By means of a hierarchy, of man above animal, man is therefore given the right to experiment with the animal. With this in mind, how might the National Socialist project be thought of as a humanism, which operated within the same logic as that used to determine the animal, in an abso-lutely horrific and irreducible way, on humans? When Lacoue-Labarthe says, 'National Socialism is a humanism' in relation to the complexity of art and politics in Heidegger, we should really give thought to the utopian dangers of any humanist project and how it perhaps coincides with fascism. Of course, these are just cursory remarks, and would need further and rigorous investigation.
6. For and excellent and rigorous etymology of the Greek oracle's phrase to Diogenes, 'Deface the currency', see Navia (1998, 16–17)

Works cited

Deleuze, Gilles. *The Logic of Sense*, trans. Hugh Tomlinson. New York, 1990.

Derrida, Jacques. 'The Animal That Therefore I Am (More to Follow)', *Critical Inquiry* (Winter 2002): 369–414.

Derrida, Jacques. '"Eating Well," or the Calculation of the Subject: An Interview with Jacques Derrida', trans. Peter Connor and Avital Ronell, in *Who Comes After the Subject?* eds Eduardo Cadava, Peter Connor and Jean-Luc Nancy. London, 1991, 96–119.

Derrida, Jacques. 'Economimesis, *The Derrida Reader: Writing Performances,* ed Julian Wolfreys. Edinburgh, 1998, 263–93.

Derrida, Jacques. 'Geschlecht II: Heidegger's Hand', *Deconstruction and Philosophy: The Texts of Jacques Derrida*, ed John Sallis, trans. John P. Leavey, Jr. Chicago, IL, 1987, 161–96.

Derrida, Jacques. *Of Spirit: Heidegger and the Question*, trans. Geoffrey Bennington and Rachel Bowlby. Chicago, IL, 1989.

Derrida, Jacques. 'Faith and Knowledge: the Two Sources of "Religion" at the Limits of Reason Alone', trans. Samuel Weber, in *Religion, eds Jacques Derrida and Gianni Vattimo. Stanford, CA, 1998, 1–79.

Guevara, Ernesto Che. *Episodes of the Cuba Revolutionary War 1956–58*, ed. Mary-Alice Waters. New York, 1996.

Heidegger, Martin. *Being and Time*, trans. Joan Stambaugh. Albany, NY, 1996.

Heidegger, Martin. *The Fundamental Concepts of Metaphysics: World, Finitude, Solitude*, trans. William McNeill and Nicholas Walker. Bloomington, IN, 1995.

Kostelanetz, Richard (ed.). *A Dictionary of the Avant-Garde*. New York, 2001.

Lacoue-Labarthe, Philippe. *Typography: Mimesis, Philosophy, Politics*, trans. Christopher Fynsk et al., ed. Christopher Fynsk. Cambridge, MA, 1989.

Navia, Luis E. *Diogenes of Sinope: the Man in the Tub*. Westport, CT, 1998.

Nietzsche, Friedrich. *Philosophy and Truth: Selections from Nietzsche's Notebooks of the Early 1870's*, ed. and Trans. Daniel Breazeale. Atlantic Highlands, NJ, 1990.

Plotnitsky, Arkady. 'Postmodernism and Postmodernity', *Introducing Literary Theories: A Guide and Glossary,* ed. Julian Wolfreys. Edinburgh, 2001, 261–89.

Ronell, Avital. *Finitudes' Score: Essays for the End of the Millennium.* Lincoln, NE, 1994.

Sloterdijk, Peter. *Critique of Cynical Reason,* trans. Michael Eldred. Minneapolis, MN, 1987.

biotechnologies | *CHRISTOPHER JOHNSON*

Without doubt, one of the most startling achievements of twentieth-century science will have been the discovery of the biochemical basis of life, encoded in the double helix structure of deoxyribonucleic acid, or DNA. Since the groundbreaking work of Crick and Watson in the 1950s the development of molecular biology has been a dramatic one, culminating most recently in the completion of the Human Genome Project, the mapping of the 100,000 or so active sequences of genes found in the human body. The unprecedented speed of such developments owes something at least to the remarkable convergence of disciplines around the question of what we call 'life' – physics, biochemistry, information theory, cybernetics – , but is also, and increasingly, dependent on what will have been one of the defining technologies of the twentieth century, the digital computer. Indeed, a gulf seems to separate Crick and Watson's primitive modelling of the structure of DNA from the powerful and sophisticated computing technology used today. Perhaps even more crucial is the speed at which the initial advances in genetic science have been followed by the possibility of their application, in the form of what is now generically referred to as biotechnology. Here, it is difficult to escape the impression that everything has happened too fast, that we have been, quite literally, overtaken by events. If human technics has irreversibly transformed the face of the earth, then the advent of biotechnics promises or threatens an even more radical transformation of our environment and, indeed, of ourselves. From now on, we are told, it is we who hold the keys to our future as a species, it

is we who are in charge of our own evolution. Inevitably, the advent of a biotechnics brings with it the demand for a bioethics, in which the identity and responsibility of this collective subject, 'we' (nations, governments, corporations, research institutions, scientists, etc.), are both defined and questioned. Important as these issues are, they will not be the primary concern of the following discussion. At most, my approach to them will be a lateral one, addressing the question of technology in biology – more precisely, the technological metaphor in biology – and using the example of a particular fictional representation of genetic science in an attempt to identify what might be some of our primal responses to the biotechnological.

An interesting feature of the history of molecular biology is the fact that a number of its early protagonists, in addition to their contribution to this particular branch of biological science, were also concerned to communicate something of that science to a wider public. The result was books such as Francis Crick's *Of Molecules and Men* (1966), or James Watson's more autobiographical *The Double Helix* (1968). In France, François Jacob and Jacques Monod, who together with André Lwoff had been awarded the Nobel Prize in 1965 for their research on RNA 'messenger', produced accounts of their subject that were both more historical and more philosophical than those of their Anglo-Saxon counterparts: *The Logic of Living Systems* and *Chance and Necessity* were published in 1970. I will be focusing on the latter two texts not simply because of their greater intellectual depth, but because they seem to share a common language of description in their exposition of some of the fundamentals of molecular biology. This common language could be qualified as 'idiomatic' in the sense that it has partly to do with the linguistic peculiarities of a national language, French, and within that language the choice of a particular set of figures to delineate the object of a relatively new science.

The original French title of Jacob's book, *La logique du vivant*, is difficult to translate into English, not because of any intrinsic semantic complication, but because of what one might term its linguistic effect or performance. The singular 'logic' is in fact plural, to the extent that Jacob's book, being as its subtitle indicates a history of heredity, is about the different logics or paradigms that in different historical periods have determined our conception and representation of the living world (Jacob, 1971, 49). At the same time, the singular is appropriate because it describes the essential logic of scientific practice and scientific discovery, which is that in the final analysis the only logic which counts is the logic which resumes and supersedes – replaces – all other explanations of living processes. This single logic is that of the combinatorial and informational science that biology has now become, thanks to the recent advances of molecular biology. In the sense that it is stored information, the genetic code could be compared to a *script* or *text* – Jacob reminds us of the heuristic role played by the linguistic metaphor in the development of molecular biology (Jacob, 1974, 195–205).

In the English translation of Jacob's book, the second term of the title, *le vivant*, is rendered by the phrase 'living systems'. While this is perfectly serviceable as a translation – in fact, is probably the *only* possible translation – , as is often the case with translation, it ends up saying both more and less than the original term. The translator has avoided the most direct and literal of translations, for example, 'The Logic of Life' or 'The Logic of the Living', which are clearly not appropriate, but it is impossible to reproduce in English the *articulation* of the French title, its alternation of feminine and masculine genders (la *logique*, le *vivant*), and especially, the essential overdetermination of the term *le vivant*. Because what this masculine term has replaced, in the discourse of the so-called 'life' sciences in France, is a more general and more inclusive term, the feminine noun *la vie*. According to Jacob, the traditional notion of 'life' (*la vie*) no longer possesses any scientific value for the contemporary biologist:

> *Today the concept of life [*vie*] no longer plays any operational role in the biologist's analysis. In their research, biologists don't consider there to be any particular mystery concealed behind the word 'life' [*vie*]. But of course, the word itself remains a highly charged one, loaded with all sorts of emotional and mythological connotations.*
>
> (Jacob, 1971, 48; my translation)

In a kind of diacritical play, *la vie* therefore subsists as the virtual counterpart of *le vivant*, the old ghost or demon of vitalism, the sacralization of life as being of another order than the material components of our earthly incarnation. What the term *le vivant* designates, without being a concept as such, is a semantic or conceptual field which is not exactly that of life as we know (or intuit) it, but which is the essential condition of life in the common sense of the term. For Jacob, the principle of *le vivant* is the genetic code, the digital information which survives the organism and ensures the reproduction of all species, from bacteria to humans: 'For the biologist, the living [*le vivant*] begins only with what was able to constitute a genetic programme' (Jacob, 1973, 304 [325]).[1] If it is neither concept nor model, as a word *le vivant* nevertheless possesses a certain performative force, in that it comes to designate the very *object* of the new biology, giving a kind of hard scientific validation to what had been the softest of the natural sciences. For Jacob and Monod alike, the strength and the success of molecular biology lies in its reduction of life and its elimination of old notions of vitalism. As Jacob remarks, life – *la vie* – is a term saturated with connotation, whereas its diacritical counterpart, *le vivant*, indicates the more certain and more neutral terrain of scientific analysis. (For a more extended discussion of Jacob's title, see Johnson, in Mallet, 1999, 353–68.)

If *le vivant* begins only with the information encoded in DNA, the double helical structure discovered by Crick and Watson accounts for how genetic information is encoded but not how it is translated into the three-dimensional structure of the protein. The crucial work of Jacob and Monod was to isolate the molecule RNA 'messenger' as the mediator between DNA and proteins. What is interesting here is how Jacob and Monod conceptualize this process of transcription, how they represent the passage from DNA to RNA to protein. On the one hand, it is represented as a process of information transfer, as the expression or translation of a code – this is the linguistic or informational metaphor mentioned above. On the other hand, because information is not a zero quantity, because there must be a material substrate or support to carry this information, and because all of this involves a *kinematics* of biochemical reactions, there is a second level of figuration in Jacob and Monod's texts, that of the *machine*. The metaphor used here is not that of the translating machine, for example, but rather the industrial machine of mass production: a constant figure in both texts is that of the *factory*. This metaphor conveys both the high level of precision involved in molecular replication and the mass production

of identical proteins. Of the two biologists, Monod appears to be most attached to this metaphor, marvelling at the perfection of the microscopic reactions involved:

> *The highly mechanical and even 'technological' aspect of the translation process merits attention. The successive interactions of the various components intervening at each stage, leading to the assembly, residue by residue, of a polypeptide upon the surface of the ribosome, like a milling machine [machine-outil, machine tool] which notch by notch moves a piece of work through to completion – all of this inevitably recalls an assembly line in a machine factory.*
>
> (Monod, 1972, 106–7 [143])

In one sense, the metaphor of the factory and of the production line could be said to fulfil simply a didactic role, part of the attempt in Monod and Jacob's texts to mediate the results of a highly specialized branch of science to a more general public. At the same time, the metaphor is not an entirely innocent one, as it plays a part in the constitution of *le vivant* as a field of connotation, as a complex of associated concepts. Because precisely, the machine is not life. The *perfection* of molecular replication, the intricate and microscopic machinery which makes such replication possible, suggest an implacable automatism associated not with the living but with death: perfect replication, the iteration of the identical, is death; *le vivant* is *le mort*. (On the becoming-science of biology and the concept of *le mort* ('the dead'), see Derrida, 1985, 6.) On the other hand, this mechanism possesses a kind of life, as there is no external or 'vital' force which endows it with motion. The machine is auto-mobile and auto-poietic, a microscopic cybernetic system, as Monod describes it (1972,

65–81 [85–107]). At the molecular level, life in the everyday sense of the word has no sense. As Jacob remarks in *The Logic of Living Systems*, the concepts of reproduction and of natural selection mean nothing to an isolated molecule (1973, 320 [341]).

If the technological metaphor informs biological description of the micro-level of molecular interaction, then it has also, from the beginning, informed the discourse of evolution. The ensemble of traits, physiological and anatomical, which make up the phenotype of a given species, are seen as the assembled product of a process of selection operating over thousands or even millions of years. Despite the illusion of design, the principle of natural selection, as it is called, operates a posteriori, on emergent traits, rather than a priori, in anticipation of them. The metaphor Richard Dawkins uses in *The Blind Watchmaker* (1986) is a variant of the classical, mechanistic image of the divine creator:

> Natural selection is the blind watchmaker, blind
> because it does not see ahead, does not plan con-
> sequences, has no purpose in view. Yet the living
> results of natural selection overwhelmingly
> impress us with the appearance of design as if by
> a master watchmaker, impress us with the illusion
> of design and planning.
>
> (1991, 21)

Again, Dawkin's choice of metaphor is doubtless influenced by the pedagogical intent of his book, his desire to mediate a relatively specialized knowledge to a lay audience. Yet while this metaphor dispenses with teleology – the illusion of design – it retains, perhaps *needs* to retain, the illusion of production, the simulacrum of an *agent* of production. Even if we accept that this retention of agency

is a kind of logical necessity, a virtual requirement of our being able to conceptualize evolution, then the metaphor of the watchmaker, the *master* watchmaker, suggests a form of technological perfection, a machine of perfectly adjusted parts, which should continue to impress us even in the absence of a divine artificer. In this connection, it is interesting to note another variant on the metaphor of production in François Jacob's *The Possible and the Actual* (1981), one which dispenses with the idea of perfection and instead proposes a nature whose products are ad hoc and approximate. Jacob borrows Lévi-Strauss's notion of *bricolage* to describe the process of natural selection:

> The action of natural selection has often been
> compared to that of an engineer. This comparison,
> however, does not seem suitable. First, in contrast
> to what occurs during evolution, the engineer
> works according to a preconceived plan. Second,
> an engineer who prepares a new structure does
> not necessarily work from older ones . . . To
> produce something new, the engineer has at his
> disposal original blueprints drawn for that particu-
> lar occasion, materials and machines specially
> prepared for that task. Finally, the objects thus
> produced de novo by the engineer, at least by the
> good engineer, reach the level of perfection made
> possible by the technology of the time. In contrast,
> evolution is far from perfection, as was repeatedly
> stressed by Darwin, who had to fight against the
> argument from perfect creation. In The Origin of
> Species, Darwin emphasizes over and over again
> the structural and functional imperfections of the
> living world . . .
>
> In contrast to the engineer, evolution does not
> produce innovations from scratch. It works on

what already exists, either transforming a system to give it a new function or combining several systems to produce a more complex one. Natural selection has no analogy with any aspect of human behavior. If one wanted to use a comparison, however, one would have to say that this process resembles not engineering, but tinkering, bricolage *we say in French. While the engineer's work relies on his having the raw materials and the tools that exactly fit his project, the tinkerer manages with odds and ends. Often without even knowing what he is going to produce, he uses whatever he finds around him . . . to make some kind of workable object.*

(1982, 33–4 [63–4])

As in Lévi-Strauss's original formulation of *bricolage* in *The Savage Mind* (1996, 16–32 [26–33]), part of Jacob's exposition relies on a counterpointing of the term with what it is not, distinguishing the *bricoleur* from the engineer. One immediately thinks of Derrida's interrogation of this distinction in *Writing and Difference* (1967), his questioning of the absolute difference between the two categories of production (1978, 284–6 [417–19]). Jacob is evidently not aware of Derrida's essay, nor perhaps would he be interested in the kind of problematic it explores. Like Lévi-Strauss, his use of the notion of *bricolage* is itself a form of *bricolage*, a temporary and makeshift expedient, a conceptual tool to be used and discarded as and when necessary. In a recent interview, he explains how he first came to use the term in the 1970s, as he and his colleagues began to establish a systematic inventory of gene and protein sequences. At that time, one of the central dogmas of neo-Darwinian theory was the idea that there was a qualitative difference between the molecular constituents of different organisms,

that the proteins making up a cow, for example, were not the same as those found in a penguin. A single protein had a single function. What the research of the 1970s revealed was that within a single organism a given protein could have the same structure but different functions, and that the same structure, or a similar structure, could be found in other organisms. Moreover, it was found that there were sections of different proteins which also exhibited a similar structure. It was this combinatorial nature of gene and protein structure which suggested to Jacob the metaphor of *bricolage*. Like *bricolage*, the evolution of different forms of life is based on the principle of making up the new with the debris of the old. Jacob himself thinks the analogy an appropriate one not only for its explanatory potential, but also for its capacity to provoke and disturb those who are unduly attached to the idea of a certain *integrity* of life, and especially of human life, who are unable to accept the notion of life as a jerry-built structure (Jacob, 1999, 20). Indeed, the dogma that his metaphor is intended to expose (one protein, one function; the organic specificity of individual proteins) supports what might be seen as a basic psychological resistance to the disparate, the dispersed and the dis-integrated, the psychological requirement that the organism, and especially the human organism, should retain a certain unity of essence. The example Jacob gives of more recent research, which shows that the same genes that describe the body structure of the fly or worm are also involved in the genetic blueprints of mammals, and therefore humans, confirms this sense of the *uncanny*, that is, our hesitation and our oscillation, our fundamental uncertainty when confronted with the familiar at the heart of the different, structural similarity beneath the phenomenally distinct.

Jacob himself later recognizes the limitations of the metaphor of *bricolage*. Whereas in *The Possible and the*

Actual he is suitably vague as to the *bricoleur's* sense of project, in the interview discussed above he qualifies that while the *bricoleur* will always know where (s)he wants to go, evolution is a process which proceeds blindly (*à l'aveugle*), without any predetermined plan (Jacob, 1999, 20). One is therefore tempted to combine the two personifications of evolution found in Dawkins and Jacob into a single, hybrid term – that of the *blind tinkerer*, for example – , to get a more precise idea of the process they are describing.

The question of agency, of project, of the *subject* of evolution should of necessity be a central question in any discussion on the subject of biotechnologies. Because the epistemological adjustments which the findings of modern biology have forced upon us, their dissolution of the different myths surrounding the question of the essence of 'life', have been accompanied, almost simultaneously, by the ethical question of the power such knowledge gives us. The decade Jacob designates as having revolutionized our understanding of the structure of proteins is also the decade in which the technical application of the two previous decades of pure research is finally made possible. One early manifestation of the moral reservations among scientists regarding gene manipulation technology was the conference held in Asilomar in 1975, where researchers called for a moratorium on the use of such technology, and discussed what risks its use might effectively entail. In *The Possible and the Actual*, Jacob refers to the popular hostility that genetic engineering has aroused, along with other contentious practices such as foetal research, behavioural control or psychosurgery. He considers fears about the possible unintended consequences of this new technology to be greatly exaggerated, and sees these fears as arising less from the inherent dangers of biotechnology as from the basic affective response it provokes in us:

If this work has raised endless debates, it is not so much because of the dangers that have been argued about . . . but because the idea that genes can be taken out of one organism to be inserted into the genetic makeup of another is by itself upsetting. The very notion of recombinant DNA is linked with the mysterious and the supernatural. It conjures up some of the old myths that have their origin in the deepest kind of human anxiety, the primitive terror associated with the hidden meaning of hybrid monsters, the revulsion caused by the idea of two beings unnaturally joined together.

(Jacob, 1982, 45–6 [84])

Jacob cites the paintings of Hieronymous Bosch as an example of the different visual representations of the monstrous which over the centuries have been designed to frighten and impress the spectator. (A detail from the right wing of Bosch's *The Garden of Delights* illustrates the front cover of the French edition of the book.) Typically, Bosch's monsters are hybrids, the unnatural products of diverse and incompatible species: 'Such hybrid monsters presuppose a dislocation of the animal bodies followed by a reshuffling of the pieces, as if, in order to cause anxiety, Bosch was opposing the disorder of an anti-world to the harmony of our own world' (Jacob, 1982, 46 [85]).

It is difficult to disagree with the substance of Jacob's diagnosis, which is that the popular reaction to biotechnology is derived less from a rational assessment of its dangers than from certain primordial fears concerning what is proper to the human and what is, properly speaking, *in*human. At the same time, it is difficult to avoid the impression that his evocation of these anxieties and the myths that give them form is rather one-dimensional, that the affective *and* cognitive complex underlying our response to the biotechnological is somewhat more complicated and altogether more profound than the simple fear of the monstrous. The example of Bosch is a convenient illustration of the delirium of recombination, of a *bricolage* of body parts run wild. But as a representation, it belongs to another century and another aesthetic, and while there may be survivals of that aesthetic in our present age, I would prefer to concentrate for the remainder of this discussion on a more contemporary medium of representation, the cinema, as a means of thinking the biotechnological and the effects/affects of the biotechnological.

The film I wish to take as an example is an obvious choice, and it has the advantage of being well known to virtually everyone, something like a contemporary myth. Ridley Scott's *Blade Runner* was initially released in 1981, and is one of the first science-fiction films in which the possibilities of genetic engineering are explicitly represented. The novel on which the film is based, Philip K. Dick's *Do Androids Dream of Electric Sheep?* (1968), as its title suggests, uses the conventional science-fictional label of 'android' to designate the renegade individuals the bounty hunter (in the film, 'blade runner') Rick Deckard is commissioned to track down and terminate. As an author, Dick is economical on the detail of the technology involved in the construction of the androids. The reader's overall impression is that they are some kind of artificial construct manifestly not human, and in any case devoid of normal human emotion. There are few indications in the novel that they are in fact neither mechanical nor electronic but organic in nature, as when Deckard replies to the statement by Rachael (one of a new generation of androids) that she is not alive: 'Legally you're not. But really you are. Biologically. You're not made of transistorized circuits like a false animal; you're an organic entity' (Dick, 1993, 149). It

is not necessarily the case that Scott's film is more detailed than Dick's novel in its explanation of the android characters' construction – the cinema is in any case not the ideal medium for this kind of exploration. And yet, as a historical document, the film bears the indelible trace of the thirteen or so years separating it from the book, in the way it reflects the ambient technology of the period. This is evident in Scott's rejection of the traditional science-fictional tag of 'android' and his search for an alternative, more appropriate term. David Peoples, who had been called in to rewrite Hampton Fancher's original script for the film, had a daughter doing research in microbiology and biochemistry, who explained the term 'replicating' to him, and it was from this that he derived the word 'replicant' (Sammon, 1996, 61). In the workprint for the film, a dictionary definition, absent from the two final versions, is given after the opening credit sequence:

> REPLICANT\rep'-li-cant\n. See also ROBOT (antique): ANDROID (obsolete): NEXUS (generic): Synthetic human, with paraphysical capabilities, having skin/flesh culture. Also: Rep, skin job (slang): Off-world use: Combat, high risk industrial deepspace probe. On-world use prohibited. Specifications and quantities – information classified. New American Dictionary. Copyright © 2016.
>
> (Sammon, 1996, 342)

As replicants, the synthetic or quasi-humans represented in Scott's film do seem more *possible*, more plausible, in the light of the recombinant DNA technology developed in the 1970s. The question of their construction, or confection, is no longer that of an assembly of parts, as in the now obsolete machinery of the android, but of *growth* – the

29

constitution of a 'skin/flesh culture'. And yet, as always, in the film as in the book, it is necessary to differentiate between human and quasi-human. Strictly speaking, replication is not reproduction, it is 'the production of exact copies of complex molecules, such as DNA molecules, that occurs during growth of living tissue' (Hanks, 1986 (on the distinction between replication and reproduction, see Dyson, 1997, 123)). The replicants are not the result of conventional bisexual reproduction, and lack the elementary structures of kinship and socialization which make the human adult such a unique complex of traits. The replicants are 'born' fully-grown adults, and so lack a childhood. They have a life span of only four years, so they also do not experience old age. They lack the normal affective responses of the average human, in particular the emotion of pity, the empathetic impulse which in Rousseau's human animal counterbalances the basic (selfish) impulse of self-preservation. This fact is particularly underlined by Dick but is also present in the film. Because the replicants simulate the human so perfectly, the only effective way of distinguishing them from humans is to submit them to what would be the affective equivalent of a Turing test. The Voigt-Kampff test blade runners Holden and Deckard administer to the replicants Leon and Rachael is an empathy test, measuring the degree of dilation of the eye in response to a standard set of questions. Characteristically, the replicant will not show the same range of emotional responses to the questions that a human will.

All of these privatives – lack of familial and social ties, truncated life span, emotional/affective deficit – mean that the replicant can be treated as being substantially less than human, and therefore as a means rather than an end, an instrument, a slave. The different replicant individuals portrayed in the film are all designed for specific functions, in a sort of pre-programmed division of labour: combat model, pleasure model, etc. The pejorative slang word, 'skin' or 'skin job', recognizes the replicant's humanity as being only skin-deep. As Deckard's voice-over in the first version of the film dryly comments, his boss, detective Bryant, who uses the term is the kind of man who once would have used the word 'nigger' to describe blacks (see Bukatman, 1997, 74–5). At the same time, the replicants' subservience to human ends is matched by their *superiority*, both physical and mental, in comparison with the capacities of the average human. Although they are not manufactured or assembled in the same way as their robot/android predecessors, they are designed in parts. Just as the automaton Olympia in Hoffmann's *The Sandman* is the product of a division of labour between Coppelius and Spalanzani, the one making the eyes, the other the mechanism, in *Blade Runner* the confection of the replicants is contracted out to different parties. The scientist-entrepreneur Dr Tyrell is responsible for the overall design of the product, it is he who holds the key or code to their conception, but the eyes (again) and brain unit are designed by others – 'I designed your eyes' (Chew), 'There's some of me in you!' (J. F. Sebastian). Whereas our merely human frames are the result of millennia of blind *bricolage*, the biotechnology of the near future, as represented in *Blade Runner*, is capable of selecting and perfecting the traits it wishes to express in its synthetic organisms, thus short-circuiting the laborious processes of evolution, reproduction and socialization. Infinitely more precise and more powerful than natural or (even) artificial selection, the kind of bioengineering we witness in Scott's film might be said to reflect the essence of technology, which is perfection. As the genetically defective J. F. Sebastian confesses to Pris and Roy, he is able to distinguish them as non-human precisely because they are 'too perfect'.

Jacob's explanation of our anxieties about genetic engineering is therefore too limited, too specific in its attribution of our fears to the unknown, the mysterious or the monstrous. There is nothing mysterious or supernatural about the replicants depicted in Scott's film, and they are certainly not monsters. The *bricolage* to which they have been subjected is not the phenomenal recombination of body parts found in Bosch's paintings, but the invisible, microscopic recombination of the human genotype. On the contrary, what does provoke anxiety and apprehension is the fact that the replicants are all *too* human, that ultimately there will be no shibboleth, Voigt-Kampff test or otherwise which will be able to distinguish the human from the bioengineered. This is the horizon of possibility that the fiction – Dick's book and Scott's film – plays with, simulates and speculates on. The eventuality of convergence between human and replicant could be said to elicit certain primordial fears concerning the integrity of human life and the regime of reproduction which supports it. Briefly, these fears may be summarized as follows:

- *The fear of obsolescence.* As the designation Nexus-6 indicates, the replicants represented in *Blade Runner* are the product of an ongoing process of research and development the goal of which is to fabricate ever more faithful approximations of the human organism. The implication is that this model will in its turn be superseded by a more perfect approximation, and so on. In Dick's narrative, this process threatens to outpace the corresponding efforts of the police department to devise more sophisticated methods of detecting renegade replicants. Ultimately, it would seem that the only trait distinguishing the replicant from the human is its reduced life span of four years. Rather than representing a limitation of near-future technol-

ogy, this would seem to reflect the need for a fail-safe device, should the slave one day threaten to replace the master. The replicant's built-in obsolescence is therefore the reverse projection of the fear of our own obsolescence. (See Bukatman, 1997, 65.)

- *The fear of miscegenation.* As was noted above, the biotechnology imagined in *Blade Runner* short-circuits the normal routes of human reproduction – replicants are not born and do not grow in the same way human or other life forms do. However, there is a taboo on intercourse between human and replicant – in Dick's book there are strict laws forbidding sexual relations between the two groups, master and servant, in the off-world colonies. Of course, the taboo and the law exist because the desire and possibility of sexual relations exist – indeed it is known that such relations take place. Though Deckard assures Rachael that she is alive, that she is not a machine, this is his delayed reponse to her assertion that she is sterile, that she cannot reproduce (Dick, 1993, 146). There is no such assurance given in the film version, in fact it seems that a subtext of the film is the question of Rachael's uniqueness, the possibility that she is one of a new generation of replicants superseding the Nexus-6 model. Could it be said, then, that the prohibition of sexual relations between human and replicant is due to an innate fear of miscegenation, of the imperceptible *perversion* of the human genotype, of dis-semination? This would explain the need to detect and terminate the replicants, genetically modified organisms who are able to pass unnoticed in human society, assimilate – and, perhaps, reproduce.

- *The fear of social dis-integration.* Reproduce or replicate? The two preceding categories of fear may well coexist in our affective response to the possibilities of biotechnology, but it may be that logically they are mutually exclusive. In other words, why should one resort to reproduction if replication is a more efficient and more economical means of self-perpetuation? But this short-circuiting of nature and nurture, of the normal structures of reproduction and socialization, would inevitably bring with it the transformation of the social infrastructures which for millennia have supplemented and relayed human reproduction. The replicants portrayed in *Blade Runner* have no parents or siblings, and as such lack the affective and cognitive reference points that would ensure their integration into a wider social sphere – in Dick's novel they are described as *solitary* animals, whose only loyalty is to their individual self-preservation, a little like Rousseau's pre-social human, minus the essential affect of pity (Dick, 1993, 28). At the same time, however, in both film and novel there are indications that despite their lack of normal human ties, the replicants are capable of group consciousness, that in their short existences they are able to experience an elementary sense of kinship with their own kind. The question is, how would the genealogical tree of a self-conscious species based on replication differ from one based on reproduction? And what would be the corresponding mode of social organization?

Finally, to these different categories of fear or apprehension may be added another response which is perhaps more complex, indeed more *evolved* in its constitution. The confrontation of slave and master (or maker), which happens a number of times, and in different modalities, in the film (and which, it should be emphasized, does not happen in the novel) produces not a movement of revulsion – the perfect cannot be abject – but the flicker of cognitive uncertainty which is always a feature of the uncanny, the recognition of the familiar at the heart of the different, of the self in the other, of the living in the artificial and the artificial in the living. Or, as J. F. Sebastian proudly declares, 'There's some of me in you!'

Note

1. Page references for original French texts are in square brackets.

Works cited

Bukatman, Scott. *Blade Runner*. London, 1997.

Dawkins, Richard. *The Blind Watchmaker*. London, 1991.

Derrida, Jacques. *Writing and Difference*, trans. Alan Bass. London, 1978.

Derrida, Jacques. *The Ear of the Other: Otobiography, Transference, Translation*, ed Christie V. McDonald, trans. Peggy Kamuf and Avital Ronell. New York, 1985.

Dick, Philip K. *Do Androids Dream of Electric Sheep?* London, 1993.

Dyson, George. *Darwin Among the Machines*. London, 1997.

Hanks, Patrick (ed.). *Collins Dictionary*, 2nd edn. London and Glasgow, 1986.

Jacob, François. 'Interview with François Jacob', *La Nouvelle Critique*, 47, (October–November 1971): 46–55.

Jacob, François. *The Logic of Living Systems*, trans. Betty E. Spillman. New York, 1973.

Jacob, François. 'Le modèle linguistique en biologie', *Critique*, 322 (March 1974): 195–205.

Jacob, François. *The Possible and the Actual*. New York, 1982.

Jacob, François. 'Interview with François Jacob', *Magazine Littéraire*, 374 (March 1999): 18–23, 20.

Johnson, Christopher, 'La vie, le vivant: biologie et autobiographie', in Marie-Louise Mallet (ed.), *L'animal autobiographique. Autour de Jacques Derrida*. Paris, 1999, 353–68.

Lévi-Strauss, Claude. *The Savage Mind*. Oxford, 1996.

Monod, Jacques. *Chance and Necessity: An Essay on the Natural Philosophy of Modern Biology*, trans. Alfred A. Knopf. London, 1972.

Sammon, Paul M. *Future Noir. The Making of Blade Runner*. London, 1996.

chora | *GREGORY L. ULMER*

Plato introduced 'chora' in *Timaeus*, one of his most influential dialogues, best known now as the first telling of the story of Atlantis. In it he explains the cosmology of the natural order within which exists the social order of the ideal city (*Republic*). *Timaeus* is a major source for the doctrine of correspondences in the western tradition – the idea, captured in the phrase 'as above, so below', that the microcosm repeats the macrocosm. A sticking point for Plato in working out the 'scientific' description of this theory concerned how the pure forms or Ideas in the mind of the Deity (being) interacted with the material substances of the world (becoming). He reasoned that there is a third fundamental nature – a receptacle – that mediates and enables the instantiation of the forms in things. This receptacle he called space (chora).

> *My verdict is that being and space and generation, these three, existed in their three ways before the heaven, and that the nurse of generation, moistened by water and inflamed by fire, and receiving the forms of earth and air, and experiencing all the affections which accompany these, presented a strange variety of appearances. And being full of powers which were neither similar nor equally balanced, was never in any part in a state of equipoise, but swaying unevenly hither and thither, was shaken by them, and by its motion again shook them, and the elements when moved were separated and carried continually, some one way, some another. As, when grain is shaken and winnowed by fans and other instruments used in the threshing of corn, the close and heavy particles are borne away and settle in one direction and the loose and light particles in another. In this manner, the four kinds of elements were then shaken by the receiving vessel, which, moving like a winnowing machine, scattered far away from one another the elements most unlike, and forced the most similar elements into close contact.*
>
> (Timaeus, 52d–53a)

What is the relevance of chora to contemporary thought? Since chora (space) is a third nature, neither intelligible nor sensible in itself (neither a concept nor a percept), it must be communicated by a kind of dream logic of metaphor, myth and story. Chora supplements concept and percept as a means of contact and interaction with reality (Walter, 1988, 122). Choral thought is 'intuitive', experienced as 'feeling' and 'insight', correlated with memory and imagination. There are three modes of apprehension then: concept, percept, recognition. There is nothing 'new' about choral knowing in itself. What is new (what is motivating the return of chora in contemporary theory) is the hypothesis that 'electracy' (which is to the digital imaging apparatus what literacy is to alphabetic writing) favours and enhances it, and hence that it may be introduced into the schools as part of the 'skill set' of an educated person. This memorial imaging is called 'chorography' (Ulmer, 1994), related to but distinct from 'chorography' (with an 'o'), referring to the branch of geography that applies plastic arts to cartography (Nuti, 1999).

Some of the other metaphors Plato used to characterize the relations among the three kinds, in addition to the winnowing device noted above, included 'family' – the eternal Forms as father, the created copies as offspring, and chora if not 'mother' then at least 'nurse'. Various modern thinkers have taken up and championed one or the other of Plato's metaphors for chora: Heidegger took up the 'tuning of the strings of a lute' in exploring *Stimmung* (attunement) (Spitzer, 1963). Julia Kristeva took up the 'mother or nurse' in distinguishing the 'semiotic chora' of the body and its 'drives' from the symbolic semantic dimension of language (Kristeva, 1984). Jacques Derrida foregrounded the winnowing basket or seive relative to the *mise en abyme* operation (transducing cosmological correspondences into rhetorical homologies) in his collaboration with Peter Eisenman on a 'folly' design for the Parc de la Villette (Kipnis and Leeser, 1997). The works of these and other critics justify the study of 'chora', but they are not my theme, since explications already abound in each case. Rather, the goal is to build on these readings by opening a new line of credit in relation to one of Plato's metaphors that has been neglected by the commentators: chora as liver.

The function of chora in the cosmos is compared with that of the liver in the body. In Plato's analogy between the city and the individual person the hierarchy of value equates the mind or reason with the ruling elite, and the heart with the guardian soldiers. The viscera are equated with the workers, and within these lower organs the liver is singled out as the seat of divination.

And knowing that this lower principle in man would not comprehend reason, and even if attain-

ing to some degree of perception would never naturally care for rational notions, but it would be especially led by phantoms and visions night and day – planning to make this very weakness serve a purpose, God combined with it the liver and placed it in the house of the lower nature, contriving that it should be solid and smooth, and right and sweet, and should also have a bitter quality in order that the power of thought, which proceeds from the mind, might be reflected as in a mirror which receives likenesses of objects and gives back images of them to the sight, and so might strike terror into the desires . . . For the authors of our being, remembering the command of their father when he bade them create the human race as good as they could, that they might correct our inferior parts and make them to attain a measure of truth, placed in the liver the seat of divination. And herein is a proof that God has given the art of divination not to the wisdom but to the foolishness of man.

(Timaeus, 71a–71e)

The mirror allusion connects the liver/divination analogy to chora, the mirror being a metaphor for chora as a receptacle that displays entities without participating in them. As part of bootstrapping literate practices out of orality, Plato retained some features of religious ritual while rejecting or demoting others. Divination is a ritual practice that is repositioned within literacy. Thus the setting of *Phaedrus*, the first discourse on method in the western tradition, is just outside Athens, near the sanctuary of Agrai on the banks of the river Ilissos. 'Agrai was the scene of the Lesser Mysteries, which served as a preparation for the Great Mysteries of Eleusis' (Kerenyi, 1967, 45). The Lesser Mysteries, the 'myesis', celebrated love, and were distinguished from the hidden mysteries given only to initiates in a revelation, the 'epoptika'. The Eleusinian Mysteries were based on the myth of Demeter's search for her ravished daughter Persephone. The myth associated the harvest with love or fertility in general. Plato's contemporaries would have recognized as an allusion to Eleusis the use of the winnowing fan or basket as a metaphor for chora. Scenes from the ceremony preserved in urn carvings show a priestess holding a *liknon* or winnowing basket over the head of the initiate: 'a plaited winnowing fan, an instrument with which the grain was ordinarily cleansed and in which the accessories of the Dionysian rites were kept and carried about: the phallus or the mask. Infants, divine as well as human, were placed in such baskets' (57).

To communicate in an image the relationship of being, becoming and space, Plato alluded to this ritual and familial scene of the nurse carrying the infant in the *liknon*. As it happens, the *liknon* was used in divination, not only in Greece but in other civilizations as well.

> *Nedembu diviners 'shake the basket' to 'cut a trail'*
> *to and from the dark springs of malice, hatred and*
> *the desire to hurt and control. . . . The basket diviner*
> *uses a winnowing basket and a set of 20–30 small*
> *objects that he makes or finds. These tell the story*
> *of misfortune, loss, and death, and the revengeful*
> *motives responsible for them. They articulate the*
> *disturbances and conflicts that surround the*
> *society's values. The story they tell explains suffer-*
> *ing as a breakdown in human relations.*
>
> (Karcher, 1997, 79)

The diviner 'sees' the situation of the querent by shaking the basket repeatedly and noting the relationship among the objects that come to the top each time. The harvesting symbolism in this context represented the winnowing of information to find the solution to the querent's problem.

Topos

Plato's *Timaeus* in the context of the history of writing (grammatology) is read as a step in the process of inventing literacy. This history serves as an analogy for the present moment, relevant to the task of inventing an institutional practice for electracy (a language apparatus or social machine includes a matrix of interdependent elements: technology, institutional practices and identity formation). Plato is credited as the inventor of philosophy since he brought to completion a long process in which alphabetic writing was used to extract from the oral epics a new mode of knowledge, a new manner of category formation – the concept. In short, he invented the institutional practices of the literate apparatus: school and method.

Aristotle continued Plato's literate project in his own school, the Lyceum, where he and his fellow peripatetics invented the 'thing'.

> *In two of his early works – in the* Categories *especially, but also in the* Topics *– Aristotle presents a*
> *revolutionary metaphysical picture. This picture*
> *has had a peculiar fate. Its revolutionary theses*
> *are so far from being recognized as such that they*
> *have often been taken to be statements of*
> *common sense, or expressions of an everyday,*
> *pretheoretical ontology. The most stirring and far*
> *reaching of those theses is the claim that included*
> *among what there is, among the entities, there are*
> things. *Aristotle, famously, goes on to maintain*
> *that these things are ontologically fundamental.*

All the other entities are by being appropriately connected to the things, for examples, either as their features (their qualities, sizes, relations-to-each-other, locations, and so on), or as their genera and species, that is, the kinds under which the things fall. These claims and their interpretation have received considerable discussion. Yet the fundamental one has gone virtually unnoticed. To formulate it most starkly: before the Categories *and* Topics, *there were no things.*

(Mann, 2000, 3–4)

When he isolated things in the world Aristotle was inventing a discourse, a way of talking (theory). 'Ontology was born when someone realized that any view of this sort implies a distinction between individual things, on the one hand, and their properties, on the other' (Grossman, 1983, 3). Aristotle criticized the Presocratics for treating entities as if they were mere heaps of stuff. 'Both a heap and a thing are one – for each is unified such as to be one heap, or one thing – the kind of unity characteristic of things is much stronger than that of heaps . . . Things are genuine unities, whose cause of being one is intrinsic to them, while heaps are merely accidental unities, whose cause of being one is wholly extrinsic to them' (33–4). Aristotle famously brought Plato's Forms down to earth, and in the process abandoned choral space. His refinements on Plato included a preference for 'topos' over 'chora' to theorize 'space'. Topical space is determined by its outer form and volume located in a certain place, which in turn must be in 'an encompassing but delimited portion of choric space' (Casey, 1998, 35). Edward Casey traced Aristotle's rejection of Plato's chora – the amplitude of the receptacle – in favour of a more stringent container, as he passed from cosmology to physics. What constituted 'place' was its

capacity as a vessel independent of any body in it or passing through it.

The reason for going into this classical context of 'chora' is to establish the nature of what must be invented to make chora the electrate equivalent of the literate topic. What has to be invented is not 'only' a new kind of category, but an institutional practice for learning and applying this category. The task is posed as a return to chora, prior to the formalization of predicate logic, in order to open a new direction that exploits the capabilities of digital imaging. Chora is not 'against' topic, but supplements it in a collaborative integration of literacy into electracy (re-establishing in rhetoric the geographic relationship between place and space). Aristotle extended his insights into place (topos) from physics to logic, with the invention of the dialectical topic as a school practice. The topic, based on Plato's dialogues, is a mnemonic system for classifying and deploying arguments. 'A topic is a "head" under which are grouped arguments, or lines of arguments; in a *topos* ("place", *locus*, "region") the speaker has a stock of arguments to which he may turn for a particular need' (Cooper, 1960, 154–5). The work entitled *Topics* is a handbook that taught students how to argue in a structured debate (Slomkowski, 1997, 3).

A fundamental aspect of topic formation is 'definition', the procedure of producing 'predicables' for the topoi – what may or may not be said of a thing, concerning its proper attributes. The definition, that is, establishes essence. There are four kinds of predicates admitted: definition, property, genus or accident. An accident is that which may or may not belong to a thing (a given horse may be awake or asleep, brown or white, large or small, without altering its essence, its true nature). 'To define a substance means to establish, among various accidental attributes, the essential ones, particularly that one which causes the substance to be as it is' (Eco, 1984, 57). The difficulty confronted by those who undertook this work in the western tradition, Eco noted, is to distinguish essence from accident: 'who really knows which differentiae are strictly essential or specific?' (67).

Vortex

The challenge of choragraphy is to formulate a school practice that does for electracy what topos did for literacy (serve as the 'places of invention'). The heuretic premise is that the principles of image reason have already been invented within the experimental and vanguard arts, participating in the 'paideuma' of the emergent apparatus that began forming early in the nineteenth century. In this grammatological frame modernism looks somewhat different from the story that it tells about itself. Or rather, the artists who invented collage-montage composition did the right thing but not necessarily for the purposes of electracy. The exemplary figure among the many possible candidates is Ezra Pound, because of his choice of 'logo' to represent his poetics: the Vortex. He got the idea for this image (which lent its name to the Vorticist movement in England) from reading scholarly accounts of classical Greek cosmology, such as John Burnet's *Early Greek Philosophy*. The passage that was the source of Pound's inspiration was by Leukippos, but we recognize in it the allusion to *Timaeus* and Plato's most important metaphor for chora.

> The worlds came into being thus. There were
> borne along by 'abscission from the infinite' many
> bodies of all sorts of figures 'into a mighty void',
> and they being gathered together produced a
> single vortex. In it, as they came into collision with

one another and were whirled round in all manner of ways, those which were alike were separated apart and came to their likes. But as they were no longer able to revolve in equilibrium owing to their multitude, those of them that were fine went out to the external void as if passed through a sieve; the rest stayed together, and becoming entangled with one another, ran down together, and made a first spherical structure. This was in substance like a membrane or skin containing in itself all kinds of bodies. And, as these bodies were borne round in a vortex, in virtue of the resistance of the middle, the surrounding membrane became thin, as the contiguous bodies kept flowing together from contact with the vortex. And in this way the earth came into being.

(Bell, 1981, 152)

The Greek word for 'vortex' is *dine*, but the allusion to the *Timaeus* is clear. The original context of the image of the sieve or winnowing basket – as part of a divination ritual in the Eleusinian Mysteries – is also specifically relevant to Pound, who used the scene of the *nekuia* or descent into Hades from Homer's *Odyssey* as the framing structure for the *Cantos*. The ritual of descent was the mystery celebrated at Eleusis.

> The conclusion one can draw from these
> Eleusinian references is that Pound's decision to
> begin the CANTOS with a translation of Homer's
> nekuia involves the adoption of the Eleusinian
> ritual of spiritual death and rebirth in the form of a
> journey to the Underworld. In other words, the
> CANTOS require of the reader a reinterpretation
> of the ODYSSEY if the parallel between the two

works is to be properly understood. For in the CANTOS Odysseus is a spiritual voyager whose principal acts are the conquest of Circe and the visit to the Underworld. These acts parallel the central ritual acts of the hierophant at Eleusis, but are by no means Odysseus' most important actions in Homer's ODYSSEY.

(Surette, 1979, 55)

With this context Pound evokes perhaps the key turning point in the origins of the literate apparatus – the moment when Plato borrowed the Eleusinian scene to represent chora within an ontological (literate) mode of categorization. Pound 'makes it new' by returning to this moment in order to take chora in a different direction. In doing so he is participating in the anti-Platonism of his own milieu. He is just one among the many philosophers and artists attempting to escape from the limits of Western metaphysics in the early twentieth century – specifically from the confines of abstract conceptual and topical categories. 'The opposition between abstraction and sensation is a prominent feature of Modernist poetics. Pound and Eliot, like the philosophers [Bergson, James, Nietzsche], assume that instrumental conventions displace us from immediate experience. Pound incessantly attacks our propensity to substitute conceptual abstractions for concrete sensations, and makes the precise rendering of immediate experience a cornerstone of his poetic program' (Schwartz, 1985, 6).

Again reflecting the spirit of his age, Pound turned to non-western sources for help with inventing his alternative practice. His reading of Ernst Fenollosa's studies of the Chinese Ideogram (undertaken during the Vorticist years) provided the relay for a non-conceptual, non-topical, image-based way of gathering heterogeneous materials into sets.

In tables showing primitive Chinese characters in one column and the present 'conventionalized' signs in another, anyone can see how the ideogram for man or tree or sunrise developed, or 'was simplified from', or was reduced to the essentials of the first picture of man, tree, or sunrise. [Thus, man + tree + sun = sun tangled in the tree's branches, as at sunrise, meaning now the East.] But when the chinaman wanted to make a picture of something more complicated, or of a general idea, how did he go about it? He is to define red. How can he do it in a picture that isn't painted in red paint? He puts (or his ancestor put) together the abbreviated picture of

   ROSE   CHERRY
   IRON RUST   FLAMINGO

That, you see, is very much the kind of thing a biologist does (in a more complicated way) when he gets together a few hundred or thousand slides, and picks out what is necessary for his general statement.

(Pound, 1960, 21–2)

The analogy with biology, alluding to Louis Agassiz, is misleading to the extent that it suggests that Pound's ideograms are inductive. Their mode of inference rather is 'conductive', an inference based on aesthetic coherence operating with the holistic gest of epiphany. The more apt analogy is with cinema, especially the montage methods of Sergei Eisenstein, which were invented out of a similar exposure in his case to Japanese arts and writing. Fenollosa's description of the Chinese ideogram as a 'verb', an action, rather than as a thing, included reference to photography that clarifies the connection of Vorticism with the emerging image apparatus. 'Things', wrote Fenollosa about 1904, are 'cross-sections cut through actions, snapshots' (Kenner, 1971, 146). Kenner also described Joyce's epiphany as a 'snapshot', related to the 'aesthetic of glimpses' at work in Pound (35).

The point in our context is that the Vorticist engages in the same process that Aristotle undertook when he invented the 'thing' as a certain kind of entity, structured by essences and properties. The modern poet now is looking for something else in experience, and produces a different coherence, another kind of entity – the Vortex. 'By tying the concept to its constituent particulars, the ideogram keeps us from detaching the abstract form from concrete sensation – the "leaf" from individual leaves, or "redness" from particular red objects. And by displaying its own etymology, the ideogram prevents us from assuming an absolute distinction between concept and figure, metaphysical truth and metaphorical imagination: we are less prone to forget that our abstractions arise from the swift perception of relations' (Schwartz, 1985, 89). Photography makes ideogrammic reason practical; chorography makes it available as a school practice.

'Vortext'

Apparatus theory is not a technological determinism (there is nothing 'new' about 'images'). Rather, it is a matter of efficacy. Pound's logic of the 'Luminous Detail', which he said already existed among the best scholars and historians, supplies a logic to go with the equipment – the imaging equivalent of 'definition'. 'Luminous Details are the transcendentals in an array of facts: not merely "significant"nor "symptomatic" in the manner of most facts', but capable of giving one 'a sudden insight into circumjacent conditions, into their causes, their effects, into sequence,

and law' (Kenner, 1971, 152). Among the multitude of facts available just a 'few dozen' of these 'interpretive details' give the intelligence of a period: '"They govern knowledge as the switchboard governs an electrical circuit"' (Pound, cit. Kenner, 153). Pound learned from Fenollosa how to arrange the details in a way that made them luminous. 'For the ideogram sketches a process, seizes some continuous happening – the movement of attention through an eye, the flow from roots to branches within a tree – and fixes it, like Buckminster Fuller's knot, with three or four minimal vigorous spatial gestures. Thus the word, freed from evanescent sound, transcends the moment of utterance and reutters itself in a vibrating field of force where, augmented by neighboring words, particulars rush *from* and *through* and *into*' (160).

Pound returned to the moment of chora before Aristotle constructed 'things' out of 'mere heaps' of properties. Pound described the *Cantos* as an epic, but in fact he jettisoned for all practical purposes every conventional organizing schema except one – the 'heap'. The great difficulty of the *Cantos* is ascribed to their lack of the conventional sources of coherence – exposition, plot, character, even musical form. Instead, it is an epic structured by a haiku-esque juxtaposition of disparate fragments. It is an enormous heap of precisely observed details.

Pound reverses the process [of essentializing] by juxtaposing phenomena in order to reveal through their relations the invisible idea. From the relations of the seen arises the unseen form, 'the forma, *the immortal* concetto, *the concept, the dynamic form which is like the rose pattern driven into the dead iron-filings by the magnet itself, but separate from the magnet. Cut off by the layer of glass, the dust and filings rise and spring into order'. The force of*

the magnet is akin to that force which orders
sphere, great bass, monad, and right reason . . .
The important point is that the accumulated data
will at one point cease to be just a 'heap' of detail.
As in a flash, the whole subject or phenomenon
will appear, in the form of an image, in the
reader's consciousness. What Pound avers here
is that revelation is a process, the final state of a
cumulative agglomeration of detail.

(Gefin, 1983, 38)

This reduction to a minimum level of literate order is at the
same time a turn in a new direction. The Vortex image is a
step in the direction of an electrate categorization (chora).

By the 'image' I mean such an equation [one that
'causes form to come into being']; not an equation
of mathematics, not something about a, b, and c,
having something to do with form, but about sea,
cliffs, night, having something to do with mood.
The image is not an idea. It is a radiant node or
cluster; it is what I can and must perforce call a
Vortex, from which, and through which, and into
which, ideas are constantly rushing. In decency
one can only call it a Vortex. And from this necessity came the name 'vorticism'.

(Pound, 1965, 152)

The updating of vortex as chora within grammatology might
be expressed in the term 'vortext'.

The Internet, with its digital tools supporting asynchro-
nous, distributed, collective interaction, offers a technology compatible with vortextual (choral) category formation.
A choral category may be constructed by a group, 'on the
fly', witnessing a 'history of the present', since its coherence is a result, not an intention. 'Every link in hypertext
creates a category. That is, it reflects some judgment about
two or more objects: they are the same, or alike, or func-
tionally linked, or linked as part of an unfolding series. The
rummage sale of information on the World Wide Web is
overwhelming, and we all agree that finding information is
much less of a problem than assessing its quality – the
nature of its categorical associations and by whom they
are made' (Bowker and Star, 2000, 7). A vortext does not
define but discovers (invents).

The Web of changes

What about the school practice in which to apply vortextual
memory? The answer is in the choral metaphor of divination.
Pound's ideogram suggests that a good relay for understanding the divination metaphor for chora is the Chinese
Book of Changes, the *I Ching*. Placing divination in a grammatological frame means considering divining as a mnemonic practice, central to the oral apparatus, but also to
written cultures, especially in the manuscript phase of the
technology. The practical function of divination is to relate
individual experience to collective cultural memory. It is a
cognitive map that enables individuals to bring to bear on
personal difficulties the stored wisdom of the civilization.
The strategy of choragraphy is not to reproduce a particular
divination system but to extrapolate from the general opera-
tional logic of divination as well as from a particular example,
to design a divining practice informed by our modern values
and beliefs. The basic elements of oracular knowing include
a symbol, chance and a critical situation, whose combination produces an image of fate (Karcher, 1997, 107).

The considerable attention paid to the *I Ching* in the
twentieth century was part of the modernist history of syn-

cretism in which vanguard artists and intellectuals sought alternatives to western positivism in all manner of non-western forms and modes. In a grammatological frame the problematic 'primitivism' is replaced by the project of elec-trate 'secondary orality'. The aim is not access to traditional wisdom, but a hybrid practice drawing upon features of wisdom and science (Varela, 1999). The *I Ching* is a relay with a possible poetics for making a contemporary divination system. This system would serve as an interface for accessing Internet resources. Espen Aarseth expresses the fit between the *I Ching* and the Internet in strictly formal terms.

> *Possibly the best-known example of cybertext in antiquity is the Chinese text of oracular wisdom, the* I Ching. *Also known as the* Book of Changes, *the existing text is from around the time of the Western Chou dynasty (1122–770 b.c.) and was written by several authors. The* I Ching *system also inspired G. W. von Leibniz, who developed the binary mathematics used by today's digital computers. The* I Ching *is made up of sixty-four symbols, or hexagrams, which are the binary combination of six whole or broken ('changing') lines. A hexagram contains a main text and six small ones, one for each line. By manipulating three coins or forty-nine yarrow stalks according to a randomizing principle, the text of two hexagrams are combined, producing one out of 4,096 possible texts. This contains the answer to a question the user has written down in advance.*
>
> (Aarseth, 1997, 9–10)

The choral connection is the fact that the *I Ching* demonstrates an alternative solution to the metaphysical and methodological problem that Plato solved by inventing chora in *Timaeus*.

> *Why this logical necessity for a third principle conceptualized as a 'substratum or subject'? As Aristotle declared, contraries 'cannot act upon each other', 'do not change into each other', and 'are mutually destructive', In logical terms, they are mutually exclusive. In contrast, the entire Chinese tradition insists that contraries both oppose each other and 'contain each other mutually: within yin there is yang, just as within yang there is yin' . . . They together form all that exists. There is thus no need to posit a 'third term' to support their relation. Even the regulating principle does not exist over and above the two contraries; it simply expresses their harmonious relation. The two contraries form on their own a self-sufficient configuration; the propensity that stems on its own from their interdependence orients the process of reality.*
>
> (Jullien, 1995, 251)

Another account of Chinese cosmogony, however, blurs the clear distinction posed by Jullien by describing 'emptiness' as functioning in a choral manner.

> *This median emptiness, itself a breath, issues from the original emptiness, from which it draws its power. Median emptiness is necessary for the harmonious functioning of the yin-yang pair; it attracts the two vital breaths and draws them into the process of reciprocal becoming. Without it, yin and yang would be in a relationship of frozen opposition. They would remain static substances*

and be formless. It is clearly this ternary relation-
ship between yin and yang and median emptiness
that gives birth to, and also serves as a model for,
the ten thousand existents.

(Cheng, 1994, 50)

The important point is that the Chinese demonstrate a categorical practice different from the conceptual and topical
ontology invented by the Greeks. 'The matter of interest
seems to be the configuration formed by chance events in
the moment of observation, and not at all the hypothetical
reasons that seemingly account for the coincidence. While
the western mind carefully sifts, weighs, selects, classifies,
isolates, the Chinese picture of the moment encompasses
everything down to the minutest nonsensical detail,
because all of the ingredients make up the observed
moment' (Wilhelm, 1967, xxiii). That which resisted measure
and hence control the Greeks called 'necessity' – 'residue
that belongs to the irrational – accident, fortune, monstros-
ity, or any other unintelligible manifestation of necessity.
Becoming is once and for all identified with "matter" and
there is no escape from this fixing of essences' (Lee, 1984,
217). The value of the accidental detail is a major point of
difference between Greek and Chinese cosmology.

Hexagrammatology

The chief insight to emerge from Jullien is that the fundamental organizational unit of Chinese thought expressed in
the *I Ching* is the *situation*, with a certain tendency or propensity. The world is approached as a continuously changing or flowing series of circumstances manifesting *shi* – a
configuration of energy, such that Chinese metaphysics is
frequently used as an analogy to explain Quantum physics,

that is, a world in which 'things' are not essences or substances but secondary, emergent features of a holistic
background field (Peat, 1987). The divination system is
structured as groups or 'piles' of lines – trigrams first – that,
in the manner of archetypal ideograms, figure eight 'germinal situations' which contain virtually every possible
arrangement of circumstances in experience. The emphasis here was not on predicates but predicaments. The eight
trigrams extended by a combinatorial pairing produced
sixty-four archetypal situations. 'It would seem impossible
to deal with today's life situations through the use of only
sixty-four hexagrams. However it is a mistake to identify
the sixty-four hexagrams with sixty-four actual situations.
The hexagrams do not represent actual or phenomenal situations (in Kantian terms), but germinal situations, each of
which might be actualized in many different ways' (Lee,
1984, 98).

The germinal situations are 'categorical' in that they
are identified by a set of attributes and properties.
Handbooks explaining the system include a chart providing
the following information for each of the eight germinal trigrams (with just one example tracked here to illustrate):
'*Name*: Ch'ien; *Trigram* [three solid or yang lines]; IMAGE,
Heaven; *Qualities*: creative, strong, light of day, firmness;
Direction: Northwest; *Relations*: Father; *Parts of Body*:
Head; *Time of Year*: Early Winter; *Time of Day*: Daytime'
(Wing, 1982, 15). The trigrams were arranged into two different sequences historically, one moving from a configuration to its opposite (Heaven is followed by Earth), and the
other following the cycle of the seasons. The importance of
the sequences is that a situation has a direction, a 'grain',
a tendency. The 'enlightened person' is one who is able
intuitively to discern this propensity in its earliest stages
(when it is still possible to influence it).

To extract a poetics that may be used to generate

equivalents for an Internet 'memoria' interface requires itemizing the parts of the *I Ching*, condensing into a 'genre' a set of features that evolved over many generations historically. Formally a hexagram consists of: a name; a combinatorial code (hexagram); the primary judgement (the text defining the overall situation and interpreting what action is appropriate); the subordinate judgements specific to the position of each of the six lines. In some editions there is also a picture selected from Chinese art to illustrate the situation. In addition to the immediate features of the hexagrams, there are several commentaries, adding layers of philosophical interpretation, and other documentation. There is also the claim that the yin-yang exchange references a historical conflict between two dynasties of ancient China.

A sense of 'hexagram formation' is readily induced from an example. Hexagram 52, for example, is 'Meditation' ('Stillness'). 'Meditation is to turn one's back so there is no consciousness of the Self. Should he go into the courtyard without noticing anyone, it is not a mistake. / Stillness (mountain) upon stillness (mountain) forms the condition for Meditation. An enlightened person, therefore, does not allow his thoughts to go beyond his situation' (Wing, 1982, 125). The editor comments on the painting used to illustrate the mood of the situation, a depiction of a boat on a river: 'The occupant of this "Boat on a River" seems heedless of his surroundings in his relaxation and meditation. Yet we see that the boat is not floating aimlessly on the water but tied firmly to the shore' (Wing, 1982, 124). Part of the point of the illustration depends upon its historical context. 'Art historians date this album leaf to the Ming Dynasty of the fifteenth century, a time when China was withdrawing from external contact. The Imperial Court delighted itself with a life full of splendors, wherein closeness to nature, detachment and contentment were the rule of the day'. The first

ten situations include: Creativity, Quiescence, Birth Pangs, Inexperience, Biding One's Time, Strife, The Army, Unity, Restraint By The Weak, Treading.

One difficulty of the interface vortext is to decide how to extrapolate from the relay to a modern system. A first step would be to design an interrelated set of germinal (arechetypal) situations. The germinal situations codified in the hexagrams achieve their coherence through a unifying mood (Wing, 1982, 14). The hexagrams gather materials into sets not by means of logic and definition but by means of art or style. 'Through the dynamism produced by this configuration, a wider meaning emerges from the theme and spreads like an aura, pervasive yet elusive. What both the Chinese and Westerners call the 'poetic atmosphere' is for them created by *shi*' (Jullien, 1995, 130). The choral connection becomes clear when these 'situations' are recognized as 'vortexts'.

Situations

The proposal of choragraphy is to base a school vortextual practice on divination by creating a 'Web of Changes' for the Internet. A first step is an analysis of situation comedies (and the TV series in general) as resources for locating and isolating a set of modern 'germinal situations'. A preliminary system could be formed by converting such hit series as *Leave It To Beaver*, *All In The Family*, *Twin Peaks*, *The Fugitive*, *Star Trek*, *Seinfeld*, *Frazier*, and the like into hexagram format, abstracting them into a specific mood, expressing a specific lifeworld condition. Divination systems are activated when a user — a 'querent' — poses to them a 'burning question' related to a personal problem or dilemma. In oral civilizations, the entire collective knowledge of the society is accessed through the randomizing procedure of the system. The germinal sitcoms similarly would be programmed to access online resources relevant to their attributes as vortexts.

At the same time, such a project could not be confined to existing pop culture situations, but would require the composition of new vortexts, reflecting the new categories enabled by choral imaging. A prototype for creating situations is already available in the relay provided by the group that formalized the creation of 'situations' as a response to the 'society of the spectacle' of which the TV sitcom is a major example. One of the chief responses of the Situationists (SI) to the commodification of everyday life was to develop a new behaviour out of the poetic tradition of the *flâneur* – the drifter – leading to the creation of situations in urban life. In protest against the rationalized urbanism of modernist planners, the drift (*dérive*) cut across the established circulation patterns and zoning of the city in order to seek out places that possessed a specific *ambiance*, mood, atmosphere, aura. Such energy nodes they dubbed 'plaques tournantes', which they registered for Paris in perhaps their best-known works – the collage maps, 'The Naked City' (the title borrowed from a film), and 'Guide psychogéographique'.

> The situationist maps described an urban navigational system that operated independently of Paris's dominant patterns of circulation. THE NAKED CITY helpfully explained itself on the reverse: 'The arrows represent the slopes that naturally link the different unities of ambiance; that's to say the spontaneous tendencies for orientation of a subject who traverses that milieu without regard for practical considerations . . . The earlier of the two situationist maps, the GUIDE PSYCHO-GEOGRAPHIQUE, had taken the situationist inter-

> est in charting each unity's 'exits and defenses' and 'fixed points and vortices' to obsessive lengths. Its arrows restlessly danced between, in, and around specific streets . . . THE NAKED CITY evoked beautifully the way in which some unities of ambiance acted as stations on the drift, junctions in the psychogeographic flow of Paris. The situationists coined a term for these junctions: plaques tournantes. *The term punned on so many meanings that it is not possible to translate it straightforwardly. A* plaque tournante *can be the center of something: it can be a railway turntable, or it can be a place of exchange (in the same way that Marseilles is sometimes described as a* plaque tournante *for trafficking, or that Paris as a whole has been celebrated as a* plaque tournante *of culture). As a center for markets, drinking, prostitution, and drugs, Les Halles was clearly a* plaque tournante *in all these senses.*

> (Sadler, 1992, 88–9)

The maps with their whirling arrows indicate that the turntable or hub is a Vortex (a chora). The maps are expressive, relational, not mimetic. 'Debord and Jorn pasted down the chunks of map at some odd angles, as much as forty-five degrees from the mean. Reorienting the chunks in this way helped to represent the drifters' passages across the city as smooth flows' (Sadler, 1992, 90). In one exemplary drift Debord and Wolman set out across Paris, choosing their path intuitively, spontaneously, arriving finally and 'unexpectedly' at the ruins of a rotunda designed by Ledoux, next to an elevated subway line.

> Upon studying the terrain the Lettrists felt able to discern the existence of an important psychogeo-

graphic hub [plaque tournante] – its center occu-
pied by the Ledoux rotunda – that could be defined
as a Jaures-Stalingrad unity, opening out onto at
least four significant psychogeographical bearings
– the canal [Saint-]Martin, boulevard de la
Chapelle, rue d'Aubervilliers, and the canal de
l'Ourcq – and probably more. In conjunction with
the concept of the hub, Wolman recalls the inter-
section in Cannes that he designated 'the center of
the world' in 1952. One should no doubt link this to
the clearly psychogeographic appeal of the illustra-
tions found in books for very young school children;
here, for didactic reasons, one finds collected in a
single image a harbor, a mountain, an isthmus, a
forest, a river, a dike, a cape, a bridge, a ship, and
an archipelago. Claude Lorrain's images of harbors
are not unrelated to this procedure.

(Debord, 1989 138).

The combination of the methods of Pound the *I Ching*, and Debord provide choragraphy with the means to image situations derived from both discourse and place.

Information infrastructure

What are the implications of an Internet Web of Changes for applied knowledge? Most commentators on public policy agree that many parties to the process are unaware of the role of the apparatus (of metaphysics) in the construction of problems.

Problems come into discourse and therefore into
existence as reinforcement of ideologies, not
simply because they are there or because they

are important for well-being. They signify who are
virtuous and useful and who are dangerous or
inadequate, which actions will be rewarded and
which penalized. They constitute people as sub-
jects with particular kinds of aspirations, self-con-
cepts and fears and they create beliefs about the
relative importance of events and objects. They
are critical in determining who exercises authority
and who accepts it. They construct areas of
immunity from concern because those areas are
not seen as problems. Like leaders and enemies,
they define the contours of the social world, not in
the same way for everyone, but in the light of the
diverse situations from which people respond to
the political spectacle.

(Edelman, 1988, 12–13).

In other words, within literacy problems are conceived to be 'things'. What might be the implications of also restructuring them as 'vortexts'?

Bowker and Star warn that this inevitable interdependence of policy and metaphysics becomes dangerous in a condition of 'convergence' – when the system disappears as such. 'This blindness occurs by changing the world such that the system's description of reality becomes true . . . It will be impossible to think or act otherwise' (Bowker and Star, 2000, 49). A community will not notice when it has reached convergence until there is a breakdown in the system (34), when its solutions fail to pass a reality check. The single greatest determinant of policy formation is 'the dominant value paradigm'. 'For any problem at the regime or macro-level of discussion and analysis there are remarkably few alternatives actually under debate. In the United States a powerful and enduring political culture (as distinct from an arguably much more variegated popular culture) helps to whittle down the range of "legitimate" alternatives to a pitiful few long before any quasi-pluralist "conflict" over problem definition ever ensues' (Bosso, 1994, 184). 'The sanctity of private property and the deification of the "free market"' – the values that Bosso names as the 'cornerstones of the American value system' – would have to be included among the defining attributes of the 'wisdom' of an American Web of Changes. The purpose of creating a contemporary divination system, however, is not only to reproduce the dominant values but to raise awareness about how these values govern collective identity and behaviour.

The Marxist critic Theodor Adorno's analysis of the astrology column of the *Los Angeles Times* showed that the divination systems found in popular culture gave only advice supportive of the status quo (Adorno, 1994, 49). 'The overall rule of the column is to enforce the requirements society makes on each individual so that it might "function"' (59). While it appears that pop divination systems simply transfer the conservative metaphysics of the ancient or oral world views to modern consumer culture, an advantage of divination as an interface metaphor for electracy is its familiarity due to the New Age movement in contemporary culture, making its operation more or less intuitive. An answer to the ideological limitations of public policy is to make students or netizens into virtual 'diviners' by inviting them to create germinal situations to be included in the Web of Changes. An effect of helping to design a divination system over simply using one that exists is an insight into how the 'dice' are ideologically loaded.

The situations comprising the Web of Changes cut across literate categories with electrate ones. The assumption is that 'problems' no less than the policies devised to address them are special cases of Western metaphysics in general, meaning literacy and the ontology of categories, concepts and topics. However, it is not that easy to think 'outside the box' of one's national culture, and that is where chora as generator comes in. The constraint on imagination is addressed in the fundamental challenge posed by electracy – to introduce into schooling the categorical image (vortext).

Works cited

Aarseth, Espen J. *Cybertext: Perspectives on Ergodic Literature*. Baltimore, MD, 1997.

Adorno, Theodor W. *'The Stars Down to Earth' and Other Essays on the Irrational in Culture*, ed. Stephen Crook. New York, 1994.

Bell, Ian F. A. *Critic as Scientist: The Modernist Poetics of Ezra Pound*. New York, 1981.

Bosso, Christopher J. 'The Contextual Bases of Problem Definition', in Rochefort (ed.) (1994), 182–203.

Bowker, Geoffrey C. and Susan Leigh Star. *Sorting Things Out: Classification and its Consequences*. Cambridge, MA, 2000.

Casey, Edward S. *The Fate of Place: A Philosophical History*. Berkeley, CA, 1998.

Cheng, François. *Empty and Full: The Language of Chinese Painting*, trans. Michael H. Kohn. Boston, MA, 1994.

Cooper, Lane. *The Rhetoric of Aristotle*. New York, 1960.

Cosgrove, Denis (ed.). *Mappings*. London, 1999.

Debord, Guy-Ernest. 'Two Accounts of the Derive', in Sussman (ed.) (1989), 134–9.

Eco, Umberto. *Semiotics and the Philosophy of Language*. Bloomington, IN, 1984.

Edelman, Murray. *Constructing the Political Spectacle*. Chicago, IL, 1988.

Gefin, Laszlo. *Ideogram: History of a Poetic Method*. Austin, TX, 1983.

Grossmann, Reinhardt. *The Categorial Structure of the World.* Bloomington, IN, 1983.

Gusfield, Joseph R. *The Culture of Public Problems: Drinking-Driving and the Symbolic Order.* Chicago, IL, 1981.

Havelock, Eric A. *The Muse Learns to Write: Reflections on Orality and Literacy from Antiquity to the Present.* New Haven, CT, 1986.

Jullien, François. *The Propensity of Things: Toward a History of Efficacy in China,* trans. Janet Lloyd. New York, 1995.

Karcher, Stephen. *The Illustrated Encyclopedia of Divination.* Rockport, MA, 1997.

Kenner, Hugh. *The Pound Era.* Berkeley, CA, 1971.

Kerenyi, Carl. *Eleusis: Archetypal Image of Mother and Daughter,* trans. Ralph Mannheim. Princeton, NJ, 1967.

Kipnis, Jeffrey and Thomas Leeser (eds). *Chora L Works: Jacques Derrida and Peter Eisenman.* New York, 1997.

Kristeva, Julia. *Revolution in Poetic Language,* trans. Margaret Waller. New York, 1984.

Lee, Jung Young. *Embracing Change: Postmodern Interpretations of the I Ching From a Christian Perspective.* Scranton, PA, 1994.

Mann, Wolfgang-Rainer. *The Discovery of Things: Aristotle's Categories and their Context.* Princeton, NJ, 2000.

Nuti, Lucia. 'Mapping Places: Chorography and Vision in the Renaissance', in Cosgrove (ed.) (1999), 90–108.

Peat, F. David. *Synchronicity: The Bridge Between Matter and Mind.* New York, 1987.

Pound, Ezra. *ABC of Reading.* New York, 1960.

Pound, Ezra. 'Vorticism', in *The Modern Tradition: Backgrounds of Modern Literature,* eds Richard Ellmann and Charles Feidelson, Jr. New York, 1965.

Rochefort, David A. and Roger W. Cobb (eds). *The Politics of Problem Definition: Shaping the Policy Agenda.* Lawrence, MA, 1994.

Sadler, Simon. *The Situationist City.* Cambridge, MA, 1998.

Schwartz, Sanford. *The Matrix of Modernism: Pound, Eliot, and Early Twentieth-Century Thought.* Princeton, NJ, 1985.

Slomkowski, Paul. *Aristotle's Topics.* New York, 1997.

Spitzer, Leo. *Classical and Christian Ideas of World Harmony: Prolegomena to an Interpretation of the Word 'Stimmung'.* Baltimore, MD, 1963.

Surette, Leon. *A Light from Eleusis: A Study of Ezra Pound's Cantos.* Oxford, 1979.

Sussman, Elisabeth (ed.). *On the Passage of a Few People Through a Rather Brief Moment in Time: The Situationist International, 1957–72.* Cambridge, MA, 1989.

Ulmer, Gregory L. *Heuretics: The Logic of Invention.* Baltimore, MD, 1994.

Varela, Francisco J. *Ethical Know-How: Action, Wisdom, and Cognition.* Stanford, CA, 1999.

Walter, Eugene Victor. *Placeways: A Theory of the Human Environment.* Chapel Hill, NC, 1988.

Wilhelm, Richard. 'Introduction', *The I Ching, or Book of Changes,* 3rd edn, trans. Richard Wilhelm. Princeton, NJ, 1967.

Wing, R. L. *The Illustrated I Ching.* New York, 1982.

difference | *ARKADY PLOTNITSKY*

Introduction

Difference is one of the oldest concepts and a much older, primordial mode of the workings of the human (and perhaps animal) mind. It has also been arguably the most dominant rubric of recent (during the last thirty-some years) theoretical and political discussions in the academy and beyond, to the point of pervading the whole contemporary intellectual, cultural and political landscape. It is true that the overt appeal to difference has somewhat subsided during the last decade, as the term gradually became over-familiarized. Besides, to cite Marcel Proust, 'fashions change, being themselves begotten by the desire for change', which is to say, the desire for difference (1982, 1: 467). It may indeed be said that we are now 'beyond difference', which might well be a more appropriate title for this essay. It is not that we have transcended the necessity of using 'difference' (i.e. the corresponding cluster of concepts, metaphors, strategies and so forth). 'Difference' has less disappeared (the actual frequency of its use has hardly diminished) than become 'invisible', in so far as we do not notice or thematize it. Nor could one say that we have sufficiently, let alone fully, mastered the meaning(s) of 'difference', as the concept has developed during the last few decades, assuming that a determinate set of such meanings or concepts (or at the limit the very concept of meaning or of concept) could apply when we approach the limits of the question of difference. For the moment, I am using the phrase 'beyond difference' in the sense that at this point we may in greater measure assess and historicize the particular role and impact of 'difference' as it has functioned in recent intellectual history. Yet another sense of 'beyond difference', more significant for my argument and more entangled with the idea of difference itself, will appear presently. It is also true that such rubrics as 'otherness' and 'alterity', on the one hand, and 'heterogeneity', 'multiplicity' and 'singularity', on the other, have been equally prominent in recent years (the qualifications just given concerning difference also apply to these terms). These, however, could be seen as species of 'difference' or, at least, as reciprocally interactive with it. In any event, if figures such as Emmanuel Levinas, Mikhail Bakhtin, Maurice Blanchot, Jacques Lacan, Gilles Deleuze, Michel Foucault, Jean-François Lyotard, Jacques Derrida, Paul de Man and Luce Irigaray, and their more or less immediate precursors such as Friedrich Nietzsche, Sigmund Freud, Ferdinand de Saussure, Martin Heidegger, Georges Bataille, Walter Benjamin and Theodor Adorno, have been dominant in recent decades, it is in large part because the question of 'difference' (or 'heterogeneity', 'multiplicity', 'singularity' and so forth) was their primary concern. There are of course equally significant earlier figures, certainly both Kant and Hegel, or Leibniz and Spinoza, or indeed most major figures in the history of western philosophy, beginning with the pre-Socratics.[1] The history of western philosophy cannot be dissociated from the history of the idea of difference. Reciprocally, however, the significance of these figures is defined by how they transformed the concept of difference by taking it beyond 'difference', to a 'beyond-of-difference' and beyond any conceivable conceptuality or indeed beyond anything, any form of 'beyond-ness' included.[2]

This last proposition defines the second sense of 'beyond-difference', to which I alluded above and which is especially significant for my argument. This 'beyond-difference' is more, indeed irreducibly, entangled with 'difference' and its avatars, which are in turn entangled with their 'beyond' ('beyond-alterity', 'beyond-multiplicity' and so forth). This 'beyond-ness' neither absolutely departs nor, rigorously pursued, remains within what it exceeds, which is in part why it is beyond any conceivable 'beyond-ness', and is, in this sense, a step beyond, which, in Maurice Blanchot's words, is also 'a step not beyond' [un pas au-delà] – a step both 'beyond' and 'not beyond'. This traversal does, however, require the most rigorous pursuit of the 'within', a pursuit equally crucial to the work of the figures listed above. Contrary to the common and even dominant view of the work of these figures, the last point could be extended to their relationships with most concepts or fields of inquiry – we may call them 'classical' – within which these figures are critically or deconstructively engaged. I use the term 'critical' in its Kantian sense of a rigorous investigation of the conceptual and textual architectures in question, such as that of various concepts of difference. This architecture may involve certain hidden or unperceived elements. The analytical exposure and investigation of such elements may be seen in terms of 'deconstruction', such as that pursued in Derrida's work, or that of his key precursors, such as Nietzsche and Heidegger.[3]

The theories of difference and of 'beyond-difference' themselves in question will be here defined as 'non-classical'. A detailed explanation of the concept of non-classical (or, conversely, classical) theories will be given in the third section. In a summary definition, non-classical theories are defined by the constitutive irreducibility of the 'beyond-of-difference' – a radical alterity of or 'difference' from difference – or anything else, any form or concept of 'beyondness' included, in considering the relationships and, specifically, the difference between what is and could possibly be subject of representational, phenomenal or otherwise cognitive encounter. In other words, non-classical theories preclude us from ascribing any given form or concept of difference, identity or anything else, including any form of 'beyondness' itself, to that which is 'beyond' what is knowable or that through which, such as difference, the knowable could emerge. As this formulation suggests, however, difference and its avatars, such as alterity, exteriority and otherness, become crucial elements of any non-classical theory, even though and because such concepts must themselves be taken to their non-classical limits. By contrast, classical theories allow that the difference between the knowable and the unknowable, specifically the unknowable that is responsible for the knowable, could, at least in principle if not in practice, be reduced or analytically compensated for. Classical theories may be associated with what Derrida calls 'the metaphysics of presence' (or its versions and proximates, such as 'logocentrism' and 'ontotheology'). Certain classical theories may also be seen as 'naive' (or 'common sense') theories, that is, as falling short of a rigorous elaboration of the possible philosophical content of their concepts and propositions even at the classical, let alone non-classical level. Neither type of theory, naive, classical or non-classical, is dispensable; and non-classical theories, as here defined, depend on classical and naive theories, and deploy them in non-classical regimes.

Difference and intervening in metaphysics

Difference is, as I said, a very old concept. It extends to the known origins (at least) of western thought, especially to pre-Socratics, such as Anaximander and Heraclitus, to whom several of the thinkers listed above are indebted. It extends even further into the past and undoubtedly into the future (such appears to be the general (en)closure of our thinking or even perception) as part of our way of thinking about, well, anything, even when this thinking is not seen or thematized in terms of difference. It is certainly (ontologically) older than and (operationally) usually precedes concepts, since concepts themselves and the concept(s) of concept are made possible only by engaging (and sometimes by repressing) difference and differences.

Consider, for example, Heidegger's famous appeal to the *difference* between (ontological) Being [*Sein*] and (ontic) beings [*Seiende*], crucial to his early ontological project in *Being and Time*. 'Ontological' is reserved by him only for the domain of Being and *Dasein* (a form of existence defined by its relation to Being), while 'ontic' relates to the existence of things around us, or as we, naively, conceive of such existence. This latter way of thinking is also a form of forgetting of Being, which, nonetheless, reveals itself also in this forgetting. Evidently difference is necessary for conceiving of Being as *different* from 'beings', and hence precedes, is 'older', than even Being, in the pre-logical rather than ontological (or ontical) sense.

Naturally, one should not see this precedence merely in naive terms. This particular difference may itself be seen as part of both the relation to Being and the forgetting of Being and, as such, needs to be conceived *differently* from more naive conceptions of difference, in particular between two different (given or present) things or what could be, naively, seen as such, say 'apples' and 'oranges'. In his later works, Heidegger would sometimes speak of 'dif-ference' at this type of juncture, or certain forms of 'sameness' pertaining to it, for example, the sameness of thinking (in turn, in Heidegger's special sense) and being, whereby 'sameness', too, needs to be radically rethought, in part as a form of difference. At the same type of juncture, Derrida (deconstructing Heidegger's earlier works, closer to Heidegger's later works) speaks of a 'difference' and a certain 'beyond-of-difference' as that which precedes or is 'older' than (again, pre-logically rather than ontologically) Heideggerian difference in still more radical terms of *différance*, arguably his most famous concept or 'neither term nor concept'. In both cases, however, we witness the rethinking and refiguring difference into something that is 'beyond difference' and, at least in Derrida's, if not Heidegger's (borderline) case, beyond anything, including, again, beyond any conceivable 'beyond'. These conceptions are ultimately unavailable to any naive conception of difference or any naive theoretical treatment, but only ultimately, since, as I said, within certain limits naive theories are not only applicable but are also unavoidable. In particular, they appear to be necessary in order to reach the limits that are 'beyond' both those of naive theory and of (the sophistication of) the metaphysics of presence, in other words, those limits that are beyond classical theories. Indeed both naive and classical theories may need to be exceeded reciprocally through a non-classical deployment of both, sometimes by using naive theories *against* classical ones.

To illustrate this point I shall consider Derrida's remarkable elaboration on Nietzsche, crucial to his analysis of writing in *Of Grammatology*. One might see Nietzsche as the first philosopher of difference, in the radical sense here in question. Hegel, while 'the last *philosopher* of the book', may well have been 'the first *thinker* of writing' (possibly in Derrida's radical sense) and, correlatively, of difference, as Derrida contends.[4] No longer a 'philosopher of the book', but a thinker and a philosopher of writing (in Derrida's sense), Nietzsche made difference the primary theme and vehicle, theoretical and strategic, of his philosophy and of his critical interventions. He also took it to a limit beyond that reached by Hegel or even Heidegger (this assessment may of course be a matter of reading, especially as concerns Heidegger's late works) and that thus far remains unsurpassed. Beyond (non-classically) entailing that which is beyond any concept of difference, but of which every concept of, and actual workings of, difference are effects, at this limit, 'difference' could no longer be figured or inscribed in terms of a single concept or even a single theme, or by means of a single text.[5] Both these non-classical conceptions – the irreducibly unknowable and the irreducibly, uncontrollably multiple – may be shown to be themselves linked or indeed correlative. Thus Nietzsche also exposed and actively deployed the irreducible differentiation and plurality of philosophical writing, including his own, or, in Derrida's terms, of the dissemination of writing, which makes writing into writing in Derrida's sense.[6] These concepts of writing and dissemination are thus also concepts (to the degree this denomination applies) of difference. This Nietzschean strategy was subsequently deployed by a number of key figures mentioned here, in particular Deleuze, Foucault, de Man, Derrida and Irigaray. As Derrida writes:

> *Radicalizing the concepts of* interpretation, per-
> spective, evaluation, difference, *and the 'empiri-*
> *cist' or nonphilosophical motifs that have*
> *constantly tormented philosophy throughout the*
> *history of the West, and besides had nothing but*
> *the inevitable weakness of being produced in the*
> *field of philosophy, Nietzsche, far from remaining*
> *simply (with Hegel and as Heidegger wished)*
> *within metaphysics [i.e. the metaphysics of pres-*
> *ence], contributed a great deal to the liberation of*
> *the signifier from its dependence or derivation*
> *with respect to the logos and the related concept*
> *of truth or the primary signified, in whatever sense*
> *that is understood. Reading, and therefore writing,*
> *the text were for Nietzsche 'originary' operations*
> *(I put that word within quotation marks for*
> *reasons to appear later [i.e. Derrida's deconstruc-*
> *tion of the concept of single or unique, absolute,*
> *origin]) with regard to a sense that they do not*
> *first have to transcribe or discover, which would*
> *not therefore be a truth signified in the original*
> *element and presence of the logos, as* topos
> noetos, *divine understanding, or the structure of*
> *an a priori necessity. To save Nietzsche from a*
> *reading of the Heideggerian type, it seems that we*
> *must above all not attempt to restore or make*
> *explicit a less naive 'ontology', composed of pro-*
> *found ontological intuitions acceding to some*
> *originary truth, an entire fundamentality hidden*
> *underneath the appearance of an empiricist or*
> *metaphysical text. The virulence of Nietzschean*
> *thought could not be more profoundly misunder-*
> *stood. On the contrary one must* accentuate *the*
> *'naiveté' of a breakthrough which cannot attempt*
> *a step outside of metaphysics, which* cannot *criti-*
> *cize metaphysics radically without still utilizing in*
> *a certain way, in a certain type or a certain style*
> *of* text, *propositions that, read within the philo-*
> *sophic [metaphysical] corpus, that is to say,*

according to Nietzsche ill-read or unread, have
always been and will always be 'naivetés', inco-
herent signs of an absolute appurtenance.
Therefore, rather than protect Nietzsche from the
Heideggerian reading, we should perhaps offer
him up to it completely, underwriting that interpre-
tation without reserve; in a certain way *and up to*
a certain point where, the content of the
Nietzschean discourse being almost lost for the
question of being, its form regains its absolute
strangeness, where his text finally invokes a dif-
ferent type of reading, more faithful to his type of
writing: Nietzsche has written what *he has*
written. He has written that writing – and first of
all his own – is not originally subordinate to the
logos and to truth. And that this subordination has
come into being *during the epoch whose meaning*
we must deconstruct.

(Derrida, 1997, 19)

Obviously, the very concepts of *interpretation, perspective* and *evaluation*, or of course *difference* itself, and even 'empiricist' are those of or are fundamentally linked to the motif of difference and its avatars, here especially multiplicity, ultimately as the irreducible, uncontainable plurality of Derrida's 'dissemination', often coupled to the irreducible singularity, uniqueness of each element of such multiplicity. By making writing no longer originally subordinate to the logos and to truth, Nietzsche showed difference to be irreducible and, furthermore, he showed that this irreducibility required taking the concept of difference to its radical limit of 'beyond-difference' and 'beyond-beyond-ness' – 'the-beyond-difference' of difference and 'beyond-the-beyond' of the beyond.' This limit equally defines Derrida's own 'differential' or, as the case may be, 'dif-

férantial' [*différantielle*] concepts or structures announced in *Of Grammatology* and related early texts – writing, différance, dissemination and so forth. This list cannot, by definition, be closed, by virtue of the dissemination that invades the network of these concepts or structures themselves, sometimes, again, giving each instant at which either one of them (or any given combination of them) is deployed the character of irreducible singularity. For the moment, my main concern is the complexity of the interaction, mutual deployment and, sometimes, a mutual critique or deconstruction of naive and metaphysical theories (or texts) as they appear in the deconstructive field, specifically as concerns the possibility of superceding metaphysics, or rather reaching a more radical field of critical and conceptual work.

First, there is a Heideggerian destruction and overcoming of metaphysics (of the ontic metaphysics of beings [*Seinde*]), at least in early Heidegger up to *Being and Time* and its ontological project, the ontology of Being [*Sein*]. This is what Derrida questions when he speaks of 'a less naive "ontology" [of Being], composed of profound ontological intuitions acceding to some originary truth', such as 'the truth of Being'. Beyond missing Nietzsche's (intervening) strategy and (non-classical) way of thinking (and indeed misunderstanding 'the virulence of Nietzschean thought'), ultimately this 'overcoming' of 'Heideggerian thought' remains within the metaphysics of presence. According to Derrida:

Heideggerian thought would reinstate rather than
destroy the instance of the logos and of the truth
of being as 'primum signatum': the transcendental
signified ('transcendental' in a certain sense, as
in the Middle Ages the transcendental – ens,
unum, verum, bonum – *was said to be the 'primum*

cognitum') implied by all categories or all deter-
mined significations, by all lexicons and all syntax,
and therefore by all linguistic signifiers, though
not to be identified simply with any one of those
signifiers; the transcendental signified allowing
itself to be precomprehended through each of
them, remaining irreducible to all the epochal
determination that it nonetheless makes possible,
and thus opening the history or the logos, and yet
itself being only through the logos, that is, being
nothing *before the logos and outside of it.*

(1997, 19–20; translation slightly modified)[7]

This reinstatement, however, becomes apparent only
through a deployment, specifically a deconstructive deployment, of Nietzsche's writing as writing in Derrida's radically
differential or différantial sense of the term. The reinstatement takes place 'in this direction . . . but only in this direction, for read otherwise [e.g. short of reaching the field of
writing in Derrida's sense], the Nietzschean demolition
remains dogmatic and, like all [unproblematized] reversal, a
captive of that metaphysical edifice that it professes to
overthrow' (1997, 19). By the same token, such a reading
could never be sufficient to leave the limits of Heidegger's
critique of Nietzsche, whose conclusions would remain
'irrefutable' short of reading Nietzsche's writing as writing
in Derrida's sense. This may also be the primary reason why
a rigorous traversal of the Heideggerian reading, appealed
to by Derrida, is necessary.

In any event, we may differentiate the two types of
overcoming of the metaphysics of presence. One, such as
that employed by Heidegger, retains or reinstates it at a
more profound (in either sense) level. The other, such as
that of Nietzsche (or Derrida's own), while retaining the
metaphysics of presence or even naive theory within

certain limits (and while more rigorously establishing these
limits), also uses it – it appears impossible to do it otherwise, specifically without a deployment of naive theory – to
reach a more radical, non-classical, regime of difference
or writing, including theoretical writing. As Derrida also
points out in *Of Grammatology* (his specific contexts are
Louis Hjelmslev, on the one hand, and Edmund Husserl, on
the other):

It is to escape falling back into this naive [scientif-
icist] objectivism . . . that is, another unperceived
and unconfessed metaphysics [such as that found
in Hjelmslev's school] . . . that I refer here to a
[metaphysical] transcendentality [such as
Husserl's] that I elsewhere put into question. It is
because I believe that there is a short of and a
beyond of transcendental criticism. To see to it
that the beyond does not return to the within is to
recognize in the contortion the necessity of a
pathway [parcours]. This pathway must leave a
track in the text. Without that track, abandoned to
the simple content of its conclusions, the ultra-
transcendental [e.g. deconstructive] text will so
closely resemble the precritical text as to be
indistinguishable from it.

(1997, 61)

Elsewhere, in considering Hegel, Derrida speaks of a difference that is both infinitesimal and radical ('Différance',
1984, 14).[8] (We may observe that 'difference' itself continues to play a major role and requires a non-classical
understanding at this meta-theoretical level.) One must rigorously establish the difference here in question, in part by
using various forms of metaphysical theories and texts,
including those of naive theories (and re-delimiting their

fields of functioning along the way), against each other, and against themselves. This is what Nietzsche's, ultimately nowhere naive, 'naiveté' accomplishes.

Now, what is this difference from the point of view of difference itself? Roughly, or naively, it is in the non-classical impossibility of an ultimate ontology, however profound intuitions of such ontology may be, as they are in the case of Heideggerian ontology of Being or yet more profound conceptions of his latter works, which may never escape it even as they also reach the ultimate limit of this possibility. The non-classical 'beyond-difference' within difference and (since difference and its avatars remain crucial concepts here) correlatively, 'beyond-the-beyond' within the beyond suspend this possibility irreducibly. In other words, Heidegger's aim is to overcome the naive or (less naive, but never sufficiently profound) ontic 'ontology' with a more profound and more rigorous ontology of Being, which, however concealed or even inconceivable in all of its specificity, remains an instance of the logos and the metaphysical truth, according to Derrida's argument under discussion. By contrast, rather than overcoming metaphysics, Nietzsche deploys naive theory, as well as more profound metaphysical theories or indeed intuitions, in order to establish, with an equal and, it follows, ultimately greater analytical rigour, the impossibility of such or ultimately any conceivable ontology, any ultimate ontology of the inconceivable included. Nietzsche does not miss or arbitrarily renounce ontology, either naive (such as ontic) or profound, such as that Heidegger pursues, but argues that such ontology is, *in principle*, excluded at the ultimate level of analysis. As will be seen, a similar situation obtains in quantum mechanics in Bohr's interpretation.

This argument is what Heidegger's reading of Nietzsche misses; this possibility, the possibility of this impossibility, that which is ultimately missed by his philos-ophy (here one can make a broader claim), from *Being and Time* to *Time and Being*, even though much of his thought should have directed him otherwise. There is no beyond metaphysics because, in the first place, there is no beyond or no 'beyond-of-the-beyond'. Or, reciprocally, to assume or postulate any beyond or beyond-of-the-beyond, however complex or profound, however non-metaphysical (vis-à-vis any more naive metaphysics), could only be another form of metaphysics. Metaphysics, however, even naive metaphysics, can be deployed to intervene in it and most crucially so as make a step not beyond, a step beyond and not beyond, to discover this situation and the non-beyond-ness that is the beyond of all beyond.

Elements of naive theory

It is not my aim here to offer a comprehensive naive theory of difference, although one can build such a theory out of four basic types or concepts of difference that I shall consider. My goal is to introduce these conceptions as entrance points for my main discussion and use them with regard to the irreducibility of the naive theory of difference. These concepts are the 'differentiation' difference; the 'alterity' difference; the 'multiplicity' difference; and the 'singularity' difference, a form of the 'multiplicity' difference. (From here on I shall use hyphenation, e.g. differentiation-difference.)

The first, differentiation-difference, refers primarily to a transformation of a given entity, or to 'the same differing (from) itself', to use Heidegger's terms. Heidegger would, of course, give this type of phrase a meaning that reaches beyond any naive theory. Derrida, in part by deconstructing Heidegger's conception, arrives at his non-classical concept of the same as différance (with an 'a'), which endlessly or at least interminably differs from and defers itself. We exceed a naive theory (we cannot, again, transcend it and need not to) by rigorously exploring the limits of such terms, concepts or propositions, along various (classical or non-classical) lines of investigation. Reciprocally, sometimes we need to move beyond the limits of naive theory in order to use it. It may be observed that differentiation-difference philosophically defines differential calculus in mathematics, which, further extended to Riemannean mathematics (which also extends differentiation-difference to multiplicity-difference), was a major inspiration for Gilles Deleuze's concept of difference, especially as developed in *Difference and Repetition*.

Alterity-difference would refer to that which is the other of a given entity. If differentiation-difference may be seen in conceptually 'temporal' terms of change, alterity-difference is conceptually more 'spatial' (using these terms naively).[9] Differentiation-difference is also often linked to or emerges as continuity (or, often via continuity, as causality), as in its manifestation in differential calculus, or in Deleuze and (differently) in Irigaray. By contrast, alterity-difference could be more naturally linked to discontinuity (and the lack of causality), as in quantum physics. The Kantian 'things-in-themselves' (even if naively read) is arguably the most immediate model of alterity-difference and, certainly, is something that extends from naive alterity-difference. A (perhaps) more radical and, at least at its limit, non-classical model could be Levinas's concept of radical alterity of the (ethical) Other (*Autrui*).[10] Freud's 'unconscious', Lacan's 'the Real', several of Blanchot's key concepts, Derrida's différance (which proceeds via Levinas, Freud, Lacan and Bataille), Lyotard's 'differend' (which has complex links to Levinas's conceptuality) and, with more emphasis on discontinuity, de Man's allegory are all examples of conceptions of difference and of 'beyond-

difference' that have fundamental dimensions of alterity-difference.

Levinas's conception also suggests a helpful 'ethical' or 'ethical-political' model of all four types of difference considered here, for the moment, a naive model, to be sure, but one that could be given a rigorous classical and ultimately non-classical meaning. If differentiation-difference relates primarily to the One, the 'I', alterity-difference would refer to the Other, ultimately to the singular, unique Other. Once these considerations are extended to that which would be the Other of both the 'I' and the Other, multiplicity-difference would arise. Ethically, this extension, a certain 'third-ness' to Levinas's Otherness, appears to be inevitable, thus establishing certain (more) 'political' dimensions of the 'ethical' (the reverse is obviously true, as well). In so far as the singularity of any given relation within the multiple is retained (it is irreducibly linked to alterity-difference), multiplicity-difference is singularity-difference. The latter thus could be double or multiple as well, and, in all rigour, may always need to be extended beyond any third-ness, or any containable multiplicity, towards something like Derrida's dissemination. These connections between multiplicity and singularity, either along more specifically ethico-political lines or in more general conceptual terms, are crucial to (but also differently configured by) Deleuze, especially in his earlier works, such as *Difference and Repetition*, and Derrida, in this case, especially in his later works, and de Man. On the other hand, Derrida's dissemination or différance-dissemination (a complex form of multiplicity-difference, in which other forms of difference here considered are engaged in a complex interplay) becomes crucial from the outset of these works, and thus also establishes a crucial link between his earlier and later writing. Heterogeneity-difference could be another related rubric, especially in connection with Bataille's work, crucial for Derrida as well, including this particular context. When multiplicity-difference is combined with more continuous forms of differentiation-difference, certain conceptions of plenitudes emerge, of which both Deleuze's and Irigaray's conceptions of difference, or earlier those of Spinoza and Leibniz (and perhaps, along certain lines, that of Hegel), would be examples or extensions.[11] By contrast, the more heterogeneous conceptions of multiplicity-difference found in the work of Bataille, Levinas, Derrida and de Man irreducibly involve singularity-difference, although they are not restricted to it and thus in turn introduce a certain heterogeneity of singularity-difference and more connected forms of multiplicity-difference.

While, however, it is tempting and often useful to define the work of these figures in terms of a given type of difference, or a determinable combination of different types of difference, it is difficult and ultimately impossible to do so. Some figures crucial to the history of the concept of difference or of 'beyond-difference' were not invoked in the above elaborations for these very reasons – Hegel, Heidegger, Nietzsche and Foucault, or for that matter Descartes, or Plato and Aristotle, leaving aside pre-Socratics or many literary figures that may be mentioned here. While Heraclitus could be seen as a philosopher of differentiation-difference, the latter would hardly suffice to define his thinking concerning difference and a possible 'beyond-difference', in spite or because of the interpretive problems his fragments pose. Many thinkers here mentioned appeal to his work as a primary example of different types of difference, or particular combinations of such types. Heidegger speaks of Hölderlin, Hegel and Nietzsche as the three great Heracliteans (and he sees all four as precursors of his own thought). But could one exclude Kant (or Fichte and Schelling) from this Heraclitean lineage or,

keeping the difference in mind, Leibniz and Spinoza, or Hume, or indeed Descartes, from this genealogy? Heraclitus is certainly a philosopher of difference, however conceived. But then, tempting and common as the juxtaposition may be, could one see Parmenides, the philosopher of the One, as a philosopher of identity, of the absolute Oneness, alone, even given that, if there could be one such philosopher, it would likely be Parmenides?[12] We can only trace balances of difference and non-difference, or what is and is not naive, classical and non-classical, balances that are often further shifting – differentiated – from one point to another in each of these cases.

Classical and non-classical theory, classical and non-classical (theory of) difference

As here understood, all non-classical theories entail, as their constitutive part, a non-classical theory of difference – of a concept of difference that is beyond difference and beyond anything, any form of beyondness included. This concept defines the non-classicality of non-classical theories, and their manifest – representable – *difference* from classical theories. Indeed this difference is *classical* on the definition adopted here.

I define classical theories as the theories that consider their principle objects as, at least in principle (it may not be possible in practice), available to conceptualization and, often, to direct representation in terms of particular properties of these objects, their behaviour, and the relationships between them. This availability defines such objects as objects of classical theories, since these objects may be idealized from some other objects, whose other properties are disregarded, in the way, for example, classical physics abstracts certain key physical properties (e.g. mass, momentum, or energy) from other properties (e.g. colour and shape, in most cases) of material bodies it studies.

Classical physics and specifically classical mechanics, the part of classical physics that deals with the motion of individual physical objects or systems composed of such objects, is or may be interpreted as such a theory. It fully accounts, at least in principle, for its objects and their behaviour on the basis of physical concepts and abstracted or idealized measurable quantities of material objects corresponding to them, such as the 'position' and 'momentum' of material bodies. While, however, in general an idealization, within its proper limits classical physics offers an excellent approximation of the behaviour of material bodies in nature. Rigorously grounded mathematically in differential calculus and its extensions, classical mechanics may also be seen as a classical theory of difference, primarily of the differentiation-difference type. Classical statistical physics, dealing with the behaviour of multiplicities of individual mechanical objects of the differentiation-difference type would be a multiplicity-difference theory of difference. Most of classical physics, extending to Einstein's relativity (a borderline case), may be seen as combining these two types of difference. Riemann's theory of manifolds, and differential topology and differential geometry, based on it (as is Einstein's general relativity, his theory of gravity), may be seen as extensions of differential calculus, including as concerns bringing together mathematically differentiation and multiplicity, differentiation-difference and multiplicity-difference. This combination makes both differential calculus and Riemann's theory central for Deleuze's work, but one might also argue that, ultimately, it makes Deleuze's conception of difference classical.[13] Differentiation-difference and multiplicity-difference may, as in quantum physics, also be taken to and combined within a non-classical regime,

which involves a deployment of a non-classical version of alterity-difference and thus converts mutiplicity-difference into singularity-difference. On the other hand, alterity-difference is found in classical physics, too, but it may be treated as classical there.

The (epistemologically) classical nature of classical physics is primarily due to the fact that it is a refinement of our perceptual and representational machinery, which appears to be classical. This point was often stressed by Niels Bohr and Werner Heisenberg, and was anticipated by Kant's argument concerning the relationships between the conditions of Newtonian physics and the general conditions of the phenomenal experience vs. a possibly noumenal nature of the actual physical or even mental world. It is a separate issue how far toward non-classical limits Kant's alterity-difference reaches. Classical physics has often served as a primary model for epistemologically classical theories elsewhere, which determines its significance for the present argument, just as the non-classical nature of quantum physics determines its significance for this argument.

In contrast to classical theories, the *ultimate* 'objects' of non-classical theories are irreducibly, in practice and in principle, inaccessible, unknowable, unrepresentable, inconceivable, untheorizable and so forth by any means that are or ever will be available to us, for example, as objects in any conceivable sense. Hence they cannot be assigned any conceivable attributes, such as those conceived by analogy with objects of classical theories. For example, it may not be, and in Bohr's interpretation is not, possible to assign the standard attributes of the objects and motions of classical physics to those of quantum physics. Thus it may no longer even be possible to speak of objects or motions, which, however, does not imply that nothing exists or, as is sometimes argued, that everything stands still, which is of course itself another classical physical attribute of the behaviour of material bodies.[14]

It may be useful to consider this situation in terms of classical vs. non-classical concepts of chance, defined by the two respective epistemological perspectives in question. The non-classical character of chance defines twentieth-century thinking about it, mathematical-scientific (for example, in addition to quantum physics, in post-Darwinian biology and genetics) and philosophical, specifically in Nietzsche, Bataille, Blanchot, Lacan, de Man and Derrida.

Classically, chance or, more accurately, the appearance of chance is seen as arising from our insufficient (and perhaps, in practice, unavailable) knowledge of a total configuration of forces involved and, hence, of the lawful necessity thus postulated behind a lawless chance event. If this configuration becomes available, or if it could be made available in principle (it may, again, not ever be available in practice), the chance character of the event would disappear. Chance would reveal itself to be a product of the play of forces that is, at least in principle, calculable by man, or at least by God. The classical view of probability is based on this idea: in practice, we have only partially available, incomplete information about chance events, which are nonetheless determined by, in principle, a complete architecture of necessity behind them. This architecture itself may or may not be seen as ever accessible in full (or even partial) measure. The *presupposition* of its existence is, however, essential for and defines the classical view as causal and, on the definition given earlier, realist. On this point, classical (there is no other) reality and causality come together, although it is the assumption of such an architecture as such, whether causal or not, or, conversely, a suspension of this assumption, that defines respectively the classicality and non-classicality of a given theory. One might also express the point by saying that, when classical theories involve alterity-difference, they configure this difference classically. Subtle and complex as they may be, all scientific theories of chance and probability prior to quantum theory and many beyond it, such as chaos theory, and most philosophical theories of chance are of the type just described. In short, they are *classical*, and in so far as they relate to multiplicities, they represent the classical multiplicity-difference.

The *non-classical* understanding of chance is fundamentally different by virtue of the fact that it uses the concept of alterity-difference in its non-classical limit. Non-classical chance is irreducible not only in practice (which may be the case classically as well) but also, and most fundamentally, in principle. There is no knowledge, in practice or in principle, that is or will ever be, or could in principle be, available to us and would allow us to eliminate chance and replace it with the picture of necessity behind it. Nor, however, can one postulate such a (causal/lawful) economy as unknowable (to any being, individual or collective), but existing, in and by itself, outside our engagement with it. This qualification (correlative to the suspension of realism at the ultimate level of description) is crucial. For, as I explained above, some forms of the classical understanding of chance allow for and are indeed defined by this type of (realist) assumption. By contrast, non-classical chance is not only unexplainable in practice and in principle but is also irreducible in practice and in principle. It is irreducible to any necessity, knowable or unknowable. It is, in David Bohm's words, *irreducibly* lawless (1995, 73). To cite de Man's elaboration in 'Shelley Disfigured': '[Shelley's] *The Triumph of Life* warns us that nothing, whether deed, word, thought or text, ever happens in relation, positive or negative, to anything that preceded, follows, or exists elsewhere, but only as a random event whose power, like the power of death, is due to the randomness of its occurrence' (de Man, 1990, 122). The formulation reflects and defines a *non-classical* concept of chance, correlative to the irreducible lawlessness or singularity of individual entities, such as the random and discontinuous events one encounters in quantum mechanics, a non-classical form of multiplicity-difference as singularity-difference. Quantum-mechanical multiplicities are, accordingly, also multiplicities of singularities, which makes the multiplicity-difference involved non-classical.

Thus, non-classically, the suspension of realism entails the impossibility of not only *describing* physical properties of quantum objects and processes, but also the impossibility of *ascribing* such properties to them and the impossibility of applying any hitherto available concept of reality to quantum objects themselves. Indeed, in the absence of classical reality (and perhaps there is no other reality) one can hardly speak of causality. The point was well expressed by Erwin Schrödinger, who, like Einstein, never accepted quantum mechanics, to the creation of which he contributed so much, as earlier did Einstein. 'If a classical [physical] state does not exist, it can hardly change causally', Schrödinger said in his famous 1935 'cat paradox' paper (1983, 154). Causality, however conceived, is merely one such attribute, as are 'change', 'process' and so forth, or their opposites, such as 'permanence' or 'system'.

Ultimately, no concept of reality that is, or ever will be, available to us might be applicable to our description of the 'quantum world', or to the 'objects' in question in non-classical theories elsewhere. The quotation marks become obligatory, since the terms, however conceived, of this sentence ('quantum', 'world', 'object', 'things', even if seen as 'things-in-themselves') may be no more applicable than those of the preceding sentence. 'Ultimately', however, is in turn a crucial qualifier here, since all these terms and classical theories or ways of thinking in general apply and are extraordinarily effective across a broad spectrum of theoretical thinking and other human endeavours, or indeed in everyday life. They are also necessary for the functioning of non-classical theories, since the latter must work with the classical (knowable) effects and, hence, rely on classical ways of thinking in handling these effects, even though their (non-classical) 'efficacity' remains *ultimately* unknowable.

I use the term 'efficacity' in its dictionary sense of power and agency producing effects but, in this case, without the possibility of ascribing this agency causality. This point is especially significant in quantum theory and in Bohr's work, but equally so in Bataille, Althusser, Foucault, Lacan (especially in the case of the register of what he calls 'the Real') and Derrida. Indeed, the very use of the term efficacity here corresponds to the French '*l'efficace*', deployed in Louis Althusser's reading of Marx, and then, in part following Althusser, by Derrida who appeals to the efficacity of *différance* (difference, temporality, spatiality and so forth would not be seen as effects of this efficacity). Foucault's 'power' could also be seen as this type of efficacity and, hence, is a concept of 'difference' (its place between classical and non-classical conceptuality would require a separate discussion).[15] Bohr appeals to quantum-mechanical 'effects' throughout his writing (e.g. 'the peculiar individuality [i.e. singularity] of typical quantum effects'). Such effects themselves (for example, 'wave' effects or 'particle' effects) are seen as classical and specifically as manifest in our (classical) observational technology. By contrast, the efficacity of these effects, defined by the (quantum) interaction between quantum objects and measuring instruments, is as irreducibly unknowable as are quantum objects, including as 'objects' or as 'quantum'. In Bataille's words, 'it would be impossible to speak of unknowledge [ultimately even as 'unknowledge'] as such, while we can speak of its effects'.[16] Reciprocally, 'it would not be possible to seriously speak of unknowledge independently of its effects' (Bataille, 1962, 219). The conjunction of both propositions equally defines Bataille's and quantum-mechanical epistemology, as well as a number of other non-classical or near non-classical conceptions, just mentioned.[17]

It follows that, in Bohr's words, 'in quantum mechanics [as complementarity] we are not dealing with an arbitrary renunciation of a more detailed analysis of atomic phenomena, but with a recognition that such an analysis is, *in principle,* excluded' (1998, 2: 62; Bohr's emphasis).[18] This impossibility, however, does not preclude, but instead enables, a rigorous analysis of the effects of this unknowable efficacity. Thus we cannot ascribe conventional properties (such as 'position' and 'momentum' of classical mechanics) or any physical properties describing their spatial-temporal behaviour to quantum objects qua quantum objects, such as elementary particles, which we now see as the ultimate constituents of matter. Being a particle or, conversely, a wave (quantum objects are capable of producing both types of effects) would itself be defined by a set of such properties. Accordingly, the terms 'particle' and 'wave' cannot be applied to quantum objects otherwise than provisionally (Bohr, 1998, 1: 56–7). Nor, again, can we apply the term 'quantum' or 'objects', or, ultimately, any conceivable term or concept. Nor, thus, can we speak of 'the quantum world' itself (for example, as 'the quantum world'), but only of the *effects* of the interaction between 'quantum objects' and measuring instruments, which is the ultimate efficacity of these effects. (It also follows of course that the term 'efficacity', or 'effects', is as provisional as any other term in these circumstances.) This interaction is itself quantum (and thus depends on the

quantum aspects of the constitution of the measuring instruments) and hence is unavailable to classical or, again, any treatment, even though the effects of this interaction are available to classical physical and epistemological treatment. All quantum-mechanical predictions are enabled by this interaction, even though quantum theory can only predict the outcome of experiments (effects) rather than describe the physical behaviour of quantum objects, in the way classical physics describes that of classical objects.

As a result, the role of technology becomes constitutive and irreducible in quantum mechanics (and, by implication, giving the term 'technology' its broader meaning, closer to Derrida's writing) and in non-classical theories elsewhere, while it may be seen as merely auxiliary and ultimately dispensable in classical physics. Indeed, one could define non-classical theories through the irreducible role of technology in them and, conversely, classical theories by the auxiliary and ultimately dispensable functioning of technology there. By contrast, in 'classical' situations the role of technology is, at least in principle, reducible, as in the case of measurement in classical physics, since measuring instruments play only an auxiliary role there so as to allow us to speak of the independent properties and behaviour of classical objects.

A more phenomenological (rather than 'technological') example of this situation is Emmanuel Levinas's phenomenology of ethical otherness, a difference of the alterity-difference type, of the relationships to what he calls the Other [*Autrui*], which has been the subject of many recent discussions. In a rough outline, following primarily his *Totality and Infinity* (1961), arguably his most influential work, Levinas's phenomenology and epistemology of the radical alterity of the Other may be viewed as follows. This radical alterity, the emergence of the (effect of the) Other in, or even on the horizon of, the phenomenal on the radar of our thought, radically restructures the latter by the power of its effects, especially in the ethical context. Indeed one may see the effects in question as the opening of the possibility of ethics, according to Levinas. The ultimate locus of the Levinasian alterity may remain indeterminate, rather than, for example, merely identified, as is commonly (mis)understood, with *others* (other individuals, cultures and so forth), even though the role of the latter may be decisive in the emergence of these effects. Accordingly, some form of 'technology' would have to emerge, more phenomenological in character but ultimately material in nature.

The ultimate objects of non-classical theories are not their objects in so far as one means by 'objects' anything that can actually be described by such a theory. They are beyond anything a theory that deals with them could approach and beyond any conceivable conception, any conceivable conception of 'beyondness' included. This is what makes any non-classical theory defined by a non-classical theory or concept of difference, in so far as even the term 'difference' could apply. At the same time, however, the efficacious impact of such objects on what the theory can describe or at least relate to and account for is crucial, and this impact cannot be explained classically, which is what makes a non-classical theorizing of the situation necessary in such cases. The character of the (knowable) effects in question irreducibly precludes the knowledge or conception, specifically on any model of what is knowable, of their ultimate efficacity or, at least, the ultimate nature of their efficacity. Thus the (irreducibly) unknowable itself in question is no more available to non-classical theories than to classical theories. Non-classical theories, however, allow us rigorously to infer the existence of this unknowable (rather than merely imagine its existence) on the basis of the phenomena that they consider, and to explain its significance for what we can know, and utilize the (manifest) effects of this interaction, while this cannot be done by means of classical theories.

It also follows, however, that non-classical epistemology does not imply that what, in certain circumstances, gives rise to the effects in question does not exist. The point is that this efficacity or the corresponding 'materiality' (which also designates something that exists when we are not there to observe or otherwise interact with it) of whatever we can observe, represent, conceive of, formalize and so forth is inconceivable in any terms that are or perhaps will ever be available to us. Derrida speaks of materiality as a radical alterity of *différance* (*Positions*, 1988, 64). Naturally, 'existence' and 'nonexistence', or 'materiality' (or, again, 'efficacity') are among these terms, along with the possibility or impossibility to 'conceive' of it, or 'possibility' or 'impossibility', or 'it' and 'is', to begin with.[19]

Non-classical theories change both the nature of the unknowable itself, making it irreducible, and of the relationships, including 'difference', between the unknowable and what we can possibly know, in so far as the ultimate nature of these relationships is itself subject to the same regime of the irreducibly unknowable. It cannot, accordingly, be seen in terms of causality, continuity, any conceivable form of connection and so forth, or their opposites. From this viewpoint, theoretical economies, such as those developed in the work of the figures here mentioned, are not incomprehensible (obscure, mystical, and so forth), as some of their critics contend. If anything, they are, in Bohr's words, 'rational generalizations' of classical conceptions, such as causality or reality, and indeed any mysticism or obscurantism is deeply foreign to them (1998, 2: 41). Non-classical theories do, however, deal with that which is irreducibly incomprehensible, unknowable, inconceivable and so forth in the sense here outlined, while at the same time shaping the efficacity of anything we can possibly know. This unknowable is mysterious in that it is beyond any available or conceivable comprehension, although not mystical in so far as it cannot be assigned any mystical, unknowable agency governing it, such as, say, the God of mystical or negative theory, anymore than it can be assigned any other classical character, idealist or materialist. All such conceptions, strictly theological (negative or positive) or not, in short all classical theories, share the ontotheological determination of the ultimate efficacity of knowledge. Classical theories do involve things that are unknowable and inconceivable to them. They are, however, not concerned with, and indeed cannot conceive of, the irreducibly unknowable or its effects (as the unknowable) upon the knowable. The unknowable, if allowed, is either ontotheologized by them or is placed strictly outside their limits (and, as it were, philosophically mastered so as to shelter the knowable by this placement), rather than being seen as a constitutive part of knowledge.

This point is crucial to Derrida's reading of Kant in 'Economimesis', which reading, thus, becomes an investigation of the possibility of non-classical difference, exteriority, alterity and so forth, and, no less crucially, of how the knowable comes about through the ultimately unknowable non-classical process defined through this possibility or indeed necessity (1981). This process conforms more closely to Derrida's *différance* and its satellite structures, or related conceptions in Nietzsche, Bohr, Bataille, Lacan and de Man. Similarly, Levinas places the radical alterity of the Other [*Autrui*] in the position of something that fundamentally shapes and even defines, or at least is the ultimate efficacity of subjectivity, rather than something that is absolutely excluded from it, is an *absolute* other of it. In other words, as crucial a move as Kantian exteriority or alterity-difference, such as that of 'things-in-themselves', was (and I shall return to its historical significance later), we must take this type of exteriority, in part via Hegel, to its rigorous non-classical limit. If not spirit, *Geist* or perhaps the letter of Hegel's philosophy, what can help us is the *nature* (in either sense of the double genitive) of quantum mechanics.

This point is equally, but for a different reason, crucial to Deleuze's argument in *Difference and Repetition*, when he juxtaposes the approach of Niels Henric Abel and Evariste Galois (he might have also mentioned Joseph-Louis Lagrange and Karl Friedrich Gauss) in mathematics to that of Kant. Abel and Galois introduced the 'radical reversal in the problem–solution relation'. Roughly, they replaced the 'Kantian' relation, of the alterity-difference type, of exteriority between a given problem and a potential solution (or conversely, insolvability) with a differential process of the differentiation-difference type, which may in fact be argued to be more 'Hegelian'. Deleuze would be likely to see it as closer to Leibniz than to Hegel, who may, however, be closer on this point than Deleuze suggests, although Hegel may be ultimately closer to the non-classical view of the situation than Leibniz, if not Deleuze. In any event, in this process, which also combines difference and repetition (in Deleuze's sense), a reformulation, or a sequence of successive reformulations of the problem 'progressively specify the fields of solvability in such a way that "the statement contains the seeds of the solution"'. Deleuze sees this type of approach as 'a more considerable revolution than the Copernican' and as 'inaugurat[ing] a new *Critique of Pure Reason*, in particular going beyond Kantian "*extrinsicism*"'. In view of the fact that 'this [e.g. thus redefined] non-knowledge is no longer a negative or an insufficiency but a rule or something *to be learned* which corresponds to a fundamental dimension of the object . . . the whole pedagogical relation is transformed – a new Meno – but many other things along with it, including knowledge and sufficient reason . . . With Abel and Galois, the mathematical theory of problems is able to fulfill all its properly dialectical requirements, and to break the circle in which it was caught' (Deleuze, 1994, 180). The reference to Plato's *Meno* is singularly appropriate here. The dialogue deals with the diagonal of a square, the first irrational quantity ever discovered. This discovery led to a crisis of Greek mathematics and philosophy alike, a kind of 'Gödel's incompleteness theorem' of Greek mathematics, establishing, to give a generalization (schematic, rather than fully rigorous, but applicable to both of these findings), the insufficiency of a given system of axioms to ascertain either truth or falsity of all propositions derivable from those axioms. The argument is further developed in Deleuze and Guattari's *A Thousand Plateaus* and elsewhere in Deleuze. It is of further significance that Deleuze (rightly) sees 'differential calculus' both as a crucial mathematical or indeed philosophical expression of the situation and as a model of the dynamics involved, specifically as the dynamics of difference and, interactively, repetition in Deleuze's sense of the latter term (1994, 179–82).

On this point, Hegel's argument in the first, greater, *Logic* and elsewhere in his works, especially the *Phenomenology*, or Kant's argument in *The Critique of Pure Reason* (or again elsewhere), or for that matter Deleuze's argument just considered, must be re-examined. Abel's and Galois's work in mathematics (algebra and analysis), the discovery (equally relevant here) of non-Euclidian geometry, first in the work of Gauss (who made momentous related contributions to algebra and analysis as well), and Lagrange's work on algebra, differential calculus and mechanics, to which he gave its properly analytic form in terms of differential equations, which we still use now,

were all contemporary to the emergence of Hegel's philosophy. These developments may also be seen as the opening of the possibility of non-classical dimensions of mathematics or even of classical physics.[20] Lagrange's (re)formulation of differential calculus became central for Hegel's logic and his analysis of the concept of continuity in general there. The re-examination in question would proceed along non-classical lines, closer to those of the epistemology of Derrida's *différance* or de Man's allegory (or their precursors in the work of Nietzsche and Bataille), or Bohr's epistemology of quantum mechanics (in this case applied at the meta-theoretical level), whereby more 'Kantian' 'extrinsicism' and more 'Hegelian' interiorization of exteriority intermix so as to reach non-classical 'exteriority' and 'difference'. As I said, Deleuze's argument just cited and his philosophy overall may ultimately remain classical, and specifically grounded in the notion of continuity in the broader sense, but are ultimately modelled on differential calculus and its extensions, especially in Riemann's work.[21] By contrast, in other cases just mentioned neither 'continuity' nor 'discontinuity', nor any other conceivable notion, such as, again, 'difference', could apply at the ultimate level, although, as will be seen, Derrida's *différance* may still retain too much differential continuity. This assessment of Deleuze (or, even more so, of Derrida) may need further qualification, no less than that of Kant's and Hegel's work as concerns their classicality or non-classicality (in either direction, discontinuity or continuity). It may, accordingly, be more prudent to leave it at the level of a question, rather than to make a definitive claim. Certainly, one should not underestimate Abel's and Galois's revolution in question, or Deleuze's own insights here, even where they proceed strictly along the classical lines of continuity, and not only on account of their alternative to 'extrinsicism'.

Beyond Bohr's epistemology of quantum mechanics, elements of non-classical epistemology are found in most theories of difference invoked in this essay: Nietzsche's epistemology, on which he bases his radical critique of classical (in either sense) philosophy; Bataille's epistemology, sometimes developed by him under the rubric of general economy; Blanchot's understanding of literature; Levinas's epistemology of ethical alterity and singularity; Lacan's epistemology of the Real; Foucault's economy of power; Deleuze's conceptuality of difference and repetition, or related conceptions developed in his later works, both with Guattari and on his own; Derrida's epistemology (of *différance* and related formations and structures, such as trace, dissemination, supplementarity, writing and so forth, or of conceptions, such as 'singularity', that he develops in his later works); Lyotard's concept of 'differend'; and de Man's epistemology of allegory. At least some non-classical elements are found in Kant's and Hegel's philosophy, as well as in the work of earlier figures, beginning with the pre-Socratics. The degree and aspects of non-classicality or, conversely, classicality of all the theories just mentioned is a matter of complex interpretive decisions.

The trajectories leading to non-classical limits may in turn be different and have been different, sometimes significantly different, in different cases, such as those cited here. They extend from what we have to confront in physical nature, as in the case of quantum mechanics, or sometimes in mathematics, to where literary works and philosophical argument, or political situations may lead us (it may be shown that our confrontations with nature or mathematics are not free of philosophical or political, and sometimes literary considerations either). As Nietzsche observes in *The Birth of Tragedy*, while meditating on Socrates's case: 'the periphery of the circle of science [in the broader sense of German *Wissenschaft*] has *an infinite number of points* . . . from which one gazes into what defies illumination [and sees] how logic coils up at these boundaries and finally bites it own tail' (1996, 97–8, emphasis added). Nietzsche, at this early juncture, speaks of 'art as salvation and remedy' (1996, 98). This, as Nietzsche came to realize rather quickly, is hardly possible. If anything, art may take us to these limits. At these limits what defies illumination can no longer be gazed at, even though it shapes what we can gaze upon, either with our actual physical eyes (as in the case of quantum physics, which would indeed *see* the eye as an observational technology) or our mind's eye.

As the preceding discussion suggests, however, the alternatives are not as desperate as it might seem, as Nietzsche's own work and the work of most other figures here discussed would demonstrate. First, one could also pursue different approaches to and different points 'at the periphery of the circle of science' that Nietzsche invoked, which may take place even within a work of a single author, as in the case of several figures here discussed, Nietzsche, among them. Secondly, one can also engage with an analysis of the very nature (unavoidably complex and diverse) of such limits, which analysis is, in principle, interminable. One might also pursue both or all three types of projects jointly in view of their reciprocity, which pursuit indeed takes place in the work of most figures here mentioned. The possibility of new knowledge often depends on our exploration of those limits. Finally, most crucially, new knowledge, new (there may be no other) *classical* knowledge and even illumination are made possible and enhanced by non-classical ways of thinking and only by them, in so far as only the latter enable us to explore the architecture of the effects of non-classical efficacities, or the architecture of the information these effects provide.[22]

Kant redux

We can now see why Kant's conceptualization of 'difference' and 'alterity' was so crucial a move. I would argue these terms to be most fitting here, even those that are not Kant's and may not be usually applied to Kant, in contrast to (leaving aside obvious post-Nietzschean references) Hegel, or indeed Leibniz and Spinoza, against whom, or away from whom and closer to Hume, Kant makes his key moves. But Kant also makes these move *from them*, and *via them*, takes them as his points of departure, especially Leibniz, to the point of famously making some of his contemporaries attribute key elements of Kant's philosophy to Leibniz. Fundamentally linked to discontinuity, a discontinuity more discontinuous than discontinuity itself (e.g. any form of discontinuity we could conceive of), non-classical difference and non-classical theory also *continue* Kant's work even though and because they also break away from him, discontinue this work, sometimes radically, along other lines or even this line (itself of course a concept of continuity). If one is permitted a little trivial pun here, they are dis-Kantinuous Kantinuities. Nietzsche, no friend of Kant, understood the situation best, even though it was also Nietzsche who made the first truly radical move toward a non-classical theory of difference and, thus, also of anything else he considered. Or it might well have been because Nietzsche has done so. Astutely 'sandwiching' Kant between Hegel and Leibniz and their tremendous question marks, Nietzsche speaks of '*Kant's tremendous question mark* that he placed after the concept of "causality" – without, like Hume, doubting its legitimacy altogether. Rather, Kant began cautiously to delimit the realm within which this concept makes sense (and to this day we are not done with this fixing of limits)' (1974, emphasis added).[23] The same, indeed correlatively or interactively, may be said

about the concept of reality. Bohr brings both together and jointly questions them non-classically in the case of quantum mechanics. In the non-classical case these limits are, as we have seen, defined by the classical level at which whatever is available to phenomenalization appears (in either sense, as it can only appear through phenomenalization). Without perhaps quite realizing the nature of his move and without giving this question a non-classical answer (in the way Nietzsche and Bohr did later), Kant posed a (and even *the*) non-classical question, perhaps for the first time, at least in post-Cartesian philosophy.[24]

Leibniz's and Spinoza's philosophy (or, following them, that of Deleuze) is the philosophy of plenitude, of plenitude-difference and difference-plenitude, while Kant's was, against them and closer to Levinas, that of insufficiency, of insufficiency-difference (arising by virtue of alterity-difference) and singularity-difference, even if short of its non-classical limits.[25] One could use the former not only (deconstructively) against the metaphysical aspects grounding the latter, but also, and more crucially, in order to take Kant's alterity-difference to its more radical limits, as Hegel realized and, to some degree, accomplished (in part, one could argue, via Leibniz and possibly Spinoza). Naturally, a converse or reciprocal deconstruction is equally possible. One can consider, for example, the closing elaborations of the *Phenomenology*, where a very complex mixture and multiple mutual deconstruction (or proto-deconstruction) of the Kantian (more Kantian than it is often perceived) alterity-difference, differentiation-difference, multiplicity-difference and singularity-difference emerges or is, at least, inscribed in the movement of Hegel's text (1979, 491–3). As in Kant's case, it is a matter of reading whether Hegel, even if against himself, reaches non-classical limits of difference or how close he approaches them.

It is hardly in question that Nietzsche reaches that far.

Nietzsche (reading Kant's argument as classical), first of all, argues that Kant cannot really speak of 'things-in-themselves' or distinguish them from 'appearances' in the way he does, or, more accurately, that the ultimate rigour of analysis of the situation would require non-classical argument. Nietzsche's argument that one must simultaneously 'abolish' [*abschaften*] both the 'true' and the 'apparent' world [*die wahre und die scheinbare Welt*] arises from the non-classical view of the non-classical alterity-difference inhabiting and inhibiting a classical view of the situation (Nietzsche, 1976, 486). That is, we must abolish them at the level of the ultimate and ultimately non-classical efficacity of the apparent world (the efficacity classically seen in terms of the 'true' world), which indeed can no longer be seen in these or, again, any terms. Nietzsche's epistemological argument, pursued throughout his work, becomes not only analogous but equivalent to Bohr's argument for quantum epistemology.

Much of Derrida's critique of the metaphysics of presence or, more accurately, of the limits of its claims follows Nietzsche's argument and refers to it at the most crucial junctures. At the same time, Derrida often translates Nietzsche's argument into more Heideggerian terms, for the reasons considered earlier. In particular, he aims, jointly, to reach, via exploring Heidegger's reading of Nietzsche, the rigorous limits of Nietzsche's analysis and to deconstruct Heidegger's own ontic-ontological difference (that between Being [*Sein*] and beings [*Seinde*]) and different, if related, metaphysical arguments emerging in Heidegger's later writing, such as that in 'The Anaximander Fragment'. Derrida considers the latter in closing 'Différance' and makes it a pathway to one of his most rigorous articulations of différance itself (*Margins of Philosophy*, 1984, 22–7). Parallel arguments are offered in 'Form and Meaning: A Note on the Phenomenology of Language' (a discussion of Edmund Husserl) and, especially, '*Ousia* and *Gramme*: Note on a Note from *Being and Time*' (*Margins of Philosophy*, 1984, 154–6, 65–7).[26]

Derrida argues, first, that, as conceived by Heidegger or as inscribed in Heidegger's text, 'presence, then, far from being, as is commonly thought, *what* the sign signifies, what a trace refers to, presence, then, is the trace of the trace', and indeed 'the trace of the erasure of the trace' (66). It follows that no denomination or (conception of) determination can be applied to such an efficacity (or these trace-like effects), in particular any determination in terms of presence (assuming indeed that any determination is possible otherwise). The latter, Derrida argues, is ultimately never abandoned by Heidegger's thought, either early, such that of *Being and Time*, or later, such as that of *Time and Being*, even as the latter almost reaches, in present terms, non-classical limits, and perhaps makes them inevitable. These are the limits of the inconceivable and of that which is 'beyond-the-inconceivable' (rather than only 'beyond-the-conceivable'), the limits of difference beyond difference, and beyond of the beyond itself, which Derrida himself approaches through différance. It may be argued that one reason, perhaps the most important one, for the famous 'a' of différance is this beyondness or un-beyond-ness. Derrida concludes:

> There may be a difference still more unthought than the [Heideggerian] difference between Being and beings. We certainly can go further towards naming it in our language. Beyond Being and beings, this difference, ceaselessly differing from and deferring (itself), would trace (itself) (by itself) – this différance would be the first or last trace, if one could still speak, here, of origin and end.
> Such a différance would at once, again, give

us to think a writing without presence and without absence, without history, without cause, without archia, without telos, a writing that absolutely upsets all dialectics, all theology, all teleology, all ontology. A writing exceeding everything that the history of metaphysics has comprehended in the form of the Aristotelian gramme, in its point, in its line, in its circle, in its time, in its space.

(1984, 67)

'Our language' may specifically refer to French. We recall that the 'a' of *différance* is inaudible in French, and, short of Derrida's chain of inscription, would appear only in writing. But then, beyond the fact that it cannot appear (only its effects, for example, those of difference with an 'e' can), it, its non-appearing included, is meaningless short of these inscriptive chains in any events. Accordingly, 'our language' here would extend at least to all Indo-European languages and (the complexity of translation notwithstanding) possibly beyond. It would be impossible to contain *différance* even by the complex differing-deferring efficacious dynamics suggested here, let alone, as is done sometimes, by some naive (e.g. undeveloped in terms of Derridean chain) conception that *différance* is something that simultaneously both differs and defers, which are merely effects of *différance*, crucial as they might be. It is also worth noting a subtle but crucial distinction between the '*différance*' of the first and the 'writing' of the second paragraph just cited. It indicates that inevitable and irreducible incisions of *différance* can only be comprehended through writing (written or spoken) in Derrida's sense, rather than through the 'speech' or 'thought' (spoken or written) of metaphysics. Rigorously speaking, one could only speak in non-classical terms of 'effects of *différance*', rather than *différance* itself, which is beyond difference (or deferral)

and beyond any beyondness, and could only manifest 'itself' (the latter being *itself* a metaphysical conception, hence Derrida's parenthesis) in terms of such effects, difference and deferral among them. The fact that the emergence of these effects, individual or collective, or their overall architecture, are unavailable to a metaphysical treatment is nicely captured by Derrida's invocation of Aristotle's geometrical language (a subject that would require a separate discussion). On the other hand, each effect as such is available to a metaphysical treatment and indeed only appears by virtue of the possibility of such a treatment. In other words, it is classical in present terms. Hence, writing would suspend the metaphysical elements invoked by Derrida only at the ultimate level of the efficacity, while retaining them within classical limits, where they are necessary in order to infer and engage, via certain effects, with the non-classical efficacity in question.

These considerations are equally significant for reading Derrida's arguably most crucial proposition here: 'this difference, ceaselessly differing from and deferring (itself), would trace (itself) (by itself) – this *différance* would be the first or last trace, if one could still speak, here, of origin and end'. A properly non-classical reading of this proposition or, at least, a properly non-classical (in the present sense) understanding of this type of efficacity would correspond to the view that any possible conception of this efficacity would ineluctably 'miss' and forever 'defer' it. In other words, it is ultimately impossible even to relate, however obliquely, to this efficacity, let alone represent it in any way. On the other hand, it is possible to read this proposition as indicating that this efficacity is dynamically represented by the process of differing-deferring or (taking the multiplicity-difference into consideration, via différance-dissemination) differing/deferring/multiplying. This view would (re)institute a more continuous dynamics to this efficacity, somewhat analogous (but not identical to) to the Deleuzean continuity, as considered above, as opposed to the irreducible (beyond all continuity and discontinuity alike) 'discontinuity' entailed by the non-classical view of the relationships between such efficacities and effects. One may also read this proposition as posing (deliberately or in spite of itself) this type of question concerning this dynamics.

A similar set of questions could be posed as concerns the epistemology of de Man's allegory (and related concepts, such as irony). De Man often associated allegory (or irony) with discontinuity, also in juxtaposition to the continuity of the symbol. In accordance with the argument of this essay, however, we may more properly think of this relation as neither continuous nor discontinuous, or in terms of any conceivable combination of both concepts, or, again, in any given terms. De Man's emphasis on the discontinuity of allegory strategically points in this direction, away from the continuity of the symbol or of classical thought in general, for example, aesthetic ideology. Both continuity and discontinuity are retained at the level of 'effects', and the effects of discontinuity are indeed more crucial to allegory (or irony), just as they are to quantum mechanics, to which the overall situation of allegory in de Man is parallel. In both cases, discontinuity is important, especially in disrupting the applicability of classical theories to such situations. It must in any event be seen as an effect (in either sense) of a more complex efficacious machinery, which is itself neither continuous nor discontinuous.[27]

I am, however, less concerned with making definitive claims concerning Derrida's or de Man's argument than with the non-classical epistemological limits of the situation, the limits of 'difference' that is 'beyond-difference' and 'beyond-the-beyond'. At the very least, both arguments ineluctably direct us to these limits, and by so doing also continue Kant's work and move it forward, in part by their own reading of Kant, in part by making Kant read them, that is, by making us reread Kant via their work.

Conclusion

Non-classical theory brings our thinking of 'proximity' to a very radical form of alterity-difference (both non-classical differentiation-difference and non-classical multiplicity-difference, especially as singularity difference, may be seen as defined by or, in any event, as correlative to this conception of alterity-difference). It is not and indeed, by definition, may not be possible to know how close such a proximity, or how distant such a distance, can be. It is conceivable, as Nietzsche (or rather Zarathustra), who urged us to love that which is most distant, realized that distance is the only way to approach this unknowable or this impossible, although, as Nietzsche also realized, both these concepts or any concept may again be fundamentally-structurally, irreducibly-insufficient here.

Is it possible, is it conceivable, then? Is it possible to conceive of something that neither connects nor disconnects, is neither connected nor disconnected, that is indeed neither conceivable nor inconceivable, is never fully, or even in any way, inside or outside any conceptual or perceptual enclosure, as all such questions are themselves the products of enclosures, beyond some of which one must move and within others of which one must remain in order to approach this radically, but never absolutely, unrepresentable, *different*? It may or may not be possible, as the very concepts of conception, representation or indeed possibility may need to be further scrutinized, transformed or abandoned, including 'questioning', a seemingly irreducible form of inquiry, which of course is not to say that it must be abandoned, either in nihilistic fashion or in favour of some atheoretical alternative. Nietzsche is certainly hardly less critical of such alternatives than he is of the traditional, classical, philosophical modes of inquiry, and yet questioning may not be a really dominant mode for him, in contrast, for example, to Heidegger, although even in this case 'questioning' already takes a very different form. It is not altogether inconceivable (it is another question how likely) that, in physics or elsewhere, non-classical theorizing will no longer be necessary at some point, as Einstein, for example, hoped in the case of quantum theory. Some of course argue that it is not and has never been necessary (how successfully is, again, another question). Non-classical theory does not in itself preclude this view or this type of argument, although one might see it, with Nietzsche, as, at least in some cases, an indifference to difference. The point and the very nature of non-classical theory, however, is that this inconceivability is structural, necessary, is an irreducible part of knowledge, and indeed an outcome of its rigour and, hence, also of the disciplinarity of the respective fields involved, such as physics or (admittedly a more complex case) philosophy. In this case, to return to Bohr's defining statement, 'we are not dealing with an arbitrary renunciation of a more detailed analysis of atomic phenomena, but with a recognition that such an analysis is, *in principle,* excluded'.

This would also mean, however, that, at least for now, the suspension of non-classicality of theoretical thinking is not necessary for knowledge and rigour of knowledge, or one might say, the progress of knowledge, although this suspension might be desirable (and seem necessary) to some. Non-classicality does not in any way inhibit knowledge or the rigour of knowledge, but enables them. And it does so, in part and indeed primarily, by providing an extension and generalization, one might say with Bohr rational extension and generalization, of the concept and practice of difference, arguably the oldest instrument of knowledge and thinking, and of much more in our theory and practice, in our lives, perhaps in all life.

Notes

1. It would be difficult to cite all the relevant works even by the primary figures do be discussed here, and my references will be limited to certain (far from all!) works especially germane to my argument. There is a recent collection of Heidegger's, Deleuze's, Derrida's and Irigaray's 'sample' writings on difference, *The Theory of Difference: Reading in Contemporary Continental Thought* (ed. Donkel, 2001), which also includes a selection of Maurice Merleau-Ponty's writings. They cannot be addressed in this essay. Nor could those of a number of other figures I have mentioned. This is unfortunate, since my argument would be considerably enriched by so doing, but it would also have to be extended well beyond its present limits. This essay contains a minimal amount of references to the secondary literature on these figures, which has by now reached Tower of Babel proportions. I permit myself to refer to some of my own works because, in addition to extending those parts of my argument that could not be accommodated within my limits here, they contain more extensive references to both primary and secondary literature. Other essays in the present volume and related works by their authors would serve well to the reader of this essay as well. In addition, one could refer (still by way of a very incomplete list) to the works of Jonathan Culler, Hélène Cixous, Rodolphe Gasché, Philippe Lacoue-Labarthe and Samuel Weber.

2. Derrida's '*différance*', seen by him as neither a term nor a concept, may immediately come to mind as an example of placing the concept of difference both beyond difference and beyond conceptuality. Derrida's writing on or (also if one uses 'writing' in Derrida's sense) of *différance* inevitably involves conceptualization and conceptual effects, including in Gilles Deleuze and Félix Guattari's special sense or concept of (philosophical) concept in *What is Philosophy?* (1993). This sense would also apply to Deleuze's concept of difference, indeed more directly (rather than in terms of 'effects' involved).

3. Each of these cases has further specificity, while the term 'deconstruction' itself has by now differentiated and disseminated into an uncontrollable diversity of meanings.

4. On the relationships between Derrida and Hegel, I refer the reader to Derrida's well-known works. See also Plotnitsky (2001, 66–84), and references there.

5. See Derrida (1988, 42; 1990).

6. On Nietzsche via Heidegger, see, again, Derrida's *Spurs* and, on 'writing', see Derrida's well-known earlier works, including many of

those already cited, such as *Of Grammatology* and *Positions*, or *Writing and Difference* (1980). All these works also elaborate on Derrida's other key operators, such as trace, supplement, dissemination or of course *différance*. On dissemination, see especially Derrida, *Dissemination* (1983). Heidegger's life-long encounter with Nietzsche, comprising several volumes of his work, is a massive subject in its own right with its own (Babel-like) towering secondary literature.

7. Derrida further links this instance of logocentrism to phonocentrism, and specifically to the privilege of 'the *voice* of Being', which subject I shall bypass here.

8. See also Derrida (1988, 43–4).

9. The temporality, or spatiality (spatial representation), of time and spatiality, or temporality, of space may be seen as effects of the dynamics that is approached by 'beyond-difference' concepts of difference here in question, such as Derrida's *différance* or, especially as concerns temporality, de Man's allegory.

10. I refer especially to Levinas (1990).

11. Henri Bergson, a major inspiration for Deleuze, and Alfred North Whitehead could also be mentioned here.

12. See Nietzsche's remarkable early lectures, *Philosophy in the Tragic Age of the Greeks*, trans. Marianne Cowan. Chicago, IL, 1996; and of course Heidegger's numerous works, specifically the essays assembled in *Early Greek Thinking* (1984). Plato's *Parmenides* could in fact be read as a gigantic meditation on difference, of effects of difference and of identity, and of their intermixtures.

13. For a supporting argument, specifically dealing with Gilles Deleuze and Félix Guattari's *A Thousand Plateaus* (1987) but applicable elsewhere in Deleuze, see Plotnitsky (1993, 56–66).

14. This type of argument for the existence of a realm without difference or change, 'Platonia', in physics has been recently offered by Julian Barbour (1999).

15. I refer most especially to the analysis of power in Michel Foucault (1990).

16. This sentence is omitted from the text published in '*Conférences 1951–1953*', in Volume VIII of Bataille, *Oeuvres complètes* (1970–88). I have considered Bataille's work in this set of contexts in Plotnitsky (1994; 2001, 16–28).

17. This confluence may not be coincidental, even beyond the more general influence of quantum physics on Bataille, who refers to it on several occasions. One of the figures involved in the discussion of Bataille's ideas in 'Conférences 1951–1953' was Georges Ambrosino, an atomic physicist, whom Bataille even credits with a partial co-authorship of the contemporary *Accursed Share* (1988, 191 n. 2).

18. The term phenomena in this statement should be given Bohr's special sense, necessitated by his non-classical view. On this point and on the relationships among Bohr's work, the epistemology of quantum mechanics and non-classical theory I permit myself to refer the reader to Plotnitsky (2002) and *Complementarity* (1994).

19. Cf. Derrida's analysis of Heidegger's Being in several essays in *Margins of Philosophy* (1984, 26–7, 65–6, 169–73) and, via Nietzsche, in *Spurs* (1990). See also, Plotnitsky (1994, 249–60).

20. On this point, I again refer to Plotnitsky (2002).

21. See Plotnitsky (1993, 56–66).

22. From this viewpoint quantum mechanics may be seen as a form of information theory, rather than as anything conceived on the model of classical (Galilean or Newtonian) physics as the mathematical science of motion of material bodies. This view has major implications for, as it became known, quantum information science, a new and rapidly developing field.

23. See Nietzsche (1974, 305), de Man on Kant, phenomenality and materiality, and Derrida on Kant.

24. But then a very different reading of Descartes may be in order as well, bringing his thought in mathematics and philosophy alike (or in their complex and sometimes conflictual interplay) much closer to Kant or even to non-classical thought.

25. This view has been developed by de Man in his readings of Kant (1997). See also Plotnitsky (2000, 49–92). A number of essays in this collection are relevant here. See also Rodolphe Gasché (1997).

26. These thematics are explored by Derrida throughout *Spurs*.

27. I have considered these aspects of de Man's work in 'Algebra and Allegory'.

Works cited

Barbour, Julian. *The End of Time: The Next Revolution in Physics*. Oxford, 1999.

Bataille, Georges. 'Conférences sur le Non-Savoir', *Tel Quel*, 10 (1962): 5.

Bataille, Georges. *Oeuvres complètes*, 12 vols. Paris, 1970–88.

Bataille, Georges. 'Conférences sur le Non-Savoir', *Oeuvres Complètes*, Vol. VIII. Paris, 1970.

Bataille, Georges. *The Accursed Share: Volume 1*, trans. Robert Hurley. New York, 1988.

Blanchot, Maurice. *The Step Not Beyond* [*Le pas au delà*], trans. Lycette Nelson. Albany, NY, 1992.

Bohm, David. *Wholeness and the Implicate Order*. London, 1995.

Bohr, Niels. *The Philosophical Writings of Niels Bohr*, 3 vols. Woodbridge, CT, 1998, 2: 62.

de Man, Paul. *The Rhetoric of Romanticism*. New York, 1990.

de Man, Paul. *Aesthetic Ideology*, ed. Andrzej Warminski. Minneapolis, MN, 1997.

Deleuze, Gilles *Difference and Repetition*, trans. Paul Patton. New York, 1994.

Deleuze, Gilles and Félix Guattari. *A Thousand Plateaus*, trans. Brian Massumi. Minneapolis, MN, 1987.

Deleuze, Gilles and Félix Guattari. *What is Philosophy?* trans. Hugh Tomlinson and Graham Burchell. New York, 1993.

Derrida, Jacques. *Writing and Difference*, trans. Alan Bass. Chicago, IL, 1980.

Derrida, Jacques. 'Economimesis', *Diacritics,* 11.3 (1981): 3–25.

Derrida, Jacques. *Dissemination*, trans. Barbara Johnson. Chicago, IL, 1983.

Derrida, Jacques. 'Différance', *Margins of Philosophy*, trans. Alan Bass. Chicago, IL, 1984.

Derrida, Jacques. *Positions*, trans. Alan Bass. Chicago, IL, 1988.

Derrida, Jacques. *Spurs: Nietzsche's Styles,* trans. Barbara Harlow. Chicago, IL, 1990.

Derrida, Jacques. *Of Grammatology*, trans. Gayatri Chakravorty Spivak. Baltimore, MD, 1997.

Donkel, Douglas (ed.). *The Theory of Difference: Reading in Contemporary Continental Thought.* Albany, NY, 2001.

Foucault, Michel. *The History of Sexuality: An Introduction. Vol. 1*, trans. Robert Hurley. New York, 1990.

Gasché, Rodolphe. *The Wild Card of Reading: On Paul de Man*. Cambridge, MA, 1997.

Hegel, Georg W. F. *Phenomenology of Spirit*, trans. A. V. Miller. Oxford, 1979.

Heidegger, Martin. *Being and Time: A Translation of Sein und Zeit*, trans. Joan Stambaugh. Albany, NY, 1996.

Levinas, Emmanuel. *Totality and Infinity*, trans. Alphonso Lingis. Pittsburgh, PA, 1990.

Nietzsche, Friedrich. *The Birth of Tragedy and The Case of Wagner*, trans. Walter Kaufmann. New York, 1966.

Nietzsche, Friedrich. *The Gay Science*, trans. Walter Kaufmann. New York, 1974.

Nietzsche, Friedrich. 'Twilight of the Idols', *Portable Nietzsche*, ed. Walter Kaufmann. New York, 1976, 486.

Nietzsche, Friedrich. *Early Greek Thinking*, trans. Frank Capuzzi and David Krell. San Francisco, CA, 1984.

Nietzsche, Friedrich. *Philosophy in the Tragic Age of the Greeks*, trans. Marianne Cowan. Chicago, IL, 1996.

Plotnitsky, Arkady. *In the Shadow of Hegel: Complimentarity, History, and the Unconscious*. Gainesville, FL, 1993.

Plotnitsky, Arkady. *Complimentarity: Anti-Epistemology After Bohr and Derrida*. Durham, NC, 1994.

Plotnitsky, Arkady. 'Algebra and Allegory: Non-classical Epistemology, Quantum Theory and the Work of Paul de Man', in *Material Events: Paul de Man and the Afterlife of Theory*, eds Barbara Cohen, Tom Cohen, J. Hillis Miller and Andrzej Warminski. Minneapolis, MN, 2000, 49–92.

Plotnitsky, Arkady. 'The Effects of the Unknowable: Materiality, Epistemology, and the General Economy of the Body in Bataille', *Parallax*, 18 (Winter 2001): 16–28.

Plotnitsky, Arkady. 'Points and Counterpoints: Between Hegel and Derrida', in *Questioning Derrida (With His Replies on Philosophy)*, ed. Michel Meyer. Aldershot, 2001, 66–84.

Plotnitsky, Arkady. *The Knowable and the Unknowable: Modern Science, Non-classical Thought, and the 'Two Cultures'*. Ann Arbor, MI, 2002.

Proust, Marcel. 'Within A Budding Grove', *Remembrance of Things Past*, trans. C. K. Scott Mocrief, Terence Kilmartin and Andreas Mayor. New York, 1982.

Schrödinger, Erwin. 'The Present Situation in Quantum Mechanics', in *Quantum Theory and Measurement*, eds John Archibald Wheeler and Wojciech H. Zurek. Princeton, NJ, 1983.

event | (EPOCHALYPSE [NOT] NOW) | *JULIAN WOLFREYS*

Events 'take place.' And again. And again.

Bernard Tschumi

. . . occurrences . . . take place in language, as occurrence to which language – never quite reducible to itself – gives place.

Gil Anidjar (emphases added)

If it be now, 'tis not to come. If it be not to come, it will be now. If it be not now, yet it will come.

Hamlet, V.ii.166–8

In a tangential and elliptical manner, difference always causes a deviation in repetition. I call this iterability, the sudden appearance of the other (itara) in reiteration. The singular always inaugurates, it arrives even, unpredictably, as the same arrival crossing repetition.

Jacques Derrida (emphases in original)

I

Interrupting the beginning with a reflection on examples, and thereby registering a suspension or hiatus, which might also be available as an unfolding or revelation: the several epigraphs to this essay address and reiterate in singular fashion matters of repetition or, rather, iterability, having to do with that which takes place, in principle and in effect. Each speaks of the possibility of an event and of an unguaranteeable eventuality, either directly or in an encrypted fashion. They do so through the implied relation of such instances of recurrence to both a spacing that ruins identity's self-presence, and a disordered temporality admitting of no present, both of which are allied, in turn, to a certain insistence on the possibility of unpredictable arrival. A disturbing, haunting logic is at work here: something has taken place for there to be repetition's difference; something could take place, but this will not have been known beforehand. If, therefore, temporality is in disarray, if identity is displaced from within itself, an arrival might have already taken place or might yet take place. But this might never have been known, nor might it ever be known, and, even supposing we believed this to be so, in any event it would be impossible for us to know, for sure. Supposing this to be the case, we are placed, as Geoffrey Bennington informs us, 'in a situation of radical *indecision* or of undecidability of the case in question . . .' Anything that can be said of the example of the epigraphs (of each epigraph as example or of the example of the grouping of the epigraphs), of what they appear to imply, of whatever possible relation they may be read as bearing towards one another; or, indeed, any effect that may chance to occur through their concatenation, would involve us in a response and a responsibility to make a decision, the grounds for which, to cite Bennington again, cannot be known. Such a responsibility entails a risk, as Bennington asserts; he continues, in the same passage just cited, that any 'decision must . . . involve a measure of *invention* [which] entails both an uncertainty and an affirmative projection of a future'. Here we are faced, therefore, with the 'essential undecidability of the event as it arrives and calls for decision' (Bennington, 2001, 15). Moving from the example of the epigraphs to a more general supposition, what is revealed here all the more distressingly for some, and perhaps uncannily for others, is that language makes possible the event, if there is one, before or without the subject. This point is suspended for the moment, though it is one to which it will have been necessary to return. And it should also be remarked: the use of the future anterior here serves to intimate, if not enact, an iterable 'looping', a kind of 'vicus of recirculation', to recall Joyce (1939, 3). As we seek to respond to the various epigraphs, to decide upon whatever fragmentary filiation might be read as haunting them, it is necessary to register a certain motion always already underway. Such movement is also what Andrew Benjamin calls a 'reworking', which is particular to language, and 'which if it is more successful means that what is given, given in being reworked, is the event. The event can never be commensurate with itself since the "itself" will already have been a plural possibility' (Benjamin, 1993,191).

So to start again, a single hypothesis and several questions: supposing for the moment that we think we know what an event is, given what has already been remarked, will the advent of a book either have been or have caused an event? And will the advent of a book, named after an unceasing heteroglossic babble, leave any mark in an otherwise indefinable 'age' during – and by – which the end of the book has been signalled, over and over again and again, like the endless appearance of the same obituary? Does the very idea of a profusion of uncontrollable speech, announcing the *anarchitecture*[1] within the insatiable desire for architectonic order, admit to an endless, virtual excess remarked by and through language, by which an event may take place and have been recognized? And, in the event of its appearance, does any book, but especially a book named *Glossalalia*, despite its form as book, despite those formal constraints which signal its being just another book (the same and yet different, already out of date, allegedly), disclose or confess to the impossibility of speaking by the book, or being brought to book on the illusory subject of the state of criticism or theory, *today*?

Let us pause, and possibly digress, here: this *today* is unstable. It admits of no present, even as it appears to consign itself to such a fate. Rather, it appears as the sign, the shadow or phantasm, of a singular-universal. It resounds with its own phantom overflow, marking and re-marking, signing itself as never simply 'it-self', but as the sign of otherwise innumerable not-selves through a constant coming, a serial becoming as well as the becoming-serial. There is, perhaps, and 'all appearances to the contrary', the admission ghosting, and spoken through, the title, *Glossalalia*, that the arrival of this book is just the latest in a number of responses to the death of the book, which is also the announcement of 'nothing but the death of speech', which 'is of course a metaphor here', where a multiplicity of writings, organized only by that minimal structure, the alphabetical pro-gramme, acknowledge and announce 'that the concept of writing exceeds and comprehends that of language' (Derrida, 1976, 8). Henceforward then, the possibility of an irreversible transformation, whereby the heterogeneity of multiple articulations is apprehended as the ineluctable overflow of necessary critical intervention and inscription: the *gloss* of *glossalalia* would remind us of the practice of interpretation, translation, commentary. That which, previously collected in some marginal place such as an appendix or glossary, situated according to the alphabetical programme, or otherwise located in the margin of the page, appears stage centre, though without any centre as such. Consider *Glossalalia*, therefore, as that 'hauntological' figure, a figure without delimitable or determinable form or identity troping itself excessively and irrecuperably beyond any ontology of the glossary, beyond any subordinating gesture of mere explanation. Consider this as twenty-seven margins, if you will, without a centre or ground.

But this is, as yet, a dream, a mere hypothesis, *encore une fois*. If there is the possibility of such an event, which would signal in its arrival both a suspension *and* a revelation, as well as an irreversible translation, it has to be understood that the event is not simply commensurate with the book, but has its chance despite the very idea of the book as a result of the multiplicity of languages that the idea of the book pretends to corral. While it is accepted by many that, today, text or writing exceeds the book, all ontology burst open and scattered irreversibly from the emergence, the becoming-visible of some other within, nevertheless, the desire to interpret remains. In the words of John Sallis, 'the confusion of tongues/lips imposes the necessity of translation. It imposes also a certain impossibility of translation, or, more precisely, a limit that prevents translation from overcoming the mutual disjointedness of languages and thereby reclaiming in effect the common language, compensating without residue for the confusion of tongues'

(Sallis, 2002, 3–4). Thus we come face to face with the experience of the aporetic: necessity *and* impossibility, disjointedness *and* confusion. In the face of the undecidable, and as a possible means of being able to move forward, we turn back to our questions, asking, in addition: are these the loci or co-ordinates of the event? And do such problems speak to the arrival and reception of a book?

Such questions should, of course, give us pause on the very threshold of introduction or inauguration, even as they announce themselves as both advent and response to that beginning. For, it has to be admitted from the outset, that an event, if there is one, will only have been recognized after the event, as the saying goes. It will have been glimpsed or otherwise perceived, felt perhaps as a singular intensity emerging through the constellated chance gathering of so many erstwhile invisible traces, through the after-effects and remainders, if the event is or will have been seen at all. Perhaps the difficulties faced in seeking to think the strangeness of the event through the singular example of the book's advent are caught in the following summary of the event's nature:

> *Events are neither already meaningful and conceptually determined entities given by the structure of thought, nor are they radically anterior conditions which produce thought's structure. Neither condition nor conditioned, neither genesis nor structure, events are the singularities of existence, moments of sense that exceed already constituted concepts but which opens the problems that concepts will answer.*
>
> (Colebrook, 2000, 114)

Without wishing to make unjustifiable leaps between distinct notions, and yet seeking to trace a spectral connection by the force of analogy, it may be said with caution that the book, its appearance in material form, can be said to be analogous with the event. It may be read, according to Colebrook's terms, as one such singularity of existence that answers to, and yet exceeds in unforeseeable ways, the concept or idea of the book. The idea of the book is neither meaningful nor determined until it has the chance of its material singularity. Nor does the idea of the book provide some anterior abstract condition, which in turn translates seamlessly into the singular form, and which, once opened, opens itself beyond any intention or will. Irreducible to any ontology, to any controllable programme or pro-ject, what chances to come about occurs only on the condition that it not only 'happens, but [as] that which surprises – perhaps even surprises itself' (Nancy, 1998, 91). Given this, and despite the irresolvable impossibilities with which we are faced here, other questions concerning the book and the event appear, arriving to give us pause, once more. (There is to be read perhaps a necessary repetition as performative gesture here: disabling-enabling interruption within ordered procedure.) Such questions not only reiterate a gesture in which this essay has already partaken, they also restage particular concerns or anxieties already announced. If they are articulated once more, this has to do, perhaps, with a certain perception within the experience of the aporetic of what Jean-Luc Nancy, apropos of the event, has described as an 'excess of truth – not the truth about the truth but the truth of the taking place of the true . . . the opening [which, here, we would wish to read, however violently, as the sign of apocalypse] of thought to the event as such, to the truth of the event *beyond* all advent of sense . . . the event opening thought to that excess that originally overflowed it' (Nancy, 1998, 93). Around the question of the event is a certain 'agitation', as Nancy puts it, pertaining to 'the logic

of the "happening" [*arriver*]', in which we are interested (Nancy, 1998, 94) but about which we can say nothing *in the event*. So, we find ourselves asking once more: is it legitimate to think, as has been intimated already, of a book as one would an event? Does the appearance of the one relate, albeit in the manner solely of the strangest non-relation, to the disclosedness of the other? Is it possible to think the book and the event as being of the same order, within the same register of translation, each perhaps as the non-synonymous substitution for, or of, the other (at least within a highly delimited context)? Are these 'ideas' – book, event – and whatever might be expressed through them, commensurable to any degree, even though they are never *simply commensurable*? To put such questions in a slightly different manner, to disorder them while ordering their implications according to different formulae and the demands of other implicit resonances: is it possible that, as a result of a book's arrival (again, there is a hypothetical supposition at work here, the validity of which is far from being assured), an event will (have) taken place?

It is the situation, of course, that 'there is always the chance of event as soon as *there is* something rather than nothing' (Kronick, 1999, 33). Moreover, the 'coming about' of the event, in being 'unique and repeatable, promises a future that is something like an invention *and* an apocalypse' (Kronick, 1999, 33). The book, and every book, is, simply put, this something; and something moreover which is both singular and a repetition, the singular instance of the singular-universal, acknowledging its singularity only by its reinscription into a law, and yet marked by a tension that is advertised, through the diacritical mark of the hyphen, in the grafting of the one onto the other. Every singular instance of the book reiterates and is haunted by the 'idea of the book', even though there is no book as such, merely the idea. In this, there is always to be read a relation without relation, even as the possible relation of book and event is one, in turn, of non-relation. We might suggest that the singular advent of the book, in figuring the becoming-book of its iterable premise, is an event in that it bears with it, in its becoming, 'the necessary transgression or contamination that leaves no event in the purity of its singularity' (Kronick, 1999, 33). Yet simultaneously and as has just been admitted, as an 'event of writing', while the instance of the becoming-book is 'unique' it must, perforce, 'each time be reappropriated by a law' (Hobson, 1998, 132); and this is no less the case even if it is also true that the book, and every singular instance of the book *just is* the disclosure of the appropriation of language by given laws, even while such appropriation could always be frustrated in the action of appearance, where the logic of that which comes to pass announces, once again, the inappropriable nature of the event. Thus the book, as the manifestation of a literary work 'must come back toward the past, toward a set of conventions and laws that allow us to recognize it as unique. Therefore, act and archive meet in the literary work because it links the advent of the new with its reinscription in a system, in generality' (Kronick, 1999, 34) There is, in the possibility of the becoming-book, the possibility of its arrival, the potential for an event 'that seems to produce itself by speaking about itself, *by the act of speaking of itself*' (Derrida, 1989, 29), even if, and especially, this speaking-of-itself is made possible – is only possible – by the not-itself. Arguably, there is little that is more obviously self-advertising than a book that speaks of itself – speaking itselves, its countless arrivals and traces, its undecidable pasts which have never been present and futures which will never arrive in the present – than a book that announces explicitly its constant glossalalic becoming, in contravention to the appropriative law that *glossary* names and seeks to enact, to enforce as the injunction

implicit in its pro-gramme and structure. Such a likelihood makes it the most typical book in the world, its singularity paradoxically announced in the event of its naming itself, its title making visible that which, in effect, produces any book.

Given this chance of arrival, taking it for granted at least for now and admitting that it is never more than a chance, the advent of a book is therefore both singular and never solely singular. What goes for an event of writing or a literary work holds also for the book. All books arrive according to some principle of their transmission, their iterable dissemination – processes of translating 'book' to 'text' – as well as with the unprogrammable expectation that some transformation, that is to say perhaps some event, might take place. A book's arrival*s*, its publication and all the subsequent 'inventions', those responses and non-responses, receptions and resistances – and reception may equally be a form of resistance, rather than its opposite – that go by the name of reading; all belong together, however irreducibly different from one another, as occurrences of that which is 'never quite reducible to itself' (Anidjar, 2002, 2). Such arrivals of the book are instances, at least hypothetically, of what takes place again and again, as that to which, obviously, language, in an overdetermined instance, 'gives place' (Anidjar, 2002, 2). The book and its ghostly double, the idea of the book (which are infinite numbers of books, endless affirmations of books-to-come), is, therefore, a momentary becoming: a becoming-visible, a becoming-material, where the endless give-and-take of memory is mis-recognized as having solidified into a static, monolithic entity. Language gives place to the semi-visible staging of the spectral, but what takes place as a performative interruption all too often comes to pass, and keeps coming to pass, invisibly, so that recognition is necessarily that misrecognition we name afterthought (which is to say simply nothing other than thought, as it will be necessary to remark once more, further in the essay). The book in lieu of memory, the material taking-place of immaterial memory perhaps, is in this sense only the analogical manifestation, one possible, possibly recursive apparition of some otherwise unpresentable other that still remains to arrive, and yet which has always already haunted us from the past, retreating and fleeing ahead of our perception, and conceivable as one of those *lieux de mémoires* spoken of by Pierre Nora. While Nora is speaking of memory in relation to historical sites, when he remarks that 'there are sites, *lieux de mémoire*, in which a residual sense of continuity remains' (Nora, 1993, 1), surely, there can be no doubt, that one such site, at least by analogy, is the book, as – to use this term once again – a recursive, untimely gesture seeking to gather together the fraying edges of some irrevocable rupture. The idea of the book can, in principle, fulfil the three criteria established by Nora for a *lieu de mémoire*. The *lieu*, the site or place, is defined according to its being 'material, symbolic, and functional' (Nora, 1996, 14). The book is the material place of imaginative investment; it is functional in that it exists to be received, to be read; it is symbolic in Nora's sense, in that, disrupting time, it concentrates memories, those of its ideas and intertexts, of its authors, and its readers, all of which supposes an 'interaction resulting in a mutual overdetermination' (Nora, 1996, 14), always already immanent in the idea of the book, and in every material experience of the book. The book is a hybrid place, to paraphrase Nora, 'compounded of life and death, of the temporal and the eternal'. Books, like *lieux de mémoire*, are 'endless rounds of the collective and the individual . . . the immutable and the fleeting. For, although it is true that the fundamental purpose of a *lieu de mémoire* [and, in its singular fashion, a book]'

is to stop time, to inhibit forgetting, to fix a state of things, to immortalize death and to materialize the immaterial . . . it is also clear that lieux de mémoire *thrive only because of their capacity for change, their ability to resurrect old meanings and generate new ones along with new and unforeseeable connections.*

(Nora, 1996, 15)

Thus, language gives place to the taking place that we call the book, albeit in unexpected ways despite all efforts to programme or control the outcome. As a singular locus of language, engaged in resurrection and generation, the book proffers a stage on which an event might be enacted. The event might thus be said to be both a suspension of unobserved flows and, simultaneously, a revelation of that suspension and those flows. Or, in short, an *epochalypse*, though not something taking place in the present, in any present. And this event, one form of which is the initial incision of a mark, cannot come to pass except from the experience of the undecidable (Derrida, 1986, 15).

II

Language marks the place, the taking place, where language will have been, though never as such, never as a presence. This is its irreducible, haunting strangeness, uncanny presence without present in the event of its unstoppable arrivals, where all that remains is, in every moment, in every invention of language, a transformation as well as a momentary suspension in the coming-to-pass of a revelation, a making felt or making visible. This is what I have sought to signal, albeit awkwardly, in the neologism and portmanteau word comprising *epoch* and *apocalypse*, which appears in the title of this essay, various meanings of which two words I have been employing on occasion, and which pairing of 'strange attractors' I have just given again: *epochalypse*. The strange, wilfully distorted nature of this word might have arrested the reader's attention, giving her pause on the very threshold of reading. Hypothetically (to work this figure yet again), and to risk a certain temporal disorder as an impossible hope, it will therefore have given one pause, perhaps, though this is far from being certain. However much I might be playing on the possibility of interruption, of hiatus or suspension on the very point of getting things going, I cannot actually programme such a disruption, for, as must now be apparent, the event itself remains absolutely unpredictable, surprising even to itself and the very idea of an 'itself'. It remains outside, before any conscious intention. All temporality is disordered between what might have taken place and any consideration of what could take place. The gap between the very possibility and all talk about the possibility is unclosable, and leaves one, yet again, with the experience of the undecidable. And here I am then, after and before, repeatedly – 'I' as the sign of a spatio-temporal *itara*, without a present, without presence (analogous, and yet markedly not the same as, that other figure already announced, *today*). 'I' signs, as you know. It tongues as well, in an erotics of transference, where the reader (my favourite fantasy) might come to mouth my phantom articulations, my ghostly figure fluttering across his or her tongue, before and after, coming and going repeatedly. In gestures of afterword and foreword, the one always read within the other as the other of the one, there being traced and anticipated the potential for relation without relation; and I, never being able to say what will have arrived, and yet, strangely enough, reflecting after the fact on a desired intent which is also an unfulfilled desire, a futurity without

guarantee. In the double gesture overwriting a single word and inaugurating – inventing? – both suspension and opening in a single inscription, I wish to signal however obliquely the idea of the book as advent and eventuality of contesting traces, if not ending the book then irreversibly placing 'it' under erasure, by the conceit of putting order and programme to work against themselves.

The neologism appears tortuously playful and punning, allusive and stuttering, self-consciously self-advertising. Look at me, it demands, on the one hand. Read me if you can, it implies, on the other. So, apparently, a typical, and typically, awkward writing gesture, typical because so transparently and archly overwritten by 'one of those critics'; you know, one whose writing makes you 'faint from *ennui*', whose writing is typified by 'epigonal dilution', by the 'dense fog' of his prose, or, allegedly, a 'wild deconstructive abandon'. (I cite, from memory, my own anonymous reviews; these are the best.) I would rush to assure you that I'm not being defensive or anxious, but that seems futile. The best I can do – the *only* thing I can do – is to aver that signalling such responses admits that an effect has occurred, despite all absence of conscious intention to produce the responses in question. Such responses, and such effects, have taken place repeatedly, and, doubtless, will continue to do so. And again. And again. However, despite the air of *gaucherie* to be read here, to be read without any sense that this odd word is or will have been read, my vulgar, blatant efforts in the construction of this word seek, against all experience, to enact particular concerns in this essay by weaving crudely particular threads. Indeed, it may even be the case that the word and phrase in parentheses following the title evinces a writing style that 'is not a mannerism at all', in the condemnatory words of Stanley Fish, 'but a self-consciously employed strategy that is intended to produce among other things, impatience and irritation' (Fish, 1989, 63). Among other things indeed, though concerning what those other things might be, Fish is notoriously vague and, therefore, irritating. But then I cannot control the effects any more than I can control whatever it is that I thought or believed that I had intended. If anything has taken place at all this is not solely governable by any intention on the part of the writing subject. Surely, the point is, *pace* Fish, that, whatever 'I' does or does not intend, there is no way in which the title's work is received at all, or, indeed, supposing it to be received, is received as anything other than the kind of mannerism to which Fish is alert, and of which he is, I suspect, rightly suspicious.

Thus, the notion of the event is not to be neutralised 'by referring it to the subject', as Geoffrey Bennington avers in his commentary on Derrida's *Politics of Friendship* (Bennington, 2000, 27). The event's relation to decision is effected through what seems a profound dismissal of the subject: 'nothing ever happens to a subject, nothing deserving the name "event"' (Derrida, 1997, 68). My language, what I call *my* language, in all truth precedes and exceeds my particular instances of articulation. I inhabit – 'I' inhabits – the uncanny place called language, where every utterance takes place because language gives place to that re-mark, never quite itself. With every utterance, 'my' speaking is haunted by the articulation of the other, that 'irruptive event of the gift' that gives itself to be thought and thereby disrupts and displaces all primacy of being, which does not await my conscious decision to speak, and which resonates with a revenant force 'before everything, before every determinable being' (Derrida, 1986, 242a).

Something strange and estranging is occurring here. What takes place is the staging of a 'between', a performative movement which, in making possible the articulation of any supposedly separable notion of event or sign, or

event or citation, for example, nevertheless collapses any systematic stability of such categorial absolutes. The collapse takes place through the event '*as* it out-comes . . . *as* it happens . . . The mode of the event is time itself as the time of the coming up' (Nancy, 1998, 99). And this temporality is not related to historical sequence but to 'its arising, as the arising it is' (Nancy, 1998, 98). The motif of 'between' is also a figure of becoming, which acknowledges a performative transport, a transference-between which establishes no relation or connection, except through the motion of what passes and crosses borders, moves across thresholds and, in so doing, erases and overflows the boundaries of any ontological category. The event cannot be thought without the sign, without that which takes place through signification as reading and memory; and yet the sign or any chain of signifiers is never simply a substitution for, or a representation (in any straightforward, ontological or mimetological sense) of, the event. The event cannot be represented as event but, if an event occurs, it generates those traces by which it is only ever acknowledged belatedly in an act of response, and without which response the marks or signs go unremarked. Perception of the event is therefore irreducible to any simple representational or mimetological function as already implied, and it is perhaps a sign of the radicality of 'eventness' that representation is left in ruins, while all that remains, as the remains of the event, are the anachronic ghostly traces that haunt the subject, the *après-coup* having always already fallen, and falling again and again in endless iterability. And it is all the more spectral in that, in the surprise of revelation, one encounters and responds to the 'there is' of the event, while being forced to recognize that 'what there is (*il y a*) there (*là*) does not exist' (Caputo, 1997, 36).

Clearly, all stable categories of presence/absence, visibility/invisibility, priority/secondarity are disrupted by the phantasmic traversal or trans-lation with which we are concerned. Michel Foucault draws out the relation without relation of the phantasm and event, acknowledging its haunting disinterrance and disruption of categories and locations: 'As for the phantasm, it is "excessive" with respect to the singularity of the event, but this "excess" does not designate an imaginary supplement adding itself to the bare reality of facts . . . This conception of the phantasm [appears] as the play of the missing event and its repetition . . . it presents itself as universal singularity' (Foucault, 1998, 352). He then proceeds to address the implications of thinking the non-relation of the phantasm and the event in a performative register that accounts for the haunting strangeness of the other within thought, in a manner suggestive for thinking that which haunts the book in its relation to event: 'If the role of thought is to produce the phantasm theatrically and to repeat the universal event in its extreme point of singularity, then what is thought itself if not the even that befalls the phantasm and the phantasmatic repetition of the absent event? The phantasm and the event, affirmed in disjunction, are the object of thought [*le pensé*] and thought itself [*la pensée*] . . . Thought has to think through what forms it and is formed out of what it thinks through' (Foucault, 1998, 353). Derrida of course notes such estrangement in 'Signature Event Context', when he cautions:

> . . . one must less oppose citation or iteration to
> the noniteration of the event, than construct a dif-
> ferential typology of forms of iteration, supposing
> that this is a tenable project . . . Above all, one
> then would be concerned with different types of
> marks or chains of iterable marks, and not with an
> opposition between citational statements on the

> one hand, and singular and original statement-
> events on the other.
>
> (Derrida, 1982, 326)

It will be noted from the outset that one should avoid any fall into habits of thought reliant on dialectical structures. The question cannot be one simply of thinking 'event' on the one hand and iterability or citationality on the other, but of recognising that other which is in place, which takes place within the same, as 'a distribution of difference . . . a performance of *sense* . . . an articulation and a movement' (Colebrook, 2000, 114). Derrida's notion of a differential typology is proposed around the active reinscription, the rereading of the notion of intention, whereby, as is well-known, intention remains to be considered but without that consideration assuming that intention can govern or master all utterances. The idea of the differential typology is one which accords with the motif and motion that is named 'between' above, an infinitely subdividable, self-differentiating and self-differencing disarticulation that dismantles the stability of either the sign/event binarism or that proposed as the citational statement/statement-event pairing. Furthermore, the very conceit of the differential typology is itself unstable, if not performative and undecidable, for it operates around the possibility of imagining the speech act ungovernable by any typology that would remain programmatically constant across any range of utterances. A differential typology names and proposes a typology that transforms itself from within itself, overflowing any merely machinic or programmatic model in order to account for every singular and exemplary speech act, of which there is no ordering model except for that which is peculiar to the 'statement-event'. Yet more than this occurs. For Derrida's proposition, and of course the essay from which we are citing, alters the comprehension of the speech act and its Austinian typology irreversibly. Derrida's text performs an irreversible troping of the speech act and what might be called its 'typology' in a manner that resounds with its own performative event, even as Derrida is responding to that which is other within Austin and which surprises the Austinian text, exposing even as it trespasses its limits. Suspending conventional wisdom concerning speech acts in an epochal fashion, Derrida thereby brings about *in stricto sensu* an apocalyptic dismantling of the ontology – possibly an onto-typology – of speech acts. Or, more precisely, Derrida's reading traces the marks of an encrypted event within speech act theory which has always already contaminated its coherence, and to which Derrida merely responds in a belated fashion, as is only befitting any subjective reaction to an event. Derrida thus witnesses that which has arrived and retreated, to which he responds after the event. The event taking place is then revealed in its dismantling temporal force, in the wake of which reading and the reading subject can only follow. For the event, any event, always implies an impossible and vertiginous multi- and hetero-temporality, articulating the not yet which already is.

III

It is necessary to retrace certain steps. A book's publication is often referred to as its 'coming out', as if to signal, albeit tacitly, that book and *e-vent* (*e-venire*: to come out) are invisibly linked in some uncanny or phantasmic manner. Speaking analogously, it is *as if* there were some spectral bond between dissimilarities, or *as if* there were to be read between the one and the other a form of non-synonymous substitution, to use a phrase already posited in an earlier question. The 'coming out' is also a disclosed-ness, a becoming-visible. The material manifestation of a book might, in these terms, be understood as a particular embodiment of that which is otherwise immaterial, that is to say thought. In this, the book's publication could be said to materialize, and to order momentarily thought, in a peculiar, uncanny – because neither alive nor dead, yet somewhere in-between – manner. Thought disclosed, appearing before the eye in the guise of the book as the simulacrum or phantasm of thought. The book as *Ereignis*, then, as happening or event, the book neither commensurate with nor the same as the event, yet readable according to the logic of the 'happening', to recall the words of Jean-Luc Nancy? Perhaps, however fanciful this might seem. For the notion of *Ereignis* is haunted by its earlier form, *Eräugnis*, meaning to place before the eye, to be disclosed. At the same time, as readers of Heidegger will doubtless be aware, the notion of *Ereignis* invokes *Eigen*, 'one's own' and 'appropriating'. However, in 'coming out', in being countersigned by the inauguration of its public availability for some future-conditional exhausting, unending iterability, a book is haunted. It arrives and promises to arrive repeatedly, disclosing thought through the 'simulacrum and effect of language' / 'simulacra et effet de langue' embodying 'the thing as other and as other thing come to pass with the allure of an inappropriable event (*Ereignis* in abyss)' / 'la chose en tant qu'autre et en tant qu'autre chose peut advenir dans l'allure d'un événement inappropriable (*Ereignis* en abîme)' (Derrida, 1984, 102/103). Derrida is speaking here of the name and work of fiction, and 'allure' names for him 'the action of something that comes without coming, the thing that concerns us in *this strange event*' / 'la demarche de ce qui vient sans venir, ce deont il y va dans cet étrange événement' (Derrida, 1984, 102/103; emphasis added). I want to suggest that a book is nothing other than this constant arrival of thought, of that something which is not a thing, which comes without coming. And the book figures this *strange event*, always already traced as it is or will have been, not only by the remainders of memories but also by its endless arrivals to come. A book's publication, its coming out, to use that phrase once more, or otherwise what might be termed its *eventiality*,[2] is always dated (and in more than one sense). However, though dated – even before publication, before the date intended or assigned for its appearance, a book is dated, traced through by countless dates, acts of dating, *data*, and, therefore always late, hopelessly so – it never ceases arriving. And this is the situation even if it never arrives, either in some intended manner or, indeed, ever. The book therefore names that which exceeds any idea of the book conventionally understood, and this not least in part as a result of work of language.

In the end, or in the beginning, then, the only possible answers to any of the questions so far posited throughout this essay are those that acknowledge the inauguration, the advent, or what is termed a 'rhetorical event' (Anidjar, 2002, 3) *in* language and *by* language, of an unsettling, a destabilization, as well as an erasure, of 'contexts, whether literary, historical or cultural' (Anidjar, 2002, 3). All of which effects are – to insist on this once more, and so to have got no further than the torque of the title and the ghosts by which it is caused to tremble – both the suspension of contexts in the instant of singular intensity that we call 'book' and a revelation through language of the event we call language. Suspension and revelation; give and take; epoch and apocalypse. Such effects find themselves encrypted in the very principle of the book and its appearance, despite the fact that a book, considered as a work, is a finite form supposedly imposing limit and order, bringing the play of writing to an end. Thinking the book in this fashion, as spectral countersignature to its material self, there emerges as somewhat traceable the notion of an ineluctable resonance within any identity, any determination already addressed repeatedly, which, as just this ghostly give and take, is irreducible to and yet in excess of simple form, stable structure, fixed meaning. The material event of a book's advent only serves to advertise the event of its 'spectral – and potentialized – encounter' (Massumi, 2002, 32). The book or, more accurately, the idea of the book as an '"implicit" form is a bundling of potential functions, an infolding or contraction of potential interactions . . . The playing out of those potentials requires . . . extension as actualization; actualization as *expression . . . The limits of the field of emergence are in its actual expression.* Implicit form may be thought of as effective presence of the sum total of a thing's interactions minus the thing' (Massumi, 2002, 34–5). Or, the book itself, advent as event, the material limits of which do nothing, or next to nothing in limiting the rhetorical events in language not yet having taken place by always already arriving. In its occurrence, language itself is the performative and irreversible event, 'every sentence . . . part of a chain of performative utterances opening out more and more' (Miller, 2002, 30). Given this opening out, an opening which is also an endless coming, invention and advent, might we not name this give and take – which has troubled this essay from the outset, preventing it from proceeding and causing it always to turn and return upon itself –, this unending arrival and withdrawal of the other within the same, *Glossalalia*? And in response to this word might we not register that which Walter Benjamin has described as the 'somewhat provisional way of coming to terms with the foreignness of all languages' (Benjamin, cit. Anidjar, 2002, 3)?

Notes

1. I first coin this term, as a figure for the anarchic disordering inherent within, and in excess of any structure or 'architecture' of knowledge, discourse or discipline, with specific reference to Lewis Carroll's *Alice* books, in my *The Rhetoric of Affirmative Resistance: Dissonant Identities from Carroll to Derrida* (1996).
2. While, earlier in the essay, I have referred to 'eventuality', there seems in this term the insistence or implication, at least, of something to-come which can be guaranteed. I have used *eventiality* to suggest the notion of the event-ness of an event, without indicating certainty of this possibility.

Works cited

Anidjar, Gil. *'Our Place in al-Andalus': Kabbahlah, Philosophy, Literature in Arab Jewish Letters*. Stanford, CA, 2002.

Benjamin, Andrew. *The Plural Event: Descartes, Hegel, Heidegger.* London, 1993.

Bennington, Geoffrey. *Interrupting Derrida*. London, 2001.

Caputo, John D. *The Prayers and Tears of Jacques Derrida: Religion without Religion*. Bloomington, IN, 1997.

Colebrook, Claire. 'Is Sexual Difference a Problem?', in Ian Buchanan and Claire Colebrook (eds). *Deleuze and Feminist Theory*. Edinburgh, 2000, 110–27.

Derrida, Jacques. *Of Grammatology*, trans. Gayatri Chakravorty Spivak. Baltimore, MD, 1976.

Derrida, Jacques. 'Signature Event Context', *Margins of Philosophy*, trans. Alan Bass. Chicago, IL, 1982, 307–30.

Derrida, Jacques. *Signéponge/Signsponge*, trans. Richard Rand. New York, 1984.

Derrida, Jacques. *Parages*. Paris, 1986.

Derrida, Jacques. 'Psyche: Inventions of the Other', trans. Catherine Porter, in Lindsay Waters and Wlad Godzich (eds), *Reading de Man Reading*. Minneapolis, MN, 1989, 25–65.

Derrida, Jacques. *Politics of Friendship*, trans. George Collins. London, 1997.

Fish, Stanley. *Doing What Comes Naturally: Change, Rhetoric, and the Practice of Theory in Literary and Legal Studies*. Durham, NC, 1989.

Foucault, Michel. 'Theatricum Philosophicum', trans. Donald F. Brouchard and Sherry Simon, in Michel Foucault, *Aesthetics, Method, and Epistemology: Essential Works of Foucault 1954–1984 Volume Two*, ed. James D. Faubion, trans. Robert Hurley et al. New York, 1998, 343–68.

Hobson, Marian. *Jacques Derrida: Opening Lines*. London, 1998.

Joyce, James. *Finnegans Wake*. London, 1939.

Kronick, Joseph G. *Derrida and the Future of Literature*. Albany, NY, 1999.

Massumi, Brian. *Parables for the Virtual: Movement, Affect, Sensation.* Durham, NC, 2002.

Miller, J. Hillis. *On Literature*. London, 2002.

Nancy, Jean-Luc. 'The Surprise of the Event', trans. Lynn Festa and Stuart Barnett, in *Hegel After Derrida*, ed. Stuart Barnett. London, 1998, 91–104.

Nora, Pierre. 'General Introduction: Between Memory and History', in *Realms of Memory: Rethinking the French Past*, 2 vols, under the direction of Pierre Nora, English-language edition ed. and foreword Lawrence D. Kritzman, trans. Arthur Goldhammer. New York, 1996, I: 1–20.

Sallis, John. *On Translation*. Bloomington, IN, 2002.

Wolfreys, Julian. *The Rhetoric of Affirmative Resistance: Dissonant Identities from Carroll to Derrida*. Basingstoke, 1996.

flirting | *RUTH ROBBINS*

Algernon to Jack: *My dear fellow, the way you flirt with Gwendolen is perfectly disgraceful. It is almost as bad as the way Gwendolen flirts with you.*

Oscar Wilde

Shoshana Felman . . . distinguishes between Lacan and contemporary French 'deconstructive' philosophy on the grounds that philosophy, no matter how deconstructive, remains 'discursive', whereas Lacan's writing is 'poetic': allusive, contradictory. The ladies' man is an expert at flirtation. Unlike the man's man, the philosopher or hunter, the ladies' man is always embroiled in coquetry: his words necessarily and erotically ambiguous. The ladies' man is looked at askance by the 'real man' who suspects the flirt of effeminacy.

Feminists have been hard on the ladies' man, presuming that his intentions are strictly dishonourable. They're right . . .

Jane Gallop

Most of our exchanges are regulated by game strategies . . . defined as a capacity to foresee all of one's opponent's moves and check them in advance.

Jean Baudrillard

On the face of it, flirting is an old-fashioned activity, apparently more at home in the pages of Restoration Drama or the late eighteenth-century comedy of manners than in our cynical millennial world.[1] And, indeed, many of the definitions of the word in the OED are marked with the tell-tale sign '*obs*' for 'obsolete'. It is, though, quite interesting to note which definitions are no longer usable, and which remain apparently untouched by time. The obsolete meanings are the terms to do with sudden movements in the physical world, and unexpected motions in conversation – a smart tap or blow, a rap, a fillip, a sudden jerk or movement, a quick throw or cast, a darting motion, a gust of wind; and in conversation, a smart stroke of wit, a joke, a jest, a gibe, a jeer, a scoff. On the other hand, the meanings that appear to still be current are those to do with sexual behaviour. A flirt is 'a fickle, inconstant person': so far so neutral/neuter. But a flirt is also 'a woman of giddy, flighty character', 'a pert young hussey' (the quotation is in the definition, not in the illustrative quotations) and 'a woman of loose character'. A flirt is 'one who flirts, or plays at courtship' and is usually 'said of a woman'. Just in case the OED is slow-moving – hardly flirtatious at all, with its strict nineteenth-century morals still intact – Chambers Dictionary, up-to-the-minute in every way, tells us that to flirt means: 'to play at courtship, to indulge in light-hearted amorous or sexual banter (with); to trifle, toy or dally (with)'. In Chambers a flirt, however, is 'a pert giddy girl; a person who behaves flirtatiously'. Somehow, wherever you look, there is more at stake in flirting for women than there is for men. But the men are almost absent from the definitions, parenthetically existing only in the '(with)' that makes the verb transitive: flirting has to have an object, and that object appears to be a man.

One of the things that this short etymological diversion points out, as Michel Foucault has shown us with reference to words such as 'criminal' and 'homosexual' and their use at the end of the nineteenth century, is that there is a qualitatively different way of seeing the world and its inhabitants when a verb or an adjective becomes a noun (1984, 43). Someone who flirts – well, that's fine, it's good clean fun, and it does not define a person in his/her entirety. But *to be a flirt* means something quite different. In particular, *being a flirt* seems to be something that women are, and it is threatening because it reverses so many of the conventional assumptions about normative sexual behaviour (the man pursues, the woman is pursued). The flirt is a menace because she is articulating her own desire – precisely the desire that western cultures have been at so much pain to deny the existence of. After all, a flirtation is only the beginning of something. Presumably sex itself is the endpoint. Flirtation is the opening gambit in the game of seduction. On the rare occasions where it is the man who is 'a' flirt, he is misplaying the game, fighting with woman's weapons of fickleness and flightiness, rather than playing it straight with his undiverted purpose and his coherent discourse.

Would that it were so simple. What I want to suggest is that flirting is a highly liminal activity, existing on the margins of acceptable sexual behaviour. There is a clear sense in which the social intercourse of banter and laughter is supposed to lead to the *telos* of sexual intercourse. Flirting has its serious side, but it is also clearly a game, with rules more or less well understood by its players. It is based on laughter and repartee. Repartee, however, is a

fencing term to do with the ritualized exchange of blows during a contest. In fencing the rules of repartee exist in order to protect the players from serious injury. The rules of flirting, however, might be a code, but they are not so completely codified. The relationship between flirting and repartee exposes that both are rituals; but it also exposes that both are rituals that divert or avoid violence. The incompetent fencer, like the incompetent flirt, might just get hurt.

Writing about 'writing', J. Hillis Miller argues that writing is unlike thinking about your beloved, and absolutely unlike touching, holding or kissing him '(or her)' (1999, 288). Although 'nothing is easier than writing – a letter, for example', writing enacts a dislocation of the selves involved in the so-called communication:

> *Writing is a dislocation in the sense that it moves the soul itself of the writer, as well as of the recipient, beyond or outside itself, over there, somewhere else. Far from being a form of communication, the writing of a letter dispossesses both the writer and the receiver of themselves. Writing creates a new phantom written self and a phantom receiver of that writing. There is correspondence all right, but it is between two entirely phantasmagorical or fantastic persons, ghosts raised by the hand that writes. Writing calls phantoms into being . . .*
>
> (289)

These comments depend for their force on the paradox that it is a myth that speech precedes writing, that social intercourse precedes literate exchange, that orality is primary and literacy merely a poor second. Miller then moves on to discuss the ways in which letters do utterly violent things to our sense of coherent self, and to expectation, referring to Jacques Derrida's discussions of the performative nature of writing:

> Derrida speculates on the performative power a letter (in the epistolary sense) may have in order to bring into existence an appropriate recipient. If a letter happens to fall into my hands I may become the person that letter needs as its receiver, even though that new self is discontinuous with the self I have been up till now . . . [T]he performative power of the letter is not foreseen or intended.
>
> (289)

It seems to me that one might make a similar argument about the ritualized exchanges of social intercourse even when it is *in person* rather than in a written communication. In other words, flirting is also performative in that, like writing, it calls into existence the very interlocutor it requires. The binary opposition of writing and speaking is not secure. Both are codes that are open to misinterpretation.

There are other kinds of *in person* exchanges that demand a particular response. Notable among them is the so-called 'primitive' tradition of potlatch, where gifts of increasing extravagance are exchanged, the second gift being called into being by the prior existence of the other, and by the participants' knowledge of the rules of the game. Similarly, the ritual insult of the tradition of 'flyting', still existing today among young, usually Black, men and boys in British and North American cities (in British cities they call it 'y'mutha' and because it is the ritualized exchange of abuse about the participants' mums) works by one insult calling another into existence in a heady and foul-mouthed accumulation of gratuitous vulgarity. As Baudrillard puts it, potlatch and flyting are 'a symbolic altercation or duel of words. By these ritual phrases and palavers without content, the natives were still throwing a challenge and offering a gift, as in a pure ceremonial' (1990, 164). What differs here from flirting is that these are plays without ostensible purpose beyond the immediate need to establish contact – 'phatic' exchanges. Flirting, however, is game with a function, an endpoint that will ideally take place in the bedroom. If flirting works as both ritual and mutual exchange the result will be pleasure all round; if not, if the interlocutor is improperly called into being, or if one of the players does not really know the rules of the game, flirting risks rape rather than seduction. The potential violence of flyting and potlatch are only more extreme versions of what is going on in flirtatious exchange, or the passes (interesting word) made in fencing.

This is a point made abundantly clear by Aphra Behn's *The Rover; or, The Banished Cavaliers* (1677). The situation of the play is that the Banished Cavaliers, Belvile, Willmore, Frederick and Blunt, are in Naples for the Carnival. The licence of carnival allows abundant opportunity for mistaken identity and failed flirtations, for often in the course of the action, the 'wrong' cavalier will court the wrong woman. Carnival, of course, is a time of ritualized licence but, as Derek Hughes puts it:

> The male and female body stand in different relations to the signs by which they are publicly represented, and for this reason the carnival masquerade offers them liberation and danger in different proportions. The carnival is not so much an inversion of the typical as a special case of the typical, and its function, therefore, is less to suspend established order than to expose the elemental patterns of power which underlie it:

patterns in which the woman is likely to become victim or commodity.

(2001, 89)

The play will end with the three heroes appropriately married to the commodified heroines Florinda, Hellena and Valeria respectively, whose worth is in their fortunes as much as it is in their faces; and the 'Essex moon-calf', Blunt, equally appropriately will have been tricked and robbed by the whore Lucetta. But although the ending speaks of ritual – it is neat, symmetrical and somehow 'just' – the process by which this outcome is reached exposes the potential violence of flirtatious exchange.

The least interesting of the men are Belvile and his pale shadow Frederick. Belvile is a generally honourable and chivalrous cavalier, playing more or less by the rules of courtly love. When we first meet him he is sighing for his forbidden beloved, Florinda, and is unwilling to participate in any other act of seduction such as the Carnival makes possible. And Frederick is only slightly less squeamish. Blunt, on the other hand, an escapee from Puritan England, is only too willing to chance his arm in the game of love. Unfortunately for him, he does not know its rules. The whore, Lucetta, calls him into being as a handsome young man whom she cannot resist, and despite the evidence of his mirror, he is only too happy to believe her:

> LUCETTA: *This is a stranger, I know by his gazing; if he be brisk, he'll venture to follow me; and then if I understand my trade, he's mine; he's English too, and they say that's a sort of good-natured loving people, and have generally so kind an opinion of themselves, that a woman with any wit may flatter 'em into any sort of fool she pleases.*

> [She often passes by Blunt, and gazes on him, he struts and cocks, and walks and gazes on her.]
> BLUNT: *'Tis so – she is taken – I have beauties which my false glass at home did not discover.*

(Behn, 1992, 170)[2]

The result of her being 'taken' is that he is taken in. He is tricked into bed in a darkened room, stripped of his clothes and money, and flushed into the sewers for his self-deception. The price of claiming the role of 'cock of the walk' when it has not been earned is that he ends up as easy prey.

Blunt is unusual as the male victim of flirtation. On the other hand, all he has lost is his clothes and his dignity. The stakes are very much higher for a woman, as the various female characters' encounters with Willmore the rover attest. Willmore – probably named for the real Restoration rake, John Wilmot, Second Earl of Rochester (1647–80) – plays flirting games with an intention of seduction that is scarcely veiled at all. He declares on his first entrance that 'love and mirth are my business in Naples' (166), and is clearly very anxious to unload his libido without much discrimination as to where he does so. Indeed, there is a sexual desperation about him. He importunes the prostitutes of the street as well as the much more expensive courtesan, Angellica Bianca, and the virginal lady of honour, Hellena. He tries to take his opportunities wherever he finds them, with almost no disguise of his highly dishonourable purpose. In a most telling scene, he enters Florinda's walled garden at night – it is unlocked to facilitate her escape to Belvile – and when he finds her there in her nightgown, he regards this as a positive invitation:

> FLORINDA: *Oh I am ruined – wicked man, unhand me.*

WILLMORE: *Wicked! – egad child, a judge were he young and vigorous, and saw those eyes of thine, would know 'twas they gave the first blow – the first provocation – come, prithee let's lose no time, I say – this is a fine convenient place . . .*

FLORINDA: *I'll cry Murder! Rape! or anything! if you do not instantly let me go.*

WILLMORE: *A rape! Come, come, you lie, baggage, you lie, what, I'll warrant you would fain have the world believe that you are not so forward as I. No, not you – why at this time of night was your cobweb door set open dear spider – but to catch flies? . . .*

(202)

Willmore is an expert reader of the signs of courtship: a young woman, alone, at night, in an open garden, in a state of undress, with youth and beautiful eyes to recommend her. What else can she possibly be thinking of? She is, one might say, asking for it. And, of course, it is true that Florinda is in this state precisely in order to get to Belvile, her beloved. The interlocutor she has called into being by her flirtatious actions, however, is not the interlocutor she desires. The mismatch of their expectations could result not in seduction (the desired outcome, licensed by marriage), but rape, seduction's much nastier other half. (Interestingly, Florinda never learns. Later in the play, she throws herself on the chivalry of Ned Blunt, desperately trying to construct him as a decent honourable man, and herself as an honourable maid as she tries to escape from her brother – '*as you seem a gentleman*, pity a harmless virgin that takes your house for sanctuary' (225); but Ned refuses to play ball, and just like Willmore, threatens her with a barely evaded rape.)

The rules in Willmore's relationship with the courtesan Angellica Bianca can scarcely be described as flirtation. The whore knows her own business, and declares: 'I am resolved that nothing but gold shall charm my heart' (178). Only, Willmore has no gold, and charms her nonetheless. Quite how he does so is something of a mystery. It can't be good looks alone, since he is certainly rather worn by the misfortunes of the Royalist cause in England – 'I believe those breeches and he have been acquainted since he was beaten at Worcester' (184). And his speech to Angellica is hardly flirtatious. He insults her by bringing the commercial nature of her transaction to the fore; 'madam, my stock will not reach [your price], I cannot be your chapman – yet I have countrymen in town, merchants of love like me; I'll see if they'll put in for a share, we cannot lose much by it, and what we have no use for, we'll sell upon Friday's mart at – "Who gives more?"' (184–5). He scorns her for the commodification of her person and the commercial taint of her business, yet nonetheless ends up in her bed. He then betrays her by falling in love with Hellena, showing that when women like Angellica are constructed into a generous mode, the giving is all one way. She had hoped he would love her and 'paid him . . . a heart entire' (193), which she expected to be reciprocated. The constant woman – even if she is a courtesan – has no hold on the flirt, whose motions are swift and sudden, and whose heart is inconstant.

With Hellena, however, Willmore quite literally meets his match. She is a woman who knows her own worth in physical, moral and material terms (she has a fortune of 300,000 crowns). As she says to her sister:

> *. . . prithee tell me, what dost thou see about me that is unfit for love – have I not a world of youth? a humour gay? a beauty passable? a vigour*

desirable? well shaped? clean limbed? sweet
breathed? and sense enough to know how all
these ought to be employed to the best advan-
tage; yes, I do, and will . . .

(160)

She is, despite her charms, supposedly destined to go into a convent. She makes the best of the carnival time to escape this fate and spends much of the play in disguise – as a gypsy, one on the very margins of society, and in travesty, enacting her equality with any man in her masculine attire. Her 'humour gay' matches Willmore's, and although she falls in love with him before he falls in love with her, she manages her flirtation in such a way as to bring it a satisfactory end. Recognizing that Willmore is a libertine, unlikely ever to be bound by the rules, she decides to play him at his own game. She tells him:

we are both of one humour; I am as inconstant as
you, for I have considered, captain, that a hand-
some woman has a great deal to do whilst her
face is good, for then is our harvest-time to gather
friends; and should I in these days of my youth
catch a fit of foolish constancy, I were undone; 'tis
loitering by daylight in our great journey: therefore
I declare, I'll allow but one year for love, one year
for indifference, and one year for hate – and then
– go hang yourself – for I profess myself the gay,
the kind, and the inconstant – and the devil's in't if
this won't please you.

(193)

Nonetheless, she insists on the 'bug word' marriage before she will sleep with him because she requires its protection from the consequences of sexual liaison – 'a cradle full of noise and mischief, with a pack of repentance at my back' (242). What kind of marriage it will be is hard to know, but it is clearly implied that it will be a severely modified version of 'happily ever after'; if Willmore strays from his vows, then Hellena will be licensed to do the same. As Willmore says near the end of the play: 'I am of a nation that are of opinion that a woman's honour is not worth guarding when she has a mind to part with it' which Hellena regards as 'well said' (244). Only in this case have the flirtatious plays of wit called into being the proper recipient of them. Apparently innocent Hellena renames herself Hellena the Inconstant, and learns quickly to be more 'knowing' than Willmore with his roving eye.

The aristocratic manners of seventeenth-century Naples, even in their representation in a play on the English stage, provide a very different context for flirtation than, say, the rustic world of late-nineteenth-century Wessex – though both locations are equally fictional. In the seventeenth-century play, flirtation is a way of life; it is a ritual expressing desire and a method for managing its violence. In Hardy's nineteenth-century novel, *Jude the Obscure* (1895), flirting makes the sex much more apparent. In a book that is often presented as resolutely tragic and gloomy, there are nonetheless some comic moments, and none more so than Arabella's flirtation with Jude, using a pig's pizzle as the emblem of her desire. (This takes us back, by the way, to some of the older meanings of the word, where a flirt is a tap, a blow, a rap, or a fillip, a smart stroke – if not of wit, then of pregnant meaning – a joke, a jest, a jibe, a jeer, a scoff.) As Jude wanders round the countryside in Chapter 6, trying to think great thoughts about the intellectual and spiritual world, about 'Euripides, Plato, Aristotle, Lucretius, Epictetus, Seneca, Antoninus' and planning how he will master 'Bede and ecclesiastical history', three women at work washing out pigs' innards across the way shout 'Hoity-toity' at him, and he does not hear them (Hardy, 1998, 37). 'Hoity-toity' is hardly subtle or witty as an opening gambit. But then, the subtle and the witty would be carried away in the wind of the open rural landscape. Urban courtship – even when it takes place outside on the city streets at carnival time – is a much less earthy business, and can hold its own with subtler signs. Rural courtship must cut to the chase.

Jude's complete unconsciousness of the women across the stream is a kind of challenge to the presumption that men and women are made for each other and ought to try to come together. It is also a reversal of the usual order of desire where masculine sexuality is predatory and feminine sexuality is – where it exists at all – passive and preyed upon. Jude, unlike Willmore, has entirely sublimated the needs of his material body into his desire for learning. How can he be brought down a peg or two into the solidity of the real world and its pressing desires?

> In his deep concentration on these transactions of the future, Jude's walk had slackened, and he was now standing quite still, looking at the ground as though the future were thrown thereon by a magic lantern. On a sudden something smacked him sharply in the ear, and he became aware that a soft cold substance had been flung at him and had fallen at his feet.
>
> A glance told him what it was – a piece of flesh, the characteristic part of a barrow-pig, which the countrymen used for greasing their boots, as it was useless for any other purpose. Pigs were rather plentiful hereabout, being bred and fattened in large numbers in certain parts of North Wessex.
>
> (38)

A pig's penis, I suppose, is as good a way of drawing attention to the sexual nature of the world as anything missive/missile. It also makes Miller's point that whatever is sent to the beloved is open to (mis)interpretation: is a pig's penis a love trophy or an insult? Given that pigs are bred and 'plentiful' in the area, its 'uselessness' is surely in doubt. Whether throwing it at your intended quite counts as flirting is perhaps a moot point. Certainly the conversation the pig's pizzle engenders is hardly an exemplar of scintillating wit, and its presence, 'a limp object dangling across the handrail of the bridge' where the lovers finally meet (40), seems scarcely an aphrodisiac. But then, Arabella's intentions and her charms are both of a very fleshly kind. Flesh, not words, is what is at stake here, and limp flesh can become firm. The comedy of their courtship is that she pretty much seduces Jude against his will and without his conscious consent: he turns to Arabella in the first place 'for no reasoned purpose of further acquaintance, but in commonplace obedience to conjunctive orders from headquarters, unconsciously received by unfortunate men when the last intention of their lives is to be occupied with the feminine' (39). When he walks out with her the next day, neglecting his Greek testament to do so, he discovers that he quite likes the feeling of her firm flesh against his. On their next meeting, she tries to get him to lie down with her on the ground using the pretext of an interesting caterpillar in a tree (pizzles, caterpillars – she's an inventive girl in the rural wilderness) to get him stretched out next to her: Jude misunderstands, and the day ends in failure with Jude lamenting 'I expect I took too much liberty with her, somehow' while Arabella is annoyed precisely because he took too little (54).

When she finally gets him into her bed, it is because she has called him into being as a man of flesh and blood by the calculated use of her own physical charms. She teases him with her unavailability because she is nestling a delicate egg in her ample bosom. She leads him on and puts him off by turns, not with a linguistic flirtation, but with a bodily one; and eventually she leads him upstairs to his doom, for, unlike Willmore again, Jude is an honourable man, and feels obliged to marry Arabella when she tells him she is pregnant as a result of this encounter. For all the tragic context of *Jude the Obscure*, these scenes of flirtation and courtship are comic in the way that Carry On films (Jude as a nervous Kenneth Williams to Arabella's voracious Hattie Jacques) or Donald Gill's postcards are comic. The same situation with the genders reversed – as in Tess's seduction by Alec D'Urberville – lacks the humour. The difference lies in the balance of power between the sexes. The woman who is flirted with and seduced against her will is tragic because her desires have not been consulted; the man who is flirted with and seduced against his is a figure of fun because his desires have not been consulted, but they have been fulfilled. Or, as Jane Miller has put it:

> There are obvious reasons . . . for women's concern with seduction . . . It has . . . been women who were most often seduced, and it has usually been men who asserted, in one way or another, that a woman had given her consent to what may thereafter be thought of as a seduction . . . surrender to desire and to pleasure is not only more complex and dangerous for women, it is riskier to represent, always anomalously admitted to. Seduction comes to stand for the tensions and the dynamic inherent in the unequal relations between women and men.
>
> (1990, 22)

Arabella makes use of this inequality. It is the woman that takes the risk in the bedroom. She takes the risk of pregnancy – faked in Arabella's case, but a real risk all the same – as a way of trapping Jude into matrimony. Not for her, any more than for Hellena, the possibility of 'a cradle full of noise and mischief, with a pack of repentance at my back'. But at least Jude got some pleasure, even if he didn't know he wanted it.

Jude and Arabella's marriage is obviously a disaster. It lasts next to no time, and each of them returns to their own preoccupations – Jude initially to his books, Arabella to a new flirtation/seduction scenario on a different continent. But Jude is again diverted from his intentions by a second woman. Sue might be a very different proposition from Arabella; her flirtations take place in the mind not the body, and they appear to have no *telos*. Indeed, it is Sue whom Jude, rather sadly, describes as a flirt (Hardy, 1998, 204) because their relationship, which Sue pursues and encourages, can have no proper outcome (because at this point in the novel she is still married to Phillotson). If Arabella seduces by bodily wiles, Sue appears to transcend the material body, indeed scarcely to inhabit a body at all: 'There was nothing statuesque in her; all was nervous motion. She was mobile, living, yet a painter might not have called her handsome or beautiful' (90). Her fear of the body is perhaps the very reason that Jude sees her as a flirt, in the sense used in the juvenile discourse of the playground – she is a prick-tease, arousing emotions and physical responses (in both Jude and Phillotson) that she has no intention of satisfying. After all, she marries Phillotson, but jumps out of her bedroom window to avoid even the possibility of any sexual relation with him. Her first relationship with the unnamed student is also unconsummated:

> We shared a sitting room for fifteen months . . . till he was taken ill, and had to go abroad. He said I

was breaking his heart by holding out against him
so long at such close quarters; he could never
have believed it of a woman. I might play that
game once too often, *he said.*

(148, my emphasis)

And with Jude, when they first run away together, she does
play that game again, denying Jude the physical relationship on which he had believed their love was to be based.
Finally, on her last return to Phillotson, she again withholds
her sex from him, until, in a truly grotesque scene of repentance, she begs to be taken into his bed as a penance for
still loving Jude. Sue cannot relate feelings to her body at
all, and feels that there is something wrong with making the
object of her affections into the object of her desire. Her
flirtation is to make men love her, not to sleep with her;
Arabella's is to make men sleep with her, not to love her. '*If
you want to love me*', Sue writes to Jude, '*you may*' (155,
emphasis in original). But the desire she calls up in him is
not reciprocated: 'I've let you kiss me, and that tells
enough' (240), she says to Jude in the early stage of their
elopement, though a kiss is clearly not enough. And when
Jude calls her a flirt, she responds with the following
explanation:

> *I should shock you by letting you know how I give*
> *way to my impulses, and how much I feel that I*
> *shouldn't have been provided with attractiveness*
> *unless it were meant to be exercised! Some*
> *women's love of being loved is insatiable; and so,*
> *often, is their love of loving; and in the last case*
> *they may find that they can't give it continuously*
> *to the chamber-officer appointed by the bishop's*
> *license to receive it.*
>
> (204)

Marriage, the proper end of flirtation and seduction, seems
sordid to her, like running a pub (which, of course, Arabella
has done – no wonder she is so good at 'it'): 'I should begin
to be afraid of you, Jude, the moment you had contracted
to cherish me under a Government stamp, and I was
licensed to be loved on the premises' (259). In the end, flirting has to be about bodies as well as about speech. The
physical response is the endpoint. Sue's tragedy is her
failure to act upon this truth, her failure is the inability to
reciprocate the physical desires her speech calls up in the
other.

Successful flirtation need not, however, be as physically realized as Arabella's is. There is another way,
brought into sharp focus by Hardy's contemporary, Oscar
Wilde. (Both *Jude the Obscure* and *The Importance of
Being Earnest* first come to public notice in 1895.) The epigraph quotation from *Earnest* with which this essay began
is an articulation of successful flirtation as mutual recognition. Jack flirts with Gwendolen; Gwendolen flirts back.
Both play the game and both know the rules. It is, perhaps,
a much purer version of the game than is found in Hardy,
and probably purer than that found in Behn's play. Jean
Baudrillard has lamented the fact that games these days
seem to have to have a purpose, and wishes for a form of
play that is not end-determined:

> *We have already witnessed the debasement of*
> *play to the level of function – in play therapy, play*
> *school, play-as-catharsis and play-as-creativity.*
> *Throughout the fields of education and child*
> *psychology, play has become a 'vital function' or*
> *necessary phase of development. Or else it has*
> *been grafted onto the pleasure principle to*
> *become a revolutionary alternative, a dialectical*
> *overcoming of the reality principle in Marcuse, an*

ideology of play and the festival for others. But even as transgression, spontaneity, or aesthetic disinterestedness, play remains only a sublimated form of the old directive of pedagogy that gives it a meaning, assigns it an end, and thereby purges it of its power of seduction. Play as dreaming, sport, work, rest, or as transitional object – or as the physical hygiene necessary for psychological equilibrium or for a system's regulation or evolution. The very opposite of that passion for illusion which once characterized it.

(1990, 158)

It seems to me that Wilde's play comes pretty close to functioning as pure play – as flirtation without outcome. Although, as Neil Bartlett has pointed out, the play 'celebrates the triumph of marriage over all adversity, and brings down the curtain on a trio of engagements' (1989, 34), these are not to be marriages in the traditional happily-ever-after joining of individuals. Jack and Algy, Gwendolen and Cecily are virtually indistinguishable from each other. In the case of the men, this is signalled by the fact that they both appropriate the name Ernest (sign of sincerity and authenticity) in order to deceive. And both Cecily and Gwendolen fall in love with that name. In almost identical words, they tell their respective suitors: 'my ideal has always been to love someone with the name of Ernest. There is something in the name that inspires absolute confidence'.[3] Cecily, at least, is right in her confidence. Her beloved may not really be called Ernest, but in every other way, Algernon Moncrieff lives up in the flesh to the figure her words have conjured.

Cecily has created her version of Ernest in her patently fictional diary. Never having met him, but having heard him much discussed, she fabricates the object of her own desire in her journal; she sends herself love gifts from him, and even writes letters from Ernest to herself. When Algy protests that he has never sent her any letters, she retorts:

You need hardly remind me of that, Ernest. I remember it only too well. I grew tired of asking the postman every morning if he had a London letter for me. My health began to give way under the strain and anxiety. So I wrote your letters for you, and had them posted to me in the village by my maid. I always wrote three times a week, and sometimes oftener.

(394–5)

Talk about conjuring up the image of one's beloved. When Algy, aka Ernest, finally does turn up, the preliminaries of courtship have already been completed. Indeed, Cecily and Ernest have been engaged for three months despite never having met each other, and despite Algy's utter ignorance of the girl's existence. Here indeed is desire without bodies, play for its own sake.

The exchanges between Cecily and Algy might suggest something very profound in Wilde's play – that one constructs one's beloved in one's own image of the ideal, that the beloved is a phantom not a person. Or it might just be an extended joke. And in a sense, that might just be the point about flirting too. It can be read two ways – often simultaneously. It is the fun that leads to serious intentions, to seduction and/or to marriage; or, it is the fun that leads precisely nowhere. Both possibilities must exist, or else it's not flirting. Those original meanings of the word that have to do with sudden physical movements – or with fickleness and flightiness (old-fashioned words, both, like flirting itself) – are played out in the interpretations of the actions of flirtation. Will Hellena and Willmore really be inconstant to each other? We cannot quite decide. We have a set of interpretative rules that suggests that marriage is forever and ought to be happily-ever-after. We read those rules and we read the play together, and come up with an oscillating interpretation. There may be lots of marriages at the end of *Earnest*, but what kinds of marriages are they? Not quite fairytale, surely. Not fixed and utterly stable.

In her discussion of Lacan's 'Encore' seminar, Jane Gallop discusses and analyses Lacan's flirtatious performance at length. She *almost* admires that performance – to paraphrase, she is impressed by his cockiness even as she cocks a snook at it (after all, she describes him as 'a prick') (Gallop, 1982, 36). But, his intentions are 'strictly dishonourable' because he 'is not always seductive and elusive. His coy flirtation continually tends to freeze into a rigid system' (36). Flirtation ends – the kissing has to stop – at the point when it becomes necessary to fix things; erotic ambiguity freezes into facts. In the two plays I have discussed, this does not happen. Marriages are projected into the future beyond the end of the staged action. We do not see the end of flirtation, its fixity, played out before us.[4] In *Jude*, though, 'the letter killeth',[5] the fixed significance of marriage – whether legally enacted or not – where one is licensed to be loved on the premises, destroys the sudden movements on which flirtation depends. It leaves no space for ongoing processes of spontaneity. In the plays we – like most of the characters – know the rules of the games they play, and the rules of the genre within which they play them. In the novel, however, as John Goode has argued, genre is precisely what's at stake, and Hardy plays fast and loose with the rules, not for flirtatious purposes but to expose the 'offensive truth' of the way they fix people into particular roles. How can we have a novel that has 'carry-on scenes' juxtaposed with a child hanging his siblings? These things ought not to inhabit the same textual universe (1988, 142). In the end, Hardy is perhaps the more radical writer in that he flirts with his reader's expectations, but not because he wants to seduce us. That damp, limp pig's pizzle stands for the reader's ungratified desires, as well as for the gratuitous insult he offers our cosy view of the world: flirting as scoffing and jeering even as we have also been led on. The plays offer a happier version, one in which we are free and even content to be deceived and seduced and led astray. The ideal reader/spectator who is called into being by the spectacle of flirtation is exactly the one who is happy to believe in flirtation's happy endings. What else could be the point of flirting?

Notes

1. Not that flirting has died out, of course. In university campuses and playgrounds across Britain, young people flirt with the modern technology of the mobile phone, text-messaging their desires to each other. They have found ways of writing a smile and a wink. But what, I wonder, is the graphic equivalent of fluttering one's eyelashes?
2. My emphasis in the speeches.
3. These are the words of Gwendolen to Jack; Cecily's words to Algy are: 'You must not laugh at me, darling, but it had always been a girlish dream of mine to love someone whose name was Ernest . . . There is something in the name that seems to inspire absolute confidence' (395).
4. A sequel to *The Rover*, *The Second Part of the Rover* (1681) does exist; but it does not treat of Willmore and Hellena's marriage; at the opening of the play, he is already a widower, setting out once again with his newly liberated roving eye.
5. 2 Corinthians, 3: 6. The quotation is used as the title-page epigraph to the novel.

Works cited

Bartlett, Neil. *Who Was That Man? A Present for Mr. Oscar Wilde*. London, 1989.

Baudrillard, Jean. *Seduction*, trans. Brian Singer. London, 1990.

Behn, Aphra. *Oroonoko, The Rover and Other Works*, ed. Janet Todd. Harmondsworth, 1992.

Foucault, Michel. *The History of Sexuality, Volume 1*, trans. Robert Hurley. London, 1984, 43.

Gallop, Jane. *Feminism and Psychoanalysis: The Daughter's Seduction*. London, 1982.

Goode, John. *Thomas Hardy: The Offensive Truth*. Oxford, 1988.

Hardy, Thomas. *Jude the Obscure*. Harmondsworth, 1998.

Hughes, Derek. *The Theatre of Aphra Behn*. London, 2001.

Miller, Jane. *Seductions: Studies in Reading and Culture*. London, 1990.

Miller, J. Hillis. 'Thomas Hardy, Jacques Derrida, and the "Disclocation of Souls"', *Literary Theories: A Reader and Guide*, ed. Julian Wolfreys. Edinburgh, 1999.

Wilde, Oscar. *The Importance of Being Earnest, Complete Works*, ed. Merlin Holland. Glasgow, 1994.

genetics | STEPHANIE A. SMITH

The magic of gene therapy. Cloning. The Human Genome Project. DNA. This language of genetics, so much a part of the daily environment in the twenty-first century, may seem, at first glance, to have nothing to do with Herman Melville's nineteenth-century 'inside narrative', *Billy Budd*. And yet I have often heard the title character diagnosed as suffering from a genetic disorder – far more of a visceral 'inside narrative' than the author could have imagined.[1] It seems, however, that Billy's 'vocal defect . . . [that] his voice . . . was apt to develop an organic hesitancy, in fact more or less a stutter or even worse' (*Budd*, 53) points to a cognitive disorder. So does his illiteracy, and the fact that 'of self-consciousness he seemed to have little or none, or about as much as we may reasonably impute to a dog of Saint Bernard's breed' (*Budd*, 52), so that 'to deal in double-meanings and insinuations of any sort was quite foreign to his nature' (*Budd*, 49). All of these 'facts' are deemed evidence of a diagnosable genetic disorder – usually autism. His abandonment by his biological parents is only icing on this particular cake because they must have known he'd be 'defective' and couldn't deal with it so they left him 'in a pretty silk-lined basket hanging one morning from the knocker of a good man's door in Bristol' (*Budd*, 51).

Gone is the notion of irony. Gone, deadpan sarcasm. Gone the tried-and-true narrative of mysterious but noble heritage, which Melville clearly invokes when he says, 'Yes, Billy Budd was a foundling, a presumable by-blow and, evidently, no ignoble one. Noble descent was as evident in him as in a blood horse' (*Budd*, 52). Gone is the (racist and sexist) logic of naturalized distinctions that accompanied the class fantasy of noble blood, eighteenth- and nineteenth-century distinctions which would later subtend the logic of twentieth-century eugenics, a 'science' that gave rise to what we currently understand as genetics. But the troubling historical lineage of genetics is not at issue for this kind of 'genetic' interpretation, in part because invoking a genetic disorder as the source of the problems presented by the 'inside narrative' appears to resolve the ethical, legal and moral dilemmas of this text. Made over into a case that would, today, have proper medical remediation, Billy can be pitied; his murder of Claggert, mitigated, and Claggert's resemblance to Billy – his unknown origins, his 'natural' but unnamed depravity – also assigned to bad genes; even Billy's execution can be explained away: since 'genetics' had not yet been discovered, how could Captain Vere (whose own status as a blooded 'gentleman' never seems to figure into this equation) have known he'd condemned a disabled person? Poor Cap'n Vere. If only he'd known the real (genetic) truth.

Genetics is often invoked as a final, even as an ideal truth: in the courtroom, where DNA evidence puts to rest doubt about guilt, sometimes decades after the crime; in disasters, when lost relatives can be identified using DNA evidence from the smallest of fragments. Genetically enhanced or designed food has been heralded as a solution to global famine. But each narrative is also accompanied by anxiety: DNA evidence has been questioned and challenged; if a tissue sample is degraded enough, DNA cannot be reliably determined; no one yet knows the long-term effects of genetic engineering.

Still, whatever heated legal, ethical, moral public debates arise because of such anxieties (and others: the possibility of human cloning, stem-cell research or the patenting of genes) genetics is generally regarded as a promising science, one that ought to have broad support. Because whatever the public fears about genetics, gene therapy still promises to cure us of disease; cloning and the Human Genome Project promise to prolong life; DNA evidence promises to free the innocent, and so the fact that 'genetics' and 'eugenics' are essentially the same science, used to justify state-sponsored human breeding, sterilization and extermination projects, isn't readily recalled by such promising discourses – or if it is, it comes out as an act of disavowal, as in: no, no, genetics is not like eugenics! Nazis practised eugenics! Of course, the American Eugenics Society had a broad-based, popular support before the Second World War. But that's the past ...

Certainly the importance of 'blood', a concept far older than the discourses made available by genetics – as Melville's wry comparison of Billy Budd to a blood horse shows – hasn't vanished into the past. Family law still valorizes 'blood' relations; parents seek to conceive their 'own' offspring. This desire is couched in the language of parental love: to have one's own biological child can only help that child, in the event, say, of illnesses associated with DNA, or should a transfusion, or organ donation become necessary. Indeed, geneticist Lee Silver once said that all parents seek the best for their child (the best being, in this particular instance, soon-to-be-available, if not already available to those who can afford it, genetically enhanced immune systems) because such a desire is part of the genetic script of parenting.[2] But how, then, to understand child labour, torture, murder, prostitution, child-abuse, abandonment and the marketing of babies? Do all parents of abused children suffer from a flaw in their parenting gene?

Leaving that question aside, however, it might be prudent to note, as Drucilla Cornell does, that 'the idealization of genetic ties is intertwined with the most profound racist fantasies, including the desire for racial purity' (Cornell, 1998, 110).[3] Yet by law and custom, we still valorize blood, and understand DNA as the 'master molecule' (Keller, 1994, 89–98; see also Haraway, 1997) capable of endless good. Which is also to overlook, at least temporarily, the capacity for a logic of genetics to underwrite genocide. Eugenics is not simply the 'past' while genetics the 'future'. Ethnic cleansing is a contemporary political euphemism for genocide, and besides there are any number of bloody conflicts being fought or political policies being made to fit recalcitrant myths about race, ethnicity and gender. For example, a persistent myth about AIDs claims that 'having' a virgin (girl) is a cure. Such a myth contributes to kidnapping, child prostitution and infant rape. It deepens the worldwide AIDs epidemic.

Still, the idealization of genetics and the potential for that idealization to lend itself to genocide isn't an awareness that is particularly stressed when profit is at stake. Genetics is, rather, the locus of an ideological idealization of the natural as a fantasmatic site of the real, the authentic, and the good. For example, as I've noted elsewhere, on 27 May, 1992 the FDA gave its unconditional approval to the production and distribution of genetically engineered fruits and vegetables (Smith, 1999). No labelling or disclosure of said engineering by the parent company need be offered the consumer. The FDA can find nothing dangerous in these products because the genes are 'natural' and therefore not in need of oversight because genes are 'organic' not artificial, like an additive or a controlled substance. As if 'nature', being 'natural', cannot also and always spell 'death', too. Recent research suggests that a particular genetically altered corn, a strain that produces its own natural pesticide, is quietly killing off the monarch butterfly. This insect has no deleterious effect on corn whatsoever, but is vitally necessary to other pollination processes. And thus, as the monarch dies out, so too do other forms of plant life.

Indeed, the idealization of genetics as 'natural' and therefore 'good' bypasses, or at least pretends to forget, the fact that genetics is a code, and as such is subject to variable interpretation, to slippages, duplicities, reversals and complications, depending upon how DNA sampling is done, who is doing it and what the goal is. Indeed, the convergence of genetics and linguistics, according to semiotician Thomas Sebeok, demonstrates that the genetic code must be considered the most fundamental of all the semiotic networks (Sebeok, 2001). But if nature, then, 'speaks' to us through a (linguistic) code and if what she says is mediated by it, how can she be reliably understood and programmed? Few, it seems, stop to wonder whether she might just as soon speak in tongues.

Biotech corporations certainly continue to claim that they can reliably 'rewrite' DNA in both medical and agricultural research. The Human Genome Organization (HUGO) – or 'project' as it is known in the United States – has produced a masterscript of DNA sequencing that supposedly spells out the overarching category of the 'human' in a universally understood biological 'language'. Yet this standardization model HUGO has employed has been criticized from within the scientific community. The Human Genome Diversity Project, first proposed in 1991 by an alliance of geneticists in the United States, was a counter-organization to the Human Genome Project; these geneticists wanted to show how the diversity of human population was being neglected by those who were in hot pursuit of a masterscript.

So if, as Jacques Derrida has noted, when 'the contemporary biologist speaks of writing and *pro-gram* in relation to the most elementary processes of information within the living cell' (Derrida, 1976, 9), he or she also should indicate that the processes of interpretation are vital. DNA is a mode of inscription, and as with all forms of inscription or mediation, what is 'expressed' by the code may not, in the end, ever be coterminous with the 'intention' of the 'author', no matter how ethical, moral, righteous or deeply felt that intention may have been. Reading, and thus interpretation, intervenes. Despite all the popular, profit-oriented promises that a genetic story will always be a happy one, fatality remains embedded, if neglected, in the most idealized of genetic stories, something that *Billy Budd*, indeed, might be said wryly to comment upon.

In the last stages of Melville's 'inside narrative', there occurs a curious conversation between the purser and the surgeon. The purser demands of the surgeon, who sees himself as a scientific man, why the supposedly invariable muscular spasm – i.e. orgasm – of a hanged man's body did not occur in Budd's case. The purser believes that the lack of spasm is a 'testimony to the force lodged in will power' (*Budd*, 124). Billy willed himself not to spasm (ejaculate). The surgeon ridicules the idea that Budd could've 'willed' such a thing; indeed he bridles at the purser's invocation of will-power, then dodges the question until the purser asks instead: 'was the man's death effected by the halter, or was it a species of euthanasia?' (*Budd*, 125). The surgeon says he doubts the scientific authenticity of the term 'euthanasia' which he calls 'something like your will power . . . it is at once imaginative and metaphysical – in short, Greek' (*Budd*, 125). But the surgeon's own 'scientific' authority has been breached, thus leaving the purser's questions open:

107

could the peculiarities surrounding Budd's hanging have been effected from the operation of an 'inside' narrative? Will-power and/or euthanasia?

As Eve K. Sedgwick argues, one answer – and I would argue the answer the 'genetic' interpretation lends itself to – would be a deadly 'yes'. According to Sedgwick, *Billy Budd* turns upon a western cultural fantasy that the world can be purged of perversity:

> Following both Gibbon and the Bible, moreover, with an impetus borrowed from Darwin, one of the few areas of agreement among modern Marxist, Nazi, and liberal capitalist ideologies is that there is a peculiarly close, though never precisely defined, affinity between same-sex desire and some historical condition of moribundity, called 'decadence', to which not individuals or minorities but whole civilizations are subject.
>
> (Sedgwick, 1990, 130)

Read as she reads the story, not only does *Budd* have the chilling implications she narrates, i.e. that '. . . the trajectory toward gay genocide was never clearly distinguishable from a broader, apocalyptic trajectory toward something approaching omnicide' (Sedgwick, 128), but, if we extend the genetic logic with which I opened this essay – the idea that Billy suffers from an unnamed genetic disorder – then surely he can also be read as 'flawed' by the so-called (fantasmatic) gay gene? Whether as an autistic child or a gay man, Billy becomes his own worst enemy. Questions about the morality of social laws, the ethics of military tribunals, the misuse of power fall away.

Infamously, of course, the questions about Budd – who he was, how and why and if he should have died – are never resolved by the narrative itself, for, as Barbara Johnson notes, the story has not one ending, but four conflicting ones.[4] Captain Vere claims, at the drumhead court he convenes, to be warding off the possibility of mutiny or mass revolt among his men. But Vere then dies murmuring 'Billy Budd, Billy Budd' (*Budd*, 129). Yet not in 'the accents of remorse' (*Budd*, 129) but rather in an accent (of desire?) left unnamed although one provocative enough to make the *Bellipotent*'s senior officer uneasy. Meanwhile, according to a naval chronicle, Budd was 'no Englishman but one of those aliens adopting English cognomens' who 'vindictively' stabbed the master-at-arms, John Claggert to death (*Budd*, 130). Yet to his fellow sailors, Budd is the Handsome Sailor, incapable of crime, and their (homosocial) love for him, their identification with him, is recorded in a ballad, 'Billy in the Darbies' (*Budd*, 132).

Melville's voice, of course, is not absent from these endings, for he insists of his 'inside narrative' that it is 'Truth uncompromisingly told' and will therefore 'always have its ragged edges; hence the conclusion of such a narration is apt to be less finished than an architectural finial' (*Budd*, 128). A nice touch. One can never say which ending is 'the' end, nor easily resolve the question: is the narrative fact or fiction? The author claims fact. We read it as fiction. Moreover, it is a notoriously unfinished tale, fact or fable, because 'the manuscript was in a heavily revised, still 'unfinished' state when [Melville] died on September 28, 1891' (*Budd*, 12), a state of such disarray that the first editor of the manuscript, Raymond Weaver, wrote in 1928 that 'such is the state of the *Billy Budd* manuscript that there can never appear a reprint that will be adequate to every ideal' (*Budd*, 12).

Yet the sparkling promise of an authentic 'genetic' truth was unveiled in 1962, when editors Harrison Heyford and Merton Sealts, Jr. produced a Genetic Text of this unfinished story. They say their text represents 'the most obvious editorial ideal . . . to put before the reader precisely what the author would have published' (*Budd*, 12–13). Through painstaking (DNA) detective editorial work, these editors have deciphered the 'genesis' of production, teasing out Melville's revisionary process so that one 'text' emerged from another in a seamless genetic sequencing of stages A, B, C, D, X, E, F, G, with sub-stages like Bc. This editorial genetics was not a new process in the 1950s but it does reflect a perceived readerly need for a viable, stable, accurate, pure 'text', an ideal text, representing what the author intended: messy, unruly, unfinished 'defective' or stuttering texts like *Billy Budd* require editorial gene therapy. (See, for example, Bowers, 1959, and Greg, 1951.)

Since 1962 and the advent of the so-called 'postmodern' such editorial practices have been called into question (see, for example, McGann, 1983); even Heyford and Sealts understood their project as a multivalent one, given that the Phoenix edition, is an abridged 'reading text' separate from the full, scholarly Genetic Text which allows any interested party to see the 'genetic' manuscript in fragments. Indeed, depending on the publisher's interest, the 1928 Weaver version and the 1948 F. Barron Freeman version, as well as the Heyford and Sealts Phoenix edition, are all still in circulation. Given this situation, the fungible, fragile, complexities of the narrative remain very visible – and troubling. For example, when some of my students realize the text is unfinished and exists in multiple forms, differently organized, often they refuse to interpret the text at all. Or else they staunchly view the Phoenix text as the real *Billy Budd*. Heyford's and Sealts' genetic logic is persuasive to them because they regard genetics as 'scientific'. To focus on the gnarled, unsettling slippages and complexities of an 'unfinished' text is unrealistic at best and folly at worst.

Yet language is as complex as genetics, and since genetics is also a language, language is as much a part of the structure of who we understand ourselves to be, as DNA. Language, like genetics, can radically alter reality – but not always in happy, comforting, predictable ways. One must keep on 'reading' and 'writing' – for example, those who 'wrote' the pesticidal corn into existence never intended genocide for the lovely monarch butterfly. Nor does the process of 'reading' ever quite end, except, perhaps, in death. And yet there remains a cultural fantasy that sees genetics as 'real', while language is 'unreal', a fantasy that refuses to acknowledge the link between the two, for fear that such an acknowledgement might – what? Show that r/Evolution is never predictable or controllable? Show that truth, uncompromisingly told, is and can never be complete?

Notes

1. The subtitle, 'An Inside Narrative' was settled upon by Hayford and Sealts as a result of their 'genetic' editorial work. Prior to their 1962 version of this story, the title was not 'as the author gave it' because previous editors failed 'to recognize Mrs. Melville's hand in the manuscript . . . For the title of the story two versions survive. One occurs in pencil draft on a slip attached to a separate leaf: 'Billy Budd/Foretopman/What befell him/in the year of the/Great Mutiny/&c'. The other occurs as a pencilled addition at the top of the first leaf of the story proper: 'Billy Budd/Sailor/(An inside narrative). That the second of these was in fact Melville's final intention for the title is made clear by all *genetic* evidence' (19, emphasis added).
2. In a lively debate at the Einstein Forum, Potsdam, Germany, 4–6 June, 1999 for their forum on 'Genetics and Genealogy'. See also Silver (1997).
3. Cornell is paraphrasing Dorothy Roberts, *The Genetic Tie*, University of Chicago Law Review, 62, 1 (Winter, 1995).
4. And that the novel is an elaborate commentary about reading itself is addressed by Barbara Johnson (1979).

Works cited

Bowers, F. *Textual and Literary Criticism*. Cambridge, 1959.

Butler, Judith. *Gender Trouble*. New York, 1990.

Cornell, Drucilla. *At the Heart of Freedom: Feminism, Sex and Equality*. Princeton, NJ, 1998.

Derrida, Jacques. *Of Grammatology*, trans. Gayatri Chakravorty Spivak. Baltimore, MD, 1976.

Greg, W. W. *The Editorial Problem in Shakespeare: A Survey of the Foundations of the Text*. Oxford, 1951.

Haraway, Donna J. *Modest Witness@Second Millenium.Female Man© Meets OncoMouse™*. New York, 1997.

Johnson, Barbara. 'Melville's Fist: The Execution of *Billy Budd*', *Studies in Romanticism*, 18 (Winter, 1979).

Keller, Evelyn Fox. 'Master Molecules', in *Are Genes Us? The Social Consequences of the New Genetics*, ed. Carl F. Cranor. New Brunswick, NJ, 1994, 89–98.

McGann, Jerome J. *A Critique of Modern Textual Criticism*. Chicago, IL, 1983.

Melville, Herman. *Billy Budd (An Inside Narrative)*, eds Harrison Hayford and Merton M. Sealts, Jr. Chicago, IL, and London, 1962.

Sebeok, Thomas. *Global Semiotics*. Indianapolis, IN, 2001.

Sedgwick, Eve K. *Epistemology of the Closet*. Berkeley, CA, 1990.

Silver, Lee M. *Remaking Eden: Cloning and Beyond in a Brave New World*. New York, 1997.

Smith, Stephanie A. 'Cyber(genetics)', in *Genealogie und Genetik*, series *Einstein-Bücher*. Berlin (under contract, 1999).

hypertext | *TERRY HARPOLD*

'Let me introduce the word "hypertext",' writes Ted Nelson in 1965 – it is the first occurrence of the term in print[1] –

to mean a body of written or pictorial material interconnected in such a complex way that it could not conveniently be presented or represented on paper. It may contain summaries, or maps of its contents and their interrelations; it may contain annotations, additions and footnotes from scholars who have examined it. Let me suggest that such an object and system, properly designed and administered, could have great potential for education, increasing the student's range of choices, his sense of freedom, his motivations, and his intellectual grasp.

(96)

He adds in a footnote:

The sense of 'hyper-' used here connotes extension and generality; cf. 'hyperspace'. The criterion for this prefix is the inability of these objects to be comprised sensibly into linear media, like the text string, or even media of a somewhat higher complexity.

(98)

Hypertext is then, first, a practice of composition: hypertexts comprise other textual objects or forms. Among these, Nelson proposes, are summaries and maps, and annotations, additions, and footnotes. That series does not exhaust the set of hypertext's possible parts – these will proliferate in the later literature – but it is sufficient to mark, from the beginning, the fundamentally liminal character of the hypertextual. Maps and summaries describe, contain and displace; conceptually and procedurally, they operate beyond the peripheries of the objects they gather and abstract. (A map whose extension is identical to the territory it represents would be something . . . more *and* less . . . than a map.)[2] The places of annotations, additions and footnotes with regard to the texts they mark are more varied (Genette, 1997), but still they operate within one periphery: complete maps or summaries of those texts would take notice of them.

In Nelson's initial formula, hypertext begins by being spread over the gamut of textual practices: joined to and depending on prior habits of writing and reading, especially those derived from print and marked by its limits or dissatisfactions; and reaching beyond them, into conjectural habits of a new technical regime, more fluid and more varied. What distinguishes *hyper*texts from the others, suggests Nelson, is the efficiency with which they combine their parts and represent this combining: hypertexts include other texts more *sensibly* than they may include . . . yet other texts. They differ in the qualities of their effects; they do something more or else; they present and *re*present in ways other kinds of texts cannot. This formal and referential play – something more than textual recursion and self-citation, and less than textual antinomy (a consequence of hypertext's lack of a general theory of the textual field it aims to encompass and exceed) – has shaped the contours of the hypertext imaginary from the beginning. Nearly four decades after its introduction, Nelson's neologism has preserved all the methodological and performative ambiguities of its first use.[3]

> *The simplest way to to define hypertext is to contrast it with traditional text like this book. All traditional text, whether in printed form or in computer files, is* sequential, *meaning that there is a single linear sequence defining the order in which the text is to be read. First you read page one. Then you read page two. Then you read page three. And you don't have to be much of a mathematician to generalize the formula which determines what page to read next.*
>
> (Nielsen, 1995, 1)

Hypertext is a kind of text inconveniently realized in print. In 1991, Nelson proposed that this is the most general trait of hypertext: 'The best current definition of hypertext, over quite a broad range of types, is 'text structure that cannot be conveniently printed'. This is not very specific or profound, but it fits best' (253). Such a definition raises at least two stumbling blocks for a theory of hypertext's difference from other textual forms. First, there is all the awkwardness of a negative economic model: how little convenient must the printing of a text or texts be to be judged . . . *in*convenient, and thus to merit a hypertextual approach? (This is not so trivial an objection as it may appear. The many, varied and indisputably valuable projects to convert existing print or graphic scholarly archives to digital-hypertextual forms have required at some point a definite response to this question. 'Convenience' may differ in degree or meaning according to the requirements of a discipline or an institution, or the habits of the individual reader: Vannevar Bush's Memex will embody this varying expediency in all its operations.) Second, what assumptions regarding the characteristics and operations of textual forms, it must be asked, are encoded in the choice of a severely restricted category of those forms as the normative model, against which hypertext is presumed to deviate?

No one is compelled to read a printed text in the way that Jakob Nielsen claims; readers seldom read any but a small and banal category of texts (assembly instructions, travel directions, shopping lists) with so fixed and programmatic a method. (Even in these cases, one can easily imagine skipping over items in a list or taking them out of turn because of changing conditions of use, or perversely, just to see what might come of it.) Novice and seasoned readers alike treat print's presumed rules of engagement with equal impertinence: they begin and end where they please; they read against every prescription of order or integrity (Barthes, 1975).

Moreover, even when she elects to read a text in the designated order of its lines and pages, the reader will have to also parse its paratextual regimes: formal, graphemic and material traits that direct the pursuit of sequence without being fully absorbed into it.[4] One can multiply these traits seemingly without end: the chapter title; the running foot or head; the page number; the choice of paper stock, typefaces and page layouts; binding methods (and faults in binding); typographical errors, stains, folds and tears; an earlier reader's marginalia; etc. All, as Jerome McGann has repeatedly noted, are *marked* and observed to varying degrees in any given reading encounter. Reading is always a contingent, multiple and multicursal performative event, potentially engaging all the specific traits of the printed artifact. The visible and material language of the page will thus always extend beyond serial procedures of the letter and the line, to include structures and scansions those procedures activate but do not limit (McGann, 1993; 2001). One reads any book – *this book, for example* – in constant, if not always conscious, relation to structures and orders, cycles and pericycles which exceed any strictly serial model of discovery.

In addition to all of the above, one must take into account the suppleness and adaptability of the codex and page. Whole traditions of typographic and bibliographic practice have been founded on exceptions to formal and procedural conventions of the page. In many printed texts, a degree of procedural difficulty and material resistance – that is, of some *inconvenience* of print and paper – is crucial to their method and aesthetic aims.[5] Rather than representing outliers of textual practice, these traditions have operated across and within conventions of print culture from its inception, anticipating and advancing its development and diversity (Adler and Ernst, 1990; Massin, 1970; and Rasula and McCaffery, 1998).[6]

The 'traditional' seriality and definite order of the printed page invoked by Nielsen – much of hypertext theory has embraced the supposed tidiness of print as an axiom of system design – is definable only in relation to the persistence of counter-serial and otherwise disorderly practices of writing and reading with paper and ink.[7] Repression of these practices – reflected in the design of hypertext applications in their generally poor support for control over graphemic traits of the displayed document (choice of typefaces, position and size of windows, appearance and behaviour of interface controls, etc.), and in the critical literature in the near-absence of analysis of their effects[8] – has resulted in a systematic blindness within design and criticism with regard to the obvious. At least for the moment, as McGann notes, the hypermedia powers of the codex easily exceed those of the digital text (McGann, 2001, 168).

By 'hypertext', I simply mean non-sequential writing. A magazine layout, with sequential text and inset illustrations and boxes, is thus hypertext. So is the front page of a newspaper, and so are various programmed books now seen on the drugstore stands (where you make a choice at the end of a page and are directed to other specific pages).

Computers are not intrinsically involved with the hypertext concept. But computers will be involved with hypertext in every way, and in systems of every style . . .

Many people consider these forms of writing to be new and drastic and threatening. However, I would like to take the position that hypertext is fundamentally traditional and in the mainstream of literature.

(Nelson, 1990, 1/17)

Hypertexts are all around us, familiar and even unremarkable; like Molière's bourgeois gentleman, we may be well-pleased to discover we have been writing and reading them all our lives. Hypertext, Nelson proposes, is simply textuality in its most flexible application, limited only (though this is only implied) by material attributes of a given document and the conventions of its use. Nelson's appeal thus to a general economy of textual operations, prior to their embodiment in a specific media technology, skirts difficulties of a definition of hypertext based on differences between strictly serial and non-serial reading practices, or presumed limits of print and their relaxing in the digital field. In Nelson's more general definition, print and digital hypertexts differ from other species of text only in that they approach the potential fluidity and connectivity characteristic of all textual forms. They differ from each other in that digital hypertext is the more flexible implementation of this ideal, because of its increased opportunities for linking, shuffling and transmission of textual units. ('Is this a technology?' Nelson asks in public lectures – 'No – it's the design of literature!' Xanadu, Nelson's famously unrealized scheme for a universal digital hypertext, aims to be the most ambitious attempt to realize that design.[9])

But this assertion of an absolutely general foundation for hypertext's difference raises other and greater difficulties, especially with regard to its abstraction of textual operations from media technologies and the specific practices they require. All of the ambiguities and endless linkages of the textual supplement (Derrida, 1974) are marked here, in the joint of the prefix and the substantive: *hyper*-text as text's liberated possibility; *hyper*-text as text's overexcited, pathological mode (Birkerts, 1994; Heim, 1993); *hyper*-text as text, more or less.

> Consider a future device for individual use, which is a sort of mechanized private file and library. It needs a name, and, to coin one at random, 'memex' will do. A memex is a device in which an individual stores his books, records, and communications, and which is mechanized so that it may be consulted with exceeding speed and flexibility. It is an enlarged intimate supplement to his memory.
>
> (Bush, 1991a, 102)[10]

The word 'hypertext' cannot be found in Vannevar Bush's 1945 essay, 'As We May Think' – Nelson will not invent it for more than three decades – but the research problem and the methods for its solution Bush describes seem to provide an opening for Nelson's proposal of a new scheme of textual practices, such that critical or historical reflections on hypertext must always chain Memex to Xanadu.[11] The orthodox genealogy of hypertext has, as Michael Joyce has wryly observed (2000, 242), the feel of latter-day scripture: prior to and between Memex and the Xanadu SilverStand, there are generations, begettings and further begettings, cycles of influence and divergence.[12] I will repeat portions of this genealogy here. My aim, however, is not to emphasize the continuities of design and thought that join Memex to Xanadu, but rather to draw attention to a crucial turn in their respective representations of the textual imaginary. In Memex, this imaginary is chiefly directed inward, though the device's methods hint inconsistently at other possibilities. In Xanadu and hypertext schemes influenced by it, the textual imaginary is directed outward, recasting a prior interiority as a potentially pure extensivity. Historical and critical analysis of these systems and their significance in the digital field must take this turn into account.

The passages in the essay concerning Memex, probably the best-known of any Bush wrote in a long history of academic research and public service, describe it as a new kind of writing-desk specially outfitted for the needs of the coming age (Figures 1 and 2).

> In one end is the stored material. The matter of bulk is well taken care of by improved microfilm. Only a small part of the interior of the memex is devoted to storage, the rest to mechanism. Yet if the user inserted 5,000 pages of material a day it would take him hundreds of years to fill the repository, so he can be profligate and enter material freely.

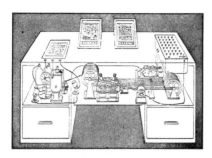

Figure 1. *Bush's Memex. 'Memex in the form of a desk would instantly bring files and material on any subject to the operator's fingertips. Slanting translucent viewing screens magnify supermicrofilm filed by code numbers. At left is a mechanism which automatically photographs longhand notes, pictures and letters, then files them in the desk for future reference' (*LIFE, *19.11: 123) Image reproduced with permission of Alfred D. Crimi, the* Atlantic Monthly, *and Richard Bush, MD.*

Figure 2. *Bush's Memex. 'Memex in use is shown here. On one transparent screen the operator of the future writes notes and commentary dealing with reference material which is projected on the screen at left. Insertion of the proper code symbols at the bottom of right-hand screen will tie the new item to the earlier one after notes are photographed on supermicrofilm' (*LIFE, 19.11: *124). Image reproduced with permission of Alfred D. Crimi, the* Atlantic Monthly, *and Richard Bush, MD.*

Most of the memex contents are purchased on microfilms ready for insertion. Books of all sorts, pictures, current periodicals, newspapers are thus obtained and dropped into place. Business correspondence takes the same path. And there is provision for direct entry. On the top of the memex is a transparent platen. On this are placed longhand notes, photographs, memoranda, all sorts of things. When one is in place, the depression of a lever causes it to be photographed onto the next blank space in a section of the memex film, dry photography being employed.

There is, of course, provision for consultation of the record by the usual scheme of indexing. If the user wishes to consult a certain book, he taps its code on the keyboard, and the title page of the book promptly appears before him, projected upon one of his viewing positions. Frequently used

codes are mnemonic, so that he seldom consults his code book; but when he does, a single tap of a key projects it for his use. Moreover, he has supplemental levers. On deflecting one of these levers to the right he runs through the book before him, each paper in turn being projected at a speed which just allows a recognizing glance at each. If he deflects it further to the right, he steps through the book ten pages at a time; still further at a hundred pages at a time. Deflection at the left gives him the same control backwards.

A special button transfers him immediately to the first page of the index. Any given book of his library can thus be called up and consulted with far greater facility than if it were taken from a shelf. As he has several projection positions, he can leave one item in position while he calls up another. He can add marginal notes and

comments, taking advantage of one possible type
of dry photography, and it could even be arranged
so that he can do this by a stylus scheme, such as
is now employed in the telautograph seen in
railway waiting rooms, just as though he had the
physical page before him.

(Bush, 1991a, 102–3)

Memex is a piece of furniture at which one sits, reads and writes. In this regard, Alfred D. Crimi's illustrations of the device may be understood to belong to an older pictorial tradition centred on the desk or bookshelf of the scholar's study. The many paintings and engravings of Saint Jerome reading form the model here: the reader, deep in thought, is bent over a book on his lectern; he is oblivious to the tilting piles of papers and books surrounding him on tables, shelves and window sills, their disorder marking in inverse proportion the degree of his concentration.[13] Much of the function of Memex supports the sharing of information between individuals, but, at least in its first incarnation, exchanges in both directions seem not to be among its primary aims. These are, rather, to enable the user to consult with greater efficiency the writings of others. The 'operator of the future' works mostly alone in the corner of his lab: Memex is 'intimate' in that sense of the word, too. It *involves* its user; the 'trails' it builds from his reading – I will come to these shortly – are specific to his use of the device. Memex clears away the mess of the scholar's study and bundles it neatly in the corner of his desk.[14]

To achieve this, the device assumes a modest fivefold improvement in current technologies of microphotography, resulting in a nonetheless impressive reduction of the paper originals. ('The Encyclopedia Britannica could be reduced to the volume of a matchbox. A library of a million volumes could be compressed into one end of a desk'

(1991a, 93).) The effective capacity of the store is enormous; an entire lifetime of research will not overrun its limits. The physical dimensions of the store are, however, limited – the designated aim of the device is to apply order to disorder, boundaries to the unbounded – and so the interior of Memex is strictly partitioned and methodically controlled. As Crimi's cut-away diagram illustrates, Memex is – no more nor less – a mechanical keepsake, an orderly enclosure for tokens of disorderly memory.[15]

In its operation, however, boundaries between the interior and exterior of the device appear more ambiguous. 'Only a small part of the desk', Bush notes, is taken up with the store, 'the rest to mechanism'. This is not because Memex's reliance on optical-mechanical methods results in an inefficient partitioning of its interior (the greater part of a modern desktop computer is similarly devoted to mechanism); it is, rather, because the *mechanism*, not the store, is the real heart of the device. Despite (or, rather, because of) Memex's function as an 'intimate supplement' to its user's memory, the documents stored within it may be retrieved or transmitted to others *only through its use* – its procedures ensure that they will thus remain always dependent upon the Memex in this way. The crossing of optical and spatial thresholds is not easily reversible; images of the pages recorded on microfilm will be too compact to read without the projector's magnifying lens and the platens; the keycoding scheme by which they are marked for storage and recovery will rely upon the mechanism of the keyboard, levers and microfilm spools. The conversion from paper to film will result in copies equally as infrangible as the originals upon which they were based.

The inward pull of Memex's model of storage and retrieval thus engages procedures which must cross the boundaries of the desk's enclosure – indeed, it cannot function without these procedures. To access the record stored on the inside (the page-images), the user cannot dispense with the outside (the spools of film, the platens, the keys, the levers): the apparatus and the record are in this regard ambiguously interleaved. The prejudicial interiority of the device is drawn outward by the textual operations upon which it depends.

All of this gadgetry, Bush observes, is conventional, apart from the projected development of present-day technologies. The reduction of the record and the relative ease with which it may be consulted from the desktop are remarkable, but they are not the most innovative aspect of the device. More important, he proposes, is the higher-level procedure they might support.

This is the essential feature of the memex. The process of tying two items together is the important thing. When the user is building a trail, he names it, inserts the name in his code book, and taps it out on his keyboard. Before him are the two items to be joined, projected onto adjacent viewing positions. At the bottom of each there are a number of blank code spaces, and a pointer is set to indicate one of these on each item. The user taps a single key, and the items are permanently joined. In each code space appears the code word. Out of view, but also in the code space, is inserted a set of dots for photocell viewing; and on each item these dots by their positions designate the index number of the other item.

Thereafter, at any time, when one of these items is in view, the other can be instantly recalled merely by tapping a button below the corresponding code space. Moreover, when numerous items have been thus joined together to

form a trail, they can be reviewed in turn, rapidly or slowly, by deflecting a lever like that used for turning the pages of a book. It is exactly as though the physical items had been gathered together from widely separated sources and bound together to form a new book.

(1991a, 103–4)

If we bracket the ambiguous effects of the apparatus that produces them, the storage of the page-images does not appear to threaten to any serious extent the bounded interiority of Memex's writing-desk. Certainly, the textual operation of the device may reach outward in a restricted way, as the film spools may be exchanged with other Memex users – that is an important consequence of the device's embrace of microphotography – but even then, they must be slotted in another Memex's internal store before they can be consulted.

The trail, however, points away from the prejudicial interiority of the memex more radically than any other feature of the device. This will become clear in unpublished writings of the 1950s, where Bush speculates on a successor to Memex that would make use of new computing and telecommunications technologies, and in which the trails take on an unmistakable priority over all other aspects of its use. In Memex II, they may be created or altered by the device itself: new trails are followed, and old trails are emphasized or discounted, based upon instructions from the user or upon his reading patterns (Bush, 1991b, 176). And trails may be shared to a degree unforeseen for the first Memex (Oren, 1991; Trigg, 1991). Professional societies and publishing organizations, Bush predicts, will host libraries collecting the trails of individual Memex users, and new trails created by dedicated in-house researchers.

One may then, under proper controls, dial by tele-
phone directly into the memex of such a library,
and use it from a distance, browsing about along
trails, and transferring items of interest to the
private store . . . Many individuals may thus
consult the library store simultaneously. When
they meet on trails there will need to be special
means provided so that they can pass one another.

(Bush, 1991b, 173–4)

The mechanism is still the heart of the device, but it has been abstracted nearly away from the gears, spools and lenses of the first Memex. (Only nearly: the network of trails Bush envisions will be traversed by 'rapid facsimile transmission over the telephone wires' (1991b, 173). A global digital network that might erase all evidence of a dependence on analogue methods is still decades off.)[16]

Xanadu will advance this abstraction still further. In Nelson's system, document linking is based on an infinitely extensible scheme that manages unique numeric identifiers ('tumblers') for each span of linked content, in relation to *all* other spans of linked content in the entire global repository (Nelson, 1990, 4/15–4/40).[17] Copies of spans are permitted (copies of partial or whole documents inserted in other documents are said to be 'transcluded'), but all instances of a given span are treated as identical within the address space, whatever the physical location of the server on which they reside.

Transclusion is what quotation, copying and
cross-referencing merely attempt: they are ways
that people have had to imitate transclusion,
which is the true abstract relationship that paper
cannot show. [Once more, hypertext would be
what other kinds of text aspires to be, once freed

of antiquated media technologies – TH]
Transclusions are not copies and they are not
instances, but the same thing knowably and
visibly in more than once place.

(Nelson, 1999, 8)[18]

New items may be added to the store; new transclusions may be defined; more importantly, all addresses will always remain valid and equally accessible from any location in the network (1990, 4/19). This enables the user to travel forward or backward along the chain of linked spans, or to return to any prior state of a document, or to single out any subset of its relations to other documents in the repository (Nelson, 1990, 3/9–3/15). All of the notoriously difficult mathematics required to implement and maintain a write-once universal address space – one of the chief reasons (depending on whom one believes) for Xanadu's long, slow birth or its ultimate impossibility (Nelson, 1995, 2002; Wolf, 1995) – is directed to this end.

The tumbler is Xanadu's version of Memex's keycodes; transclusion is, more subtly, its version of the Memex's filing away of the page-image. Where the Memex store is intimate and bounded (though reaching, in a tentative way, outward), Xanalogical storage is general and extensive; linked spans are ranged in relation to the ever-changing structure of the network as a whole: storage and retrieval as a procedure of form, not location. Where the textual imaginary of Memex tends towards involvement and enclosure, Xanadu's writing-desk mirrors larger and more expansive orders.

The Xanadu stations, or SilverStands, will be the
local outposts of the network, parlors with a
homey futuristic atmosphere, staffed by an atten-
tive crew in perky uniforms. Besides being an

actual storage and transmission depot, the
SilverStand will serve as an induction and training
office, a 'drop-in center', a place for advertising,
promotion, public relations, goodwill . . .

(Nelson, 1990, 5/6)

'Quieter carrels', away from the hustle and bustle of the foyer of the Xanadu franchise ('where the true Xanies hang out'), are available in the back of the building, for those of a more scholastic temperment (Nelson, 1990, 5/6).

All the ambiguities of memory's role and location in the psychic apparatus apply here. If, as Freud concluded as early as the unfinished *Project for a Scientific Psychology* (1895; Freud, 1954), the media of perception, memory and consciousness must be exclusive of one another, a materialist theory of their mutual engagement is at pains to account for differences in their localized functions. This problem will remain critical for psychoanalysis for nearly thirty years, until the essay on the 'Mystic Writing Pad' (Freud, 1925; Derrida, 1978, 1996; Kittler, 1997). Only then – and only haltingly – is Freud able to rewrite the engram within the regime of structure. Even so, Kittler observes, he can go only so far as information technologies of his era: the Freudian engram cannot account for regimes introduced by the intervention of the computer program (1997, 135). It will take Lacan, Kittler argues, to make the crucial conceptual break that frees psychoanalysis from the confusion of psychic interiority with the magnetic charge of the signifier.[19]

The enigmatic question of the Project concerning
'an apparatus which would be capable of the
complicated performance' of simultaneously
transmitting and storing, of being both forgetting
and memory, finds its answer at last. In circuit
mechanisms, a third and universal function – the

algorithm as the sum of logic and control – com-
prehends the other two media functions.
Computers release theory from an age-old con-
straint of having to conceive of storage as an
engram – from cuneiform characters in sound
through sound-grooves in vinyl.

(1997, 144)

A homologous development marks the trajectory from Memex to Xanadu: from the prejudicial interiority of the record, via the apparatus of storage and transmission, to a mnemonics of extensive form, supported by program methods. Distinctions between the textual record and its methods are inconsistent in Memex from the start: the procedures of the device traverse their boundaries; the trail, as record of the record's form, points memory away from enclosure to a more general structure, within which enclosure is at most a conceptual moment in the overall operation of the system.

In Xanadu, the algorithmic support of mnemonic practice is further generalized, and the record, while the ostensible rationale for the system, will be progressively obscured by the complexity of the apparatus required to maintain it. 'Everything', says Nelson, 'is deeply intertwingled' (1974, 45). To grasp the relation of that formula to the legacy of Memex, and more generally to the media technics of memory, one must be read it, not as a description of the textual field as its exists, but rather as the principle of a program by which it may be reconstructed (Figure 3). The cross-connections can't be divided up neatly; they are too numerous, and you couldn't identify them all. You need procedures for tracking the important information, a dependable box to put it into, but also: an algorithm to repeat its arrangement, in case something should happen to the box. Such an algorithm, Nelson

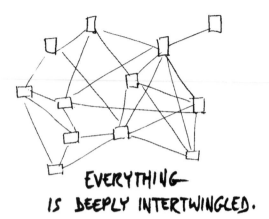

EVERYTHING
IS DEEPLY INTERTWINGLED.

In an important sense there are
no "subjects" at all; there is only
all knowledge, since the cross-
connections among the myriad topics
of this world simply cannot be
divided up neatly.

Hypertext at last offers the possibility
of representing and exploring it all
without carving it up destructively.

Figure 3. *Illustration from Nelson's* Dream Machines *(Nelson, 1974, DM45). Copyright © Theodor Holm Nelson. Reproduced with permission of Theodor Holm Nelson.*

proposes, 'at last offers the possibility of representing and exploring it all without carving it up destructively' (1974, 45).

Mislaid, however, in this faith in the salvivific force of the algorithm is an acknowledgement of its dependence on the structure of oblivion that it aims to circumvent. Psychoanalysis's trajectory from interiority to structure did not signal the supersession of interiority, but rather its incorporation into the function of the algorithm as its alibi or guarantee, and a concurrent recognition of the deeper problem of the limits of the algorithm's capabilities. One of the lessons of hypertext's vexed relations to the technics of memory lies in the orientation by this problem. The multiplicity and subtlety of the textual operation is discernable at its points of contact with the real matter of textual memory, *in so far as they signal aspects of the operation which are addressable by code but not exhausted by it.* Much of later hypertext design and theory has drawn on Xanadu's insistence on an absolute transmissability of the textual unit as the precondition of its survival – that is, on a repression of aspects of the textual encounter for which there is, as yet, no encoding scheme. Hypertext's celebrated triumph over the limits of print depends on this repression, and on an impoverishment of textual operations resulting from it.

Notes

1. Nelson had used the term 'hypertext' in lectures and unpublished papers as early as 1963 (Nelson, 1999).
2. As in Borges's famous fragment (1972, 131).
3. A comprehensive account of the development of hypertext systems is beyond the scope of this essay. The essays collected in Nyce and Kahn (1991a) provide excellent background on Bush's pre- and post-Second World War careers and his work on Memex and related technologies. Subsequent developments in hypertext lack so comprehensive a historical treatment. Barnes (1997), summarizes the contributions of Douglas Engelbart's oNLine System (NLS, 1968) to the development of human–computer interface (HCI) methods, many of which are crucial to methods of modern hypertext systems. (My neglect of Engelbart's role in the conceptual trajectory I sketch here, from Memex to Xanadu, is a regrettable consequence of space limitations.) Nelson's autobiographical sketches (1990, 1/22–1/38; 1992) describe the early history of Xanadu. Wolf's skeptical account of Xanadu (1995) provides much information not found anywhere else, but must be read with Nelson and other Xanadu team members' responses (Nelson et al., 1995). Conklin's early article (Conklin, 1987) remains a good source on systems of the 1970s and 1980s. Nielsen (1995) offers a short history of the major systems, ending in the early 1990s. Landow (1991, and to a lesser extent, 1997) is substantially based on the methods of Intermedia, an important hypertext environment of the 1990s, now no longer in use. Bolter (1991b) discusses early versions of Storyspace (he was one of the program's developers), a hypertext system for desktop computers used by many of the best-known authors of hypertext fiction. Berners-Lee (1999) offers an autobiographical account of the development of hypertext protocols and methods that would become the foundation of the World Wide Web (WWW).

4. Genette (1997) is the classic statement of this problem. Jackson (1999) offers a more informal taxonomy of these regimes. No analogous investigation of paratextual forms of the graphical user interface (GUI), used by most contemporary hypertext systems, has yet been written. (Mullett and Sano's treatment of visual conventions of the GUI (1995) is perhaps a first step in this direction.) This is not surprising. The rapid evolution of computer operating systems and GUI techniques, the frequent inconsistency of those techniques within a given release of a GUI and the ability of application programmers to apply interface 'standards' in any way they deem appropriate mean that such a project inevitably will be caught up in a morass of exceptions and one-off efforts. More significantly, as I suggest below, the general inattention within the disciplines of HCI to deep problems of the interface's materiality has meant that its paratextual traits are generally treated as conceptually transparent, strictly peripheral elements of the digital artifact, noteworthy only for their service of stated objectives of the artifact.

5. See, for example, the essays and exemplars collected in Rasula (1998) and Rothenberg and Clay (2000); Drucker's histories of the contemporary artists book (1997) and Modernist experimental typography (1996); and Saper's analysis of contributions of twentieth-century visual poetry and performance art to contemporary media practices (Saper, 2001).

6. Theorists of digital hypertext often propose that its *narrative* methods seem to have been anticipated by twentieth-century print works of generative or combinatorial fiction and poetry – Cortázar's *Hopscotch*; Queneau's *Cent Mille Milliards de Poèmes*; Saporta's *Composition No. 1*, etc. – (Bolter, 1991b; Landow, 1997; Douglas, 2000). But extra-narrative aspects of the reader's operation of these printed texts have not been addressed in this context. She must flip back and forth between numbered sections of Cortázar's novel; she must take the unbound leaves of Saporta's novel into her hands and shuffle them before reading; Massin's famous edition of Queneau's text requires of the reader that she fold and collate individual lines of the sonnet database, etc. These embodied actions on the printed text are not easily transposed to actions of the user interface, as material and dimensional cues crucial to the printed forms have no direct analogue on the screen. Similarly, when Bolter compares a digital hypertext to 'a printed book that the author has attacked with a pair of scissors and cut into convenient verbal sizes' (1991a), he effaces – perhaps the problematic, unexamined concept is *convenience*, again – effects of the resistance and irreversibility of the scissor's action on paper – which, for example, Tzara and Burroughs considered essential to this literary technique. Missing in these assertions of the printed form's anticipation of the digital form is an account of what, in the digital encounter, corresponds to the embodied activity and spatial consciousness of encounters with printed forms. If, as Drucker (1996) and McGann (2001) have observed, critical-theoretical models of the visible and material resources of print are still in their infancy, even less work has been done toward developing a corresponding theory of digital text. Rosenberg's essays on spatial hypertext (Rosenberg, 2000 and 2001), Glazier's discussion of electronic poetry (Glazier, 2001) and McGann's recent work on questions of text encoding and digitization (McGann, 2001) have opened promising lines of enquiry in this regard.

7. Aarseth's taxonomy of dynamic and performative texts ('cybertexts') is a significant contribution to the study of these practices (Aarseth, 1997). However, as McGann notes (2001, 148), Aarseth's reliance on a zero-degree category of textual form ('ordinary textuality'), from which cybertexts may be distinguished, elides the contribution of cybertextual functions of the most mundane texts.

8. The lack of authorial control over the display of documents is, in fact, considered one of the strengths of HTML, the mark-up language used by the WWW (Berners-Lee, 1999). Visual attributes of HTML documents, including the typeface of text and the position and dimensions of document windows, are most often determined by settings of the user's web browsing application. Katherine Hayles's influential essay on the 'importance of media-specific analysis' is a striking example of the neglect of these aspects of digital text in the current critical literature. Hayles's essay, which focuses primarily on Shelley Jackson's hypertext fiction, *Patchwork Girl*, does not mention significant differences between the Macintosh and Windows releases of the text, or even which release Hayles is using as the basis of her analysis. Hayles cites from multiple nodes of *Patchwork Girl*, and describes images embedded within the text, but her essay does not include any images showing how these objects might appear on the reader's computer screen.

9. See Nelson (1974, 1990, 1999, and 2002) for descriptions of Xanadu and its technical methods, many of which have changed over the course of the system's development. 'Xanadu™' is a registered trademark of Theodor Holm Nelson.

10. 'As We May Think' was originally published in July 1945 in *The Atlantic*. In September of that year, a condensed version of the essay, with illustrations and different subheads, appeared in *LIFE* magazine. The passages cited in this essay include material from both versions, as reprinted in Nyce and Kahn (1991a, 85–110). In Bush's earliest writings on Memex, he does not capitalize the first letter of the device's name. In later writings, he uses the capitalized form, 'Memex', without the definite article, and most of those writing on Bush and Memex have followed this example. I have done this here, retaining the lower-case form only when Bush used it.

11. See, for example, Conklin (1987), Landow (1997) and Nielsen (1995). Nelson has frequently cited Bush's essay as an inspiration for the design of Xanadu (see, for example, Nelson, 1991); lengthy citations of 'As We May Think' are included in Nelson (1974) and Nelson (1990). The degree to which Bush's essay can be said to *anticipate* the technical procedures of later hypertext theory and systems is, as I suggest here, not so sure as re-readings of the essay by later hypertext theorists propose. (On this question, see Nyce and Kahn, 1991b.) Tim Berners-Lee appears to have been unaware of Bush's writings on the Memex

(or of Nelson's earliest work on hypertext) until late in the development of hypertext mark-up language (HTML) (Berners-Lee, 1999, 4–6.)

12. Nelson (1990, 5/6–5/7). 'SilverStand™' is a registered trademark of Theodor Holm Nelson. Were this essay a hypertext, this footnote would direct the reader back to footnote 3, where I defer the task of outlining a history of hypertext systems, and ahead, to a quote from Nelson's *Literary Machines* in the body of this essay, describing the SilverStand. But the directions 'back' and 'ahead', workable in relation to the flow of the printed page, seem insufficiently robust to capture the coincidence of these parts. In a hypertext of the kind envisioned in Xanadu, this footnote, footnote 3, and the passage from *Literary Machines* – that is, the corresponding passage of Nelson's book, distinct in every other way from its citation in *this* book – would be one and the same block of text.

13. See Petroski (1999, 100–28). Perec's observation regarding Antonella da Messina's painting of Jerome, that the space of the painting is organized around a piece of furniture, and the furniture around a book, is also relevant here. All that is peripheral to Messina's depiction of Jerome's carrel – the 'glacial architecture' of the church; the distant landscapes visible through the window and a vaulted corridor on either side; the lion, birds and potted plants of the painting's allegorical codes – is cancelled out, says Perec, by the centripetal pull of the desk and the open book at the painting's centre. 'They are there solely to lend scale to the piece of furniture, to enable it to be *inscribed* [*lui permettre de* s'inscrire]' (1997, 87; 1974, 118). In Crimi's illustration of the Memex, this pull of the centre is so powerful that the operator is nearly cancelled out, appearing only as an accessory hand, reaching in from outside of the frame to annotate the pages projected on the screen (Figure 2).

14. This is, in a narrow sense, what Memex aims to do: straighten up the mess that confronts the knowledge worker of the modern era. Readers familiar with Bush's essay may note that I have skipped over much of the argument leading up to the introduction of Memex, and thus Bush's justification for the development of it and similar devices: the scientific record, he complains, is growing too fast for the researcher to take in even the small portion that is directly relevant to his research. 'The summation of human experience is being expanded at a prodigious rate, and the means we use for threading through the consequent maze to the immediately important item is the same as was used in the day of square-rigged ships' (1991a, 89). Nearly half a century later, Tim Berners-Lee will cite the burgeoning record as the principal justification for new protocols for document access, annotation and transmission that will form the foundation of the World Wide Web (Berners-Lee, 1989; 1999.)

15. In this, the Memex evokes an array of related cultural forms and practices: the closet, the cupboard, the strongbox, the trousseau, the casket, the wardrobe, the *Wünderkammer* – the public, private and disciplinary enclosure, and all the varieties of furniture-as-intimate-exteriority that

Bachelard includes among the 'organs of the secret psychological life' (1994, 78). Much as for its relation to the pictorial traditions of the scholar's study and lectern, a proper genealogy of the Memex would also situate Bush's writing desk in relation to these container objects and their correspondences; to the phenomenology of domestic interiority signalled by Bachelard; and to the 'glossary' of objects, actions and events Derrida links to the coffin, the cartouche, the tomb, *tire, tirer, tiroir*, etc. – all of which must creep conceptually from the interior to the frame and its supplemental effects (Derrida, 1987, 192).

16. Even so, the transmission of trail information by fascimile in Memex II appears to mark a new level of distinction between the page-images and trails that is not present in Memex I.

17. The address of a Xanadu document thus differs from addresses of documents on the WWW. In the latter system every copy of a document has a different URL ('Universal Resource Locator'), based upon a unique name assigned to the host machine (Berners-Lee, 1999). Moving a document to a different location on the network will change its URL and break any direct links to it.

18. Transclusion was originally called 'quote-windows' (Nelson, 1975, 24).

19. Freud's letter to Fliess, 15 October 1897 (Freud, 1954, 221–25); Freud (1901, ch. 4.).

Works cited

Aarseth, Espen J. *Cybertext: Perspectives on Ergodic Literature*. Baltimore, MD, 1997.

Adler, Jeremy and Ulrich Ernst. *Text als Figur: Visuelle Poesie von der Antike bis zur Moderne*. Weinheim, 1990.

Bachelard, Gaston. *The Poetics of Space*, trans. Maria Jolas. Boston, MA, 1994.

Barnes, Susan B. 'Douglas Carl Engelbart: Developing the Underlying Concepts for Contemporary Computing', *IEEE Annals of the History of Computing*, 19.3 (1997): 16–26.

Barthes, Roland. *The Pleasure of the Text*, trans. Richard Miller. New York, 1975.

Berners-Lee, Tim. 'Information Management: A Proposal'. Geneva, Switzerland: CERN, 1989. <http://www.w3.org/History/1989/proposal.html>.

Berners-Lee, Tim. *Weaving the Web: The Original Design and Ultimate Destiny of the World Wide Web by Its Inventor*. San Francisco, CA, 1999.

Birkerts, Sven. 'Hypertext: Of Mouse and Man', *The Gutenberg Elegies: The Fate of Reading in an Electronic Age*. Boston, MA, 1994, 151–64.

Bolter, Jay David. 'Topographic Writing: Hypertext and the Electronic Writing Space', *Hypermedia and Literary Criticism*, eds Paul Delany and George P. Landow. Cambridge, MA, 1991a, 105–18.

Bolter, Jay David. *Writing Space: The Computer, Hypertext, and the History of Writing*. Hillsdale, NJ, 1991b.

Borges, Jorge Luis. *A Universal History of Infamy*, trans. Norman Thomas di Giovanni. New York, 1972.

Bush, Vannevar. 'As We May Think', in James M. Nyce and Paul Kahn (eds), *From Memex to Hypertext: Bush and the Mind's Machine*. New York, 1991a, 85–110.

Bush, Vannevar. 'Memex II', in James M. Nyce and Paul Kahn (eds), *From Memex to Hypertext: Bush and the Mind's Machine*. New York, 1991b, 165–84.

Conklin, Jeff. 'Hypertext: An Introduction and Survey', *IEEE Computer*, 20.9 (1987): 17–41.

Derrida, Jacques. *Of Grammatology*, trans. Gayatri Chakravorty Spivak. Baltimore, MD, 1974.

Derrida, Jacques. 'Freud and the Scene of Writing', trans. Alan Bass, in *Writing and Difference*. Chicago, IL, 1978, 196–231.

Derrida, Jacques. 'Plato's Pharmacy', trans. Barbara Johnson, in *Dissemination*. Chicago, IL, 1981, 61–172.

Derrida, Jacques. 'Cartouches', *The Truth in Painting*, trans. Geoff Bennington and Ian McLeod. Chicago, IL, 1987, 183–254.

Derrida, Jacques. *Archive Fever: A Freudian Impression*, trans. Eric Prenowitz. Chicago, IL, 1996.

Douglas, Jane Yellowlees. *The End of Books – Or Books Without End?: Reading Interactive Narratives*. Ann Arbor, MI, 2000.

Drucker, Johanna. *The Visible Word: Experimental Typography and Modern Art, 1909–1923*. Chicago, IL, 1996.

Drucker, Johanna. *The Century of Artists' Books*. New York, 1997.

Freud, Sigmund. 'Project for a Scientific Psychology', in *Standard Edition of the Complete Psychological Works of Sigmund Freud*, ed. James Strachey. London, 1950 (1895), 1: 295–391.

Freud, Sigmund. 'The Psychopathology of Everyday Life', in *Standard Edition of the Complete Psychological Works of Sigmund Freud, Vol. 6*, ed. James Strachey. London, 1960 (1901), 6: 1–290.

Freud, Sigmund. 'The Theme of the Three Caskets', in *Standard Edition of the Complete Psychological Works of Sigmund Freud*, ed. James Strachey. London, 1958 (1913), 12: 291–301.

Freud, Sigmund. 'A Note Upon the "Mystic Writing Pad"', in *Standard Edition of the Complete Psychological Works of Sigmund Freud*, ed. James Strachey. London, 1961 (1925), 19: 227–32.

Freud, Sigmund. *The Origins of Psychoanalysis. Letters to Wilhelm Fliess, Drafts and Notes, 1887–1902*, trans. Eric Mosbacher and James Strachey, eds Marie Bonaparte, Anna Freud and Ernst Kris. New York, 1954.

Genette, Gérard. *Paratexts: Thresholds of Interpretation*, trans. Jane E. Lewin. New York, 1997.

Glazier, Loss Pequeño. *Digital Poetics: The Making of E-Poetries*. Tuscaloosa, AL, 2001.

Hayles, N. Katherine. 'Flickering Connectivities in Shelley Jackson's *Patchwork Girl*: The Importance of Media-Specific Analysis', *Postmodern Culture*, 10.2 (2000).

Heim, Michael. *The Metaphysics of Virtual Reality*. New York, 1993.

Jackson, Kevin. *Invisible Forms: A Guide to Literary Curiosities*. New York, 1999.

Joyce, Michael. *Othermindedness: The Emergence of Network Culture*. Ann Arbor, MI, 2000.

Kahn, Paul and James M. Nyce. 'The Idea of a Machine: The Later Memex Essays', in James M. Nyce and Paul Kahn (eds), *From Memex to Hypertext: Bush and the Mind's Machine*. New York, 1991, 113–44.

Kahn, Paul and Krzysztof Lenk. *Mapping Web Sites: Digital Media Design*. Mies, Switzerland, 2001.

Kittler, Friedrich A. 'The World of the Symbolic – A World of the Machine', trans. Stefanie Harris, in *Literature, Media, Information Systems: Essays*, ed. John Johnston. Amsterdam, 1997, 130–46; 185–8.

Lacan, Jacques. *The Seminars of Jacques Lacan, Book II: The Ego in Freud's Theory and in the Technique of Psychoanalysis (1954–1955)*, trans. John Forrester. New York, 1991.

Landow, George P. *Hypertext: The Convergence of Contemporary Critical Theory and Technology*. Baltimore, MD, 1992.

Landow, George P. *Hypertext 2.0: The Convergence of Contemporary Critical Theory and Technology*, 2nd edn. Baltimore, MD, 1997.

McGann, Jerome. *Black Riders: the Visible Language of Modernism*. Princeton, NJ, 1993.

McGann, Jerome. *Radiant Textuality: Literature After the World Wide Web*. New York, 2001.

Massin, Robert. *Letter and Image*, trans. Caroline Hillier and Vivienne Menkes. New York, 1970.

Mullet, Kevin and Darrell Sano. *Designing Visual Interfaces: Communication-Oriented Techniques*. Mountain View, CA, 1995.

Nelson, Theodor Holm. 'A File Structure for the Complex, the Changing and the Indeterminate', *Association for Computing Machinery, 20th National Conference*. Cleveland, OH, 1965, 84–100, Vol. P-65.

Nelson, Theodor Holm. *Computer Lib/Dream Machines*. South Bend, IN, 1974.

Nelson, Theodor Holm. 'Data Realms and Magic Windows', *Meeting of the Association of Computer Programmers and Analysts (ACPA)*, 1975, 23–6.

Nelson, Theodor Holm. *Literary Machines 90.1*. Sausalito, CA, 1990.

Nelson, Theodor Holm. 'As We Will Think', in James M. Nyce and Paul Kahn (eds), *From Memex to Hypertext: Bush and the Mind's Machine*. New York, 1991, 245–60.

Nelson, Theodor Holm. 'Opening Hypertext: A Memoir', *Literacy Online: The Promise (and Peril) of Reading and Writing with Computers*, ed. Myron C. Tuman. Pittsburgh, PA, 1992, 43–57.

Nelson, Theodor Holm, et al. (1995) 'Xanks and No, Xanks'. <http://www.wired.com/wired/archive/3.09/rants.html>.

Nelson, Theodor Holm. 'Xanalogical Structure, Needed Now More than Ever: Parallel Documents, Deep Links to Content, Deep Versioning, and Deep Re-Use', *ACM Computing Surveys*, 31.4es (1999).

Nelson, Theodor Holm. 'Xanadu® Technologies – An Introduction'. 2002 <http://xanadu.com/tech/>.

Nielsen, Jakob. *Multimedia and Hypertext: The Internet and Beyond*. Boston, MA, 1995.

Nyce, James M. and Paul Kahn, eds. *From Memex to Hypertext: Bush and the Mind's Machine*. New York, 1991a.

Nyce, James M. and Paul Kahn. 'A Machine for the Mind: Vannevar Bush's Memex', in James M. Nyce and Paul Kahn (eds), *From Memex to Hypertext: Bush and the Mind's Machine*. New York, 1991b, 39–66.

Oren, Tim. 'Memex: Getting Back on the Trail', in James M. Nyce and Paul Kahn (eds), *From Memex to Hypertext: Bush and the Mind's Machine*. New York, 1991, 319–38.

Perec, Georges. *Espèces d'espaces*. Paris, 1974.

Perec, Georges. *Species of Spaces and Other Pieces*, trans. John Sturrock, ed. John Sturrock. New York, 1997.

Petroski, Henry. *The Book on the Bookshelf*. New York, 1999.

Queneau, Raymond. *Cent mille milliards de poèmes*. Paris, 1961.

Rasula, Jed and Steve McCaffery (eds). *Imagining Language: An Anthology*. Cambridge, MA, 1998.

Rosenberg, Jim. 'A Prosody of Space/Non-Linear Time', *Postmodern Culture*, 10.3 (2000).

Rosenberg, Jim. 'And *And*: Conjunctive Hypertext and the Structure Acteme Juncture', *Hypertext 2001*. Århus, Denmark, 2001, 51–60.

Rothenberg, Jerome and Steven Clay. *A Book of the Book: Some Works and Projections about the Book and Writing*. New York, 2000.

Saper, Craig. *Networked Art*. Minneapolis, MN, 2001.

Trigg, Randall H. 'From Trailblazing to Guided Tours: The Legacy of Vannevar Bush's Vision of Hypertext Use', in James M. Nyce and Paul Kahn (eds), *From Memex to Hypertext: Bush and the Mind's Machine*. New York, 1991, 353–67.

Wolf, Gary. 'The Curse of Xanadu', *Wired*, 3.06 (June 1995): 137–52; 94–202.

126

the story of I/i | *THOMAS PEPPER*

For Paula Rabinowitz, *à un degré éminent*

Il y a le nom et la chose; le nom, c'est une voix qui remerque et signifie la chose; le nom, ce n'est pas une partie de la chose ny de la substance, c'est une piece estrangere joincte à la chose, et hors d'elle.

Dieu, qui est en soy toute plenitude et le comble de toute perfection, il ne peut s'augmenter et accroistre au dedans; mais son nom se peut augmenter et accroistre par la benediction et louange que nous donnons à ses ouvrages exterieurs. Laquelle louange, puis que nous ne la pouvons incorporer en luy, d'autant qu'il n'y peut avoir accession de bien, nous l'attribuons à son nom, qui est la piece hors de luy la plus voisine. Voilà comment c'est à Dieu seul à qui gloire et honneur appartient; et il n'est rien si esloigné de raison que de nous en mettre en queste pour nous: car, estans indigens et necessiteux au dedans, nostre essence estant imparfaicte et ayant continuellement besoing d'amelioration, c'est là à quoy nous nous devons travailler. Nous sommes tous creux et vuides; ce n'est pas de vent et de voix que nous avons à nous remplir; il nous faut de la substance plus solide à nous reparer. Un homme affamé seroit bien simple de chercher à se pouvoir plutost d'un beau vestement que d'un bon repas: il faut courir au plus pressé. Comme disent nos ordinaires prieres: 'Gloria in excelsis Deo, et in terra pax hominibus.' *Nous sommes en disette de beauté, santé, sagesse, vertu, et telles parties essentieles; les ornemens externes se chercheront après que nous aurons proveu aux choses necessaires. La Theologie traicte amplement et plus pertinement ce sujet, mais je n'y suis guiere versé.*

(Montaigne, 1962, 15–16)

There is the name and the thing. The name is a sound which designates and signifies the thing; the name is not a part of the thing or of the substance, it is an extraneous piece attached to the thing, and outside of it.

God, who is himself all fullness and the acme of all perfection, cannot grow and increase within; but his name may grow and increase by the blessing and praise we give to his external works. Which praise, since we cannot incorporate it in him, inasmuch as he can have no accession of good, we attribute to his name, which is the part outside him that is nearest him. That is why it is to God alone that glory and honor belong. And there is nothing so remote from reason as for us to go in quest of it for ourselves; for since we are indigent and necessitous within, since our essence is imperfect and continually in need of betterment, it is this betterment that we should work for. We are

129

all hollow and empty. It is not with wind and sound that we have to fill ourselves; we need more solid substance to repair us. A starving man would be very foolish to try to provide himself with a fine garment rather than with a good meal: we must run to what is most urgent. As our ordinary prayers say, Glory to God in the highest, and on earth peace toward men. *We are in want of beauty, health, wisdom, virtue, and suchlike essential qualities; external ornaments will be sought after we have provided for the necessary things. Theology treats this subject amply and more pertinently, but I am hardly versed in it.*

(Montaigne, 1965, 468)

Remarking, signifying, accruing honor and interest, praising, glorying, starving, being empty, mourning, praying: I am hardly versed in it. The I is hardly versed in it. The I is entirely versed in it. Every I is versed in it. The I is it. I is it: 'We must run to what is most urgent.'

1. I, 'I,' not I, and i, materially, conceptually and analytically considered

Not *ego* – as Valéry and the English Freud translators would have it – but *I*, a simple, single letter, unmixed. (About this question of mixity, methexis, hybridity, hubris, I have much to say anon, inasmuch as this moment of this letter-which-is-more-than-just-one touches precisely on the simple and undivided phenomenological core of the transcendental ego, which of course turns out to be as impersonal and as third person as can be, and thus quite contaminated by something else, impure, not at all

unmixed.)[1] *Ego* and *Id* are not the same as I and it; and it is a lamentable accident of what happened to some of the greatest thought of the last century that this is how we Anglos got it – in Latin. And nor shall I treat here of those librarians, Benveniste and Jakobson, of whom, in this context, I am bored.

The tack of *I* is different, in our mother tongue (to whom, by the way, am I speaking, is I ever speaking?): English has the distinctly random privilege of being the major language in which this apparently innocent, but in fact quite guilty letter (guilty since it has precisely to do with the very origins of sin – Kierkegaard: as soon as there is a word, there is anxiety)[2] is the shifter name of the first person personal pronoun. And yet, of course, after the advent of this random stupidity or brilliance of the signifier, we may indeed speak of the becoming necessary of the contingent; for I as sound and as pun has become a topos in this, 'our' language.[3]

Even in order to be the indefinite article to accompany I, *a* itself must bow and submit to its nasal prosthesis and gain a letter, losing its right to primacy or alphabetic primogeniture, its single-letter-hood. What is an aleph, an alpha, that no longer stands alone? Zukofsky could and did write an epic poem, *A*, but 'an' would not serve the same function, leaning as it would on a vowel to come, an absent noun – although *And* is a possibility for a novel with which I have been flirting now for some time. (After all, isn't the novel [*Roman*] the name of F. W. Schlegel's *progressive Universalpoesie* precisely because anything can be incorporated within it? And hence is not *And* the perfect title?)

Unlike a, however, I is only a word in 'our' 'language' if it remains a majuscule. As *i* it merely reminds us of cummings, beloved of early adolescents. And yet . . . There is something else to be said for *i*: given that *j* really is nothing

130

but a smeared *i* anyway, the minuscule of our chosen letter is the only letter in the Roman – see how I like to stretch the boundaries of 'our' 'language' for my purposes? – alphabet to have a *detachable part*. I/*i* has at least two bodies, majuscule and minuscule; and *i* itself also has two: the detached *caput* and its stumpy support. The dot of *i* floats, hovering, like the ball bouncing from syllable to syllable on a video screen in a karaoke bar; or like the piece of foreskin cut off in male circumcision in order to indicate that the non-bearer is forever on the culture side of the nature–culture distinction; or like the jism of the phallic geyser; or like the little part of the real that gets thrown out there into the world when the subject arrives on the scene, and which object we call the little object a. So the dot of *i* is, in Lacanian algebra, its *a*, just as *i* has usurped *a*'s primacy (revenge!) – or at least claims equiprimordiality: i(a). Think the ego *as* the totality of the mechanisms of defence, hence of reactivity, spite, resentment.

On the question of whether *I* is a concept, this matter is quite serious and must be elaborated, pushed to the max. Does *I* delimit a space – jagged or geometrical? – on what Deleuze and Guattari would call the plane of immanence? If so, certainly it is a porous space, a concept which thus not only borders on other concepts but commingles with them, converses with them, is contingent upon them, shot through with them, as they with *I*-it. (See Deleuze and Guattari, 1994.)[4] Through my choice of verbs it is clear that I have sex in mind. Converse, let us remember, is intercourse; and intercourse is conversation; commingling is intimacy; and being contingent not only means touching but also contamination.

Yes: we must think about the sexual intercourse of concepts, the wonderful offspring they beget, and as monsters. Are they all monsters? Is the I a monster concept, something that can be shown, but not said, mute? Or – I hate the cheapness of what chiasmata such as this have become, but here it is necessary – is the concept a monster, the very headbirth of the headbirth, so to speak? (I don't trust reduplication, either, as a trope: it is getting old.) In asking these questions, I already poses the answer: Yes.

But to come back to a matter from which I would constantly be the one who digresses, a question about the topology of the I, or its geometry: the cliché concerning the matter would have the I as a point, dimensionless, the (0, 0, 0) of a Cartesian coordinate system. Obviously, what happens to a point when it has the kinds of truck, transport or sex (*Verkehr*) of which I have already spoken is that it becomes, if you will, pregnant, distended, obtunded. Soon it will be seen to have dehisced, yawned open, as it is now, gaping: 0.

The fiction of the I as a point, at this point in time, is intrinsically caught up with the fiction of a free market or any economy conceived as functioning according to purely utilitarian rules.[5] But we are not in a Newtonian-Cartesian universe of point masses and point consciousnesses anymore; and if we do rely on those versions of the shape of this differently enabled concept, I, then we have to recognize that we are dealing, precisely, with fictions (Bentham, Lacan on Bentham's theory of fictions. When Foucault thought the panopticon he was, as so often, leaning on Lacan's intuition here). The point has smeared – but into what?

I recur to this little point about the detachable part: foreskin, teardrop-ejaculation (zero, zero, zero), the beheaded, minuscule *i*, a medusa of sorts, the *kephale* of its acephalic podium, the dot through which the headless stump mediates its relation to 'the world', if world there even be – one. Everything depends on the matter of this *detachable part*, of which Montaigne has spoken under the name of the name.

Excursus: Imperial I[6]

But there is more to be said here about this '"our"' in 'our' 'language' (Blanchot, *The Last Man*: 'This "we" that holds us together and in which we are neither one nor the other?'; '. . .this drunkenness that always says We'; Blanchot, 1987, 26, 73).[7] In the context of Empire, and of the concomitant globalization of the English language, 'our' language is rotting at its core. The nihilistic instrumentalization of English has impoverished the language – I could just say language, zero article – not to mention the conception of language as such, and to a degree the Romans could never have dreamed of achieving. As more and more people grow up into an English ever more resembling the 'primitive language[s]' described as heuristic devices by Wittgenstein at the opening of his *Philosophical Investigations* ('Slab!', 'Brick!', 'That!', etc. (Wittgenstein, 1958)), the language becomes more and more hollow. For a language worker who also happens to be a university professor in the middle of the American Empire – precipitously waning as it is, but violently and reactively so (I is pure reaction, a masculine protest of itself) – this is most evident: it is not non-native speakers, who take the time to *learn* the language as a second language, whose words are poor. It is the language of 'my' American students, these 'native speakers', – it is precisely these terms of propriety I am trying to interrogate, to push here; for to whom does anything, let alone do or does I belong in the ghettos of Empire? – who don't know either the syntax or the lexicon of their 'own' language, which is progressively levelled, flattened.

To be an immigrant from another linguistic community (what does this even mean in face of global English?) and to have to make do in a language not one's 'own' is, at least, by comparison, to have an idea of what different pieces of language (not only at the sentential-grammatical but also in the metaphrastic dimension) *do*. Monolingualism is the sin of America, where students arrive at the university without knowing what a noun is, a verb, a subject, an object: only 'I'. It is as though nobody in the United States can say anything but 'I': 'this is how *I* feel'; 'this is *my personal* opinion'; 'this is where *I* hurt'; 'this is where *I* was touched'; '*I* saw this'; '*I* was so moved'; 'they have done this to *me*'. Hence the post-11-September-2001 irony of 'united we stand', or, even more shocking (hilarious?!), 'army of one'.

I: in its ownmost tendency essentially fascistoid. (Foucault, in his preface to the English translation of *Anti-Oedipus*: the fascism lurking inside all of us.)

In the state of nature that is the root fiction of the ideology of the free market of Empire, in the venerable war of all against all – in other words in the regnant ideology – 'our' 'language' has, in fact, been, is constantly being reduced to a series of ever more animalistic grunts and groans. And let us make no mistake: the goal of the free-marketeers is nothing short of the bringing into existence of the fiction of the state of nature, with all the worst Darwinist implications. To revise Pierre Clastres's title, we could say that what we are seeing is culture-society against the Empire State (see Clastres, 1987). This is the reign of death, for, inasmuch as 'we' are at war with our own very real projections, we are also on a suicide mission.

Here I disavow any relation to the right wing, except that of enemy: it is right-wing ideology which has produced a society that cares not at all about education, whose leaders themselves are inarticulate morons backed up by profiteering technocrats (think Enron). The agenda of our current 'education president' and the recrudescence, with his administration, of so many – alas – no longer forgotten, and so often indicted, elements of previous Republican administrations (Adorno: one can never imagine the death of the truly evil), is now more than ever involved with mass destruction inflicted so as to secure the profits of oil and heroin (or cocaine: white is white) trade routes – and not for the American economy, but only for the oleogarchy. This is the reign of one who cannot speak, much less think, except with his human-toy soldiers and bombs. And it is also the reign of the monstrous, that is to say, of the unspeakable.

Pace the critique of humanism we have witnessed, are still witnessing in – what is still – 'our' time, we are forced to admit that human animals are now more present in their animality than ever before. 'Our' 'language' is the index of our world poverty (think the middle of Heidegger's middle thesis: the animal is poor in world, it has the world in the mode of not having it, precisely because it has no names for what surrounds it, thus poor access to the ontological difference, thus a vague horizon of the not-quite worldhood of the not-quite-and-ever-less world; see Heidegger, *Die Grundbegriffe der Philosophie*). Glob. English, especially in the United States of America, is ever more an animal language. Now more than ever must we strip ourselves of all humanist illusions. Note the ambivalence of Heidegger: man is world creating; the animal is world poor; and the inert object, worldless. What I am speaking of here is the man-animal, or the bionic man-animal-thing.

The 'language' 'we' 'speak' is a borderline man-animal language; what look like 'words' are, in fact, word-grunts, word-groans, *Wehen des Eigenen*, the groans of the own. The They, itself the borderline imaginary projection of the subject onto what is actually structure, hence has no face, – this They, made up of all those Is, wants the human race back firmly on the other (nature: itself a fiction) side – now this side – of the nature–culture distinction. 'Language', at least in the regnant ideological representation – for of course the truth is the opposite – becomes dispensable,

along with 'art', 'culture' and any other promise of happiness not based on obscene financial gain (preferably by theft) and total conformity.

The truth of Heidegger-Derrida's critique of humanism is materialized today – even if thus ironically, ideologically speaking – all around us in the sounds made by the hominids of *homo sapiens non sapiens*. When we walk on the street, or read the headlines of the 'news' papers in the kiosks, we see faces and words, the faces of words 'seized by the seismic tremors of the unconscious', which is outside, all around us.[8]

Our 'smart bombs' have difficulty killing *them* (= aggregates of evil not-Is, the *Them* – the They in the oblique) because the Afghans (or whatever placeholder stands in for Them in the eternal now of perpetual war) – what should they be doing, living in nice, destructible, disposable suburbs and skyscrapers, like 'people', like 'us'? – are hiding out – living, staying alive – in caves. Imperial I goes, like the corporate residents of Babel's twin towers, for the sky, whereas those others running the war machine (in Deleuze-Guattari's sense) against Imperial US(a) are living in caves. On the ideological distinction – between 'US' superhumans – who build towers, planes and 'smart bombs' (each of us a mobile army of one, because in the United States, one can only count to one) and subhumans, who live in caves and use knives – betrayed here in this kind of 'news', – concerning these kinds of 'facts', I shall say no more.[9] Even during the few turns of breath of the writing of this essay, the enemy-evil-function has already shifted to a new array of states, poor and starving as they are (like so many in the fourth world, at the heart of the so-called first world), in what resembles by cheap parody Orwell's switching the enemy from Eurasia to Eastasia (or vice versa: does it make a difference?) during a rally in *1984*.

End of excursus. The I, an excursus, the time of a digression.

1. Continued

To resume: one of only two letters in our language to serve as a word in its own right (*i* and *a*: both vowels, of course. Of course!? – Precisely: only with vowels can letters be *voiced*), I proclaims its primacy from the start: I is A, the alpha-aleph. It, too, comes first, at least since the ordering of our classical Indo-European grammars (different of course from the Tibetan and concomitant Buddhist-philosophy-generating grammars, in which our first person is their third, and vice versa: Protestantism would not have worked so well in Tibetan, I guess).

That the second person (maintaining its numerical position, but not capable of trying any harder) in both aforementioned systems is largely irrelevant to the I-he/she/it, being, as *you* is, at the level of the pure imaginary reflection of the I, says something profound about its ontological weakness and fragility. And this in turn tells us something about the weakness of the vocabulary of dialogue.

Dialogue is, after all, a misrecognition or miscovery [*méconnaissance*] between two subjects, each of which is itself built on its own – but what does 'own' mean here? – miscovery in the mirror. I is not talking to you. It is not for you that I is speaking or writing. This is not a dialogue. The *you* is the weakest person in the same way that the imaginary is the weakest of Lacan's three registers, despite the fact that one must work through it in order to perform a bypass operation if one wants to do anything at all, for

[w]hat is a praxis? It seems doubtful to me that the term be considered an improper one concern-

ing psychoanalysis. It is the most ample term to designate a concerted action by man, whatever it might be, which puts him in the position of treating the real by the symbolic. That he encounters the imaginary to a greater or lesser extent here is a matter of only secondary importance.

(QCF, 15)

I is, in fact, a derived power, but one which reinvents itself as primordial in a *coup d'état* or a *coup de lalangue*, which is the nonsense field of any natural language once syntax and logic have swept their part away. *Lalangue* is thus the stuff of which slips, puns, and dreams are made.[10] Thus (would) (the) I pretend(s) to be, as Lacan called himself – in English – on French television in 1972, a 'self-made man'. This letter from the middle of the set – the ninth, to be precise, and the third of the vowel set – usurps the role of the first and sets itself up as His Majesty the I.

And if Montaigne speaks first of god and then of himself, he is still in the polite world in which the premier reference, in the very gesture of praise of which he speaks, must belong to the first, the most important, and highest principle. God, not I. Let us here remember to remember what we always forget not to forget: god is unconscious, it is not an I. I is sleeping in the dream, where the subject – not I – does not lead, but is led. (QCF, 88). Consciousness is a quality of a finite being, not of a being unlimited by being within being. 'I am that I am' is itself an anthropomorphism: however empty a husk I is, however little ontological consistency it may have, it is still too much to say of god that it has an ego that might say I.

The subject, like god's name for Montaigne and just as man was created in god's auto-miscovery in its (god's) mirror stage, is unconscious god's little piece of the real, *his* object a, through which the all-demanding Father gets what he craves and needs and desires: praise, love, unqualified and limitless adoration and submission. This is how, in the divine name, the real – god's little piece, what comes off in the creation, his auto- (not self-) circumcision – touches upon the symbolic: god's name is the touching, contamination or contingency of the real and the symbolic. It is its (god's) little piece of the rock, his real, the substance of us as subject. The imaginary misrecognition that we are made in his image is precisely the ego-self-censored version of this fact of our being god's little piece of shit, his foreskin, his trash. That handles the matter of how it stands from god's side of things.[11]

And from the humanoid subject's side of things, too, god's name is the nodal point of the real and the symbolic: it is his little piece of the rock, his real, his name; and there it enters the symbolic (dis)order of the finite subject – a pleonasm. In our taking god's piece, his name, a stone, into and letting it out of our mouths, it also thus participates in our desire, our real and, simultaneously, in our own symbolic order. 'That he [man] encounters [– better: that it is encountered –] the imaginary to a greater or lesser extent here is a matter of only secondary importance'.

2. The Difference between Paranoia and Neurosis, or between Modern Subjective Philosophy and Criticism

Now, the intellectual cliché of a majusculized Modernity would have it that Descartes's discovery of the *cogito* is a reply to the drift of Montaigne's poverty and necessitousness, to his melancholic-almost-baroque collecting of the available fragments of classical learning. Montaigne, *bricouleur*; Descartes, engineer. But a simple reading of the source text upon which this old saw is founded will suffice

to tell us that the novelty of Descartes perhaps inheres in his impolite and perhaps impious gesture of discussing I finding itself as a thing, the thing, the thing that thinks – or things – before he reveals, in the set-piece of the *Meditations*, that the whole thing still depends on god, anyway. The good god will be trotted out as one of Descartes's stage props, in order to back up the I in its certainty, thus in a counter-gesture to that of Montaigne.

Montaigne is what we would call a critic, an obsessional neurotic, who worries over the status of his object, worries that object, as I do here my object *a, i*; and, as such, he realizes that he always begins *in medias res*, in the midst of things or of the world, even if it looks, superficially, as though the first principle is mentioned first (this is why he says that theology treats of this, but that he is not versed in it). Essays are, after all, just that: they are attempts, and attempts in a genre Adorno will call precisely hybrid – 'Mischling' – mestizo.[12] The I is an essay.

Descartes, on the other hand, the engineer who brushes away all the facts in order to begin the world anew, is the regressed, anal-sadistic philosopher, the one who, in the very repudiation of his object, forecloses reality and has only his 'own' object come back to him from the field of the real. Even if it *looks like* he begins his bracketing operation in a room, by a fire, dressed in a robe, and, most importantly, at night, this too is just a set-up for his levelling operation. It took god six days to create the heavens and the earth; it takes Descartes the six nights of the *Meditations* first to undo and then to redo the whole job – but this time with his own subjective certainty.[13] That the Cartesian operation is an extremely violent one, a kind of war of the I against the world, is confirmed by Michel Leiris, in his essay 'On Literature Considered as a Bullfight', the envelope of his first volume of autobiography, translated as *Manhood*:

*Le Havre is now largely destroyed, as I can see
from my balcony, which overlooks the harbour
from such a height and distance to give a true
picture of the terrible* tabula rasa *the bombs made
in the center of the city, as if there has been an
attempt to repeat in the real world, on a terrain
populated by living beings, the famous Cartesian
operation. On this scale, the personal problems
with which* Manhood *is concerned are obviously
insignificant: whatever might have been, in the
best of cases, its strength and its sincerity, the
poet's inner agony, weighed against the horrors of
war, counts for no more than a toothache over
which it would be graceless to moan; what is the
use, in the world's excruciating uproar, of this faint
moan over such narrowly limited and individual
problems?*

*Yet even in Le Havre, things continue, urban
life persists.*

(Leiris, 1968, 11)

In any of Descartes's I-books, the distance from the I as
thinking substance is no distance at all from the I as total
war, a state in which the I lives – 'persists' – in its own path
of destruction. Of the same generation, if in a very different
vein, mode, and genre, Levinas knows this as well. The
second sentence, and the first of the second paragraph, of
the Preface to his *Totality and Infinity*, reads: 'Lucidity – the
opening of spirit upon the true – does it not consist in fore-
seeing the permanent possibility of war?' (Levinas, 1961, 5;
my translation). And now we see how the story of I, in its
self-interested narrative of primal-sadistic machismo,
becomes the story of O, of a passive hole, to be filled only
by the destructive desire of the I. (This is I's story of O, not
mine – keep reading.)[14]

Heidegger, of course, will call this nihilism, in its
Modern phase. Levinas gives us the kernel of this thought in
one lapidary sentence: 'Descartes thought that by myself, I
would have been able to account for [*se rendre compte de*,
literally *to realize*] the heavens and the sun despite all their
magnificence' (Levinas, 1982, 188; my translation).[15] Call it
nihilism or hubris, the fact is that the *coup d'état* of man
over god fails because of the leftover of magnificence,
which – Levinas clearly asserts here, just as Montaigne
does – is not our province. Magnificence is reserved for the
very sublimity of the trace of the other's passing, of which
trace the creation itself is an index. Think Kant: 'The starry
heaven above me, the moral law within me'.

Here let us recall that other twentieth-century reader
of Descartes's gesture, the paradigm-paranoid Dr
Schreber, who dreams of the end of the world, of the lower,
bad god and the upper, good god.[16] In this, after all,
Schreber is not so far from Descartes, who, off on the
night-errant quest for certainty, asks if there might not be a
being, the evil genius, whose purpose is to use all power at
his disposal to trick René himself, or me, or I – any I as pure
thinking substance. It is the *entirety* of the power of this
being which tells us of the paranoid essence of the I which
thinks this thought. This is the very good-god-bad-god, the
good-cop-bad-cop routine, which will give Schreber so
much trouble two-and-a-half-odd centuries down the line
in all his struggles with the lower (bad) god and the upper
(good) god. It is he who must struggle against losing his
identity as a man: given that his phantasy is that for the
world to be saved, he must be turned into a woman and
fucked by god, we get a sense of the degree to which the
first René is struggling, like his later counterpart – no
longer a 'philosopher' but rather a 'paranoid' autobiogra-
pher, who maintains the pretense of knowledge brought by
theological revelation – not to be turned into a Renée.

The figure of the modern philosopher, essentially paranoid in the quest for certainty, is the one who dreams of system and that everything is related to *him* or *her*. At least Socrates-Plato had the dignity and the tact to avoid thinking everything was all about him or them. The megalomania of philosophical modernity is something else again. And we all know not to try to reason with a paranoid. Watch, some time, the violence with which people trained in the engineering schools of philosophy attack those who worry philosophical texts – not only as thoughts, but primarily as texts – in 'our' critical, obsessional mode. Anyone who has ever witnessed this embarrassing spectacle will recognize that of which I speak (see Kernberg, 1992, 159–74).

This scene, of the obsessional confronting the psychotic and vice versa, can even take place among psychoanalysts. Perhaps it could be allegorized or dramatized as one between medical psychoanalysts – who, by virtue of their medical training, with its silly obeisance to the voodoo I-doll of natural science, are not at all necessarily capable of thinking or of anything resembling it, but more of a kind of insurance-and-drug-company-related engineering and administration – and analysts, whether medical doctors or not, who recognize that the tree of science does not have merely one trunk (QCF 17). Witness, on 24 November 1975, Doctor Jacques Lacan, speaking with and against various members of the Western New England Psychoanalytic Institute in New Haven, Connecticut (USA), here in intercourse with Marshall Edelson, *inter alia*:

> Doctor Edelson: *The logical constructions we make in order to understand unknown reality become in their time reality. What has been a logical fiction in physics is today reality.*
> J. Lacan: *Logical constructions – I said that I considered them psychotic . . .*

> The interpreter, Professor Felman: *He's making a joke; at the beginning of his presentation, he said that a perfectly coherent logical construction was what he defined as psychosis.*
> Doctor Edelson: *Hmm.*
> Professor Felman: *It was a provocative assertion.*
> Doctor Edelson: *I'm provoked.*
> Professor Felman: *But he said that, thus, in this sense, he himself was psychotic, because he was trying to be rigorous. Thus he is not against rigor, but it [alone] doesn't add up to science. I think that is the main point. Coherence as such would only be the proof of psychosis, and not of truth.*
> J. Lacan: *Psychosis is full of meaning.*
> Doctor Edelson: *In my experience, psychosis is called stereotypy and is deprived of meaning.*
> J. Lacan: *But the stereotypes obtain for the psychotic only by virtue of their meaning [ne tiennent pour le psychotique que pour leur sens].*
> (See Lacan, 1976, 29)[17]

And so on. The stereotypy of psychotic phantasy has precisely the function of massively confirming the relations I am attempting to describe between paranoia and the very structure of the subject itself.

Sometimes I is a philosopher, when it bops along at the level of the concept, and sometimes I is a critic, when – inevitably – it gets lost in the words and their order and their letters, such as I do with *i*: but I, the I, is, in its systematic and systemic tendencies – or, better yet, at the limit of what I might call its event horizon – a philosophical psychotic, asserting its being-in-control against the despair that it might not be entirely in control.[18] This is the very structure and function of His majesty the I, as Freud says, parodically, though unfortunately not only: remember Al Haig, on the occasion of Reagan's being shot: 'I'm in control here!'[19]

Now, in truth, things are even more complex than this tendentious, if useful, distinction between the neurosis of the critic and the psychosis of the Modern philosopher – preoccupied with subjectivity and with its idealized correlate, certainty – would allow. For, as we know from that thinker of the last century, Freud-Lacan, there are gradations in the twilight zone between lack of certainty about what I am seeing and certainty in the paranoid foreclosure of reality. There is disavowal [*Verleugnung*]; there is, of course, fetishism [*Fetischismus*]; and, in addition, there is foreclosure [*Verwerfung*], in which the subject goes for the All and tries to deny everything-as-one-thing, replacing reality (the realm of being together, of relation, of the imaginary character of the social bond, whether conceived of as positive or negative) with his or her own object, which comes back to the paranoid as though from the field of the real – which is also the place of the gods for precisely this reason.

The gods belong, god belongs to the field of the real – not to reality – because they and it belong to the projective-identification space of a desire. And the replacement of reality with the object of one's desire and the concomitant mistaking of that desire (the kernel of one's being, the real) for reality is the definition of psychosis. One might indeed say that project*ive* identification is project*ile* identification. In the emblems of which we have spoken – Descartes, Schreber – this involves a revealing split between the good other and the bad other, a fact in which the key concept of ambivalence, in its primitiveness and its overwhelming importance, is revealed. The ambivalence, in both cases, is ambivalence toward the father. The Father, like Darth

Vader, cannot be dissociated from his insatiable and infanticidal dark side.

3. On the Psychotic Phantasy Structure Known as Monotheism

What might we say about the invention of this figure, the Father, the one and only Father, the one and only god? Certainly the unity of this figure – the very core of monotheism – holds together this very deep and strong ambivalence on the part of the subject of the father – an expression I deliberately leave ambiguous. Look at the relationship between the Old and New Testaments: Christianity is a whitewashing of the Father(,) who so loved us that he gave us his only begotten son and allowed him to be sacrificed for all of our sins – forever.

What is this if not the very manifestation of psychotic, or at least borderline, ambivalence? Things get nasty, though, when this ambivalence cannot admit as much to itself, and the making of the Father into only Goodness itself – because the ambivalence is too much to bear – has to efface the bad side. Thus the Good News not only supplements the Bad News, but actually, in effect, represses it, replaces it. This is the very structure of Christian antisemitism, which is thus the ownmost tendency of Christianity itself: let us get rid of the Jews, because, as long as they are around and in our midst, they remind us of the other, castrating side of Daddy, and embody the return of the repressed, of the indestructible. Hence, if we get rid of them we shall have expunged the memory of the fact that Father is not, and was not always all good.[20] And besides, didn't the Jews get us into this mess in the first place by inventing, or better yet, *synthesizing* the Father function (think Foucault: author function) in the first place, thus producing our ambivalence toward him, which we cannot bear; and so mustn't we therefore hate them for destabilizing us with this truly terrible invention?[21]

Here it is worthwhile to make some observations on Kafka, who understood better than anybody just about everything having to do with the Father and his administrative apparatus, with the world in which we live as well as with the I and the you and the he-she-it. In a set of notebooks known as *The Blue Octavo Notebooks* and kept separate from his journal, Kafka, most likely at the end of February or the beginning of March 1918, writes the following aphorism, one of several concerning Abraham written in this time during which the writer is deeply impressed with his recent reading in Kierkegaard:

> *Abraham is captive of the following illusion or disappointment [*Täuschung*]: he cannot bear the monotony of this world. But the fact is that the world is obviously and uncommonly manifold, which can be tested at every moment one takes up a handful of world and looks at it a little more closely. Of course, Abraham himself knows this. So the complaint about the monotony of the world is therefore really a complaint about insufficiently deep commixture with the manifoldness of the world. And thus actually a springboard into the world.*

> (Kafka, 1983, 92; my translation)

The illusion or disappointment under which Abraham suffers, namely that of and at the uniformity, the monotony of the world (in Edelson's words, its stereotypy), is certainly related to being the father of monotheism, of being its founder, first believer and witness. So, if he is caught up in

dis-illusion [*Täuschung*] at the monotony of the world, and yet the diversity of the world is everywhere in evidence around him, then Abraham's plaint must be about something else, namely a complaint about his being insufficiently involved with, caught up in the evident variegatedness of the world. And thus, in articulating his complaint, which expresses the desire for something other than the dis-illusion in which he is caught, the complaint itself serves as a springboard, a diving board out of the illusion of monotony into the manifoldness of the world.

For in *complaining* of monotony, when differentiation is everywhere to be found, one is, in a sense, giving oneself a way out – of the illusion or of the disappointment – of the dis-illusion, the privative illusion that keeps one separated from the rest of the world. One gives oneself a way out by virtue of the *act*, of the *plaint*: for if the monotony of the world is the paranoid-melancholic's (is this combination even possible?), the psychotic's projection of his or her 'own' inner poverty, monotony, and bad immanence onto the world itself, it is nonetheless the case that in *addressing* this plaint to another, the paranoid enacts, acts out a relationship *to* that other, which relationship is precisely denied by the totalizing narcissism of the represented constructions that link all elements of the world to him or her. And, given the ambivalence of the situation, this plaint toward the other, which might be the last vestige of the possibility of relation and of a way out of the paranoid-totalitarian phantasm, is itself a manifestation of deep anxiety concerning contamination, whether by another subject (inmixing, transference), fluoridated water, radioactivity, those who are HIV positive, food additives, African Americans, anthrax, communism, Jews, Muslims, women, homosexuals, or just dirt.

That Kafka speaks of monotony and of lament only underscores the burden monotheism imposes upon its servant, who has to sit there all the time, as does the man from the country ('ein Mann vom Lande', a *Lanzmann*, a Jew) does before the law, waiting for the call from the Father, a call which is only going to demand some horrible and jealous act of total fealty. God's jealousy is so strong that Isaac is too much competition for Abraham's attention. So something has to be done.

After all, doesn't the insatiable god, whom Lacan called the dark god, demand a payback for sustaining the world at every instant? And, as Pascal notes, isn't man's duty, in the face of Christ's abandonment by god, to pay attention by staying awake for the rest of time: 'Jesus will be in agony until the end of the world. One must not sleep during this time'? (Pascal, 1963, 620; my translation) 'Vater, siehst du denn nicht, dass ich verbrenne?'[22]

There can always be only one competitor at a time: Hagar and Ishmael had to be sent out into the desert, but only when Isaac came along to prove that lawfully wedded Sarah was not barren. Now the next face-off has to come, because the Father is so jealous that he cannot admit any distraction to the one who worships him.[23] And Abraham's lament about monotony also reminds us that, while god has promised him revering descendants numerous as the monotonous grains of sand – the very monotonous variegations in any handful of world – in the sea or as the stars in the firmament, these are, in fact, just as many reasons for lamentation – lamentation that this Father business got him into something neither he nor his descendents will ever be able to get out of. Therefore it is god himself who thus has made for the psychotic melancholic depression (Luther: *Anfechtung*, Kierkegaard: *Anfægtelse*) in which everything will only ever be monotonous; for it is the synthesis of him – of that which cannot be gotten rid of – which is enough to make anyone with a conscience crazy and see everything in grey forever, think life as nothing but the endless

living out of the agony of this imposed predicament. If the lament, as Kafka asserts, is the beginning of a way out of this terrible situation – is this, too, not the fulfilment of Kafka's wish to be able to ditch the father? Kafka's work, destined, as its posthumous part was, to be burned, is, in its constant assertion of the authority of the Father, also the instrument of his execution. This is the sense of the lament which might serve as a springboard out of psychosis and into the world. Not only did Abraham draw the knife out of and for faith and despair; so did Mohamed Atta.

4. The Threat and Promise of Silence

This is why Levinas insists that all philosophy tends toward idealism, for the thinking of the one – father, universe, world, subject, being – all of these are projections that attempt to efface the arrival of the other, the one who left magnificence as a trace of its passing. And let us not forget Heidegger's own massive, ambivalent rage here: It is he, after all, who is on the line between what he puts down but cannot live without – metaphysics – and thinking, about which we know precious little except that *it* thinks, or lets thinking happen or occur – to me, to us, to a generation, but always to something in an oblique case – or not. The self-interested representation of the *I* as 'all there' as such has nothing essential to do with it.[24] As a *reader* of the history of philosophy, Heidegger is obsessional. As the one who dreams the regressed phantasy of *Gelassenheit,* of letting thinking happen, he is an obsessional who expresses the wish not to be so.

Think of all those battles with Nietzsche, whether he is mentioned in the immediate context in Heidegger's writing or not: every philosopher thinks one thought, i.e. his or her unthought; all of metaphysics thinks the same; all metaphysics thinks the same thought, i.e. the or its unthought. Heidegger's ambivalence of mood vis-à-vis Parmenides's own one-thought, that being and thinking are the same – this on the part of the one who proclaims the closure of metaphysics, this *Wechsel der Töne* or of *Stimmung*, betrays everything. But what is betrayed?

First of all, what is betrayed is Heidegger's anxiety: am I inside or outside (of metaphysics, of ontotheology)? Was he (Nietzsche) outside before I got there – if I am there? Is there a there there? This is the very battle of the giants concerning being to which Heidegger refers in the opening pages of *Being and Time*.

What is also betrayed is death: what it means to live being toward it; what it means to live for the liberation of after it; what it means to live with it; what it might mean – such is philosophy, so much philosophy – to try to forget it. If Being and Thinking are the Same, and if thought is verbal, even if silently so, as in a monologue, unspoken aloud even to oneself, then Being is Speaking, and the ultimate threat to thinking would be silence.[25] And who is to say that literature, or writing in the eminent sense, are not names for the space that thinks silence, whether it is a question of Homer as commented by Longinus, of Shakespeare, of George Eliot, or of Mallarmé, or of the dying Clarice Lispector, who writes, just before it's all over, a few lines before the end of her last work, *The Hour of the Star*:

> *Silence.*
> *Should God descend to the earth one day there*
>   *would be a great silence.*
> *The silence is such, that thought no longer thinks.*
>   (Lispector, 1986, 85)

'The silence is such, that thought no longer thinks': a cruel and devastating sentence and a cruel and devastating

thought, especially for thought. This sentence threatens thought in its very being, at its very core, in a manner quite similar to the way in which Lacan often refers to the dehiscence or gaping open, the endless yawn of the parakenotic, emptied subject, leading to the navel of the dream. And yet, as I have said about literature or writing: there are modes of thinking, perhaps of the subject at the cost of the I, and which can and do think silence. They are risky thoughts, lurking, on the prowl.

What I would assert is that, having witnessed the unspeakable things we have toward the end of this last millenium, and which have not ceased, but seem only rather to intensify day by day – I assert that thought, henceforth, can only think on the basis of silence. Let the I be silent. Let it be impersonal. Let us get away from the need the self-reassuring, defensive ego has to destroy silence, to neutralize it, to deny it, to foreclose it, to prevent it from *happening*. Even war today – the bombs falling elsewhere, the anthrax of the media at 'home' (where the horror is) – is nothing but the repression of silence, the perpetual suspension of silence. The perpetual war of the imperial – or better: *Gesellschaft mit beschraenkter Haftung – socius*, is, in fact, the very coming together of this body in and as its fated, autoimmune dissolution. Empire is the drive consigned under its attribute of death. Duras: 'You announce the reign of death' (Duras, 1982).

When Hannah Arendt writes that one of the most salient features of what she calls totalitarianism is its conversion of solitude, which is elected, into loneliness, which is enforced, she is prescient of the intensification of the ways in which the current media of mass communication have virtually eliminated silence (Arendt, 1973).[26] At this time, if there is silence, it means that something essential to the functioning of the current imperial regime of global capitalism is not working, has broken down. Silence today can only be uncanny, as when, during the days immediately following 11 September 2001, one noticed, on going to sleep, say, the eerie silence of the lack of civilian aviation in the metropolitan skies of the United States – and the concomitant foreboding with which one did hear aircraft, knowing that they had to be military.

5. The Many Lies of and about Modernity

What is also betrayed is everything we say whenever we – despairing over our lack of control of it – try to codify the Modern. Is the modern what began in ancient Greece, and which, Heidegger thinks, is a big cover-up? Is it the advent of lyric subjectivity in the Troubadours, who invented, *in a certain way*, what we today call Modern lyric? Is it stilnovism? Is it the famous modernity of Descartes, which, as I have suggested, consists not in some radical, new departure for knowledge, contained within the human I itself, but rather in the shamelessness of speaking (of) itself first, and then of bringing god in as a fulcrum, of pulling god's strings to make him dance in this philosophical marionette theatre of subjectivity for the purpose of the philosopher's own convenience, in this *outrecuidance*, this *geste sans vergogne*, this shameless going beyond all caution? Is it what Foucault means when he writes of the break-up of the classical episteme between 1790 and 1810, and speaks of the transformative movement that turns, for example, grammar into philology, classification into evolution, and the analysis of wealth into political economy? Is it an aesthetic style to which we refer when we speak of the New, whether in relation to Rilke's *New Poems*, to the International Style, to De Stijl, or to the Modern Breakthrough, itself a Kierkegaard-effect in Northern European literature?

This, in short, is the problem of periodization, to which

the silliness of contemporary criticism has returned for now, in a pathetic and reactive gesture, a gesture that denies the critique of time we have witnessed throughout the last century, from Heidegger's vulgar time consciousness to Freud's timelessness of the unconscious, along with Lévi-Strauss's and Althusser's glosses thereupon. The task of the coming intellectual history will be to deal with the crisis that has already happened in the thinking of time, and which is intimately linked with the structure of consciousness. The I *is* vulgar time consciousness; but Heidegger's Dasein is not, nor Freud-Lacan's subject.

'I' was not invented in any of those 'places', at any of those 'times'. The unities described there are merely tendential and projective, as Lévi-Strauss says of the unities of his reference myths. We can use examples from so many periods, so many epochs, so many genres, modes, styles in order to make our point. There is no modern. And yet, there is a modern, by which I mean, there are moderns, there are modernities. But they are anachronic to and with each other, and do not correspond to and with each other according to some unilinear – progressive (Blumenberg, for example) or regressive (Leo Strauss, for example) – scheme. And anyone who reifies any of these into *one* which would purport to have some kind of ontological consistency in terms of the time or the objects described does so at his or her own peril.[27]

6. Of I in its Relation to Everything, Nothing, and Song

Let us watch the surgence of one of these modernities in the arrival of I as lyrical song, accompanied by nothing. Watch the emergence of the world in the song, *canso* 3, of Guillaume IX, Duke of Aquitaine, the first Troubadour:

Farai un vers de dreyt nien:
non er de mi ni d'autra gen,
non er d'amor ni de joven,
ni de ren au,
qu'enans fo trobatz en durmen
sobre chevau.

No sai en qual hora·m fuy natz:
no suy alegres ni iratz,
no suy estrayns ni sui privatz,
ni no·n puesc au,
qu'enaissi fuy de nueitz fadatz,
sobr' un pueg au.

No sai quora·m fuy endurmitz
ni quora·m velh, s'om no m'o ditz.
Per pauc no m'es lo cor partitz
d'un dol corau;
e no m'o pretz una soritz,
per Sanh Marsau!

Malautz suy e tremi murir,
e ren no sai mas quan n'aug dir;
metge querrai al mieu albir,
e non sai tau;
bos metges es qui·m pot guerir,
mas non, si amau.

M'amigu' ai ieu, no sai qui s'es,
qu'anc non la vi, si m'ajut fes;
ni·m fes que·m plassa ni que·m pes,
ni mo m'en cau,
qu'anc non ac Norman ni Frances
dins mon ostau.

Anc non la vi et am la fort,
anc no n'aic dreyt ni no·m fes tort;
quan non la vey, be m'en deport,
no·m pretz un jau
qu'ie·n sai gensor et bellazor,
e que mais vau.

No sai lo luec ves on s'esta,
si es en pueg ho es en pla;
non aus dire lo tort que m'a,
abans m'en cau;
e peza·m be quar sai rema,
ab aitan vau.

Fag ai lo vers, no say de cuy;
e trametrai lo a selhuy
que lo·m trametra per autruy
lay vers Anjau,
que·m tramezes del sieu estuy
la contraclau.

I will make a vers of exactly nothing:
there'll be nothing in it about me or anyone else,
nothing about love or youth
or anything else.
It came to me before, while I was sleeping
on my horse.

From exactly nothing, the poet brings forth an agent – still hiding here, sleeping in the verb, the first word of the poem (more in a moment)[28] as well as *vers*, nothing, anyone else, love, youth, anything else, before, sleep, horse. In the following three stanzas, through exactly the first half of the poem, we watch the similar emergence of birth, cheer, moroseness, stranger, here, night, fairy, peak, waking, heart, someone, grief, Saint Martial, mouse, illness, shivering, death, doctor, wellness:

> I do not know the hour of my birth.
> I am not cheerful or morose,
> I am no stranger here and do not belong in
>   these parts,
> and I can't help being this way,
> I was turned into this, one night, by some
>   fairy
> high on a peak.
>
> I don't know when I slept
> or wake, if someone doesn't tell me.
> My heart is almost broken
> from the grief in it,
> and I swear by Saint Martial, to me the whole
>   thing
> isn't worth a mouse.
>
> I am sick and shiver at death
> and don't know it except when I'm told.
> I will look for the doctor I have in mind,
> I don't know who he is.
> He's a good doctor if he can make me well,
> but not if I get worse.

Now I have attained this poem, the true object of my desire for many years, and about which I hope someday to write an entire essay of this scope, which is the least it deserves. But, even in the context of this short and all-too-inadequate gloss, certain distinctions must still be made. For in the eight stanzas of this *vers*, not all the objects conjured forth into this sublimely intricate simplicity are equal. The major

prestation is reserved for one thing only, and to which three entire stanzas are devoted:

> I have my little friend, I don't know who she is,
> because I've never seen her, so help me God;
> she's done nothing to make me feel good, or bad,
> and I don't care,
> because there's never been a Frenchman or a
>   Norman yet
> inside my house.
>
> I have never seen her and love her a lot,
> she has never done right by me, or wrong.
> When I do not see her, I enjoy myself.
> And I don't care a cock,
> because I know a nicer one, better looking,
> and worth more.
>
> I do not know the region where she dwells,
> Whether it's in the heights or on the plains.
> I dare not tell how she wrongs me,
> it hurts me in advance.
> And it pains me to stay on here,
> and so I go.

At the beginning of this last quotation, exactly after the break between the fourth and fifth stanzas, the dead centre of the poem, we witness the arrival on the scene of the *belle dame sans merci*, the *domina* of this discourse, in a negative theology of the eternal feminine worthy of a Mallarmé. But that is hardly all that happens at this moment, in this line; for at the same time as the construction of the female friend happens, so does the first use in a non-oblique case of the first person pronoun: *ai*. And indeed I is not the *first* word here in this first line of the fifth stanza, which is 'M'amigu', 'my little friend' (compare the modern French *mamie*, which is a contraction of *ma amie*),[29] it is the next. The pronominal I awakens from its captivity in the conjugation of the first person singular verb *here*, when it speaks of its friend, whom 'I have'.

My discussion above of Lacan's word concerning the un- or aconsciousness of god comes home here. The creator of the world in the first half of the poem lacks company (other than someone, who may or may not wake me up, and a doctor, who may or may not heal me). The first four stanzas of the poem are the creation of the world, or of a poetic miscellany of and as the world, constructed, *trobar*ed, invented(?)[30] fashioned, made, found, discovered, as though out of the first chapter of the Book of Genesis. If the first person pronoun occurs in this first part of this poem, its very obliqueness of case underscores the fact that the agent is still in the verb. But to push the comparison with the first chapter of Genesis further (and why not, as a point of comparison? Is it here, the heresy of the Troubadours, the reason why the Church wiped them out?), the lack of the nominative of the first person pronoun in the first half of this poem re-enacts – but in human song – the way in which god, in the beginning, is either described as doing something in the third person ('and he created . . .'), or as being present in an exhortation ('lux fiat').

But let us remember that in that hortatory subjunctive, so pre-eminent as a manifestation of god's infinite power, the power to create (rather than the limited power of discovery or of invention), has, as its subject, *lux*, light, and not god 'himself'. It is not until god creates man (1:26) that even he – god – gets a first person pronoun in an oblique case, ('Let us make man . . .'), and not until 1:29 that he actually gets to say I in the nominative ('I have given you . . .').

Chapter two exposes, of course, similar complications, inasmuch as god, once again, says I when he announces that he will create woman ('I will make him an help meet for him . . .', 2:18). And Adam will not use a first person possessive adjective until he speaks of woman ('This is now bone of my bone . . .', 2:23), nor will he actually say I until after the eating of the forbidden fruit, when he responds to god's 'where art thou?' with his own 'I heard thy voice' (3:10). Woman (unnamed as Eve until 3:20) says 'we' in 2:2, and, quoting god, in 2:3. But she does not say I until she confesses to the transgression (3:13): 'The serpent beguiled me, and I did eat . . .'

In a minute or so, let us find out what happens, then, after they eat.

Excursus: 'Poem'

Today, in what I take here as a gloss on the topos of both Guillaume and Mallarmé, we have Louise Glück's poem, significantly enough entitled 'Poem':

In the early evening, as now, a man is bending
over his writing table.
Slowly he lifts his head; a woman
appears, carrying roses.
Her face floats to the surface of the mirror,
marked with the green spokes of rose stems.

It is a form
of suffering: then always the transparent page
raised to the window until its veins emerge
as words finally filled with ink.

And I am meant to understand
what binds them together
or to the grey house held firmly in place by dusk

because I must enter their lives:
it is spring, the pear tree
filming with weak, white blossoms.

(Glück, 1975)

A reading of this poem, which is not what I offer here, would have to deal with the intimate commingling of fictions, and of their inmixation in the world, of which they compose the most important parts, and through which they move, ceaselessly, like atoms, causing all the things they bump into to swerve, derailing and debunking the falsehood of the immanence of nature in relationship to an entirely pretended – and poisonous – transcendence by man. Here too a world is brought into being, but it is not dreamed: it is written – and in the early evening, which is once present as itself and yet again as dusk. I must enter their lives because they are already in mine; and it is not at all clear whether the page is a page or a mirror or a window.

Dusk, in its very seeming, is what holds all these elements in place. Hegel may indeed provide the critique of the immediacy of sense perception as certainty – house, tree, dusk, all those things outside – but we do know for sure that he wrote such a critique, because we have it.[31] It is part of a book, and it is printed and widely disseminated.

The very form of Glück's 'Poem' – sestet, quartet, two triplets in another sestet – takes us close to the realm of the sonnet. But this is not a sonnet. I – a degenerate sonnet.

But is this a love poem? Or is it rather that the speaker here can only observe the man conjuring the feminine, and wonder what she (or he) is to do with this bizarre situation, in which they are all bound together in an erotic triad? This is a poem about love and knowledge – that is for certain. But there is much more to be fleshed out here, including

the speaker's relation to its counterpart in Sappho's 'phainetai moi'. End of Excursus.

6. Continued

We must return to Guillaume, at and as the end:

I have made this vers, *I don't know what about;*
and I shall send it to someone
who will send it for me with someone else
to someone in Anjou there;
let him send me from his little box the key
to what we have here.

(Goldin, 1973, 24–7)

The key, *contreclau*, counter-key, is the last word of the poem, which itself is what we have 'here'. The box, 'estuy', in modern French *étui*, is a nominalization of a verb the senses of which include 'taking care [soigner]', 'watching over [veiller sur]', as well as of 'prison', or 'an empty object for the purpose of containing something' (Rey et al., 1992, I: 1336).

I has made this *vers*, and I has filled it with all sorts of worldly things, as well as with a diminutive feminine (we speak of grammatical terms) friend here. But I doesn't know what it's about. So I sends it off, through a series of relays – I think of Molloy out on the strand with his stones: 'sucks and transfers' – to someone down in Anjou – 'Anjau' – there, who will send us back the counter-key to what we care for, watch over, keep hidden here, in and as *our* box.

The I creates the world in a demiurgic or – why not? – para-divine *vers*, a furrowed line of writing, a line pointed in its towardsness toward the verses of courtly love. It doesn't know what it's about. It needs, this verse-box, to be deflowered by its counter-key from the box in 'Anjou', 'Anjau'. This place – *Anjau* – of the penultimate addressee of the poem – before I itself – is at least partially determined by sound parallelism, as well, perhaps, as by other factors of which I am ignorant. (The rhyme scheme of the entire song is consistent from the first stanza to the last [111212]; but while 1 may vary in sound value from stanza to stanza, 2 is rigidly fixed: it is always *au*.) So we might say that, by virtue of the sound pattern alone, all the final words in the fourth and sixth lines of each stanza make a kind of loose series, including: *au, chevau, au, au, corau, Marsau, tau, amau, cau, ostau, jau, vau, Anjau, contreclau*. A rather interesting series in and of itself, including (some of them I don't recognize, being a non-native speaker in 'my' Provençal, but therefore also capable, even if only a little bit, of seeing its idiocies): other, horse, high, Saint Martial, worse, care, house, cock, worth, hurt, Anjou, counter-key – the last word, and notably the only trisyllabic one in the group.

And of all the *au*s in this series, only one, 'un jau', a cock (sixth stanza, line four, final position), is a minimal variation on the toponym *Anjau* (last stanza, same position, same line). *Un jau*, a cock; *Anjau*, Anjou. Only one letter changes. The most minimal variation always says something important. Here the problem is solved if we read the cock's significance as an emblem of male rivalry, as in the practice of cockfighting. So *un jau* helps to force the imposition of the toponym *Anjau*, which otherwise is motivated only by the necessity of its being in the *au* series. Always look for overdeterminations.

And why does it have to be a counter-key? 'Ferai un vers . . . Fag ai lo *vers*': 'I shall make a verse . . . I have made this verse'. *Vers*: line, verse, furrow. From the future to the past, from the indefinite to the definite, from no first person pronoun to its occurrence, this last change somehow mediated – or not? – by the first emergence of I/*ai* in

tandem with the arrival of I's little friend, his dear one. From the first word to the last: 'Ferai . . . contreclau': 'I shall make the counter-key'. To make the *vers*, to scratch it down, to write a poem, to furrow a field, is to make the counter-key, that is, to give oneself a beloved and a pronoun, to give oneself the verse and its key.

But again: why the *counter*-key instead of just the key? Certainly there are the furrows of a field, plowed alternately in the opposite direction – but also because the *counter* – that which answers, comes back or against, conceals, watches over, hides, keeps safe and in protective custody – also contains the word *con*, 'cunt'. This is what is in the box – the secret gift hidden in the exchanges of Freud and Dora – it is in the verse, in these lines, these furrows of the plow. The thing, the matter, *res*, is concealed in the furrowed lines in and as the box.

The traces have already been inscribed within and on and as the poem-box, in its hollow self-protection, just as I has come to gape open: O. The Troubadour sends the box to Anjou-*Anjau*, where whoever he is – that one down there – might send back to me, from his *Schatzkammer*, the room in which he keeps what is dear to him, the *cunt-key*, the key that opens up cunt, but also the cunt itself as key. At the moment of the greatest force of I-phallic joying, in the very creation of the poem, there is *con*, cunt, also stupidity. Or is it idiocy, the idiocy of Provençal in this case, the *lalangue* of the Troubadours, of the perfection of the lyric search for and of the eternal feminine, leading us on?

The long and the short of it is not the cliché of this lock-and-key hypothesis of the enzymes of love, but the fact that *our* box *is itself* the graven furrows of the writing, and the key is at least partly also a cunt. One may think that these cocks – I, the ones running the relays, and the one down there in Anjou – traffic in 'cunt'; but what they send back and forth, the 'clau' in 'contreclau', certainly also looks like a classic detachable part to me, the fetish object, that which stands in for the mother's penis, for that which is hallucinated into being, dreamed, 'while I was sleeping on my horse', precisely because it is indeed so very dear.

These guys traffic, they trade in poetry (remember the institution of pastoral?), and the poetry opens up the space of the phantasy of the feminine. Yet the *con*-text and signification of the last word of the poem are about as bisexual as can be. To figure out the riddle of this poem, which might have been entitled, with Courbet, *L'Origine du monde*, what one must understand is that, at the limit of the *i*'s jism, in the very act of creation of the poem-box, there is: femininity.

When it's said and done and dreamed – and *written*, furrowed – it becomes a box. And a box requires a key. And this key, made partially of 'con', and just as bisexual as its locked box, turns out to be – for it is not only a key – the key? – to cunt, Guillaume's main subject.

> These songs are funny in different ways, and in different meters, but they all have a common theme:

> > Dirai vos de con, cals es sa leis,
> > *(I shall tell you about cunt, [its law])*
> > > (Goldin, 1973, 6)

– is this key not also a cunt, *the* cunt, *cunt*? Am I a cunt? Is *I*?[32]

At the limit of the masculine there appears – the feminine.[33] This riddle has been hanging around for a long time. We may have thought that the I was 'His Majesty', 'the Phallus', 'the Gaze' (itself precisely related to castration, and to the mother *and* father), or any one of the things in *that* column. *I* is what nice people of the pro-war and anti-abortion variety call a very 'dirty' word, and it brings forth a dirty world. At the tip of the sword, the scabbard begins.

(Baudelaire, cited by Claudel, cited by Celan: 'À la pointe acérée de l'infini', 'at the sharpest point of infinity', where the 'German' twentieth century writes to the French nineteenth:

> They lie bare the ores, the crystals,
> the geodes
> What is unwritten,
> hardened into language, lays
> a sky free.
> > (Celan, 1983, 251–2; my translation)[34]

And when Heidegger himself wants to place *place*, *Ort*, he too refers to the tip of the rapier. That very dimensionless point – Descartes's I, the dot of *i* – spaces itself out into a no-place place, the place of the subject, an empty space destined to hold contents.)

But the origin of the world has more consistency than this mere point. Of the counter-key sent from Anjou by that other guy (*autruy*) – his missing piece might be our missing piece. The I: its missing piece, a missing piece.[35] In any case, we come together over the missing piece.

Cunt is not the vagina, the scabbard. Cunt has more ontological subtlety, and does not simply represent the resting place of I's supposed sword – which is, let us remember, an always detachable part. The origin of the world is no mere sheath for nothing, for the little nothing, for somebody's thing. I find this missing piece much more privative than cunt. The reason 'cunt' is such a dirty word is that it names a positivity, and, a positivity which the male order, posing, thanks to the Bible, Plato and Paul, as the only essence, must not allow to come into being. For it is the ground of their being, and it'self', therefore, not a being – not an essence in the way the phallus poses as one, anyway. It has its own way of being and of not being. These fighting cocks try to efface cunt in the same way His Majesty the *ich* comes along and proclaims itself to have always already been there, and whence they issue the taboo: one does not speak of the origin of the world.

Even in the phantasy of the phallic mother, in the denial of castration, there is still the problem that cunt is not touched; it is only hidden by a wishfully undetached detachable part. Castration covers over a secret, yes it does, and a secret that protects, via projective hallucination, the pride of the fighting cocks. And the secret is that there might be something different, something other behind the mother's phallus, behind the fetish – not just the nothing (just?!), the very object of anxiety of the hallucinating, paranoid, male ego. No wonder Lacan insists that woman doesn't exist: the woman of the fighting cocks certainly doesn't: it is the ultimate unreal object, the essence of the riddle (*Rätsel*:[36] also something terrible) of the empty box, which stands as an enigma (think Turing), both treasure chest and key, while at the same time neither. But there might be something else supporting the phantasm: 'The real serves as support for the phantasm, the phantasm protects the real' (QCF, 50).

The I as phallus -ihilates as soon as it pronounces its barest name. 'Verschwindet heute das Subjekt, so nehmen die Aphorismen es schwer, dass "das Verschwindende selbst als wesentlich zu betrachten" sei'. 'If the subject today be vanishing, aphorisms take it heavily upon themselves "to regard that which is disappearing itself as essential."'[37] The disappearing subject, the aphanisis (QCF, chapter XVII, 'Le sujet et l'autre (II): L'aphanisis') of the I: this fadeout is the time of an aphorism. Pascal, Nietzsche, Adorno: Aphoristic I.

Today all of this amounts to the absolute necessity to consider tone, *Stimmung*, the tone of mourning – 'world-finitude-loneliness' – with which the last century has

bemoaned the empty place of the I, even in the defensive-aggressive assertion of its power.[38] The I *as* I, is what has always been vanishing, coming together again in new dominants, formations and constellations: the pronoun, the subject of Freud-Lacan, the subject of lyric, the non-personal subject of free indirect discourse, the subject of the law, of empire, the subject of the treatise, essay, aphorism, narration, silence, cunt: '. . . the calm center of measureless excess, the silent Yes at the center of every storm' (Blanchot, *L'Espace littéraire*, 261, cit. Frey, 1998, 265). The I is the disappearance in its appearing of 'this *thought*':

Moi-même, je n'ai pas été le messager malheureux d'une pensée plus forte que moi, ni son jouet, ni sa victime, car cette pensée, si elle m'a vaincu, n'a vaincu que par moi, et finalement elle a toujours été à ma mesure, je l'ai aimée et je n'ai aimé qu'elle, et tout ce qui est arrivé, je l'ai voulu, et n'ayant eu de regard que pour elle, où qu'elle ait été et où que j'aie pu être, dans l'absence, dans le malheur, dans la fatalité des choses mortes, dans la nécessité des choses vivantes, dans la fatigue du travail, dans ces visages nés de ma curiosité, dans mes paroles fausses, dans mes serments menteurs, dans le silence et dans la nuit, je lui ai donné toute ma force et elle m'a donné toute la sienne, de sorte que cette force trop grande, incapable d'être ruinée par rien, nous voue peut-être à un malheur sans mesure, mais, si cela est, ce malheur je le prends sur moi et je m'en réjouis sans mesure et, à elle, je dis éternellement: 'Viens', et, éternellement, elle est là.

I myself, I have not been the unhappy messenger of a thought stronger than I, nor its plaything, nor

149

its victim, because this thought, if it has conquered me, has but conquered through me, and finally it has always been my equal, I have loved it and have loved only it, and all that has happened, I wanted it, and having had regard only for it, wherever it might have been or wherever I might have been able to be, in absence, in unhappiness, in the fatality of dead things, in the necessity of living things, in the fatigue of work, in these faces born of my curiosity, in my false words, in my lying vows, in silence and in the night, I gave it all of my strength and it gave me all of its, with the end that this too great strength, incapable of being ruined by anything, perhaps consigns us to a boundless unhappiness, but, if this is the case, I take this unhappiness upon myself and I take joy in it infinitely and, to it, I say eternally: 'Come,' and eternally, it is there.[39]

'This *thought*' is, of course, feminine in the original: 'cette *pensée*'. So all the 'it's in the translation are 'elle's in the French. This thought is not I; it is she. If I bring this up, it is not only to show how much the English cuts off in its privation of the feminine, but to draw attention to the following:

The contrast between [the last two examples] permits a surprising hypothesis. The tendency of the novel of point of view to represent otherness through sexual difference has its basis not simply in an extralinguistic reality, but in the fact that once the first person has been eliminated (and the second person along with it), the difference of 'I' and 'you' or 'I' and '(s)he' must be replaced by some other of the remaining features. Number is ruled out, however, since the 'privacy' of the Cartesian subject seems to exclude its being a

plural pronoun. There remains the difference of gender. How the feature of gender comes to the pronoun from its role as Self is a question that awaits crucial evidence.

(Banfield, 171)

If I were to worry, as I has been doing for some time now, about the tendency of male writers to construct an elusive feminine entity, which I call, for the purposes of shorthand and after Goethe, 'the eternal feminine', I would like to begin again with this remarkable, if not yet pursued, suggestion by Ann Banfield. But with the proviso that 'the novel', that vehicle of 'progressive universal poetry', extend to other genres – for example, the lyric – and to other times of literary history.

This is what I would like to announce here. Beyond the phantasm, the real. The evidence is, indeed, crucial.

Minneapolis–Paris
September 2001–February 2002

Notes

1. For an excellent account of this problem of the impersonality of the thinking substance in Descartes's text, see Guéroult (1984, 57–74). For the uncensored, non-ego-ideal version of the way in which I is rent at its core by it, see de Man, 'Sign and Symbol in Hegel's *Aesthetics*' (1996).

2. The (massive) reference is to Kierkegaard's *The Concept of Anxiety*, which is still the best phenomenological treatment of the subject in the literature. But it is indeed much more, for its subtitle reads: 'A Simple Psychologically Orienting Deliberation on the Dogmatic Issue of Original Sin'. The problem and its solution proceed thus: if anxiety is objectless, has the nothing as its object, how is this object possible, since everything that exists is, by definition, good, and that which exists the most, i.e. god, is the eminent good? Therefore, how did anxiety, which has as its object something with no existence, come into being as a basic mood? In other words, when did the nothing

enter the world? Well, it has to have been with original sin, of which anxiety is the hereditary proof of existence. Benjamin's 'On Language as Such and on the Languages of Man' and *The Origin of German Tragic Drama* are unthinkable without this thought, as are Heidegger's *Being and Time* and 'What is Metaphysics?' Kierkegaard is the *conditio sine que non* of late Wilhelmine and Weimar discourse. This is one of the objects of my current work.

3. For a landmark study of the relations between stupidity and idiocy, see Avital Ronell (2001). On the becoming necessary of the contingent, as for so many important things, see the long interview published under the name Louis Althusser, *Sur la philosophie* (1994); and for the brilliance and stupidity of the signifier, see Jean-Claude Milner, *For the Love of Language* (1990). For another powerful philosophical treatment of 'grammatical death' in and as disjunction between the first and third persons, see 'Dreadful Reading: Blanchot on Hegel', in Warminski (1987).

4. I do not wish to pursue the implied reference to Buber here. He will assume his proper place in Weimar.

5. See Mary Douglas, 'No Free Gifts', her introduction to the new translation of Marcel Mauss, *The Gift* (1990).

6. Who can use or mention 'Empire' today without referring to Hardt and Negri's massively imposing *Empire* (2000)?

7. These citations, which I take from Hans-Jost Frey's most careful and caring 'The Last Man and the Reader', in *Yale French Studies* 93 (1998): *The Place of Maurice Blanchot*, would have to be articulated with the question of 'we' in Duras's *La Maladie de la mort* and in Blanchot's *La Communauté inavouable*, a constellation I am pursuing elsewhere.

8. For the definitive discussion of animality in our time, see Derrida (1987); for seismic tremors, see Lacan (1974); for outsideness, see Lacan (1990 [1973]), chapter X, henceforth referred to in the text as QCF, followed by page number. A note to and on Derrida: the treatment of the animal in *Télévision* undoes any simple accusation of Lacan as the last cry of a dying humanism. I say this not because Derrida himself doesn't know it, but because we American academic animals still labour under the silly phantasms of Derrida versus Lacan versus Deleuze versus Foucault versus Althusser, etc. *This* is stupidity. The future generations will have to ditch all of the partisan discourse of the last decades – the petty polemics – and put together a much finer map, not one that says all of these thinkers are saying the Same, but that they are not simply opposed to each other, either. They stand in an anoppositional relation to each other, which is to say they stand in the most intimate relation. The story of what happened in and to thought in France between the end of the Second World War and 'now' has yet to be written in any manner worthy of its subject(s).

9. Except that, as Agamben shows in his seminal study, this is precisely the creation of bare, naked life (*vita nuda*) as the equiprimordial remainder of the emergence of the sovereign power of the Imperial I. 'We' make sacrifices, are sacrificers; Afghanistan and its caves are now Empire's camp, the space of bare life, which can only be killed –

by 'our' 'smart' bombs. See Agamben (1998). 15 November 2001: The Vice-President and the Attorney General of the United States of America both said yesterday that resident aliens who are suspected of being terrorists are no longer covered by the rights of the Constitution – this in case anybody thinks that the production of bare life – that which can merely be killed, without being sacrificed – is confined to a military battlefield 'somewhere else'. There is now no longer any somewhere else: this is the meaning of Empire. In the immortal words of Buckaroo Banzai: 'Just remember: no matter where you go, there you are'. Here is now contained in every there, and vice versa.

10. The term emerges in 1972 in Lacan's seminar on feminine sexuality. See Lacan (1975). The parallel between what Lacan means by 'lalangue' and what Paul de Man means by 'rhetoric' in his famous essay of the same year, 'Semiology and Rhetoric', is extraordinary.

11. Levinas makes this point in a lecture given during the Fall of 1983 at the Ecole Normale Supérieure, rue d'Ulm, Paris, entitled 'Piété et kénose dans la lecture de Chaim de Volozhine'.

12. In 'The Essay as Form', the introduction to his *Notes on Literature*.

13. Foucault locates Descartes at night and Zarathustra at dawn. The degree to which Foucault's power as a thinker has so much to do with his encounters with so-called literary texts is indeed manifest in his strong review essay, 'Guetter le jour qui vient', 'To await the coming day' (now in Foucault, 1994) of Roger Laporte's first book, *La Veille*. (1963). Let the social scientists eat their hearts out: until they are capable of reading Foucault's 1966 essay on Blanchot, 'La Pensée du dehors', 'The Thought of the Outside' (now also in the aforementioned volume of the *Dits et écrits*), and of understanding the way in which, for example, the apparatus of the discursive formation comes from Foucault's meditation on Blanchot's oeuvre, they will understand nothing important of where Foucault comes from or of what makes him tick. *Mutatis mutandis* for the historians. Fortunately for the history of thought, and by virtue of his constant prowling at its edges, Foucault was neither. He was, along with Derrida and among other things, one of the most important readers of Heidegger of his generation.

14. 'Where is *The Story of O* in all of this?' was one of the guiding questions during a wonderful evening – Sunday, 13 January 2002 – in Athens, Georgia, at the home of Kate Tremel and Joshua Cole, with a group interested in French cultural studies, and supported by the Humanities Center of the University of Georgia. That evening I had the pleasure and the honour of hearing the thoughts of some very careful readers of an earlier draft of this text. I thank my hosts, as well as their company, which included Christine Haase, Beatrice Hanssen, Katarzyna Jerzak, Jay Lutz, Catherine Parayre and Miranda Pollard, for an excellent workout.

15. The essay from which this citation is taken, 'The Trace of the Other', was first published as a kind of abstract of *Totality and Infinity* in 1963.

16. If the dream of the end of the world is not merely a contingent, but rather an essential moment or feature of the paranoid scenario (and it

is), it is because the paranoid thus miscovers his or her own rageful and anxious gesture – of brushing away the facts, of effacing reality – and projectively identifies this act as being that of the other, who persecutes the paranoid subject. What have the last decades, what does the present moment teach us, if not that there is an *essential* relation between paranoia and war? The email flying around after 11 September 2001 suggesting that Osama bin Laden be stopped by turning him into a woman by means of a sex-change operation, so that thus he might experience the everyday degradation to which women were (are) exposed under the Taliban, only reinforces my thought here about paranoia's essential relation to war. In this scenario, for the world to be saved from this conflict, the enemy must be humiliated by being turned into a woman and raped. (Catherine Parayre tells me of a January 2002 expedition to Atlanta, where she saw t-shirts saying, 'Osama, yo Mama'.) And since, as I claim here, bin Laden is us, *ergo* this 'joke' reveals precisely the innermost kernel of America's desire. Given the USA's worse-than-pitiful record of treating other countries and their governments over the last half century, and given the poisoned recycling of the same people who are in control now as through the interim, I take a wait-and-see attitude as to how women, or anyone else for that matter, may fare under whatever 'new' government Empire chooses to impose. Where is Stanley Kubrick now that we really need him?

17. The professional identifications of the contestants appear here as they are found in the text. My translation.

18. One can always fill a room of critics with castration anxiety (sometimes manifested as anger and resentment at being made to feel ignorant) by manifesting some fluency with basic or advanced topics in philosophy, but the reverse is not true. The very fact that literature, something that might not be capable of being entirely controlled, exists, is precisely at the root of the terrible anxiety that makes the structure of philosophical thought psychotic in the form of its mentation, and of which this psychotic thinking, in order to assert its being in control, must deny or subjugate the existence – sometimes even the very possibility of existence. How could a philosopher *as* philosopher consciously acknowledge that literature exists, or even that it might exist? Forms of reactive avoidance can, of course, go either in the direction of catatonia, the withdrawal of perception from what is right out there, or of rageful, destructive acting out. The fact that philosophers will happily use examples from prose fiction in their arguments only underscores my point: the literary genre dominated by the device of realism precisely reassures them that what they are dealing with is a matter of the clear and direct representation of reality and that there is no linguistic hanky-panky involved. It is enough to realize this in order to sink much of the contents of the current law-and-literature discourse. Of course, it is entirely the case that various commixtures of philosopher and critic – let alone novelist or poet – can coexist within the same given, empirical human subject. But that does not mean that all these modes of thinking belong to the same structure. Lawyers may be something else altogether.

19. Here I remember Michael Rogin, with whom, as with Ann Banfield, I had the anxious pleasure of discussing some of the ideas in this essay in Paris one evening in July 2001, before Mike's untimely death. After a long, postprandial walk through the Faubourg St Antoine, we said goodbye, they and I, under the new plaque commemorating those who died at La Charonne. We planned to see each other again around now, here in Paris, where I write this last note (5 February 2002). So too was I supposed to see Naomi Schor and Howard Bloch here and now. Naomi's cruel death, one week after and along with Mike's, robbed so many of heres and nows and wes, – wes not merely aggregates of Is. How can I not remember how Naomi, when I was first getting to know her and otherwise going through the worst, thought to invite me out for a consultation on the wily distinctions between and among universality, particularity, and singularity in reference to Sartre's Kierkegaard essay and *Anti-Semite and Jew*? I sent her the first draft of this essay the week before she died. Winnicott, dreaming, after leaving the Athenaeum: 'my club'.

20. Speaking of I in its relation to rage, paranoia (and its stereotypy), Jewish-American machismo, homophobia, the denial of castration, hatred of women: Philip Roth *almost* got this right in *The Counterlife*. But given the matter of stereotypy, one might just as well read anything by him in order to get the same points.

21. Yom Kippur – the Jewish day of atonement, the holiest day of the Jewish calendar – 27 September 2001 (in Christian reckoning): not even three weeks after 11 September, which brought so-called Western so-called Judeo-Christian (read: Christian) so-called culture into a holy war with the object of its own psychotically disavowed image. I am getting off the bus at one of the major entrances to the University of Minnesota campus, where town meets gown in a major, four-cornered commixture site, in order to teach my freshman seminar, 'The Truth in Fiction'. A member of the Gideons, whose colleagues are also standing on all the other corners of the same intersection, hands me a little green book containing *only* the New Testament. Is this not the very aggressive, psychotic disavowal of origins I described above, the very instantiation of antisemitism as the ownmost possibility of Christianity?

22. I have written about the relation between this moment in Pascal and Freud's Dream of the Burning Child in 'Nights on Earth' (1999).

23. On the matter of God's constant and hectoring *testing* of Abraham I am thinking with the recent work of Avital Ronell.

24. For the finest statement about the fate of the I in twentieth-century European discourse, see Ann Banfield (1998), henceforth Banfield, followed by page number. Here Banfield, one of the few and most original critical minds in America, provides not only an extremely sophisticated account of first person-third person relations, she also explains the way in which the linguistics of free indirect discourse, that great

triumph of the novel, has the most serious philosophical implications for the theory of the subject and of the I, let alone of the text. The assimilation of the importance of Banfield's thinking is one of the most urgent tasks for the coming generations of critics and thinkers of language. This assimilation may not be an easy task, for her thought blinds with its elegance and lucidity. Check out her *The Phantom Table* (2000), too.

25. This is precisely the place at which Jacques Derrida's *Speech and Phenomena* asserts itself as an event in the history of philosophy, that is to say, in history. Compare Gottlob Frege: 'But, isn't thinking a kind of speaking? How is it possible for thinking to be engaged in a struggle with speaking? Wouldn't that be a struggle in which thinking was at war with itself? Doesn't this spell the end of the possibility of thinking?' These sentences are taken from 'Sources of Knowledge of Mathematics and the Mathematical Natural Sciences' (1924–25; Frege, 1979). Certainly Derrida (as well as Foucault, Freud-Lacan, Deleuze) is much more the heir to these simple and profound questions than so much of what calls itself philosophy – and denounces the aforementioned French – in the Anglo-American sphere today.

26. Thank you, George Kateb.

27. And likewise, anybody who transposes these temporal categories into national ones – as Heidegger did speaking to the *Spiegel* in 1966, published only on the occasion of his death ten years later, or as Martin Jay does, in his symptomatic misunderstanding of the French twentieth century – only makes nation instead of time into essence. Who would have thought it, but Martin Jay's *Downcast Eyes* is just as entirely a symptomatic repudiation of the French, in favour of German, Enlightenment, as Heidegger's Black Forest provincialisms, which, in comparison, are neither as ignorant nor as silly as those of the intellectual historian who works under the superego of his German intellectual godfather, a member of the original Frankfurt Group. What one is up against in Jay's book is the blind prejudice of at least two generations: that the Frankfurt School was one thing, univocally opposed to the barbaric collaboration of the Heideggers and the Schmitts, whose avatars in thought, but not in political practice, are the postwar French. Today, anyone who turns a courageous eye, both to the texts as to the thoughts, can see that hidden elective affinities of thought put Benjamin and Adorno on one side of this group, and the sociologists on the other. There are the ones who read Kierkegaard on the one side, and the ones who don't on the other. And Jay doesn't. If one thinks in Jay's manner, how is one to account for a figure such as Kantorowicz, whose involvements with the George Circle – not with the Frankfurt School – and with the brutal putting down of the German soviets at the end of the First World War seem, otherwise, to be in complete contradiction with his fight against the Regents of the University of California in the 1950s, and his subsequent move to the Institute for Advanced Study at the invitation of J. Robert Oppenheimer? The image of the so-called Frankfurt School must be destroyed as the false icon of what was in fact quite a disunified

entity, so as to be thought – finally! – in its divisions and tensions and cleavages. And the same holds, *mutatis mutandis*, concerning the word 'poststructuralism', whether used by those who think of themselves as friends or enemies of this phantom, the haunting effect of which must be accounted for in different ways.

28. Many warm thanks to Howard Bloch, who pointed out to me that there is no I, no first person pronoun, in the first verse of the poem, and reminded me as well of the historical problem of the emergence of the non-emphatic first person pronoun out of the conjugated verb. Thus 'my' Bloch made a crucial intervention on the route of the following analysis, when I called him to discuss what I had seen in the last stanza. I think here too of Claire Nouvet, who introduced me to Troubadour poetry, and, in memory, of Roger Dragonetti, who encouraged me to keep reading in the path of the letter.

29. I am grateful to François Brunet for this point, as for so much else.

30. I cannot not speak here of Derrida's magnificent essay, 'Psyché', to be found in his collection of essays of the same title (1986). The essay itself was written in December 1983–January 1984, immediately upon the death of Paul de Man.

31. I owe this point to Paul de Man and Andrzej Warminski. See, respectively, de Man, 'Hypogram and Inscription', in his *The Resistance to Theory* (1986), and Warminski, 'Reading for Example', in his aforementioned *Readings in Interpretation*. My comment to them both is: in discussing what is *certain*, you have already allowed Descartes to lure you into his paranoid world system. Their response, likewise, would be, so, do you really think that there's anything outside? Here we would have to come to terms with a discussion over the relations between the Lacanian real and what de Man and Warminski mean by event or inscription. It is a worthy discussion, but the Lacanian side wins out, because, in its description of the subject, and of its waking self and defences, it describes the structures of what is called reading avoidance, which de Man and Warminski themselves can name, but cannot account for.

32. I think here of Bataille's *Madame Edwarda,* as well as of Diderot's *Indiscreet Jewels.*

33. Andrzej Warminski's seminar, Street Hall, Yale University, New Haven, Connecticut, USA, one or two days after the death of Jean Genet (16 April 1986), and also around the day of Simone de Beauvoir's death. Jacques Derrida visits this seminar to answer questions about *Spurs*, which has been assigned for that class meeting. Having mentioned Genet's death to me in the elevator on the way to the classroom, Derrida says, at one point, that at the limit of the most masculine, the most phallic, the most active, macho, penetrative activity, he finds passivity and femininity – this in questioning the existence of these as essences. I ask him: In *Otobiographies* (1984), you cite two sentences from Nietzsche, one being 'Als mein Vater bin ich tot, aber als meine Mutter überlebe ich', and 'Vielleicht ist es nur ein Vorurteil, dass ich lebe'. What is the relation between these two sentences? Derrida

responds: In the funeral cortège, the wife (mother?) follows the bier of the husband (son?). My parentheses indicate my doubt concerning my memory, although I'm not sure it makes a difference.

34. For the definitive reading of this poem, and of its stance in literary history, see Werner Hamacher (1996, 384–7). Note, with Hamacher, that the severed head of Apollo in Rilke's *Neue Gedichte anderer Teil* also makes its appearance at the moment exactly after part one, thus exactly after an absent centre.

35. We are not at all far from Sartre's early conception of the other as a hole in the structure of the world. Today we would say a black hole. It is this very conception from which Lacan too set out on his own quest – perhaps for the feminine? Jacques-Alain Miller's affirmation of the Sartrean position as Lacan's point of departure (at the conference of the American Lacanian Link, UCLA, March 1999) is a kind of liberation from the silly – and ignorant – partisanship of so many American people who think they are reading Lacan, but are ignorant of the perhaps not-as-fashionable intellectual context. This context is no surprise at all, given the presence of both figures at Kojève's lectures in the 1930s on Hegel. No one ever begins a career with a radically new conception of the other. Toward such a conception one works one's whole life, or longer.

36. Freud, *Jenseits*, chapter II, the emergence of *fort-da*. A sentence that stunned me when I was 19, and left itself inscribed within me. The author watches his grandson: 'Und es dauerte ziemlich lange, bis das rätselhafte und andauernd wiederholte Tun mir sienen Sinn verriet'. The narrative tension of this sentence, its projection of *Unheimlichkeit* onto Sophie's child's play, the afterwardsness of the 'ziemlich lange' (what brought it all back? – Sophie's death?) – all of this demands . . .

37. For-ihilation, see Michael Hamburger, 'Introduction', in Celan (1980, 19–20). For the disappearing subject, see Adorno (1951, 9), my translation.

38. For 'Stimmung', see Leo Spitzer's last and unfinished book, *Classical and Christian Ideas of World Harmony: Prolegomena to an Interpretation of the Word 'Stimmung'* (1963). 'World-Finitude-Loneliness' is the subtitle of Martin Heidegger, *Die Grundbegriffe der Metaphysik*.

39. This is the last sentence of the second version of Blanchot's *L'Arrêt de mort* (1948, 127), my translation. This second version bears no new copyright; its only difference from the first is the elision of a detachable part, that is two paragraphs following the sentence cited above.

Works cited

Adorno, Theodor W. *Minima Moralia*. Frankfurt am Main, 1951.

Agamben, Giorgio. *Homo Sacer: Sovereign Power and Bare Life*. Stanford, CA, 1998.

Althusser, Louis. *Sur la philosophie*. Paris, 1994

Arendt, Hannah. *The Origins of Totalitarianism*. New York, 1973.

Banfield, Ann. 'The Name of the Subject: the "il"?', *Yale French Studies* 93 (1998).

Banfield, Ann. *The Phantom Table*. Cambridge, 2000.

Blanchot, Maurice. *L'Arrêt de mort*. Paris, 1948.

Blanchot, Maurice. *The Last Man*, trans. Lydia Davis. New York, 1987.

Celan, Paul. *Gesammelte Werke, I*. Frankfurt am Main, 1983.

Clastres, Pierre. *Society against the State*. Cambridge, MA, 1987.

de Man, Paul. 'Semiology and Rhetoric', *Allegories of Reading*. New Haven, CT, 1979.

de Man, Paul. 'Hypogram and Inscription', *The Resistance to Theory*. Minneapolis, MN, 1986.

de Man, Paul. 'Sign and Symbol in Hegel's *Aesthetics*', in *Aesthetic Ideology*, Andrzej Warminski. Minneapolis, MN, 1996.

Deleuze, Gilles and Félix Guattari. *What is Philosophy?* New York, 1994.

Derrida, Jacques. *Otobiographies*. Paris, 1984,

Derrida, Jacques. *Psyché*. Paris, 1986.

Derrida, Jacques. *De l'esprit*. Paris, 1987.

Douglas, Mary. 'No Free Gifts', in Marcel Mauss, *The Gift*, trans. W. D. Halls. New York, 1990.

Duras, Marguerite. *La Maladie de la mort*. Paris, 1982.

Foucault, Michel. *Dits et écrits I*. Paris, 1994.

Frege, Gottlob. *Posthumous Writings*. Chicago, IL, 1979.

Frey, Hans-Jost. 'The Last Man and the Reader', *Yale French Studies* 93 (1998).

Glück, Louise. *The House on Marshland*. New York, 1975.

Goldin, Frederick (ed. and trans.). *Lyrics of the Troubadours and Trouvères*. New York, 1973.

Guéroult, Martial. *Descartes' Philosophy Interpreted According to the Order of Reasons*. I: *The Soul and God*, trans. Roger Ariew. Minneapolis, MN, 1984.

Hamacher, Werner. *Premises*. Cambridge, MA, 1996.

Hamburger, Michael. 'Introduction', in Paul Celan, *Poems*. New York, 1980.

Hardt, Michael and Antonio Negri. *Empire*. Cambridge, MA, 2000.

Heidegger, Martin. *Die Grundbegriffe der Philosophie. Gesamtausgabe* 29/30. Frankfurt am Main, 1976–91.

Kafka, Franz. *Hochzeitsvorbereitungen auf dem Lande und andere Prosa aus dem Nachlass*. Frankfurt am Main, 1983.

Kernberg, Otto. 'Projection and Projective Identification: Developmental and Clinical Aspects', in *Aggression in Personality Disorders and Perversions*. New Haven, CT, 1992, 59–174.

Lacan, Jacques. *Télévision*. Paris, 1974.

Lacan, Jacques. *Le séminaire XX: Encore*. Paris, 1975.

Lacan, Jacques. 'Conférences et entretiens dans des universités nord-américaines', *Scilicet*, 6/7 (1976).

Lacan, Jacques. *Les Quatre concepts fondamentaux de la psychanalyse*. Paris, 1990 [1973].

Laporte, Roger. *La Veille*. Paris, 1963.

Leiris, Michel. *Manhood*, trans. Richard Howard. London, 1968.

Levinas, Emmanuel. *Totalité et infini: Essai sur l'extériorité*. Paris, 1961.

Levinas, Emmanuel. *En Découvrant l'existence avec Husserl et Heidegger*. Paris, 1982.

Lispector, Clarice. *The Hour of the Star*, trans. Giovanni Pontiero. New York, 1986.

Milner, Jean-Claude. *For the Love of Language*, trans. and intro. Ann Banfield. New York, 1990.

Montaigne, Michel de. *Essais*, ed. M. Rat, Vol. 2. Paris, 1962.

Montaigne, Michel de. *The Complete Essays of Michel de Montaigne*, trans. Donald Frame. Stanford, CA, 1965.

Pascal, Blaise. *Oeuvres complètes*, ed. Louis Lafuma. Paris, 1963.

Pepper, Thomas. 'Nights on Earth', Danish trans. Marianne Baht Jensen and Mads Madsen, in Møller Lis and Cecilia Sjöholm (eds), *Ny Poetik* 9(1999).

Rey, Alain et al. (eds). *Dictionnaire historique de la langue française*. Paris, 1992.

Ronell, Avital. *Stupidity*. Chicago, IL, 2001.

Spitzer, Leo. *Classical and Christian Ideas of World Harmony: Prolegomena to an Interpretation of the Word 'Stimmung'*. Baltimore, MD, 1963.

Warminski, Andrzej. 'Dreadful Reading: Blanchot on Hegel', in *Readings in Interpretation*. Minneapolis, MN, 1987.

Wittgenstein, Ludwig. *Philosophical Investigations*. New York, 1958.

jouissance | *JULIET FLOWER MACCANNELL*

Jouir: Derived from Latin gaudere – to rejoice, be glad, be joyful, take pleasure, be pleased, delight, to give joy and to receive it; to be in a joyous state, to have free use of or for one's lot, to have one's will of a woman, gratification, pleasure, use of something that affords pleasure or advantage, profit, delight, pleasure, sensuality, voluptuousness, usufruct.

A *sensation, a legal right, a capital pleasure, a delight given to another. Jouissance* is the French word for an extreme pleasure, with notable overtones of the bliss of sexual orgasm. The verb *enjoier* was originally either intransitive or transitive, meaning to enjoy and also to give enjoyment to. Its highly subjective nature would seem to preclude any easy translatability. Nevertheless, jouissance achieved worldwide currency in critical discourse during the latter half of the twentieth century. For good cause – the cause itself of desire.

Jouissance more practically and more modestly also means the usufruct or surplus value of goods. *'Jouir de'* implies that one has the right to and/or the power to profit from a good, whether one officially owns it or not. Revolutionaries took up the cause of jouissance over the property-owning classes (Saint-Just comments: 'Happiness has become a political factor') and capitalism rallied around it under the banner of unfettered profit. Both revolution and capitalism have sometimes taken their jouissance to excess and that is also an integral part of the

story of Jouissance, which is surplus or excess value itself, par excellence.

There is yet one more twist in the meaning of jouissance. It is of such extreme etymological amboceptivity that it eventually comes (particularly after Sade, Freud and Lacan) to be inmixed with its presumptive opposite: *pain.* The pleasure in Pain: the perverse pleasure to be had in suffering. The peculiar jouissance of death drive (lethally preferred above symbolically shared 'human' life). The sublimely sacrificial submission to an Other who is invasive and violating in taking its Jouissance from your portion of it (*'la Jouissance de l'Autre'*).

Jouissance is completely subjective and individual and it is also what everyone holds in common. As such it has seemed to many a special vantage point for critiquing communal structures that fail to recognize or attempt to ban jouissance in both the personal and the communal domains. The spectral utopia of an unalloyed enjoyment has haunted western culture at least since the industrial revolution, where it became the regulative ideal that contrasted with an increasingly restrictive socio-economic order. One comes to rebel and even do murder in the name of jouissance (Saint-Just again). Fredric Jameson, who does not himself use the term much, tells this plausible tale: of sensual enjoyments ruined by the accelerated rationalization of capitalist culture (1981).

Such neo-Blakean historical narratives ('binding with briars my joys and desires') of a pure Jouissance that Rational, Oedipal, Industrial or Capitalist society has

banished fall short, however, of capturing the more enduring flavour of jouissance, its permanent subjective allure.
Jouissance appears as the horizon beyond every logical
distinction, as the mythic sublime unitary substance which
everyone is invested in keeping undivided but that nevertheless each demands a fair share in. Jouissance is the
secret, but true objective of every intersubjective struggle:
whoever appears to possess an outsize portion of 'it'
becomes a target of unconscious envy and deadly competition, even though everyone consciously knows that no
human subject could ever *really* have 'it'. It is conceptually
incorrect (though understandable) to regard jouissance
nostalgically, as a lost utopia of undivided enjoyment in
which everyone nonetheless shared.

From a strictly theoretical rather than historicist viewpoint, jouissance is better defined as the way the subject
(unconsciously) represents its 'real, true' substance to
itself – the 'stuff' of its very being which has been extracted
from him by the effects of language, reason and the entire
range of social dictates. Jouissance appears (in the unconscious) as a singular whole; a complete and indivisible
thing which belongs entirely and uniquely to the subject
and is coextensive with its being. It represents what the
subject has a fundamental right to, what it can uncontest-
ably claim for itself. Jouissance as the substance of one's
being stands in stark contrast to one's *meaning*. Meaning is
what language alone is capable of promising the subject as
a recompense for its lost being.

Jouissance, according to Jacques Lacan, is the only
real substance in psychoanalysis – the supreme pleasure
the subject unconsciously treasures for its own. Jouissance
is what remains absolutely resistive to analysis, what
cannot be broken down by conceptual language, which is
otherwise the instrument of choice for rational analysis.
Lacan thus chose 'jouissance' to translate Freud's sense of

what it would mean to 'satisfy' a drive. Not the quaffing of a
thirst, a natural need, but the satisfaction of an insistent
constant inner pressure on the subject. It is a pressure to
discharge dammed up energies, but these are energies that
have arisen from no organic source. They derive from
something at work in the subject's body, something that
functions *in* the organism from *beyond* it. Drive is the unre-
lenting surge of energy in surplus over and above a body's
physical construction, an excess that endlessly assails,
rather than supports the natural body, the organic constitution it inhabits and that nourishes it. Drive is what threatens
to overwhelm this body with a raging tide of jouissance
unless mental faculties are roused to work at fending it off.[1]

Drive, Freud said, is 'a demand made on the mind for
labor'. This is another way of saying that Drive urges us to
a satisfying discharge but that it also stirs us to the mental
exertion required to resist it. It forces us to invent alternative pathways to direct its flow of jouissance – into other
objects, alternate aims (i.e. sublimation, repression, et al.).
Freud theorized early (in the *Project*) that Drive must
remain *unsatisfied* if culture is to work its many miracles:
the miracle of forging social coexistence, the miracle of
compensating for our loss of animal (blind, unthinking)
jouissance. While it once seemed that Freud meant we
must sacrifice our pleasures for the sake of society, after
Lacan recast *Jouissance* in the role of the 'satisfaction' of
a drive, the process appears in a strange new light. In
Lacan's revision, Jouissance is the very idea of an indivisible substantiveness that is opposed to alienation and distinction. Jouissance is now seen as a thing – adamantly
resistive to meaning, to language and to elaborated symbolic culture[2] – that appears beyond the borders of life, that
takes on the allure of a chimerical, shimmering substance
that encompasses and transcends all conceptual distinctions, all natural divisions.

The later twentieth century, like other anti-classical eras, rejected the partitioning of the communal from the subjective, the physical from the psychical, the intimate from the extimate. Jouissance came to the fore, an after-effect of the secularizations and liberalizations that have taken place since the eighteenth century. Today jouissance unmistakably sits enthroned alongside all the distinctions of logic and language – enthroned as their absolute other, their indivisible remainder (Žižek), their dangerous supplement (Derrida), the accursed share (Bataille). Jouissance has steadily emerged from the unconscious shadows to which it was formerly relegated and fantasies built around it have made themselves increasingly visible and audible in our affairs.

Jouissance certainly now contests the strictures of social order with formidable commandments of its own. 'Enjoy!' has become an articulation to reckon with.[3] Do we yield to the clamour for Jouissance (the satisfaction of the Drive), or do we bestir ourselves to inventing new ways of channelling it? 'Satisfying the drive' – Jouissance – is not, that is, of the same order as simply giving in to primal 'natural' urges. Jouissance is, after all, not a natural substance; it is the byproduct *of* cultural differentiation and linguistic splittings (of what Lacan called 'castration' by language).

Jouissance represents the secret, unified essence of our being, like the ooze that finally issues from the corpse of Poe's M. Valdemar – what is hidden inside the legible shape of the body: its jouissance. Yet this sense of jouissance as the secret core of our being depends, entirely, of course, on the prior shaping, tailoring and trimming away of real, animal jouissance that language performs on amorphous, natural substance. The second jouissance produced by language is inaugurated by the aftermath of conceptual operations. It is the unintended derivative of the working of the signifier that 'carves' a human body, as Lacan phrases it, out of an animal substance (i.e. that figuratively 'castrates' it).[4] As Deleuze put it, the body created by the cutting, divisional power of language gets born again as a 'body without organs', i.e. as a body made of signifiers rather than organic substance. This body is, however, open to the return of the jouissance it has spurned, in fantasmatic form. It enters through the gaping wound that language has inflicted on the body. Castration strives to exclude jouissance from the body it forms so that it can insert that body into the human community, yet the very energy put into excising jouissance inevitably ensures its second coming to haunt the body from which it has been carved away.

Language reshapes the original organic logic of life to suit its own necessarily *social* bias (for there is no language without society; no society without language, the common coin of social intercourse and exchange). This eminently social bias of the signifier turns around on itself, however, when, in the very act of closing off the avenues for jouissance, it inadvertently produces an opening for its return. This return of jouissance (in the unconscious) is in effect the return of the *anti-social* element to the subject, who in practice cannot actually dispense with society. Jouissance as the after-effect of the civilization and culture that opposes it and that it opposes is thus rather more interesting and compelling a concern than its comparatively simpler natural model. It means that in fact it is language and its correlate, society, that have energized drive (and the jouissance that fuels it): they are the excess it had thrown away come back from the outer darkness stronger than before. That this remainder over language (Derrida's 'reste') created by the operations of language itself makes its credible claims on the subject, purporting to be the very 'stuff' of life itself, is perhaps one of the most pungent enigmas critical thinking has faced in our time.

'Might jouissance be the key to unlocking the secret of our mighty collective pain?' 'Might that pain possibly have had its origin in some particular person's flawed relation to enjoyment (say, that of a Hitler who was a catastrophe for so many)?' Indeed, to a century rife with painful memories, jouissance has proved an understandably compelling term. Jouissance did in fact begin to shape the agenda of critical questioning as the twentieth century drew to a close. Criticism has now begun to wrestle with the implications of a jouissance (the pleasure in pain, the indivisible substance we all want a piece of) that can no longer be naively assimilated to natural urgings, and that makes its presence and its claims felt far more strongly than natural ones have ever done.

Jouissance in the Unconscious

In most 'bodies without organs' that house the subject, the 'return of jouissance' takes place in 'erogenous zones' located in their familiar, unmentionable places – in their eroticized body parts called the genitals. However, certain bodies without organs, bodies inhabited by particular kinds of subjects (e.g. hysteric and perverse), experience fantasmatically redoubled jouissance as an overflowing of 'the genital zone [which in them] is relatively less prominent than the other erotogenic zones'. (This last citation is from Freud, who is describing that jouissance fails to be genitally delimited in hysterics and perverts.)[5]

Such jouissance-effects surface in all 'normal' and in all 'deviant' bodies alike; there is a universality to the process. Every single body has a unique, unconscious point at which jouissance inserts itself as the supreme model of satisfaction. (It is, to be sure, a satisfaction no reasonable creature could ever withstand – not without

losing its reason.) Yet even the most rational person has such a point of opacity, of resistance to cultural education. What is more, he deeply (if unconsciously) holds this point to be the very 'kernel' of his being. The secret place where jouissance makes its dwelling in the subject is what Lacan calls the 'fundamental fantasy', a space where the subject's unconscious interpretation of what constitutes its absolute jouissance is permanently being staged.

Even though the fantasy might be thought to precede the differential language of reason, it is in fact generated solely out of its effects. As such this most 'intimate' portion of our beings – our fantasy of jouissance – is (ironically enough) tied umbilically to what ought to be most purely exterior to our being – it is tied to language and thus to other subjects. Fantasy, the unintended byproduct of language which is formed against language, is where the subject stages again and again the narrative of how symbolic culture wounded it and how it can repair that wound. The fantasized object – jouissance is the very heart of the subject's discontent in civilization. Jouissance is what he feels cheated of, what he imagines others possess to excess simply because he goes without it.

Clinically, the *cause* of a patient's suffering is always determined to be a fantasized jouissance: the cause of his desire, the cause of his being, the cause he unconsciously 'fights for' against the strictures of civilization.[6] Lacan's theses regarding unconscious jouissance grew out of his clinical treatment of patients who suffered from the fantasy, from the impossibility of bearing jouissance even in fantasy.

In time, however, Lacan began making theoretical moves that reconnected jouissance (the jouissance generated by the differential operations of language itself) to another aspect of satisfying the drive that Freud, almost in passing, had mentioned with a certain puzzlement. Freud had noted in 'Civilized Sexual Morality and Modern Nervousness' that art mysteriously engineered things so that a certain measure of 'direct satisfaction' could be experienced by its means – a direct satisfaction he judged to be occasionally necessary to human life. Art managed jouissance so that it not only escaped conscious moral censure and unconscious repression alike, it also caused art to be socially valued precisely because it permitted the roundabout satisfaction of drive, in sublimated/sublime form. Art, then, was like unconscious fantasy, a way to stage jouissance; but like analysis, it was also a way to articulate and thereby defuse that jouissance as well. Fantasies, Lacan said, cannot, after all, withstand being articulated.

Lacan built upon Freud's initial insight that art was a special and unique way of satisfying the drive in two late seminars, one on James Joyce and the other on 'Lituraterre' (not to forget the purloined and insistent letters of earlier work). In the Joyce seminar he devised the term *sinthome* to designate a signifier that was more than the cardinal instrument of deleting jouissance's metaphorical but also its metonymic support and conveyance as well. The late Lacan rediscovered the 'enjoyment' of letters in a somewhat different way from the earlier Lacan and that he began to spell 'jouis-sens' or 'enjoy-meant' – a supplemental jouissance taken from and in the very freeplay of differential language as such.

Once it was critically deployed by Lacan, *jouissance* gained prestige in a variety of domains, winning a name for itself as a precision tool for cultural critique, political and economic analysis and for the clinic of psychopathology. While such socio-culturally focused concerns might seem extraneous to the 'aesthetic' work of art and of literature, the fact is that Freud (and later Adorno) felt it crucial to link aesthetic theory to Jouissance. After all we should not forget that art first enunciated its emancipation, its *autonomy* in the guise of Kant's *aesthetic delight*, enjoyment without practical, economic or moral purposiveness. To grasp how Kantian aesthetics becomes replayed through the modern lens of jouissance requires following the socio-cultural vicissitudes of jouissance and the critical transgression that art brings to their repression of it.

Lacan elaborated a set of what he called the 'discourses' (of the master, the hysteric, the university, the analyst) – the forms of the social tie. Later he thought of adding the discourse of capitalism, and he virtually created a discourse of perversion in 'Kant avec Sade'. Each graphed the way a particular social arrangement imagined it could handle or 'treat' excess jouissance. Even the most 'totalizing' system, like global capitalism, generates a surplus jouissance, a remainder that the 'system' cannot contend with because it has itself generated this excess which now insists on making itself heard and felt. In critical practice, certain authors have treated Lacan's discourses as works-in-progress that offer supple and flexible tools for analysing contemporary formations. Slavoj Žižek's books, The *Sublime Object of Ideology* and *For They Know Not What They Do: Enjoyment as a Political Factor*, gave enormous currency to 'unbearable jouissance' (the kind of jouissance that was inimical to social and subjective balance) as a way of reading cultural objects and group psychologies. His work was followed by many younger, psychoanalytically inclined practitioners of cultural critique. Žižek focused in these early books on the moments in social and cultural life where the obscene enjoyment that hides within the official symbolic makes itself felt, if not seen.

Jacques-Alain Miller, in his classical essay on 'Extimité' (1994, 74–87), utilized jouissance as a way to uncover the root form of racism. It was, he explained, a question of how the subject responds to the jouissance it imputes to others.

Privation of jouissance is a necessary precondition of social coexistence, something automatically foregone in any social being. The prohibition against contact with one's own inmost 'good' (jouissance), however, gets unconsciously projected outward onto others who, especially when their mode of life differs evidently from your own, *seem* to be enjoying everything you feel you are forbidden to enjoy. The actions of your foreign neighbour, who 'enjoys' *his* kind of music, food, sex differently from the way you do, evokes your unconscious surmise that the neighbour is enjoying what you cannot because he must have thieved it from you. Thus is racism born.

Joan Copjec ('Locked Room, Lonely Room', in *Read My Desire*, 1994) ably depicts the paradoxical consequences of something of the reverse of Miller's analysis. Copjec speaks of what happens when the cultural actor feels commanded to adopt jouissance as a 'cure' for the discontent inherent to life in that culture – and to display that adoption openly. To force a human being shaped by language to acquiesce in reopening his original wounding by culture (and displaying the excess it inserts in him) runs counter to every instinct of symbolic make-up: jouissance must be relegated to the privacy of unconscious repression. Jouissance as a command to enjoyment is formally and structurally unbearable for a human, social being. When such commands take on a public and official character horror often ensues: critics Willy Apollon and Juliet Flower MacCannell have each used jouissance to dissect analytically the unconscious of fascism and colonialism as instances of how the command to jouissance overwhelms the subject.

Following upon jouissance's explanatory success in cultural and clinical critique, aesthetic inquiry has begun to deploy it for the criticism of art, literature and film, particularly through the vehicle that conveys the subject's 'right to jouissance' to him: the Superego. The Superego represents that point in the unconscious where society enters into the subject and where the subject enters into society and skews the subject's relation to sexual enjoyment. Ironically, the Superego is also the crucial portal through which Jouissance itself 'returns'.

Superego and the Command to Jouissance

The Superego proved to be a splendid device for unifying critical applications of jouissance. The Superego so used has many variants: the Freudian (moral) Superego, the Lacanian (obscene) Superego, the Kleinian (cannibalistic/maternal) Superego, and the Sadistic Superego. Freud first outlined the life-history of the Superego in his essay on the passing or the 'Waning of Oedipus Complex'.

The child has learned to pleasure itself. When the Father places a ban on his masturbation, the child (avid for the gratification the banned action brings) is old enough to be sceptical of the Father's threat. How could the Father who loves him so ever exercise his brute *real* power over the child to cut his pleasure short? The child's first sceptical inklings deepen until they induce the more or less complete 'fall' of the magisterial, authoritative, Oedipal Father in favour of the supremacy of the unlimited pleasure the child realizes it can grant itself, by itself.

A certain nagging guilt toward the fallen Father persists, however. This guilt eventually reintroduces the voice of paternal authority but in peculiarly altered form. The dictates that once emerged from the Father now issue from a disembodied voice, internally heard, that spews strange, malevolent and often contradictory commands. The new vocal imperative is wholly different in character from the clear-cut negations of Paternal speech. The Superego speaks, as it were, with forked tongue, for on one side it claims to be entirely on the side of jouissance and therefore of the child. It urges the child to enjoy! by sceptically voicing the question, 'Who is really going to stop you?' Yet it seems to be equally on the side of the severe social sanctions toward the jouissance that it presses on the child: 'Go ahead and try – see how far you'll really get!' Superego pressure is almost unbearable. The Father had represented the constraints on jouissance as part of the requirements of living with others. The superegoic voice that inundates the child evokes (and invokes) an inflated battery of rules and regulations, bans and prohibitions, censure and censorship at the same time it urges jouissance upon the child. The Father stands for society's demands, but tempers their harshness with his love. The Superego commands the child to enjoy! but effectively menaces him with the punitive social humiliation the jouissance would inevitably bring. It is thus that the Superego can be called the psychical representative of the paradoxical point of entry for jouissance into the subject, the correlate of the fundamental fantasy. The Superego stands for the point where the communal seizes the subject and tells it 'You must not!' and where asocial, wild jouissance makes the opposing demand, 'You must!'

The Superego figure comes to the fore in post-Oedipal contexts where political events seem to be the corollaries of the subjective scepticism toward patriarchal, paternal and parental authority – toward the Master – events like the regicide and Terror in the French Revolution. It is perhaps no accident that the venerable Marquis de Sade, contemporary to the capitalism that was dawning at the same time Saint Just pronounced his judgment on jouissance, would forge his own superego-driven compromise. Sade elaborated his political and sexual theories of jouissance which he takes primarily to mean the freedom to exploit others sexually without exercising mastery over them. Sade writes (*Philosophy in the Bedroom*): 'Never may an act of possession be exercised upon a free being; the exclusive possession of a woman is no less unjust than the exclusive possession of slaves?' He then adds a note:

> *Let it not be said that I contradict myself here, and that after having established . . . that we have no right to bind a woman to ourselves, I destroy those principles when I declare we now have the right to constrain her; . . . it is a question of jouissance and jouissance only, not of property . . . I have no real right of possession over such a woman, but I have incontestable rights to the jouissance of her; I have the right to force from her this jouissance, if she refuse me it for whatever the cause may be.*

(de Sade, 1965, 537)

Sade tried (in vain, some say) to fuse the two faces of jouissance – extreme pleasure and extreme pain – coldly recommending that pleasure-be-taken-in-pain as a way to guard against the full force of either. Psychoanalysis remains unconvinced by his plan. His coldness, Lacan decided in the end, turned Sade himself into the perfect object-instrument of delivering pain. In refusing the phallic limits placed on jouissance Sade becomes the object-instrument, acquiescent, pliant, of the abusive Jouissance of the Other.

There is another way than the Superego solution for the subject to deal with jouissance. It is neither oedipal/phallico nor sadistic in character. It resists Superego strictures, yet is nonetheless a way of handling excess jouissance from a subjective (rather than Sadean-objective) position. Its two names are feminine (the 'other jouissance' – as distinct from the 'Other's Jouissance') and aesthetic. Each marks the arrival of *transgression* – a transgression, in effect, of the Superego's commands (Lacan, 1992, 222).[7]

The Feminine: the Other Jouissance

Most of the feminists who were influenced by the French tradition found jouissance of great practical critical value. Jouissance appears in Julia Kristeva in the guise of the 'semiotic' that contests the differential values of language (1980, 242, 247–9). It appears in Cixous' dramas, where an excessive horror and terror rains down on peoples formerly subjected to extreme regulation. It appears in the fondness Juliet Mitchell and Jacqueline Rose have for Lacan's 'Other Jouissance' (feminine Jouissance), the jouissance he delimited by contrasting it to 'phallic jouissance', in his graphs of sexuation (1998).[8] Feminism has understood 'woman's' *jouissance* quite diversely. Irigaray portrays a 'hysterical' *jouissance* not shaped by the 'paternal', and that is therefore 'unrepresentable' (1985, 357–360). Cixous employs the alternative strategy in 'The Laugh of the Medusa', of creating vivid images of feminine *jouissance* as wild, invincible, unconstrained by phallic limits. Kristeva assigns *jouissance* to the portion of woman that escapes the limits of Oedipus, the laws of language. For Lacan, 'woman' does not ex-sist from the perspective of the masculine logic and its particular discursive relation to jouissance. She only in-sists from outside the totalizing, phallic world of masculine things ('jouissance devices' Lacan calls them in *Encore*) for defusing Jouissance and its threat of overwhelming the subject.

That Woman and her jouissance exceed the phallic fantasy that enumerates and counts every possible woman and generates 'the' Woman from its repeated experience

of them is not to be doubted. Ah, but this Other Jouissance, this feminine one . . . in what does it consist? Analysts, like poets and lovers everywhere, have wondered this from time immemorial: '*Ever since we've been begging them . . . begging them on our knees to try to tell us about it, well, not a word!*' (Mitchell and Rose, 1982, 146).

The 'other' jouissance – what is it? Well, it is something that exceeds the phallic imaginary, invoking a 'beyond' adumbrated long ago by Rousseau:

> *Had all my dreams become realities, they would not have been enough for me; I would have imagined, dreamed, desired still [encore]. I found in myself an inexplicable void that nothing could have filled; a certain launching of the heart towards another sort of jouissance of which I had no idea and of which I nonetheless felt the need . . . This in itself was jouissance because I was transpierced by it with a very vivid feeling and an attractive sadness that I would not have wanted not to have.*
>
> (Rousseau, I: 1140–1)

Aesthetic Jouissance

Jouissance seems perfectly suited to any post-classical context, to the art that opts to defy classicism's measured divisions and distinctions, that favours dissonance and even chaos over harmony and balance.

Yet consider what it really means to have an art that refuses to obey the dictates of social harmony – that transgresses its careful limits? Kant, following Rousseau, broke a founding distinction made by Augustine (*De Doctrina Christiana*) between the *uti* and the *frui*, between the things that are to be used and the things that are to be enjoyed for their own sake (though only, of course, because they brought us nearer to perfect, divine Joy). Kant refused the distinction, and left art swimming in jouissance.

Here, then, is the next twist in the story of Jouissance. Yes, the image of a utopia of unalloyed, unfettered, unrestricted Jouissance has long been held out as distant prize to compensate for the accelerating fractionalizations of modernity. Jouissance as that unique substance capable of resuturing all that is fragmented is a pure hypothesis that has acquired its status as a quasi-natural, quasi-mythical, uniquely undivided substance only where fantasy is redoubled (and undone) by the articulated work of art. Gilles Deleuze devoted much of his later work to trying to occupy the field of jouissance that only ever really opens in poetic art. *Milles Plateaux* speaks of a courtly poetry that becomes a 'permanent plane of consistency of desire' – a consistency that looks a lot like what Jouissance is supposed to be: indivisible, refractory to linguistic distinctions and logical partitionings. Language alone can convey the promise of so much bliss. It does so in an act of promising that becomes itself an other sort of jouissance.

Notes

1. Drive [translated 'Instinct' by Strachey] is 'a measure of the demand made on the mind for work', in 'Three Essays on Sexuality' (Freud, 1953, 168).
2. Copjec, in *Read My Desire* (1994), says that Drive has shifted its topological position in our culture, and is now manifestly audible and visible. Ours is a climate of 'duty' to enjoy; instead of disrupting speech, then, in classical Freudian fashion, Jouissance sits enthroned beside speech as its equal. This is an apparent change from Freud's sense that we always place obstacles in the way of complete satisfaction. But the change is only apparent. Below I will show how the simulation of jouissance operates. Lacan devised the notion of the partial drive and its circuit – it circulates around and thereby avoids the object of jouissance (the object a).
3. See my 'Fascism and the Voice of Conscience'.
4. Lacan's remark in *Television*: '[Man] thinks as a consequence of the fact that a structure, that of language – the word implies it – carves up his body, a structure that has nothing to do with anatomy' (1990, 6); see MacCannell (1996, 105–25).
5. From his analysis of 'A Phobia in a Five-Year-Old Boy' (1909) *SE*, X, 109.
6. Today, the Lacanian clinic worldwide operates with typologies that analyse the patient's relation to jouissance: the modalities of psychopathology (neurotic, psychotic and perverse) are the positions the subject takes up toward jouissance.
7. 'I have thus brought together for you two cases which Kant does not envisage, two forms of transgression beyond the limits normally assigned to the pleasure principle opposed to the reality principle considered as a criterion, namely, the excessive sublimation of the object, and what is commonly called perversion. Sublimation and perversion are both a certain relation of desire which draws our attention upon the possibility of formulating, in the form of a question, another principle opposed to the reality principle. For there is a register of morality which is directed from the side of what there is at the level of *das Ding*, namely the register which makes the subject hesitate at the moment of bearing false witness against *Das Ding*, that is, the site of his desire, be it perverse or sublimated'.
8. Also previously published in English as Jacques Lacan, 'A Love Letter' ['Lettre d'amour'] (Mitchell and Rose, 1982).

Works cited

Copjec, Joan. *Read My Desire: Lacan against the Historicists*. Cambridge, MA, 1994.

de Sade, Marquis. T*he Complete Justine, Philosophy in the Bedroom, and Other Writings*. New York, 1965.

Freud, Sigmund. *Standard Edition of the Complete Psychological Works of Sigmund Freud*. Vol. VII, trans. James Strachey. London, 1953.

Irigaray, Luce. *This Sex Which is not One*. Ithaca, NY, 1985.

Jameson, Fredric. *The Political Unconscious: Narrative as a Socially Symbolic Act*. Ithaca, NY, 1981.

Kristeva, Julia. *Desire in Language*, trans. Leon Roudiez. New York, 1980.

Lacan, Jacques. *Television: A Challenge to the Psychoanalytic Establishment*, ed. Joan Copjec, trans. Denis Hollier, Rosalind Krauss and Annette Michelson. New York and London, 1990.

Lacan, Jacques. *The Seminar. Book VII. The Ethics of Psychoanalysis*, trans. Dennis Porter. New York, 1992.

Lacan, Jacques. *Encore: On Feminine Sexuality: The Limits of Love and Knowledge. The Seminar of Jacques Lacan XX (1972–1973)*. New York, 1998.

MacCannell, Juliet Flower. 'Jouissance Between Clinic and the Academy: The Analyst and Woman', *Qui Parle*, 9: 2, (1996). 105–25.

MacCannell, Juliet. 'Fascism and the Voice of Conscience', in *Supposing the Subject*. New York, 1994, 106–32; rpt. in MacCannell, *The Hysteric's Guide to the Future Female Subject*. Minnesota, MN, 2000.

Miller, Jacques-Alain. 'Extimité', *Lacanian Theory of Discourse*, eds Mark Bracher, Marshall Alcorn, Ronald Corthell and Françoise Massardier-Kenney. New York and London, 1994, 74–87.

Mitchell, Juliet, and Jacqueline Rose (eds). *Feminine Sexuality: Jacques Lacan and the école freudienne*. New York, 1982.

Rousseau, Jean-Jacques. *Oeuvres Complètes*. Paris, 1964.

knowledge | K IS FOR KNOWLEDGE | *MARGARET RUSSETT*

'Knowledge' is not a word we expect to find in a glossary of cultural theory, even one as diverse as this. It has an unfashionable sound; when mentioned, it may be qualified almost beyond recognition, as in Arkady Plotnitsky's rigorous account of 'unknowledge' in his essay on 'Difference'. We may think that knowledge belongs to a different sort of endeavour: to the empirical sciences, or to the kind of philosophy that frowns on the vagaries of theory. Alternatively, the term might be associated with the extra-academic 'knowledge work' characteristic of the post-industrial economy. Among literary critics, only the naive and the polemically anti-theoretical call for a grounding in 'knowledge'. In so far as theory is aligned with literature, knowledge may even be regarded as a necessary exclusion: the term against which literary/theoretical discourse defines itself. A relic of western culture's longstanding debate between the philosophers and the poets, this antipathy finds exemplary expression in the nineteenth-century essayist Thomas De Quincey, who – groping for a definition of literature that did not reduce to the insipid idea of 'books we read for fun' – divided the world of print into the 'literature of power' and the 'literature of knowledge', only the first of which counted as literature *per se*. Equating knowledge with measurable facts, De Quincey contends that 'it [i]s a mean or subordinate purpose of books to give information', and illustrates this claim by contrasting a cookbook with Milton's epic poem *Paradise Lost*. 'What do you learn from *Paradise Lost*?' he asks rhetorically, and replies:

Nothing at all. What do you learn from a cookery-book? Something new, something that you did not know before, in every paragraph. But would you therefore put the wretched cookery-book on a higher level of estimation than the divine poem? What you owe to Milton is not any knowledge . . . what you owe is power *– that is, exercise and expansion to your own latent capacity of sympathy with the infinite.*

(Masson, 1897, 55–6)

We might quibble with many facets of De Quincey's argument, beginning with the assumption that we learn nothing in the way of facts from Milton's poem. What about the ideal of reason Milton advocates? Or the cosmology and mythology on which he draws? We might also consider the contextual framework needed to make sense of the plot. I am reminded of an admired senior colleague's frequent device for initiating discussion: 'What must you know to be able to read this?' Already, the question of how 'knowledge' relates to what De Quincey calls 'power' appears more complicated, or at any rate more dialectical, than the initial distinction allows.

Leaving such objections aside for the moment, however, we can see that De Quincey attempts to distinguish a communicative use of language from an affective one. The first conveys facts; the second, whose function is to 'move', evokes what De Quincey calls our 'sympathy'. The question of sympathy relates to a well-established tradition in aesthetics, as old as Aristotle's perception of the terror and pity with which we contemplate tragedy. Rather than review that tradition, let us notice the assumptions that accompany De Quincey's rhetorical foil, the 'steps of knowledge' along which we slog in pursuit of the mundane.

One has already been pointed out: that is, knowledge exists outside of language, which communicates but does not create it. It follows that knowledge is independent of our ability to acquire it: in other words, De Quincey's statement preserves the common-sense division between subject and object (knower and known). Objective knowledge, or the possession of information, is furthermore opposed to the *subjective* sensation of power which is cultivated through literature.

But power to do what? Power over whom? Rather than answer such questions, De Quincey turns them back on the reader (implicitly characterizing his own work, we may note, as literature of power rather than knowledge):

> *When in* King Lear, *the height, and depth, and breadth, of human passion is revealed to us – and for the purposes of a sublime antagonism is revealed in the weakness of an old man's nature, and in one night two worlds of storm are brought face to face – the human world, and the world of physical nature – mirrors of each other, semichoral antiphonies, strophe and antistrophe heaving with rival convulsions, and with the double darkness of night and madness, – when I am thus suddenly startled into a feeling of the infinity of the world within me, is this power? or what may I call it?*
>
> (Burwick, 2000, 71)

The revelation to be gained from *King Lear*, which we might be tempted to call *knowledge* of human nature, is redefined as a perception of space within the reading subject; power *is* subjectivity, circularly construed as the capacity for infinite response. The technical word for the experience De Quincey describes is 'sublime', a sensation of self-expansion derived, paradoxically, from the frustration of our discursive reason (the faculty of *knowledge*). What De Quincey calls the literature of power, and what aestheticians call sublime writing, may then be redefined as that class of works whose function is to demonstrate the superiority of subject over object by making us aware of our capacity to transcend factual concerns.[1] Thus, our *subjective* power is experienced in direct contrast with our power over the known physical world. Literature gains in prestige what it loses in empirical reference; rather than being disabled by its division from knowledge, literature becomes a means for expanding inner space – the place where, presumably, knowledge may then lodge.

I have called De Quincey's discussion exemplary, by which I mean that it both typifies a certain kind of thinking and exaggerates it. Percy Shelley couched the relationship between literary and empirical discourse in less sharply antithetical terms when he called poetry 'the centre and circumference of knowledge'. In both cases, however, we see that the perceived need to defend the value of literature leads to a denigration of 'mere' knowledge, even while, by articulating this value, the two writers construct a new *field of knowledge*, i.e. the knowledge of literature, or what we now generally call the 'humanities'. That such knowledge (as instanced by De Quincey's facility in citing a 'canonical' text) does indeed constitute a form of power is suggested by his excited slip from what *King Lear* shows 'us' to his assertion of the infinity within '*me*': it is De Quincey who is aggrandized by the sublime experience that he both discovers and, in his role as teacher, inculcates in his reader. Further, while De Quincey seems to regard this mode of power as a purely private affair, we may reasonably question how his experience translates into expertise, or social authority. The fact that this knowledge purports *not* to be knowledge – or, more precisely, that what De Quincey 'knows' is a 'feeling' he characterizes as the opposite of knowledge – neatly encapsulates the ongoing dialectic of authority that has defined humanistic studies in academia. What do we talk about when we talk about literature? What knowledge do we gain from such reading?

The philosopher Jean-François Lyotard focuses this problem when he argues that modern society is characterized by a rigid division between scientific or 'denotative' knowledge (roughly, knowledge as defined above) and 'narrative' knowledge, which includes stories, proverbs, etc. – and would, clearly, encompass *King Lear* as well as *Paradise Lost*. We might, therefore, choose to recast De Quincey's distinction in terms of two *kinds* of knowledge. Doing so would at least let us revise our initial definition of knowledge (as inert and external to language), to account for its generation through the exercise of linguistic *power*, if power is understood in De Quincey's sense as the ability to elicit 'sympathy with' what is known. We might even decide that the term 'knowledge' is an abstraction so large as to obscure what it purports to describe. These parallel insights were in fact central themes of Anglophone philosophy during the first half of the twentieth century. Bertrand Russell, for example, argued that the inherent vagueness of the word 'knowledge' had led previous philosophers to imagine 'an intimate and almost mystical contact between subject and object' (1948, 430), whereas knowledge can more usefully be described after the fact, as the cause of successful actions. Gilbert Ryle similarly contended that 'knowing what' (i.e. '*possessing* knowledge') is just a special case of 'knowing how', rather than the model for all

mental operations. In the most profound such critique of traditional metaphysics, Ludwig Wittgenstein pointed out that the attempt to understand what knowledge 'is' puts the cart before the horse: this mode of inquiry falsely assumes that there was first such a thing as knowledge, and then a word that named this thing. Rather than asking the real knowledge to stand up, or attempting to outline its necessary preconditions, Wittgenstein would have us understand that different *kinds* of knowledge are produced by different ways of using language, including the verb 'to know'. (We 'know' other people, how to tie shoelaces, the answers to a quiz, the state of our feelings, the ideas explored in *King Lear*, and so forth.). We become confused about the nature of knowledge when we try to infer a coherent entity from a variety of sometimes incompatible 'language games'.

By resituating epistemology within the context of language, Wittgenstein goes a long way toward making knowledge – De Quincey's antithesis to literature – a literary problem after all. Returning to De Quincey's discussion of *King Lear*, then, we see not only that he reserves the word 'knowledge' for one kind of language-game; he produces the knowledge of literature by recognizably literary means: that is, through the devices of direct address (apostrophe), rhetorical questions, and the metaphor of an inner world whose vastness 'mirrors' the cosmos without. He even tropes these 'two worlds' as the *strophe* and *antistrophe* of an ancient Greek ode. While a scientist might find this mode of definition illegitimate, and the consequent 'knowledge' spurious, we can say, echoing Wittgenstein and Lyotard, that the game of literary knowledge rests on a *narrative* of its distance from knowledge. Or better: literary knowledge is constituted as the suspension of claims to 'real' knowledge. Such a definition has the advantage of turning our attention from the object in question (be it *King*

Lear or *The Joy of Cooking*) toward the rules of the game we play with it. It is also generally in line with the tradition of academic literary studies, from the New Criticism forward, that focuses on how poetic language interrupts the attempt to extract knowledge (aka 'paraphrase' or 'doctrine') from a text. We might also notice, however, that the literary *displacement* of knowledge-claims has the effect of turning Knowledge into a mystical object of desire, to echo Bertrand Russell.

Modernist authors made this desire explicit, in such famous questions as Virginia Woolf's 'Who knows even at the moment of intimacy, This is knowledge?' or W. B. Yeats's 'How can we know the dancer from the dance?' The critic Paul de Man parses Yeats's question – itself capable of being understood in at least two contradictory ways – as a meditation on the difficulty, but also the necessity, of distinguishing the dance/signifier from the dancer/signified. In what remains perhaps the most convincing definition of 'literariness' (De Quincey's 'power'), de Man identifies 'the rhetorical, figural potentiality of language' with the unknowns that persist in the communication of truths. (It should be noted that de Man also identifies this 'figural potentiality' in texts usually classified as philosophical, i.e. oriented toward knowledge.) Joan Retallack, a contemporary poet cited in the entry on *Poetics*, similarly describes her work as poised 'on the Know Ledge'. We might add that the interrogative form suggests how desire (the wish to *know* knowledge linguistically) functions to maintain the literary suspension, or distance from the desired, that de Man claims to describe. It is this claim of objective *knowledge* about literary language – often interpreted, in a reversal of De Quincey's terminology, as a claim of *powerlessness* in the face of what we do, after all, 'really' know – which inspired much of the hostility toward de Man that followed his period of greatest influence in the 1970s.

To summarize the argument so far: literary discourse, which for our purposes includes discourse *about* literature, knows itself as a structural ambivalence toward knowledge. We might even appropriate Lyotard's account of 'postmodern' knowledge to claim that literary study 'produc[es] not the known, but the unknown' (1984, 60). What I wish to stress here is not only the tendentiousness of such a claim (i.e. how it is motivated by competition with other disciplines), but also the conceptual mutation which it represents. The remainder of this essay will briefly sketch certain parallels between this literary sense of knowledge-as-'unknowledge' and some influential developments in contemporary thought which, by virtue of sharing a paradoxical account of knowledge, may be understood – in a somewhat different sense than usual – as 'literary' theory. A secondary theme in this account will be the role of power in the redefinition of knowledge, so that the opposition with which we began will become thoroughly confounded by our conclusion.

The idea of knowledge as its own lack probably first calls to mind the institution of psychoanalysis. Freud proposed, in effect, that we cannot know what we know because our knowledge may be unconscious. Psychoanalytic therapy was presented as a technique for making this unknowledge known by analysing verbal and other signs. While Freud himself generally described this as an achievable task, however, his disciple Jacques Lacan characterized the unconscious as 'a corpus of knowledge . . . which must in no way be conceived as knowledge to be completed, to be closed' (1973, 134). By depicting the achievement of full understanding as a chimera, Lacan emphasized the literary structure of psychoanalytic knowledge, which he indeed modelled on the study of language. This characterization also makes explicit the asymmetrical distribution of power involved in the construction of knowledge. For if we cannot know our own minds 'in themselves', knowledge becomes a matter of projection and ascription; in the analytical relationship, which for Lacan models all others, 'there is established a search for truth in which the one is supposed to know, or at least to know more than the other' (137), and the father-analyst knows best. Our relationship to what Lacan calls 'the symbolic order', or the social structure as a whole, is predicated upon the existence of such an 'other', which – though the role may be occupied by any number of individuals, serially or at once – determines the articulation of knowledge as a form of subjection. In other words, the power *to know*, which can never lodge absolutely in one person (to believe otherwise would literally be psychotic) is continually projected upon others, whose power may thus be said to originate in 'fantasy' – but only if it is understood that fantasy has real social effects. (The political implications of Lacanian theory have recently and strenuously been explored by Slavoj Žižek and the Slovenian school of Marxist psychoanalysis) (Žižek, 1989). In his own work as analyst and teacher, Lacan was well aware that he occupied the role of knowing 'other' vis-à-vis his students and patients. However ironic this awareness, however, Lacan chose to dramatize rather than to mute it; to know that one does not *know*, he thereby suggested, does not diminish the authority-effect that accrues to the analytical or pedagogical position. (Anyone who has ever been silenced by the retort 'Who knows?' can grasp the truth of this insight.)

The synonymy of knowledge and power has been most forcefully argued in, and most consistently associated with, the writings of Michel Foucault. Rather than describe Foucault's debts to and disagreements with psychoanalysis – probably the best known feature of his work, and accessibly presented in his *History of Sexuality* – we will focus on one corollary of his core insight that modern power operates by *producing* knowledge *in and as discourse*. Foucault may be said to extend the implications of the 'language game' theory, with his contention that knowledge is constructed rather than discovered in particular uses of language. Thus sexuality, to take his most famous example, is not a fact of human nature so much as it is the conceptual horizon of many different, overlapping genres of writing and speech. Foucault's is a literary view of knowledge in its indifference to De Quincey's generic distinction; both novels (literature of power) and medical treatises (literature of knowledge) contribute to making sexuality *real*.

The *power* of novelistic as well as medical discourse consists in its hold over thought (and, hence, our experiential reality) as well as the different relations to authority that it makes possible: patient, analyst, deviant, normal and so on. Thus Foucault criticizes the quest-structure of knowledge that Lacan describes as a fact of existence. 'Knowledge', observes Foucault, 'is also the space in which the subject may take up a position and speak of the objects with which he deals in his discourse' (1972, 182). It is not simply wielded *by* subjects, as De Quincey assumes, but makes individuals *into* subjects. The power that De Quincey finds in evoking the experience of reading is, by this account, the same *kind* of power a legislator or expert witness possesses. For our purposes, however, Foucault's most remarkable claim is that, whatever we may think we know about sex (or criminality, or madness), we cannot know the foundation of this knowledge. As Foucault writes, 'it is not possible for us to describe our own archive, since it is from within these rules that we speak' (1972, 130). The point is not that our knowledge is false, or even limited; rather, it exists within a system of signification that, by making certain statements possible, excludes even the possibility of formulating others.

(The content of the unconscious, by this account, is a form of knowledge particular to our own 'archive'.) Knowledge rests, then, on a certain constitutive ignorance – the silence that dictates the available forms of utterance.

For a cultural analysis that takes seriously Foucault's conflation of power and knowledge (as well as the continuity between literary and empirical discourse) we may turn for a moment to Eve Kosofsky Sedgwick's *Epistemology of the Closet*, which – tellingly, for a book with 'epistemology' in its title – includes no index headings for 'knowledge' or 'know', though it does list several entries for 'knowingness'. Sedgwick notes that sexuality in general, and particularly homosexuality, has throughout western culture been intimately entwined with the metaphorics of knowledge as such, to the extent that 'epistemological pressure of any sort . . . [is] saturated with sexual implication . . . [w]hat we now know as sexuality is fruit – apparently the only fruit – to be plucked from the tree of knowledge' (1990, 73). Foucault's account of power-as-knowledge becomes, for Sedgwick, the more pointed equivalence of knowledge and sexuality (both knowledge *of* sex and knowledge 'as' sex, or *epistemophilia*). Sedgwick goes on to argue that such 'knowledge' is often masked by a disingenuous *refusal* to know, as in the don't ask/don't tell attitude toward gay identity. 'Knowingness' is entirely consistent with an empowering ignorance, as we perceive in the literary structure of the 'open secret' – what he who runs may read, so long as he's in the know. Thus Sedgwick reintroduces an ethical dimension into the (purportedly neutral) literary displacement of knowledge. She refuses, however, to speculate on the epistemological limits of her own inquiry, contending that 'no one *can* know *in advance* where the limits of a gay-centered inquiry are to be drawn' (53), as though the invocation of knowledge could never shed its association with oppressive exercises of power.

Sedgwick's account of 'knowingness' may be taken as a critique of Lacanian analysis, even while she shares a generally Lacanian view of how self-knowledge and its 'other', the unconscious, are constituted by the subject's relation to the symbolic order. Sedgwick apparently believes, unlike Foucault, that we can in fact 'describe our own archive' by subjecting texts to a scrutiny that makes their unconscious assumptions speak. For a sociological perspective on the relationship between a culture's silent assumptions (what 'goes without saying') and its material power structure, we may conclude with a glance at the work of Pierre Bourdieu, particularly his *Outline for a Theory of Practice*. Assuming, with Foucault and Shelley, that a culture's 'deep truth is imageless' (*Prometheus Unbound*, II.iv.116), Bourdieu posits the concept of the 'habitus' as the set of behaviours that we perform unthinkingly – and well – precisely because they are so ingrained as to seem natural. The habitus can thus be understood as a culture's collective knowledge, but only in the paradoxical sense that this knowledge eludes discursive grasp. For example, we all know how to flirt, without following a consciously elaborated set of rules. Such knowledge might therefore be described as 'unconscious', but for Bourdieu, this description is valid only in so far as the 'unconscious' is understood as the way a given social structure – i.e. gender roles, class hierarchy and so on – has been internalized by its subjects. 'It is because subjects do not, strictly speaking, know what they are doing', contends Bourdieu, 'that what they do has more meaning than they know' (1986, 79). An ethnographer may infer a great deal about a culture's power structure from analysing its courtship rituals, but as Wittgenstein argued in a different context, the knowledge embodied in practice ('just act natural!') is of a fundamentally different kind from the statements that can be made about it. Bourdieu's project bears some resemblance, then, to the anthropologist Clifford Geertz's interest in 'local' as opposed to 'totalizing' knowledge, but attends more closely to the relations of authority involved in analytical translations from one language-game to another. Bourdieu's book *Distinction* is in fact devoted to redefining both know-how and more formal knowledge as 'cultural capital' – the charismatic form of authority that, seemingly natural, is reflected in such spontaneous judgments as De Quincey's 'cultured' reaction to *King Lear*.

Bourdieu's dialectical account of the relationship between knowledge and practice (another version of unknowledge) offers a case in point for Lyotard's argument that postmodern investigations challenge the very concept of knowledge, at least in the way we first defined it. One of the most important recent developments in this process has barely been touched on here, although it would merit an essay in itself: as computers transform (individual) knowledge into (exchangeable) information, 'we may . . . expect a thorough exteriorization of knowledge with respect to the "knower", at whatever point he or she may occupy the knowledge process' (4). Information technologies, that is, promise to enact *in practice* the 'decentring' of knowledge theorized, for example, in Foucault's impersonal 'archive'.

With Lyotard, we come full circle from De Quincey's opposition between the communicative and the affective, acquisition and expansion; for while, according to Lyotard, science has traditionally asserted the superiority of abstract, denotative statements about the world, it now concerns itself with 'such things as undecidables, the limits of precise control, conflicts characterized by incomplete information, "*fracta*", catastrophes, and paradigmatic paradoxes' (198, 60) – in other words, with the kind of phenomena which, posing radical challenges to cognition, were once called 'sublime'. And with this preoccupation,

says Lyotard, science has borrowed from literature the technique of the 'little narrative' through which an imaginative challenge may be posed. (Geertz likewise sees no contradiction in acknowledging his debts to literary criticism while asserting the scientificity of interpretive anthropology.) Lyotard's 'literary' view of contemporary science as producing the 'unknown' is echoed in Paul Feyerabend's equally paradoxical argument that prolonged periods of conceptual 'stability', rather than confirming the progress of knowledge, actually calls its very status into question (73). In light of such developments, the literary critic Alan Liu goes so far as to posit a utopian 'ethos of the unknown'. The point of the present essay is not to celebrate conceptual instability for its own sake, but merely to note the ways in which literature, traditionally both honoured and distrusted for not knowing, offers an analogy for postmodernism's incorporation of unknowledge into the structure of knowledge. This conceptual adjustment also allows us to notice the ways in which effects of power precipitate from the game of distinguishing knowledge from its opposite (as De Quincey illustrates). Whether we conclude, with Plotnitsky, that unknowledge is 'irreducible', or with Stanley Fish – the most eminent epistemologist among literary scholars – that we simply can't help knowing what we know, we might keep asking: what motivates either the denial or the assertion of knowledge? How do the shifting boundaries between knowledge and its 'other' map differing relations to power? And if this other is not knowledge, then what may I call it?

Note

1. For an excellent account of sublime aesthetics, including a reading of Kant's Third Critique (which I paraphrase and from which De Quincey borrows his imagery), see Thomas Weiskel (1976).

Works cited

Bourdieu, Pierre. *Distinction: A Social Critique of the Judgement of Taste*, trans. Richard Nice. Cambridge, MA, 1984.

Bourdieu, Pierre. *Outline of a Theory of Practice*, trans. Richard Nice. Cambridge, MA, 1986.

Burwick, Frederick (ed.). *The Works of Thomas De Quincey*, Vol. 3. London, 2000.

de Man, Paul. *Allegories of Reading: Figural Language in Rousseau, Nietzsche, Rilke, and Proust*. New Haven, CT, 1979.

Feyerabend, Paul K. *Problems of Empiricism: Philosophical Papers, Volume 2*. Cambridge, 1981.

Fish, Stanley. 'Commentary: The Young and the Restless', in *The New Historicism*, ed. H. Aram Veeser. New York, 1989, 303–16.

Foucault, Michel. *The Archaeology of Knowledge and the Discourse on Language*, trans. A. M. Sheridan Smith. New York, 1972.

Geertz, Clifford. *Local Knowledge: Further Essays in Interpretive Anthropology*. New York, 1983.

Lacan, Jacques. *The Four Fundamental Concepts of Psycho-analysis*, ed. Jacques-Alain Miller, trans. Alan Sheridan. New York, 1973.

Liu, Alan. *The Laws of Cool: The Culture of Information*. Chicago, IL, 2003.

Lyotard, Jean-François. *The Postmodern Condition: A Report on Knowledge*, trans. Geoff Bennington and Brian Massumi. Minneapolis, MN, 1984.

Masson, David (ed.). *The Collected Writings of Thomas De Quincey*, Vol. 11. London, 1897.

Russell, Bertrand. *Human Knowledge: Its Scope and Limits*. New York, 1948.

Ryle, Gilbert. *The Concept of Mind*. London, 1949.

Sedgwick, Eve Kosofsky. *Epistemology of the Closet*. Berkeley, CA, 1990.

Shelley, Percy Bysshe. 'A Defence of Poetry' and 'Prometheus Unbound', in *Shelley's Poetry and Prose*, eds Donald H. Reiman and Sharon B. Powers. New York, 1977.

Weiskel, Thomas. *The Romantic Sublime: Studies in the Structure and Psychology of Transcendence*. Baltimore, MD, 1976.

Wittgenstein, Ludwig. *Philosophical Investigations*, trans. G. E. M. Anscombe. New York, 1958.

Wittgenstein, Ludwig. *The Blue and Brown Books: Preliminary Studies for the 'Philosophical Investigations'*. New York, 1960.

Woolf, Virginia. *To the Lighthouse*. San Diego, CA, 1927.

Yeats, William Butler. 'Among School Children', in *Selected Poems and Two Plays of William Butler Yeats*, ed. M. L. Rosenthal. New York, 1962.

Žižek, Slavoj. *The Sublime Object of Ideology*. London, 1989.

love | *DANIEL COTTOM*

Professor Loveless

When Allan Bloom declared that 'the eroticism of our students is lame', he made it clear that loveless teachers, especially of the 'theoretical' sort, were to blame (1987, 133). This image of the unloving theorist has now become widespread. Historians such as Gertrude Himmelfarb, critics such as Roger Shattuck and Alvin Kernan, and novelists such as Stephen Dobyns are among the many who have echoed Bloom's accusation (Himmelfarb, 1994, 2; Shattuck, 1999, 3–8; Kernan, 1990, 145, 70–1; Dobyns, 2000, B10). They do not always anathematize the name of theory as such, but they are as one in their judgment that the love of learning is mortally threatened by theoretical approaches supposed to have become dominant across the humanities in the last thirty years: feminism, deconstruction, African-American studies, cultural studies, and so on. Even scholars once associated with radical new approaches to theory, such as Harold Bloom and Frank Kermode, are now lending a hand to this accusation. Bloom tells us that his 1994 tome, *The Western Canon*, 'is not directed to academics, because only a small remnant of them still read for the love of reading'. Kermode warns that university teachers 'can read what they like and deconstruct or neo-historicize what they like' but must prove their love of books if they are not to be accounted 'failures and frauds'. A related case in this Erotic Rearmament Campaign is that of Robert Scholes, who has prefaced a recent book, which is 'critical of much that has been going on recently in the name of "theory", by introducing himself as a former 'boy who loved language' and as a professor who now hopes that his students may 'learn to love it' as he did (Bloom, 1994, 518; Kermode, cit. Ellis, 1997, 59; Scholes, 1998, ix–xi).

What is this thing called love?

Clearly, this accusation of unlovingness is some sort of *cri de coeur*, and only a brute would dismiss it out of hand. For we who have been engaged in theory are not simply disputed, dismissed or derided by these critics; there would be nothing particularly remarkable in that sort of collegial treatment. Instead it would seem that I and persons with whom I feel more or less intellectually affiliated have all been beseeched, lovingly, and have refused to requite this love.

Yet I cannot be persuaded that I and all these others are as hard-hearted – or, for that matter, as dominant in academe – as all that. What then are we to make of this ever-more-beloved image of our unlovingness?

Academics are a touchy lot, and one need not be especially perspicacious to detect a note of personal grievance in this *fin-de-siècle* rhetoric. (We can see, for example, that Harold Bloom's bullying characterization of other scholars as members of 'The School of Resentment' neatly exemplifies what it deplores.) And perhaps a personal note is not only inevitable but positively desirable in any discourse on love. In any case, I would not wish to seem unloving in my approach to this topic, and so rather than dismissing these arguments on the grounds of their evidently personal motivation, I shall take this motivation as providing all the more of a reason to pursue my analysis further.

In this charitable spirit, I will freely stipulate that love may indeed appear to be an apt type and token of the metaphysical idealisms undone in recent theory. Theorists have certainly critiqued love for what they see as its mystification of bourgeois values, its misrecognition of the object of desire, its legitimation of patriarchy, its enforcement of compulsory heterosexuality and its essentializing of identity, among other dubious accomplishments. So we can see how people may have come to the conclusions before us. After all, if a celebrated theorist such as Roland Barthes could maintain, in 1977, that the lover's discourse had come to be so 'ignored, disparaged, or derided' as to be driven 'into the backwater of the "unreal", why should these others not feel justified, some ten or twenty-odd years later, in saying something similar? (1978, 1).

At the same time, I must acknowledge that these critics of the current state of academe are all intelligent and erudite persons, and so they all must know that love in western traditions has always been defined in and through social agendas of various sorts. They certainly know that when Socrates discussed eros, one of his marked concerns was to advocate a regulation of erotic behaviour, especially in the form of pederasty, that was at odds with the customary practices and understandings of some of those with whom he spoke. For his part, Aristotle maintained that while love of the highest sort was neither to be expected nor particularly desired between husband and wife, it ought to serve specific social, political and economic values where it did appear, as between male friends (1926, 503). Later, when figures such as Augustine, Aquinas

and Dante came on the scene and invoked the essence of love in their writings, they put it in the service of concepts of natural and divine law as defined by Catholic dogma, outside of which, they maintained, it could have no legitimate existence. Going rather beyond Plato and Aristotle alike, Andreas Capellanus maintained that since a husband's and wife's legal possession of each other in matrimony eliminated the quality of gratuitousness necessary to its definition, love could exist only in an adulterous or extra-marital liaison – wherefore the third book of his treatise on love abruptly condemns the passion lovingly analysed in the first two and proselytizes for the virtue of Christian chastity. The neoplatonic platitudes in Pietro Bembo's discourse on love in *The Book of the Courtier* (1528) by Baldesar Castiglione, the court of Urbino's Emily Post, were expressly designed to teach persons of rank and fortune how to comport themselves with grace in their social world. In the seventeenth century, John Milton represented as Christian dogma woman's subordination to man in matters of love: 'He for God only, she for God in Him' (Castiglione, 1959, 354–6; Milton, 1998, 238). Throughout the entire course of western literature, in other words, love has been a proxy for all sorts of political, religious, economic, scientific and sexual matters.

In fact, love has been the proxy par excellence. Those who 'love love', in the phrase of Marsilio Ficino, have always done so in the express service of formalized conceptions of power beyond any particular experience of love (Pico della Mirandola, 1984, 97 [5: 8]). Nothing could be more contrary to the whole fabric of western tradition, as it has traditionally been woven, than the notion that it is possible, much less desirable, to love reading, literature or learning simply for themselves. It was precisely for this reason that Dante provided us with eloquent testimony from a certain Francesca of Rimini. In his *Inferno*, she is the whirligig who pauses in her rounds long enough to explain how a beloved literary classic – in this case, a volume telling the romance of Lancelot – may pander to self-deluding and self-destructive desires, as by leading one to kissing one's brother-in-law and thence to eternal damnation (1973, 1: 55).

But the critics with whom we are concerned here are intelligent and erudite spokespersons for western tradition, and so they are intimate with this literature, I am sure. They must know perfectly well that love has always been articulated in the form of social agendas and, moreover, that it has always been the subject of dispute and debate, as in Plato's *Symposium* and Renaissance *dialoghi d'amore*. Otherwise Pico della Mirandola would not have bothered to note that 'since it is common for the word *love* . . . to mean different things, it is necessary, before we talk about love, to explain what we mean by this word, thus eliminating everything else which it can mean' (1984, 95). Even more challengingly, Plato had portrayed Socrates as emphasizing that love does not put one into possession of the truth – in fact, that it does rather the opposite, dislodging us from the sense of values and knowledge of which we are inclined to boast. Socrates' erotic pedagogy, in which 'Eros is necessarily a philosopher', teaches us nothing if it does not teach us, first and foremost, that love is a non-obvious, tricky, cunning power – a 'clever hunter ever weaving some new device' – that can be followed only through a process of questioning in which tradition and the established agendas of society, like every other mortal thing, are put at risk (1991, 145–7). In a commentary on the *Symposium*, Plotinus drew attention to this point when he said that love 'includes within itself an aspiration ill-defined, unreasoned, unlimited' (1956, 197).

What we talk about when we talk about love

At least from Sappho on, literature has registered the philosophical nature of love – which is to say, its philosophically questionable nature – through its characterization as a pre-eminently paradoxical experience. In literary as in philosophical and religious tradition, love is a power that knows us in a way that we cannot know it, and so it is typically condensed into a paradox of defect and perfection. A defect in so far as it is manifested in desire and so presupposes a lack of wholeness, it is perfection in so far as it yet suggests a presumptively divine origin and end. Or a defect in so far as it is an 'excessive state of emotion', as Aristotle put it, it is perfection in so far as this excess may be redeemed in the service of society (Aristotle, 1926, 473; on this topic, see Derrida, 1997). All you need is love, and all's fair in love and war; love is our salvation, and numberless are the crimes committed in the name of love. To put it as succinctly as possible, 'I hate and I love', Catullus wrote (1970, 105).

So Sappho tells of Eros 'with his gift of pain', or of 'bittersweet' love, as Ovid evokes the 'co-existence of hope and fear' in lovers, as Guido Cavalcanti recounts love's 'anguishing delights', or as Giordano Bruno cites the motto '*hostis non hostis*' to designate the enemy/non-enemy borderline along which love arises (Sappho, 1928, 213; Ovid, 1968, 210; Cavalcanti, 1986, 23; Bruno, 1964, 129). Today the poetry of popular music continues to traffic in such images. One might think, for example, of how Tina Turner's rending voice plays out this sort of paradox in 'What's Love Got To Do With It?' (1984), fiercely reiterating La Rochefoucauld's suggestion that love is nothing but 'a second-hand emotion' while just as urgently conveying the conviction that this has ever been love, pure love, love precisely as real as literature, song and other forms of cultural representation. 'Should I order cyanide or order champagne?' was Cole Porter's wry question in 'I Am in Love' (1953).

Love in this tradition is simultaneously bondage and deliverance, suffering and ecstasy, the wound and the cure. The thematics of *Liebestod*, fatal love, develop out of this tradition, as does the folk etymology that sees *mors*, death, in *Amor* (as recorded, for instance, in Mario Equicola's *The Nature of Love* [1525]) (1983, 29). Hence the statement of Philo in the *Dialogue of Love* (1535) written by Leone Ebreo, who was an eminent scholar and a physician to the royal court of Spain: 'Love continually makes the lover's life die and death live' (1929, 55). Cut from the same cloth is Perottino's observation, in Pietro Bembo's *The Asolani* (1505), that there is more than a passing resemblance between the words *amore* (love) and *amaro* (bitter) (1991, 90). In recent centuries as in ancient times, we do not lack for testimony to this mutually constitutive intimacy of love and hate.

Those who promulgate the stereotype of the unloving theorist must certainly know all this. As surely as they know that love is the desire said to comprehend all others – *omnia vincit amor*, 'God is love', and so on (see Virgil, *Eclogues*, 10: 69, and 1 John 4: 8) – they know that it does so only in so far as it divides itself in the rhetoric of paradox or in other forms that simultaneously promise and frustrate its comprehension. Love's bittersweetness is then the very image of that shocking, even terrifying uncertainty we are taught to value by Socrates' erotics, in which love is intermediate between wisdom and ignorance, goodness and badness, beauty and ugliness, mortality and immortality (Plato, 1991, 145–7).

Love stinks

To adapt the case to the present: nothing could be more untraditional than the assumption that a focus on issues such as gender, race, class, sexuality or imperialism is necessarily exclusive of love or is even to be suspected of such a dereliction. Traditionally, love does not take a self-evident form, and the beauty that may lead us by it, through it and to it certainly is not to be taken at face value. (Socrates, we are pointedly told, was not a handsome man.) And since those who promulgate the stereotype of the unloving theorist surely know all this, now I begin to suspect a greater love in them than I had previously divined. I begin to see that their displays of seeming irrationality, their efforts to compel our submission before their own blatant and yet formally disavowed political agendas, are in fact meant to awaken me, and all of us, to an esoteric meaning in their words. They are not beating up on those other profs, such as myself, to whom they are opposed. Paradoxically, they themselves are both the agents of and the sacrifices to their rhetorical violence.

I have been far too hasty. After all, one of the recurrent features in the dialogues on love that figure prominently in western literary, philosophical and religious tradition is the dramatic use of counterintuitive sophistical arguments. One model for such arguments is the speech given in Plato's *Phaedrus* by Lysias, who contends that the best lover is an older man who is *not* in love with the younger object of his attentions. With such precedents in mind, I have to reformulate my question about the popular image of the loveless theorist. Could it be that this image is actually a rhetorical device designed to invite a more beautiful discourse on love in contemporary academia and popular culture? Such a hypothesis would go far toward explaining how such a badly reasoned and fundamentally absurd argument has come to be taken as seriously as it has by intelligent persons.

And now I feel ashamed of my earlier imperceptiveness. It is as if all the world has been transformed. Initially, to be sure, this love that dares shout its name appears self-contradictory in every respect. Flouting its proclaimed premises in western tradition, this militant love of certain critics of academe seems ridiculously mistaken in its apparent assumptions that love unequivocally defined learning in the past, that love clearly does not move learning now, and that western tradition will be at an end if love fails in the future to regain the aforementioned power it never in fact had. But as I now come to see, all this is just an invitation into a dialogue of love completely at odds with its initial appearance. *Of course* these scholars know that love's rhetoric is characteristically paradoxical, and so their motive in labouring to popularize the stereotype of the unloving theorist has been that of awakening us all to the stupidity, moral danger and political irresponsibility of *untheoretical love*. Like Socrates, they have been willing to seem ignorant, to sacrifice their pride in themselves, so as to bring us toward this greater wisdom.

Now all is changed for me. *Of course* these critics know that love's paradoxical nature – in psychological terms, its ambivalence – is a condensed expression of the historical fixations, social conflicts and incompatible imaginings of the future that divide our languages and our selves. They have read their western canon, and so of course they know that we are social beings whose affective relations are bound to embody the historical suppositions, propositions and demands to which we are committed by the lives we lead. They value reason, and so they recognize the consequence: that wherever we encounter it, the notion of love will be shattered by the conflicting demands of the hypothetical, the propositional and the imperative modes, which may be precariously correlated with one another in particular cultural forms but which in any case are irreducible to a formal logic or semantic simplicity. If love takes pride in bringing a community together, they know it must also take responsibility

for the hostilities between communities. If it is the glue between couples and among the members of families, it is also the detachment with which we turn away from an annoying student, colleague or passerby.

Who wrote the book of love?

The age-old trope that puts love beyond expression, or beyond the comprehension of anyone but the lover, is another way the theoretical nature of love has been registered in everyday experience. Similarly, the question Jane Austen put into the mouth of Elizabeth Bennet – 'Is not general incivility the very essence of love?' (1993, 93) – is a reminder that the presumptive universality of love is precisely what makes it endlessly provoking in any specified circumstances. Austen's wit thus comes from the same tradition as Herbert Marcuse's longing for 'the destructiveness of the liberated Eros', which he saw as missing in the citizens of the contemporary West. 'In their erotic relations', Marcuse sneered, 'they "keep their appointments" – with charm, with romance, with their favorite commercials' (1996, 95). Yet Austen was surely wiser in this matter than was Marcuse, whose contempt for the popular expression of love was very much like Allan Bloom's. Even though Marcuse celebrated the youth culture whose alleged products were later castigated by Bloom, both men sought to prescribe to society a supposedly superior form of eros that seems unwittingly designed to prove to their readers just how out of touch these profs were with the impassioned lives of those to whom they were offering their prescriptions. In contrast, Austen's novel mocks the notion of a philosophical 'essence' of love in the same words that convey to us the undeniable passion of philosophical tradition. Casually, it shows us this passion in the formation of popular consciousness while also clueing us into the ideological aspects of any debate over the theory and practice of love. Coming immediately after her Aunt Gardiner's objection to the phrase 'violently in love' – an 'expression . . . so hackneyed, so doubtful, so indefinite' – Elizabeth's statement is remarkable for its recognition that love does not allow for any more certain, or any less ideological, form of expression. She thus anticipates a statement offered by Martha Nussbaum, the contemporary classicist and philosopher, in a discussion of the *Symposium*: 'Uttered about ordinary passion by an ordinary mortal, the claim to have a general understanding of love is as good an example of the self-refuting proposition as anything philosophy has to offer' (1990, 317).

But what then of Aristotelian tradition, in which the general understanding of love has its origins in one's self? One's own love for oneself 'is the beginning of all other loves, as anyone can see', Dante wrote in his *Convivio*, treating Aristotle's doctrine as a truism (1990, 88). Like Aristotle, Dante did not refer to 'self-love of the ordinary kind', in the sense of selfishness or vanity, but rather to a good man's love for what is 'lovable in his nature', for what is 'the dominant part of himself'. The good man, Aristotle explained, then 'feels toward his friend in the same way as toward himself (for a friend is another self)' (Aristotle, 1926, 551, 539, 553, 535). It is crucial to note that it is 'the good man', specifically, who appreciates this truth; as Tasso would proudly note, 'the vulgar' regard as 'the lies of poets' the idea that the 'miracles of love' have the effect of making lovers 'not two, but one' (1935, 253). For those truly in the know, though, the beloved is said to be that paradoxical being, the *alter ipse* or *heteros autos*, the self-same other or other self.

As one's second self or as one's own self divided from oneself, the beloved is then a model for the intersubjectivity presumed to constitute sociality, or humanity, in general.

Therefore, in writing of the friendship born of love, Cicero concluded, 'But if you should take the bond of goodwill out of the universe, no house or city could stand, nor would even the tillage of the fields abide' (1971, 135). Yet this is not an easily conceptualized perception – Nussbaum's caution on this score is entirely traditional. The distinction between the popular and the philosophical senses of self-love, like the distinction between the vulgar and the elite, the common members of society and the good man, the Christian and the pagan, or man and woman, point out to us that this model is specific to cultures in which only a relative few, and those only within the one culture as distinguished from others, are imagined as being capable of participation. (Thus, when Oscar Wilde had one of his characters say, 'To love oneself is the beginning of a life-long romance', his satire was political as well as literary and philosophical) (1989, 522; the speaker is Lord Goring). Even for those few, moreover, the paradoxical nature of love remains an occasion for fear and confusion.

In so far as one recognizes a duplication of the self in the other, this amazing, miraculous or ecstatic experience is likely to seem a kind of death, as all sorts of traditions tell us. One goes beyond mortal boundaries, one's seemingly discrete self loses itself to another, and so society is figuratively instituted through an incorporation of death that is also a consciousness of profound division within and multiplication of the self – a bittersweet experience indeed. Hence the pedagogical caution that the physician and humanist Symphorien Champier addressed to the imagined readership of his *Book of True Love* (1503): 'Ladies! Be pleased to be lovers of true love and do not fear what Plato says when he states that one who loves dies in himself and has life in the other. For he lives in the thing that he loves and dies in himself when he abandons himself to serve the one he loves' (1962, 66–7).

Through paradox, a rhetorical figure that seems to break with ordinary time and space, with the grammar of experience as it is commonly formulated in our schools and other institutions, we are offered a portal onto the historical specificity of love. We are made witness to its material texture, which is the excitation in which it discovers itself in its alienation from itself and hence in confusion, fear, violence and misapprehension. The simultaneous constitution and fragmentation of the self in identifications formed through desire, in imagination, articulate the social body love would demand. In one such world of love, the good man may enjoy an unequivocal dominance; in others, the poet may lord it over the vulgar; a scholar at the University of Chicago may find his love for himself reproduced in his students and peers; a professor at Yale may thrill to his conviction that the image of himself he most treasures, in which he is the object of others' resentment, is affirmed by those hateful others, those dears.

In any event – and these are of course the merest sketches of my point – the claim to have a general understanding of love is a self-refuting proposition not because such claims are impossible to establish but because they are *too* possible. Traditionally, the assertion of love is a self-refuting proposition because love divides and multiplies the self through the apprehension of a society imagined to exist not only in the present but also in the past and the future. As our poems and songs and stories testify, love undoes us.

Love among the ruins

And so once again I am forced to revise my impressions. Having arrived at this point in the discussion, I now see that the stereotype of the unloving theorist is not only a rhetorical device but also an object lesson in the wily ways of love.

Having first seen this stereotype as an abuse of others and then as critical self-abuse, I now can see that these critics are actually pleasing themselves. The problem is that they can neither accept nor overcome this pleasure. They are trapped in a volatile structuring of supposition, proposition and demand according to which love is imagined to have defined learning in the past, is declared to have now abandoned learning and is ordered to return. Within this scenario, we can see that these critics' abuse of others as unloving is a way of confessing, in an inverted form, how much pleasure they take in loving themselves. They cannot openly admit to this pleasure because doing so would entail the further confession that the image of self one cultivates and loves also implies an image of a polis and of all the policies and institutions appertaining thereto – and to make *that* confession would be to put their pleasures, and their ideologies, on the same level as others', where they would have to suffer the democratic fate of a discussion without a predetermined outcome. Being learned and erudite persons, they must know perfectly well that love has always been articulated in and through social agendas, but because they cannot suffer this knowledge that what makes their loves also makes their politics – even though everybody does it that way – they must obscure their own knowledge, belie their own understanding of tradition, and displace onto the fantasy-figure of the victimized university the delicious misery they are really inflicting on themselves. To such lengths will moonstruck people go.

So theirs is the love of the lawbreaker for the law, but they are not to be blamed on that account. True, even in the most charitable estimation, this love may seem perverse. If love has been unable to teach us anything else, however, it has taught us the necessity of such perversity.

As love goes, beyond reason, beyond itself, so go we, theorists all.

Works cited

Alighieri, Dante. *Inferno, The Divine Comedy*, 3 vols, ed. and trans. Charles S. Singleton. Princeton, NJ, 1973.

Aristotle. *The Nicomachean Ethics*, trans. H. Rackham. London, 1926.

Austen, Jane. *Pride and Prejudice*, 2nd edn. Donald Gray. New York, 1993.

Barthes, Roland. *A Lover's Discourse: Fragments*, trans. Richard Howard. New York, 1978.

Bembo, Pietro. *Gli Asolani*, ed. Giorgio Dilemmi. Florence, 1991.

Bloom, Allan. *The Closing of the American Mind: How Higher Education Has Failed Democracy and Impoverished the Souls of Today's Students*. New York, 1987.

Bloom, Harold. *The Western Canon: The Books and School of the Ages*. New York, 1994.

Bruno, Giordano. *The Heroic Frenzies*, trans. Paul Eugene Memmeo, Jr. Chapel Hill, NC, 1964

Castiglione, Baldesar. *The Book of the Courtier*, trans. Charles S. Singleton. Garden City, NY, 1959.

Catullus. '#85', *The Poems of Catullus*, trans. Frederic Raphael and Kenneth McLeish. Boston, MA, 1979.

Cavalcanti, Guido. 'If Favor were friendly to my desires', *The Poetry of Guido Cavalcanti*, ed. and trans. Lowry Nelson, Jr. New York, 1986.

Champier, Symphorien. *Le livre de vraye amour*, ed. James B. Wadsworth. The Hague, 1962.

Cicero. *De Amicitia. De Senectute, De Amicitia, De Divinatione*, trans. William Armistead Falconer. London, 1971.

Dante. *Il Convivio*, trans. Richard H. Lansing. New York, 1990.

Derrida, Jacques. *Politics of Friendship*, trans. George Collins. London, 1997.

Dobyns, Stephen. 'A Pretty (Not True) View of Creative Writing', *Chronicle of Higher Education*, 46 (24 March 2000): B10.

Ebreo, Leone. *Dialoghi d'amore*, ed. Santino Caramella. Bari, 1929.

Ellis, John M. *Literature Lost: Social Agendas and the Corruption of the Humanities*. New Haven, CT, 1997.

Equicola, Mario. *La Natura d'Amore*, ed. Neuro Bonifaci. Urbino, 1983.

Himmelfarb, Gertrude. 'On Looking into the Abyss', in *On Looking into the Abyss: Untimely Thoughts on Culture and Society*. New York, 1994.

Kernan, Alvin. *The Death of Literature*. New Haven, CT, 1990.

Marcuse, Herbert. *Eros and Civilization: A Philosophical Inquiry into Freud*. Boston, MA, 1966.

Milton, John. *Paradise Lost*, 2nd edn, ed. Alistair Fowler. London, 1998.

Nussbaum, Martha C. 'Love and the Individual: Romantic Rightness and Platonic Aspiration', in *Love's Knowledge: Essays on Philosophy and Literature*. New York, 1990.

Ovid. *Ovid's Amores*, trans. Guy Lee. New York, 1968.

Pico della Mirandola, Giovanni. *Commentary on a Canzone of Benivieni*, trans. Sears Jayne. New York, 1984.

Plato. *Symposium. The Dialogues of Plato*, 4 vols, trans. R. E. Allen. New Haven, CT, 1991.

Plotinus. *The Enneads*, 2nd edn, trans. Stephen MacKenna, rev. B. S. Page. London, 1956.

Sappho. *Poems and Fragments, Lyra Graeca*, 3 vols, ed. and trans. J. M. Edmonds. London, 1928.

Scholes, Robert. *The Rise and Fall of English: Reconstructing English as a Discipline*. New Haven, CT, 1998.

Shattuck, Roger. 'Nineteen Theses on Literature', in *Candor and Perversion: Literature, Education, and the Arts*. New York, 1999.

Tasso. 'Il Cataneo o vero de gli Conclusioni', in *Prose*, ed. Francesco Flora. Milan, 1935.

Wilde, Oscar. *An Ideal Husband, Complete Works of Oscar Wilde*. New York, 1989.

music | SOUNDING DESIRE – ON TRICKY[1] | *SIMON CRITCHLEY*

Does art still have a critical function? Several theses

1. The question whether art should still be critical is the same question as whether art still has an *emancipatory* intent. Is art concerned with liberation understood in the broadest terms, that is, emancipation understood as both an affective, cognitive and, most importantly, social process? What I mean is that the critical function of art is a critique of praxis, of actually existing praxis (say the pragmatics of capitalist globalization), as varieties of more or less unfree or systemically distorted praxis, with a view to how a critique of praxis might allow us to become emancipated from a condition of unfreedom. Thus, critical art asks us to look at the world from a utopian standpoint. Critical aesthetic praxis, in its intention and action, traces the outline of a utopian praxis, of the world otherwise imagined, otherwise seen, 'a completely new set of objects' (Wallace Stevens). I understand utopia simply as the demand to look at things from how they might appear otherwise, from that hair's breadth that separates things as they are from things as they might otherwise be. This is what Adorno, in the final fragment of *Minima Moralia*, calls adopting the standpoint of redemption. For Adorno, we have to adopt this standpoint precisely because there is no guarantee of redemption – hence it is not at all a question of religion. Thus, in this minimal sense, art is utopian not because it might be seeking to articulate a direct social or political content (although it might well also be doing that),

but because it is engaging the spectator, reader or auditor in some sort of transfigured relation to the world they inhabit. In other words, critical art describes the common features of our being-in-the-world by pulling us out of that world – for a moment, an instant, an epiphany. *The mundanization of art is its demundanization.* To anticipate a little, this will be one of my claims about music. To summarize, the critical function of art is indistinguishable from its utopian moment, however minimal and thin that utopia might prove to be. To put this in a formula, *critique without utopia is empty, but utopia without critique is blind.*

2. But if the critical function of art is the critique of praxis with a view to the emancipation from or transformation of that praxis, then this is hardly a simple matter. That is, the business of critique must also be based upon a description, a more or less accurate description, at least a description that *resonates* with us (and maybe the resonation of the artwork is its truth content – I will come back to this), of the structural features of contemporary praxis that block emancipation. I want to call these structural features, following Axel Honneth, *social pathologies* (1994, 9–69). That is, critique must proceed from a description of social pathologies, from a certain diagnosis of the time *(Zeitdiagnose)*, a grasping of the present in thought. This *zeitdiagnostisch* linking of critique and emancipation to the social pathologies that block emancipation explains, in my view, the significance of the philosophical critique of modernity, a critique that arguably begins in Rousseau's

Second Discourse and continues in Hegel, the early Marx and Nietzsche. The philosophical critique of modernity begins from a descriptive diagnosis of what blocks emancipation in the modern world. It is this philosophical critique of modernity that passes over into the classical sociological critique of modernity in Weber and Durkheim, and into the aesthetic critique of modernity that arguably defines the whole logic of the avant-garde from Jena romanticism to the Situationist International, from 1798 to 1968.

3. Without an account of the social pathologies that block emancipation and thwart human freedom, the question of the critical function of art remains so much empty posturing, the formal vapidity and abstraction of good conscience. I am not suggesting for one minute that art or artists have, or should have, or should provide, a good conscience. I would rather encourage artists to be as wicked as possible, in Tricky's words 'to fight evil with evil'. Art is not like Guinness – it is not necessarily good for you. Much of the critical power of art consists in the fact that it offers a critical description or exaggerated elaboration of the social pathologies, structural features, of what passes for life at the present time. If the description of the pathology resonates, then the subject might begin to be afforded a glimpse into the modes of representation and subject-construction within which we move and have our being. For an example here, I think of Cindy Sherman's *Untitled Film Stills* series that begins in the late 1970s, where something like the pathologies of femininity are critically redescribed. The question of the critical function of art, to refine it once more, is whether and to what extent art provides some sort of redescription or exaggerated elaboration of the social pathologies of contemporary praxis, with a view to an emancipation or transformation of that praxis.

4. It seems to me that there is a moment of clarification in art, a clarification which often simply sets us before *the obscure as obscure*. The obscure in what passes for our life, the sheer intricacy, density and banality of the everyday routines within which we move and have our being, is clarified in being set before us – by looking, by reading, by listening. I am not saying that this clarification is clarifying; on the contrary, the moment of clarification in art presents us with the thickness and opacity of experience. If anything, it has the quality of an enigma. But a confrontation with the obscure as obscure is still liberating, that is, it still permits what Wittgenstein would call aspect-change with respect to the forms of life that we inhabit.

5. Does what I have said so far amount to a defence of aesthetic modernism? Certain of the claims that I have been making about critique, praxis and utopia were advanced by the first generation of the Frankfurt School. The exemplary case here is Adorno's *Minima Moralia*, where the question of emancipation is perhaps all too obscurely linked to the various social pathologies being described that block it; but it is still decisively there. Elements of this Frankfurt School approach were obviously influential in classic statements of aesthetic modernism, such as Greenberg. But let me stay with Adorno and put my cards on the table: I want what Adorno wanted. That is, an emancipation from domination towards forms of social, economic and political organization that would be more free, more equitable, more just, etc. However, as is also well-known, Adorno was – to put it mildly – rather pessimistic about the possibilities of emancipation after Auschwitz, and in particular the resources of rationality that would bring about emancipation (*incipit* Habermas's reformulation of the theme of rationality in terms of communicative action). It seems to me that this pessimism has to be respected, at least initially and strategically, particularly if one wants to avoid the rather easy optimism of some representatives of contemporary critical theory which makes their position difficult to distinguish from mainstream political liberalism. Such is what I have described as 'Left Rawlsianism' (1998, 27–39).

6. But if we stay with Adorno's and Horkheimer's description of the social pathologies of modernity, I would want to take issue with a couple of important matters. Firstly, I would take issue with the unmitigating bleakness and darkness of their social diagnosis, particularly in *Dialectic of Enlightenment,* which risks leading into a philosophical and political cul-de-sac, sparsely populated by a few *précieuses* delighting in the endless negativity of a free-floating jargon. Although the account of the inversions of Enlightenment into ideology proceeds with an understandably hyperbolic gusto which is not without a certain admirable jouissance – even a comic brio – the sociological descriptions are empirically highly questionable. After Auschwitz, the *Lebenswelt* is not completely evacuated in the way described by Adorno, and on this point I would tend to side with Habermas against Adorno. But, more specifically, the bleakness of the social description is linked to the notion of the culture industry as the compromised aesthetic experience of an unfree society – bread and circuses. Or as Adorno puts it in his essay on Beckett, in a typical and delightful exaggeration, the dream of social reconciliation is reduced to 'pap and pralines' (1991, 275).

7. Aesthetic modernism in Adorno, but also in Greenberg, goes hand in hand with an elevation of certain forms of high modernist aesthetic production (Schoenberg, Beckett, abstract expressionism) and a denigration of mass art in all its forms. The easy accessibility and technological availability of mass art is understood as compliance to domination or, at best, kitsch. The battle lines of the now strangely *démodé* conflict between modernism and postmodernism were often drawn in terms of how one evaluated the phenomena of mass art (cinema, television, pop music, etc.). Now, I like mass art. Despite its perplexingly mixed metaphors, I even cried when Elton John sang 'Candle In The Wind 97' at the funeral of our glorious princess. So, how can I reconcile what I want to claim about the critical and emancipatory function of art with an evaluation of mass art that avoids both the inexcusable ignorance and elitism of an Adorno without collapsing into some sort of vapid postmodernist inversion of the high into the low?

8. In response, I am tempted simply to ignore the distinction between high and low culture in the same way as I would like to sidestep the modernism/postmodernism debate. What I mean, following Simon Frith in his important book *Performing Rites*, is that it is not so much a question of accepting a priori a distinction between high and low culture, but rather of investigating this distinction as a social fact, of dismantling it a posteriori as a social construction (1996, 18–19). It is then a question of using and analysing the particular experience of aesthetic evaluation (of what you like) as a way of disrupting the distinction between high and low culture. For example, I can read Milton and listen to Massive Attack in the same evening, and undergo similar or at least analogous aesthetic experiences and experiences of evaluation. How different – affectively and cognitively – is the experience of reading Satan's seduction of Eve in *Paradise Lost* from listening to Massive Attack's 'Unfinished Symphony'?

9. A general question is at least beginning to take shape: namely, *what are the critical and emancipatory possibilities* *of mass art, that is, of art intentionally aimed at a mass audience, employing the technologies of the modern media?* The issues of critique and emancipation in relation to the phenomena of mass art can be bracketed out in a number of ways. For example, one might follow Baudrillard's depoliticized extension of the work of Henri Lefebvre and Guy Debord and view the phenomena of mass art as simulacra in the general play of simulation that defines the alleged hyper-reality of the contemporary world. Alternatively, one might assess mass art in terms of the endless mirror plays of ideology and subjection, which is the risk of a certain cynicism that I see in the cultural Lacanianism of Slavoj Žižek and Renata Salecl. In distinction from such approaches, my claim would be that the phenomena of mass art, or at least certain examples of them, might serve the vocations of critique and emancipation more powerfully than the advocates of high modernism would ever have dreamt possible. Obviously, this is a large claim which I cannot hope to substantiate in a single talk. In order to begin to address it fully, it would be necessary to look to what Noel Carroll, in a helpful recent book, has termed 'celebrations of mass art' (1998). Namely, Walter Benjamin's meditation on the work of art in the age of mechanical reproduction and Marshall Mcluhan's peculiarly optimistic evaluations of the transformations in aesthetic experience offered by the mass media.

10. How to proceed, then? Rather than continuing to make these rather abstract theoretical generalizations, I want to look at a specific example of mass art and exercise judgement in relation to that example. In this way, I hope to give some sort of performative elaboration of the more general claims I have been advancing. The choice of example in such discussions strikes me as absolutely essential, but also essentially contingent. It is a question of trying to find an example that *resonates* and there is no guarantee of

that – there is no accounting for taste. However, I want to focus on an example of contemporary popular music – Tricky – and explore the ways in which such music can illuminate questions of cultural identity and sexual identity.

11. The choice of an example and its evaluation are essential to the claims I want to advance. Let me insert a final caveat. It is not my intention to provide either a general description or overall defence of mass art. Thus I am not in the business of providing an ontology of mass art, in the manner of Noel Carroll. Incidentally, the real weakness of his book is his unwillingness to evaluate mass art, which for him is a critical rather than a philosophical task. I simply do not accept this distinction, particularly keeping in mind what I said above about the function of critique. Although the claims I have advanced so far aspire to a certain generality, what it comes down to in the end is an experience of critical evaluation, of judgment in relation to a singular example, and the peculiarly local character of what that example illuminates. I simply want to show what *an* example of mass art *can* do when thinking through the issues related to the critical potential of art. What I would see myself calling for from you is analogous experiences of evaluation, which will also have a local character and will therefore not coincide with mine. As I will emphasize presently, music *places* us, *locates* us, within time and within a culture. But – and this is both the pleasure and the paradox of the experience – it does this by momentarily *displacing* us, by *dislocating* us, by dislocating our experience of the 'us'. Music roots us by uprooting us and by uprooting the 'us'.

12. I want to make two claims about Tricky. Firstly, I want to claim that Tricky's music, in Simon Frith's words, gives 'cultural confusion a social voice' (Frith, 1996, 278). That is, it offers some sort of idealized picture of the cultural mongrelism or bastardy that defines and will hopefully more and more come to define 'Britishness'. It gives us one profile of *a post-colonial acoustic*. In this sense, Tricky's music has a certain utopian function in so far as it enables us to imaginatively inhabit an emergent form of cultural identity, of ways in which culture is being made and remade. Through the utopian displacement of musical expression we come to inhabit what we are, or what we have come to be on our curious little island, what the 'we' has come to be and might come to be. This will be the easier claim to advance. The second claim is more problematic, but probably for that reason also more interesting. For what I think is going on in Tricky is something rather strange, what I see as an articulation of the demundanizing workings of sexual desire, something like the contradictions and complexities at its heart. To speculate, perhaps what is being made and remade in Tricky's music is the terrifying solitude of our being, a solitude opened by the ever-obscure workings of sexual desire. This is what Freud would call the life of the drives, a life which is culturally mediated and ultimately orientated towards something deathly. In my recent work, I have tried to give voice to this deathly desire with Lacan's Freudian notion of the Thing (*la Chose, das Ding*), and Levinas's and Blanchot's notions of the *il y a,* the neutral murmuring of existence stripped of all diurnal comfort.[2] But to put things more plainly, I think there is something like an experience of transcendence in relation to desire taking place in Tricky's sounds and words, or rather *transcendence as desire*. Such transcendence gives us a different experience of the social forces that make up our desire, that code it as gender. So, to avoid one possible confusion, I don't at all want to say that rock and roll is about getting your rocks off, which is not really as self-evident as one might imagine and ultimately ends up replaying certain racist identifications of black music with

sexuality. Rather, I want to try and show that what is being voiced and *sounded* – sounded in the way in which a ship sounds the sea for submarines – in Tricky is something like the beautiful destructiveness of sexual desire, the suffocating physicality of eros, a suffocation where the frontiers identifying what we think of as our gender identity begin to blur, to decode and recode in new ways. There is something like a musical description of the pathology of desire being articulated in Tricky's music, and the imagined tracing of what desire might come to be.

Culture

Let me now turn towards the music and begin with a few biographical and bibliographical details, which most of you might know, but might serve as enlightenment to the musically challenged. To date, Tricky has released three albums under his own name. *Maxinquaye,* which came out in early 1995, *Pre-Millenium Tension*, which came in autumn 1996, and *Angels With Dirty Faces*, from May 1998.[3] I shall only be dealing with the first two of them. *Maxinquaye* is not some gnomic, new age neologism, but is simply the name of his mother, Maxine Quaye. As you might know, Tricky is part of the Quaye family, and Finley Quaye is Tricky's uncle. *Maxinquaye* is, I think, perhaps the most significant piece of musical innovation to come out of the UK in the last few years. It is a stunning piece of work, which had an overwhelmingly positive critical reception and sold surprisingly well. After making an album that everyone liked, it seemed that Tricky was determined to record something that no one could listen to. Such is *Pre-Millenium Tension*, whose title is a word play of rather questionable taste. This album is hard listening. It is extraordinarily intense, and wicked in all senses of the word; at times rhythmically recalcitrant, lyrically counter-intuitive, and deliberately difficult to access and assess. But I think it is nearly the equal of *Maxinquaye*, which is really saying something. *Angels With Dirty Faces* is a much more mixed bag. The main innovation is that Tricky drops his synthetic cocktail of noises, sampling and drum programming and uses acoustic instruments, natural drums and far too much tinny, unconvincing, electric guitar. As a result, the wonderful claustrophobic unity of sound and voice on the first two albums begins to sound like Tricky singing with a band. There are some undoubted highlights, such as the duet with P. J. Harvey, 'Broken Homes', and two fine and sparsely arranged concluding tracks, 'Taxi' and 'Peyote Kills'. But I don't really think the experiment works, the production is too clean and certain of the lyrics – witness 'Analyze Me' – are monomaniacal and vapidly narcissistic. In places, sadly, the whole thing actually sounds quite tired.

Tricky began his career guesting and rapping with the glorious Massive Attack. You can find his first pieces on *Blue Lines* from 1991, itself a real watershed album in contemporary British music. If you have that album, then listen to the title track, 'Blue Lines', 'Five Man Army' and 'Daydreaming', where Tricky is rapping with 3d and Horace Andy. You can also find two pieces with Tricky on Massive Attack's second album, *Protection*, from 1994: 'Karmacoma', which is then remixed and reworked as 'Overcome', the first track on *Maxinquaye*, and 'Eurochild', which is wonderful. Snatches of lyrics from the latter appear on 'Hell Is Round The Corner' from *Maxinquaye*. Tricky came out of that rich Bristol musical tradition that goes back to Rip, Rig and Panic, and the Pop Group in the 1970s and which has also produced Portishead and made Nellee Hooper one of the most sought after producers in the world. To see the link between Portishead and Tricky, listen to 'Glory Box', the final cut on Portishead's *Dummy*, which is the same backing track as Tricky's 'Hell Is Round The Corner'. But although the Portishead album came out before *Maxinquaye*, the backing track and the Isaac Hayes string sample were Tricky's before they were Portishead's. Tricky's track is much better and rougher, particularly for the scratch record effect that he uses with the sample, an effect that has been widely imitated, recently by R. Kelly and Lauren Hill.[4]

However, although Tricky belongs to this Massive Attack/Portishead/Bristol Sound constellation, what takes place with *Maxinquaye*, I think, goes beyond this tradition, transposing, extending and deepening it. This has something to do with the mysterious, aethereal voice that Tricky uses as a foil and cover on his albums, namely Martina Topley-Bird, but we will also come back to her. Let me venture a few words, in passing, on Portishead. Simon Frith concludes his *Performing Rites,* by claiming about *Dummy* that, 'no record better captures the pop aesthetic at this time, at this place' (277–8). Although we should put emphasis on the clauses 'at this time, at this place', which is Frith's way of signalling the fundamentally evanescent character of popular music – the joy of its instant – the strength of the evaluation is clear and the judgement persuasive. However, I think what is going on in Tricky, at least in the first two albums, is stronger, deeper, darker, more original, innovative and experimental than Portishead. This is a point that can be reinforced by listening to Portishead's eponymous second album released last year, which although excellent, simply doesn't extend aesthetically beyond their earlier work, and Beth Gibbon's whining feminine melancholia begins to wear a little thin after a while. In May 1998, Massive Attack released *Mezzanine*, only their third album in seven years, where Tricky doesn't appear at all. However, many of the tracks, 'Risingson', 'Inertia Creeps' and the wonderful title track, show a more than passing resemblance with Tricky, although Massive

Attack's use of soaring, grinding electric guitars is much more successful than anything achieved on *Angels With Dirty Faces*. The tracks 'Teardrop', 'The Man Next Door' and in particular the wonderfully minimal 'Exchange' – which also features an Isaac Hayes sample – are outstanding. I wish we could play all these tracks right now, and of course this is the point. If God loveth adverbs, then music requireth adjectives. As Frith wrties, music is *adjectival experience* (263). The experience of music is bound up with the need for evaluation and for such evaluation to be inter-subjectively shared. How often do you want simply to sit someone down and say 'Now listen to this, it's really good'?

To complete the bibliography, a collection by Tricky, modestly entitled *Nearly God*, came out in summer 1996, and features some nice guest vocal pieces from Terry Hall, Alison Moyet, Neneh Cherry and Björk. Of particular interest on this album are the tracks 'Poems', 'I be the prophet', 'Bubbles' and 'I sing for you'. Apparently for some obscure legal reason, which restricts Tricky to releasing one album a year, Island Records did not allow him to release *Nearly God* under his own name.

Having done a little sleeve note scholarship, I would like to let Tricky introduce himself. The first track I want to discuss is 'Tricky Kid' from *Pre-Millenium Tension*, which I will now imagine you have just listened to: 'They used to call me Tricky Kid, I live the life they wish they did, I live the life don't own a car, and now they call me superstar'. Of course, this is a massively self-ironical presentation, 'Everyone wants a record deal, everyone wants to be naked and famous, everyone wants to be just like you Tricky Kid, naked and famous'. This self-lacerating irony also explains the use of religious imagery, 'Here comes the Nazarene, look good in that magazine, Haile Selassie I, they look after I, god will receive us, got me like Jesus, Mary Magdalene that'd be my first sin, in with this temptress'. An acute little *Selbstdarstelling,* then. But what is really important is the movement of the bass in this track, the way it comes in and hits you after about 20 seconds and whips around in a two-second loop.

'Look deep into my mongrel eyes', Tricky says. The whole question of mongrelism is fascinating in Tricky. Picking up on an argument I made a few years ago with regard to the question of race and the philosophical tradition, I would want to describe cultural identity as a *mongrel assemblage*, a patchwork of diverse historical threads (Critchley, 1999, 122–42). The British are bastards. They always have been and are now more than ever. British cultural identity has always been a series of interpolations from other regions and other shores, most recently from the Caribbean and the Indian subcontinent.

My thesis here would be that contemporary British music is the aesthetic expression of this radical impurity, this cultural mongrelism. A post-colonial acoustic, then. You can see this in Tricky both through his biography, but best of all by simply tracing the influences on his sound: Jamaican sound system dub reggae, punk, R&B and hip-hop. There is something culturally absolutely specific about Tricky and that is very important for the following reason. For me, the real danger of the interest in Techno, particularly somewhere like Germany, is that this music can create the illusion of some sort of contact and immediacy with an international culture. Think of the German outfit Sash, who began as a passably interesting DJ project, but quickly degenerated into stale, predictable, dance pap. They emphasize this sham internationality, by featuring a different language on each of their hits, from the rather good 'Encore Une Fois' to the depressingly awful 'La Primavera'. In this music, one's own past, tradition and identity are erased in some fantasy of identification with an international scene. The desire here is to use music as a means not to be where one is, but to be where it is really happening, whether that is London, New York or wherever. For me, on the contrary, the great virtue of contemporary popular music is its local character, its particularity, which emerges out of a specific cultural assemblage. In Britain, this is a post-colonial assemblage, in Germany, struggling as it is with multiculturalism, there is a fascinating Turkish-German hip-hop scene, in France the dance scene has taken a slightly different, extremely interesting route, where one can detect strong *Maghrebin* influences. It is only through this conscious assumption of particularity that music can hope to be a little utopian and engage in some sort of critical engagement with one's local culture. In this sense, music can lead to a decoding and recoding of cultural identity. The very mongrelism of contemporary music is itself some sort of description of social pathologies, a description that already presupposes a refutation of all forms of ethnic essentialism. My point here is that such musical mongrelism or bastardy is at its most powerful when it is at its most local. Therefore, it is not a question of imitating it in other contexts, of producing a German or Norwegian Tricky, say, but of *transposing* that mongrelism to meet and resonate with local conditions.

Music places you, socially, temporally, spatially. It dates you in relation to a specific place. Hence one's tastes in popular music can easily be dated and – therefore – outdated. Even dance styles among those who no longer regularly dance can date you (think of the saddening phenomenon of post-conference academic dancing as an illustration, where – their hips loosened by a little alcohol – one can determine an academic's date of graduation by their more or less antiquated dance style). I can remember literally hundreds of dated and placed musical experiences: listening to Bowie's 'Suffragette City' on my mother's stereo in 1972 and not understanding my excite-

ment; in a friend's bedroom in Letchworth Garden City in 1976, listening to the first Ramones album with a sense of joyful disbelief; hearing Public Enemy's *Fear Of A Black Planet* on a walkman at 6.00 a.m. travelling on a train in Tuscany; hearing the first Tricky single on a portable CD-player in a hotel on the Leidesplein in Amsterdam; listening to R. Kelly's 'When A Woman's Fed Up' driving north through Louisiana, etc. etc. etc. And it is the *etcetera* that is the point. One's sense of cultural and even personal identity can be literally assembled, or composed, from a bundle of tunes. Memory is a record collection and you can learn who you are from sleeve notes. For most of us mere mortals, narrative identity is much more deeply rooted in a record collection than in a reading of Proust, Joyce and Musil. The unanswerable question is: what is it about song, about words and rhythm that is able to do this, to connect together the pieces of a life?

Sex

Let me now turn to my second claim and talk about sexual identity, and in particular the sounding of sexual desire in Tricky. For this purpose, I would like to look closely at another track from *Maxinquaye*, the best track on the album, called 'Suffocated Love', which I will once again imagine that you have just heard.

Here is a first theoretical approximation. We are all Freudians now. And if this is true then it means the following: that human consciousness, this strange awareness taking place between our ears, is the effect, the aftershock, the deferred resonance, of unconscious desire, a desire that is fundamentally sexual, and which is culturally and discursively coded as gender and gender differentiation. This desire is undoubtedly and obdurately social or discursive, but it keeps bumping its head against the reality of something that resists the discursive, however it is thematized and approximated: the Real in Lacan, the Semiotic in Kristeva, Wild or Savage Being in Merleau-Ponty, natural history in Adorno, or whatever. It is that obscure limit between the social and a real that seems to resist it that Freud names with his limit-concept of the drive, *der Trieb.*

Of course, to recognize the operation of unconscious sexual desire is also to acknowledge that we cannot recognize this recognition, for that we require some sort of intersubjective mediation, for example that offered by psychoanalysis itself in the pact of transference. Some sort of mediation is required to bring about what Hegel would call 'self-recognition in absolute otherness', a self-recognition that does not annul or assimilate otherness into self-consciousness, but which struggles with an other that resists the self. If Socratic wisdom is viewed through a Lacanian lens, then psychoanalytic knowledge consists in the fact that we do not know who we are, it consists in the deposing of *le sujet supposé savoir.* Psychoanalysis recalls us to this sheer cognitive modesty. That which permits us to acknowledge this modesty is what Freud calls the work of sublimation, letting the drive become displaced onto a new object. This is the place of art in psychoanalysis – it sublimates. We might say that *art traces the obscure limit between what we can know and the working of unconscious desire.* Art traces that limit and allows us to transgress it, just for a moment, in the sheer elongation of instant. From time to time, here and there, in depressed boredom and in manic joy, we are turned around to face the Thing that flickers and burns at the heart of desire.

Maybe, as Schopenhauer thought, and Nietzsche after him in crucially different ways, *music* traces this limit more powerfully than any other art form. For Schopenhauer, as is well known, music is the direct objectification or representation *(Vorstellung)* of the Will, the world understood as the expression of Will. That is, music is a mimesis of the will. For Nietzsche, rightly, without music life would be an error. However, for him, and this is the thought that I would like to retain, music is not mimetic, that is it is not a symbol of the symbolized, or a representation of the ultimate reality. Such is the Schopenhauerian position that Nietzsche criticizes in *The Birth of Tragedy.* It is the position that Nietzsche calls, in his attempted self-critique in the 1886 Preface to *The Birth of Tragedy,* an 'artist's metaphysics'. Music, then, in all the complexity of this formulation, is a *phenomenon of the Dionysian,* a phenomenon of the *unphenomenologizable,* a redemptive *Schein* for the pain and contradiction of what he calls the *Ur-Ein,* the primal unity from which we are torn by that detour we all too easily call 'life'.[5] Thus, beyond the mimetic theory of the relation of the will to music, music permits us to glimpse the springs of desire in a moment and movement of Dionysian excess, and music saves us from contact with that excess, because contact would destroy us, suffocate us. Otherwise said, *music is a work of sublimation that leaves the sublime sublime,* something that it somehow does through the work of rhythm, through drum and bass rather than through Apollinian melody and harmony, what Nietzsche calls 'the architecture of sound'. Rhythm: the resounding, pounding throb of drum and bass, breaking through the floorboards in the house of being. Had Nietzsche had the good fortune to live to hear James Brown and the JB's invention of funk in the 1969 classic 'Cold Sweat' rather than the empty teasing of Bizet's *Carmen,* I think he would have been forced to agree, despite all the undoubtedly silly remarks he would have made about Black music, slave morality and slave culture. I dream of seeing Nietzsche getting down in the Apollo Theatre in Harlem on one of those enormous nights in the 1960s when James Brown was screaming his divine heresies over the sliding, percolating bass of Bootsy Collins.

Let me return to Tricky. My suggestion is that music traces the obscure limit between what we can know and the working of unconscious desire, it is a work of sublimation that leaves the sublime sublime. In Tricky, this is something achieved through the compulsive fusion of rhythm and voice. However, as rhythm is spectacularly difficult to talk about with any precision, let me look at how this effect is achieved in the lyrics to 'Suffocated Love'. The first thing to note is the careful and disorienting use of antithesis to both familiarize and estrange the sexual scene being described: 'she's so good, she so bad . . . is it love, no not love . . . she says she's mine, I know she's lying . . . you understand, I can't stand . . .' What these antitheses, whispered like heresies, evoke is a suffocating picture of sexual passion, of the playful destructiveness of eros, 'She suffocates me . . . I think ahead of you, I think instead of you, will you spend your life with me and stifle me, I know why the caged bird sings, I know why.' The picture of sexual desire here is described in terms of suffocation, stifling, containment and imprisonment. As if to overstate his point, the last line in the above-cited lyric contains an allusion to Maya Angelou's autobiography, *I Know Why the Caged Bird Sings*, itself a tragic picture of rape and sexual abuse in childhood, an abuse also sublimated into a work of art.

What is sex? Here is another approximation: sex is skin, nerve endings, the laying down of memory traces whose recollection is a physical reverberation, a resonance which is olfactory and tactile before being visual and auditory. Sex is a series of distensions of the instant somehow invisibly tattooed on the surface of the body, where the body surface is the membrane of memory. In sex, the privilege of eye and ear gives way to nose and body surface. Sex is a smell: sweat, dirt, latex, sperm, mucous, sundry products. Becoming if not an animal, then some sort of subtle variant of humanity. There is a struggle for recognition here, a sheer physical suffocating play of and for recognition. And love, oh yes, love.

But on this point Tricky is – well – tricky, for the suffocating vision of eros that is being expressed is not nice, not nice at all. It is menacing and dark. As Tricky says on 'You don't' from *Maxinquaye*, 'I fight evil with evil'. In this connection, let's also imagine you have listened to 'Abbaon Fat Tracks' from the same album. This piece is an example of extraordinary and ambivalent sexual intensity. It is the coupling of Tricky's and Martina's voices here that is so powerful, 'fuck you in, tuck you in, suck you in with me'. 'I am she', say both voices simultaneously. But who is 'she'? Martina says, 'I fuck you in the ass, just for a laugh, with the quick-speed, I'll make your nose bleed'. But who fucks who in the ass? It is, as we philosophers say, not at all clear. It is a kind of suffocated and suffocating love, then. Bodies pressed close together to the point of asphyxiation, stifling each other, 'I think ahead of you, I think instead of you, will you spend your life with me and stifle me'. One imagines bodies pressing together in the half light, their frontiers vague, their contours indistinct. One imagines – and the point here is to let the obscure but overwhelming affect of the music induce imagination – a certain freezing and stretching of time, of taking up a space withdrawn from the world, the epiphany of a transgression that leaves you speechless, language becoming beautifully profane, becoming incantation, gossip becoming truth, truth leaving you speechless, and still you speak, often in adjectives. As I said, this is not nice? 'Hell is round the corner, where I shelter'.

To go back to 'Suffocated Love', the line I always keep thinking about is 'she cuts my slender wrists'. 'Slender wrists' is such an odd formulation, it is spoken by Tricky, and this is strange because in English a man would rarely, if ever, describe his wrists as slender. There is a continual blurring and transgression of gender divisions in Tricky, which is enacted through the way the words are swopped between Tricky and Martina. They continually seem to exchange gender roles, which adds to the completely disorientating sexual intensity of the music. This swopping can be seen in the cross-dressing that Martina and Tricky enagage in on the sleeve to their first single 'Overcome', with Martina dressed like Charlie Chaplin and Tricky in a wedding dress, smeared red lipstick, a baseball cap, and Adidas trainers. But this is no mere Bowie-esque gender-bending, but something altogether more macabre.

A particularly clear example of this staged sexual ambivalence is a track called 'Black Steel' from *Maxinquaye*. This track is a cover of Public Enemy's 'Black Steel In The Hour Of Chaos' from their seminal 1988 album *It Takes A Nation Of Millions To Hold Us Back*. Once again, let me imagine that you have listened to both versions of this track. What should be noted here is the curiously direct feminization of Chuck D's particularly macho rap about an African-American draft dodger locked up in the state penitentiary. Martina mumbles, almost indifferently, 'cos I'm a black man and I could never be a veteran'. More subtly, this gender ambivalence can be seen in a quite beautiful song from *Pre-Millenium Tension,* the best track on the album, 'She Makes Me Wanna Die'. It is sung by Martina as a woman or a man or something in between. The pronouns flip and slip back and forth between masculine and feminine. She makes me wanna die; but who wants who to die exactly? The way the voices play together here is fascinating, Tricky's voice anticipating and rumbling beneath Martina's, like a series of obscene whispers, 'who do you think you are, you're insignificant, a small piece, an "ism"'. The effect is extraordinary and all the more stunning because of its utter musical simplicity, just a guitar and a rhythm track.

Let me try and pull together the various strands of what I have said and conclude. Music roots us in uprooting us, places us in displacing us, locates us in dislocating us. It dislocates the 'us' of our cultural identity and lets us imagine another way of being 'us', another way of inhabiting these roots, not as roots that tie us to the earth, or back to some pregiven ethnic essence, but rather as routes that open over a vast geographical surface and reactivate previously sedimented strata of history. The utopian dimension to music offers other, imagined and yet to be imagined, ways of inhabiting these strata. It is what Paul Gilroy calls 'a changing same' (1993).

In a more Heideggerian register, with Béatrice Han, it can be said that music lights up our being-in-the-world through affect and mood, through *Stimmung*. But there is an essentially reflexive movement at work here: the *Stimmung* of music lights up the way in which being-in-the-world is always already understood affectively, that is, pre-reflectively and pre-cognitively. Yet, music calls for – demands even – cognition, reflection and judgement. Music is no simple lapse back into the pre-discursive, or the supposed authenticity of silence, it rather produces an endless effort of evaluation, cognition and judgement, what I have called 'adjectival experience'. Musical experience is both pre- and post-reflective.

But this is not the whole story. For it seems to me that there is, at least in relation to the figuring of sexual desire in music, not so much a recalling of *Dasein* to the pre-established harmony of *In-der-Welt-sein*, but rather a *deworlding* of the world through eros. In eros, the world somehow withdraws, and the lovers withdraw from the world into a mute or whispered privacy. Perhaps this is music's *Grund-Stimmung*, its basic or fundamental mood, where the destructive play of eros shows that all in the world *stimmt nicht*, where eros achieves a certain *de-mundanization,* a withdrawal from the world that allows a certain abyssal, pre-linguistic Thing to flicker and burn within us, something like the vibration of a guitar's sound-box after the chord has faded, like a ship sounding the sea for submarines . . . but at this point the similes and the approximations have to stop.

Notes

1. This is the text of a talk presented at the Momentum conference on contemporary art and the function of critique in Moss, Norway, May 1998. I would like to thank Tarjei Mandt Larsen, Birgit Bærøe, Lars Svendsen and Ståle Finke. Conversations with Sarat Maharaj in Norway were also clarifying and hugely entertaining. However, the idea behind this text is a little older, and goes back to some radio shows on contemporary British music that I gave in Germany on Frankfurt City-Radio X in March 1997. Many thanks to Felicia Herrschaft and to the responses from some listeners. In both cases, the lecture was accompanied by extensive musical excerpts, which can – sadly – only be imagined in written form.
2. See Chapters 8, 9 and 10 of my *Ethics – Politics – Subjectivity* (1999); and Lecture 1 of *Very Little . . . Almost Nothing* (1997).
3. All released by Island Records Ltd, London.
4. 'Everything Is Everything', from *The Miseducation of Lauren Hill*

(Ruffhouse, New York, 1998); 'When A Woman's Fed Up', 'Don't Put Me Out' and 'Suicide', from *R* (Jive, New York, 1998).
5. I owe these formulations to my colleague Béatrice Han, in her excellent essay 'Au delà de la métaphysique et de la subjectivité: musique et Stimmung' (1997, 519–39).

Works cited

Adorno, Theodor W. 'Trying to Understand *Endgame*', in *Notes to Literature*, trans. S. Weber Nicholsen. New York, 1991.

Carroll, Noel. *A Philosophy of Mass Art*. New York and Oxford, 1998.

Critchley, Simon. *Very Little . . . Almost Nothing*. London, 1997.

Critchley, Simon. *Ethics – Politics – Subjectivity*. London, 1999.

Critchley, Simon and Axel Honneth. 'Philosophy in Germany', *Radical Philosophy,* 89 (May/June 1998): 27–39.

Frith, Simon. *Performing Rites. Evaluating Popular Music*. Oxford, 1996.

Gilroy, Paul. *The Black Atlantic*. London, 1993.

Han, Béatrice. 'Au delà de la métaphysique et de la subjectivité: musique et Stimmung', *Les Etudes Philosophiques* (Oct.–Dec. 1997): 519–39.

Honneth, Axel. 'Pathologien des Sozialen. Tradition und Aktualiät der Sozialphilosophie', in *Pathologien des Sozialen. Die Aufgabe der Sozialphilosophie*. Frankfurt am Main, 1994, 9–69.

nation | *JOHN BRANNIGAN*

If nation-states were widely conceded to be 'new' and 'historical', the nations to which they give political expression always loom out of an immemorial past, and, still more important, glide into a limitless future.

It is the magic of nationalism to turn chance into destiny.

Benedict Anderson (1991, 11)

Theorizing the nation

The nation remains an obscure, treacherous concept in contemporary thought, despite the surge of interest in the study of nations and nationalism since the early 1980s. The prevailing tendency among social and political scientists, critical theorists, historiographers and anthropologists is to demythologize the nation as a romantic, idealist construct, to divest the nation and nationalism of their apparent 'magical' charms. Benedict Anderson (1991) emphasized the nation as an 'imagined' identity, behind which lay the materialist and historical causes of nationalist movements and beliefs. Ernest Gellner (1983) argued that nations and nationalism were entirely modern constructions, which had no foundation in pre-modern histories or ethnicities. Eric Hobsbawm (1990), Paul Brass (1991) and John Breuilly (1982) have tended to stress the nation as an instrument of ideological and political manipulation, manoeuvred into play by interested power elites in modern societies. Tom

Nairn (1977) and Michael Hechter (1975), influenced by Gellner's early work on the relationship between national formations and capitalism (1964), see the nation as the inevitable by-product of uneven capitalist development, and thus the outcome of thoroughly modern economic structures. In all of these conceptions of the nation, which focus attention particularly on the conditions for the emergence of nationalist movements, the predomination of materialist methods tends to result in a bias towards analysing the more 'objective' elements of the nation-state, political institutions and territories, rather than the more abstruse concepts of will, memory and energy which characterize the lived and imagined experience of the nation. In highlighting the fundamental modernity and political instrumentality of nationhood, they tend to dismiss as myth the claims to longevity or popular emotional appeal which surface continually in nationalist conceptions of the nation.

The materialist, anti-romantic emphasis in contemporary studies on demythologizing nationalism and the nation emerged for understandable reasons. Nazism in Germany had shown the horrific, logical outcomes of nineteenth-century romantic nationalism. The political cartography of postwar Europe reflected a withdrawal from the primacy of nationalist concerns, and was instead swept into the globalized politics of the 'cold war', in which nation-states acted routinely as the pawns of global power blocs. Nationalism was clearly on the agenda of postwar global politics, however, most visibly in the waves of colonized countries which fought or campaigned for independence.

But the results of such processes were sometimes violent, sometimes unstable regimes, which suggested to the western observer that nationalism was a regressive force, and that the emergent nation-states were the dying, imitative gasps of European modernity. As John Hall notes, in practice the troubled fate of nationalism in the postwar world meant that it was more or less neglected in the academy, until Gellner and others represented its re-emergence as the subject of widespread public concern (Hall, 1998, 1). Nationalism exists in the pages of such studies as a distinctly modern ideological formation, produced out of the particular conditions of industrialized, mass-conscious society, while 'nation' remains a more opaque myth, to which people demonstrably subscribe *en masse*, but for which there is no basis in economic, political, cultural or social fact *other* than that of the functional state apparatus. With the disintegration of the Eastern European power bloc since 1989, the unexpected return of ethnic conflict in the Balkans, and a perceived rising tide of nationalist violence in various parts of the globe, the ethno-symbolist arguments of John Armstrong (1982), John Hutchinson (1987) and Anthony D. Smith (1986; 1999) have seemed more prescient reminders of the mythic potency of ethnic and national identities. Even in these arguments, however, the burden of defining the nation has tended to be displaced onto other collective forms of identity, such as ethnicity or culture. Much contemporary critical engagement focuses not on what forms the nation takes, or how the nation functions, but on the conditions of its emergence into state institutions, so that the historiography of the nation-state or ethnic culture substitutes for theorization of the nation.

This is hardly surprising given the notorious complexity of the nation as a formation. According to different critical perceptions, and according to its various historical manifestations, the nation has been defined through language,

territory, cultural identity, race and ethnicity, and religion. It is consequently susceptible to being confused with various other collective forms of identity, which in turn makes it impossible in many cases to determine when, how and in what forms a nation can be said to have existed. Many of the debates prompted by Gellner's work focus on the criteria we might use to determine the moment at which a nation emerges into being, in terms both of identifying the several kinds of relationships which integrate large groups of people (historical, political, economic, cultural, linguistic, geographical, ethnic, religious) and of a less tangible marker of a collective consciousness of belonging. The difficulty of this process of analysis has been remarked upon by Hobsbawm, who observes that 'The "nation" as conceived by nationalism, can be recognized prospectively; the real "nation" can only be recognized *a posteriori*' (Hobsbawm, 1972, 387). The nation for Gellner, Hobsbawm and other materialists tends to be the product of nationalism and national movements, the effect of their labour, but what is obscured in this conception is what Hobsbawm calls 'the real nation', which must exist in some rough shape in the minds of those whom nationalist movements are attempting to mobilize. The nation has some imaginative and symbolic force, in other words, prior to the emergence of modern nationalist movements and agitations. (Otherwise, as Miroslav Hroch suggests, we might 'persuade the Irish, for example, that they were in fact Germans, or . . . win over the Hungarians to the notion that they were actually Chinese' (Hroch, cit. Hall, 1998, 99)). Nationality might therefore be a myth, might indeed be an imagined community, but it is not arbitrarily imagined. The materialist emphasis on tracing the emergence of nationalism neglects the larger issue of how and in what forms the nation emerges initially as an imaginative force. As Gellner rightly insists, 'nations are not inscribed into the nature of things' (Gellner, 1983, 49); they are not given, immemorial entities, but they are not simply the product of modern nationalism either. I want to suggest here some of the ways in which we might theorize the nation outside of nationalism, in which we might understand the *force* and *energy* of 'nation' as an imaginative construct. It is uncertain in contemporary studies whether the nation is given or acquired, ancient or modern, myth or reality, designed or accidental. We can be unsure of everything about the nation, I would argue, except its cultural, political, economic, social and, perhaps above all, psychological force.

The force of 'nation'

How might we conceptualize the compelling force of the nation, as an idea, as an imaginative construct, as the projection of a collective cultural will? If nationalism mobilizes the idea of the nation into a set of political and cultural institutions, what accounts for the prior existence of (albeit inert) notions of national identity? Our experience of the nation may be radically different from its conception prior to modern discourses and ideologies of political nationalism, and we might even argue, like Gellner and others, that there is no uninterrupted, unmediated connection between us and premodern conceptions of national identity, but this does not mean that there is no connection at all. The idea of the nation, once embodied in collective forms of representation (it exists, arguably, in no other fashion), outlives the historical conditions of its initiation because of what I will call, after Stephen Greenblatt's formulation of cultural representations (1988), the 'social energy' encoded in it. 'Energy', I would argue here, is a more appropriate paradigm to describe the longevity and appeal of the nation than 'identity':

But what is 'social energy'? The term implies something measurable, yet I cannot provide a convenient and reliable formula for isolating a single, stable quantum for examination. We identify energia *only indirectly, by its effects: it is manifested in the capacity of certain verbal, aural, and visual traces to produce, shape, and organize collective physical and mental experiences. Hence it is associated with repeatable forms of pleasure and interest, with the capacity to arouse disquiet, pain, fear, the beating of the heart, pity, laughter, tension, relief, wonder.*

(Greenblatt, 1988, 6)

Greenblatt argues that certain forms of representation are invested with sufficient imaginative and symbolic energy to 'enable them to survive at least some of the constant changes in social circumstance and cultural value that make ordinary utterances evanescent' (7). This is certainly the case with representations of national belonging, which not only survive historical change, but which also possess an extraordinary capacity to lay dormant for long periods of time, only to be reawakened in altered political circumstances. This is perhaps the most salient lesson of the resurgence of ethnic nationalism in the Balkans, in which long-forgotten, or sometimes never realized, forms of national identification have been re-energized. In such situations, the political primacy of nationalist sentiments triggers a chain of mythic and symbolic representations and images of a vaguely defined national identity, which have survived through history because of prior acts of cultural investment or attachment. Those acts may not even have taken 'national' shape in their original contexts, but they come, in altered contexts, to have profound significance in the emotional and symbolic topography of the nation.

'Nation' is produced first in 'verbal, aural and visual traces', as Greenblatt suggests of social and cultural identities in general. The conditions for this production, we might assume, must entail a proliferation of publicly accessible forms of representation, such as the theatre, and, more importantly, mass print culture. The newspaper, with its assumption of a shared time and shared culture, especially enables the production of a myth of mass community consciousness. This would bring us close to Anderson's argument that imagined national communities acquire material shape through the institutional forms of what he called 'print-capitalism' (1983). But this overstates the degree to which national identity, a consciousness of national belonging, is only made possible by these modern technologies of cultural production, for oral and manuscript cultures have proved surprisingly adept at forging their own senses of collective identity, their own senses of ethnic and national genealogy. It underestimates the degree to which the cultural productions of pre-print societies – say, for instance, *Beowulf*, Chaucer's tales, the *Táin Bó Cuailgne* or the *Vinland Sagas* – may find significant resonance in a shared consciousness of national history, language and culture. It is no accident that literary and cultural histories often serve to piggyback ideas of national identity and history, and even that we find the formative discipline of philology heavily involved in shaping ideas of a national tradition. These 'traces' of older expressions of cultural identity, of the lore and myth of large groupings of people, acquire sufficient imaginative force or social energy in their own societies to enable their transmission, albeit often in altered and rewritten forms, to the cultural nationalisms of the modern era. That such traces are consciously mobilized through mass media and mass educational institutions in the modern era does not mean that we should nullify the historical processes of transmission and empowerment through which

these cultural representations have survived; rather, it means that we need to take account of the various acts of investment and re-investment which have continued to make them visible and accessible throughout their histories.

To understand how cultural representations of ethnic and national identity continue to find expression and resonance in various different times and contexts, we need to conceptualize the process of energization and re-energization. How do myths of national identity acquire and continue to attract the acts of faith and attributions of belonging which are necessary to their perpetuation? How, in other words, does the nation become a self-perpetuating myth, with its own discursive and ideological force? What forms does the relationship between modern nationalism and premodern representations of ethnic and national identities take? And, is it the case, as Gellner, Anderson and others imply, that the nation as an idealist construct has found material expression in the institutions and cultural productions of the nation-state? Is the nation entirely concomitant with the nation-state? To answer these questions, we need to theorize the role of cultural memory in the construction of national identity, the structural forms of national belonging and the rhetorical tropes of discourses of nationhood.

The territorialization of memory

The word 'nation' owes its roots to notions of birth, home, beginnings. Its etymology does not tie it necessarily to collective identity or memory, but in cultural practice it has become routinely associated with a sense of belonging to a particular people in a particular territory. Nation, in the modern sense, is, above all else, a geographical space, a landscape physically and imaginatively inhabited by *its* people; and nationalist movements always entail staking a political claim to a particular piece of land. It is also a historical space, however, one which necessarily involves a sense of temporal continuity and genealogy. In Renan's conception of the nation in his renowned lecture, 'What is a nation?' (1882), the nation is defined as 'a soul, a spiritual principle', which contains two parts. The first is 'the possession in common of a rich legacy of memories'. The second is the articulation of consent, 'the clearly expressed desire to continue a common life. A nation's existence is, if you will pardon the metaphor, a daily plebiscite' (Renan, cit. Bhabha, 1990, 19). In Benedict Anderson's conception, in *Imagined Communities* (1983), however, it is this latter formulation of the daily consent of the nation which takes precedence over the sense of a shared history or past. Anderson argues that the temporal mode of the nation is best conceived as the 'empty, homogenous time' of the present, a concept he borrows from Benjamin's 'Theses on the Philosophy of History' (1950). Anderson distinguishes between a medieval sense of genealogy, in which the kin or nation could be identified by its 'simultaneity-along-time', and the modern sense of community, in which the nation is experienced as the temporal coincidence of people living in the same space (1991, 24). What this conception ignores, however, is the degree to which the geographical space of the nation is already heavily invested with cross-temporal meaning and representation. It erases what Anthony Smith calls 'the territorialization of memory' (1999, 151).

The sense of a common past, the 'rich legacy of memories', in Renan's terms, is communicated not just in narratives of national history, but is embedded in the landscape. The landscape, or, what becomes known as the national territory, is the repository of collective history. The symbolic sites of the national past – its borders, fields of con-flict, architectural treasures, historical monuments, sacred places and scenic resources – signify the long story of inhabitation, survival and achievement of the national community. The landscape thus appears to write the identity of the nation, just as it bears the inscribed ancestry of its inhabitants. The history of the changing landscape testifies to the history of the people who have lived on it. 'The land as a historically unique and poetic landscape', Smith writes, 'as a decisive influence over historic events and as the witness to ethnic survival and commemoration over the *longue durée*; these are all components of a general process of "territorialization of memory"' (Smith, 1999, 151). Two interrelated processes are at work here: the landscape functions as the memory of the nation, in the sense that it bears witness to the evolution of the national community; and, at the same time, memory is divided into territories, so that each national community has its own mnemonic rituals and structures, which differ in practice and form from other nations.

The primary characteristic of the relationship between the nation and landscape, however, is imaginary, or, more properly, attributive. The landscape tells stories of the nation only when the cultural cartography of the nation is superimposed on it, and yet, at the same time, there is no time when the landscape is not the product of cultural and political projections. The landscape functions to tell the story of the national community *because* it has been affected, shaped and produced by the cultural energy invested in it by the national(ist) projections of its inhabitants. Once the land becomes the grave, it is invested with emotional, psychological and mnemonic significance. It becomes the 'home' of a community. We cannot simply dismiss the idea of the national landscape as myth, for in a very visible sense landscape and nation are inseparable. The landscape is made habitable, readable and meaningful within the discursive constructions and representative practices of the national community. In this sense, the geographical and architectural structures of the landscape, like the political structures of the state, are effects of the energy invested in the idea of the nation. What we are dealing with in examining these effects, it might be argued, is the extent to which the nation is a psychogeographical space or phenomenon. Debord defined psychogeography as the study of 'the precise laws and specific effects of the geographical environment, consciously organized or not, on the emotions and behaviour of individuals' (1981, 7). The nation is imagined primarily as a territorial construct. It is the fiction of a delimited geographical and architectural space, which exercises itself forcefully and continually on the behaviour and attitudes of individuals who see themselves as living or belonging within that imaginative space. Moreover, it is the historical longevity of the emotional investment in the nation as an idea which lends it such symbolic and cultural force, and which imbues it with such powerful psychological effect in the present. It is when the nation can be reproduced as memory – through landscape, architecture or other cultural productions – that it acquires the power to shape and maintain our sense of belonging. The 'here and now' of Anderson's sense of nation, in other words, is premised upon (and only possible through) prior acts of memorializing the nation in its landscape.

The architectonics of the nation

The central difficulty in theorizing the nation lies in the constant elision of the interrelated concepts of nation, nationalism and nation-state. Too often in contemporary conceptions of the nation, the nation-state is imagined as the complete fulfilment of nationalist demands, which in turn are manifestations of a cultural or ethnic ideal of the nation. But this is to ignore the very different architectural structures of each of these formations. The nation-state is, put simply, an institutional mode of social organization, comprising, in Rogers Brubaker's words, 'a standardised scheme of social accounting, an interpretive frame for public discussion, a dense organisational grid, a set of boundary markers, a legitimate form for public and private identities' (Brubaker, cit. Hall, 1998, 287). In most cases, the initial legitimacy of a nation-state derives from the compelling force (cultural, political and perhaps also military) of nationalism. It is important not to treat nationalism simply as the means of creating political, state institutions, for some nationalisms may seek to express a sense of national belonging in cultural or social forms only, or may have very different political goals. Thus, nationalisms can survive the formation of the nation-state and take the form of critical, even subversive, opposition to the state's institutions. The nation-state is an institutional and territorial form of organization; it is a form of settlement, of consolidation. Nationalism, on the other hand, is structured according to the itinerant logic of aspiration, nostalgia and discontent.

The architectonics of the nation differs from either the nation-state or nationalism. The nation precedes and continues to exist outside of, or adjacent to, nationalism and the nation-state. It is the condition which brings about organizational and institutional forms of national belonging, but it is not to be confused with its bureaucratic manifestations. Nation is not an identity, but an attitude of collective relationship, of collective belonging. It is a commitment to what Derrida calls 'traces of writing, language, experience – which carry anamnesis beyond the mere reconstruction of a given heritage, beyond an available past' (1998, 60). It is the attribution of power, of force, to an idea of belonging and a myth of 'being-together', which may have no material existence. The nation is most visible when it takes institutional form, but it is, *in itself*, defined and organized around absence. To think through the idea of the nation outside of philosophies of nationalism and the nation-state is to recognize that the nation has no discernible origins, no essence, no destiny or end-point. It is mutable, contingent; we may argue that it takes on different forms at different times or in different contexts – through notions of ethnicity, language, culture, regionalism and so on – but these are the multiple faces of national belonging, the signs of its constant fluctuation and reinvention.

Nation follows the logic of connection, not being. It is the relation between individuals who assign to it the function of expressing the collective being. In this sense, it is a theological construct, akin to the ascription of the face and name of 'God' to the fiction of creation and omnipotence. Nation is the face and name we give to the fiction of a shared past and sense of belonging. To attribute power to the idea of the nation is, thus, an act of prosopopoeia, of giving a face or voice to the absent, as Anderson's concept of the imagined community implies. It is a relationship with the absent dead and the unfamiliar living, with whom we believe we are intimately connected, a relationship to which we choose to give expression in the concept of nation. These absent others are *our* dead, *our* people, related to us through the attributed energy of the nation, whom we commemorate and identify with through our continued allegiance to the idea of nation. Such communion involves a particular sense of ethical responsibility, to recover the memory of the dead, to share in the burden of caring for and supporting the living, which takes on a variety of institutional forms (e.g. national libraries and galleries, commemoration ceremonies, the welfare state).

Nationality is not inherited, not innate, so much as it is inculcated, passed on and energized through both formal and informal processes of education and acculturation. It is acquired as the result of the propagated awareness of traditionality, of a relationship of indebtedness and communion with the dead, which continues to exercise and forge a relationship with the living. We experience 'nation', then, as a form of haunting, as the continual presence of a relationship with the absent and the dead. Like haunting, nation is a form of social and cultural figuration which serves to activate the traces of past memory and experience, of connection to otherness and absence. It gives expression to the desire for durable meaning, through the notion of historical and spatial interconnectedness. The spatial and temporal architectonics of the nation, I would suggest, owe something to the logic of spectrality. If nationalism and the nation-state are organized through teleological narratives of origin, destiny and progress, and are thoroughly historicist formations, the nation, in contrast, is structured around the temporal modes of recurrence and disappearance. It is the vehicle through which the dead are continually brought into relationship with the living, in which the past folds into the community of the present. For Homi Bhabha, this means that the time of the nation is radically disruptive of the linear, monologic narratives of nationalism, for the slippage between temporal continuity and cultural mutation produces the possibility that residual forms of national identity, or minority discourses within the nation, may return to haunt its present formation: 'How does one encounter the past as an anteriority that continually introduces an otherness or alterity within the present? How does one then narrate the present as a form of contemporaneity that is always belated?' (Bhabha, 1990, 308). The disruptive time of the nation indicates to Bhabha its ambivalent formation, its constant divergence from the logic of nationalism and the state. The temporal discontinuity between nation and its institutional forms, in other words, has the potential to reintroduce the nation as a critical, antagonistic practice, to return to the nation-state the memory of its repressions and exclusions.

To think the logic of nation outside of its institutional forms, outside of the specific practices and interdicts of nationalism, is to encounter the impossible dream of community, of a virtual coming-together, which is emphatically not the mythic 'common being' of nationalism. It is the dream of connection, of community, of losing identity and entering a relation with otherness, difference and limits. The nation is, as Julia Kristeva argues, the *'symbolic denominator*, defined as the cultural and religious memory forged by the interweaving of history and geography' (Kristeva, 1986, 188), which oscillates between *'identity* constituted by historical sedimentation' and *'loss of identity*, which is produced when the relational logic of the nation causes it to disappear under the sign of other identities. The nation is at once a mode of presence and absence, continuity and discontinuity, longevity and instantaneity, visibility and invisibility, community and dissolution. It is perpetually imminent, yet constantly mourned.

The Energy paradigm

The nation is constantly represented in contemporary society as a threatened form of community. It is either too weak to check the reckless tendencies of global capitalism (Habermas, 2001), and therefore in need of reconfiguration or realignment into power blocs. Or, as Partha Chatterjee argues, it is depicted as the 'dark, elemental, unpredictable force of primordial nature threatening the orderly calm of civilized life' (Chatterjee, cit. Balakrishnan, 1996, 215). In Habermas' account of the contemporary predicament of

global politics, the nation is effectively redundant, since it privileged an economic sovereignty which has since been overtaken by global markets and systems of communication, while, for Chatterjee, the nation functions ambivalently in western discourse as its return from colonial and marginal regions in the form of violent nationalism represents the dark side of the western construction of popular democratic sovereignty. Yet, despite the widespread notion that we live in a postnational era, the nation-state continues to be the most powerful and pervasive form of political organization, and nationalism continues to exercise its presence in various forms throughout the globe. The nation as an idea, in other words, persists in generating political and cultural effects, and remains a potent representation of the desire for community and historical memory. This, my argument goes, is the consequence of the energy invested in 'nation' as a force of collective belonging. Even, and perhaps especially, in the postnational constellation, the nation as a form of social and cultural energy will continue to mobilize notions of historical and cultural belonging and serve to counterbalance the triumphant reign of multinational capitalism. 'Nation' embodies the aspiration to community, to connection, which may yet function to check the construction of the individual as the sole locus of sovereignty and power. Thus to think the nation outside of the structures of state government or nationalism is to begin to imagine the oppositional and aspirational forms which we might invent in its name in response to the pressures of 'globalization'. This is not to turn to the illusory comforts of retreating inside the shell of national sovereignty, but to reimagine the nation as a desire for historical and cultural connectedness. In such a revisioning, the nation might regain the idealist sense of ethical responsibility to others, and shared historical and cultural memory, which it has occasionally, fleetingly, promised.

Works cited

Anderson, Benedict. *Imagined Communities: Reflections on the Origin and Spread of Nationalism*. London, 1991.

Armstrong, John. *Nations Before Nationalism*. Chapel Hill, NC, 1982.

Benjamin, Walter. 'Theses on the Philosophy of History', in *Illuminations*, trans. Harry Zohn. London, 1992, 245–55.

Bhabha, Homi (ed.) *Nation and Narration*. London, 1990.

Brass, Paul. *Ethnicity and Nationalism*. London, 1991.

Breuilly, John. *Nationalism and the State*. Manchester, 1982.

Brubaker, Rogers. 'Myths and Misconceptions in the Study of Nationalism', in *The State of the Nation*, ed. John A. Hall. Cambridge, 1998, 272–306.

Chatterjee, Partha. 'Whose Imagined Community?' in *Mapping the Nation*, ed. Gopal Balakrishnan. London, 1996, 214–25.

Debord, Guy. 'Introduction to a Critique of Urban Geography', in *Situationist International Anthology*, ed. Ken Knabb. Berkeley, CA, 1981, 7–8.

Derrida, Jacques. *Monolingualism of the Other, Or, the Prosthesis of Origin*, trans. Patrick Mensah. Stanford, CA, 1998.

Gellner, Ernest. *Thought and Change*. London, 1964.

Gellner, Ernest. *Nations and Nationalism*. Oxford, 1983.

Greenblatt, Stephen. *Shakespearean Negotiations: The Circulation of Social Energy in Renaissance England*. Oxford, 1988.

Habermas, Jürgen. *The Postnational Constellation: Political Essays*, trans. Max Pensky. Cambridge, 2001.

Hall, John A. (ed.). *The State of the Nation: Ernest Gellner and the Theory of Nationalism*. Cambridge, 1998.

Hechter, Michael. *Internal Colonialism: the Celtic Fringe in British National Development*. London, 1975.

Hobsbawm, Eric. 'Some Reflections on Nationalism', in *Imagination and Precision in the Social Sciences*, eds T. J. Nossiter et al. London, 1972, 385–406.

Hobsbawm, Eric. *Nations and Nationalism since 1780*. Cambridge, 1990.

Hroch, Miroslav. 'Real and Constructed: the Nature of the Nation', in *The State of the Nation*, ed. John A. Hall. Cambridge, 1998, 91–106.

Hutchinson, John. *The Dynamics of Cultural Nationalism: The Gaelic Revival and the Creation of the Irish Nation State*. London, 1987.

Kristeva, Julia. 'Women's Time', in *The Kristeva Reader*, ed. Toril Moi. Oxford, 1986, 187–213.

Nairn, Tom. *The Break-up of Britain: Crisis and Neo-Nationalism*, Rev. edn. London, 1981.

Renan, Ernest. 'What is a Nation?' in *Nation and Narration*, ed. Homi Bhabha. London, 1990, 8–22.

Smith, Anthony D. *The Ethnic Origins of Nations*. Oxford, 1986.

Smith, Anthony D. *Myths and Memories of the Nation*. Oxford, 1999.

origins

ORIGINS: OF DECONSTRUCTION FOR EXAMPLE? OR, DECONSTRUCTION, THAT WHICH ARRIVES (IF IT ARRIVES)[1]

JULIAN WOLFREYS

A (metaphysical) thought, which begins by searching for origins or foundations and proceeds to a reconstruction in order, infallibly finds that things have not happened as they ought . . . The more naive believe in a paradise lost, the more cunning restore order by claiming to think, in order, the absence or loss of order. For Derrida, as for Heidegger . . . one is constructing things on an unquestioned value: presence.

Geoffrey Bennington

. . . (but what is more problematic than this concept of an original base for a fictional work?) . . .

J. Hillis Miller

Men can do nothing without the make-believe of a beginning. Even science, the strict measurer, is obliged to start with a make-believe unit, and must fix a point in the stars' unceasing journey when his sidereal clock shall pretend that time is set at Nought. His less accurate grandmother Poetry has always been understood to start in the middle; but on reflection it appears that her proceeding is not very different from his; since Science, too, reckons backwards as well as forwards, divides his unit into billions, and with his clock-finger at Nought really sets off in medias res. *No retrospect will take us to the true beginning.*

George Eliot

I

Thinking the very notion of an origin is impossibly fraught, untraceable to any roots we might assume it to have. It is not possible to speak of origins with any certainty in any example. Thus, this essay will explore the problem of the origin in relation to a specific example, which serves to expose the limits of any discourse of the origin: deconstruction. With this in mind, let me begin with a number of questions: what does this phrase, *origins of deconstruction*, imply, name or state? What do those who make such an impossible demand wish to identify, or otherwise believe they can locate? In whose interests is such a remark? What, in the articulation of this strange phrase, remains either silenced and unread or otherwise remains to be said? Does it give us to read a disabling and impossible temporality in the same place as the desire for an identity? Who is interested in pursuing 'the origins of deconstruction'? What haunts the structure of this expression? Does it amount to an idiom or axiom? Of what order are the motifs of this phrase? What 'concepts' does anyone believe to be mobilized in whatever this phrase stages or puts on stage? What is going on *between* 'origins' and 'deconstruction'?

— Everything takes place between. (Everything, that is, and all the rest.)

To hypothesize about or otherwise to inquire into the 'origins of deconstruction' is to repeat, whether intentionally or otherwise, the age-old metaphysical demand or desire for foundation, for Logos and, from such a location, to reiterate the desire for discernible order or progression as the historicity of that founding originary site or concept. Accompanying such an inquiry in search of an ideality, at once 'supratemporal and omnitemporal' (Derrida, 1989, 148) would be the assumption of or search for an absent presence or identity, which, in itself, is comprehended as complete, undifferentiated, homogeneous, full, simple and self-sufficient. Yet, as Michel Foucault has it, in a 'response' from 1968 to the Paris Epistemology Circle, such activity is always fraught from the very start by its own premises and practices because any such 'analysis of discourse [is always] . . . a quest for and repetition of an origin that escapes all determination of origin' (Foucault, 1998, 306). Still, one behaves as though there were both beginnings *and* a traceable continuity between those beginnings and the point at which any such inquiry begins with the injunction to turn back, as though one could offer, in Jacques Derrida's words, the reconstitution of 'the pure tradition of a primordial Logos toward a polar Telos' (Derrida, 1989, 149). Indeed, as Foucault in the article already cited points out, such behaviour is, if not a manifestation of institutional power, then the institution, the singular *inauguration*, of a power the purpose of which is to effect a kind of self-reflective, self-interested discursive maintenance of that very continuity. It is, in turn, the function of the metaphysical demand to delineate that continuity, thereby maintaining the very same continuity. Such a gesture 'function[s] to guarantee the infinite continuity of discourse and its secret presence to

itself in the action of an absence that is always one stage further back' (Foucault, 1998, 306). As Foucault's remarks make plain, the processes in question are, of course, not restricted either to the immediate or previous interests in a supposed 'history', 'historicity' or 'genealogy' of 'deconstruction' (which I place in quotation marks in order to suspend the possibility of a ready assumption of meaning, value or identity for this word). There is identified, therefore, the work of a certain procedural thinking, as is explicit in Foucault's comments, and as already addressed at the beginning of this paragraph; and, again, before that particular starting point, in the initial epigraph to this chapter (see Bennington, 1993, 15–16). I thus find myself retracing my steps in the very process of seeking to get underway.

As is well known, Jacques Derrida has in a number of places addressed the logic of a search such as the one just sketched, and, equally, its fruitlessness. It is tempting to suggest that this 'major concern of Derrida's analysis', as Arkady Plotnitsky sums it up (1993, 238), has been with Derrida from the beginning of his published works in 1962, with the 'Introduction to *The Origin of Geometry*'. 'The Time before First' offers another example (Derrida, 1981, 330–40). While the motif of 'origin' or 'origins' (and the plural, at least, initially, does nothing in any drastic manner to 'origin-singular', at least not unless we call into question the concept and thinking of 'origin') as starting points appear to promise a beginning in being called to our attention, such a gesture only '"begins" by following a certain vestige. *I.e.* a certain repetition or text' (Derrida, 1981, 330). In 'Qual Quelle' (Derrida, 1982, 273–306), the impossibility of assigning either origin or source is also considered, as Derrida responds to these motifs in relation to questions of identity and consciousness in the text of Paul Valéry. The source, we read, 'cannot be reassembled into its originary unity' (1982, 279). In addition, we learn it is the philosopher, as exemplary representative of the laws of the institutional search outlined above, who (according to Valéry), always in search of the origin, of an originary voice or presence, voice as the guarantee of presence, reproduces what Derrida calls the 'crisis of the origin' (Derrida, 1982, 291, a crisis acknowledged in Bennington's remarks, above) in the very act of writing on such a theme, whereby there is to be perceived '[d]iscontinuity, delay, heterogeneity, and alterity . . . a system of differential traces' (Derrida, 1982, 291) that get both the idea and the motif of the origin going. It is, we might propose, the very errancy of the motif as performative trope that haunts and motivates the very search or, more accurately, re-search, the always too-late recovery, for the always already *retrait* of origin.

The procedures by which the search for origin get underway and by which crisis comes to be reproduced take place repeatedly around the name of 'deconstruction' also. Whether within the limits of an institutionalized programme of analysis, proceeding by all the protocols that such a programme prescribes or, more generally, in posing the ontological question that concerns itself with determining 'deconstruction' and, specifically, 'origins of deconstruction', as though the terms and the concepts they appear to name are taken as understood; in such gestures, it must be admitted that nothing will have been comprehended concerning what has been said, for example, by Derrida and others with regard to the figure of 'deconstruction'. As Derrida has remarked,

> [d]econstruction, in the singular, is not 'inherently' anything at all . . . the logic of essence . . . is precisely what all deconstruction has from the start called into question . . . Deconstruction does not

> exist somewhere, pure, proper, self-identical, outside of its inscriptions in conflictual and differentiated contexts; it 'is' only what it does and what is done with it, there where it takes place . . .
> (Derrida, 1988a, 141; emphases added)

That 'deconstruction' only 'is' – without being anything as such – that it only has some momentary, provisional figuration (if this can be said) where and whenever it takes place, if it takes place as that which announces both singularity and iterability, suggests that it is impossible to speak of 'deconstruction' 'in the singular'. This is well known. This also suggests, furthermore, that because 'deconstruction' can only be discerned where 'it' takes place – without assuming an *ipseity* for deconstruction – and because every instance will necessarily be perceived as differing from every other in the various 'conflictual and differentiated contexts', 'deconstruction-in-the-singular' cannot be assigned origins other than the 'origin', if we can use this term in this fashion, of its taking place on every occasion. Moreover, that 'it' can only be reflected on 'in the singular' as an event both inappropriate to and unappropriable for any 'univocal definition' (1988a, 141) or totalizing determination signals that fact of 'its' instability, as announced in the destabilizing motif of différance, and, therefore, 'its' undecidability, the undecidability of any 'it' for deconstruction. Certainly, in the light of this, it would be an act of misrecognition or misappropriation to attempt to gather together the work of various deconstructions, if in such a gathering there took place the erasure of differences between them (regardless, for the moment of the 'system of differential traces' making up any 'deconstruction') in order to produce the 'univocal definition'.

Several contiguous remarks need to be made: (1) whatever goes by the name 'deconstruction' simultaneously *exceeds* and *lacks* any ontological or metaphysical determination; (2) 'deconstruction' is irreducible to any statement or formula beginning 'deconstruction is . . .' or 'deconstruction is not . . .' (i.e. any modality producing identification as stabilization, whether of an ontological or negative theological condition); (3) deconstruction (and here I will abandon the quotation marks), if it *is* anything, is that which necessarily *takes place* within any manifestation of structure *as* necessary to and yet radically incommensurable with or irreducible to that structure's identity or meaning, or indeed the horizon of any such possibility. As Derrida remarks of deconstruction, it is '*firstly* this destabilization on the move in, if one could speak thus, "the things themselves;" but it is not negative' (Derrida, 1988a, 147; emphasis added). It is thus provisionally figurable as the non-identity *of* and *within* yet also other than any identity, where 'non-identity' is comprehended not as negation or dialectical opposite, but as the sign of *différance*. Deconstruction thus provides a provisional 'name' for the trace of an alterity by which the perception of identity is made possible even as otherness remains invisible, unacknowledged. If it is anything at all, it does not in fact require or await a subject's cognition or consciousness (as Derrida remarks in 'Letter to a Japanese Friend', 1988b, 4) to determine what is called deconstruction by assigning an undifferentiated or universal meaning to, or identity for, a 'singular event', for want of a better phrase.

One of the problems, then, surrounding the misunderstanding and misappropriation of deconstruction, so-called, is ontological specifically, as well as being more generally metaphysical. If we turn to Martin Heidegger briefly, on the problem of determining Being, the procedures by which deconstruction as an institutionally domesticated term is made to operate in some quarters, or otherwise to dwell unproblematically in analytical or critical discourse, comes into focus. To recall a point just made, it appears as if deconstruction functions as a name, yet what it names is not this precarious trait but something determinate and delimitable; it is, therefore, a name used to identify a 'certain sameness in differentiation'. The phrase is Heidegger's, and he employs it to determine particular ontological approaches to the apprehension of Being: 'we understand being . . . in such a way that it expresses a certain sameness in differentiation, even though we are unable to grasp it' (Heidegger, 1995, 28). From this awareness, Heidegger concludes that, with regard to Being, 'there is no genus in itself' (1995, 29). The same can – or *must*, of necessity – of course, be said of deconstruction.[2] This is insufficient, however. The definition of genus must, necessarily, be raised. Heidegger asks (and answers) thus:

What is a genus? That which is universal and common to the many and can be differentiated and organized into species by the addition of specific differences. Genus is inherently related to species and thus to species-constituting differentiation.

(Heidegger, 1995, 29)

It is instructive to watch Heidegger construct an apparently circular logic here. In admitting to differentiation, he determines genus according to a range of species comprising differences that are relational rather than of the order of radical, heterogeneous difference. Being relational, such differences are also subordinate, appurtenances in the order of the self-same, in accordance, and of a piece, with the notion of genus. Thus the analysis of genus, proceeding by the acknowledgement of differentiation according to which the architectonic is delineated, makes a gesture by which it can fold back on itself, whereby 'species-constituting differentiation' is the connective fibre that allows us to know or assume genus. Such 'species-constituting differentiation' is only that belonging to the order of the same: that which constitutes the species and, from that gesture of folding back, to the implicitly circular reconstitution of the genus as an identity comprising so many genus-constituting species. In turn, the genus then becomes of the order of the self-same called the universal: '[t]he universal, comprehended and defined as species-enabling genus, is usually called "concept"' (Heidegger, 1995, 30). However,

> If being is not a genus, then it cannot be comprehended as a concept, nor can it be conceptualized . . . If the delimitation of a concept . . . is called definition, then this means that all definitional determinations of being must on principle fail.
>
> (Heidegger, 1995, 30)

Quite simply – though I do have the feeling that this is all far from being simple – all misunderstanding concerning deconstruction has little to do with any 'deconstruction'. Rather what takes place around the name deconstruction and the impossibility of assigning it an essence is the exposure of a crisis in thought that remains to be read fully. Such misrecognition arises from an ontological imperative, as it were, a will towards a particular manifestation, time and again, of a certain kind of seamless, undifferentiated conceptualization. Being is not available to ontological inquiry, it is not a category or entity like others, and can only be known, as Heidegger makes clear in *Being and Time*, through beings and through a recognition of the irreducible difference *between* beings, which in turn allows for the thinking of being to arise as an *après-coup*. Similarly, deconstruction. Irreducible to either concept or origin

(whether singular or multiple), deconstruction can only be known, if it can be known at all, as that which is already underway, already at work and within ontological inquiry and conceptualization as that which disorders, from the beginning, all such investigation.

In the face of these statements concerning this peculiar name 'deconstruction' and the potential itineraries for reading that they might be imagined as generating, it has to be said that there are no 'origins of deconstruction' as such.

Such a response must give the reader pause, however. For, even though this statement situates itself in relation to the question or demand concerning origins-of-deconstruction and it does so, moreover, by pointing out the ways in which such a question might be construed as being articulated within and by wholly conventional parameters, its articulation is made possible only by those same conventions. It is given according to the very programme identified as the limit of the question itself. Responses, therefore apparently in opposition, announce a role already assigned in the structure of identification described as speculative dialectics. Situated in opposition to and subordinated by the instituting violence of the demand, the assumption in this response is that the question (or demand) with reference to origins-of-deconstruction is to be read in an entirely predictable way, and that this is the only reading available for that which calls this and other essays into being, a title which is not posed as a question as such but, instead, is simply stated: origins of deconstruction. The banal conventionality of the retort is clearly apparent in its resistance to the assumptions seeming to motivate the phrase in question. Furthermore, the reply – and this clearly is a reply, even if no question or statement were present, given a reading of the conventions of its various remarks – is markedly unoriginal, in all senses of that word.

For not only does it say nothing that has not been said before, many times in a number of different ways, it presents nothing 'original', it has nothing of an 'origin' about it. It belongs to the predictable academic gesture – or genre, the response or remark or, rather, re-mark, this being the re-statement, the re-situation of more or less established, if not canonical, positions or locations within some manifestation of that dialectical structure, repeated again and again, without the adequate or necessary consideration of the concepts, motifs, tropes or terms herein employed.

– It seems we're caught in the middle, without being able to locate where we are. So, let's begin again.

II

Supposing the impossible. This is what is called for in the issuing of a request or command to write on 'the origins of deconstruction': a speculation on the possibility of the impossible, specifically in the guise of mapping or determining so-called 'origins'. At the same time what is required in at least one reading of the injunction that causes this essay to be written is a gradual delimitation of the proper, of what is or might be proper allegedly to so-called deconstruction 'in the humanities', 'in the university, today', 'in the history of western thought'. What is demanded in effect is a response involving the work of cartography. It is necessary to recognize though that such labour would have to proceed in the face of the unmappable, as though the inscription of every topographical co-ordinate invoked or implied countless others, in a constellation that, far from being exhaustible, would moreover enervate in the face of its own generative powers. Before – such a fantasy! – the location of any origin as such there would take place inevitably and inesca-

pably multiplicity and multiplication, a fraying even as one seeks to tie together loose ends. One has, therefore, to turn back, to define the starting place of this chapter not as a starting point at all, but instead as a necessary response, a reaction, to the impossible injunction and the impossibility that the injunction addresses and comes to proliferate. Doubtless, there is more to say about this imaginary scenario.

The impossible attempt to consider the concept of origins, the origin, the very idea of an origin or origins *for* or *of* the notion of the origin (*an* origin, *some* origin) or, in fact, considering origins in all their impossibility, clearly becomes even more impossible when the question concerning the location of origins is linked to this strange word, deconstruction. It appears then that I am asked to think with supposition and with speculation, supposing for the moment supposition or speculation to be modalities of thinking rather than the suspension of thought narrowly conceived in favour of some process of projection or conception, and asking for some impossible answer. The answer is impossible, strictly speaking, because the very idea of an answer implicitly assumes a moment of finality. There is implicit, often all the more marked for being so tacit, in the idea of an answer the assumption of speculation, projection and conception as modalities of thought that are perhaps related to but not wholly consonant with the rigorous thinking of a concept. There is furthermore in the assumption of the speculative project the idea that its problems can come to rest so that, teleologically or hermeneutically, where one ends is the origin itself, unfolded and refolded onto itself, a supplementary doubling of what had been there all along. As though the end were the beginning, as though destination were origin. The logic of circularity and the circularity of logic here inscribed are clearly haunted. And what haunts the effect of closing the circle is this phantom or phantasm of the origin, an origin, from the very elusiveness of which one must start all over again, fulfilling the promise of that Foucauldian assessment to which I had earlier alluded. What disturbs therefore, to return to where I began, is a barely submerged desire, all the more compulsive for being so caught up with the impossible and masquerading as some institutionally authorized archaeological or archival retrospect. Believing one can begin at all reveals in any such inaugural gesture the call of the institution, and the subjection of subjection interpellated by that call. Assuming I can assume any such question automatically leaves me with the impossible task, even or especially if I believe I can engage in a demystification of the premises by which such a call gets underway.

The very idea of the origin is thus that which arises inevitably and the search for the origin or origins belongs to a question or family of questions impossible to answer – *what if? What if* there were origins *for* deconstruction, *what if* there were an origin or origins *of* deconstruction? This is the phantasm of the starting point, the illusion of a beginning, and, it has to be added, *a beginning all over again*. Such a start, such an 'origin', begins and can only begin then as a response to a response.[3] Such circularity concerning origin is observed, once again, by Heidegger, in 'The Origin of the Work of Art' (Heidegger, 1971, 15–89). At the very beginning of the essay, Heidegger, stating that the 'question concerning the origin of the work of art asks about the source of its nature', offers the predictable answer – 'the usual view' – to that question: the artist (Heidegger, 1971, 17). Immediately after, however, the question and answer are folded back on themselves, as Heidegger continues by pointing out that the determination of the artist as artist only arises as a result of the work: 'The artist is the origin of the work. The work is the origin of the artist' (Heidegger, 1971, 17). Thus, 'origin here means that

from and by which something is what it is and as it is' (Heidegger, 1971, 17). On this understanding, no absolute origin is either possible or conceivable, given the enfolding and regenerative reciprocity of the structural schema proposed by Heidegger; a schema, I would add, which propels itself in a double act: that of a doubling of any singular locatable place of origin outside or before any event, and also a dismantling, not only of the traditional conceptualization of origin, but also of the stabilizing separatism of the binary calculation: artist/work. Interestingly, Heidegger's gesture also disturbs the temporal priority on which any notion of origin is founded. More than this, however, there is in Heidegger's instituting complication a performative element. Clearly displacing itself as a response to a question arriving from some other place, Heidegger's beginning, in Dennis J. Schmidt's words, 'must not be taken as an excuse for an awkward or misfired beginning to the text but as a comment on the character of the beginning as such' (Schmidt, 1988, 102).[4] However, I would argue for risking a stronger reading than Schmidt's: as just stated, Heidegger's gambit works so startlingly precisely because he does not merely *comment on* his subject, as would the philosopher on the source, issuing what he or she believes to be a constative statement. Rather, the performative dimension has to be insisted on here. It is precisely this performativity which destabilizes logical calculation from within, radicalizing the thinking of origin from the start. And yet, of course, it is not so simple to decide on whether Heidegger's argument or the way in which he states it are simply *either* performative *or* constative. For, similar to the suspensive operation at work in Heidegger's scandalous assertions concerning a disseminative reciprocity between artist and work (or work and artist), so too, before any determination, his own discourse materially suspends the possibility of identification through its redoublings and divisions, especially in the first page, but also, arguably, throughout the entire essay. As J. Hillis Miller remarks apropos of this suspension between the constative and performative, '[t]he tension between the two functions means that the performative aspect of the text makes it produce deceptive, illusory knowledge, or the illusion of knowledge' (Miller, 2001, 153).

III

But this is merely an illustration and a detour. If I attempt to imagine an origin or more than one origin, or even no more origins either for or of deconstruction, deconstructions, my response is then not a beginning as such (but this is already announced and is hardly original). I find myself entering into or, perhaps more accurately, locating myself within and in relation to a self-reflexive circularity which disrupts the certainty of the metaphysical demand, while engaging with the possibility that such an encircling 'opens up its own conditions'. Reflexive engagement clearly identifies itself as a response to the call, the demand, the injunction to speculate. In turn, such an injunction arrives or arises, coming to be seen as not, itself, an instituting formulation but, rather, a response within itself, to the other in itself, to that speculative *what if*. Speculation hides itself and yet returns in, thereby exceeding the violence and logic (the violent logic) of institution and demand. This is where we are.

Imagine though for the moment the impossible, imagine that this is the place to begin: that it is possible to start to speak of 'origins of deconstruction'. One might start, cautiously and conventionally enough, with a quotation.

Necessarily, since it [deconstruction] is neither a philosophy, nor a doctrine, nor a knowledge, nor a method, nor a discipline, not even a determinate concept, only what happens if it happens [ce qui arrive si ça arrive].

(Derrida, 2000, 288)

It is perhaps noticeable that the bracketed French – and it seems that, if there is a history or even an origin, or origins of deconstruction, one is always enjoined, silently, invisibly or otherwise, to bracket the French, to demarcate some boundary, some location or idiom – appears in other words in my title. As one beginning, I have let go the more normative, more conventional translation (what happens if it happens) in the title, in order to emphasize arrival, a certain unexpected, yet inevitable phantom insistence, a certain idiomatic interruption or eruption of arrival, as though arrival, and, specifically, the *arrival of an origin*, never happened only once, for the first time, but could be spectralized, taking place over and over again, and in a manner moreover irreducible to, uncontrollable by, any taxonomy or conceptualization of arrival. Which, of course, takes place already in the name of deconstruction. [A parenthesis: it is not going too far perhaps to suggest another translation, one redolent, inadvertently or not, with what might be called a 'biblical' resonance: that which comes to pass (if it comes to pass). Such a phrase appears to acknowledge, to comment on, a simple event – *and it came to pass*. However, it might more appropriately be considered a performative statement the rhythms of which are pertinent to the present consideration. The articulation or inscription of the line, whether in the present, past or infinitive forms – it comes to pass, it came to pass, to come to pass – delineates a movement, the first part of which, coming toward a location or point of reference (such as the subject) and arriving from a future, the second part, departing from the point of reference, traversing it, and moving into a past. Writing or speaking this phrase traces materially – performs – that on which it is the purpose of the phrase to comment. Such a motion in the materiality of the letter marks and is marked by a disorientation of spatial and temporal assurances, announcing as it does a 'destabilization on the move'.] The spectral figure of an unanticipatable arrival, the ghostly arrival of such a figure, might be said to figure – possibility of the impossible – origins-of-deconstruction. That which cannot be anticipated concerning the arrival thereby speaks of the undecidability of deconstruction/s, if I can say this, and therefore, perhaps, of 'deconstruction's origins' (do deconstructions 'originate'? do deconstructions cause origins to arrive, to happen or to come to pass? are deconstructions original?) even as origin takes place, in the chance of deconstructions. How do we do justice to this?

In the face of the experience of the undecidable which the idea of the 'origin' names, it has to be recognized and stressed, again and again, that the very idea is enigmatic, *auto-occlusive* perhaps; all the more mystifying even, precisely because these names, *origin*, *origins*, are all too often deployed as though what was being named were blatant, all too obvious and self-evident, as though nothing could be clearer than the possibility of the origin. And also hieratic and encrypted. For the mere sign of an origin or origins blares the promise, the illusion of a secret. And it is in such illusory certainty, a rhetoric, if not a hegemony, of certainty,[5] that one encounters precisely the obscurity which is situated at the obscure heart of any notion of origin. Take the example and notion of tradition, as Foucault suggests:

it is intended to give a special temporal status to a group of phenomena that are both successive and identical (or at least similar); it makes it possible to rethink the dispersion of history in the form of

the same; it allows a reduction of the difference proper to every beginning, in order to pursue without discontinuity the endless search for origin . . . Then there is the notion of influence, which provides a support . . . which refers to an apparently causal process . . . [in which there is to be seen] the phenomena of resemblance and repetition . . . There are the notions of development and evolution: they make it possible to . . . link [events] to one and the same organizing principle . . . to discover already at work in each beginning, a principle of coherence and the outline of a future unity, to master time through a perpetually reversible relation between an origin and a term that are never given, but which are always at work.

(Foucault, 1972, 22; emphases added)

Tradition both authorizes and is authorized by origin. The one-and-only time of origin is what tradition (or racial purity, or the destiny of a nation) both needs and by which it keeps up the game. Influence, identity, succession, causality, resemblance, repetition, development, evolution: in short, the delineation of that which amounts to a genetic purity. This is the secret, a secret out in the open, promised by the idea of origin and yet also hidden by that very idea, which obscurity justifies the inquiry into origin, and which deconstruction arrives, if it arrives at all, to interrupt.

IV

So, to return to the question of what happens, what arrives, what comes to pass, what takes place, what passes (if it passes), what arrives (if it arrives at all) *and also* what also cannot pass or come to pass, before which I am immobilized, in the face of the impossible, impossibility itself: the demand, the call of the title, this impossible title, *origins of deconstruction*. This title arrived, as such things often do these days, in e-mail, a demand and a request, an invitation from a friend, at one and the same time, then, both friendly *and* threatening. Its arrival recalled a question concerning arrival, concerning that strange figure of the *arrivant*, asked by Derrida: 'What is the *arrivant* that makes the event arrive?' (Derrida, 1993, 33) Derrida continues:

> *The new* arrivant, *this word can, indeed, mean the neutrality of* that which *arrives, but also the singularity of* who *arrives, he or she who comes, coming to be where s/he was not expected, where one was awaiting him or her without waiting for him or her, without expecting it* [s'y attendre], *without knowing what or whom to expect, what or whom I am waiting for – such is hospitality itself, hospitality toward the event.*
>
> (1993, 33)

Neutrality *and* singularity. Bearing this in mind – and returning to the first citation from Derrida, above, the one appearing, it should be noted, after the title (both titles, that which arrived via e-mail, unexpectedly, and my own) and yet being one source, though not the only origin, for my title – it is no doubt possible, however reckless, to suggest different titles for this chapter, if only so as to disrupt any sense of priority or origin: *deconstruction, that which arrives or happens (if it arrives or happens at all)*; or *deconstruction, who arrives (if s/he arrives) or happens (if she or he happens at all)*. Whatever, or whoever, arrives unexpectedly might just cause an event to happen perhaps; this is the hope; and, in anticipation of this originating arrival, I must wait without expectation concerning the form such

an arrival might take; what is wholly, radically, original or, perhaps, ab-original here is that which takes place *between* the *arrivant* and the subject. It is here, if anywhere, smallest of chances, that deconstructions, origins, will, therefore, have occurred. *Origins-of-deconstruction coming to pass in between.*

A note of caution. Everything takes place in 'between' (between beings, for example, or between the artist and the work of art). Yet, in the words of Jean-Luc Nancy, '[t]his "between", as its name suggests, has neither a consistency nor continuity of its own. It does not lead from one to the other; it constitutes no connective tissue . . . From one singular to another, there is contiguity but not continuity' (Nancy, 2000, 10). It therefore follows that one cannot speak even of an origin (as such) *of* or *for* whatever chances to present itself *in* or *as* the figure of *between*, let alone *of* or *for* whatever one thinks one means when one speaks of *deconstruction*. *Between*, therefore, a motif without motive, the name of in-difference, intimate proximity *and* unbridgeable spacing – deconstruction, in other words, at the origin (one is tempted to say) of any search for origins or foundations, as Geoffrey Bennington has it (1993, 15).

V

This is still to be too precipitate, however. Forestalling the illusion either of a beginning or any supposedly 'original' starting point as the beginnings of a tracing, consider the following consideration of Nancy's on the subject of origins:

> *. . . meaning can only be right at [à même] existence . . . It is the indefinite plurality of origins and*

their coexistence . . . we do not gain access to the origin: access is refused by the origin's concealing itself in its multiplicity . . . The alterity of the other is its being-origin. Conversely, the originarity of the origin is its being-other, but it is a being-other than *every being* for *and in crossing through [à travers] all being. Thus, the originarity of the origin is not a property that would distinguish a being from all others, because this being would then have to be something other than itself in order to have its origin in its own turn . . . the being-other of the origin is not the alterity of an 'other-than-the-world'. It is not a question of an Other . . . than* the world; *it is a question of the alterity or alteration of* the world.

(2000, 10–11)

Alterity, inaccessibility. There is inscribed here a response to, as well as in recognition of, the priority and primordiality of alterities, heterogeneous and illimitable, irreducible to a negative theology governing or desiring to determine finally any conceptualization of an other. Such a determination would still imply an origin or source 'beyond' or 'other than', as the extract makes clear. If origin is an other, to place for the moment Stéphane Mallarmé's tongue in Jean-Luc Nancy's mouth, this is to comprehend origin radically as *différance* rather than source. Origin, therefore, nowhere as such, has always already returned not as itself but as a trace within any being as the non-identity of beings irreducible to any dialectical stability. There is, then, never the possibility either of an hypostasized Origin, or even multiple Origins, if by such a figure (and 'Origins' still is the name of figure-singular, if it is understood as indicating so many 'species' belonging to a genus aspiring to the universal concept of 'Origin') there is implied merely the polyva-

lent possibility of several sources for deconstruction. Rather, it is necessary to stress, in order to conclude this 'make-believe of a beginning', and following Nancy, that the idea of origin is incorrectly assumed if by this notion one believes one can identify or locate that to which deconstruction can be traced and yet which is separable from deconstruction, and thereby delimitable. At the same time, and to turn back to the beginning of this essay, it is also incorrect to assume that 'deconstruction' is a given, that the meaning of this word has been resolved epistemologically, which the presumption of origins would appear to announce. Indeed, one might risk the proposal that, if origin *is* an other, is every other and wholly other, and is only perceived through the trace of *différance as* that irreducible disjunction and 'what makes every identity at once itself and different from itself' (Royle, 2000, 11), it is also possibly the case that deconstruction*s*, having to do with traces, 'with the logic of the "nonpresent remainder"', as Nicholas Royle puts it (2000, 7), are the crossings-through of that sign of the being-other of origin, an origin, origins. Or, to put this in another's words, in other words, 'what emerges is in fact the very "origin" of [deconstructions], the material trace or the material inscription that would be the condition of possibility and the condition of impossibility' of *origins* (Warminski, 2001, 28). Comprehending the materiality and singularity of an inscription or articulation always already taking place, and recognizable only after the event as having taken place in every singular instance, we are forced to acknowledge also the impossibility of determining an essence or being. Any act of naming deconstruction must affirm this differentiation-at-the-origin, as it were, of deconstructions. In conclusion, we might illustrate this through indirection and detour, by citing Philippe Lacoue-Labarthe's anti-essentialist analysis of the relation between language, alterity and being:

223

*Existence . . . [is] language, or more precisely, the faculty of language, which, in the being (*étant*) that is man, does not come under the heading of being – so that man 'is' not only the being that he is. The faculty of language, the ability to name, is in reality intimacy itself, the intimate differentiation of the being . . . For this reason, language is not, in its essence, purely and simply being (*étant*); yet there is language, or language exists . . . Language is the other in man; it constitutes him as man* himself. *Man does not* have *language . . . man is constituted beginning with language . . . Thus language can be considered man's origin.*

(1999, 96)

No absolute originary articulation therefore, but radical origination in every utterance. Every time there is language, every time difference and deconstruction take place, every act originates, originating itself as other than itself, and this can and does only take place, repeatedly, *between*.

Notes

1. This essay had its 'origins' as a paper presented at the annual conference of the IAPL (International Association of Philosophy and Literature), at one of two panels entitled 'Origins of Deconstruction', terms which this chapter, clearly, takes as its title.
2. An obvious, though instructive, difference being that Being has been subject to inquiry, speculation and attempted definition for far longer than deconstruction. What is instructive, however, is that approaches to the absolute or universal determination of deconstruction are 'contaminated' by the same logic, the logic which makes the demand 'What is . . . ?', and which also, sooner or later, desires to pursue the matter of origins.
3. Arguably, the relentless structure I am describing can be seen in the

situation of Foucault's comments cited at the beginning of this essay, which belong to a response to a demand on the part of the Paris Epistemology Circle, a demand to define 'the critical propositions on which the possibility of his theory and the implications of his method are *founded*' (1998, 297; emphasis added), coming as the Circle's response to *Madness and Civilization*, *Birth of the Clinic* and *The Order of Things*. The words quoted here are those of the Circle, not Foucault's interpretation.

4. Schmidt's reading continues in the same passage by pointing out how 'Heidegger opposes the figure of circularity to the traditional metaphysical admiration for . . . syllogistic straight lines'. Such straight lines, such unbroken linearity in general are, doubtless, those that would trace the continuity between a discourse, subject or concept, and its origin.

5. Not to sound too certain about this, but it is perhaps a feature of many 'discussions' of or, more accurately, polemics concerning origins (let us say, for example, those on the part of particular fundamentalist Christian constituencies) that certainty is hegemonic inasmuch as there is no place available for the possibility of discussion, debate, challenge, uncertainty, scepticism, speculation or, indeed, any form of discourse, dialectical or otherwise, which would be able, according to the laws and rules of the discourse on origin, to question or call into question any article of faith. Nothing perhaps is more certain about a discourse which asserts certainty when nothing could be less certain than origin.

Works cited

Bennington, Geoffrey. 'Derridabase', in Geoffrey Bennington and Jacques Derrida, *Jacques Derrida*, trans. Geoffrey Bennington. Chicago, IL, 1993, 3–310.

Derrida, Jacques. *Dissemination*, trans. Barbara Johnson. Chicago, IL, 1981.

Derrida, Jacques. 'Qual Quelle', in Jacques Derrida, *Margins of Philosophy*, trans. Alan Bass. London, 1982, 273–306.

Derrida, Jacques. 'Afterword: Toward an Ethic of Discussion', trans. Samuel Weber, in Jacques Derrida, *Limited Inc.*, trans. Samuel Weber and Jeffrey Mehlman. Evanston, IL, 1988a, 111–54.

Derrida, Jacques. 'Letter to a Japanese Friend', trans. David Wood and Andrew Benjamin, in *Derrida and Différance*, eds David Wood and Robert Bernasconi. Evanston, IL, 1988b, 1–5.

Derrida, Jacques. *Edmund Husserl's Origin of Geometry: An Introduction*, trans. with preface and afterword John P. Leavey, Jr. Lincoln, NE, 1989.

Derrida, Jacques. '*Finis*', in Jacques Derrida, *Aporias*, trans. Thomas Dutoit. Stanford, CA, 1993, 1–42.

Derrida, Jacques. 'Et Cetera . . . (and so on, und so weiter, and so forth, et ainsi de suite, und so überall, etc.)', trans. Geoffrey Bennington, in *Deconstructions: A User's Guide*, ed. Nicholas Royle. Basingstoke, 2000, 282–305.

Foucault, Michel. *The Archaeology of Knowledge*, trans. A. M. Sheridan Smith. London, 1972.

Foucault, Michel. 'On the Archaeology of the Sciences: Response to the Epistemology Circle', in Michel Foucault, *Aesthetics, Method, and Epistemology: Essential Works of Michel Foucault 1954–1984 Volume Two*, ed. James D. Faubion, trans. Robert Hurley et al. New York, 1998, 297–334.

Heidegger, Martin. 'The Origin of the Work of Art', in Martin Heidegger, *Poetry, Language, Thought*, trans. and intro. Albert Hofstadter. New York, 1971, 15–89.

Heidegger, Martin. *Aristotle's Metaphysics Θ 1–3: On the Essence and Actuality of Force*, 2nd edn, trans. Walter Brogan and Peter Warnek. Bloomington, IN, 1995.

Lacoue-Labarthe, Philippe. *Poetry as Experience*, trans. Andrea Tarnowski. Stanford, CA, 1999.

Miller, J. Hillis. *Speech Acts in Literature*. Stanford, CA, 2001.

Nancy, Jean-Luc. *Being Singular Plural*, trans. Richard D. Richardson and Anne E. O'Byrne. Stanford, CA, 2000.

Plotnitsky, Arkady. *In the Shadow of Hegel: Complimentarity, History, and the Unconscious*. Gainesville, FL, 1993.

Royle, Nicholas. 'What is Deconstruction', in *Deconstructions: A User's Guide*, ed. Nicholas Royle. Basingstoke, 2000, 1–13.

Schmidt, Dennis J. *The Ubiquity of the Finite: Hegel, Heidegger, and the Entitlements of Philosophy*. Cambridge, MA, 1988.

Warminski, Andrzej. '"As the Poets Do It": On the Material Sublime', in *Material Events*, eds Tom Cohen, Barbara Cohen, J. Hillis Miller and Andrzej Warminski. Minneapolis, MN, 2001, 3–31.

poetics | *GEOFF WARD*

The term 'poetics' is one that has been stolen by theory. In seeking to return the term to poetry, to particular poets and therefore to a poetomachia, this essay is not a rebuttal of theory but rather a reminder that the practice of writing poems does itself and of necessity signal a theoretical dimension, a poetics, and one whose current condition is at times livelier than the narcotized offerings of official culture would have us believe. Crucial growth-points for theory, such as the 1980s debates surrounding postmodernism, were both powered and deformed by a hangover from marxism that chose always to focus on the point of cultural consumption rather than the point of artistic production. The causes of this lopsided approach go back to a nervousness about literary creativity as being corrupted by discredited, romantic notions of 'genius', or other forms of self-glorifying solipsism such as the bohemian, which appeared skewed towards male privilege and away from social commitment. This suspicion gained unexpected support from certain attempts by poets themselves to depress the aims and ambitions of poetry; the insistence on provincialism, conservatism and brevity by Philip Larkin and others who trumpet the virtues of a regional cul-de-sac is a case in point. Since the years of modernist rupture, poetry has frequently been caught in a pincer movement between forces of conservatism that detested its traditions of emotional largesse, permissiveness and fantastic artifice and a residual marxism which (apart from hating all those things as well) has bequeathed to recent theory its queasiness over subjectivity. The sub-

jective is supposedly a real zone of self-indulgence, plumping up bourgeois narcissism ready for another leeching by the consumer industries, and yet delusory, conjured into hallucinatory half-life by the voodoo of individualism. To the marxist tradition, all these tendencies in poetry have to be contained, dumbed down into a safe preference for the rousing ballad (and even so agile a theoretician as Terry Eagleton can still fall for this one). Alternatively poetry is chimerized as the always-as-yet-unwritten, one of those models of unalienated labour in whose pleasures we will bask without guilt once the struggle for everything else in this world has been won.

In the massiveness, the totalizing – as distinct from the undoubtedly totalitarian – ambitions of marxism lay its grandeur as well as its undoing. In our less grand times a different kind of conformity holds sway, and a neo-Lyotardian mistrust of metanarratives has itself become the new master-narrative, the art of carping. The combined effect of these forces on the assessment and discussion of poetry, particularly in the American university and its career-oriented conferences, has been to dismiss out of hand categories such as value or aesthetics in the rush to award poetry a certificate of approval on the basis of its author's membership of a particular ethnic or disenfranchised group, so as to avoid having to read, with all the risks that that entails. (I recall a remark by Leo Bersani to the effect that Humanities students suffer from a condition known as Fear of Poetry, forcibly induced in high school. He might have added that if those particular shots have worn off, the MLA Conference will be happy to arrange a lethal dose.) Comparable points are argued forcefully by Marjorie Perloff, a critic who, in the twenty years since she wrote the first book on Frank O'Hara, has not wavered in her support for avant-garde American poetics against the successive orthodoxies that have masked themselves as liberation movements. In a recent essay she contrasts the stultifying conformism of postmodernism's *fin de siècle* with the genuine, albeit imperilled vitality of that much-derided decade, the 1970s:

> In 1972 Art with a capital A still mattered and it
> mattered that Jasper Johns was 'better' than a
> second-generation abstract expressionist like
> Norman Bluhm. Merce Cunningham was judged to
> be more 'interesting' than Murray Feldman. And
> so on . . . Within a decade, a curious reversal had
> set in . . . (The) concept of difference, as it
> seemed in the 1970s, has now been replaced by a
> bland diversity that, as the poet Charles Bernstein
> observes in A Poetics, harks back 'to New Critical
> and liberal-democratic concepts of a common
> readership that often . . . have the effect of trans-
> forming unresolved ideological divisions and
> antagonisms into packaged tours of the local
> color of gender, race, sexuality, ethnicity, region,
> nation, class, even historical period: where each
> group or community or period is expected to come
> up with – or have appointed for them – represen-
> tative figures we can all know about'.
>
> (1999, 181, 183)

There will be more to say shortly about Charles Bernstein and the adversarial poetry and criticism with which he has opposed the packaging of what he terms elsewhere

America's edgy and inconsolable adjacencies of class, of origin, of loss. What interests me in Perloff's overview is not only its broaching of major issues of evaluation and aesthetics as they relate to recent history, but the role that the ideology of nationhood is shown to play in soothing 'divisions and antagonisms' into 'bland diversity':

> Indeed, despite the lipservice paid to multicultural-
> ism, one often has the sense that the only thing that
> matters in US culture . . . is US culture. True, that
> culture is divided up into dozens of marginalised,
> disempowered, and minority subsets: African-
> American, Chicana/o, Native-American, Asian-
> American, gay and lesbian, and so on. But the
> requisite for all these groups turns out to be US cit-
> izenship: the 'other', it seems, does not include the
> literatures of other nations or in other languages.
>
> (1999, 197–8)

While it is often possible to feel that transatlantic poetic relations generate a conversation, or at least (to revive a term used by Thom Gunn) establish a *détente*, such ease is borne out only for the Anglo-Saxon hegemony and via the major publishing houses of London and New York, Oxbridge and the Ivy League, commerce between Chicana and Gaelic poets being scant, at least at the time of writing. Moreover a crucial divergence between British and American literary culture is triggered by reference to particular ethnic or other sub-sets, so that, while for example the designation 'Scottish' can currently be read as carrying a threat to the United Kingdom, however unresolved and open to discussion, the designation 'African-American', however unresolved and (alas) closed to discussion, poses no ultimate threat to American powers of containment.

Questions of freedom and limit have been central to

modern American poetics, no more so than in the poetry of Frank O'Hara (1926–66), from whose *Collected Poems*, published in 1971, flow lines of descent to much of what holds the interest in current American practice. Like many of his generation, whose work was gathered first for wide attention in an important anthology, Donald Allen's *The New American Poetry* (Allen 1960), O'Hara was an experimental writer who detested career-conformists. However, one side-effect of the experimentalism, and one that shows a divergence between American and European attitudes to the nineteenth century, is shown by the subtle ways in which the new poetry worked not to bury but to praise and perpetuate the founding father, Walt Whitman. The Allen generation modernized Whitman's booming prophecies of union between the individual psyche and America en masse through their attention to the work of William Carlos Williams, whose more earthbound poetics centred on such dicta as 'No ideas but in things'. One of the resultant insights of O'Hara's poetry is that what an American stumbles over, negotiating the leaves of grass, may be not only material things but ideological, indeed fully internalized, perimeter fencing. The permission to a collective negative capability that the nation gives itself is counterbalanced by the ineluctable containment of misrule. This is one of the discoveries of 'In Memory of My Feelings' (1956), Frank O'Hara's most famous poem, in which a Whitmanic acceleration of successive, surrealistic and transnational identifications is slowed to a moment of mingled pathos and bitterness at America's failure to live up to its promises:

> Grace
> to be born and live as variously as possible. The
>   conception
> of the masque barely suggests the sordid
>   identifications.

> I am a Hittite in love with a horse. I don't know
>   what blood's
> in me I feel like an African prince I am a girl
>   walking downstairs
> in a red pleated dress with heels I am a champion
>   taking a fall
> I am a jockey with a sprained ass-hole I am the
>   light mist
>   in which a face appears
> and it is another face of blonde I am a baboon
>   eating a banana
> I am a dictator looking at his wife I am a doctor
>   eating a child
> and the child's mother smiling I am a Chinaman
>   climbing a mountain
> I am a child smelling his father's underwear I am
>   an Indian
> sleeping on a scalp
>   and my pony is stamping in the
>   birches,
> and I've just caught sight of the Nina, the Pinta
>   and the Santa Maria.
>   What land is this, so free?
>   (O' Hara, in Allen, 1971, 256)

The quasi-Whitmanian motto 'Grace / to be born and live as variously as possible' gains an inflection more particular to Frank O'Hara if we know not only that it would be chiselled on his gravestone but that the poem was dedicated to a friend, the painter Grace Hartigan. Such a touch of 'Personism', to adopt the term used by the poet in his mock-manifesto of that name, is characteristically intimate while avoiding the confessionalism developed by Robert Lowell and others that was coming to prominence at this time. The surrealism that animates other lines shows a European influence but is distinctively American in the particular kinds of loss it registers, as well as in its poetics. Indeed poetics and loss are intertwined, not only here but in modern poetry generally. If then we are to re-steal fire from the Prometheus of theory to give it back to the poetic Orpheus, that will entail following the orphic trail down into crepuscular zones of non-meaning and absence. The first of these opens its gates with the death of a poet.

William Bronk, American poet, died on 22 February 1999 at the age of 80. I am not going to dwell on his poetry as such, though it repays attention, and an exploration of its affinities with and departures from the kinds of work anthologized by Donald Allen would bring salient shading and detail to anyone's map of modern American poetry. What interests me in the present context is the obituary material, posted on the website of the *Electronic Poetry Journal* at Buffalo, a superb ongoing archive of the American avant-garde, and one in which Charles Bernstein is an important presence. The intention, I must insist, is not to bring out anything critical or curious, let alone macabre from this material, but simply to notice that the death of a poet is immediately a matter of poetics (among other things), and that those poetics are immediately bound up with tropes of loss; not simply of the expected kind, registering the world's loss of a writer, but loss as intrinsic to poetics in its self-assertion within the poetomachia.

The obituary material for William Bronk included a reminiscence by Robert Creeley, again a poet from the Don Allen generation and along with John Ashbery the most eminent practitioner the nation has currently to offer:

Although one saw him but rarely, there was a strong sense of bond between us two who had begun together back at the close of the 40s, in Cid Corman's Origin *. . . I recall those early poems had*

often a humor, neither droll nor necessarily relieving. It was a humor of situation, that one was in this world indeed, just so . . . Our first meeting was at a reading I'd had in New York, and he came up to introduce himself just after, but really to tell me with a look of real consternation, that he would never have imagined I'd read my poems as I did, stuttering, seeming almost in pain – why? I had no answer. He read his own thoughtfully, firmly, considering. When, a few years ago, he was unable to attend a festival we were both to be at, a tape of his reading was provided, and so I sat with others listening to that dependable, quiet voice speak through the lines of an age old human wondering. Why indeed, I thought – it was a good question . . . Finally, there was no one else quite like him, so large in his singleness, so separate yet enclosing. One will not see his like again.

(http://wings.buffalo.edu/epc/)

The generosity and perceptiveness of this obituary notice are entirely characteristic of Creeley. So is the judicious use of cliché, employed not at all in an automatic or unreflecting way, but precisely because reflection shows that the well-worn phrase is – as on other occasions the wildly original phrase is – the true. One will not see his like again. The main thrust of the reminiscence is towards the singular wholeness, the reliability and the unrepeatability, of Bronk's 'dependable, quiet voice'. One was in this world, just so, and being thrown into it, daily and without so much as a by your leave, the thing might then be neither to recoil nor to fight, but to attain a certain balance that would recur in the poetry's factors of statement, the author's physical vocalization and his attitudes. In respecting the particularity of this poet, Creeley's obituary becomes an obituary for human presence itself, in its singularity and dependability an anchor those of us remaining in this world, just so, are sad to lose.

It is not so as to unpick any of the above that I draw out some contradictions in the prose, but rather to show how deep the implications of a poetics can run. Take Bronk's 'dependable, quiet voice'; not there, actually, in the one public instance of its vocalizing that Creeley chooses to recall, but represented by a tape recording when the poet fails to show. Not that dependable, then. And what about all the emphasis on Robert Creeley's own, famously diffident if not tortured delivery of his poems? 'Stuttering, seeming almost in pain' he is the opposite of Bronk, almost upbraided by him for an overly expressionist delivery: 'he would never have imagined I'd read my poems as I did . . . why? I had no answer.' It is clear not only that Creeley lacked an answer, but that he is not particularly interested in looking for one, as his reading style has not altered significantly over a half century's life in poetry. The voice is open to experience, and trembles, at times almost choked; just so, the poetics of the line-break with which Creeley has been associated since his days at Black Mountain College in the company of Charles Olson, Ed Dorn and John Wieners, have had to do with lyrical fracture and the furtherance of attempts to interestingly wreck and go beyond the pentameter, attempts begun by the 'first heave' of Pound's *Cantos*. This is very different from Bronk's steady, meditative flow, chanelled somewhat in the wake of Wallace Stevens, but not Pound. Such a division between the traditionalist and the avant-garde has been played out in American poetry for nigh on a hundred years. Bronk, among the traditionalists, is perhaps one of the most engaging to a reader taken with Creeley, Ashbery or O'Hara. Creeley, along with Ashbery, can appeal to readers otherwise more at home in safer waters. So some *détente* is possible, not just across the Atlantic but within the rival traditions of American poetry.

Opposition between a conservative tradition and an avant-garde implies a pugilistic stance on the part of the latter. This goes back to the well-attested bad behaviour of male artists in the early decades of the twentieth century in Europe; Gaudier-Brzeska sculpting knuckle dusters for Wyndham Lewis, André Breton and Benjamin Péret thumping academicians determined to hang on to their alexandrines, and all that. On the British side there was an anxiety not to appear unmanly in the wake of the Wilde trial and its effect on public perceptions of the artist, and the self-conscious hooliganism of course picks up resonance from the militarism of the times and streetfighting between fascists and socialists. These shenanigans are easily put down as laddish tribalism from feminist or other contemporary perspectives, though something is lost by so doing. A time when people took poetry so seriously as to be ready to get into a fight over it can't have been all bad. By the time Robert Creeley was at Black Mountain or visiting New York, it was the painters who were up for it, with Willem de Kooning a noted brawler when drunk and Jackson Pollock prone to legendary and rapid feats of furniture-removal when similarly aroused. The poets tended to stand aside from all this, a posture with an obvious relationship to market leverage, though the shared culture of cigarettes, alcohol and trashed motor vehicles (again, vulnerable to moralizing from the squeaky-clean present but telling, as reality always does, a complicated tale) suggests that what the painters exhibited, the poets introjected. Here the American male poets of the time showed some prescience vis-à-vis our own, and the closing lines of O'Hara's 'In Memory of My Feelings' can be pulled towards a context unavailable historically to its first readers:

I have forgotten my loves, and chiefly that one, the cancerous

statue which my body could no longer contain,
                                        against my will
                                        against my love
become art,
                    I could not change it into history
and so remember it,
                    and I have lost what is always and
                                        everywhere
        present, the scene of my selves, the occasion
of these ruses,
which I myself and singly must now kill
                    and save the serpent in their midst.
                                        (1971, 257)

As it was for Shelley, the snake amid the leaves of grass is the self that makes poems, and even he who gains the grace to live as variously as possible had better have the savoir-faire to know when to slip away, make space for the serpentine lines of the printed voice, and click on Save. Notwithstanding Whitman's singing the body electric, the mind is too acute to really believe in its inseparability from the body, and in O'Hara's lines the one slips quietly away from the other with memory as its bridge to a possible history. The scattered use of the word 'hero' throughout the poem suggests that Emerson's formula, 'Love of the hero corrupts into worship of his statue', – or at least its forms of attention – might hang fatefully behind these lines, warning the poet into his subtlest skill, and the one that most looks forward: sloughing his skin. The murders of sundry selves, often comic or urbane in O'Hara, leave an interesting selection of survivors. The winner in his greatest elegy 'The Day Lady Died' (for Billie Holiday) is O'Hara the shopper. His openness about his sexuality and his joyful consumerism look forward to more modern versions of male identity at least as much as they look back to a tra-

dition of the literary dandy. Just so there are articulations of male selfhood in the poems of John Wieners for which even the present climate is barely ready. Robert Creeley's lyric attentiveness to the opposite sex, so finely articulated and questioning as well as questing, looks forward to a more wondering and less possessive sense of maleness.

All of this operates at some distance from Wyndham Lewis's getting acquainted with T. E. Hulme by way of a fist-fight that left him hanging upside down from the railings of a square in Bloomsbury. The retention of avant-garde pugilism in the titles of manifestos, the little magazines echoing *Blast* and Pound's injunction to make it new, coexist with an ambivalent, frequently ambiguous and difficult expressivism of the introjected, negotiation of the line-break being the crucial point of presence, as in Creeley's early poem 'The Whip':

I spent a night turning in bed,
my love was a feather, a flat

sleeping thing. She was
very white

and quiet, and above us on
the roof, there was another woman I

also loved, had
addressed myself to in

a fit she
returned.

                                        (1982, 162)

Words like 'flat', 'white' and 'quiet' limit our sense of the first woman's reality and so propose the second on the roof as apparition, that is as a version of the first, or projection of what may be the man's sleeplessness, his dream, or some white night of the two. Despite the poem's insistence on the singularity and centrality of experience to poetics – look at the 'I' hanging by a thread to line six, its swerve into white space recalling the stammered, tortured vocalization which William Bronk had questioned – it knows identity to be fractured, projected, at times a double (or triple) exposure of what we address among ourselves, a kind of life-long pun on 'fit' speaking to the aptness and madness of all we get up to. There is, as has often been noted, a New England wryness to Creeley's spaced-out poetry, and the big gaps are various and questioning in both their music and their phenomenology.

Similarly and yet differently, another master of the broken line, James Schuyler, can break it for the sake of accurate representation, as in this early and Carlos Williams-influenced poem 'Flashes', depicting a dark rainy day:

> hanging dissolving forming going renewing
>   mixed with cloud
>   steams
>   and darks
>   a bird
>   snapped by
>   it's raining
> just in one spot
>   flashes
> in puddles
>   on a tar roof
>
>   (Schuyler 1993, 22–3)

But of course in poetry there is no depiction, no description, that isn't simultaneously and often primarily an articulation of the self, and one involved with a particular poetics. In the wake of Carlos Williams' poetics of observation, this relatively upbeat piece catches things on the turn, decides to see perception of the world as 'flashes'. But where then do things go? Is the white space, the nothing around the event a death, or a confirmatory location of events in time? Like Creeley's 'The Whip', Schuyler's lyric comes from the age of the improvisers, when individualistic gesture and performativeness dominated the American arts from abstract expressionist painting to poetry, dance and jazz. That puts the emphasis on the temporal, and the happy unrepeatability of each moment. Yet the darkness that presses in on Schuyler's poetry, as in this later fragment from a poem called 'This Dark Apartment', links the line-break to loss, to a diffidence analogous to Creeley's stutter, and to the careful or infirm moves of someone physically or emotionally hurt:

> Coming from the deli
> a block away today I
> saw the UN building
> shine and in all the
> months and years I've
> lived in this apartment
> I took so you and I
> would have a place to
> meet I never noticed
> that it was in my view.
>
> I remember very well
> the morning I walked in
> and found you in bed
> with X. He dressed
> and left. You dressed
> too. I said, 'Stay

five minutes.' You
did. You said, 'That's
the way it is.' It
was not much of a surprise.

(Schuyler 1993, 227)

Nothing in Schuyler's view can really be relied on to 'stay' longer than 'five minutes', be it rain on the roof or a lover, not really. And so the line is broken at that point. That fact was there to be seen, all the time, as plain to the eye and yet as veiling of identity and intention as the letter 'X', but one didn't see it, like the skyscraper that was shining there all the time: 'I never noticed / that it was in my view'. Although the breaking of the line goes back to a time of manifestos and an American avant-garde more inclined to doctrinal fisticuffs than today's, it is clear that the resulting poems associate changing form with an increased ability to enact pain and difficulty at least as much as a heroics of content, à la Ginsberg's *Howl*. The importance of loss to poetics is bequeathed by the Creeley-Schuyler-O'Hara generation, born by and large in the 1920s, to contemporary American poetry in its liveliest formations.

Chief among these has been the Language grouping. The first published use of the term 'Language Poetry' may have occurred in 1975, when Ron Silliman edited a selection of work by such poets as Bruce Andrews, Clark Coolidge, Robert Grenier and Silliman himself for *Alcheringa* magazine. Silliman wrote there of a small-press poetry culture associated with now defunct journals such as *This*, *Tottel's* and *Big Deal* as 'called variously "language centred", "minimal", "nonreferential formalism", "structuralist" . . . a *tendency* in the work of many' (1986, 742). By this time Stephen Rodefer, a quondam pupil of Charles Olson and a writer influenced by the New York School, was beginning to compose poems that ironized

those influences, while Steve McCaffery had begun to publish poems resulting from 'a calculated action *upon* a specific word-source or "supply-text"', a use of found materials clearly derived from the cut-ups of William Burroughs and the work of composer John Cage (1975, n.p.). 1975 was also the year in which various projects of the earlier generation were brought to a moment of historical fruition; Creeley published his *Collected Poems*, Ed Dorn completed his epic sequence *Gunslinger*, John Wieners published his last full-length collection and *The Collected Books of Jack Spicer*, an influential figure who had died like O'Hara prematurely and in the mid-1960s, appeared. This was therefore a critical moment of transition which in a sense has not truly been superseded, as the post-1975 names (some of which have already faded and been replaced) continue to mine a poetics that either perpetuates or defines itself by a critical stance towards the earlier generation. That said, the acidic reaction of elders such as Dorn to the new poetry left no doubt that a smooth generational handover was not exactly what was happening. And there were immediate signs of difference in Language poetry and poetics, one of which was typified by the use of words such as 'signs' and 'difference'. As Silliman's critical vocabulary of tendencies, formalism and structuralism makes clear, this was the first generation of American poets to be influenced by the discourse of marxism and the the impact of literary theory post-1968 on the university syllabus. The initial assertion of this essay that theory has stolen poetics has to be revised in memory of the late 1970s, when poets stole theory from the universities and used it as part of a poetics.

The new poets came to prominence with the bimonthly journal *L=A=N=G=U=A=G=E*, appearing first in 1978 and edited by Charles Bernstein and Bruce Andrews. Its somewhat squat and unprepossessing format was doubtless an economic necessity, but also recalled (as did the staccato hyphenation of the title, which Wyndham Lewis had used throughout the first version of *Tarr*) an adversarial modernism. This feature was consolidated by the historical aspect of the new poetics, that brought the achievements of Russian Formalism or Gertrude Stein back into prominence, revived interest in an early, experimental work by John Ashbery – *The Tennis Court Oath* – that Harold Bloom, then top dog in the critical food chain, had savaged, coupling this in some ways frail and unlikely company to a revolutionary marxist manifesto. If Language in this first phase crashed on the rocks of its own ambition, it still engendered some intriguing poetry by, *inter alia*, Steve Benson, Lyn Hejinian, Bob Perelman, Joan Retallack and Charles Bernstein, and it is worth saluting the ambitiousness of the latter's project, announced in the journal, which drew attention to:

> *our analysis of the capitalist social order as a whole and of the place that alternative forms of writing and reading might occupy in its transformation. It is our sense that the project of poetry does not involve turning language into a commodity for consumption; instead, it involves repossessing the sign through close attention to, and active participation in, its production.*

> (1984, x)

While this reads initially like a happy marriage of poetry and theory engendering a poetics, it was not to be. Critics and theorists, as has already been noted, turned out only to be interested in poetry in so far as it could be treated as 'a commodity for consumption' and with a few honourable exceptions such as Marjorie Perloff and Michael Davidson have shown no interest in the repossession of the sign by poets, the creative agents of its production. Once again American poetics would be bound up with loss, this time following the collapse of marxism worldwide, and with it the failure of all revolutionary aspiration excepting certain manifestations of feminism. The first phase of Language had placed equal emphasis on poems and poetics in its publications. It became in time the first vanguard grouping in American poetry to promote work by equal numbers of female and male authors. At a significant gathering in 1997, the *Assembling Alternatives* conference and poetry festival held at the University of New Hampshire, Bernstein had more the air of an *eminence grise* than a *chef d'école*, most of the male poets appeared to have retreated into a New York School-derived ironic mode, and it was women such as Carla Harryman, Rae Armantrout, Joan Retallack, Marjorie Welish, Lisa Robertson, the Québec separatist Nicole Brossard and English poets such as Denise Riley who were steering their craft into more bracingly choppy waters.

Retallack offers, if that's the word, a take-no-prisoners poetry that pushes bravely and to unsurpassed extremes the stylistic tendencies traditionally-minded readers find most inimical in Language production. A recent poem, 'The Earlier N'Ames Are Almost Forgotten -bladed -eyed' begins as follows:

> *nabja- beak nipple nibba bib (see Gesture and Gaze) [He] scop him Heort naman Time does go (stuck so fast) fast er as you (none of it that would agree) age .nana. called by the child that name she said since each year (the particular) (combination of sounds) that passes passed nant- through us Kore mended from several pieces now fardi- journey see per-2 taken unbeknownst to FERDI-Nand becomes a*

smaller fraction *per- haps (if we or they had
not) through many centuries of oral and
scribal transmission corruptions bound to
occur (even as they say) in the simplest text of
which this frayed (even they say) is not of
one's life almost forgotten . . .*

(1996, 18)

I find it impossible wholly to dislike a poem that begins 'nabja- beak nipple nibba bib' (and that several pages later goes on 'niger nike rapids nitron nizdo nobh nogh nogw') not merely for its nice negotiation of the nonsensically neo-dadaist, nor for some austere opposite that would win praise for having stopped making sense in order to uncover the means by which sense is made – though both these aspects have, and both resist, which is their mode of occupancy, an important place in the poem. Also to be saluted is the intellectual generosity of a text so willing to make of its writer a laboratory, less controller or even author than a nexus – beak, nipple and bib – where sociolinguistic matrices converge. The poem is the explosion that follows convergence, the poet being not so much the eye of the storm as, to use Retallack's own attractive phrase, the Eve of the swerve, an appellation used in a recent statement of poetics, done indeed for the excellent *Poetics Journal*, and titled 'Blue Notes on the Know Ledge'. Perched on the ledge of the known, Retallack gives the unknown that had already produced us a knowing look, but then language is always 'attached to practice and to interests', poetics being the space that can be cajoled out of accident and possibility:

> *Is this then to be yet another poétique terrible?*
> *Or better or worse yet, another retreat from*
>   *poétique terrible?*

*One, for instance, in which Duchamp is Fred
    Astaire with Marceled hair, Gertrude Stein's
    Kate Smith comes over the once in a blue Mt.
    Wittgenstein
(Witt. played by Gary Cooper playing Ed Dorn).
    Come on, real poets cast
off those Prussian Cowboy blues! See how the
    women come and go
casting off their incognito?*

(1998, 47)

In poetry's room the women come and go, shedding their incognito, a veil inside which a form of the cogito (I think 'therefore I am') can be discerned, though that too has to go, nudged by Retallack from the know-ledge into a poetic freefall that ends in an exploded diagram of how we got here. It is a risky procedure, to move beyond the theft of poetics by theory, and Language's retrieval of the second, to a point of social analysis where there is no division at all between poetry and poetics. Here the historical distance between the gestural expressivism of the Creeley, poetry and jazz generation and the Eve of the swerve is quite marked.

An important anticipation of the conjoining of poem and poetics, and one that continues to influence Language and neo-Language writing, occurs in the work of the English poet Tom Raworth. The title of his first book *The Relation Ship* (1967) is drawn from Creeley, as is the title of one of the poems, 'My Face Is My Own, I Thought'. The title of his second book *The Big Green Day* (1968) quotes Ted Berrigan, a second-generation poet of the New York School. Along with the early poetry of Lee Harwood, these were unusual gestures of affiliation for an English poet of the time. While Raworth's poems to some extent free themselves from the shackles of Movement and Larkinesque formalism by adopting American-style expressivism, this is not a transatlantic poetry, and Raworth's was and is a singular trajectory. A slightly later book *Moving* (1971), at the time apparently his most minimalist and withdrawn work, now seems the most prescient of Language poetry and poetics that were only nascent five to ten years later. The section entitled 'Stag Skull Mounted' consists of a sequence of poems not merely dated but timed, a precision matched by their attention to micro-detail at the level of event and syllable. '1.31 pm. June 5th. 1970', dedicated to Berrigan, retains a degree of lyrical impetus, a tension and release that are quasi-musical, albeit sparse:

> *my up*
> *is mind made*
>
> *absolutely empty*
>
> *now here comes thought thought*
> *is laughing at language language*
> *doesn't see the joke the joke*
> *wonders why it takes so long*
>
> *but it's friday*
> *and it's a long way down*

The 'absolutely empty', absolutely characteristic of Raworth's minimalism and interest in thought-from-scratch, implies a Zen-like indifference to the theoretical consensus that human identity is 'always already' (a motto sure to bring a stab of nostalgia in decades to come, like The Commodores singing 'always and forever') produced. Here by contrast the poem is the record of its own emergence, is its own poetic. A sceptical self-awareness, also entirely characteristic of Raworth, allows the sequence to dwindle

to parodic degrees of sparsity, culminating in '10.26 pm. June 5th. 1970', which in its entirety runs as follows:

> *word*

That piece seems however extravagantly prolix when compared to '10.59 pm. June 5th. 1970', the shortest poem in English, which runs as follows:

> (1971, n.p.)

Charles Bernstein's writing contrasts markedly with Tom Raworth's at the level of style, approach and temper. There is a shared insistence nonetheless on ideal inseparability of poem and poetics. Bernstein's most recent book *My Way* (1999) offers each in the guise of the other, together with an interview and other immediately hybrid forms by which one rhetoric of purpose can be set up in order for other things to be accomplished. Thus, an essay analysing the statistical recurrence of water images in poems published by *The New Yorker* between 30 January and 15 May 1989 begins comically but ends by making a serious point about which cultural additives both its manufacturers and its purchasers believe the mainstream American poem should contain. An earlier piece, *Artifice of Absorption,* published separately in 1987, was collected in *A Poetics* (1992) and is one of the major statements of linguistically innovative poetics in this period. Appropriately, its lines are broken in a way recalling poetry:

> *. . . there is always an unbridgeable lacuna*
>   *between*
> *any explication of a reading & any actual*
> *reading. & it is the extent of these lacunas –*
> *differing with each reader but not indeterminate –*

that is a necessary measure of a poem's meaning.

(1992, 12)

Bernstein cuts to the centre of what this essay is about. There is no poetics that is not linked to loss, to the 'lacuna'. It may be the death of a poet, the breaking of form, the silent meaning of the white space pressing on words, and/or the intersubjective slippage of experience from precedent described above. To such measures of difference might be added the lacuna between the Then of a poem's being authored and the Now of reading; the lacuna between the macro-Then of history and the possible intentions of the writer at the point of writing: and, *inter alia*, the lacunae between and within poems, lines and words. It may well be that contemporary poetry and poetics, at least of the kind with which Bernstein is concerned, are particularly able to make of these lacunae something dizzyingly alive – poetry being, as he remarks elsewhere, a swoon that brings you to your senses. (And the life is still with the avant-garde – or if that seems too nostalgically progressive, what John Ashbery terms the other tradition. There is no reason to be interested in the tabid Robert Haas, or the downright marcid Andrew Motion.) Perhaps Bernstein's work has in historical terms partnered deconstruction in exposing the deferral of stable meaning as a defining feature of communication. More plausibly deconstruction laid claim to uncovering what modern or indeed romantic poetic practice had long known from the inside, from the actual writing of poems, that even the most careful and pointed use of language slides from its intended aim and into its own strange life. 'Could I revive within me her symphony and song . . .' Thus S. T. Coleridge, lamenting his failure to recapture poetic vision in 'Kubla Khan', an aspiration whose failure attains a Pyrrhic victory by becoming the poem's subject. There poetry was compared to song, to symphony. Its more secret home is the failure, the loss, the death, the if only.

Could I . . .

Works cited

Allen, Donald (ed.). *The New American Poetry*. New York, 1960.

Allen, Donald (ed.). *The Collected Poems of Frank O'Hara*. New York, 1971.

Andrews, Bruce and Charles Bernstein. 'Repossessing the Word', in *The L=A=N=G=U=A=G=E Book*, eds Bruce Andrews and Charles Bernstein. Carbondale, IL, 1984, ix–1.

Bartlett, Lee. 'What is "Language Poetry"?' *Critical Inquiry*, 12: 4 (1986).

Bernstein, Charles. 'Artifice of Absorption', in *A Poetics*. Cambridge, 1992, 9–90.

Big Allis 7. New York, 1996.

Creely, Robert. *The Collected Poems of Robert Creeley, 1945–75*. Berkeley, CA, 1982.

McCaffery, Steve. *'Ow's "Waif"'*. Toronto, 1975.

Perloff, Marjorie. 'Postmodernism/"fin de siècle": defining "difference" in late twentieth century poetics', in *Romanticism and Postmodernism*, ed. Edward Larrissy. Cambridge, 1999, 179–210.

Raworth, Tom. *Moving*. London, 1971.

Retallack, Joan. 'Blue Notes on the Know Ledge', *Poetics Journal*, 10. Detroit, 1998, 39–54.

Schuyler, James. *Collected Poems*. New York, 1993.

quilting | ""CRAZY QUILT(ING)(S)"" | *JOHN P. LEAVEY, JR*

Epigraph 1
'The soundness of a conception can be judged by whether it causes one quotation to summon another' (Adorno *Minima Moralia: Reflections from Damaged Life,* trans. E. F. N. Jephcott [London, 1974] 87 [#51]).

Epigraph 2
'Texts which anxiously undertake to record every step without omission inevitably succumb to banality, and to a monotony related not only to the tension induced in the reader, but to their own substance . . . Thought waits to be woken one day by the memory of what has been missed, and to be transformed into teaching' (Adorno *Minima Moralia* 80–81 [#50]).

C I collected my books, started tearing up the pieces, sometimes marking or underlining, other times attaching some sort of bookmark. Had I the letter C, I would have begun pasting all the pieces together on a paper or cardboard subjectile to produce a collage. Like marquetry, the quilt gets taken up into the order of furniture, not clothes, not aesthetics. Like parquetry, the quilt can also become a floor covering. Like montage or collage, the quilt is rarely of whole cloth.

'A quilt has to do with protection' (Jonathan Holstein The Pieced Quilt: A North American Design Tradition [Toronto, 1973] 9). Quilting:

> Almost always its purpose is protection: against blows, as in armor; against heat or cold, as in pot holders and sleeping bags; layered materials are very efficient at this. Its application to bed furnishings has been in quilts for the bed itself and curtains which surrounded those early 'great' bedsteads, to protect against both drafts and cold. (10)

I also marked out certain files on the computer, which allowed the overlay of one text by another. If the quilt is a textual citation collection, the pattern for reading the sheets becomes significant. The order of the fabric becomes not only how to write but how to specify the reading.

Hypertext would allow the specification of a limited number of paths of reading.

I also began a list of those to be omitted here (like thrums), even when one might argue that the history of, say, for instance, the fragment, would seem to require additional discussion. And yet, that discussion might distract. So I omit Blanchot, whose writing and ordering, even more than Barthes, pertains. Without reason, but with sense. Also Novalis.

The quilt can be a simple object: two layers of cloth stitched together through wadding. Its purpose: supposedly protection: from cold, from another's weapons, perhaps from the wrath of God. The origins of quilts and quilting are difficult to assess. Fabric deteriorates. Samples wear out. The lines of argument from the samples left either in fabric or in representations can be difficult to read or write. One simple agreement, even if only of convenience: patchwork, if not invented by the 'Americans', was most developed in the United States.

The letter Q in this alphabetic gloss_alalia: *incertum.*

Q

Q, the monkey letter, the 'secret' synoptic source, the dropped Greek letter, the gadget man in James Bond films, the queer, and the alternative (like *Q-news* from London on the Muslim world).

An **alphabet** could seem to be arbitrary, surely unmotivated, yet conventional. But which alphabet? Whose? Letters come and go, dropped in(to) some alphabets, seemingly waiting to be written and spoken, written or spoken. In appliqué, **SCRAPS** overrun other **SCRAPS**, like the letter Q, overlapping the C and the K in sound, application, and spelling.

Glossolalia can mean non-meaningful speech that is fabricated, perhaps like a crazy quilt. This alphabetic book desires to eschew meaning, to avoid reducing the counterpoint of counterpanes to less than the utility of **SCRAPS**. Fabric is rarely transparent or opaque.

'Upon waking next morning about daylight, I found Queequeg's arm thrown over me in the most loving and affectionate manner. You had almost thought I had been his wife. The counterpane was of patchwork, full of odd little parti-colored squares and triangles; and this arm of his tattooed all over with an interminable Cretan labyrinth of a figure, no two parts of which were of one precise shade – owing I suppose to his keeping his arm at sea unmethodically in sun and shade, his shirt sleeves irregularly rolled up at various times – this same arm of his, I say, looked for all the world like a strip of that same patchwork quilt. Indeed, partly lying on it as the arm did when I first awoke, I could hardly tell it from the quilt, they so blended their hues together; and it was only by the sense of weight and pressure that I could tell that Queequeg was hugging me." (http://www.princeton.edu/~batke/moby/moby_004.html)

Counterpane

The quiltpoint (*culcita puncta*), a counterpoint or counterpane, gets us into the history of bedding, of bedding down, of seating and catching hold. Quilting, whether as literature or sewing, involves more often than not **PATCHWORK** and padding stitched. A. Sam Kimball pointed out the immediate reference here to the opening of the fourth chapter of *Moby Dick,* which is entitled 'The Counterpane'. Kimball takes this tattoo and the counterpane to the opening reference in Derrida's 'Force and Signification' in *Writing and Difference* (trans. Alan Bass [Chicago, IL, 1978]), the epigraph of Flaubert: 'It might be that we are all tattooed savages since Sophocles'. And then on to the tattooes in *Glas* and Genet.

Che vuoi?

In his 1975 *Roland Barthes,* Barthes forgets not the order of writing (in fact he remembers the order down to the last fragment, the religion of friendship, and dates it, 3 September 1974 [165]), but he forgets the classification itself of that order:

> He more or less remembers the order in which he wrote these fragments; but where did that order come from? In the course of what classification, of what succession? He no longer remembers. The alphabetical order erases everything, banishes every origin. Perhaps in places, certain fragments seem to follow one another by some affinity; but the important thing is that these little networks not be connected, that they not slide into a single enormous network which would be the structure of the book, its meaning. It is in order to halt, to deflect, to divide this descent of discourse toward a destiny of the subject, that at certain moments the alphabet calls you to order (to disorder) and says: *Cut! Resume the story in another way* (but also, sometimes, for the same reason, you must break up the alphabet). (Trans. Richard Howard (New York,1977) 148)

Others, Condillac for instance, only discovered the order after the fact, with two sheets arriving in place only

after they were ᵈ/ₘisplaced.

Will the order of the alphabet be violated here, in this book? Or perhaps I should ask that question as follows: what order will be violated here, in this book, in this quilt?

The fragment before the last one of Barthes I just cited, is itself outside of the alphabetic order:

> Temptation of the alphabet: to adopt the succession of letters in order to link fragments is to fall back on what constitutes the glory of

language (and what constituted Saussure's despair): an unmotivated order (an order outside of any imitation), which is not arbitrary (since everyone knows it, recognizes it, and agrees on it). The alphabet is euphoric: no more anguish of 'schema,' no more rhetoric of 'development,' no more twisted logic, no more dissertations! An idea per fragment, a fragment per idea, and as for the succession of these atoms, nothing but the age-old and irrational order of the French letters (which are themselves meaningless objects – deprived of meaning). . . . This order, however, can be mischievous: it sometimes produces effects of meaning; and if these effects are not desired, the alphabet must be broken up to the advantage of a superior rule, that of the breach (heterology): to keep a meaning from 'taking.' (147–8)

In 'How this book is constructed' of *A Lover's Discourse: Fragments,* in a subsection on 'order,' which begins after the citation of Vergil's *Aeneid*'s interrupted Neptunian sentence *quos ego,* the alphabet is chosen to avoid the monster of meaning, here particularly a 'philosophy of love' to be derived from the order of the figures that Barthes names. Barthes uses the convention of the alphabet to avoid the meaning that could possibly result from 'the wiles of pure chance, which might indeed have produced logical sequences' (trans. Richard Howard [New York, 1978] 8).

NAMES OF THE QUILT DESIGNS included places, politics, nature, religion, historical movements and events, games, and common objects, to name a few categories (Holstein 59). Holstein gives examples of each: 'North Carolina Lily . . . Tree Everlasting . . . Whig's Defeat . . . Free Trade Patch . . . Leap Frog . . . New York Beauty . . . Monkey Wrench . . .' (59).

SCRAPS

,

I
NEVER
GET
BEYOND
THE
SCRAPS

.

'But the rags, the refuse – these I will not inventory but allow, in the only way possible, to come into their own: by making use of them' (Benjamin *The Arcades Project* N1a,8 [trans. Howard Eiland and Kevin McLaughlin (Cambridge, MA, 1999) 460].

Another **voile,** this time the soft palate in Genet (who says he never learned how to sew) in *Glas:*

> the glue of chance [*aléa*] makes sense, and progress is rhythmed by *little jerks,* gripping and suctions, patchwork tackling [*placage*] – in every sense and direction – and gliding penetration. (Trans. John Leavey and Richard Rand [Lincoln, 1986] 142b)

French letters, like quilts, can also be **prophylactics.**

The **SCRAP** can be applied to the surface of another subjectile, then stuffed again 'above' the top and the wadding that is between the top and the bottom; it can also be stitched on top of another larger piece of fabric rather than to another smaller **SCRAP** to continue the fabrication begun. 'PATCHWORK' technically applies to both kinds of quilting, (1) the pieced or 'peaced' (Holstein 56) together, often into blocks that are pieced together again, then stitched or tacked through the wadding onto the back, and (2) the 'applied', *l'appliqué.*

I learned to sew when I attended a German Kindergarten. Each student was given a cardboard image with perforations through which colored yarns were passed with a needle. The yarns outlined a completed figure. We learned other skills and played other games; for me it certainly was a German **ABECEDARY.**

Alphabetic

SCRAPS:
Adami, counterpoint, not fragments
Bernini's quilt
Deleuze, PATCHWORK
Derrida, placage
Fabric as citation of fabric
Text
Translation as pieced work (a rereading of Benjamin and Derrida on translation and poetics): no whole of which this language is a part

Bernini's Quilt, a sixteenth-century subjectile for the hermaphrodite.
In Smollett's *Travels through France and Italy* (Edinburgh, 1796; http://www.ku.edu/history/index/europe/ancient_rome/E/Gazetteer/ Places/Europe/Italy/.Texts/Smollett/Travels/31.html), in Letter 31 from Nice of 5 March 1765, Smollett writes of this marble bed:

> Among the exhibition of art within the [Villa Pinciana, 'at Rome'], I was much struck with . . . the famous hermaphrodite, which vies with that of Florence; though the most curious circumstance of this article, is the matrass, executed and placed by Bernini, with such art and dexterity, that to the view it rivals the softness of wool, and seems to retain the marks of pressure, according to the figure of the superincumbent statue.

'1803. Napoleon I not only thrust his sister, Pauline Bonaparte, on the weak Prince Camillo Borghese, but also relieved the Prince's father of much of his ancient statue collection, sending it to the Louvre in Paris. In exchange, he gave him land, of little consequence, in the north of Italy'. (http://web.tiscali.it/romaonlineguide /Pages/eng/rbarocca/sBHy8.htm)

The quilt and its superincumbent statue were taken to the Louvre in 1807, the year of the publication of *The Phenomenology of Spirit*.

From the bed to the coverlet, from the bed to its cover, the quilt covers the question of literature. The wadding between bed and cover is the body – not only the ideology that the stitch of Žižek holds tight but also what disrupts, rubs against, wears down and out of the stitch. The tripartite structure of two fabrics and padding (sometimes reduced to two by leaving out the wadding) needs to be examined – what protection (against weather and weapon) is required? Why the thickness for the memorial, the signature, the art of the quilt? What is its materiality – for Deleuze, for instance? Striation and smoothness. The quilt as smooth because fragment. But also, what is the absence of the wadding?

What of the sleeping bag? Usually not of the crazy quilting kind, it encircles the body as do clothes. The portable bedroom. And the question of how to differentiate clothes from the bed becomes more finely sketched here. Not between inner and outer garments, but between garments and bedding. The tallith too is to be worn in bed. One could argue for the following thesis: we have begun to wear our beds. Certainly an uncertain thesis. *Incertum*. But the prohibition of transvestism would be difficult to discern or to follow in this situation (see *Veils* trans. Geoffrey Bennington [Stansford, CA, 2001] 66). What determines the difference between men's and women's clothes? And how will the properness of such a determination be maintained in the bed? Does this split of gender apply to the animal, from which the clothes are made? Is there such a thing as the gender of wool? Or silk?

The problem of the **FRAGMENT**

Given no totality, given no pure language, the whole of the fabric in its fabrication cannot remove thrums. Signatures stop and start as the discontinuity signing any continuity. Hence the blocks and remnants of the pieced **PATCHWORK**, crazy quilt.

Adami's quilt
The blood-red *sang* of his text: *sang, sans, sens*. Of what colour inks to write of here . . .

The briefest history of the quilt
The quilt survives in wearing out. Technology as the condition(ing)(ed) of . . . memory and remains. Against total recall (whether a man as war or movie), there are the **SCRAP** and the quilt.

Fabric diaries

(See Roderick Kiracofe, *The American Quilt: A History of Cloth and Comfort 1750–1950* [New York, 1993] 8–12.)

Like the veils and sails of Cixous and Derrida, the veil of the eyes and the shawl of remembrance, fabric diaries recall. **SCRAPS** of cloth and inscriptions remind one, entice the memory to the event of the cloth, of the textile and textual event, the remnant of which the **SCRAP** of cloth recalls. The fabric, a nubby silk, for instance, to line a new suit of a mother who dies the next day, begins to fade, in substance and in memory. Like Christ's robe in Trier, the sight of which is all that Christian pilgrims must be satisfied with, for a fabric and fabrication too delicate to touch. Now under glass. *Che vuoi?*

And perhaps also like the tallith that Derrida touches or kisses without seeing almost every evening he is at home (*Veils* 44) and that he differentiates from the veil and textiles because it may never become a **SCRAP** or a remnant. It is never to be used up, although its fringes can be used as a bookmark, should they become 'useless' (71). The 'memory' of an event to come, the tallith touches itself and encloses me 'before' I am.

Fabric diaries, however, are not quilts, not even crazy quilts, although the relation of crazy quilts and useless but existing talliths cannot be easily specified. In the recognition of the tallith to give and order, given in order to order, the commemoration of a commandment, Derrida sets out to honor another commandment with the remnants of the irreplaceable tallith, the fringes, 'signed and booked and dated' within the 'fabric diary' Derrida undertakes in *Veils*.

Hypothesis
The tallith is said to be the proper to man, although not all agree. *Incertum.* The prohibition against wearing (out) the clothes of the other gender, in this reading, would differentiate the tallith from the veil, and the commandments to wear or not wear (out) the tallith and or the veil fall under this hypothesis.

What of patchwork gathered from many genders? Does this too fall under this hypothesis?

. . . tlef, . . . leuze, . . . rrida

De

Deleuze: 'le monde comme patchwork' (*Pourparlers* [Paris: Minuit 1990] 201).

Deleuze: 'the world as a collection of heterogenous parts: an infinite PATCHWORK, or an endless wall of dry stones (a cemented wall, or the pieces of a puzzle, would reconstitute a totality)' (*Essays Critical and Clinical,* trans. Daniel W. Smith and Michael A. Greco [Minneapolis,1997] 57).

Deleuze: '. . . for the Americans invented PATCHWORK' (*Essays* 86–7). More specifically, regarding Melville and *Moby Dick:*

> The subject loses its texture in favor of an infinitely proliferating PATCHWORK: the American PATCHWORK becomes the law of Melville's oeuvre, devoid of a center, of an upside down or right side up. It is as if the traits of expression escaped form, like the abstract lines of an unknown writing, or the furrows that twist from Ahab's brow to that of the Whale, or the 'horrible contortions' of the flapping lanyards that pass through the fixed rigging and can easily drag a sailor into the sea, a subject into death. (77)

Mixture: smooth and striated space
Woven material, fabric, is striated: the grid of power. The thrums could perhaps become part of the felt, a smooth space. PATCHWORK takes the grid of power in order to speed off, movement. Fabric becomes felt in PATCHWORK, which is 'an amorphous, nonformal space prefiguring op art'.

A slightly longer history of the quilt

The story of the quilt is particularly interesting in this connection. A quilt comprises two layers of fabric stitched together, often with a filler in between. Thus it is possible for there to be no top or bottom. If we follow the history of the quilt over a short migration sequence (the settlers who left Europe for the New World), we see that there is a shift from a formula dominated by embroidery (so-called 'plain' quilts). The first settlers of the seventeenth century brought with them plain quilts, embroidered and striated spaces of extreme beauty. But toward the end of the century patchwork technique was developed more and more, at first due to the scarcity of textiles (leftover fabric, pieces salvaged from used clothers, remnants taken from the 'scrap bag'), and later due to the popularity of Indian chintz. It is as though a smooth space emanated, sprang from a striated space, but not without a correlation between the two, a recapitulation of one in the other, a furtherance of one through the other. Yet the

> complex difference persists. Patchwork, in conformity with migration, whose degree of affinity with nomadism it shares, is not only named after trajectories, but 'represents' trajectories, becomes inseparable from speed or movement in an open space. (Deleuze and Guattari, *A Thousand Plateaus: Capitalism and Schizophrenia*, trans. Brian Massumi [Minneapolis, MN, 1987] 477)

Smooth and striated are not reducible to local and global: local is the absolutely open that gets reduced to the horizon that encompasses and out of which it is thrown. The patchwork indicates that relation as follows: fabric, global; SCRAP, local. The relation of one to the other is always across the mixture of these two. The SCRAP becomes PATCHWORK, encompassing the world as the center of relation, and expels the SCRAP as SCRAP. *Incertum*. Not in the sense of uncertainty, but uncertain as to how the mixture takes. Like translation, the relation is neither simple nor secondary, always dissymetrical between smooth and striated (Deleuze and Guattari, *A Thousand Plateaus*, 486).

Remainder and fragment: the PATCHWORK crazy quilt.

> Can the nodal point totalize? Is it possible for there to be no remains? The *point de capiton* is also a counterpoint to that totalization. Yes, the quilt encompasses, but as a remains, even in the anniversary version.

Of what comfort fat?

'How now blowne Jack? How now quilt?' (*Henry IV,* IV. ii. 54). The greeting of the overblown, fat one, Falstaff, by Prince Henry. Of what protection is fat?

On felt and fat, see Beuys ('Coming to terms with his involvement in the war was a long process and figures, at least obliquely, in much of his artwork. Beuys often said that his interest in fat and felt as sculptural materials grew out of a wartime experience – a plane crash in the Crimea, after which he was rescued by nomadic Tartars who rubbed him with fat and wrapped him in felt to heal and warm his body. While the story appears to have little grounding in real events [Beuys himself downplayed its importance in a 1980 interview], its poetics are strong enough to have made the story one of the most enduring aspects of his mythic biography' [Joan Rothfuss, http://www.walkerart.org/beuys/gg3.html]).

On fat and the counterpane, see Melville's chapter 68 of *Moby Dick,* 'The Blanket' (http://www.princeton.edu/~batke/moby/moby_068.html): 'A word or two more concerning this matter of the skin or blubber of the whale. It has already been said, that it is stript from him in long pieces, called blanket-pieces. Like most sea-terms, this one is very happy and significant. For the whale is indeed wrapt up in his blubber as in a real blanket or counterpane; or, still better, an Indian poncho slipt over his head, and skirting his extremity. It is by reason of this cosy blanketing of his body, that the whale is enabled to keep himself comfortable in all weathers, in all seas, times, and tides.'

On fat and Kripke, see Žižek: 'If we refer to somebody as "fat," it is clear that he must at least possess the property of being excessively corpulent . . .' (90). Unlike the situation when we call him Peter or Falstaff. Or proffer an insult? Fathead, for instance?

The **PATCHWORK** quilt can be a literary device: the compilation of extracts to form the whole, sewn and padded together with the quilting stitch. In the US, quilting is associated with women: they get together to make the quilts. Quilting is not the business of tailors. In 'her memoirs' of 1889, Frances Willard writes about the Ohio Women's Temperance Crusade quilt:

> It must, indeed, be a women's convention that would make so curious a testimonial as a quilt. . . . Within its folds are hidden all our hearts. The day will come when, beside the death-sentence of a woman who was burned as a witch in Massachussetts, beside the block from which a woman was sold as a slave in South Carolina, and besides [*sic*] the liquor license that was issued by the State of Illinois to ruin its young men, there will hang this beautiful quilt, to which young men and women will point with pride, and say, 'There is the name of my great-grandmother, who took part in Ohio's great crusade.' (*Glimpses of Fifty Years*; cited in Clark, 153)

Point de capiton 1

In '"Che Vuoi?"' under the subsections 'Identity' and then 'The Ideological "Quilt,"' of Žižek's *The Sublime Object of Ideology* [New York, 1989]:

> What creates and sustains the *identity* of a given ideological field beyond all possible variations of its positive content? . . . the multitude of 'floating signifiers,' of proto-ideological elements, is structured into a unified field through the intervention of a certain 'nodal point' (the Lacanian *point de capiton*) which 'quilts' them, stops their sliding and fixes their meaning.
>
> Ideological space is made of non-bound, non-tied elements, 'floating signifiers,' whose identity is 'open,' overdetermined by their articulation in a chain with other elements – that is, their 'literal' signification depends on their metaphorical surplus-signification. . . . The 'quilting' performs the totalization by means of which this free floating of ideological elements is halted, fixed – that is to say, by means of which they become parts of the structured network of meaning.(87)

Point de capiton 2

Lacan's gratuitous (*à mon gré*) translation of the Stoic *lekton* (*Ecrits I* [Paris: Seuil 1971 ('Points')] 11). The incorporeal non-ideal, the fourth according to Deleuze in *The Logic of Sense,* 'neither word nor body, neither sensible representation nor *rational representation* . . . It is exactly the boundary between propositions and things. . . . the event is sense itself' (trans. Mark Lester with Charles Stivale [New York, 1990] 19, 22).

U *sure*
Usury and worn-out clothes stitched together in the quilt
The **PATCHWORK** quilt takes the worn materials, stitches them together, joins them to the quilting from both sides. The materiality of material opens up here under the cover of the irreplaceable tallith. Under the cover of all these fabrics: quilts, veils, shawls, head scarf.

On the scarf, let's read Derrida's *Fichus: Discours de Francfort* (Paris, 2002), his Frankfurt discourse upon receiving the Adorno Prize in September 2001. His travels in China delayed the usual day of the award from the 11th until the 22nd (51n).

There are 6,000 quilts being made for the families of those who died in the attacks on the World Trade Center.

In *Fichus* Derrida cites Benjamin's letter to Adorno's wife, Gretel (Letter 321, signed 'Detlef' and dated 12 October 1939 from the 'Camp des travailleurs volontaires, Clos Saint-Joseph Nevers (Nièvre), of *The Correspondence of Walter Benjamin, 1910–1940,* ed. Gershom Scholem and Theodor W. Adorno, trans. Manfred R. Jacobson and Evelyn M. Jacobson [Chicago, 1994]). The letter was written in French and in the main concerns a dream about 'reading' that Benjamin had the night before. In the relation of that 'beautiful', happiness-producing dream, Benjamin includes the following sentence he speaks aloud in the dream (and 'this is another reason to give an account of it in the same language'): 'Il s'agissait de changer en fichu une poésie.' In the English translation, this sentence is translated as follows: 'It was a matter of turning a poem into a fichu' (615). The French edition, as Derrida points out, includes the translation that Benjamin immediately gives to this phrase: '**Es handelte sich darum, aus einem Gedicht ein Halstuch zu machen**' (Fr. ed., 308). In the dream, the contiguity of beds and writing and reading recurs, and the letter d, or at least the upper parts of it are seen (Derlef, Dora, Dausse). And upon his saying this sentence, which refers to the writing and images on the material that becomes *(le) fichu,* 'something intriguing happened':

> I noticed that one of the women who was very beautiful was lying on a bed. When she heard my explanation, she made an extremely rapid movement. She pushed aside a bit of the *couverture* that was covering her as she lay in bed. It took her less than a second to do this. It was not to let me see her body, but to see the pattern of her sheet. The sheet must have had imagery similar to the kind I had probably 'written' years ago to give to Dausse. I was quite aware that the woman had made this gesture. But the reason I was aware of it was because of a kind of supplementary vision. For my bodily eyes were somewhere else. And I was not at all able to distinguish what was on the sheet that had been surreptitiously revealed to me. (615; trans. modified)

FORM: THE QUILT ITSELF.

Or that of an anthology, as J. Hillis Miller told me regarding the Heath *Anthology of American Literature,* which takes the concept of PATCHWORK from Deleuze to conceive American literature.

The quilt memorializes. The NAMES Project AIDS Memorial Quilt covers for the stone of the monument. Fabric arts are often not placed in the fine arts. What is this monument of supplemental permanence, perhaps less than writing, and this supplemental seeing, although like the postcard, it is material delivering the destinerrance of the message. See, for example, *Always Remember: A Selection of Panels Created by and for International Fashion Designers* (New York, 1996). And the Names Project website: http://www.aidsquilt.org/.

Adorno on the postcard, eventually on trash

'Great paintings and picture-postcards have in common that they have put primeval images at our fingertips' (*Minima Moralia,* 225). This is part of a maxim devoted to kitsch (#145, 'Kunstfigur') and trash. Trash and art both remain ('unrelated to any model') celebratory of the freedom from and yet still trapped in the constraint of nature that they attempt to 'forgo'. Art strains toward perfection, the removal of any traces of the contradiction between is and made. Mass production highlights the contradiction in its question What for? Seeking perfection eventually leads to fragmentation: 'the endless pains to eradicate the traces of making, injure works of art and condemn them to be fragmentary.'

Quilts were often signed (Holstein, 27), with the most interesting signature for me the embroidered phrase on a 'crazy quilt', which Holstein argues means 'crazed', 'fractured'. The phrase is cited by Holstein:

'I wonder if I am dead'. (62)

See Barbara Brackman's 'Signature Quilts: Nineteenth-Century Trends', in *Quiltmaking in America: Beyond the Myths: Selected Writings from the American Quilt Study Group,* eds Laurel Horton et al. (Nashville, 1994) 20–9, on the geography of the signature quilt in the US in the nineteenth century.

Fichu

I wonder if I am dead.

I wonder if, on this quilt, this shouldn't be translated:

Je me demande si je suis fichu.

Friendship and Album Quilts contain inscriptions, signatures, **SCRAPS** from the clothes of the signers (Roderick Kiracofe, *The American Quilt: A History of Cloth and Comfort 1750–1950* [New York, 1993] 80–3). *Fabric diaries writ memorial public social.*

The PATCHWORK, pieced quilt was **utilitarian** (Holstein, 31, 49). Yet the work on such quilts certainly would not be universally accepted as useful. Class disputes arose. In 1870, C. Wood recommends the cultivation of the mind for 'farmers wives' rather than quilting in the leisure moments. A spread will do just fine for covering the bed. The answers to her query hypothesis thesis in *Western Rural* (31 March) are less concerned with the cultivation of mind than the economy of work. Hass responds: 'Nothing . . . is neater in my opinion than a neat **SCRAP** quilt, to say nothing of economy . . .' (14 April; cited in Ricky Clark et al., *Quilts in Community: Ohio's Traditions* [Nashville, 1991] 90). And there is a letter signed 'Young Housekeeper': 'I do not think it takes as much time to piece quilts as it does to wash spreads & keep them clean . . .' (5 May; cited in Clark, 90).

from contempt to power

PATCHing runs from contempt to power. The quilt runs from mere utility to art, and PATCHWORK indicates in its differences very particular relations to labour (individual, group, men, women), power (the heritage of the family cloth as indicator of the 'rank' of the wearer), and class. For the preliminaries on this, see Schnuppe von Gwinner, *The History of the PATCHWORK Quilt: Origins, Traditions and Symbols of a Textile Art,* trans. Edward Force (West Chester, PA, 1988).

Wadding: yada, yada, yada . . .

WY The quilt stitches the ditch between aesthetics and utility. Gwinner's concluding paragraph in his introduction: 'Perhaps this book can help the

PATCHWORK quilt attain a status appropriate to it, between the demands of high art and the contempt of mere patching' (11). This categorical scheme places the quilt within the historical division of the arts, even as that division shifts or appears to be arbitrary. I am wondering if more isn't at stake here besides this division, which the museums and the academic studies continue to refine. The quilt as smooth space places it first as a model of a difference within the philosophical concepts of *A Thousand Plateaus.* One might ask about the status of the model of the difference, although that relation of model to the real has not learned of the distinctive relation the model 'entails'. If the smooth and striated are the relation of relation, then the modelling is encompassed somehow within its relation. Like fabric. Like tallith.

Striated: Interpellation
Smooth: Depellation

If interpellation is the power grid of the subject position, forms the subject position – *incertum* – then depellation would be the hailing that displaces that position before the hailing. Neither other nor same, depellation makes possible that distinction in the interpellation. Depellation is often read as the moment after that hollows out a lack in the subject position. All of this would make sense if the temporality of such statements were not already under cover.

Wadding –

What is wadding? Filler? Caught up within this question is the possibility, of course, that the quilt need only be two pieces of cloth (one, if folded) tacked together, the filler not being necessary if it's not cold or dangerous. How is this middle constituted as filler? And how is it differentiated from the top and the bottom? In Benjamin's dream, it is not the revelation of the filler, the body, that matters, but the unreadable pattern on/of the sheets. The quilt as tacked intermediary, as nomadic smoothness, takes on the wadding (closer to felt, anti-fabric), although as fabric enclosing the relation to wadding as its fabrication, the quilt is nothing but –

wadding.

Signature

●

● ritornello. The marking and remarking of territory. The repetition of the Album quilt in its difference. The same blocks signed differently.

untranslatable

Il signait toujours ainsi ses lettres à Gretel Adorno, et précisait parfois « *Dein alter Detlef* ». A la fois lue et écrite par Benjamin, la lettre **d** figurerait alors l'initiale de sa propre signature, comme si **D**etlef se donnait à sous-entendre: « Je suis le fichu », voire, du camp de travailleurs volontaires, moins d'un an avant son suicide, et comme tout mortel qui dit moi, dans sa langue de rêve: « Moi, **d**, je suis fichu. » (*Fichus*, 41)

Reading

Are quilts to be read? Signature, Album, Friendship, and Memorial quilts are usually inscribed. Their monumentality offers itself for reading. As does every quilt. Even fabric diaries intermix the material and the writing. But the question of reading must also deal with the fractals of the crazy quilt? How is one to – or should one even? – read it? Under what terms and according to what rules? Figural? Sewing? Coloristic? Memorial? Monumental? Forgery? Thievery? Historically? Within class struggles? Within the technological? Aesthetically? Pop art, for instance? As if reading could be reduced to any of these categories, even in a happy dream.

Incertum.

Neither **SCRAP** nor tallith, the quilt is its own materiality whose deterioration is loss of self. The more the quilt becomes art, the more its materiality cannot be translated. The quilt is idiomatic, without reproduction. Or, conversely, the materiality of art is the materiality of the quilt.

What for?
Fichu

Is it possible to write outside the borders of a quilt? There are writings on all kinds of subjectiles, even that of history ('The events surrounding the historian, and in which he himself takes part, will underlie his presentation in the form of a text written in invisible ink. The history which he lays before the reader comprises, as it were, the citations occurring in this text, and it is only these citations that occur in a manner legible to all. To write history

257

thus means to *cite* history. It belongs to the concept of citation, however, that the historical object in each case is torn from its context', Benjamin *The Arcades Project* N11,3 [476]). But if the **SCRAP**, the rag, the citation are de jure the quilt, then Benjamin might be read to say there is nothing but the quilt. Only the quilt has the density and the smoothness, the stitching and the padding to write history. The technological condition is the quilt condition. Fabric encloses before I am – finite – depelled. *Je suis fichu(e).*

JOHN P. LEAVEY, JR | ""CRAZY QUILT(ING)(S)"" | quilting

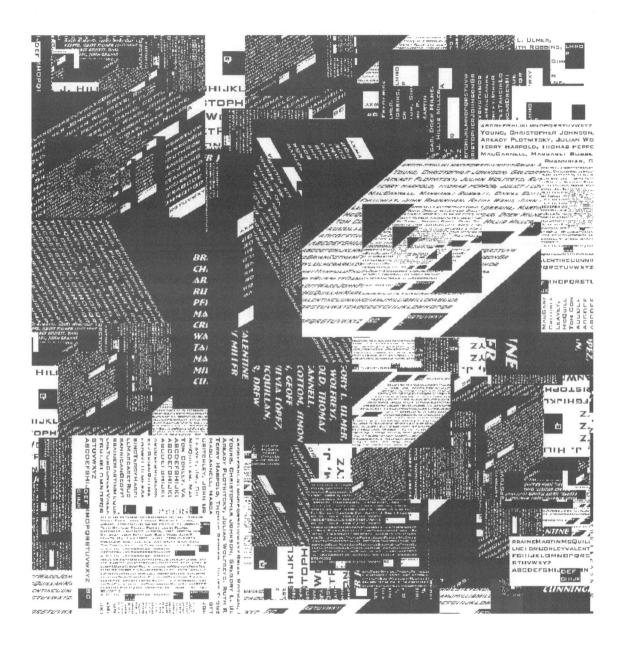

259

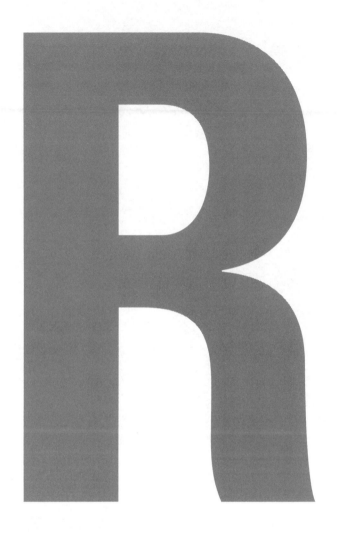

reification | ('VERDINGLICHUNG') | SILVIA L. LÓPEZ

The commodity can only be understood in its undistorted essence when it becomes the universal category of society as a whole. Only in this context does the reification *produced by commodity relations assume a decisive importance both for the objective evolution of society and for the stance adopted by men towards it. Only then does the commodity become crucial for the subjugation of men's consciousness to the forms in which this reification finds expression and for their attempt to comprehend the process or to rebel against its disastrous effects and liberate themselves from servitude to the 'second nature' so created.*

(György Lukács, 1971, 86)[1]

The appearance of György Lukács' *History and Class Consciousness* (1923) is considered the single most important theoretical contribution to twentieth-century marxism. This work owes its status as an undisputed pillar of the western marxist tradition to the fundamental transformation produced by the appearance of what, in its moment, was both the first serious philosophical grounding of marxism after Marx as well as the most powerful theoretical explanation and justification of the Bolshevik revolution. Regardless of how quickly after its formulation Lukács' interpretation of the Bolshevik revolution became unsustainable, the book inaugurated a new paradigm that forever changed marxism from what Lucio Colletti has

called 'a cosmological romance', and thus a surrogate 'religion' for the 'lower' classes' into a philosophical tradition with universal aspirations (Colletti, 1973, 178).

Reification and the consciousness of the proletariat: theorizing the revolution

In his essay *Reification and the Consciousness of the Proletariat* (included in *History and Class Consciousness*) Lukács adopts Marx's discussion of the fetishism of commodities[2] as the basis for his theory of reification. Following Marx, Lukács explains the essence of the commodity structure: 'it is that a relation between people takes on the character of a thing and thus acquires a "phantom objectivity", an autonomy that seems so strictly rational and all-embracing as to conceal every trace to its fundamental nature: the relation between people'.[3] To gain insight into the 'ideological problems of capitalism and its downfall', Lukács maintains that one must extend the discussion of the problem of the fetishism of commodities to 'an objective form and also as a subjective stance that corresponds to it'. It is this particular feature of the commodity as penetrating society in all its aspects that he considers 'the specific problem of our age'. The central question then that Lukács sets to ask himself is: 'How far is commodity exchange together with its structural consequences able to influence the *total* outer and inner life of society?'

In order to answer this question Lukács has to show

that the contemporary process of capitalist production has indeed achieved a moment in which the commodity becomes universally dominant, determining not only the fate of those who sell their labour power but of society as a whole. Lukács adopts Weber's concept of rationalization[4] to clarify how the differentiation of the capitalist economic process produces not only the fragmentation of the object of production but also how it necessarily entails the fragmentation of its subject. The fate of the worker 'is typical of society as a whole in that this self-objectification, this transformation of a human function into a commodity reveals in all its starkness the dehumanized and dehumanizing function of the commodity relation' (HCC, 92). Weber saw the paradox of societal rationalization precisely in the fact that the development of formal rationality and its institutions is by no means irrational in itself, and understood the 'disenchantment of the world', the fragmentation of a unified reality, as a condition of no return. In contrast to this, Lukács thought this process of fragmentation to be only apparent because the atomization for the individual is only the reflex of consciousness. The laws of capitalist production have been extended to cover every manifestation of life in society. By this logic, just as the capitalist system reproduces itself economically, the structure of reification penetrates the human mind further and further, to the point where it can no longer see its own predicament. In other words, the dominant form of consciousness, namely bourgeois consciousness, can only but correspond to the unified economic structure of the current moment of capitalist development.[5] While Weber's analysis of formal rationality is linked with learning processes that exclude the possibility of a return to metaphysical worldviews as well as that of establishing a dialectical connection with objective reason, Lukács attempts to insert the analysis of rationalization into the understanding of the social totality.

The concept of reification is central to the resolution of this apparent methodological contradiction.

Through it Lukács provides us for the first time with a theoretical explanation for the functioning of ideology as a system of partial laws – be this bourgeois science, philosophy or jurisprudence – for which its own concrete underlying reality lies beyond its grasp. The partiality of this system is evident in what Lukács calls the central antinomies of bourgeois thought, which he identified as the separation of facts and values; the distinction between phenomena, or appearances, and noumena, or essential things-in-themselves; and the opposition between free will and necessity, form and content, subject and object. Bourgeois thought, Lukács claimed, 'entered into an unmediated relationship with reality as it was given' (HCC, 156).

The logical question to be posed to this totalized system is: how is it possible to see through reification, or more importantly, how is it possible to change a reified reality if all means of access to it are part of reified life? The first condition for answering this contradiction is to maintain, for reasons that he can demonstrate theoretically, that the process of rationalization, as complete as it seems and as deep as reification has penetrated into all aspects of human life, must find its limit in the formal character of its own rationality. As Jürgen Habermas has pointed out with regard to this particular conceptual move, Lukács here shifts the burden of proof from the political economic terms that Marx wanted to resolve with a theory of crisis to the realm of philosophical demonstration (TCA, 361). The unity of reason and practice taken by Lukács as philosophical principle will require him to supplement his theory of reification with a theory of class consciousness.

Lukács did not believe in the idea of an 'inevitable' revolutionary outcome as an unmediated consequence of a given condition, i.e. the fact that the sheer number of workers living under certain conditions would necessarily result in revolt and revolution. The difficulty of the development of class consciousness had been explained by Marx in the *18th Brumaire*. Consciousness was much more than the empirical consciousness of individual subjects. Lukács refers to class consciousness as consisting of 'the appropriate and rational reactions "imputed" to a particular position in the process of production' (HCC, 51); he is theoretically proposing it as simply an 'imputed' subject of history. His notion of class consciousness is imbedded in a notion of totality that can be characterized as 'reflective', meaning that the whole is understood as a reflection of its own genesis and the product of its own praxis.[6] For Lukács, 'only concrete historical becoming can perform the function of that genesis and consciousness (the practical consciousness of the proletariat) is an integral part of that process' (HCC, 204). This subject of history is the proletarian class in which consciousness evolves dialectically in relation to the socio-historical process and it is only by virtue of becoming conscious of itself and by transforming itself from 'a class in itself' to 'a class for itself' that it can act successfully. It is through this act that the complete shattering of a reified existence becomes possible. Once the gap between 'empirical' and 'imputed' class consciousness narrows and eventually vanishes, the proletariat becomes the identical subject-object of the history of society. One must speak here of a metaphysics transformed into a dialectical philosophy of history that had as its ultimate goal the theoretical explanation of the events of 1917.

This theoretical proposition of Lukács did not hold up under the scrutiny of the events that quickly succeeded the Bolshevik revolution. By the time *History and Class Consciousness* appeared, the links between the masses, the soviets, and the party had practically dissolved (one can recall examples like the workers' uprising in Kronstadt crushed by the Soviet leadership in 1921 (Jay, 1981, 113)). Whether this failure followed from pre-revolutionary Bolshevik assumptions, as Rosa Luxemburg and the young Trotsky had charged, cannot be discussed here. It is relevant, however, to conclude that Lukács' model carried the burden of not only being capable of a conceptual perspective from which the unity of the abstractly separate moments of reason could be grasped, of being itself capable of identifying the subjects who would establish this unity practically and of directing them in this path. Habermas suggests that Lukács makes a decisive error 'by bringing in this "becoming practical" on a theoretical plane and representing it as a revolutionary actualization of philosophy. In doing so he has to credit theory with more power than even metaphysics had claimed for itself' (TCA, 364).

Lukács' specific achievements in this founding text of western marxism include on the one hand a materialist appropriation of Hegel that makes explicit the idea that Marx's categories refer to structured forms of *practice* that are simultaneously forms of objectivity and subjectivity and represent a powerful attempt to overcome the classical subject-object dualism. The notion of totality developed by Lukács will become the operative notion of totality with which western marxism works and wrestles from this moment on. On the other hand he brings Marx and Weber together in such a way that 'he can view the decoupling of the sphere of social labor from that of cultural and subjective contexts simultaneously under two aspects: as reification and rationalization'.[7] This insight permits Lukács to have a historically specific understanding of the totality of capitalist forms. As Moishe Postone has suggested 'his contribution points to a theory of forms of thought and their transformation in capitalism which avoids the materialist reductionism of the base–superstructure model and of the more idealist, culturalist models' (Postone, 1996, 73).[8] The concept of reification permits him to speak of processes that increase the division between culture and production, and its imbeddedness in a concept of totality guarantees the philosophical dimension. The question that too quickly arose, perhaps before the book was even finished, was: given the course that events took with the rise to power of the Soviet Union, how was a theory of reification to hold without a theory of class consciousness?

The afterlife of reification: the critique of instrumental reason or mourning the revolution

The rapid historical developments of the 1920s proved Lukács to be mistaken in his theory of class consciousness, as the gap between 'imputed' and 'empirical' consciousness only widened in the Soviet Union's process of state formation. When the book came under attack for methodological reasons by the Comintern, Lukács opted to tow the party line by denouncing his own book.[9] In spite of this, the text had caused such a ripple effect that it survived and circulated clandestinely and influenced every marxist thinker of the time. *History and Class Consciousness* presented a theoretical alternative to orthodox marxism. Its theory of reification, along with the rejection of bourgeois science, served as the foundation for what came to be known as Critical Theory as it was developed at the Institute of Social Research in Frankfurt.[10] To understand the development of Critical Theory after Lukács, specifically to explain the afterlife of the concept of reification, one must understand the historical experiences that defined the conditions of its theoretical possibility for critical theorists, like Theodor W. Adorno and Max Horkheimer.

The methodological preoccupations that defined the early proposal of the Institute of Social Research, of which Horkheimer became the director, were in accordance with a number of historical problems that Lukács could not have foreseen. The first of these challenges was the rise of fascism, which demonstrated the ability of advanced capitalist societies to respond to critical revolutionary conditions not only by absorbing the opposition but by restructuring the political system and creating consensus through a fundamentally charismatic appeal. The second problem concerned developments in the United States regarding the emergence and appeal of mass culture under non-coercive conditions. Giving a theoretical account of these pressing realities became the research imperative of the members of the Institute of Social Research.

Lukács had assumed the validity of a logic according to which the process of the reification of consciousness had to lead to its own overcoming in proletarian class consciousness. Unable to retain Lukács' theory of class consciousness, Adorno and Horkheimer nonetheless held on to the theory of reification, which in turn determined how they would explain the historical experiences that so clearly demonstrated the fact that the subjective nature of the masses was incorporated into the whirl of societal rationalization without offering resistance. Fascism and mass culture seemed to follow quite different logics even when both could be largely understood from within the theory of reification.

Adorno and Horkheimer's theory of mass culture starts from the view that the commodity form takes hold of culture and thus has a tendency to take over all of the functions of human beings; their theory of fascism involves the way in which the political elites restructure political control in light of the resistance of the population to the process of rationalization itself. A different understanding of subjectivity and its social expression, and particularly of its unconscious dimensions, becomes crucial in their critical approach. Adorno and Horkheimer radicalize Lukács' theory of reification in socio-psychological terms; they do this so as to explain the stability of advanced capitalist societies without having to give up the critique of commodity fetishism. Other socio-psychological factors complicated their understanding of the reproduction and maintenance of the status quo. The need to explain phenomena as disparate as fascism and mass culture led them to an expansion of the concept of reification. A much broader critique of rationalization became necessary: namely, a critique of instrumental reason.

Lukács used the concept of reification to describe the way in which human relations (and subjectivity) are assimilated into the world of things, a process, which comes about when social actions are coordinated through the medium of exchange value. As Jürgen Habermas has pointed out in *Dialectic of Enlightenment*, Horkheimer and Adorno:

> detach the concept not only from the special historical context of the rise of the capitalist economic system but from the dimension of interhuman relations altogether; and they generalize it temporally (over the entire history of the species) and substantively (the same logic of domination is imputed to both cognition in the service of self-preservation and the repression of instinctual nature). This double generalization of the concept of reification leads to a concept of instrumental reason that shifts the primordial history of subjectivity and the self-formative process of ego identity into an encompassing historic-philosophical perspective.
>
> (TCA, 379)

Horkheimer and Adorno see themselves forced to extrapolate the foundations of the reification critique and to expand instrumental reason into a category of the world-historical process of civilization as a whole, that is to project the process of reification to the origins of human societal organization. This expansion of the concept of reification loses its conceptual framework and leads to the following paradox: Horkheimer and Adorno would have to put forward a theory of reason before instrumental reason, which, according to their own ideas, is impossible. The dialectic of enlightenment finds itself engaged in a self-critique of reason in order to show the way to a truth that, at this stage of complete alienation, is simply not accessible.

Lukács' thesis that the complete rationalization of the world finds its limit in the formal character of its own rationality is disputed by Adorno and Horkheimer on empirical grounds, as evidenced in the forms of penetrating reification of culture and inner nature, and theoretically, by showing that even the objective idealism developed in Hegelian marxism follows the logic of identity thinking and reproduces in itself the structures of reified consciousness.[11] This distrust of the Lukácsian concept of totality combined with an expanded notion of reification leads them to denounce the whole as untrue. The aporia produced by this philosophical development in critical theory resides precisely in the denunciation of the whole as untrue, with no recourse to a conceptual apparatus of immanent critique that does not already implicate itself in the pretensions of the great philosophical tradition. A critical theory that situated itself between philosophy and social science, that is marxism as neither an empirical social science nor as speculative science but as 'critique', seemed to have outlived its own claims. Can reification, and with it a fundamentally marxist understanding of society, be rethought critically and theoretically?

The end of reification as concept? Jürgen Habermas' paradigm shift

Jürgen Habermas, inheritor of the Frankfurt School tradition, tries to answer this question by restricting the concept of reification once again and by regarding it as a distorting effect on the lifeworld, that is primarily as intersubjective alienation. Habermas shifts the problem from the subject–object paradigm of instrumental reason to a subject–subject paradigm of communicative rationality. The problem of reification, says Habermas, 'arises less from a purposive rationality that has been absolutized in the service of self-preservation, from an instrumental reason that has gone wild, than from the circumstance that an unleashed functionalist reason of system maintenance disregards and overrides the claim of reason ingrained in communicative sociation and lets the rationalization of the world run idle' (TCA, 380). The fundamental premise of this proposition is the communicative nature of social interaction. The shift brings back the sphere of action into the realm of norms, values and linguistic understanding. While reification may be the fundamental experience of our functionalized world, it is by no means regulated by a totalizing system where objective forms correspond to subjective stances nor by the instrumentality of reason imbedded in an untrue whole where social actors disappear. At stake for Habermas is the restitution of a holism in marxism with normative guarantees which would, therefore, allow for the intervention in the world of reality again.

The intricacies and theoretical presuppositions of Habermas' model are beyond the scope of this essay but invite us to think further about a paradigm shift that abandons both the idea of the revolution for that of democracy as well as the concept of totality that, in all its vicissitudes, had been at the heart of the analysis of capitalism in the marxist tradition. The idea of reification as distortion of the lifeworld is central to the survival of a Marxist project that must at the same time guarantee its normative ground in order not to be demoted to its pre-Lukácsian status of 'religion of the poor'. On the success or failure of this enterprise, Habermas thinks, marxism gambles its future.

Conclusion: Lukács reappraised

In 1967, when Lukács finally agreed to an edition of *History and Class Consciousness*, he did so with the proviso of being able to write an introduction in which he could explain the flaws of this work. Aware of the impact his text had had over the previous forty years, the point he made shortly after its publication had to be made again: this was an idealist text that 'out-Hegeled' Hegel. The historical record, however, surprised us when the CPSU in Moscow opened its archives after the collapse of the Soviet regime. A text in defence of *History and Class Consciousness*, entitled *Tailism and the Dialectic* and authored by Lukács sometime in 1925 or 1926, was found in the archives. Its recent translation into English has renewed interest in Lukács' classic text and its intellectual history, as well as illuminating a text that Lukács was thought never to have defended.

In the *postface* to *Tailism and the Dialectic*, Slavoj Žižek asserts that this recently discovered text allows us to recover Lukács against the tradition of its western reception. Against Habermas, Žižek sets Lukács apart as the philosopher of the revolution in an era in which 'no leftist dares to question the premises of democratic politics' (Žižek, 2000, 165). For Žižek, Lukács must be remembered as the philosopher who believed in the political act above all, as the thinker of the revolutionary event, of the revolutionary will. Lukács, as the philosopher of Leninism, stands as tribute to the possibility of imagining the revolutionary moment and in this light the problem of reification is turned on its head. The question becomes not where does it stand in relation to us today but, in Leninist fashion, where do we stand in relation to it?

The contestation over the legacy of György Lukács attests to a practical imperative that sets Marxist theory apart from all others: that of changing the world. Reification as concept allows for the envisioning of its negation. The form of that negation can only be determined historically, as our understanding of the concept of reification itself has been.

Notes

I am most thankful to Chris Chiappari for his thoughtful reading and indispensable comments on this article.

1. I will refer to this book as HCC from here on.
2. In section four of the first volume of *Capital*, entitled 'the fetishism of commodities and the secret thereof', Marx describes the commodity as follows:

> A commodity is therefore a mysterious thing, simply because in it the social character of men's labour appears to them as an objective character stamped upon the product of that labour; because the relation of the producers to the sum total of their own labour is presented to them as a social relation, existing not between themselves, but between the products of their labour. This is the reason why the products of labour become commodities, social things whose qualities are at the same time perceptible and imperceptible by the senses . . . It is only a definite social relation between men that assumes in their eyes the fantastic form of a relation between things.
> (Marx, 1967, 72)

3. All citations in this paragraph are in HCC, 84 and *passim*.
4. For Max Weber the process of modernization is a process of rationalization that involves the differentiation of social spheres into special-

ized spheres and quasi-autonomous institutions, and the development of a higher degree of abstraction (formal rationality) that makes possible the creation of law, the formulation of science, the standardization of bureaucracy and the disintegration of a unified reality.

5. My analysis of the relationship between reification and rationalization follows Jürgen Habermas' analysis in *The Theory of Communicative Action* (1981). I will refer to it as TCA from here on.
6. For a discussion of the notion of totality in Lukács see Jay (1981).
7. See n. 5.
8. Postone develops the most interesting defence in recent times of Marx's late social theory against the standard interpretation of orthodox marxist doctrine regarding the supremacy of labour. In his view both Lukács and Habermas err along these lines in their readings of Marx.
9. Lukács maintained this line throughout his life. In the preface to the 1967 edition of the book he recapitulates for the reader what he sees as the 'errors' in this work of his youth.
10. Hence later to be known as the Frankfurt School.
11. Adorno in particular develops a distinct dialectic of non-identity that will later on set him apart from Horkheimer. See Adorno's *Negative Dialectics* (1973).

Works cited

Adorno, Theodor W. *Negative Dialectics*. New York, 1973.

Colletti, Lucio. *Marxism and Hegel*. London, 1973.

Habermas, Jürgen. *The Theory of Communicative Action*, Volume One, trans. Thomas McCarthy. Boston, MA, 1981.

Jay, Martin. *Marxism and Totality*. Berkeley, CA, 1981

Lukács, György. *History and Class Consciousness: Studies in Marxist Dialectics*. Boston, MA, 1971.

Marx, Karl. *Capital*, Volume 1, ed. Frederick Engels. New York, 1967.

Postone, Moishe. *Time, Labor and Social Domination*. Cambridge, 1996.

Žižek, Slavoj. Postface to *A Defence of History and Class Consciousness: Tailism and the Dialectic*. London, 2000.

schizoanalysis | *TAMSIN LORRAINE*

In 1972, the publication in France of Gilles Deleuze and Félix Guattari's book, *Anti-Oedipus*, resonated with the growing challenges to structuralism and Lacanian psychoanalysis that arose with the political upheaval of May 1968. In this book, Deleuze and Guattari deride psychoanalysis for reducing the anarchic productivity of unconscious desire to the familial desires played out in the Oedipal triangle. They object to the psychoanalytic figuring of desire as lack and contend instead that desire is productive and flows according to immanent principles. On their view, understanding that desire according to an interpretative schema externally imposed upon its unfolding not only fails to capture its dynamic becoming, but literally thwarts its creative progress. Psychoanalysis is a normative, normalizing theory that would reduce the multiple forms desire can take. Schizoanalysis is their proposal for an alternative form of analysis. Instead of referring all desire to the personal identities of the Oedipal triangle, schizoanalysis pursues the breaks and flows linking elements of life according to a desire that unfolds of itself without reference to anything that transcends its own becoming. That is, schizoanalysis deliberately pursues the multiple unfoldings of desire that link the prepersonal elements of psychic life in ways too 'peculiar' to consolidate the identities of conventional familial and social life. This form of analysis would shun interpretation entirely and instead constitutes a practice with the express intent of mobilizing flows connecting the elements of psychic life across traditional 'barriers' with the hoped-for effect of enlivening individuals

and fostering energizing links that connect those individuals to one another in novel ways.

In *A Thousand Plateaus*, the follow-up to *Anti-Oedipus* first published in 1980, Deleuze and Guattari claim that the meaning pronounced by authors in a book about the world can be trapped within the signification and desire of 'dominated' subjects. While traditional theory (for example, psychoanalysis) tends to present itself as an interpretation of a world it would represent, Deleuze and Guattari describe their book as an assemblage that aspires to be an experiment 'in contact with the real'. The theory of schizoanalysis (or what they also call deterritorialization, destratification or the construction of a body without organs, among other terms) presented in *A Thousand Plateaus*, is meant not to provide 'interpretations' of life, but rather 'maps' that could lead us to new realities. Interpretations trace already established patterns of meaning; maps pursue connections, or what Deleuze and Guattari call 'lines of flight', not readily perceptible to the normative subjects of dominant reality. Their notion of a collective assemblage of enunciation suggests that a theory extracts a unified perspective from an impersonal array of virtual relations with concrete consequences for the social field as a whole. The events of language that a theory attributes to states of affairs do not simply reflect a reality they cannot affect, but rather bring about what they call 'incorporeal transformations' that are a creative participant in the heterogeneous mix of human life. The writing assemblage of Deleuze, Guattari, words and world resulting in *A*

Thousand Plateaus is meant to establish connections between fields of reality, representation and subjectivity that defy the traditional divisions of world, book and author. It is their hope that these connections will precipitate vital alternatives for living through the reading assemblages that pass them along.

Deleuze and Guattari characterize a way of doing theory in *A Thousand Plateaus* that illuminates the shift their conception of schizoanalysis takes from what started as a critique of psychoanalysis and oedipal subjectivity in *Anti-Oedipus* to the broader conception of mapping that emerges in the later work. Schizoanalysis is no more interested in maintaining its own identity as 'schizoanalysis' than it is in maintaining the personal identity of the selves it analyses. And yet, Deleuze and Guattari's proposal to understand individuation as an unfolding series of states provides an alternate means for recognizing individuals (be they theories or human subjects) without excluding the creative evolutions of their becoming. In what follows I elaborate the project of schizoanalysis that emerges in these two works in light of the conception of linguistic production (captured in such terms as 'collective assemblage' and 'incorporeal transformation') characterized in *A Thousand Plateaus*. Deleuze and Guattari's conception of theory as an evolving force actualizing the virtual-real of language with pragmatic implications for a dynamic social field suggests that we need to consider the effects of words as seriously as we consider the effects of other actions in the world. They believe that the most ethical theory is ultimately the one that is most responsive to life – even if this means being 'true' to mutating flows of desire rather than the boundaries of already established identities. Such a view, as we will see, has important repercussions for how we understand ourselves as well as how we theorize the world.

According to Deleuze and Guattari, books contain statements that are evaluated by their readers against the background of pragmatic implications, implicit presuppositions and incorporeal transformations that 'make sense' in a given time and place. The direct discourse of a book is extracted from the indirect discourse of what Deleuze and Guattari call the collective assemblage of enunciation in keeping with implicit rules of the 'operations of signifiance' and the 'proceedings of subjectification' regulating our normative notions of meaningful sentences and speaking subjects. When a man stands on the deck of a ship as he searches the horizon for a whale, there is a set of bodies – man, ship, water, whale – that act and are acted upon. Bodies (taken in the broadest sense) are affected by actions and passions (he is now walking or swimming, joyful or sad). They are also the object of non-corporeal attribution (he is now married, or divorced, or tenured). The statements, 'Ahab hunts the white whale' or 'Ahab becomes-whale', express incorporeal transformations or events that can be distinguished from the actions and passions of bodies. The collective assemblage of enunciation entails incorporeal transformations 'current in a given society' that are 'attributed to the bodies of that society' (ATP, 80). The events my propositions express – to hunt, or to become-whale – do not represent a state of affairs, but 'anticipate them or move them back, slow them down or speed them up, separate or combine them, delimit them in a different way' (ATP, 86). The event of becoming-whale implies a different set of virtual relations than the event of hunting; the assemblage expressing the former event rather than the latter attributes distinctive incorporeal transformations to Ahab's actions that will produce unpredictable effects in future assemblages of readers, book and world. Speech acts do not simply represent states of affairs, but intervene with them. Part of the goal of *A Thousand Plateaus* is to thwart the normative divisions of author, world and book that foster the illusion of a personal self commenting upon a world from which it is separate. 'Speaking in tongues. To write is perhaps to bring this assemblage of the unconscious to the light of day, to select the whispering voices, to gather the tribes and secret idioms from which I extract something I call my Self (*Moi*)' (ATP, 84).

Schizoanalysis, unlike psychoanalysis, would foster the recognition that when the subject speaks, she can never speak in her own name in the sense of producing a personal statement. Instead, there are no individual statements and it is rather 'when the individual opens up to the multiplicities pervading him or her, at the outcome of the most severe operation of depersonalization, that he or she acquires his or her true proper name' (ATP, 37). While psychoanalysis would support the fantasy of having a private, personal self, schizoanalysis would insist that the individual is not a person but a series of states that unfold out of a specific milieu. This process of individuation acquires its individuality not through a set of enduring attributes, but through the specificity of its unique unfolding. Like the name of a disease or a scientific effect (such as AIDS or the Joule or Kelvin effect), a proper name designates not a person, but a series of states that are sets of particular effects within a field of potentials. 'Mononucleosis' designates not one thing, but a set of symptoms that converge in varying patterns over the course of the disease; various symptoms may come and go, but it is not until a critical proportion of symptoms has disappeared that we can say the disease is cured. 'Gilles Deleuze' designates not one person, but a set of effects whose relationships shift over time in interaction with the surrounding world; many of these effects come and go, but a critical proportion must maintain continuity for the individual we call Deleuze to continue to exist. Personhood is the result of the 'subjectification proceedings' of the collective assemblage of enunciation of a given society (in particular, a society that prizes oedipalization). Such proceedings obliterate non-normative connections in favour of those that produce readily recognizable subjects. It is thus the individual whose statements exceed the norms regulating personhood in deference to the contingent connections of her own unfolding that can acquire 'her true proper name'.

Gilbert Simondon, an important influence on Deleuze and Guattari's thinking about individuation, argues that the individual has traditionally been defined in terms of a state of stable equilibrium. That is, the individuated being is assumed to be in 'the sort of equilibrium that is attained in a system when all the possible transformations have been achieved and no other force remains to enact any further changes' (GI, 302). This approach not only excludes the notion of becoming from our thinking about individuation, but strips the individual from the interactions with its surrounding milieu that make it what it is. Simondon suggests understanding the individual as a relative reality – 'merely the result of a phase in the being's development' – instead of a completed totality. Thus individuation could be viewed as 'a partial and relative resolution manifested in a system that contains latent potentials and harbors a certain incompatibility with itself' (GI, 300). The tensions arising from the incompatible forces of a specific phase of development precipitate the individual into its next phase of development. Each phase of the system of the individual's reality is 'replete with potentials' (GI, 316). It is in part due to the force of potentials in the process of becoming that the individual moves from one state of its being to another. Individuation entails not a synthesis that finally brings a being into a state of completion, but 'rather the being passing out of step with itself' (GI, 314). Accounts of the subject that attempt to sum up its essential attributes fail to capture the shifting movements of its unfolding;

Simondon's account suggests that any individual is a series of metastable states, no one of which captures the essence of what that individual is.

In *Difference and Repetition*, Deleuze develops a way of understanding individuals in terms of the problems inherent in a given process of individuation. Like Simondon, he contends that examining only the final states of equilibrium in which a process results (however we may define such states), gives us an impoverished understanding of the individual at issue. Individual things, including a human subject or a philosophical concept, would be better understood in terms of a self-differentiating series of states comprising virtual potentialities as well as material forms that unfold in response to the problems of life. Each state of the series is replete with the potential to move into any number of other states in concert with its surrounding milieu. The individual subject or concept, on this view, is not what remains the same throughout all the changes it undergoes, but is rather a conjunction of states that includes the dynamic force inherent in each state. The states of a process of individuation are not clearly defined but entail the infinitesimal movement of elemental particles toward a limit that marks a qualitative change in an open-ended set of particles. This limit is the virtual event or singularity that oversees the actualization of the series; it is the problem insisting in the unfolding of a series of points. For example, the point on a vector where water begins to boil (or Deleuze dies or the event of 'to schizoanalyze' begins) is a singularity. That singularity inheres in a state of non-boiling water (or the living Deleuze or a thought-movement) as a virtual possibility. Although it has not yet actually manifested, it insists in that state as a potentiality, a kind of problem that will only be resolved when the incremental movements of multiple elements coalesce in a specific way. The singularities of freezing and evaporation also inhere in non-boiling water as virtual possibilities. Any one of these singularities only become actualized given the convergence of a whole set of forces that include processes beyond those defining the individual at issue. The virtualities of boiling, freezing and evaporating constitute part of the incompossible field of virtualities that condition the next state the water actually reaches. The entire field of the virtual must ultimately include the conditions not just for a given process of individuation, but for all of life since all the forces of life ultimately affect one another. Transitions across the multiple thresholds involved in a given process of individuation happen in infinitesimal degrees that fall below the identities perceived in ordinary awareness. The psychic self and coherent body of conscious awareness (as well as boiling water or a philosophical concept), from this perspective, are the emergent effects of unstable processes in continual movement that unfold over time and that entail a field of virtual potentialities as well as the determinate configurations of material elements.

Language is a crucial factor in the processes of individuation of specific human subjects as well as of specific cultures and humanity as a whole. Like any process of production, linguistic activity unfolds with respect to problems. Just as material processes entail virtual singularities that may or may not be actualized (for example, the freezing or boiling points of a pot of water), so do linguistic processes entail events – pure becomings expressed by propositions – that may be actualized in the specific state of affairs to which they are attributed, but which can always be actualized in other states of affairs. Thus there are always other states of affairs to which the event 'to boil' (or 'to schizoanalyze') can be attributed. Furthermore, the relations of events can be distinguished from the relations of material things. The statement 'I swear!' is a different statement when said by a child to her mother, a woman to her lover or a witness in court. But according to Deleuze and Guattari, all the possible 'effectuations' of this statement are present in one of its effectuations and these virtual effectuations create a virtual line of variation which is 'real without being actual, and consequently continuous regardless of the leaps the statement makes' (ATP, 94). What they call the 'abstract machine' of language is 'not actual, but virtual-real; it has, not invariable or obligatory rules, but optional rules that ceaselessly vary with the variation itself, as in a game in which each move changes the rules'. A concrete assemblage actualizes relations that are a function of the lines of continuous variation drawn by the abstract machine. 'The assemblage negotiates variables at this or that level of variation, according to this or that degree of deterritorialization, and determines which variables will enter into constant relations or obey obligatory rules and which will serve instead as a fluid matter for variation' (ATP, 100).

An assemblage (like authors, book and world) that opens and multiplies connections approaches 'the living abstract machine' (ATP, 513). Psychoanalysis 'royally botches the real' because it interprets everything in keeping with a set of normative rules regulating significance and subjects. The continuous variations in language that are imperceptible to persons with 'common sense' – the virtual relations of events that defy the thresholds of conventional perception and thought – are ignored in deference to the established patterns of meaning imposed by psychoanalysis. The virtual relations of language are as real for Deleuze and Guattari as the relations already actualized in specific speech acts. Concrete assemblages like that of Deleuze and Guattari, *A Thousand Plateaus* and world can negotiate the virtual relations of events and actualize connections conventional assemblages would

ignore. Rather than interpret desire by representing it with reference to a preconceived structure, schizoanalysis experiments with desire, actively participating in the drawing of lines, rendering previously imperceptible lines of continuous variation perceptible. It pursues not the structures and relations of persons, subjects, and interpretations, but the lines 'running through groups as well as individuals' (ATP, 204). Schizoanalysis refuses to reduce desire to the connections established vis-à-vis persons and the phallus, and instead experiments with the lines of continuous variation that are above and below the thresholds of perception and representational thought where the boundaries delimiting the identities of persons and things are unambiguous. Theorizing, like other processes, can remain trapped in repetitive patterns or create new patterns in flow with the contingencies of thought-movements in their specific milieus. Deleuze and Guattari expect that the concepts of schizoanalysis will creatively evolve in different contexts and that those concepts will have unpredictable effects in the individuation processes of the human subjects and cultures in which they emerge.

Although Deleuze and Guattari do not use the term 'assemblage' in *Anti-Oedipus*, in this earlier work they characterize human beings as unfolding processes of individuation in constant interaction with their surroundings, and refuse the psychoanalytic notion that such interactions should be referred to oedipal positions. They describe human subjectivity in terms of three syntheses of the unconscious: connective syntheses that join elements into series ('desiring-machines'), disjunctive syntheses that resonate series in metastable states ('bodies without organs'), and conjunctive syntheses that gather metastable states into the continuous experience of conscious awareness. Deleuze and Guattari agree with the psychoanalytic account that the coherent body-image and sense of self of a sentient subject is the result of a mostly unconscious process that unfolds over time. They also agree that oedipal subjectivity is one form that human sentience can take. The syntheses they describe, however, have oedipal and anoedipal forms. Schizoanalysis is designed to foster the latter. The subject, as a process of individuation emerging from the social field, is an inevitable co-participant in the creation and mutation of social formations. Deleuze and Guattari contend that unconscious investments in the social field take precedence over conscious investments in personal identity. Schizoanalysis, rather than tracing all desire to the positions of an oedipal triangle, wants to attain 'the immediate productive unconscious' that affects and is affected by the breaks and flows of the larger social field (AO, 98).

Deleuze and Guattari claim that capitalism came into being when 'flows of production' were decoded in the form of money-capital and 'flows of labour' were decoded in the form of the worker free to sell her labour-power. Instead of coding (or overcoding) flows of desire, thus making sure that 'no flow exists that is not properly dammed up, channeled, regulated', capitalism 'has created an axiomatic of abstract quantities that keeps moving further and further in the direction of the deterritorialization of the socius' (AO, 33). That is, capitalism's emphasis on the abstract quantification of money and labour (what matters is how capital and labour circulates – not the specific form wealth takes or who in particular does what) encourages desire to permute across the social field in unpredictable ways. Capitalism as a social formation that seeks to replicate itself depends on oedipalization to manage this tendency toward deterritorialization. Oedipalization entails replacing the connection of partial objects with a regime for the pairing of people. 'Partial objects now seem to be taken from people, rather than from the nonpersonal flows that pass from one person to another. The reason is that persons are derived from abstract quantities, instead of from flows' (AO, 71). On the body without organs, desire is the only subject. It passes from one body to another, producing partial objects, creating breaks and flows, 'following connections and appropriations that each time destroy the factitious unity of a possessive or proprietary ego' (AO, 72). Oedipalization makes it appear that partial objects are possessed by a person and that it is the person who desires. The exclusive disjunctions of oedipalization designate global persons 'who do not exist prior to the prohibitions that found them' rather than intensive states through which the subject passes on the body without organs. The designations of the exclusive disjunctions differentiate among global persons and situate the ego vis-à-vis those persons (AO, 78).

The axiomatics of capitalism does not care about preserving the content of a given capitalist formation; the specific forms that places of work take with the concomitant identities of employers and employees matter much less than that capital flows and the market flourishes. Yet if capitalism is to replicate itself despite the mutating forms of the institutions and people who manifest it, it must make sure that the deterritorializing flows of capital do not mutate to the point of rendering capitalism unrecognizable to itself. As a process of individuation, capitalism passes beyond itself in a series of states of partial resolution that contain incompatibilities and latent potentials. For the tensions in these states not to rupture this process entirely (thus ending in capitalism's demise), they must be resolved from state to state. Oedipalization is useful to the replication of capitalism because by making sure desire is always constrained to the personalized triangle of oedipus, the inherent deterritorialization of capitalism is effectively managed. Oedipal subjects maintain the innovations of deterritorializing capital within the tightly bound parameters of a personal identity and familial life (or the triangulated authority relationships that mimic oedipus in the public realm). It is Deleuze and Guattari's contention that this is precisely the process that psychoanalysis would foster and support.

Schizoanalysis would encourage capitalism's inherent deterritorialization to approach and move past its limit and foster the schizo subject whose desire moves past the constraints of oedipalization. Instead of referring the body to a model of totalized body parts referred to a privileged signifier (the phallus), the schizo experiences her body as a field of multiplicities vibrating in an intensive field with no external point of reference or culmination. According to Deleuze and Guattari, oedipalization constitutes an illegitimate restriction on the syntheses of the unconscious because it emphasizes global persons (thus excluding all partial objects of desire), exclusive disjunctions (thus relegating the subject to a chronological series of moments that can be given a coherent narrative account), and a segregative and biunivocal use of the conjunctive syntheses (thus reducing the identity of the subject to a coherent or static set of one side of a set of oppositions).

Life itself is an activity of production. Whether a subject is oedipalized or not, she is a process in full participation with life as process; the elements of her body and psyche are in constant movement, making, disrupting and remaking various connections. The conscious awareness of both the oedipal subject and the schizo are the emergent effects of myriad processes. But while the oedipal subject is subjected to the dominant signifier of the phallus, the schizo is able to experience her surroundings in terms of partial objects and non-specific connections, inclusive disjunctions and non-segmentary, polyvocal conjunctions. She still experiences a sense of wholeness, a sense that

the various states through which she passes are experienced by her. But the subject of her experiences is not the global person whose identity is fixed on either one side or the other of various oppositional divides (male *or* female, white *or* black), and she designates the various pleasurable and painful states through which she passes in terms of intensities that are always becoming-other rather than as attributes of an unchanging being. Because her unconscious productions defy the constriction of oedipalization, her reality is different from that of the oedipal subject; her sensations, emotions and thoughts defy oedipal categorization. While the oedipal subject experiences the world in terms of the possibilities posited by dominant reality, the schizo is sensitive to the singularities and events that could produce alternative realities. Furthermore, given that the schizo does not come up against the blank wall of schizophrenia, alcoholism or some other form of a failed or empty body without organs, her production of this reality reverberates with and through the realities of others.

According to Deleuze and Guattari the unconscious neither symbolizes, imagines nor represents, but instead engineers. Deoedipalization would release desire from the regulated channels of oedipal desire and allow the creative proliferation of desiring and social machines. Energy, instead of encountering the blank wall of oedipalization, would produce innovative forms of subjectivity with different ways of interacting with others and the environment, and new forms for collective living. Perhaps more importantly, these fresh formations would be lived with an intensity and excitement unavailable to oedipalized subjects. Human beings as biological processes immersed in a living world would share in the joyfully creative processes of life that always moves onward, generating new forms in response to the mutating forces of becoming.

Schizoanalysis creates concepts on the fly that are

meant to map experiments 'in contact with the real' rather than to trace interpretations according to a representation of reality it cannot affect. 'The map does not reproduce an unconscious closed in upon itself; it constructs the unconscious. It fosters connections between fields, the removal of blockages on bodies without organs, the maximum opening of bodies without organs onto a plane of consistency' (ATP, 12). The question for Deleuze and Guattari is not whether their theory is right or wrong, but how effective it is in fostering the creative productions of the unconscious. They reject the psychoanalytic contention that the only alternative to oedipal subjectivity is psychosis and instead explore anoedipal flows of desire and the schizo who is a functioning subject of such desire. Their notion of the unconscious suggests ways of approaching its 'symptoms' that point to possibilities for creative transformation inevitably linked with social change. Since theory responds to problems presented by the ongoing flow of life, concepts cannot do life justice or help us to be ethical unless they themselves unfold in dynamic thought-movements, mutating as they go. In addition to refusing to endorse the normative role of a theory that would freeze life in keeping with a set of static categories, Deleuze and Guattari insist that theory consider its role to be that of a co-participant in a set of creative forces that are always evolving.

As a process that unfolds in the writing and reading assemblages of which it is a part, theory effectuates statements drawn from the lines of continuous variation of the abstract machine of language. It creates a 'personal' perspective from the heterogeneous mix of impersonal flows of the collective assemblage of enunciation. The events it expresses become forces in the unfolding processes of human and social individuation. A theory can either parrot dominant norms of signification and subjectification or it can actualize virtual relations of sense in keeping with variations of specific situations that defy personal identity and conventional perception. Rather than describing more or less accurately a world it cannot touch, schizoanalysis reveals a shifting, heterogeneous set of forces of which it is a part. Deleuze and Guattari's characterization and enactment of schizoanalysis invites us not only to remark the multiple connections we have to the world, but to open ourselves to their creative becoming. When we attribute events to states of affairs in deference to becomings that defy conventional delimitations, we co-create new realities that are in keeping with the flow of life. Schizoanalysis not only shows us a new way to do theory, it gives us a map of contemporary life that allows us to situate individual processes of becoming within a continually evolving social field. Such maps tell us more about a future toward which we could unfold than a reality that is bound to be and, in the process, challenge us to responsibly participate – in our words as well as our actions – in the co-creation of a future we can all desire.

Works cited

Deleuze, Gilles. *Difference and Repetition*, trans. P. Patton. New York, 1994.

Deleuze, Gilles and Félix Guattari. *Anti-Oedipus: Capitalism and Schizophrenia*, trans. R. Hurley, M. Seem and H. R. Lane. Minneapolis, MN, 1983. Cited as AO.

Deleuze, Gilles and Félix Guattari. *A Thousand Plateaus: Capitalism and Schizophrenia*, trans. Brian Massumi. Minneapolis, MN, 1987. Cited as ATP.

Simondon, G. 'The Genesis of the Individual', trans. M. Cohen and S. Kwinter, in *Incorporations*, eds Jonathan Crary and Sanford Kwinter. New York, 1992, 297–319. Cited as GI.

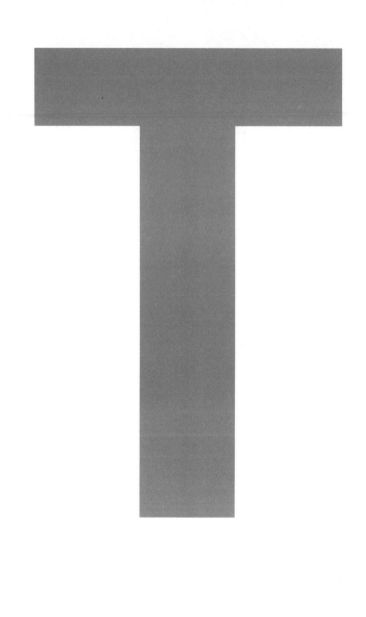

tele-techno-theology | *MARTIN MCQUILLAN*

An entire epoch of so-called literature, if not all of it, cannot survive a certain technological regime of telecommunications (in this respect the political regime is secondary). Neither can philosophy, or psychoanalysis. Or love letters.

Jacques Derrida (1987, 197)

This is still a dangerous world. It's a world of madmen and potential mental losses.

George W. Bush

T

is for telepathy, T is for tele-technology, T is for theology, T is also for the Taliban and for terrorism. In the immediate aftermath of 11 September I was asked by an Internet journal to comment on the 'Event'. Like most I was too traumatized to speak, no commentary could do justice to what happened in New York, Washington DC and Pennsylvania. It would seem that the mediatic space which reported these events, and whose images pre-figured it, was incapable of bearing the weight of analysis they demanded. The one thing that this space could not understand was the very thing that it had foreshadowed in so many filmic scenarios from the secret bases of the terrorists of SPECTRE to the Alien invasion in *Independence Day*. By this reckoning, this event is made the only thing – at this time, in this space – worth understanding, even if such an analysis runs the risk of a disproportionate response, mistaking the concentrated power of those media images for a general chal-

lenge to world hegemony. Such an analysis may only lend credence to the thinking that perpetrated the attack and the mirror-logic which responded to it as, and with, an act of War. What follows is an approach to an analysis of the War (this 'war' as the latest incident in a world war which will has been raging for the last thirty years) and telepathy (*tele-pathein*, pain at a distance).

I

I will have a foreign-handed foreign policy.

George W. Bush

Nicholas Royle has outlined the question of telepathy and psychoanalysis for us.[1] For Royle telepathy is a remainder within psychoanalysis, a stubborn stain which can be neither explained by the scientific categories of psychoanalysis (and so be accommodated within the bounds of psychoanalysis as a suitable object of study) nor excluded absolutely as belonging merely to the unscientific world of the Occult. Telepathy is something of an embarrassment to Freud who over a series of unpublished papers comes to accept the possibility of 'thought-transference' while equivocating over this belief in front of his colleagues and disciples. Telepathy then destabilizes the boundaries of psychoanalysis: inside–outside, public–private, reason–occultism, science–religion and so on. Thus, telepathy thwarts and contaminates the scientific ambitions of the

Freudian project, refusing it closure and pressuring it into an 'analysis interminable', while sending back messages to psychoanalysis telling it what it has known all along.[2] This is a persuasive deconstruction.[3] However, what interests me about Freud's 'secret lectures'[4] on telepathy is the way in which telepathy is linked in his writing to the experience of war. It has become commonplace to suggest that the elaboration of the economy of *thanatos* in *Beyond the Pleasure Principle* (and all that this means for a resituation of the Freudian topography) is closely linked with the experience of mechanized warfare in western Europe. *Beyond the Pleasure Principle* is not just any book for Freud, nor is it just any book by Freud for deconstruction. Just as telepathy leaves a stain on psychoanalysis, so does the question of war, and as we will see, by extension the issue of telepathy is marked by the experience of war.

The two lengthy studies of telepathy by Freud, 'Psychoanalysis and Telepathy' (1921) and 'Dreams and Telepathy' (1922), are characterized by their frequent references to war.[5] Freud explicitly states in his introductory remarks to 'Psychoanalysis and Telepathy' that the interest in occult phenomena tugging at the coat-tails of his science 'is a part expression of the loss of value by which everything has been affected since the world catastrophe of the Great War' (SE, 177). The injunction of telepathy is double and contradictory for psychoanalysis. On the one hand it is 'a part of the tentative approach to the great revolution towards which we are heading and of whose extent we can form no estimate' (SE, 177). Since the effects of the epistemic shift of psychoanalysis cannot be estimated, telepathy can be neither ruled in nor ruled out of its scientific realm. On the other hand, says Freud, 'no doubt it is also an attempt at compensation, at making up in another, a super-mundane, sphere for the attractions which have been lost by life on this earth' (SE, 177). Thus the interest in telepathy,

if not telepathy itself, can be quite easily explained by psychoanalytic categories as part of the work of mourning compelled by the experience of war. Freud's inquiry into telepathy is then divided within itself from the very beginning, at once attempting to rationalize the irrational and simultaneously drawn to this phenomena as an exemplary instance of the counterintuitive logic of psychoanalysis.

He writes that psychoanalysis does not have any interest in defending the scientific authority which dismisses occultism because psychoanalysis itself 'stands in opposition to every-thing that is conventionally restricted, well-established and generally accepted' (SE, 178). Where Freud and the occultists would seem to part company, for 'alliance and co-operation between analysts and occultists might [initially] appear both plausible and promising' (SE, 178), is over the question of belief. The occultist is a 'convinced believer' while psychoanalysis seeks after knowledge in an attempt 'to conquer this new sphere' (SE, 178). Thus the history of telepathy is marked by the confrontation between blind faith and colonial aspirations (the painting pink of the dark regions of the psyche). It is this binary structure which determines the system of relationships between telepathy and psychoanalysis as well as the present confrontation between a certain Islam and the West. This structure is undone in Freud's text by its movement through the questions of writing, media and the trace. As we shall see the same structure undoes itself in the present context by a similar movement through Media. Freud likens the competing claims of science and the occult to a war-zone, with psychoanalysis as a displaced person:

We have heard during the war of people who stood half-way between two hostile nations, belonging to one by birth and to the other by choice and domicile; it was their fate to be treated as enemies first by one side and then, if they were lucky enough to escape, by the other. Such might equally be the fate of psychoanalysis.

(SE, 180)

If telepathy turns psychoanalysis into a refugee, destined to wander, forever seeking asylum, one can track in these essays Freud's shift in opinion from his initial declaration that he had never come across a truly telepathic experience in any of his patients to his final refusal to rule out the possibility of thought-transference. The sceptic becomes a believer and the refugee becomes a fugitive.

Freud keeps his 'belief' secret fearing the effects that his new found faith will have on the institution of psychoanalysis. The essay 'Psychoanalysis and Telepathy' was originally prepared for a meeting of the Central Executive of the International Psycho-Analytic Association to be held in the Harz mountains in September 1921. Ernest Jones, the then President of the Central Executive, states that no such meeting took place although Freud did read a paper to a small group of close followers including Jones at this time. In the manuscript edition of 'Dreams and Telepathy' the essay is described by Freud as a 'Lecture given before the Vienna Psycho-Analytic Society'. However, the published minutes of the Vienna Society do not record the paper having been delivered. A version of the paper was, however, published in the journal *Imago* in 1922. 'Psychoanalysis and Telepathy' was not published in German until 1941. At best telepathy might be said to be something of an discomfiture to Freud, a state which is stateless; at worst telepathy is something so fundamentally unsettling for Freud that it calls for censorship and repression in order to prevent internecine fighting within psychoanalysis.

In an exchange of circular letters Ernest Jones, in February 1926, fears that his predictions regarding the threat of telepathy to psychoanalysis have come true (thus demonstrating his own telepathic powers). In reply Freud confirms his conversion to telepathy:

Our friend Jones seems to me to be unhappy about the sensation that my conversion to telepathy has made in English periodicals. He will recollect how near to such a conversion I came in the communication I had the occasion to make during our Harz travels. Considerations of external policy since that time held me back long enough, but finally one must show one's colours and need bother about the scandal this time as little as on earlier, perhaps still more important occasions.

(See Jones, II: 422)

However, Freud makes no attempt to incorporate his new-found faith into the system of psychoanalysis, it remains a matter of personal belief, difficult as such a gesture might be to reconcile with everything that psychoanalysis has to say about personal beliefs. He writes to Jones, 'the theme of telepathy is in essence alien to psychoanalysis . . . [and my] conversion to telepathy is my private affair like my Jewishness, my passion for smoking and many other things . . .' Telepathy troubles the relation between foreign policy ('considerations of external policy since that time held me back') and faith (telepathy is said to be 'like my Jewishness', one's true colours). It crosses the border between reason and religion, the media and the academy, the English periodicals and the circular letter.[6] Finally it would seem that there is a link between the wandering Jew and the refugee of (and from) psychoanalysis. Telepathy, as the fugitive within psychoanalysis itself, is doubly displaced as the refugee from the refugee, the outcast that the other refugees will not speak to, the rogue state.

These two essays on telepathy wander along a contingent path of inquiry but return frequently to the Front. It is not a matter of arriving at this no man's land between two warring nations; rather Freud seems to be unable to avoid this place. It is a place that befalls Freud, having escaped he turns a corner only to arrive back on this border, like the sense of confusion and déjà vu he writes of in the essay on the uncanny when he cannot negotiate himself out of a certain district in an Italian town. The essays take the form of analysing particular case histories, either patients of Freud or correspondents who have written to Freud with supposed telepathic experiences. A high proportion of these cases involve presentiments related to the war. In 'Psychoanalysis and Telepathy' we have the case of the man ruined by the war and the Russian Revolution whose wife later consults a fortune-teller (SE, 186). 'Dreams and Telepathy' opens with Freud's own dream of the death of his son at the front:

> I saw the young soldier standing on a landing-stage, between land and water [a liminal space surely suggestive of the borders of the Western Front], as it were; he looked to me very pale. I spoke to him but he did not answer. There were other unmistakable indications. He was not wearing military uniform but a ski-ing costume that he had worn when a serious ski-ing accident had happened to him several years before the war. He stood on something like a footstool with a cupboard in front of him; a situation always closely associated in my mind with the idea of 'falling', through a memory of my own childhood. As a child of little more than two years old I had

> myself climbed on a footstool like this to get something off the top of a cupboard – probably something good to eat – and I fell down and gave myself an injury, of which I can even now show the scar. My son, however, whom the dream pronounced dead, came home from the war unscathed.

> (SE, 197–8)[7]

Freud warns us at the start of this essay 'you will learn nothing from this paper of mine about the enigma of telepathy; indeed, you will not even gather whether I believe in the existence of "telepathy" or not' (SE, 197). His interest here is merely in the relation between so-called telepathic occurrences 'whatever their origin' (Freud maintains the public use of scare-quotes) and dreams. While Freud will later observe that 'by far the greater number of all telepathic intimations relate to death' (SE, 218) he is also able to rationalize such experiences within the Oedipal schema, 'I might, however, add the observation that the instances of telepathic messages or productions which have been discussed here are clearly connected with emotions belonging to the sphere of the Oedipus complex' (SE, 219). Thus Freud explains the dream of his son's death as a displaced account of his own childhood accident.

The dream is not truly telepathic (the son returns from the war). Rather, Freud's dream seems to connect his own castration anxiety with the scars left by the experience of war. In an inversion and re-affirmation of Oedipus the 'telepathic' message arrives, as it did from Delphi, to herald the return of the lost son, brought to manhood (by his war experiences), to enact the family drama. Of the two telepathic messages recounted by Sophocles the first presages the death of the father and the life of the son, the second foretells the price to be paid for this life by the son's own castration. For Freud this dream is more about scars than scares. The son is said to come home 'unscathed' but as Freud notes later on in his essay 'we are very proud of our art if we achieve a cure through psycho-analysis, yet here too we cannot always prevent the formation of a painful scar as an outcome' (SE, 215). Analysis leaves its scars but so does war and there would seem to be a rather obvious connection between the controversy of psycho-analysis (the controversy of telepathy within psychoanaly-sis) and *polemos* (war). It is a matter of reading the trace of the scar, which marks Freud's white skin like the trail of skis in the snow, to appreciate the accident of castration which befell Freud and the accident of telepathy which befell psycho-analysis.

If telepathic experience in Freud is heavily marked by the question of war, it is equally scarred by the problem of writing. It is not an exaggeration to say that the issue of *polemos* and the nature of writing may finally be the same thing.[8] Freud prefaces the account of this dream by saying:

> *I once dreamt during the war that one of my sons then serving at the front had been killed. This was not directly stated in the dream, but was expressed in an unmistakable manner, by means of the well-known death-symbolism of which an account was first given by Stekel [1911a]. (We must not omit to fulfil the duty, often felt to be inconvenient, of making literary acknowledge-ments).*
>
> (SE, 197)

Freud's paranthetic remark demonstrates that the meaning of this dream – its rhetorical status as the first dream ana-lysed in this essay and accordingly as an example of non-telepathic experience – has been determined in advance by its relation to other acts of writing. Stekel leaves a trace in Freud, marked by the scars of these round brackets. The question of literature is undoubtedly germane to an under-standing of telepathy, as Royle has shown. However, the more general issue here is one of media and of its tele-pathic nature. In 'Psychoanalysis and Telepathy' the wife of the man ruined by the Great War consults a medium, 'a famous fortune-teller' (SE, 187) who 'got his clients to press down a hand into a dish full of sand and foretold the future by studying the imprint'. He tells her, 'in the near future you will have to go through some severe struggles, but all will turn out well. You will get married and have two children by the time you are 32' (SE, 188). Again, Freud explains this prediction in terms of an Oedipal effect. However, one might pause here to consider the telepathic event as a reading of an imprint left in the sand. Similarly, one might dwell on Freud's suspicion that despite the woman having removed her wedding ring 'it would not have needed any great refinement of observation to dis-cover the trace of the ring on her finger' (SE, 188). As in the dream of his son Freud's analysis is concerned with the scars of castration and the traces from which so-called telepathy is discernible.

However, there is an overwhelming accretion in both these essays of the problematic nature of media and its interpretation. The telepathic occurrence recounted prior to this narrative in 'Psychoanalysis and Telepathy' also involves a medium who predicts the death of the brother-in-law of one of Freud's patients (SE, 182). Again, for Freud, the premonition can be shown to relate to an external, Oedipal, reality and so be a subjective anticipation rather than true telepathy. However, this incident is the first occasion on which Freud openly entertains the idea of thought-transfer-ence as a possibility. The issue here is double and contra-dictory. On the one hand, Freud cannot explain why the medium would be able to make a prediction (one that did not come true but which bore a striking resemblance to an incident the previous year in which the brother-in-law almost died of seafood poisoning) of his patient's death wish for his brother-in-law unless it had been transferred to her 'by some unknown means which excluded the means of communication familiar to us' (SE, 184). Freud suggests that this suppressed wish had been communicated to the medium 'by means of induction from one person to another' and the second person gives consciousness to the wish that has a special relation to the first's psychic experience. However, on the other hand, Freud views the medium's role in this event as remarkably unproblematic. He writes 'we can also, so it seems to me, leave the fortune-teller (or, as we may say straight out, the "medium") quite out of account as a possible source of deception' (SE, 184). In other words, despite Freud's intensive study of the ways in which the dream work complicates and displaces messages from the unconscious, he is prepared to believe that this telepathic message passes through the medium in a transparent fashion. He compares the experience to the development of photographic images:

> It [the case] shows that an extraordinarily power-
> ful wish harboured by one person and standing in
> a special relation to his consciousness has suc-
> ceeded, with the help of a second person, in
> finding conscious expression in a slightly dis-
> guised form – just as the invisible end of the spec-
> trum reveals itself to the senses on a
> light-sensitive plate as a coloured extension.
>
> (SE, 184–5).

The medium is a *tabula rasa* on which the young man imprints his wish, just as Freud's other correspondent left the print of her hand in the sand. The wish may go through some distortion, 'a slightly disguised form', but only in the sense that it lies just beyond the senses, in parenthesis, like 'the invisible end of the spectrum'. In other words, despite his frequent admonition that telepathy is inimical to psychoanalysis, Freud is able to entertain this experience as telepathic because he is able to offer a psychoanalytic account of it as wish-fulfilment. Just as there is a means, a technology, to view invisible light so there exists for psychoanalysis a means, a vocabulary, for explaining the invisible passage of thought-transference.

One might go straight from here to 'A Note Upon the "Mystic Writing Pad"' and to Derrida's 'Freud and the Scene of Writing' to discuss the relation between the psychic apparatus and technologies of writing.[9] Alternatively, one might proceed to the privileged relation between wish-fulfilment and writing Freud outlines in 'Creative Writers and Day-dreaming' to appreciate that although Freud protests that telepathic experience does not alter the Freudian theory of dreams (SE, 197) the question of writing certainly does (SE, IX, 144–55). In his opening remarks in 'Delusions and Dreams in Jensen's *Gradiva*' [1907] Freud, in a gesture similar to Derrida's reproach to Austin in 'Signature, Event, Context', suggests that far from being a secondary concern for a psychoanalytic understanding of dreams, dreams in literature are pointedly relevant to such an understanding (Freud, SE, IX, 7–97; see also Derrida, 1977, 172–97). While cognitive science does not believe that dreams can be interpreted Freud, the superstitious 'common people' and literature do. It is both a question of reading and a matter of telepathy. He writes:

> *The author of* The Interpretation of Dreams *has
> ventured, in the face of the reproaches of strict*

science, to become a partisan of antiquity and superstition [i.e. that dreams can be interpreted]. He is, it is true, far from believing that dreams foretell the future, for the unveiling of which men have vainly striven from time immemorial by every forbidden means. But even he has not been able entirely to reject the relation of dreams to the future. For the dream, when the laborious work of translating it has been accomplished, revealed itself to him as a wish of the dreamer's represented as fulfilled; and who could deny that wishes are predominantly turned towards the future?

(SE, IX, 7)

Many years before Freud's private conversion we find him here unable to rule out the possibility of telepathic dreams. Thus, Freud's own oeuvre demonstrates its own telepathic powers. His explanation here, in relation to the future orientation of wishes, surely presages his later account of the death wish for the brother-in-law. However, the difference in the essay on the *Gradiva* is that while the desire can be read in the imprint of *Gradiva*'s foot in the ash of Pompeii, and Norbert Hanold's wish can be accommodated within psychoanalytic parameters, Jensen's writing (the medium that relates the story) introduces the element of undecidability, what Freud calls the 'unfettered imitations' of 'unrestrained and unregulated structures'.[10] What is at stake here is the very project of psychoanalysis as a method of interpretation. Telepathy can only lie inside psychoanalysis if it can be adequately explained. Like writing, telepathy problematizes any easy notion of a transparent medium which would allow a message to arrive fully formed in the present. While, Freud sees no need to view the fortune-teller as a source of deception, he admits that

some disguise and displacement ensues. This instance of telepathy is useful to Freud, however, because despite its contortions its meaning can be determined. Moreover, it can be determined by the medium of Freud's own writing. This contradiction between the alterity of the psyche and the supposed stability of the medium which articulates its desires leads Freud's negotiation of telepathy into some confusion.

The essays on telepathy are replete with instances of messages relayed by various media. In an echo of Freud's own dream of his son, 'Dreams and Telepathy' recounts another experience related to Freud in a letter (Freud makes frequent reference in this essay to turning his correspondents letters 'to literary account' (SE, 200)):

In 1914 my brother was on active service; I was not with my parents in B——, but in Ch——. It was ten a.m. on August 22 when I heard my brother's voice calling, 'Mother! Mother!' It came again ten minutes later, but I saw nothing. On August 24 I came home, found my mother greatly depressed, and in answer to my questions she said that she had had a message from the boy on August 22. She had been in the garden in the morning, when she had heard him call, 'Mother! Mother!' I comforted her and said nothing about myself. Three weeks after there came a card from my brother, written on August 22 between nine and ten in the morning; shortly after he died.

(SE, 210)

Here the telepathic message precedes the arrival of a letter confirming the death intimated by the telepathic event. If the spirit giveth life, the letter surely kills. If the majority of telepathic experiences intimate death it is precisely because a certain idea of telepathy (the one more or less, given slight but not irremediable distortions, entertained by Freud in his explanation of the fortune-teller's prediction) presupposes that the message received in telepathy is readable and that its expression in consciousness is its only and final port of call. As with the preceding dream analysed in 'Dreams in Telepathy', in which one of Freud's correspondents dreams that his wife has given birth to twins only to receive a telegram a few days later to say that his daughter gave birth to twins at the same moment he was dreaming, this telepathic experience involves prodigious (even uncanny) doubling, an Oedipal schema and confirmation by letter. In this war-time experience the letter only arrives belatedly, its message having been received on the way by both the dead man's brother and his mother. It is this very doubleness which leads Freud to the conclusion that it will be impossible for psychoanalysis to rule out the possibility of telepathy. There would seem to be here an open contradiction between Freud's desire to explain all of these dreams in terms of a circuit of desire which is regulated by death (the death of the Father, castration as the death of desire, death wishes and so on) and the ultimate impossibility of a determination of, or by, death (voices from beyond the grave, the brother-in-law does not die, one dream is said to haunt a correspondent 'like a ghost' (SE, 209)). Sometimes the letter does not arrive, as Freud's own dream demonstrates. He did not receive a telegram confirming the death of his son. Finally, it may not be possible to determine the meaning of telepathy in this way. In fact, what Freud's essays show might be that telepathy itself is the very structure, if structure is an appropriate word in this context, of a certain experience of undecidability.

Telepathy is the name Freud gives to the undecidable, that which falls outside of the determination by interpreta-tion, while that undecidability calls forth and enables the practice of interpretation just as that practice attempts to repress it. It is perhaps for this reason that Royle calls telepathy 'a psychoanalysis beyond psychoanalysis' (Royle, 1995, 74). It is in parenthesis, after and beyond, while complementing and completing, psychoanalysis, as a problem. Telepathy as undecidability, the beyond of inter-pretation, is clearly related to the question of writing. The undecidability of Freud's two essays with their inability to close off debates within Freud's oeuvre and within psycho-analysis, their unfulfilled desires, their inauguration of a private anxiety and public embarrassment (which will no doubt have been in motion since at least the *Gradiva*), their open contradictions and obsession with marks and traces, are themselves exemplary instances of this telepathic experience. Telepathy is for Royle 'a new practice of writing and a new theory of subjectivity' (Royle, 1995, 76–7). A new mode of writing because it lies beyond the practice of interpretation, a new theory of subjectivity because its meaning cannot be determined by death and so lies beyond the subject just as much as it takes place within the subject, making any idea of the subject as a determination of fixed boundaries impossible. If telepathy then works according to the same principle of all tele and postal tech-nologies, namely the mediation of meaning through a system of exchange which results in and requires as an a priori condition the possibility of its non-arrival at a final destination, then telepathy as a new practice of writing may go some way to explaining Derrida's somewhat gnomic comment with which this essay began. Namely, that a certain idea of reading, whether it is found in litera-ture, philosophy, psychoanalysis or love letters, cannot survive when confronted by a structure of meaning which, as Freud puts it, by some unknown method excludes 'the means of communication familiar to us'. And this is the contradiction in Freud, to reverse a commonplace assumption, between his writerly desire for closure and the scientific stricture which will not allow for any easy dismissal of thought-transference.

The medium of Freud's essay finally catches up with itself and recognizes that what makes the question of telepathy undecidable one way or the other is the very nature of media itself. 'Dreams and Telepathy' closes with a return to the dream of the brother killed at the front. Freud comments:

There remains one element of the apparently intimate connection between telepathy and dreams which is not affected by any of these considerations: namely, the incontestable fact that sleep creates favourable conditions for telepathy. Sleep is not, it is true, indispensable to the occurrence of telepathic processes – whether they originate in messages or in unconscious activity. If you are not already aware of this, you will learn it from the instance given by our second correspondent, of the young man's message which came between nine and ten in the morning. We must add, however, that no one has a right to take exception to telepathic occurences if the event and the intimation (message) do not exactly coincide in astronomical time. It is perfectly conceivable that a telepathic message might arrive contemporaneously with the event and yet only penetrate to consciousness the following night during sleep (or even in waking life only after a while, during some pause in the activity of the mind). We are, as you know, of opinion that dream-formation itself does not necessarily wait for the onset of sleep before it begins. Often the latent dream-thoughts may

have been being got ready during the whole day, till at night they find the contact with the unconscious wish that shapes them into a dream. But if the phenomenon of telepathy is only an activity of the unconscious mind, then, of course, no fresh problem lies before us. The laws of unconscious mental life may then be taken for granted as applying to telepathy.

(SE, 219–20)

In other words, if telepathy can be thought of as a question of mediation by the unconscious then it cannot be ignored by psychoanalysis. Rather, the belatedness and undecideability of telepathy would be an exemplary instance of the *nachträglichkeit* which characterizes mental life. Taking Freud's final sentence in an unironic way the experience of deferred meaning in telepathy (the result of meaning passing through media) precisely characterizes the revolutionary problematic of the unconscious which psychoanalysis as an ontotheology, if not a science, at once exposes and continually attempts to repress (see Derrida, 1987, 411–97). We might note here that the argument of Freud's essay once more returns to the experience of war as a demonstration of the difficulty in determining what can and cannot be ruled out of psychic experience. It is this ambivalence within Freud's text, by which telepathy causes the certainty of scienticism to tremble, that (despite the confidence avowed above, 'no fresh problem lies before us') causes Freud to make a sudden about turn in his final sentence. Despite a clear movement towards accepting the possibility of thought-transference, Freud is keen not to be seen ruling telepathy in: 'I have been anxious to be strictly impartial'. For finally, Freud says of telepathy, and this will not be his last finally, 'I have no opinion on the matter and know nothing about it' (SE, 220).[11]

I do not need someone to tell me what to believe.
But I do need someone to tell me where Kosovo is.

George W. Bush

Much of this will depend on Derrida. Fortune-telling and telepathy are important conceits in Derrida's novel *Envois*. The essay 'Telepathy', published separately, was, according to a footnote by Derrida, accidentally excluded from the manuscript of *The Post-Card* ('There will perhaps be talk of omission through "resistance" and other such things') (Derrida, 2000a, 524 n.1). However, it would seem that 'Telepathy', the essay, is not in fact the entire remainder [*restant*] of this text, 'From this bundle of daily dispatches which all date from the same week, I have extracted *only a part for the moment*, through lack of space. Lack of time too, and for the treatment of which I had to submit this mail, sorting, fragmentation, destruction etc., the interested reader may refer to "Envois", p.7ff' [my emphasis]. Other postcards remain 'lost'. It would seem that telepathy brings out something of the private individual in Derrida as well when he also decides to hold back material for publication, if only 'for the moment'.[12] The interested reader of 'Envois' will note that its narrator suggests that the correspondence 'should all have been burned, all of it, including the cinders of the unconscious' so that '"they" will never know anything about it' (Derrida, 1987, 7). However, it is an exchange of letters which 'immediately got beyond us', as Derrida tells his addressee, and which therefore lie beyond the censoring powers of the individual. This would be the whole, if not the only, point of Derrida's rhetorical strategy by which these private letters pass through the various destinations of his readership, are countersigned by the reader en route, without ever coming to rest at a final address. A structure of writing-for-the-future which Derrida will later call 'telepoesis' (see Derrida, 1997).

The set-up of this postal technology, relay and exchange without telos through the sorting office of the medium of writing, is precisely the action of telepathy. Derrida's reading of Freud's essays and correspondence on telepathy in this text demonstrates the impossibility of closure in the circuit of telepathic exchange. Far from being an aberrant means of communication which lies outside of patterns of meaning familiar to the subject, telepathy is for Derrida the very principle by which all communication works. He notes:

The truth, what I always have difficulty getting used to: that non-telepathy is possible. Always difficult to imagine that one can think something to oneself [à part soi], deep down inside, without being surprised by the other, without the other being immediately informed, as easily as if it had a giant screen in it, at the time of the talkies, with remote control [télécommande] for changing channels and fiddling with the colours, the speech dubbed with large letters in order to avoid any misunderstanding.

(Derrida, 2000a, 504)

Derrida's commentary here is useful in two respects. Firstly, telepathy in its expanded Royle-Derrida sense describes the very act of communication because it names 'the outside-the-subject' (518). Telepathy as a structure of meaning not only lies outside of the subject, or discipline, of psychoanalysis but acts outside of communication between subjects as stable and assured identities. Rather telepathy, or the undecidable remainder of meaning, follows the structure of supplementarity, an add-on to subjective experience, at once both outside-the-subject and constitutive of the subject.[13] This is the situation that Freud simultaneously discovers and denies: as Derrida puts it, it will be 'difficult to imagine a theory of what they still call the unconscious without a theory of telepathy' (505). The essay concludes 'telepathy is the interruption of the psychoanalysis of psychoanalysis' in which psychoanalysis 'resembles an adventure of modern rationality set on swallowing and simultaneously rejecting the foreign body named Telepathy, for assimilating it and vomiting it without being able to make up its mind to do one or the other' (523). Telepathy, then, is caught in a constant battle, a war of words, between ontotheology and deconstruction. I will return to this.

Secondly, here Derrida makes explicit the link between telepathy as a structure of meaning and all tele-techno spectral media as structures of reproduction, inscription and iteration. As Derrida writes in conclusion to this particular *envois*:

> For here is my final paradox, which you alone will understand clearly: it is because there would be telepathy that a postcard can not arrive at its destination. The ultimate naivety would be to allow oneself to think that Telepathy guarantees a destination which 'posts and telecommunications' fail to provide. On the contrary, everything I said about the post-card structure of the mark (interference, parasiting, divisibility, iterability, and so on [in English in the original text] is found in the network. This goes for any tele-system – whatever its content, form or medium.
>
> (506)

If telepathy is an exemplary instance of the techne of writing, the very action of dissemination, and what goes for telepathy goes for every tele-technological system, then we are thrown back upon the original premise of our inquiry: what is the relation between telepathy and the new techno-media wars of the last decade? This is the question which occupies us here.

Three possible directions of inquiry suggest themselves. Firstly, the question of media as such. The point being not just that these wars are being fought through the presentation of media images and the *polemos* of journalism – everyone knows that.[14] Rather, that when we are dealing with media as such there is only ever a rhetorical relation of translation, transference, transposition and metaphor. Media as representation, as the aesthetic experience, is what grounds the literal by means of the figurative (see de Man, 1996). After contemporary fashion we might call the media, all and every media and so communication and representation as such, phantomatic. However, what is at stake here is a fundamental question concerning knowing and thinking, Being and beings. The ultimate naivety would be to suppose that media representation implied destination and determination. In this sense, the telepathic experience of watching War 'live' on our televisions, 'pain at a distance', lies 'outside-the-subject'. This is at one and the same time theoretically trivial and perhaps *the* most complex thing that we can be asked to think about. This is an analysis I have attempted elsewhere and calls for a commentary that I am forced to postpone for the moment.[15] However, we should note that Freud treats the idea of death as 'pain at a distance' in his 'Thoughts for the Times on War and Death'. Here he suggests that the so-called civilized man shares with the primitive a powerful death-wish for strangers, foreigners and enemies. He cites Balzac citing Rousseau:

> In Le Père Goriot, *Balzac alludes to a passage in the works of J. J. Rousseau where the author*

asks the reader what he would do if – without leaving Paris and of course without being discovered – he could kill, with great profit to himself, an old mandarin in Peking by a mere act of will. Rousseau implies that he would not give much for the life of that dignitary. 'Tuer son mandarin' has become a proverbial phrase for this secret readiness, present even in modern man.

(Freud, SE, XIV, 296)

Thus Rousseau shows how 'our unconscious will murder even for trifles'. In this essay, war is for Freud a regressive step back to the primitive state. It would seem that the new tele-technological wars of today only provide a new and more deadly opportunity for the expression of this primal wish.

Secondly, Freud's writing on the foreign-body of telepathy describes the action of a foreign-policy. As he remarks in his letter to Jones, telepathy calls for diplomacy, 'considerations of external policy since that time held me back long enough, but finally one must show one's colours'. To quote at length the letter from 7 March 1926:

I am extremely sorry that my utterance about telepathy should have plunged you into fresh difficulties. But it is really hard not to offend English susceptibilities . . . I have no prospect of pacifying public opinion in England [no peace in the polemos with England], but I should like at least to explain my apparent inconsistency in the matter of telepathy. You remember how I had already at the time of our Harz travels expressed a favourable prejudice towards telepathy. But there seemed no need to do so publicly, my own conviction was not very strong, and the diplomatic consideration of

guarding psycho-analysis from any approach to occultism easily gained the upper hand. Now the revising of The Interpretation of Dreams *for the Collected Edition was a spur to reconsider the problem of telepathy. Moreover, my own experiences through tests I made with Ferenczi and my daughter won such a convincing force for me that the diplomatic considerations on the other side had to give way. I was once more faced with a case where on a reduced scale I had to repeat the great experiment of my life: namely to proclaim a conviction without taking into account any echo from the outer world. So then it was unavoidable. When anyone adduces my fall into sin, just answer him calmly that conversion to telepathy is my private affair like my Jewishness, my passion for smoking and many other things, and that the theme of telepathy is in essence alien to psychoanalysis.*

Freud knows what is at stake here but must deny it publicly for diplomatic reasons. He knows that telepathy repeats the 'great experiment' of his life but he must act as if both telepathy and psychoanalysis were closed, 'without taking into account any echo from the outer world'. Such private affairs are only private in the sense that they lie outside-the-subject and are thus public. Freud did not choose his Jewishness, and sometimes a cigar is just a cigar. The alterity of telepathy leads Freud to cultivate a double vision ('*la diplopie*' as Derrida has it, 1987, 515) which protects the borders of psycho-analysis through an even-handed and under-handed diplomacy. This is a diplomacy which conducts 'external policy' through the exchange of letters, opening a channel of communication which at once encourages dialogue while issuing an official denial.

Psychoanalysis does not negotiate with telepathy, just as the foreign-body is causing an explosion within the house of which Freud is no longer the master.

Telepathy is diplomacy without end, an exchange without borders, in which finally showing one's colours is a private affair which will always lie outside-the-subject. No act of determination, no final ultimatum, can win this war because diplomacy is the language the other will have been speaking long before Freud's show of colours. Telepathy, pain at a distance, sympathy at a distance too, is not only the order of subjectivity but is the order of world diplomacy, of all intersubjective and international relations. It does not begin and end with single events and it cannot be abandoned in the name of a forceful response but is the interminable analysis of geopolitical events. Diplomacy is always on the inside-outside between communication and miscommunication, always calling for responsibility in the midst of irresponsibility.[16] It is always in the middle of *le subjet en proces*, as the French has it, subject-in-violence/subject-in-[peace]-process. To deny telepathy is to fail to speak the language of diplomacy, to fail to give peace a chance, even if it is Freud's private wish, and even if telepathy itself will never bring peace. The repetitive folding structure of openness and closure which characterizes telepathy also scars Peace as a self-contradictory concept. Peace is eternal, in a Kantian sense, or it is not peace at all. An armistice between acts of war is not peace, only a lull in war. Peace to be truly peace, to earn the name of a true peace, must be endlessly open and infinite. At the same time, as Kant recognizes, eternal peace only comes in the quiet of the grave.[17]

Thirdly, the endless war between ontotheology and deconstruction. Nicholas Royle remarks that telepathy is 'closely linked to the so-called decline of Christianity in European and North American culture: a belief in telepathy, in the late nineteenth century, often (though by no means always) appears to have provided a kind of substitute for a belief in God' (Royle, 1995, 72). Freud in his letter to Jones describes his belief in telepathy as a 'fall into sin'. It is not surprising then to find the twenty-first century regime of telecommunications closely associated with what has been called 'the return of the Religious'.[18] Indeed it may be the case that no religion can do without the media, from the call of Abraham and the commandments written in stone or the epistles of Paul, to the phantom presence of transubstantiation and the loudspeakers which call the faithful to prayer across the Islamic world. (On this point, see Derrida, 2001, 56–94.) It is unsurprising to find religions of all kinds deploying the available channels of telecommunication (what is unironically termed 'religious broadcasting') in order to promulgate belief in the absolute by the most phantasmatic of means. The tele-technological network, with its in-built deconstruction, is the very means by which the good news of the certainty and stability of God is announced. This will always have been the case.[19] As Derrida states in an early essay, just as 'differance is inimical to all theologies including negative ones', differance is 'the economic action of delay in which the element of the same aims to come back to the deferred pleasure of presence' (Derrida, 1982, 17). If differance initiates all and every conceptuality without itself being a concept then it must also put into play those conceptual orders, including metaphysics and ontotheologies, which seek to repress its action. Just as deconstruction renders a certain idea of God as an assured and given centre impossible, by the same token God and all that is thought in the name of God must be the only topic which concerns deconstruction. Deconstruction (and telepathy as dissemination would be a good example of this) can only ever inhabit parasitically the very textual events which attempt to close off the possibilities which deconstruction puts into play. The relation between the religions of the book and the regime of telecommunications then are merely another instance of this familiar problem. The mistake would be to believe that either could finally annul the other. Deconstruction will never defeat the occult practices of metaphysicians. This is not a war that can be won by a final decisive blow; rather it is one which calls for interminable analysis.

The present war, we are frequently told, is not about religion, but it is certainly concerned with religion, just as it is concerned with telepathy.[20] It presents to us in a concentrated form the relation between the media and religion, modernity and God, telepathy and theology. It would be possible to analyse either side: the Taliban with their satellite phones and sectarianism, the West with its stealth bombers and manifest destiny. Both follow the principle of 'in God we trust', just as the events of the war (a terrorist network with global coverage connected by cell phones and known as 'sleepers', the prosopopeiac recordings of desperate last-minute phone calls, anthrax letters which kill those who sort them but miss their targets, the FBI's use of 'remote viewers' – psychics enlisted to predict likely terrorist targets – as a supplement to its techno-scientific arsenal[21]) show that no such trust is justified. Having resisted such a strategy, I will not now introduce these examples to screen out and mediatize thinking. Rather, I will conclude by making a more general, even abstract, point. This war, if it is a war, if it has anything so clear-cut as objectives and a determinable exit point, is a war about Modernity and within Modernity. Here we can follow the structure of Freud's relation to telepathy as a negotiation between the binary structure of rationality and superstition.

Axiomatically speaking the argument could be made that the West is inseparable from Christianity and vice versa.[22] In this sense it is impossible to think of Modernity

in the West outside of a certain Christian, at least Protestant, heritage. However, Modernity – and the regime of tele-technology which predicates it – places Christianity in crisis. Just as Modernity drains Christianity from the West, it leaves the imprint of Christianity on everything that is Western and Modern. Modernity, as Jean-Luc Nancy puts it, is 'bound within the very fabric of Christianity' (Nancy, 2001, 115). In this sense, to begin to understand in what way Modernity, not to mention Postmodernity, is still Christian while simultaneously being the great impious and atheistic Satan, would cause us to think the very limits of Christianity. This would be a Christianity which was open to the possibility of its own negation and an atheism which acknowledged its Christian aetiology. Thus the West, as it moves towards the completion of Modernity, turns away from itself (i.e. its Christian heritage) just as it exposes its own limits (by thinking the limits of Christianity) in this gesture. This would be the necessarily deconstructive step in an analysis which would have to run through all the political, cultural and philosophical histories and institutions of the West (Rousseau, Kant, Hegel and Heidegger would be only the most obvious touchstones here).

The double-bind works like this. Christianity, like any ontotheology, must always already be in deconstruction. However, the very idea of Christianity as an ontotheology represents the rapid foreclosure of the possibility of deconstruction. One might recall here the repetitive folding structure of telepathy within psychoanalysis outlined above, as a model for this aporia, in which telepathy pushes us to the limits of psychoanalysis while its effacement of psychoanalysis represents the completion of psychoanalysis beyond psychoanalysis. Thus, psychoanalysis must open itself to telepathy, which as the completion of psychoanalysis, means that psychoanalysis only opens itself onto itself, without end. In this way, psychoanalysis is forced to engage ceaselessly with its own negation, and is ruined by the very opening telepathy offers to psychoanalysis. Similarly, as Nancy explains, a Christianity in deconstruction 'opens onto itself and opens only onto itself, infinitely: hence Christianity becomes nihilism, and ceaselessly engages nihilism, the death of God' (Nancy, 2001, 130). Everything is ruined, including the opening, by the opening. This is true of every politics, every ethics and every history. The difficult thing to think today is how one might imagine both a sense beyond sense which would make sense and the figure of a delimited opening which is not a determination of sense (in the case of telepathy one that was not science, in the case of Christianity and the West one that was not God). This is the problem initiated, and quickly withdrawn as a scandalous blasphemy, by the term 'Operation Infinite Justice'. As I write this final sentence the Taliban have surrendered their last stronghold, Kandahar: I wonder, how much justice will have been ruined by such a potentially infinite opening.

Sofia–Nashville–Leeds
2 October–8 December 2001

III postscript

Will the highways of the Internet become more few?

George W. Bush

As part of my researches for this essay I took with me, on a trip to Vanderbilt University in Nashville to meet with Jacques Derrida and my host Marc Froment-Meurice, a copy of Nicholas Royle's *Telepathy and Literature*. On the final day of my stay Marc and I visited the Parthenon in Nashville's Centennial Park. I bought a postcard and, before leaving Nashville, placed the card randomly within the pages of *Telepathy and Literature*. On my return home I opened the page of the book where the card had been placed. It fell on the 'postscript' to Chapter 2, the closing lines of which read:

And as a postscript to this postscript I would only like to mention a postcard, which I had no reason to expect or foresee, posted in the United States on the day, as it happens, I began writing this. It arrived in the middle, and is a photograph of the Parthenon – at night – in Centennial Park, Nashville, Tennesse.

(Royle, 1990, 27)

I am told by the author that although Jacques Derrida was not the sender of this card, when he read these lines he became convinced that he must have been the writer of this *envois*. I returned home on Halloween 2001.

Notes

1. See, Royle, *Telepathy and Literature*, (1990), 'The Remains of Psychoanalysis (I): Telepathy' (1995) and 'Memento Mori' (2000). See also the comments, *en passant*, by Bennett and Royle (1999), a book with imitators but no peers.
2. On the question of telepathy in psychoanalysis see Maria Torok's 'Afterword' to Abraham and Torok (1986).
3. On deconstruction and telepathy see also John Forrester, 'Psychoanalysis: Gossip, Telepathy and/or Science?' (1990) and Ned Lukacher 'Introduction: Mourning Becomes Telepathy', in Derrida (1991).
4. This is the phrase used by Derrida in his 'Telepathy' (1988, 3–41); rpt. in McQuillan (2000).
5. 'Psychoanalysis and Telepathy' and 'Dreams and Telepathy', SE, XVIII. See also Lecture XXX, SE, XXII and 'The Occult Significance of Dreams', SE, V.

6. In 'Archive Fever: a Freudian Impression', (1995a, 9–63), Derrida makes the connection between the Freudian project and tele-technology by suggesting that this form of circular letter follows the structure of e-mail.

7. This dream is also discussed in a passage added in 1919 to *The Interpretation of Dreams*, SE, V, 558ff.

8. On the issue of *polemos* see Jacques Derrida, 'Violence and Metaphysics' (1978). See also *parallax*, 15 (April–June, 2000).

9. See Freud, 'A Note Upon the "Mystic Writing Pad"', SE, XIX, 225–32. See also Derrida (1978).

10. The problem for Freud is in fact more interesting than my comments here seem to suggest. In fact for Freud the question of dreams in literature imply that the shimmer of meaning is an effect not of reflective transparency but of inscription, system and grammar. He writes:

> Even if this enquiry should teach us nothing new about the nature of dreams, it may perhaps enable us from this angle to gain some small insight into the nature of creative writing. Real dreams were already regarded as unrestricted and unregulated structures – and now we are confronted by unfettered imitations of these dreams! There is far less freedom and arbitrariness in mental life, however, than we are inclined to assume – there may even be none at all. What we call chance in the world outside can, as is well known, be resolved into laws. So, too, what we call arbitrariness in the mind rests upon laws, which we are only now beginning dimly to suspect.
>
> (SE, IX, 9).

This is an analysis I will have to postpone for the present.

11. Let me note in passing that the name of the racehorse bet on by Sean Connery in that most deconstructive and Freudian of films, *Marnie*, is Telepathy.

12. If we re-insert the pages of 'Telepathy' back into 'Envois' two curious coincidences arise. The *envois* for 8 July 1979, the entry before the 'Telepathy' cards, tells of Derrida's response to the rumour (spread at different times by Serge Doubrovsky and Jacques Lacan) that 'J.D. is in analysis'. The narrator claims he is not in analysis and tells the narratee: 'I'm acquainted with several people who know, support, explain to themselves that I'm not in analysis (you know who I'm talking about)'. Once again the supplement of parenthesis is significant: Derrida's wife, Margueritte, is a psychoanalyst. The *envois* breaks off from this story to close:

> Refound here the American student with whom we had coffee last Saturday, the one who was looking for a thesis subject (comparative literature). I suggested to her something on the telephone in the literature of the 20th century (and beyond), starting with, for example, the telephone lady in Proust or the figure of the American operator, and then asking the question of the effects of the most advanced telematics (la télématique la plus avancée) on whatever would still remain of literature. I spoke to her about microprocessors and computer terminals, she seemed somewhat disgusted. She told me that she still loved literature (me too, I answered her, mais si, mais si). Curious to know what she understood by this.
>
> (Derrida, 1987, 204).

Avital Ronell later took up this project in *The Telephone Book: Technology, Schizophrenia, Electric Speech* (1989).

13. On this point see Nicholas Royle's commentary on Derrida's essay (Royle, 1995, 73).

14. This conflict has truly been a 'Media War'. While the press in Europe attempts to explain the mind of terrorists, in Afghanastan – to date – more western journalists have been killed than American military personnel and the 'liberation' of Kabul was lead by the BBC journalist John Simpson.

15. See the chapter on 'Aesthetic Ideology' in my *Paul de Man* (2001) and my 'Specters of Poujade: Naomi Klein and the New International' (2001).

16. On the aporetic relation between responsibility and irresponsibility see Derrida (1995b).

17. See Kant (1996, 311–53). On this point see also Derrida (2000b, 6).

18. Derrida has written at length on the relation between religion and tele-technology (1998, 1–78).

19. This, in brief, is the plot of the film *The Matrix* in which the regime of tele-technology is at war with 'terrorist' humans who figure their struggle in explicitly theological terms. Neo, the chosen one, dies and is resurrected to save Zion.

20. The war is also concerned with the question of Palestine. In *Spectres of Marx* Derrida comments, 'the war for the "appropriation of Jerusalem" is today the world war':

> Messianic eschatologies [the Abrahamic religions] mobilise there all the forces of the world and the whole 'world order' in the ruthless war they are waging against each other, directly or indirectly; they mobilise simultaneously, in order to put them to work or to the test, the old concepts of State and nation-State, of international law, of tele-techno-medio-economic and scientifico-military forces, in other words, the most archaic and most modern spectral forces.
>
> (1994, 58)

21. Reported in *The Guardian*, Saturday, 17 November 2001, 'The Editor', 4.

22. Here I owe a debt to the more considered arguments of Jean-Luc Nancy in 'The Deconstruction of Christianity' (2001, 112–30).

Works cited

Bennett, Andrew and Nicholas Royle. *Introduction to Literature, Criticism and Theory*, 2nd edn. Hemel Hempstead, 1999.

de Man, Paul. *Aesthetic Ideology*, ed. Andrzej Warminski. Minneapolis, MN, 1996.

Derrida, Jacques. 'Signature, Event, Context', *Glyph*, 1 (1977): 172–97.

Derrida, Jacques. *Writing and Difference*, trans. Alan Bass. London, 1978.

Derrida, Jacques. *Margins of Philosophy*, trans. Alan Bass. Brighton, 1982.

Derrida, Jacques. *The Post Card*, trans. Alan Bass. Chicago, IL, 1987.

Derrida, Jacques. *Specters of Marx: the State of the Debt, the Work of Mourning, and the New International*, trans. Peggy Kamuf. London, 1994.

Derrida, Jacques. 'Archive Fever: a Freudian Impression', trans. Eric Prenowitz, *Diacritics*, 25: 2 (Summer, 1995a): 9–63.

Derrida, Jacques. *The Gift of Death*, trans. David Wills. Chicago, IL, 1995b.

Derrida, Jacques. *Politics of Friendship*, trans. George Collins. London, 1997.

Derrida, Jacques. 'Faith and Knowledge: the Two Sources of "Religion" at the Limits of Reason Alone', trans. Samuel Weber, in *Religion*, ed. Jacques Derrida and Gianni Vattimo. Cambridge, 1998, 1–78.

Derrida, Jacques. 'Telepathy', trans. Nicholas Royle, *Oxford Literary Review* 10 (1988): 3–41; rpt. in *Deconstruction: a Reader*, ed. Martin McQuillan. Edinburgh, 2000a, 496–527.

Derrida, Jacques. 'Hostipitality', *Angelaki*, 5: 3 (December 2000b).

Derrida, Jacques. 'Above All, No Journalists!' in *Religion and the Media*, eds Hent de Vries and Samuel Weber. Stanford, CA, 2001, 56–94.

Forrester, John. *The Seductions of Psychoanlysis: Freud, Lacan and Derrida*. Cambridge, 1990.

Freud, Sigmund. *The Standard Edition of the Complete Psychological Works of Sigmund Freud*, 24 vols, trans. J. Strachey et al. London, 1953–74. Cited as SE.

Jones, Ernest. *Sigmund Freud: Life and Work*, 3 vols. London, 1953–57.

Kant, Immanuel. 'Toward Perpetual Peace', in Immanuel Kant, *Practical Philosophy*, trans. and ed. Mary J. Gregor. Cambridge, 1996, 311–53.

Lukacher, Ned. 'Introduction: Mourning Becomes Telepathy', in Jacques Derrida, *Cinders*, trans. Ned Lukacher. Lincoln, NE, 1991.

McQuillan, Martin. 'Specters of Poujade: Naomi Klein and the New International', *Parallax*, 20 (July–September 2001a): 114–30.

McQuillan, Martin. *Paul de Man*. London, 2001b.

Nancy, Jean-Luc. 'The Deconstruction of Christianity', trans. Simon Sparks, in *Religion and the Media*, eds Hent de Vries and Samuel Weber. Stanford, CA, 2001, 112–30.

Parallax, 15 (April–June, 2000).

Ronell Avital. *The Telephone Book: Technology, Schizophrenia, Electric Speech*. Lincoln, NE, 1989.

Royle, Nicholas. *Telepathy and Literature: Essays on the Reading Mind*. Oxford, 1990.

Royle, Nicholas. 'The Remains of Psychoanalysis (I): Telepathy', in *After Derrida*. Manchester, 1995.

Royle, Nicholas. 'Memento Mori', in *Theorising Muriel Spark: Gender, Race, Deconstruction*, ed. Martin McQuillan. London, 2000.

The Guardian, Saturday 17 November 2001, 'The Editor', 4.

Torok, Maria. 'Afterword', in Nicholas Abrahams and Maria Torok, *The Wolf Man's Magic Word*, trans. Nicholas Rand, foreword Jacques Derrida. Minneapolis, MN, 1986.

universals | U IS FOR UNIVERSALS | *MARK CURRIE*

We are all bored with difference. We cannot bear to read another appeal to historical specificity. Fragmentation can no longer excite us. And there is no politics of pure particularity. None of these things, frankly, begin with U. They are non-U. Let us talk of what things have in common with each other, of the unity of multiplicities, the possibility of common denominators, abstractions and universals.

I could be bounded in a nutshell and count myself the king of infinite space, like every other academic who specializes in something small and yet knows everything. Perhaps it is necessary that the academic should operate in limited space but extend the significance of minute observations outwards towards something more general and more abstract. It is not only in DNA, atomic particles or quanta of light that the pattern of a larger reality can be discerned. Literary criticism has aped the microscopic developments of particle physics, quantum mechanics and genetics, in so far as it has turned away from grand, deductive and speculative theoretical models that dominated in the middle of the twentieth century and has found its recent intellectual energy in a newly rampant particularism. There are several models, perhaps the most common of which is an identity particularism, whereby the largest totalities such as humankind, or epochal totalities such as Romanticism or Modernism, are dismantled to reveal a multifarious polity of previously effaced differences of race, class and gender. But there is another model which often cooperates with particularisms of identity, whereby the literary critic focuses attention on increasingly small units of cultural meaning – objects or events which carry within them an explanation of something much larger than themselves. One no longer goes to conferences to hear papers about speech act theories of literary discourse or principles of unity in *Ulysses*. One goes to explore the cultural metaphoricity of atomic details – the history of the typewriter, telegraphy and telepathy, the cigarette in modernism, late nineteenth-century refuse collection, the gas lamp in Victorian London, skin as a cultural metaphor, or rats in literature. The point about these particularities is that they are universally suggestive. They reflect that general academic habit of mind which specializes in something tiny but which seeks to explain the whole of society, culture or indeed the universe through the lens of this microcosmic detail. There are two identifiable strategies. The first is to find tiny non-literary details which evoke a society or a culture as a whole, and the second is to find objects or moments in literary texts which can implicitly stand for the whole significance of that text, and by extension, the historical context to which it belongs. The really clever trick is to follow both of these strategies at the same time and, with the help of a little psychoanalytic theory, offer the metaphorical assemblage as the components of an idea.

It is my proposition here that these universalizing habits of mind are particularly well-developed in the new literary historicisms because critics are not primarily expert in history. They are experts in metaphor. History provides a forum for the demonstration of skills in the metaphorical, analogical and allegorical interpretation of details, their expertise in the tropes of resemblance that allow miscellaneous cultural fragments to aggregate into collectives or turn outwards towards portentous universals. The contemporary critic is unusually particularist and universalist at the same time. I know someone who sits on a publishing board for cultural historical projects who asked me to explain recently why cultural historians from history departments send in proposals with titles like *The Teacup Handle from 1760–1768* whereas cultural historians from English departments would rather write a book called *The Teacup Handle and Democratic Culture*.

There are one or two well-known objections to these new particularisms. J. Hillis Miller, for example, has called the problem that of the biological synecdoche, a kind of argument in which a small detail is seen to bear within it the pattern of a complex whole, through a relation of apparently biological necessity. Similarly Dominick La Capra cautions against what he calls world-in-a-grain-of-sand arguments in the new historicisms, and their incumbent paralogical methods which imply universals by analogy and association. LaCapra complains that the value of logic in critical argument is being steadily replaced by the importance of being interesting. The objection to biological synecdoche, or the world in a grain of sand, is partly then an objection to a new logical slipperiness, by which complex totalities once deemed unrepresentable or ungraspable by speculative reason, are rehypothesized in a mode of nervous insinuation, and can then retreat to the alibis of particularity and historical specificity if that hypothesis is questioned. These new particulars are, in short, metaphors masquerading as microcosms. They are universals in nutshells.

One of the difficulties with this kind of objection, of course, is that it might be considered to be an objection to literature itself. If contemporary criticism is characterized by an unusual degree of particularity combined with an unusual ability to imply universality, if metaphor and synecdoche are the means by which criticism can project the meaning of details beyond their particularity, it begins to look as if criticism is the reprise of its own critical object. It is, after all, about the most persistent critical view from Aristotle onwards, that literature is distinguished from history and philosophy on the basis of its equilibrium between particular and universal significance. William Wimsatt argues this in *The Verbal Icon*, that 'whether or not one believes in universals, one may see the persistence in literary criticism of a theory that poetry presents the concrete and the universal, or the individual and the universal, or an object which in a mysterious and special way is both highly general and highly particular' (1970, 71). Wimsatt is following several early twentieth-century New Critics, particularly John Crowe Ransom and Allen Tate, in borrowing from Hegel's account of the work of art as a kind of concrete universal:

> *In comparison with the show or semblance of immediate sensuous existence or of historical narrative, the artistic semblance has the advantage that in itself it points beyond self, and refers us away from itself to something spiritual which it is meant to bring before the mind's eye ... The hard rind of nature and the common world give the mind more trouble in breaking through to the idea than do the products of art.*
>
> (Wimsatt, 1970, 72)

John Ruskin, well known for his God-in-a-blade-of-grass arguments, prefers to think that natural objects might have the structure of the concrete universal on their own account, remarking in *Modern Painters* that poetry is not distinguished from history either by the omission or addition of details: 'There must be something either in the nature of the details themselves, or the method of using them, which invests them with poetical power'. It is this ambiguity, I think, between whether particular details are containers of an extended significance in themselves, or have that significance invested in them by the possessor of poetical power, that animates the new particularisms of literary criticism. If a metaphor is a figure constitutively split between its particularity and its equivalence to something else, it is the trope which allows the new cultural historicisms simultaneously to apprehend the past as past, in its particularity, and to signify beyond itself to something which transcends that particularity, such as the present.

It may be that new particularisms have something in common with poetic power conceived as the concrete universal, and it is certainly common to find the new cultural historians themselves establishing this link between creativity and criticism. One example is Terry Eagleton describing Walter Benjamin's style of microscopic sociology:

In this kind of microanalysis, the individual phenomenon is grasped in all of its overdetermined complexity as a kind of cryptic code or riddling rebus to be deciphered, a drastically abreviated image of social processes which the discerning eye will persuade it to yield up.

(1990, 329)

'What this method then delivers', he says a little later, 'is a kind of poetic or novelistic sociology in which the whole seems to consist of nothing but a dense tessellation of graphic images; and to this extent it represents an aestheticised model of social enquiry' (1990, 329–30). Eagleton also explicitly links this with James Joyce's use of myth in *Ulysses*, which he describes as a return of the Romantic symbol, a reinvention of the Hegelian 'concrete universal' in which 'every phenomenon is secretly inscribed by a universal law, and any time, place or identity pregnant with the burden of the cosmic whole' (1990, 319).

It seems to me that there is already a rich tradition of what Eagleton calls a poetic or novelistic mode of sociology, which we refer to affectionately as poetry and the novel. But it is undeniable that we have recently lived through an age in which literature and criticism have been on convergent paths. On the side of criticism, aestheticization has been underpinned by a set of theoretical positions which declare that a critic does not describe a literary text objectively, or from a position of neutrality, but rather creates it, invents it or performs it. Fundamentally this view is based in a constitutive account of language – that language does not describe or reflect reality, it constitutes reality. A much favoured terminology is that language is performative, not constative – it brings a state of affairs into existence rather than describes a state of affairs in a way that could be adjudged true or false. It is from this point of view that Barthes can declare that there are no more critics, only writers, in other words no neutral descriptions of literary objects but only creative inventions of them. On the other side of the boundary, the corollary of aestheticized criticism is literature which is increasingly critical or theoretical, in the sense that it assimilates and incorporates critical and theoretical perspectives into its discourse as self-knowledge. The most obvious example of this is metafiction, self-conscious fiction which reflects critically upon itself or on the nature of novels in general, that is self-referential, self-knowing fiction, or fiction which takes itself as one of the topics that it represents.

But is this relationship really symmetrical? 'The yarns of seamen', says Conrad's narrator in *Heart of Darkness*, 'have a direct simplicity, the whole meaning of which lies within the shell of a cracked nut. But Marlow was not typical, . . . and to him the meaning of an episode was not inside like a kernel but outside, enveloping the tale which brought it out only as a glow brings out a haze in the likeness of one of those misty halos that sometimes are made visible by the spectral illumination of moonshine' (Conrad, 1995, 18). This is an image that adapts well from the universal suggestivity of Marlow's narrative in *Heart of Darkness* to the new aestheticized models of social inquiry and cultural history. Particularities are nuts, which do not contain their meanings within them, like a kernel, but are surrounded by misty halos; they project a light outwards to glow upon a haze. My feeling is that, though this is clearly acceptable in a modernist novel, as a model for critical thought, it is a bit fuzzy. In the aestheticization or poeticization of criticism something may have been gained (mainly freedom), but it is clear to me that something has also been lost. The universal has been neglected, the ability to describe general rules about literature, the boldness of mid-century efforts to assemble a global science of literature, the attempt to theorize with any degree of precision the large totalities to which our objects of study belong. I sometimes think that the literary object itself has been lost as a result of the performativity and the metaphoricity of criticism, not only because critics have turned their attention away from literary texts to cultural history, but because any sense of transparency to the object, to the literary text has been sacrificed to the belief that neutrality is impossible. I have found myself railing against metaphor in literary criticism and theory, arguing for some kind of programme of decontamination, for what Paul de Man calls semiological hygiene (1979, 6) in the face of such excesses of metaphorical ingenuity.

What I am saying here then is that the aestheticization of criticism involves two kinds of loss – the loss of the literary object as a whole and the sacrifice of the universal to a hazy implication. And the universal does not only mean a theory of totalities. It also means the unity of much smaller things: the unity of a literary text, and the unity of a concept or a noun. This is one of the legacies of poststructuralism, which characteristically translated singularities into multiplicities. In the work of Derrida, Foucault and Deleuze there is a celebration of difference, irreducible difference and multiplicity. It is not only the big words like Modernism, but every noun that has become a little universe of differences, a multiplicity, a site of contestation. A noun is a little universal. It is, in Deleuze's words 'a machine for containing difference' and 'an absolute survey traversed at infinite speed'. The universal has, in philosophy, always oscillated between the poles of the infinitely large genus and infinitely small genus, signifying at one end the entire membership of the largest imaginable set (the set that contains everything) and at the other end the supposed referents of any general term such as the word 'red' or the word 'tree'.

I have already suggested that particularism in criticism might be thought of firstly as a replication of the microscopic sciences, and secondly as a replication of the concrete universality of literature. I would now like to consider a third possibility, that the increasing interpenetration of particulars and universals might reflect, or be produced by the process of globalization. Recent social theory of globalization has a complex tropology which imagines the world as an increasingly small place, a global village, a tiny unity by comparison with the vast complexity that it used to be. One version of this argument is what David Harvey calls time-space compression (Harvey, 1989) – the idea that as travel speeds have increased from the horse to jet aviation, the world has contracted. Similarly the imagery which describes telecommunications and the Internet is often that of the increased singularity and visibility of the globe. The largest totality therefore becomes more visible, both because the world can be seen as a single place, a small particularity (the view of earth from outer space), and because trade and tourism produce microcosms of the earth as a whole – the supermarket, and Disney World – the semiotic consumption of cultural difference. However there is a complex twist in this kind of theory. The social theory of globalization has shifted in recent decades away from the traditional view which understood the process of globalization as standardization. Many have argued that this is above all a process of Americanization, where the political and economic dominance of the United States is felt across the globe, spreading its cultural hegemony through an army of cultural forms from Donald Duck to Ronald McDonald. According to this view, globalization threatens cultural difference, threatens to homogenize diversity in the name of modernization. More recent theories of globalization have recognized, however, that cultural difference is certainly not in retreat, and that, in fact, the process of globalization might actually generate difference, or that the threat of standardization produces a counter-politics of the local. Most cultural theorists since Heidegger have recognized that if globalization is conceived as a process of compression and unification, it is at the same time a process of diversification, of an increasing awareness of diversity or an increasing individuation of cultures on the global stage. There is an idea that resistance is local, and corporate capitalism is global. The dichotomy of the universal and the particular, the cosmopolitan and the parochial, is sometimes therefore thought of as a dichotomy of power and its resistance. The proliferation of difference and the standardization of the world seem to go hand in hand, so that globalization is both convergence and dissemination. What this necessitates, then,

is an account of the interpenetration of the universal and the particular which finds its philosophical expression in Hegel and Heidegger and its political reality in the complicity of homogenization and diversification.

Robertson, for example, describes recent history as follows:

In recent world history, the universalism–particularism issue has come to constitute something like a global-cultural form, a major axis of the structuration of the world as a whole. Rather than simply viewing the theme of universalism as having to do with principles that can and should be applied to all, and that of particularism as referring to that which can and should be applied only locally, I suggest that the two have become tied together as part of a globewide nexus.

(1992, 102)

As if in homage to what Harvey calls 'the increasing interpenetration of opposite tendencies in capitalism as a whole', the social theory of globalization has come to recognize that it is no longer possible to conceive the particular and the universal as mutually exclusive poles. And nowhere is the need to reformulate the universal felt more strongly than in the corner into which left politics has been driven, that is the corner in which the left is constrained to a counter-politics of the local.

The need to break out from the limited space of difference, of particularity and of the local is no doubt responsible for the return of universality in the social theory of the left. Nowhere is this more apparent than in the recent work of Ernesto Laclau, Slavoj Žižek and Judith Butler who are each, in different ways, rereading and rewriting Hegel's concept of concrete universality. The central theme of this rereading is that the impossibility of an abstract universal is exposed whenever that abstraction is represented, since the very act of representation entails a concrete embodiment which will specify an entity which is by definition not specific. Žižek, for example, describes the Hegelian concrete universal as 'a process of particular attempts that do not simply exemplify the neutral universal notion but struggle with it, give a specific twist to it' and therefore 'decide the fate of the universal notion itself':

> Universality is concrete, structured as a texture of particular figurations, precisely because it is forever prevented from acquiring a figure that would be adequate to its notion. This is why – as Hegel puts it – the Universal is always one of its own species: there is universality only in so far as there is a gap, a hole, in the midst of the particular content of the universality in question, that is in so far as, among the species of a genus, there is always one species missing: namely, the species that would adequately embody the genus itself.
>
> (1999, 103).

In the midst of every genus, then, which presumably means every noun, collective or otherwise, there is a hole which Žižek rather pretentiously calls the absent centre of political ontology. But the exact sense in which this absent centre is a hole requires a little further reflection. For Hegel, one image of the Concept is a genus which specifies itself in its species. In other words, the concept is embodied in its own species, but not adequately embodied. The hole in the midst of a genus is therefore not an absence so much as an inadequate presence – a contingent embodiment of the concept, the genus or the universal which can only partially represent it. The partial and inadequate representation of a totality therefore gives that totality a particular set of characteristics, and in this sense, gives a particular twist to, rather than simply exemplifies, the universal.

I want to return in a moment to the idea of the internal gap because I think it posits a particular conceptual shape for the increasing interpenetration of opposite tendencies. But it will be worth considering first the much clearer formulation of the particular/universal relation that Laclau offers in *Emancipations*. For Laclau, the emptiness of a universal is not imaged as an internal gap where it fails to find particular representation. The universal is 'an empty but ineradicable place' which is always at some remove from any particular attempt to represent it. As for Žižek, particular contents of the universal genus compete with each other to fill this empty place, to embody it and represent it. For Laclau there are two major consequences of this. The first is that the relationship between a particular and a universal is a hegemonic relationship, which is to say that the unrepresentable totality is contingently represented by particular contents: the empty space is filled by particular characteristics and interests which stake a claim to be the most adequate available embodiment of the totality, where the gap between the embodiment and the universal body remains unbridgeable. The second consequence is that any particular content which attempts to represent the universal cannot then be thought of as purely particular, since it is in part constituted by its relationship to the universal. This is fundamentally, I think, a structuralist observation not only because the very idea of particularity is inhabited by its opposite, but also because any particularity is, like a linguistic sign, secretly inscribed by the systemic relationships which are the basis of its intelligibility or identity. Thus, for Laclau, a particularity is like the shell of a walnut – a unity which is constitutively split between its particular content and its systemic component, or between itself and its relationship to the whole. The next step in the argument is that if each particular is constitutively split between its own particularity and an element of universality, it follows that all the particularities which compete for the hegemonic role of representamen of the universal have something in common with each other, namely a systemic or a universal component. This is what Laclau refers to as the chain of equivalence – that principle so much neglected in the age of difference which dictates that, however much particularities may differ from each other, in the very act of differing, they have something in common. The chain of equivalence which runs between particular contents competing for the hegemonic role depends upon a shared component which is constitutive of each particularity. In other words a particularity is a crossing point between the logic of identity and the logic of equivalence. There are two significant observations which I would like to make from this scheme. The first is expressed best in Judith Butler's summary of the political potential of Laclau's scheme:

> When the chain of equivalence is operationalized
> as a political category, it requires that particular
> identities acknowledge that they share with other
> such identities the situation of a necessarily
> incomplete determination. They are fundamentally
> the set of differences from which they emerge,
> and this set of differences constitutes the structu-
> ral features of the domain of political sociality. If
> any such particular identity seeks to universalize
> its own situation without recognizing that other
> identities are in an identical structural situation, it
> will fail to achieve an alliance with the other
> emerging identities, and will mistakenly identify
> the meaning and the place of universality itself.
> The universalization of the particular seeks to

> elevate a specific content to a global condition,
> making an empire of its local meaning.

(Butler et al., 2000, 31)

The chain of equivalence therefore locates universality not only in the empty but ineradicable place above all particularity, but as an emptiness within each differential identity on the basis of which political alliance is possible. But the second observation I would like to make is that this crossing point of the logic of identity with the logic of equivalence is a time-honoured account of metaphor. Wimsatt, for example, describes this connection in his discussion of concrete universality:

> Even the simplest form of metaphor or simile ('My
> love is like a red, red rose') presents us with a
> special and creative, in fact a concrete, kind of
> abstraction different from that of science. For
> behind a metaphor lies a resemblance between
> two classes, and hence a more general third
> class. This class is unnamed and most likely
> remains unnamed and is apprehended only
> through the metaphor.

(1970, 79)

In fact the metaphor has always been, and remains conceived as exactly the crossing-point between the logic of equivalence and the logic of identity, or as the figure which is constitutively split between being itself and being something else. This is what G. B. Madison describes as the is/is-not character of metaphorical statements. 'The meaning of a metaphor', he argues, 'is not like the meaning of a straightforward referential proposition or a constative utterance; it is not what is apparently said, but is, rather, what the utterance shows in transcending itself towards what is not said in the saying, and it is what the utterance does when it leads another person to recreate for himself a meaning analogous to the intended by the maker of the metaphor' (1990, 149). It is on the basis of this structural homology between political sociality and metaphor that the new creative particularisms of literary criticism found their political metaphoricity.

What this uncovers for me is a disagreement that I have with Žižek and a greater degree of agreement with Laclau over the political salience of what Derrida, Butler and others refer to as 'performative contradiction'. Žižek seems to view the power of performative contradiction in Butler's work as the power of challenging an 'officially asserted' universality with a counter-assertion of 'the very content this universality (in its hegemonic form) excludes' (Butler et al., 2000, 102). My problem here is that Žižek's reading of Butler's performative contradiction reduces the notion to the mere counter-assertion of marginalities. Laclau comes closer in his description of Butler's related notion of parodic performance:

> One of Butler's most interesting contributions to social theory is her notion of 'parodic performance'. Butler has applied her notion only to very precise examples, and has not universalized her own notion, but my optimistic reading of her texts is that this generalization, if it is fully realized, can tell us something really important concerning the structuration of social life. My argument would be as follows: if a parodic performance means the creation of a distance between the action actually being performed and the rule being enacted, and if the instance of application of the rule is internal to the rule itself, parody is constitutive of all social action.
>
> (Butler et al., 2000, 78)

What would the universalization of this notion of parodic performance or that of performative contradiction entail? My own view is that this question is the real intersection of political and aesthetic dealings with the issue of universality. And my answer to it would be, somewhat against Butler and Derrida, that there can be a kind of formal or abstract logic for performative contradiction capable of universalizing its significance. My argument here will owe something to Alan Badiou's recently translated account (Badiou, 2000) of his disagreement with Deleuze, in which he proposed that everything that Deleuze thought about multiplicity could be accounted for in set theory. Deleuze's resistance to this propostion seems to me a rather stubborn adherence to the conviction that philosophy is no more abstract than its object, or that it is a practice as concrete as those it counts among its objects of study.

One of the things that has interested me particularly in the idea of a hole in the centre of a universal is how closely it resembles the postulation of black holes embedded in the universe. If I am remembering Hawking's *A Brief History of Time* correctly, there is a preposterous account of the danger that the gravitational pull of a black hole might become so strong that it would suck the entire universe into it, which seems like such a perfect metaphor for an egocentric academic specialism that I can only suspect it of being one. The black hole is of course already widely used to describe a spiralling sensation experienced by lecturers and students when they have had too much to drink the night before, causing a complete loss of linearity or recall of the topic under discussion. But the black hole is also an excellent metaphor for what might be called the problem of aporetic self-reference. If Žižek sees the genus, or universal, as something with a hole in it where its own self-representation is missing, he is missing the most interesting cases, namely those where the universal performatively includes itself in the membership of its own genus. A well known example is the proposition 'All generalizations are false, including this one', which expresses a contradiction or a paradox, and that this paradox emerges because the proposition refers not only to the set of all generalizations, but that, as a generalization, it includes itself in the proposition, or to put it another way, that the particular proposition renders itself false in the act of offering itself as a truth. These sorts of paradox are well known in philosophy and have troubled logicians since antiquity. The ancient liar paradox, for example, is a syllogism which simply does not work because the truth value of a sentence cannot be determined when that sentence is implicated in its own claim. Hence, the sentence 'This sentence is false' is contradictory because if it is true, then it is false, but if it is false, then its proposition appears to be true, in which case it appears to be both true and false, or neither, or either. Bertrand Russell's work on set theory throws up a more complicated example, which is particularly relevant to the question of universals. Clearly some sets are members of themselves, for example the set of all sets; but what if you take the set of all sets that are not members of themselves? If it is a member of itself, then it is one of the things that is not a member of itself and so it is not a member of itself. If on the other hand it is not a member of itself, this clearly means that it is one of those sets that are not members of themselves, and therefore it *is* a member of itself. In this paradox, it would seem that the set of all sets that are not members of themselves both is and is not a member of itself. If a universal claim is one that will be true for all the members of a set, these examples show that when the set is self-conscious, or self-referential, a kind of logical rebound will ensue. The self-referentiality of a proposition or a set in these cases means that there is one particular member of the set, namely itself, which governs the identity of the set as a whole. In Žižek's formulation, the concrete universal is the impossibility of a genus including itself among its species, whereas in these examples, the genus includes itself in its species as a black hole, or to use Derrida's words, as an internal pocket which is larger than the whole (Derrida, 1992).

So where does this line of thought go? I think what I am describing here as an internal black hole, an internal pocket larger than the whole, is a kind of algebra for a new kind of logic, a universal and abstract logic that finds exemplification on both sides of the boundary between literature and criticism, and which is both a political and a philosophical mode of reason. 'Performative contradiction' is a phrase originally used as an accusation from Habermas to Derrida to complain that Derrida could not use reason to destroy reason without implicating himself in a contradiction. And yet this formula, of using reason to destroy reason, or language to undermine the reliability of language, is exactly what this new logical practice is: a form of immanent critique for which the self-referential set provides a kind of theory. Hence, Butler finds performative contradiction in any account of universal human rights, such as the American Constitution:

Not only does a racist speech contradict the universalist premise of the constitution, but any speech that actively contests the founding premise of the constitution ought not for that reason be defended by the constitution. To protect such a speech would be to engage in a performative contradiction. Implicit to this argument is the claim that the only speech that ought to be protected by the constitution is speech grounded in its universalist premises.

(1997, 88)

The idea of performative contradiction has become an account of the universal because it is the basis of political sociality. The idea that the universalist premises of political sociality might be figured in this way as performative contradiction can also be found in Derrida's use of friendship as a metaphor for democracy (Derrida, 1997). Considering a sentence attributed to Aristotle, 'O My friends, there is no friend' (Derrida, 1997, 1), Derrida identifies a performative contradiction interpreted by Nietzsche as an account of friendship in which there is always an internal pocket capable of destroying friendship itself. In this rather chilling account of friendship and therefore democracy, there is always some unspeakable secret that must never be touched upon, and on which the possibility rests as a foundational silence.

There is no doubt in my mind that these kinds of theoretical approach to universality are thoroughly prefigured in literature. The split between particular and universal simply is, as I have argued, the structure of metaphor, but it would be possible to find analogues even for the aporetic models of universality. The liar paradox, for example finds its most complex articulations in the paradoxes of unreliable narration; the self-conscious set, which counts itself among the species of its genus is self-conscious narration; and the set with a black hole in its midst is the self-referential aporia of metafiction. In each case, the set theory is an inadequate, formal and skeletal account of something much richer in literature. Just as Derrida feels that he can say nothing about Joyce's *Ulysses* that the text does not say itself, I feel that there is little that anyone can say about the relations between fragments and universals that is not more interestingly and more entertainingly addressed in a novel such as Rushdie's *Midnight's Children*. Returning to the convergence of literature and criticism, then it seems that literature is tailing theory from the front, assimilating its perspectives and yet leading the way.

I believe that fictional narratives are the most complex expressions that we have of logical difficulties in the relationship between particular and universal significance, particularly in those cases where narrative self-consciousness and the performative contradiction seem to demolish any formal logic which might describe them. But this doesn't mean that there is no formal logic. It means that there is a formal logic more complicated and more contradictory than the models we already have. Criticism, in my opinion, should be more abstract than the particularities it describes. Whereas for Deleuze philosophy is no more abstract than its object, for me, literary criticism and theory are relatively abstract practices, and that abstraction is necessary not only for an understanding of how fictional narratives work, but what they teach us about non-fictional narratives as they operate everywhere. In a nutshell, the universal is not a thing but a relation. It adheres to the particular as the abstract adheres to the concrete. They are sutured together like the two halves of a walnut.

It was with some disappointment that I realized recently that everything I thought could be represented in a small Venn diagram made up of three overlapping sets. Set number one could be called *self-consciousness*, number two would be *paradoxes and contradictions* and the third is relations between the universal and the particular. The realization was paramount to a recognition that what had once seemed an irreducible universe of disconnected ideas was contracting into a smaller constellation. This recognition was accompanied by an anxiety that the contraction may be determined by, or metaphorically stand in the place of, the physical contraction of my brain. Projecting forward, it seems possible that the three stars of this constellation may eventually converge on a point where I can claim to know only one thing, so that it might some day be possible to compress it all into the shell of a nut. I was told of this once by a no doubt utterly bogus scientific study which claimed to have shown that an academic education was the best possible guard against the dangers of senility – that the ordering of one's concepts, ideas and arguments in a rational framework early in life could help to contain the spillage and mess associated with senility, so that the ever-contracting constellation of one's ideas might become, in later years, a conveniently portable container for everything that one once knew. Drawing this diagram is not easy, because each of the three spheres is itself the whole totality, that is I cannot give an account of what I think about anything, or the way that I think in general, without mentioning all three. There is nothing, for example, that I know about self-consciousness that could not be included inside of the set about particulars and universals, yet also nothing that I know about universals that does not belong within the idea of self-consciousness. Each set is both a universal and a subset. But this sudden recognition, that everything I thought could be contained in three sets, is itself a self-conscious reflection on what I think, and the way that I think, from some Olympian height. As such, it betrays its own immanence in what it describes, its own failure to reflect on my thinking neutrally, since it is itself a self-conscious and paradoxical reflection on the issue of universal sets. The observation affirms everything that I already think about the interconnectedness of self-consciousness, paradox and the universal. I cannot therefore reflect on the way that I think without it being an example of the way that I think, so that my attempts to think about myself from the outside turn out to be tiny particles of my interiority.

And so, for those too pressed for time, here is the nutshell in a nutshell. The universal is a nutshell that hegemonizes an empty place, it is a nut that contains a hole where it cannot represent itself, and it is a nut with a black hole in it capable of swallowing the nut itself.

Or in an even more compressed form: U is the centre of NUT.

Works cited

Badiou, Alain. *Deleuze: the Clamour of Being*, trans. Louise Burchill. Minneapolis, MN, 2000.

Butler, Judith, Ernesto Laclau and Slavoj Žižek. *Contingency, Hegemony, Universality: Contemporary Dialogues on the Left*. London, 2000.

Butler, Judith. *Excitable Speech: a Politics of the Performative*. London, 1997.

Conrad, Joseph. *Heart of Darkness*, ed. and intro. Robert Hampson. London, 1995.

de Man, Paul. *Allegories of Reading: Figural Language in Rousseau, Nietzsche, Rilke, and Proust*. New Haven, CT, 1979.

Derrida, Jacques. 'The Law of Genre', in *Acts of Literature*, ed. Derek Attridge. London, 1992, 221–52.

Derrida, Jacques. *Politics of Friendship*, trans. George Collins. London, 1997.

Eagleton, Terry. *The Ideology of the Aesthetic*. Oxford, 1990.

Harvey, David. *The Condition of Postmodernity*. Oxford, 1989.

Laclau, Ernesto. *Emancipation(s)*. London, 1996.

Madison, G. B. *The Hermeneutics of Postmodernity: Figures and Themes*. Bloomington, IN, 1990.

Robertson, R. *Globalization: Social Theory and Global Culture*. London, 1992.

Wimsatt, W. K. *The Verbal Icon: Studies in the Meaning of Poetry*. London, 1970.

Žižek, Slavoj. *The Ticklish Subject: the Absent Centre of Political Ontology*. London, 1999.

visuality | V SIGNS: THOUGHTS ON VISUALITY AS VISION IN THE EXPANDED FIELD | *STEVEN UNGAR*

Vision's trace

Writing in 1988, the art historian Hal Foster defined visuality as a set of differences among 'how we see, how we are able, allowed, or made to see, and how we see this seeing or the unseen therein' (Foster, 1988, ix). To which I would add *how we say this seeing or the unseen within* in order to convey what I hold to be at stake in the interaction of visual and verbal experiences and the kinds of understanding this interaction promotes. As a phenomenon of discourse and thus one of language, utterance and communication, visuality is grounded in – but identical to – the physical phenomena that traditional anatomy and optics study with reference to the eye and the action of light. This essay explores two models of visuality, as they have evolved over the past thirty years in conjunction with 'the new Art History' and visual anthropology, the latter in the form of filmed ethnography. My goal is to identify the nature and extent of a shift in thinking about vision, from an object of erudite study addressed in the main by art historians, psychologists and philosophers, toward an object of consideration increasingly informed by models of semiology, psychoanalysis, gender and historicisms of various stripes. In particular, I mean to examine how critical debate surrounding vision and visuality discloses changes in understanding associated with the disciplines of art history and anthropology and claims to knowledge bearing on what Michel Foucault has analysed within a broader linkage of power and knowledge. Finally, what I invoke in my title as 'the expanded field' alludes by semantic stretch to current debate on ethnographic film among anthropologists and others for whom fieldwork increasingly engages visuality in conjunction with the discipline and figurative 'field' of anthropology.[1]

Considerations of vision among philosophers, psychologists and art historians over the past thirty years have increasingly drawn on semiology, psychoanalysis and feminism in order to analyse and assess assumptions related to thinking and writing about vision. These considerations range from questions of method and critical vocabulary to those of knowledge and interpretation. As a set, they posit a shared object in traces of this thinking and writing that constitute a prime sense of the term 'visuality'. Among these considerations, Martin Jay's *Downcast Eyes* is especially clear and insightful, not in the least because of the sensitivity that Jay displays toward the ubiquity of visual metaphors such as those in the adjectives I have just used to describe his book (Jay, 1993, 1). Jay's sense of this ubiquity obtains not just in figures of speech discernible in everyday usage, but as well in models of understanding linked to intellectual figures such as René Descartes for whom vision was the noblest of the senses.

Several years before *Downcast Eyes*, books by John Tagg and Jonathan Crary on photography and early nineteenth-century technologies of the visual analysed models of perception as instances of what Jay later termed scopic regimes. They did this by extending the notion of power/knowledge Michel Foucault had developed in conjunction with practices of perception and surveillance in the medical clinic and the prison (see Crary, 1990; Tagg 1988 and Foucault, 1975 and 1979). The studies by Tagg and Crary were variants of Foucault's archaeologies, in which assumptions related to knowledge concerning vision grounded in the histories of optics and anatomy overlapped with visuality as a discursive phenomenon. For Foucault, documents disclosing how vision was thought and 'spoken' formed the material basis for analysing claims to truth about vision and the authority on the basis of which these claims were made. Each in his own way, Crary and Tagg analysed how these claims disclosed relations of power that were never equal. In fact, Hal Foster's definition of visuality already conveys this sense of power/knowledge relations in the clause where the passive forms 'allowed' and 'made' describe seeing as regulated from outside or beyond the competence (Jay might prefer 'scope' or 'purview') of the first-person plural pronoun.

Whatever one holds visuality to have been at various moments in the past, it is very much a word used in the present. My software underscores the point by underscoring it in red as a reminder to confirm its spelling. This reminder is also an electronic way of conveying that the word is non-standard in current usage and that I might need to confirm its meaning as well as its spelling. Etymology links 'visuality' to 'visualize' and 'vision', all of which derive from the Latin root *visio*, for 'sight'. *The New Shorter Oxford English Dictionary* lists its initial occurrence in the mid-nineteenth century, with reference to mental visibility and/or a mental image. Usage has evolved since the mid-1970s in conjunction with critical and theoretical work across disciplines from art history and philosophy to film and media studies. It has also responded to innovations in the technologies of electronic and digital media, some of whose applications no longer conform to the laws of physical or material

space (Sturken and Cartwright, 2001, 147). These innovations have enhanced the rate and range of visual information accessible to a public sphere increasingly cast as 'users'. They have also imposed new concerns linked to emergent models of visual culture, visual studies and virtual reality for which the critical notion of visuality is crucial.

Critical prompts from 'the new art history'

The remarks by Hal Foster cited at the start of this essay first appeared in the preface to *Vision and Visuality*, a collection of essays that helped to define debate surounding 'the new Art History' in the mid to late 1980s. The essays in *Vision and Visuality* acknowledged the relevance as well as the limitations of writings on vision, painting and aesthetics by art historians, philosophers and social critics such as Erwin Panofsky, Martin Heidegger, Maurice Merleau-Ponty, Jacques Lacan and Frantz Fanon. Taken cumulatively, the volume's essays by Martin Jay, Jonathan Crary, Rosalind Krauss, Norman Bryson and Jacqueline Rose sketched a critical programme whose ambition Foster aptly described as one of thickening modern vision by drawing on recent work in psychoanalysis, deconstruction, gender and cultural studies. Foster's choice of terms was far from incidental, since the verbal form 'thickening' drew on the title of Clifford Geertz's 1973 essay, 'Thick Description: Toward an Interpretive Theory of Culture', and to a trope of anthropology that I address in the second half in this essay.

Norman Bryson added to Foster's prefatory remarks when he defined visuality as a cultural construct that undermined the notion of unmediated visual experience by inserting between retina and world a screen of signs consisting of the multiple discourses on vision built into the social arena (Foster, 1988, 91–2). The screen in question was drawn from structural linguistics and, in particular, from the general science of signs known as semiology, first outlined in Ferdinand de Saussure's 1916 *Course on General Linguistics*. For Bryson, the shadow cast by the screen surrounded the seeing subject with codes of recognition and understanding imposed from the outside and to what a Derridean might term a fatal decentring. As a set, the essays in *Vision and Visuality* characterized attempts among proponents of 'the new Art History' of the 1970s and 1980s to question and move beyond models of centralized vision whose origins in European models of perspective and Cartesian space extended to modernisms of the mid-twentieth century. The fact that many of the contributors to *Vision and Visuality* had contributed to the journal *October* conveyed the sense of a collective statement, or *October* manifesto. As I discuss below, the affiliation was meaningful in conjunction with a questionnaire on visual culture published in the journal eight years later.

A second prompt for my thoughts on visuality came from Michael Baxandall's assertion – at the start of *Patterns of Intention* (1985) – that the explanation of pictures occurs only in so far as they are considered under some verbal description or specification. By which I take Baxandall to mean that description mediates explanation to the extent that what it purports to describe – what it is ostensibly a description *of* – is less a specific picture in and of itself than thought (or thoughts) after seeing this picture. Accordingly, he concludes that what we explain, first, through description, are thoughts we have had about a particular picture, and only secondarily the picture itself. What Baxandall termed the mediating role of description derived, at least in part, from problems involving the systematic description of a work of art, as engaged by tra-

dition in the rhetorical exercise of ekphrasis. Finding the right words with which to construct a true and accurate description of works of art is also a practical matter related by traditions of rhetoric and logic to orderly argument.

Baxandall related concerns with rhetoric and logic to those of understanding and epistemology when he noted that descriptions treating the subject matter of the picture's representation as if it were real would not enable one to reproduce the picture, but only to visualize what it was purported to represent. Descriptions based on form rather than subject-matter seemed closer to reproducing the act of looking at a picture as though all at once in its entirety. But here again, Baxandall noted an incompatibility or lack of fit between what he called the gait of scanning a picture and the gait of ordered words and concepts: 'Within the first second or so of looking we have *a sort of impression of the whole field of a picture*. What follows is sharpening of detail, noting of relations, perceptions of orders, and so on, the sequence of optical scanning being influenced both by general scanning habits and by particular cues in the picture acting on our attention' (Baxandall, 1985, 4; italicized words convey my emphasis). Furthermore, the order used to describe aspects and elements of a picture was variable much in the way that looking at a picture could vary from one instance to the next.

Baxandall's concerns with the nature and function of description opened onto broader questions of understanding and interpretation. In terms of the latter, they bore a number of similarities with the critical project Roland Barthes undertook in *S/Z* when he mixed description, analysis, and commentary in order to simulate a single instance of reading Balzac's novella, 'Sarrasine'. Comparable concerns obtained in passages of *The Pleasure of the Text* and *Roland Barthes by Roland Barthes* where Barthes wrote that Proust's *Remembrance of Things Past* was a mandala, a circular memory that he read and reread, skipping over different passages each time. In all three texts, what Barthes addressed in the act of reading addressed in terms of prose fiction what Baxandall engaged with reference to the historical explanation of pictures. Baxandall's reference to 'a sort of impression of the whole field of a picture' recalled the dynamics of reading Barthes undertook to analyse in terms of Balzac's 'Sarrasine' and Proust's *Remembrance*. In particular, the notion of 'the whole field of a picture' attributed wholeness as much to the perceiver as to the physical entity of the picture. Baxandall's use of the term 'impression' likewise touched on what others working in psychoanalysis, film studies and/or feminism since the 1970s have theorized in terms of the gaze, the visual field and the cinematic apparatus.

This is the proper moment for me to state that I take Baxandall's critical stance as cautionary on the aesthetic issue of possible parallels among the arts. By which I understand what he argues concerning the historical explanation of pictures to be at a remove from the position taken by Mario Praz in 'Ut Pictura Poesis' on the correspondence between painting and poetry (see Praz, 1970, 3–27). Baxandall's assertion in *Patterns of Intention* that what description describes is less a specific picture in and of itself than thought after seeing this picture also touched on concerns with reference subsequently addressed by critical debate surrounding virtual images. As in the passages by Foster and Bryson cited above, Baxandall and Barthes analysed the production of meaning in ways that challenged and revised earlier models of description as direct and unmediated. Finally, what Barthes contended concerning description drew directly on what Jacques Lacan had set forth as interaction between realms of the imaginary, the symbolic and the real, an interaction to which Baxandall made no reference whatsoever.

Baxandall and Svetlana Alpers were among the first art historians associated with visual culture through their respective attempts to study artistic production in conjunction with – rather than apart from – popular practices linked to everyday life in premodern societies (Moxey, 2001, 107). The breakdown of distinctions between high art and popular practices remains central to ongoing debate surrounding notions and models of visual culture. W. J. T. Mitchell has argued that 'from the standpoint of a general field of visual culture, art history can no longer rely on received notions of beauty or aesthetic significance to define its proper object of study. The realm of the vernacular and popular imagery clearly has to be reckoned with, and the notions of aesthetic hierarchy, of masterpieces and the genius of the artist to be redescribed as historical constructions specific to various cultural place-times' (cit. Moxey, 2001, 108). Mitchell's stance is coherent with those for whom the emergence of visual studies constituted a liberation from traditional histories of art grounded in large part on aesthetic criteria such as beauty and genius. It is fair to note that the breakthrough status accorded to Baxandall's *Painting and Experience in Fifteenth Century Italy* (1974) and Alpers's *The Art of Describing* (1983) did not at all mean that they were always in agreement with the tone and range of recent debate. Alpers stated as much when she wrote that the notion of visual culture was discriminating rather than encompassing and that she understood it accordingly as distinct from verbal or textual culture (VCQ, 26).

Eight years after *Vision and Visuality*, a 'Visual Culture Questionnaire' in issue no. 77 of *October* provided an update in the form of statements from nineteen respondents to whom four hypotheses (referred to as 'suggestions') had been sent in the winter of 1996. The respondents included two contributors to the earlier volume, Jonathan

Crary and Martin Jay, as well as a range of art and architecture historians, film theorists, literary critics and artists. (Because Rosalind Krauss and Hal Foster were editors of *October*, it was likely that they had at least some role in the project.) The first of the four hypotheses concerned the displacement of models of history such as those of art, architecture and film by a model of anthropology that made the interdisciplinary project of visual culture eccentric with regard to the 'New Art History'. The second hypothesis asserted the prospect of a return in the name of visual culture to medium-based historical disciplines and a breadth of practice that these disciplines entailed. The third asserted that an equation of the visual and the disembodied image was a precondition for an interdisciplinary rubric of visual studies. The fourth hypothesis asserted that pressure within the academy to shift toward the interdisciplinarity of visual culture, especially in its anthropological dimension, paralleled shifts of a similar nature within practices of art, architecture and film.

Responses to the questionnaire varied in terms of type and degree of provocation. Questions of scholarly discipline and interdisciplinarity received high visibility, along a range of positions. Michael Ann Holly welcomed the disorderliness of institutional spaces and unsettling questions that the study of visual representations produced in place of simply reproducing canonized knowledge (VCQ, 41). Tom Conley likewise acknowledged the pleasure of discovering that the study of the growth of visual culture within the academy was linked to a mobility that resisted localizing it within a disciplinary space (VCQ, 32). Jonathan Crary reiterated a distinction in his earlier work between historical problems about vision and a history of representational practices (VCQ, 33). Thomas Crow set conceptual artists against modernist critics in order to assert that preoccupation with the optical entailed a failure to recognize that

painting achieved a high degree of self-consciousness in western culture by virtue of antagonism toward its own visuality (VCQ, 36).

David Rodowick argued that visuality was a paradoxical concept linked to the historical emergence of new media whose incompatability with systems of aesthetics placed them *ahead* of philosophy. He took this incompatability, which he also noted in the historical emergence of cinema, as a challenge to visual and cultural studies to provide a genealogical critique of the aesthetic as well as a positive investigation of concepts invented or suggested by new media. Rodowick struck a Nietzschean tone, inflected via Michel Foucault and Gilles Deleuze, with reference to a conceptual untimeliness that set philosophy *behind* new media whose emergence was paradoxical in the sense that it went against received opinion. New media imposed a philosophical confrontation out of which, presumably, new concepts and new understanding would emerge: 'Our era is no longer one of images and signs. It is defined, rather, by simulacra in Deleuze's sense of the term: paradoxical series where concepts of model and copy, the Same and the One, the Identical and the Like, are no longer easily reconciled nor reduced by principles of unity and the self-same' (VCQ, 62; See Rodowick, 1998, 66–83).

Tom Gunning called for a historical and political approach to visual studies that went beyond identifying oppression in terms of specific media or even broad practices in order to pursue oppression *and liberation* (my emphasis) in actual practices and situations in which these media were deployed (VCQ, 37). Gunning took disclosure of oppression as a means of attaining liberation rather than an end in itself. Accordingly, he was reluctant to jettison the concepts of text and context, at least as long as they remained the site of contest between institutions and reception and thus the area in which the richest unfolding of visual culture in its complexity can occur (VCQ, 37–8). Where Rodowick challenged aesthetics and philosophy to overcome the untimeliness that set them 'behind' new media, Gunning's sense of the potential of visual studies to renew and transform critical understanding within the academy drew him instead – and with due reservation – to ethnography and anthropology

> Although anthropological methods and concepts of culture that erode barriers between everyday structures of experience and aesthetic domains can be extremely useful in this opening of the text, I remain as suspicious of the power relations and reification possible in the concept of ethnographical research as I would be of the master narratives of traditional historical methods. These suspicions are, of course, central to many current rethinkings of anthropology, so the relation of visual studies to anthropology would need to be clarified in terms of what anthropological models are being invoked.

> (VCQ, 38)

Gunning shared Rodowick's sense of paradox concerning visual studies, new media and aesthetics. But whereas Rodowick directed his challenge toward philosophy, Gunning looked instead toward models of description linked to anthropology whose complexity as a site of both power relations and critical self-awareness was in line with disclosing the interplay and oppression and liberation that he wanted visual studies to pursue. This stance set Gunning's response apart from that of Tom Conley, for whom anthropology was a discipline built over the nightmares of history and the redemptive violence of 'man' in the name of colonialism (VCQ, 32).

Tom Gunning went the farthest among respondents to the *October* questionnaire in elaborating, with due caution, how anthropology might contribute to what he described as a historical and political approach to visual studies, mainly from the perspective of film studies (VCQ, 37). The following section of this essay examines critical and theoretical work on ethnographic film and visual anthropology in conjunction with the challenge that the Visual Culture Questionnaire in *October* set forth in terms of attempts to anthropologize vision.

Anthropology in a new light

The assertion that anthropology has always been visual obtains in a strict sense for ethnography, where observation in the field remains a precondition for creating the accounts that purport to describe customs and habits of peoples, races and/or groups. It obtains as well with reference to human and other artifacts collected abroad and displayed in Western Europe at nineteenth-century colonial and universal exhibitions. In France, these artifacts were the material basis for an association founded in 1789 under the curious name of the Société des observateurs de l'Homme [Society for the Observers of Mankind] (Piault, 2000, 5–6). Perhaps, in the apt formulation of Ira Jacknis, many anthropologists have been doing visual anthropology without realizing it (cit. Banks and Morley, 1997, 4).[2]

But what if the process of ethnographic observation leading to word-based accounts such as field notes, articles and books led instead to image-based accounts such as photography, film, video or television in which the role of the visual was heightened? Jean Rouch and others have described an 'ethno-look' or 'ethno-gaze' peculiar to anthropologists working in the field. Johannes Fabian has defined visualism as the ability to visualize a culture synonymous with understanding it (Fabian, 1983, 106). Anna Grimshaw recently devoted an entire study, *The Ethnographer's Eye*, to ways of seeing in modern anthropology (Grimshaw, 2001a). Fatimah Tobing Rony has analysed early ethnographic and feature films such as *King Kong* in conjunction with practices of reading racialized bodies that she characterized in terms of seeing anthropology (Rony, 1996, 21–43).[3] Elsewhere, Rouch identified difference of another kind when he noted that ethnographers considered film to be like a book and that a book on ethnology appeared no different from an ordinary book (cited in Taylor, 1996, 64). In all these cases, questions concerning the status and function of film – ethnographic, documentary or feature – form the basis for considering the nature and function of the visual within anthropology.

The origins of visual anthropology overlap with the birth of cinema, as represented by the December 1895 public presentation of short films by Auguste and Louis Lumière on their newly patented cinematographe. The same year, Félix-Louis Regnault and Charles Comte filmed Wolof, Malagasy and other Africans on display at the Ethnographic Exhibition of French West Africa (Senegal and Sudan) held on the Champs de Mars in Paris. Regnault was trained as a medical doctor. His photographs and moving pictures of Africans in Paris extended the efforts of Etienne-Jules Marey to film the anatomy and physiology of human movement. Regnault worked with Marey as early as 1893. But whereas the subjects of Marey's chronophotography were European male athletes, Regnault filmed men and women from regions of Africa recently colonized by the French as well as French soldiers. This comparative dimension disclosed the extent to which Regnault's fascination with human locomotion drew on models of evolutionary relativism and a corollary notion of

transformisme that served at the time among anthropologists in France as an alternative to Darwinian evolution. As Fatimah Tobing Rony puts it, 'the desire to demarcate difference and the quest to describe pure racial types coincided with the rise of imperialism and nationalism: the discourses of race, nation, and imperialism were intimately linked' (Rony, 1996, 26).[4]

In 1900, the Cambridge anthropologist Alfred Cort Haddon advised a colleague about to undertake fieldwork in Australia: 'You really *must* take a kinematographe or biograph or whatever they call it in your part of the world. It is an indispensable piece of anthropological apparatus' (cit. Grimshaw, 2001a, 16). Two years earlier, Haddon spent nearly eight months on the Torres Straits islands, off the coast of Queensland, before returning to England with photographs, native drawings and other visual materials that he used in a six-volume report. He also returned with filmed footage including sequences of ceremonial dances and of three men lighting a fire. Haddon's efforts to make film 'an indispensable piece of anthropological apparatus' were in line with a scientism for which the kinematograph was anthropology's equivalent of the microscope, capable of documenting and preserving exotic ways of life (Henley, 2001, 35). Documentation in the form of visual recording also promoted the classification of human types that was a prime component of anthropology of the period. Yet the efforts of Haddon and others of his generation to make film indispensable to anthropology were tempered by the new medium's potential for display, spectacle and entertainment that tapped into knowledge/power relations inherent in colonial 'ways of seeing' of the period.[5]

Scepticism among anthropologists concerning the status and role of ethnographic film is linked to a model of anthropology as a word-based ('logocentric') discipline in which film and video are 'transparent representations or "research documents" rather than forms of knowledge production in their own right' (Ginsburg, 1998, 179). Along similar lines, Lucien Taylor has used the term iconophobia to describe a condition of ambivalence toward or mistrust of the visual among those for whom ethnographic film is logically inferior to anthropological texts (Taylor, 1996). As Taylor put it, this institutionalized fear of the image was anthropology's loss, figured as a failure to use what film showed – rather what than what it merely purported to say – about human experience.[6]

Against the grain of such scepticism and fear, a growing minority of anthropologists as well as scholars and producers of documentary film have begun to assess and rethink the kinds of understanding of culture and human experience to which visual anthropology can contribute. The documentary film-maker and critic David MacDougall has explored the properties of visual images that make them distinct from ethnographic writing (MacDougall, 1998, 271). Anna Grimshaw has explored the implications for teaching of a visual anthropology in which the dislodging of language from its central place in representing the world opens onto other ways of knowing (Grimshaw, 2001b, 245).

Jay Ruby argues in a recent study that ethnographic film can be a viable tool to begin a discussion of how culture can be extracted from visible behaviour. Borrowing from the notion of ethnography as thick description first set forth by Clifford Geertz, Ruby asserts that:

The central issue for the ethnographic filmmaker is to be able to find culture in filmable behaviour, and then to generalize from the specific, to make concrete the abstract, and yet to retain the humanity and individuality of those portrayed while still making a statement about culture. In

other words, ethnographers should strive to make ethnographically thick films.

(Ruby, 2000, 243)

This challenge to his fellow anthropologists culminates Ruby's review of visual anthropology as a series of attempts to record and study human behaviours in conjunction with pictorial expressions of anthropologically constructed knowledge. Ruby concludes by proposing what is less a matter of films about anthropological subjects than of films made by trained anthropologists for the express purpose of filmed ethnography; that is, a visual anthropology in which the visual is not simply incidental. To this end, Ruby advocates the practice of filmed ethnography in place of what most others designate as ethnographic film. Lucien Taylor reinforces Ruby on this point when he notes that contemporary interest in visual anthropology often posits the visual as its *object* rather than its *medium* of analysis (MacDougall, 1998, 15). The result is an equation of visual anthropology and an anthropology of vision at odds with the kind of anthropological visuality that he, Ruby, and others mean to theorize as well as practice.

David MacDougall asserts throughout the essays in his *Transcultural Cinema* that film can render the commonplace features of the world in immediately recognizable forms that verbal descriptions can only approximate. Moreover, whereas written accounts have always strained to carve out precise descriptions from a general repertoire of words, photography introduced a mode of description in which the particular appeared to ride effortlessly on the back of the general. Extending the assertion to include films as well as photographs, MacDougall links their means of depicting commonplace features of the world to a capacity to transcend and reframe their own specificity. These visual media are transcultural not only in the sense that they seemingly cross cultural borders, but also because their disclosures of affinities between ourselves and others 'apparently so different from us' remind us that cultural difference is 'at best a fragile concept' (MacDougall, 1998, 245).

MacDougall's notion of transcultural cinema does not reformulate the 'Family of Man' argument grounded in assumptions of universality that occlude or elide difference.[7] Nor is it what Hal Foster calls a 'rogue investigation of anthropology' among artists on the left who misconstrue anthropology as a practice and discipline legitimizing over-identification with the other (Foster, 1996, 182).[8] To the contrary, it is intended to counteract slippage from the appropriate recognition of difference to a compulsory imposition of difference to which practices of writing anthropology have contributed. Transcultural cinema is self-reflexive to the extent that it engages the spectator in an evocation of being-in the-world involving subject, filmmaker and spectator. This evocation, in turn, aims to replace assumptions of extreme or absolute alterity with an intersubjectivity grounded in an identification with (rather than *of*) the other. A key precursor of MacDougall's transcultural cinema is the shared anthropology developed in the 1950s and 1960s by the ethnographic film-maker Jean Rouch. Referring directly to the Rouch's *Moi, un noir* (1957) and *Jaguar* (1967), MacDougall emphasizes that the roles played by the filmed subjects arise out of their lives and, as recorded by the filmmaker's camera, become part of it. *Jaguar* adds a third element in the comments by the subjects while viewing a preliminary version of the film, comments that Rouch incorporated in the final version (MacDougall, 1998, 193).[9]

MacDougall asserts that the fundamental role of identification with others derives partly from responses to the human face, without which 'much of what matters to us in films would vanish' (MacDougall, 1998, 51). The assertion is significant because it posits the role of film within a prelinguistic contact with and awareness of the physical world whose study was the object of the phenomenology first set forth by Edmund Husserl and Martin Heidegger. Citing filmmakers (Robert Bresson, Ingmar Bergman) and philosophers (Maurice Merleau-Ponty, Gilles Deleuze), MacDougall asserts that the face is the site of individuality and expression signalling emotional states with which the spectator's identification posits the existence of parallel sensory experience in others. Accordingly, he writes that 'we reaffirm our identity not only through others' responses to us, nor merely by seeing ourselves *as* others (as in Lacan's account), but in light of others' equivalent consciousness' (MacDougall, 1998, 52).

This phenomenological dimension supports MacDougall's ambitions to link transcultural cinema to an encounter with the other in the form of an identification focused on the human face. This focus on the face of the other occurs as sensory experience removed from the conceptual alterity to which models of anthropology as a word-based discipline contribute. This is the sense in which film provides the basis for what MacDougall describes as an analogy for a single unified field for which filming provides a material trace, 'an object in which the filmmaker's interaction with the film subject is explicitly inscribed' (MacDougall, 1998, 56).

The unique interaction that film makes possible as an encounter with the face of the other conveys an ethical dimension whose formulation in the writings of Emmanuel Levinas seems to complement the philosophers, filmmakers and writers whom MacDougall invokes. Levinas writes:

The proximity of the other is the face's meaning, and it means from the very start in a way that goes beyond the plastic forms which forever try to cover the face like a mask of their presence to perception. But always the face shows through these forms. Prior to any particular expression and beneath all particular expressions, which cover over and protect with an immediately adopted face or countenance, there is the nakedness and destitution of the expression as such, that is to say extreme exposure, defenselessness, vulnerability itself. This extreme exposure – prior to any human aim – is like a shot 'at point blank range'.

(Levinas, 1989, 82–3)

To my knowledge, MacDougall does not cite Levinas. But when Levinas describes the face in terms of extreme exposure ('a shot "at point blank range"'), he reformulates what MacDougall takes to be film's unique ability to reveal in a flash the stamp of the self in an exposed nerve or emotion. Extreme exposure is the equivalent for Levinas of the revelation that MacDougall attributes to film experience.

MacDougall also uses the term 'quick' (as in the sense of cutting or going to the quick) to convey the disclosure of alterity that Levinas conveys with reference to the nakedness and destitution of the human face beneath its masks. Mixing vocabularies, one might conclude that what is disclosed by the unique focus attributed by MacDougall to the film experience is the point-blank flash of authenticity that Levinas locates in the face of the other. The 'quick' may mark the limits of the comparison I am making. For whereas the disclosure evoked for Levinas through extreme exposure sets a responsibility toward the other against his or her irreducible alterity, the revelation of 'the quick' that MacDougall attributes to the film experience entails a *destination* in others and their sense of self. 'The quick' entails

a direct interaction on the basis of which we reaffirm our identity and for which the human face serves as a synecdoche for the physicality of the other.[10]

MacDougall's emphases on interaction and the ethical dimension of transcultural cinema are in line with the importance of the physical qualities of film images that engage visuality with reference to ethnographic description. The point is conveyed less in content such as perceived differences among cultures than in representation involving the particular and the general. The relevant criterion is that of the sensory details elided or limited by ethnographic writing because, MacDougall argues, they would shock or repel us if we were to confront them directly. By contrast, pictures are 'staggeringly particular and indiscriminate in detail, but they constantly reiterate the general forms in which the particular is contained' (MacDougall, 1998, 246). For MacDougall, these forms are nothing more or other than the commonalities of being human that ethnographic descriptions often leave out. The reasons for such elisions in written anthropology range from concerns with concision and accuracy to individual descriptions that invariably include some details at the cost of others.

The selective nature of written descriptions also derives from the fact that in anthropology, writing tends to favour categorization over detailed description of observations, so that 'the visible and the physical' often slip through the net and become attenuated, if not invisible (MacDougall, 1998, 247). For MacDougall – as for Jay Ruby, Faye Ginsburg and Anna Grimshaw – ethnographic film remains an untapped resource that anthropologists committed to word-based descriptions would do well to conceptualize as filmed ethnography (Ruby's expression) rather than as a secondary means of recording work in the field. Resistance or reluctance on the part of anthropologists goes against the prospect of a serious contribution that visual recording ('an indispensable part of anthropological apparatus') held for Alfred Cort Haddon a century ago. MacDougall rightly notes that visual images threaten verbal descriptions with redundancy because most anthropologists take the excess of data conveyed by the image to be superfluous for purposes of analysis. Accordingly, they resist making central to anthropology that which they are accustomed to dismissing. Yet why should this excess drop out as superfluous when it conveys the irreducible physicality that the visual conveys with a force of detail seldom achieved by words? The designation of anthropology as a social (or human) science emphasizes the primacy – for ethnography, at the very least – of description based on observation in the field. The model sciences here are botany and zoology, in which the variety and ordering of species is grounded on systematic and exhaustive description intended to draw out the distinctive qualities of the natural phenomena in question (Laplantine, 1996, 1).[11]

The ends of vision

The transition of visual technologies over the past twenty years from analogue to electronic and digital systems has promoted the emergence of a virtual reality at odds with key assumptions related to space and subjectivity dating back in Western Europe to the sixteenth century. The shift is often read in terms of danger or a threat. Jonathan Crary notes that 'most of the historically important functions of the human eye are being supplanted by practices in which visual images no longer have any reference to the position of an observer in a "real", optically perceived world' (Crary, 1990, 2). Increasingly, Crary concludes, visuality will be situated on a cybernetic and electromagnetic terrain where abstract visual and linguistic elements coincide and are consumed, circulated and exchanged globally. I take Crary's remarks concerning virtual images and 'the historically important functions of the human eye' less as a prognosis of the eye's irrelevancy or its obsolescence than as an echo of earlier challenges in response to changes imposed by and through new technologies. In fact, virtual images can be both analogue and digital. What makes them distinct from other images is the extent to which the phenomena they represent are simulated or constructed, as opposed to actual or specific. It is also the case that the impact of virtual images is quite . . . real, in the sense of present, sustained and powerful.

What Crary writes concerning virtual images recalls Walter Benjamin's remarks in 'The Work of Art in the Age of Mechanical Reproduction' about the extent to which the emergence of photography virtually implied ('foreshadow' is the exact term used) that of sound film (Benjamin, 1969, 219). The relevant point here is that the logic or principle of technological change should properly be understood as additive. Accordingly, the advent of virtual images and virtual events imposes less of an elision or disappearance of subjectivity than a necessary shift or reconfiguration. I take ('see') the impact of this shift or reconfiguration to be best understood within a longer duration and across media. Writing in 1945, André Bazin argued that the advent of photography signalled less the demise of painting than a 'liberation and fufillment' that freed it from the obsession with realism and allowed it to recover its aesthetic autonomy (Bazin, 1967, 16). Chris Marker's 1997 CD-ROM, *Immemory*, is an example of additive logic by drawing on sources ranging from Marcel Proust's *Remembrance of Things Past* to digital media. Raymond Bellour describes Marker's unique attempt to cut across technology from the book to digital images in order to invent 'an ambiguous path, which has as much to do with the logic of the media involved as with his need to write the rules of his own game' (Bellour, 1997, 125). Much like Bazin with reference to painting, photography and film, Marker mobilizes new media in order to consider the extent to which their logic retains as well as departs from that of their antecedents. Because they promote such considerations of principle and logic, ongoing debates surrounding vision and the discursive phenomenon of visuality among art historians, anthropologists and others remain relevant to theory and critical thinking throughout disciplines in the humanities and social sciences.

Notes

I thank my Iowa colleagues Dorothy Johnson and Louis Schwartz for identifying sources that facilitated the writing of this essay.

1. Martin Jay invokes James J. Gibson's relevant distinction between 'the visual world' and 'the visual field', with the latter subject to the rules of perspectival representation (Jay, 1993, 4). My use of the expression 'expanded field' is intended as figurative.

2. Visual anthropology is often equated with the anthropology of visual systems or visible cultural forms. For Marcus Banks and Howard Morphy, the questions raised by such definitions revert to discussions of visual worlds and ways of seeing in Gregory Bateson and Margaret Mead's *Balinese Character: A Photographic Analysis* (1942):

   Theory in visual anthropology revolves around the issues of visible culture, the structuring of the visible world and how visible phenomena are incorporated within cultural process and influence the trajectory of socio-cultural systems. It is in this respect that visual anthropology must include equally the anthropology of art, of material culture, and of ritual form. Visual understanding, what we see and how we interpret it, is an important part of the way we exist as humans in the world and the ultimate justification for the discipline of visual anthropology must lie in this direction: it is the study of the properties of visual systems, of how things are seen and how what is seen is understood.

   (Banks and Morphy, 1997, 21)

The pertinence of this definition lies in its assertion of the visual as a discrete mode of understanding and being in the world, as well as an instrument of representation. Because visual anthropology questions (problematizes) both the ontology and epistemology of visual systems as well as their instrumentality, it warrants inclusion in any and all critical considerations of anthropology. The fact that Banks and Morphy relate their definition to problems raised by Bateson and Mead some sixty years ago indicates the persistence of issues involving the visual within the full history of twentieth-century anthropology.

3. See also Michel Leiris's 1930 essay, 'L'oeil de l'ethnographe' [The Ethnographer's Eye], written while he prepared for his duties as secretary-archivist of the 1931–33 Mission Ethnographique Dakar–Djibouti expedition led by Marcel Griaule. 'L'Oeil de l'ethnographe' appeared in issue no. 7 of *Documents* and is reprinted in Leiris' *Zébrage* (1992). I am unaware of any English translation of this text.

4. Critical studies of human displays are central to reconsiderations of the history of anthropology. Human zoos are the subject of a 2001 colloquium, *Zoos humains: corps exotiques, corps enfermés, corps mesurés* [Human Zoos: Exotic Bodies, Imprisoned bodies, Measured Bodies], sponsored by the Association Connaissance de l'Histoire de l'Afrique Contemporaine (ACHAC). See also Daeninckx (1999).

5. Pierre Leprohon's *L'Exotisme et le cinéma: les 'chasseurs d'images' à la conquête du monde* [Exoticism and Cinema: the 'Image-Hunters' Out to Conquer the World] (1945) remains a rich resource, not the least because it documents the persistence of colonial values in attitudes toward the exotic and the picturesque. For a more recent and critically informed perspective, see Ezra (2000).

6. Margaret Mead's classic 1975 essay, 'Visual Anthropology in a Discipline of Words', defends the potential of the camera to afford a medium of expression for the inarticulate and to record a culture for its members and for the world. But Mead tempers this defence when she adds that 'as anthropologists, we must insist on prosaic, controlled, systematic filming and videotaping, which will provide us with material that can be repeatedly reanalyzed with finer tools and developing theories' (Mead, 1995, 10). This defence reverts to an instrumentalist model in which the visual specificity of formats such as film and video is elided within concerns for systematic analysis. Jay Ruby echoes some of these concerns but does not mention this elision. Kirsten Hastrup asserts that visual and textual representations of ethnography display *different* (her emphasis) kinds of accuracy, related to different anchorages of their authority. She concludes that the iconographic knowledge that films provide is not on equal terms with ethnographic writings. The relevant criterion here is that of context-values for which, Hastrup maintains, the visual record remains 'thin' when compared to the 'thick' description of the written record (Hastrup, 1992, 15).

7. The reference is to Edward Steichen's 1955 book, *The Family of Man*, based on 500 photographs exhibited first at the Museum of Modern Art

in New York and later around the world. See Roland Barthes's critique of this exhibition (Barthes, 1972, 100–2).

8. See also Foster's 'Whatever Happened to Postmodernism?' in the same volume.

9. Rouch's practice of shared anthropology was intended to give the human subjects of his films more active roles in the process of making films. In Africa, Rouch often screened the completed film to those who had appeared in it and was reputed to have given away his camera equipment so that those whom he had filmed in the field could make films of their own. In *Chronicle of a Summer* (1961), Rouch and Edgar Morin imported an aspect of shared anthropology to their native France when they included in the film's final version a discussion among subjects interviewed in the film to whom they had shown early rushes. Manthia Diawara's *Rouch in Reverse* (1995) performed a critical twist on shared anthropology by casting Rouch in the role of native informant in a video about his work and the city of Paris in which he and Morin had shot *Chronicle of a Summer* thirty-five years earlier. On Rouch and shared anthropology, see Eaton, (1979), Feld (1989, 223–45), Russell (1999, 218–29) and Piault (2000, 211–18). Feld edited a 1985 issue of *Studies in Visual Communication* devoted to *Chronicle of a Summer*. Nancy Lutkehaus and Jenny Cool echo Jean-Luc Godard's oft-cited hommage to Rouch when they cite his early influence on 'a new wave' of ethnographic film (Kutkehaus and Cool, 1999, 117).

10. MacDougall's transcultural cinema shares a number of pertinent features with an emphasis on intersubjectivity that motivates Michael Jackson to assign priority to lifeworld (*Lebenswelt*) over worldview (*Weltanschaung*). Jackson describes his critical perspective as existential-phenomenological. His writings draw on a range of references including not only Husserl, Sartre and Merleau-Ponty but also Frantz Fanon and Milan Kundera. This perspective and range are evident in a passage where Jackson describes the origins of what he later conceptualized as an intersubjective turn:

> Fieldwork experience has taught me that notions of shared humanity, human equality, and human rights always come up against the micropolitical exigencies of ethnic, familial, and personal identity, and the dialectic between particular and universal frames of reference often dissolves into a troubled dialogue between the privileged microcosm of anthropologists and the peoples of the Third World whose voices, struggles, and claims define with far more urgency the conditions that define our global future. The reflexive dimension of this work testifies to the ways in which one's understanding of others is never arrived at in a neutral or disengaged manner, but is negotiated and tested in an ambiguous and stressful field of interpersonal relationships in an unfamiliar society.
>
> (Jackson, 1998, 5)

The passage illustrates what Jackson means by the notion of lifeworld (*Lebenswelt*) that I associate with Edmund Husserl's late writings and that engaged the physicality of daily life more than the loftier notion of worldview (*Weltanschaung*) favoured by many philosophers and social scientists. Rereading the passage in early October 2001 gives Jackson's words concerning the voices, struggles and claims of the Third World an unsettling prescience.

11. Laplantine notes the inherent pedagogy of this practice as a *leçon de chose* (literally 'lesson of the thing', perhaps also 'object lesson' in figurative usage) to develop qualities of observation. Traditional rhetoric posits a similar ambition in the exercise of ekphrasis, to which I refer above in conjunction with questions raised by Baxandall in *Patterns of Intention*.

Works cited

Banks, Marcus and Howard Morphy (eds). *Rethinking Visual Anthropology*. New Haven, CT, 1997.

Barthes, Roland. 'The Great Family of Man', in *Mythologies*, trans. Annette Lavers. New York, 1972.

Baxandall, Michael. *Patterns of Intention: On the Historical Explanation of Pictures*. New Haven, CT, 1985.

Bazin, André. 'The Ontology of the Photographic Image', in *What is Cinema?* ed. Hugh Gray. Berkeley, CA, 1967.

Bellour, Raymond. 'The Book, Back and Forth', in *Qu'est-ce qu'une madeleine?* ed. Yves Gaevert. Paris, 1997.

Benjamin, Walter. 'The Work of Art in the Age of Mechanical Reproduction', in *Illuminations*, ed. Hannah Arendt, trans. Harry Zohn. New York, 1969.

Crary, Jonathan. *Techniques of the Observer: On Vision and Modernity in the Nineteenth Century*. Cambridge, MA, 1990.

Daeninckx, Didier. *Cannibale*. Paris, 1999.

Eaton, Mick (ed.). *Anthropology – Reality – Cinema: The Films of Jean Rouch*. London, 1979.

Ezra, Elizabeth. *The Colonial Unconscious: Race and Culture in Interwar France*. Ithaca, NY, 2000.

Fabian, Johannes. *Time and the Other: How Anthropology Makes Its Object*. New York, 1983.

Feld, Steven. 'Themes in the Cinema of Jean Rouch', *Visual Anthropology*, 2 (1989): 223–45.

Foster, Hal (ed.). *Vision and Visuality*. Seattle, WA,1988.

Foster, Hal. 'The Artist as Ethnographer', in *The Return of the Real*. Cambridge, MA, 1996.

Foucault, Michel. *The Birth of the Clinic: An Archeology of Medical Perception*, trans. A. M. Sheridan Smith. New York, 1975.

Foucault, Michel. *Discipline and Punish: The Birth of the Prison*, trans. Alan Sheridan. New York, 1979.

Geertz, Clifford. *The Interpretation of Cultures*. New York, 1973.

Ginsburg, Faye. 'Institutionalizing the Unruly: Charting a Future for Visual Anthropology', *Ethnos*, 63 (1998): 173–201.

Grimshaw, Anna. *The Ethnographer's Eye: Ways of Seeing in Modern Anthropology*. New York, 2001a.

Grimshaw, Anna. 'Teaching Visual Anthropology: Notes from the Field', *Ethnos*, 66 (2001b): 237–258.

Hastrup, Kirsten. 'Anthropological Visions: Some Notes on Visual and Textual Authority', in *Film as Ethnography*, eds Peter Ian Coward and David Turton. New York, 1992.

Henley, Paul. 'Fly in the Soup', *London Review of Books* (21 June, 2001): 35–7.

Jackson, Michael. *Minima Anthropologica: Intersubjectivity and the Anthropological Project*. Chicago, IL, 1998.

Jay, Martin. *Downcast Eyes: The Denigration of Vision in Twentieth-Century French Thought*. Berkeley, CA, 1993.

Kutkehaus, Nancy and Jenny Cool. 'Paradigms Lost and Found: The "Crisis of Representation" and Visual Anthropology', in *Collecting Visible Evidence*, eds Jane M. Gaines and Michael Renov. Minneapolis, MN, 1999.

Laplantine, François. *La Description ethnographique*. Paris, 1996.

Leiris, Michel. *Zébrage*. Paris, 1992.

Leprohon, Pierre. *L'Exotisme et le cinema: les 'chasseurs d'images' à la conquête du monde*. Paris, 1945.

Levinas, Emmanuel. 'Ethics as First Philosophy', in *The Levinas Reader*, ed. Séan Hand. Cambridge, 1989.

MacDougall, David. *Transcultural Cinema*. Princeton, NJ, 1998.

Marker, Chris. *Immemory*. Paris, 1997 (CD-ROM, ISBN 2-85850-947–6).

Mead, Margaret. 'Visual Anthropology in a Discipline of Words', in *Principles of Visual Anthropology*, rev. edn ed. Paul Hockings. New York and Berlin, 1995.

Moxey, Keith. *The Practice of Persuasion: Paradox and Power in Art History*. Ithaca, NY, 2001.

Piault, Marc Henri. *Anthropologie et cinéma: passage à l'image, passage par l'image*. Paris, 2000.

Praz, Mario. *Mnemosyne: The Parallel Between Literature and the Visual Arts*. Princeton, NJ, 1970.

Rodowick, D. N. 'A Genealogy of Time: The Nietzschean Dimension of French Cinema, 1958–98', in *Premises: Invested Spaces in Visual Arts, Architecture, and Design from France: 1958–1998*. New York and Paris, 1998, 66–83.

Rony, Fatimah Tobing. *The Third Eye: Race Cinema, and Ethnographic Spectacle*. Durham, NC, 1996.

Ruby, Jay. *Picturing Culture: Explorations of Films and Anthropology*. Chicago, IL, 2000.

Russell, Catherine. *Experimental Ethnography*. Durham, NC, 1999.

Sturken, Marita and Lisa Cartwright. *Practices of Looking: An Introduction to Visual Culture*. New York, 2001.

Tagg, John. *The Burden of Representation: Essays on Photographies and Histories*. Minneapolis, MN, 1988.

Taylor, Lucien. 'Iconophobia: How Anthropology Lost It at the Movies', *Transition*, 69 (1996): 64–88.

'Visual Culture Questionnaire' (1996) *October*, 77 (1996): 25–700. Cited as VCQ.

He who has laughter on his side has no need of proof.

Theodor W. Adorno

In *The Soul of Wit: Joke Theory from Grimm to Freud*, Carl Hill claims that there is something about *Witz* which makes it 'quintessential to the project of modernity' (Hill, 1994, 9). At issue is the enlightenment and socialization of critical thought as it seeks to become the *sensus communis* or common sense of intellectual life. Hill suggests that the German *Witz* encompasses both 'wit' and 'witticism', 'both the mental faculty and the jokes it produces' (Hill, 1994, 10). By this token, *Witz* is subtly distinct from English *wit*. There is, however, many a slip betwixt wit's playful judgments and the technique of gags. From the learned wit with which Erasmus praised folly to the interpretation of jokes as symptoms of psychological process, the history of wit shadows the history of thought. The loss of wit's extended conceptual field is evident in the shift which sees Freud's work *Der Witz und seine Beziehung zum Unbewussten* metamorphosed from A. A. Brill's first English translation as *Wit and its Relation to the Unconscious* (1916) into James Strachey's *Jokes and their Relation to the Unconscious* (1960). There is more than a whiff of family resemblance among the key terms, however, not least where questions of translation sift the perception of wit through linguistic filters.

Hill suggests that '*Witz* first became an issue for German intellectuals after 1671, when Dominique Bouhours in his *Entretien d'Ariste et d'Eugene* informed them that they didn't have any. Of course, the phrase he used was *bel esprit* (beautiful spirit) and not *Witz*, but we shall see how the one later evolved into the other' (Hill, 1994, 11). The resulting feud between French and German conceptions of wit, and indeed of culture as such, continues to resonate in the different relations adopted by English-speaking thought to French and German philosophy. For all Nietzsche's cracks at the expense of German gravity, the call for free spirits to enjoy the lightness of more joyful sciences has fallen on deaf ears. The forces of seriousness have reduced wit's human intelligence to the status of the halfwit, a dealer in merely ingenious witticisms trading on ingenuity rather than truth. There is, as Nietzsche suggests, something un-Greek about *esprit*. In *The Gay Science*, Nietzsche points to a lack of sociability in the Greeks to explain the lack of spirit even in their most spirited, a lack of wit even in their wittiest. He claims that 'In good society one must never wish to be solely and entirely right, which is what all pure logic aims at; hence the small dose of unreason in all French *esprit*' (Nietzsche, 1974, 136). Strangely, the rhetoric of wit seems to have been more knowingly developed by Roman intellectuals than by Greeks. In *Wit and the Writing of History: The Rhetoric of Historiography in Imperial Rome*, Paul Plass suggests how the wit of Tacitus: 'provides what amounts to a small glossary of false language and values, defined with epigrammatic point on the pattern of anti-thesis' (Plass, 1988, 46). C. S. Lewis connects the history of *wit* to the translation of *ingenium*, going so far as to suggest that 'If a man had time to study the history of one word only, *wit* would perhaps be the best word he could choose' (C. S. Lewis, 1967, 86). The perspectives suggested by linking the fortunes of wit with the history of *ingenium*, are confirmed by the entry on 'Ingenium' in *Historisches Wörterbuch der Philosophie* (Ritter). Between the Greeks and our latter-day ironists of critical theory, the fate of wit serves to suggest how far reason has become social and how far spirits of the good society are reduced to jokesmiths and wisecracks.

If colloquial wit continues to accuse Germans of lacking a sense of humour, there is also something doggedly humourless about Anglo-Saxon resistance to the different rhetorics of French and German thought. Notable exceptions have been made for the wit with which Wittgenstein's work exists in both German and English, almost to the extent that Wittgenstein's characteristic wit seems more comfortable in its English translations. The soul of Freud, not least in the authority of the English language of the Standard Edition, continues to be fought over in a curious world of parallel translation. Samuel Beckett is perhaps the most notable modern writer to have explored the limits of wit through self-translation of his writing into English and French, to say nothing of his involvement in German translations of his work. Such exceptions nevertheless point to a rule which states that appreciation for philosophical wit gets lost in translation, not least where there is a strong predisposition to assume that, for example, German philosophy is humourless while French thought is somehow more classical, crisper and wittier. Consider the adaptation of the French phrase *l'esprit d'escalier* into Denise Riley's 'Stair Spirit' (Riley, 1993). It may only be the gossip of the playground or the academic corridor but who has not been tempted to suggest that the project of fundamental phenomenology is more persuasive in the elegantly elusive French of Merleau-Ponty than in the more cumbersome German of Husserl? Who has not heard someone suggest that the earnest communicative rationality of a Habermas lacks the more readable and playful *esprit* or philosophical wit of a Derrida? Against such gossip, we should perhaps pose Carl Hill's claim to see 'a clear connection between *Witz* and Habermas's notion of the bourgeois public sphere'. Hill's account of *Witz* presents a paradoxical sense of the difference it makes when wit is not seen as a laughing matter, but understood rather as the instrument of democratic modernization: '*Witz*, the enemy of all scholastic pedantry, stoutly refuses to collapse into an esoteric discourse designed only for the ears of the initiated, but instead seeks a wider public' (Hill, 1994, 18–19). One man's *esprit* is another man's exclusive clique. Habermas could be read as a representation of the spirit of postwar German reconstruction, suspicious of the playful and irresponsible rhetoric of French Nietzscheanism. The necessity of Derridean play nevertheless seeks to show how the play of difference conditions the possibility of philosophy's rhetorics of rigour and seriousness. Against which, in turn, there is the humourless challenge of Heidegger's apparently beguiling obscurity and the rhetoric Adorno rather violently dismissed as the 'jargon' of authenticity (Adorno, 1973). If much of Derrida's work cannot be understood outwith an understanding of Heidegger, there is nevertheless a sense that the resistance to such recognitions has much to do with the perceived *esprit* and wit of French thought against the perceived weight, pathos and piety of Heidegger. But what if Heidegger were the real joker, the truer wit?

Perhaps the most notable recent instance of wit's persuasive power would be the recognition that Slavoj Žižek's less than scientific rhetoric is at least provocatively entertaining. Wit can affront scholarly exactitude by refusing the literal-minded seriousness and rational protocols of academic argument. Wit can also reflect the preference of consumers for more easily digested matter than the linguistic precision and mathesis of scientific rigour. The fate of critical theory within the academy is bound up with the fortunes of what is supposed difficult or accessible within the philosophical rhetoric of critical theory's most popular exponents. The association of the witty digest with the perils of the market has a historical dynamic. As Hill observes, '*Witz* was deeply involved in the new economic order of the literary marketplace, reflecting the dialectic of popularization both in its democratic sympathies and its uses in playing on popular prejudices in the service of a repressive political order' (Hill, 1994, 62). What if Žižek does not so much show how Hitchcock can be used to explain Lacan, or that Lacan can be used to illuminate Hitchcock, but that Žižek is the Tony Blair of critical theory: master of the reductive soundbite, but a servant of the powers that be? Much seems to rest on the reductive paraphrases which become the currency and stock in trade of critical theory and through which students are introduced to higher learning. Need it be said that the witty introduction obscures as much as it illuminates? Wit, accordingly, is both the medium of critical theory's translation, and a fateful temptation to favour style over the content and the labour of the concept. There are nevertheless intimations of freedom in the idea that wit should not be laboured, should instead speak of free and interested cognitive pleasures, providing associative and speculative plays of language with which to shine lights on the dark forces of naturalism and literalism.

Consider the difference it would make if the understanding of 'wit' through philosophical translation saw wit itself as the medium for the recognition of philosophical differences. What if, for example, Hegel's *Phänomenologie des Geistes*, translated into French by Jean Hyppolite as *La Phénoménologie de l'esprit*, were more appropriately translated into English as the *Phenomenology of Wit*? Such a translation might alter the tone of the whole work and its reception, reworking the affinity between *esprit* and spirit, such that the evolution of *bel esprit* into wit could somehow pass through the German conception of *Geist*. Hegel's own comments suggest scorn for the aestheticians of wit and irony, part of the marked resistance in Hegel's thought to the qualities of negative capability on which wit thrives. There is nevertheless a quality of wit in the speculative agency of Hegel's thought. Hegel would doubtless have recoiled from Brecht's flippant quips to the effect that dialectical thought requires a sense of humour, but perhaps the inability to think through or read the rhetoric of Hegel's speculative sentences reflects a lack of wit's characteristic combination of associative imagination and judgment. If Hegel's systematic and scientific claims are suspended in the development of a phenomenological understanding of Hegel's work, might not Hegel be read as the wittiest idealist of them all?

Gillian Rose argued for a reading of Hegel's work as the comedy of absolute spirit, offering an understanding of the comedy of misrecognition that would position Hegel as the politician of wit's struggle for recognition (Rose, 1996). Hegel nevertheless seems to have shared Johnson's distaste for the yoking together of the heterogeneous associated with witty conceits: 'metaphor may arise from the wit of a subjective caprice which, to escape from the commonplace, surrenders to a piquant impulse, not satisfied until it has succeeded in finding related traits in the apparently most heterogeneous material and therefore, to our astonishment, combining things that are poles apart from one another' (Hegel, 1988, I: 407). Assuming that the labour of the concept can overcome the caprice of metaphor, is this not a quality of thought necessary to grasp the truth of Hegel's claim that what is rational is actual and that what is actual is rational? If dialectics is the recognition of the heteronomy of the non-identical, wit becomes the post-Hegelian art of non-identical heterogeneity. Initial scepticism might then be forced to recognize that the struggle for recognition and knowingness involved in the philosophical evolution of 'wit' is closer in spirit to some of the key themes of Hegel's conception of absolute knowledge, a conception otherwise so awkwardly translated into 'science'. The relation between 'science' and the Latin root *scientia* points to the way conflicts in the translation of wit are also about the appropriation of the classical vocabularies of philosophy. Is there a necessary priority of one or other modern vernacular language to be or become the language of modern philosophy? It might be argued, speculatively, that the conflicts of wit are born in the Babel of linguistic confusion released by the waning of Latin as the lingua franca of philosophical thought. The English word 'wit' can be traced to the Old English word 'witan' to know, cognate with the German verb 'wissen'. While 'wissen' has become central to *Wissenschaft* – the German for knowledge and/or science – comparable uses of 'wit' as the verb 'to know' or as the noun for the mind and/or understanding have become obsolete or archaic. What, then, if Nietzsche's *Die fröliche Wisssenschaft*, subtitled 'la gaya scienza', should be translated, not as *The Gay Science*, a translation with its own intriguing fate, but simply as *The Joy of Wit*? What if the spirit of joy, science, knowledge and the 'gai saber' might still cohere in a modern conception of wit?

Few of the defining gestures cast over wit's history have remained fashionable for long. This elusive quality points to the social differential at the heart of wit's progress. For some, the defining quality of wit is its sense of occasion.

Aphorisms apt for the wedding lose their savour when unleashed on the funeral party. For others, the characteristic virtue of wit unbinds language from the shackles of context, showing the way a good aphorism or joke transcends its occasion, gesturing towards utopian cognitions of the good life. The joke told once too often, however, crumbles to reveal a melancholy automatism beneath the surface of smart repartee. Wit's fragile capacity to transcend its social conditions seems comparable to the fragility of literature's claims for lasting value. If poetry is news that stays news, perhaps true wit is a joke that remains amusing, precisely because it knows how little it knows. The persistence of wit, the endurance of its esprit de corps, resists mummification, perhaps because wit's substance is so evidently human and historical. While wit's critical fortunes can serve as a historical index of how far intellection has become truly human, the gregariously diffuse spirit of wit lacks an essence or clear and distinct properties. Thus the critical task involved in characterizing the spirit of wit is to outline some of wit's contradictory energies and to suggest wit's lively resistance to specification.

Wit's conditions of possibility range from the simplest word games and conceptions of taste or good humour, through to ideas about intellectual invention and the intimation of our warmest social ideals. At different historical stages wit has been a central term within literary argument, analogous with ideas about language as such and comparable with arguments around conceptions of style, irony and beauty. William Empson's discussion of the meaning of wit in Alexander Pope's *Essay on Criticism* provides an object lesson in wit's complexity as a word and phenomenon (Empson). Empson was part of a modernist recuperation of wit's interest against romanticism's perceived devaluation of wit. The modernist reading of metaphysical wit, for example, made wit a key term in modern literary criticism and a defining ambition of modernist literature. Within the overall carapace of modernist poetry lurks the more particular recuperation of metaphysical wit associated with Donne, memorialized in Thomas Carew's elegy as the universal monarch of wit (Grierson, 1921, 178). The clarion call sounded by Herbert Grierson's 1921 anthology of metaphysical poetry juxtaposes the work of Donne with poems such as Abraham Cowley's seminal ode 'Of Wit' to suggest a new poetic programme and canon. Such claims resonate through T. S. Eliot's 1921 review and Eliot's brief sketch of the dissociation of sensibility in the seventeenth century (Eliot, 1975). Eliot helps to generate recognition within modernist writing and literary criticism of what might have been lost in the way wit took on a pejorative flavour associated with quick smartness rather than with the lively, knowing powers of poetry. The historical value of Eliot's sketch has long been contested, but much of the energy of New Criticism went into salvaging the intellectual qualities of wit that had been lost between Donne and the strictures against metaphysical wit suggested by Dryden and Johnson. The underlying revision of canons and tastes brought the wit and argumentative qualities of poetic concision into critical focus. If philosophical thought has long known the perils of argument by analogy, literary criticism has often sought to reinstate the value of the analogical and metaphorical mindset, even if only to draw attention to the ideology of such mindsets within particular literary contexts. A critical tension emerges between the wit of imaginative association or fancy, and the wit of discrimination and judgment. As if defining the problem of seriousness within criticism, the claims of the latter come to define true wit over the claims of what are henceforth seen as merely amusing or ingenious forms of cleverness. If ingenuity and judgment are held together in the conception of *esprit* evident in the work of Descartes and Pascal,

the subsequent fortunes of English wit have seen the separation of such qualities.

Within the broader range of modernism, the rhetoric of wit can be traced across the revaluation of the philosophical sentence in writers as different as Nietzsche and Wittgenstein, as well as through the reorientation of literary argument evident in texts such as Joyce's *Ulysses* or Kafka's *The Trial*. As if prefiguring positivist and empirical resistances to critical theory's modernist rhetorics, the wit of many modernist literary texts has been resisted by literary scholarship. Rather than seeing wit as the mode through which social conflicts are mediated and negotiated within the rhetorics of modernism, the texts of modernist wit have more often been rendered obscure, difficult or elitist, hedged around with cognitive references. The academic appropriation of modernist rhetorics seems to prefer such values over the awkward kinds of witty association, inter-textual allusion and collective fun which might be had with texts such as *Finnegans Wake*. More recent literary texts have perhaps retreated from the full ambition of modernist wit to the looser pleasures of irony, camp and pastiche. A gulf has emerged, moreover, between frivolous populism and avant-garde seriousness, as though the true seriousness of modernist wit were considered too knowing or too inaccessible. The fragility of wit's modernist poetics of occasion is perhaps best illustrated by the resistance of Frank O'Hara's poetry to the kind of laboured elaboration evident in the critical reception of John Ashbery's poetry.

Within modern critical argument, however, there are ongoing reverberations regarding the role of wit, not least in the way the spirit of intellectual play haunts academic seriousness. Conflicts run deep between arguments trading on wit and arguments resisting any association with the social implications of wit's struggle for recognition. Wit somehow becomes a socialized way of knowing that you are known and a way of developing recognitions that can range from particulars to more general claims about social action. Social content lurks in the forms of wit, and it is wit's historical destiny to shape the social recognition of those contents that can be shared and enjoyed. The awkward cognitive status of wit's struggle for recognition has significance for critical thought more generally, not least because wit is one of the key moods through which critical thought seeks recognition for itself. Some of the most important modern thinkers are important not because their ideas are rigorous or true but because their work is presented with such wit as to be irresistible. Recognition that wit's charisma and charm can be tyrannical extends a suspicion of the cultural physiognomy of wit from the television politician to the academic professional. Wit has become one of the unacknowledged legislators of critical reputation.

According to Egon Larsen's seductively titled book *Wit as a Weapon: The Political Joke in History*, 'jokes assume the role of the *vox populi* in countries and periods lacking free elections' (Larsen, 1980, 2). It is less clear, however, what happens when jokes are elected or when elections are more expensive than free. From George Bush senior to George W. Bush junior, or from Vaclav Havel imprisoned dissident to Vaclav Havel elected president, the speed with which history plays its little jests seems dizzy: a revolving door rather than a revolutionary process. Faced with the return of Napoleon, the nephew in place of the uncle, Karl Marx quipped in *The Eighteenth Brumaire of Louis Bonaparte* that 'Hegel remarks somewhere that all the great events and characters of world history occur, so to speak, twice. He forgot to add: the first time as tragedy, the second as farce.' (Marx, 1973, 146) It may have been Marx's own ruse to ascribe this perception of history's drama to Hegel. Even if Hegel never made such a remark, there is a

Hegelian logic at work in Marx's sense of humour. Indeed, socialism itself might be described as the attempt to tell new jokes about the history of class struggle, and to actualize the spirit of such jokes in new social relations.

The ruses of history are cunning indeed, but the thought that history itself has a sense of humour delimits a speculative agency capable of understanding the wit of history as the history of wit. Among the weapons of the dialectician, chiasmus is perhaps the lowest form of wit. It may not be possible to recognize that the history of wit *is* the wit of history, but to think such speculative identities may be no less remarkable than to think that the cost of a bottle of champagne is the equivalent of a week's wages in China. Capitalism may not yet have had the last laugh, but the shaggy dog stories told against the politicization of the economy suggest that it is laughing louder and longer. Some jokes lose their savour. Larsen retells a joke from actually disappearing socialism: some leading Soviet-style economists from the old East Germany were invited to Africa to modernize the Sahara area. Nothing changed in the first year, nothing in the second. In the third year the Sahara ran out of sand. Slavoj Žižek cites Edward Moser's *The Politically Correct Guide to the Bible*, as the source of such quips as 'Thou shalt remember the Sabbath day, *so thou can get all thy shopping done at that time*' and 'Thou shalt not take the name of God in vain, *but with gusto, particularly if you are a gansta rap artist*' (Žižek, 2000, 180). Elsewhere, Žižek trumps such jibes by speculating that modern capitalism realizes Moses's ten commandments in negative forms: 'As the experience of our post-political liberal-permissive society amply demonstrates, human Rights are ultimately, at their core, simply *Rights to violate the Ten Commandments*. "The right to privacy" – the right to *adultery*, in secrecy, where no one sees me or has the right to probe into my life. "The right to pursue happiness and to possess private property" – the right to *steal* (to exploit others)' (Žižek, 2000, 110). The pleasure of such provocations is the invitation to pursue Hegelian speculations relating religion to the spirit of capitalism. And yet the truth of such witticisms is held within a suspended disbelief that refuses the labour of historical inquiry or moral judgment, preferring instead an ironic mode of intellectual therapy. Žižek suspends academic seriousness within a form of academic performance that is knowingly attuned to the weariness of the academic consumer. As Terry Eagleton observes of Empson, 'if the intellectual's own discourse is inauthentic, it is also because his or her ideological interests are, on the whole, at one with the very society his or her ironic self-distancing seeks to shut out. Only by the *form* of the intellectual's statements can such interests be momentarily transcended; "irony" is the device whereby the modern bourgeois critic can at once collude with and privately disown the ideological imperatives of the modern state' (Eagleton, 1988, 628). Such criticisms can be returned to the sender. The critic of ironic wit can hardly escape the performative contradiction of his or her own position within the political economy of wit's linguistic forms.

Denise Riley has recently reopened such questions by defending irony as a political strategy, a linguistic and rhetorical strategy capable of developing self-reflexive interventions. Her descriptions of irony parallel some of wit's social physiognomy: 'Irony as self-scrutiny is above all conscious of its own provisionality; this is what it stages, and especially in the conspicuous provisionality of the categories of social being' (Riley, 2000, 165). Wit's provisionality also points to the historical potential for change evident within the forms of social recognition: 'that irony is alert to history, that to be able to deploy a category ironically frees you to recognize its historical formation and consequently its potential to alter and disintegrate. To recognize that

irony has in this sense an inclination towards the good is a part of acknowledging the historical vulnerability of any rhetorical language. This recognition can aid its critical reworking' (Riley, 2000, 166). The politics of irony are paralleled by the problems of knowingness and recognition evident in the perils of wit's self-criticism. The historical ruins of wit extend across different political strategies in relation to different property relations and yet reveal what become the recognizable forms and formalisms of rhetorical criticism. Consider the sentence, 'It is a truth universally acknowledged, that a single man in possession of a good fortune, must be in want of a wife.' Harvey Gross describes how Jane Austen's grammatical arrangement fashions 'a prosody of wit' (Gross, 1964, 13). As is universally acknowledged, the content to be recognized, including the formal elegance of the sentence, is not universal, but social and historical. The title of Jerry Palmer's book *Taking Humour Seriously*, labours the point that the levity of wit is still felt by the decorum of the everyday academic: 'even if we have largely abandoned the rules of neo-classical decorum in the arts (and some in everyday life), there is still a tendency to make a clear distinction between what is funny and what is serious' (Palmer, 1994, 131).

Wit's moment of recognition is, then, a moveable feast whose defining tensions are the locus for the struggle between different conceptions of cognition and recognition, and across different rhetorics of speech and writing. The grammar of argument can seem like a series of puns, difference against indifference, in which distinctions become differends only if accompanied by a sufficiently witty suspension of disbelief. Analogous with Lyotard's conception of the differend, the exchange of phrases offered by wit remains unstable, illegimate and philosophically indeterminate (Lyotard). Wit's lively knowingness would nevertheless figure itself as the recollection and revivification of dead arguments. As well as offering anamnesis of arguments so that they can be shared again in language, wit also figures itself as the bright spark of speculative association, the intellectual vitality of comparative insight. This creativity, the creativity of metaphors and jokes, comes close to the originality of creation itself, a human image of the art of God. A. J. Smith construes the metaphysical wit of John Donne's poetry in such terms: 'Poetic invention itself amounts to a rediscovery of the hidden articulation of the creation, the recovery by human wit of the infinitely subtle interconnections of all the forms of being' (Smith, 1991, 11). For every bright spark that reveals God's immanence in creation, however, another will suggest that the joke is on us. Nietzsche conceded an envy of Stendhal for beating him to it with the atheistical joke: 'God's only excuse is that he does not exist' (Nietzsche, 1974, 244). This joke takes a further twist in Beckett's play *Endgame*, when Hamm remarks on the lack of response to their prayers to God: 'The bastard! He doesn't exist!' (Beckett, 1986, 119). The fatherless originality of God also points to the kind of low blow favoured by colloquial wit. Rather than sharing in God's little jokes, the punk joker will aver that god is merely a dog spelt backwards. Many of the strangest forms of contemporary wit are those that seek witty redemptions of the witless moralism of religious thought. J. William Whedbee's book *The Bible and the Comic Vision* (Whedbee, 1998) can perhaps be read in the light of Ted Cohen's unlikely claim that: 'the Hebrew Bible presents one conception of decency in which the fully human, fully acceptable response to the mystification of the world is a laughing acceptance, a kind of spiritual embrace' (Cohen, 1999, 51). Once upon a time the realists and the nominalists fought it out to provide crushing blows against Platonists convinced that God was the great wit of the universe. More recently, conversational pragmatists wrestle with language-game sceptics to show the wrong-headedness of speech-act utopians and social idealists. Is it wittier to show the difference between grammatical coercion and fuzzy logic or to show that language is just a game? The edifiers propose a witty party while the ethical policeman call on us to abandon the slippery slopes of wit's transcendence. While wit figures in the tool box of those seeking therapy from the labour of the concept, wit also figures in the identity parade of metaphysics's metaphorical transgressions.

Even if the philosophical legitimacy of wit remains questionable, the cultivation of wit has a philosophical history, not least as a way of lending social grace to intellectual virtue. Whether true wit combines judgment with fancy or releases the play of the imagination, the key historical tensions appear to be those between pure wit and applied wit, or between abstract intellectual cognition and concrete social recognition. The acquisition of wit can appear, as it does in the work of Marcel Proust, as a necessary tool for social climbers and defensive cliques. Wit might then be understood as the negotiation between emergent bourgeois intellectuals and aristocratic nostalgia for a world in which only the leisured few had the taste for wit's refinement. The taint of aristocratic hauteur seems to cling to those, such as Oscar Wilde or Slavoj Žižek, who appear to aspire to the status of universal wits. Alternatively, the challenge posed by wit can be understood as the recognition both of the equality of the natural wit we are born with and of the dignity of mental labour. The modern division of labour throws up embarrassing contradictions for the intellectual seeking to legitimate their efforts over manual labour. The suspicion of wit as a slippery virtue more modern than courage or valour is evident in the Homeric contrast between Achilles and the wily cleverness of Odysseus. Once freed from the aristocratic pretensions of martial nobility, superior wit becomes the mark of the political leader's strategic intelligence. There is nevertheless an awkward similarity between the wit of the politician and the carping voice of seditious sarcasm. The power of wit becomes politically ambiguous when only wealth and power divides Odysseus's comic skills of observation from those of Thersites. Every Timon deserves their Apemantus, but the philosophical wit has to choose between the asceticism of the professional cynic or the enslavement of their wits to the powers that be. Just as Virginia Woolf needed a room and an income of her own, the true classical wit needs patronage or a private income. One of the triumphs of capitalism is to have released wit from the classical forms of bondage so that wit can be sold. Writing around 1604, George Chapman puts an eloquent account of the emerging market into the mouth of Monsieur D'Olive: 'Good sooth: but indeed to say truth, time was when the sons of the muses had the privilege to live only by their wits; but times are altered, monopolies are now called in, and wit's become a free trade for all sorts to live by . . .' (Chapman, 1875, 117). Market society brings social mobility to those who know how to live by their wits: court jesters, fawning bards and guttersnipes can now become entrepreneurial intellectuals.

In modern society, then, wit cuts across birthrights and the artificial refinements made possible by education or art. In the red corner can be found the prodigiously gifted natural savage, while in the blue corner can be found the hard-working intellectual accumulating the material conditions of wit like there's no tomorrow. Whereas exception might be made for musical prodigies, such as Mozart, there remains something socially suspicious if not monstrous about naturally gifted children. Perhaps a natural aptitude for art can be a source of shared wonder whereas a natural aptitude for long division merely depresses those who have to learn the hard way. Social respect seems to accrue to those skills that involve training natural aptitudes in tasteful combinations of inspiration and perspiration. Although wit needs to be shared and recognized socially, the celerity of imagining and the quickness of mind associated with wit nevertheless seems like mental faculties that cannot be laboured or worked on. The artifice of effortlessness becomes wit's defence against the perception that it is acquired through nerdy practice, from swot to pedant, or arises from the social injustice of God's gifts.

Understood as a form of cultural capital, it becomes as difficult to know the right kinds of wit to acquire as it is to tell the difference between safe investments and south sea bubbles. According to Hobbes, the causes of the difference of wits are in the passions: 'The Passions that most of all cause the differences of Wit, are principally, the more or lesse Desire of Power, of Riches, of Knowledge, and of Honour. All of which may be reduced to the first, that is Desire of Power. For Riches, Knowledge and Honour are but severall sorts of Power' (Hobbes, 1968, 139/35). If this sounds suspiciously like the seventeenth-century voice of Nietzsche or Foucault, the interest is in the political challenge to the constitutive role that might be claimed for the body or for education in the acquisition of wit. The subtlety of the formulation is the way it blurs the difference between natural and acquired wit. Wit, according to Hobbes, is not some temper of the brain or an organ of sense. The naturalist attitude that would claim wit as a birthright or as an expression of some higher intellectual quotient is collapsed into the social recognition of wit as an expression of the will to power. What becomes substantive, given the recognition that wit is about the use and abuse of social power, is the social regulation of those who arrogate wit's power. The distinction between natural wit and artificial intelligence resonates in the suspicion of computer-generated humour: 'Perhaps one day a software house will create a computer program that invents original jokes; but the computer will not be a fully human entity until it enjoys them (if then)' (Palmer, 1994, 1). Wit may be nature dressed to advantage, but the mothers of invention can also produce hideous fashion victims, to say nothing of the monsters of genetic comedy, such as the mouse sporting a human ear on its back.

The tendency of Hobbes's rhetoric is directed against metaphysical wit, arguing for the power of intellectual judgment and discretion over more fanciful or poetic conflations of meaning. Against the absurdity of scholastic ingenuity and poetic extravagance, Hobbes prefers the light of perspicuous words purged of ambiguity. The taint of wit nevertheless blossoms just where opposition to wit is most forcefully asserted: 'The Light of human minds is Perspicuous Words, but by exact definitions first snuffed, and purged from ambiguity; *Reason* is the *pace*; Encrease of *Science*, the *way*; and the Benefit of man-kind, the *end*. And on the contrary, Metaphors, and senslesse and ambiguous words, are like *ignes fatui*; and reasoning upon them, is wandering amongst inumerable absurdities; and their end, contention, and sedition, or contempt.' (Hobbes, 1968, 116/117). The simile used to compare idealist delusions with the will-o'-the-wisp or some marshy gas cannot help but wander into its own contentious metaphorical journeys. The reader needs all their wits about them to follow the chains of association and reason that might conjoin contention, sedition and contempt. Is the violence of sedition slipped between contention and contempt so as to mask the witty highlight of this deeply ambiguous call to arms? Only the wittiest thinker can hope to regulate those seditious wits who would plunge argument into punning duels and senseless war. At the same time, the judicious wit arguing for the legitimacy of the state against the perils of civil war also seeks to wrest power from the blunter instruments of social control. Duly purged of fanciful excess, wit becomes one of the forces of peaceful coexistence. Over and above the conflict of differences, wit might even offer utopian intimations of the realm of freedom and the good life.

To recognize wit in all its glory is to see it standing amid all that is most human and most sociable. What could be more pleasant, more profoundly political, than hours of Socratic banter on the way to the forum to debate the public good? Like some utopian intimation of the ideal speech-act world of democracy, wit promises an engaging and engaged play of free intelligence. The hope is that argument might be embodied as the concrete spirit of mutual recognition. Wit's critical tolerance might then bespeak a fully socialized community, a society of civilization and understanding. Wit begets freedom, and freedom begets wit, or so the aphorism goes. As Shaftesbury puts it in *Sensus communis – an essay on the freedom of wit and humour*, 'All politeness is owing to liberty. We polish one another and rub off our corners and rough sides by a sort of amicable collision. To restrain this is inevitably to bring a rust upon men's understandings' (Shaftesbury, 1709, 31). The bright lights of enlightenment are all for the polish and politesse of wit, as though our best wishes might animate the struggle between polite differences and politics. One step back from this edifying conversational spectacle, however, and wit stands accused of being a gossipy fraudulence, a trivial ornament on scientific seriousness or a footling bourgeois grace beloved of the chattering classes. The darker but no less witty forces of scepticism and nihilism suggest that wit is best turned against the poisoned illusions of language.

In *Twilight of the Idols*, Nietzsche bangs on about philosophizing with a hammer, tapping away as with a tuning fork to sound out hollow vessels: 'I fear we are not getting rid of God because we still believe in grammar . . .' (Nietzsche, 1968, 38). But who has the resources to survive his jokes? Some of the aphoristic irreverence of Nietzsche's cheerful prose style is lost in Heideggerian translation, but perhaps we cannot read Heidegger until we can see his funny side? Despite protestations to the contrary, it is hard not to hear a pejorative note and distrust of wit in Heidegger's attempt to distinguish discourse (*die Rede*) from idle talk or chatter (*die Gerede*): 'when Dasein maintains itself in idle talk, it is – as Being-in-the-world – cut off from its primary and primordially genuine relationships-of-Being towards the world' (Heidegger, 1962, ¶35). Heidegger's sublime poetics of language can be read as ways of shaking grammar and etymology to their roots, and yet the pathos of inquiry risks becoming bathetic, too serious and insufficiently sociable in its relation to language. In part the difficulty is knowing how far the conceptual roots of philosophical language amount to more than puns made possible by the historical accidents of Greek and German, and of Indo-European language more generally. The translation of Heidegger's philosophical German into Derridean French somehow reverses the struggle between Teutonic gravity and French esprit. The arch proponents of deconstructive wit seem to want their irony to be both rigorously particular and yet always already invulnerable. Being unguardedly occasional and playful becomes a way of being all the more philosophically guarded. A further mark of the problem is the earnestness with which Derrida's English translators spell out the play of meanings in Derrida's French sentences. The footnote or explanation becomes a fussy *avertissement*, a warning that speaks of *a-version,* a diverting that would avert the *advertisement* of advertising, etc. ad nauseam, and thus an advertisement of linguistic competence that inadvertently reveals an eagerness to make wit too explicit, an eagerness that empties wit of its potential energy. The problem as to whether the energy of wit is best left implicit or calls for translation, exegesis and research is also a problem for any academic enquiry into wit. Paul Lewis, for example, argues for humour criticism and humour research, but nevertheless points out that: 'The reluctance to take humour seriously is one of many problems that have troubled humor researchers' (Lewis, 1989, 1). Does this sentence *mean* to advertise its playful abyss or is this an inadvertent collapse of scholarly register?

Even amid the deserts of pure reason, Kant is capable of cracking jokes. The conventional academic injunction to eschew colourful, ironic or playful language is nevertheless motivated by the difficulty of recognizing the limits of literalism amid academic prose. Read against the standards of academic clarity, the mannered rigour of the deconstructed sentence is at once too pious and too playful, serious to the point of irrelevance. But the dry and austere voices of academic criticism can appear witless or joyless, somehow frozen amid wastes of abstraction. Market forces and a suspicious populism respond with calls for more sociable 'introductions', thawing out critical concepts to serve up chattier digests. For all the care with which philosophical discourse and critical theory have argued against reductive paraphrase, many of the most engaging critical theorists play fast and loose with the proprieties of academic prose style. The critical brio of Marx and Nietzsche seeks to polemicize against the institutions of academic philosophy, jousting with ideology, scholasticism and philological indigestion. Their rhetoric of political quips, perspectival insights and aphoristic interventions finds curious echoes that cut across the conventional ways of reading the traditions of critical theory. How seriously are we to take claims such as Adorno's aphorism that

'In psycho-analysis nothing is true except the exaggerations' (Adorno, 1974, 49)? Writers with wits as different as Freud and Adorno resonate to very different effect in the different styles of Judith Butler and Slavoj Žižek. However different, the styles and rhetorics of modern critical theorists can be characterized by the way they use wit to traverse the tensions between professional specialization, commercial accessibility and the communicative rationality of public argument. Wit becomes one of the ways in which individuals can brand and market the distinctive creativity of their work, while also being the medium capable of traversing the divisions between scientific reason, genealogical interpretation and common sense.

The highly specified conditions of divided intellectual labours are also subject to a logic of globalization in which the struggle for intellectual hegemony or public prominence necessitates different styles of presentation and wit. The performative contradictions stored up in Adorno's aphoristic provocations can perhaps be read as a strategy of resistance to publicity. Just as there is a price to be paid for the dogmatic transparency of vulgar Marxism, so the popularization and institutionalization of psychoanalysis poses new problems for its most influential exponents. Lacan's use of the seminar to develop an authoritatively anti-authoritarian resistance to intellectual transference undermines the authority of his own spoken discourse and writing. And yet the resulting opacity mystifies even Lacan's most articulate exponents, with the notable exception of Slavoj Žižek. Žižek's almost absolute confidence in his reinterpretation of Lacan points to the need to project a dogmatic schematism through which to interpret works that attempt to deconstruct their own authority. Žižek's exposition of Lacanian discourse also exemplifies the way contemporary critical wit is characterized by the use of illustrative analogies to bridge the gulf between critical jargon and so-called popular culture. Just as the clergy once domesticated theological doctrine through more or less witty homilies, so the latter-day critical theorist needs to suggest how the speculative proposition can be illustrated by the latest Hollywood product. But if philosophy, for Hegel, transcends the picture-thinking representations of religion and art, Žižek's wit comes closer to claiming that Hollywood can transcend the technical difficulties of critical thought. There is something tiresome and oppressive about the excesses of wit and its claims for the autonomy of its sparks of analogy and comparison. The prison-house of wit is a play in which all are called on to perform the role of Oscar Wilde. Sensitivity to context calls for the fiction that language is more than a game, and true wit knows the price of the freedom it claims.

The social theatre of wit is, then, animated by diverse struggles for recognition. The ancient violence of metaphor in Hill's account is revealing: 'The *bon mot* can be a rhetorical dagger thrust that finishes off one's conversational adversary, securing victory for one's own ideas with an attendant advance in social prestige and status. The public sphere becomes an arena for the gladiators of *esprit*' (Hill, 1994, 33). Wit's claims to cognitive knowledge may unleash the democratization and politicization of philosophical rhetoric, but wit's love of the cut and thrust of duelling suggests the limits of wit's claims to be more than a weapon. Wit is all too human, too fallible and too anthropormorphic to claim the dignity of primary cognition. Rather than offering foundational authority, wit's associative capacities and its powers of adaptation and translation form themselves through social recognitions, above all the recognitions disclosed by language-games. As Abraham Cowley puts it, 'In a true piece of *Wit* all things must be, / Yet all things there *agree*' (Grierson, 1921, 189). If the sublime puns of linguistic ingenuity become indistinguishable from the tricks of the crossword puzzle, the knowingness of wit needs to operate more at those levels of exchange and association which avoid the anti-social extremes of disagreement. Accordingly, the quality of wit resists generalization, working more as the spirit of dialogue than as a dialectical power or a logic of contradiction. Pushed to extremes, wit amounts to nothing, the nothing out of which comes nothing but paradoxes or the tragic absence of affable abrasions and amicable collisions. The occasional and particular moments of wit are the historically encoded remarks and remaking of perceptions whose conditions of possibility are immanent within existing social relations. In a society suspicious of anything other than the minimal force of the unstable differend or the power of isolated language-games, wit becomes the medium of philosophical indifference asserted against the claims of master-narratives and of first philosophy. But if thought remains within the medium of such sceptical knowingness, it risks becoming the nihilism which responds to all truth-claims with amused disbelief and a flurry of footnotes. Without the legitimacy of truth, modern thought becomes therapeutic, a game of two halves in which nothing can be proved, a game in which the spoils go to the most amusing interpretations. The dynamics of such interpretations begin to deconstruct all assertions of identity so as to reveal metaphysical delusions and speculative claims. But wit's finest moments are the utopian insights released by speculative propositions, the thought that God *is* love, or that God *is* dead. If wit relies too much on a shared, human sense of Being, seeking modestly to illuminate the social quality of our species-being, the immanence of wit within existing social relations makes wit a site of critical struggles. In so far as critical theory remains inaccessible to those with their wits about them, it remains a professional jargon, a disassociated sensibility whose critical perspectives are literally out of this world. In so far as critical theory actualizes and articulates our already existing recognitions of the good life, it cannot afford to ignore the use and abuse of wit.

Works cited

Abrams, M. H. 'Wit, Humor and the Comic', in *A Glossary of Literary Terms*, 7th edn. Orlando, FL, 1999, 329–32.

Adorno, T. W. *The Jargon of Authenticity*, trans. Knut Tarnowski and Frederic Will. London, 1973.

Adorno, T. W. *Minima Moralia: Reflections from Damaged Life*, trans. E. F. N. Jephcott. London, 1974.

Beckett, Samuel. *The Complete Dramatic Works*. London, 1986.

Chapman, George. *Monsieur D'Olive*, in *The Works of George Chapman*, ed. Richard Herne Shepherd. London, 1875.

Cohen, Ted. *Jokes: Philosophical Thoughts on Joking Matters*. Chicago, IL, 1999.

Eagleton, Terry. 'The Critic as Clown', in *Marxism and the Interpretation of Culture*, eds Cary Nelson and Lawrence Grossberg. Urbana and Chicago, IL, 1988, 619–32

Eliot, T. S. 'The Metaphysical Poets', *Selected Prose of T.S. Eliot*, ed. Frank Kermode. London, 1975, 59–67.

Empson, William. 'Wit in the Essay on Criticism', in *The Structure of Complex Words*. London, 1951.

Grierson, H. J. C. (ed.) *Metaphysical Lyrics and Poems of the Seventeenth Century*. Oxford, 1921.

Gross, Harvey. *Sound and Form in Modern Poetry*. Ann Arbor, MI, 1964.

Gutwirth, Marcel. *Laughing Matter: An Essay on the Comic*. Ithaca, NY, 1993.

Hegel, G. W. F. *Aesthetics: Lectures on Fine Art*, 2 vols, trans. T. M. Knox. Oxford, 1988.

Heidegger, Martin. *Being and Time*, trans. John Macquarrie and Edward Robinson. Oxford, 1962.

Hill, Carl. *The Soul of Wit: Joke Theory from Grimm to Freud*. Lincoln, NE, 1994.

Hobbes, Thomas. *Leviathan*, ed. C. B. Macpherson. Harmondsworth, 1968.

Larsen, Egon. *Wit as a Weapon: The Political Joke in History*. London, 1980.

Lewis, C. S. 'Wit', in *Studies in Words*, 2nd edn. Cambridge, 1967, 86–110.

Lewis, Paul. *Comic Effects: Interdisciplinary Approaches to Humor in Literature*. Albany, NY, 1989.

Lyotard, Jean-François. *The Differend: Phrases in Dispute*, trans. Georges Van Den Abbeele. Manchester, 1988.

Marx, Karl. *Surveys from Exile: Political Writings, volume 2*, ed. David Fernbach. London, 1973.

Miner, Earl. 'Wit: Definition and Dialectic', in *Seventeenth-Century English Poetry: Modern Essays in Criticism*, rev. edn. ed. William R. Keast. London, 1971, 45–76

Nancy, Jean-Luc. *The Speculative Remark (One of Hegel's Bon Mots)*, trans. Céline Suprenant. Stanford, CA, 2001.

Nancy, Jean-Luc. 'Menstruum Universale', trans. Paula Moddel, *The Birth to Presence*, eds Werner Hamacher and David E. Wellbery, trans. Brian Holmes and others. Stanford, CA, 1993, 248–65.

Nietzsche, Friedrich. *The Gay Science*, trans. Walter Kaufmann. New York, 1974.

O'Connor, William Van and Lowry Nelson. 'Wit', in *The New Princeton Encyclopedia of Poetry and Poetics*, eds Alex Preminger and T. V. F. Brogan. Princeton, NJ, 1993.

Palmer, Jerry. *Taking Humour Seriously*. London, 1994.

Plass, Paul. *Wit and the Writing of History: The Rhetoric of Historiography in Imperial Rome*. Madison, WI, 1988.

Riley, Denise. 'Stair Spirit', in *Mop Mop Georgette: New and Selected Poems, 1986–1993*. London, 1993, 65–71

Riley, Denise. *The Words of Selves: Identification, Solidarity, Irony*. Stanford, CA, 2000.

Ritter, Joachim and Karlfried Gründer. 'Ingenium', in *Historisches Wörterbuch der Philosophie*, Vol. 4: I–K. Darmstadt, 1971–.

Shaftesbury, Third Earl of (Anthony Ashley Cooper). (1709) *Sensus communis: an essay on the freedom of wit and humour. In a letter to a friend*, ed. Lawrence E. Klein. Cambridge, 1999.

Smith, A. J. *Metaphysical Wit*. Cambridge, 1991.

Whedbee, J. William. *The Bible and the Comic Vision*. Cambridge, 1998.

Žižek, Slavoj. *The Fragile Absolute, or, Why is the Christian Legacy Worth Fighting For?* London, 2000.

Žižek, Slavoj. *Did Somebody Say Totalitarianism?* London, 2001.

In the 1970s, a decade now viewed as the heyday of post-structuralism, few critical studies marked the French critical horizon so indelibly as Roland Barthes's *S/Z*. Published in 1971, his reading of Balzac became a turning point in the fortunes of textual analysis and, from the distance of retrospection thirty years later, a beginning for what has since become a burgeoning field of cultural studies. *S/Z* promised a close reading of a moderately sized novella by the author of the grandiose *Comédie humaine*. Until then micro-analysis of literature had generally been confined to poetry, and if at all possible, to shorter pieces whose sum and whose aspect would be held within the confines of a single page. Short forms were canonized. A classical study of that shape had been Claude Lévi-Strauss and Roman Jakobson's analysis of Baudelaire's 'Les Chats', in which principles of structural approaches to literature and an anthropology of poetry were advanced.[1] The work became such a *cause célèbre* that from American shores Michael Riffaterre crossed swords with the authors by advancing, through an alternative reading of the same poem, more modest (in his view) and more carefully drawn concepts of interpretation.[2] For critics learning the tools of the new trade – and they were many in the wholesale revision of French and continental canons in the 1960s – these readings constituted a line of divide drawn between traditions old and new.

The *Querelle des anciens et des modernes* was revived. *Modernes* affiliated themselves with Lévi-Strauss and Jakobson in order to find a path outside of the close quarters of *explication de textes* that had exploited philol-ogy to confirm what biographical criticism had advanced in compendious works about *la vie et l'oeuvre* (forever 'revues et augmentées') of given authors. The linguist and the structural anthropologist made clear the tensions inhering in the relation of images (belonging to the realm of metaphor) to narrative fragments of myth (unwinding along an axis of metonymy). These tensions, they argued, could be seen in nature and culture in general and were not of Baudelaire's copyright, even if he, better than many, was of exceptional sensitivity and talent required to bring them forward. Principles of close reading that had belonged to philology were thus marshalled for the ends of seeing where and how humans imagined themselves in the nature of things. The analysis had an uncannily salubrious effect of displacing 'man' from a self-given rung at the top of a ladder of being. It asked its readers to ponder life at large in terms of space and place: to construct a sense of who and where one is, via the compass points of metaphor and metonymy, and how to invent a sense of location when indeed in life there is none. *Where* determines *what* you are, but all the while the *where* makes the *what* as disquieting as *what* when it is staked under the effect of *where*. Where and how to mark the entry of consciousness into language and to pre-given social forms became one of the aims of literary theory.

Roland Barthes's *S/Z* rehearsed the same questions by virtue of its style and form. The task of the book entailed study of a piece of prose according to a shape in which each chapter-unit of analysis, following more or less the calendar of meetings of a graduate seminar of a year's duration, provided a sequence of reading that followed that of a novella but that splintered the object of criticism into a mosaic of reflections on criticism, reading and writing. The tradition of *explication de textes* was both followed and called into question. Bearing a serial aspect, *S/Z* aspired to 'metonymy' in its development of critical concepts that were in accord with the reading that proceeded from one sentence to the next. It was a 'metaphor' in that the whole of the operation substituted something unknown – but what exactly was it? – in place of a relation of reader to text, of critical appreciation to creative writing, or perhaps of Barthes's analytical talents to that of Balzac, the writer for semiology would have been self-evident or visible in the overarching scientific design of the *Comédie humaine*.

In this brief essay it will be argued, first, that what was unknown bore in part the effects of a letter, and that the letter in question was *x*. Second, it will be shown that *x*, a concealed letter, in *S/Z* attests to a greater and longer tradition affiliated with the same cipher. Much of it can be read between the lines of the entries for X in any major dictionary.[3] The mobilization of its force in a textual field makes it unique. It pertains to the presence of visual perspective within writing, on the one hand, where it becomes the sign of a chiasm, indeed that of a figure on a ground and not that of a grapheme transcribing speech. On the other, the *x* can be seen rehearsing for its perceiver a continuous or endless process of deixis that marks, points out, indicates, locates and shows. To draw an *x* in the field of the imagination as one reads the sign is tantamount to contemplating reiteration of the origins of writing, of a first sign made when one line crosses another. It means taking cognizance of the difference between a figure and a ground and between a mark and a sign or a vocable and its graphic inscription. In so far as the *x* is an almost unvoiced conso-

nant it shows the reader where the transcriptive agency of printed writing is betrayed, or where other modes of signification inhabit alphabetical writing.

It may be that the alterity of the *x* goes hand in hand with its iconic value as sign of the unknown. The *x* that marks the spot where riches are buried on maps in fiction (*Treasure Island*, *Les Vampyrs*, every pirate story we have known . . .) points to the convergence of the abstraction of finality, fatality and desire. On a map an *x* belongs to textual material tipped into the design as well as the recondite language of cartography. A series of *x*'s on a topographic map might represent fields of grapes grown on sunny hillsides; three or four in a cluster at the edge of a city-view could refer to a patibulary gibbet where criminals are tortured or hanged (see de Dainville, 1964). It is of the very lines determining relief and contour, but also akin to the writing in the legend below or in adjacent toponyms. In a picture constructed by perspectival means a virtual *x* resides at a point of vanishment where the physical and transcending realms of the world would intersect.[4] In a classical film an *x* is a sign that portends the demise of the personage on whom its shadow is cast.[5] In the matter of advertising it is a concealed sign said to evoke fantasies of unfettered sexual congress, death, castration and subliminal excess of every sort.[6] In a mathematic equation *x* is a function of the unknown, to be sure, but is also a point where we realize that algebra and geometry are infused with language, and that discourse is apt to reside, like a strange bedfellow, in their ostensive abstraction. In the most sublime of all sublime moments of poetry, it is, in Mallarmé, the 'ptyx', the agglutination of the 'petit-*x*', or 'little mark' of a 'little death' in a signifier that, in 'Ses purs ongles', after all is said and done, means nothing. In each of these realms the beauty of the *x* owes its force to a rich history of the art of concealment, deceit and magic.

All of these virtues are elegantly repressed in *S/Z*. The vanishing point of his study of Balzac signals to what degree Barthes's art of reading capitalizes on the stigma of this letter. We can recall at the beginning that Barthes invokes ascetic Buddhists who 'succeed in seeing an entire landscape in a bean' (Barthes, 1971, 9).[7] Therein an analogy with formal treatments of narrative (implied are Vladimir Propp, Jakobson and Lévi-Strauss) who want to discern 'all the tales of the world in a single and same structure', with the inferred logic of a model juxtaposed to an example for the purpose of disengaging pertinent references that would be the mark of individual variation. In the comparative process we can choose either to put stories in a contrastive field in order to see how they function as *copies* of a model, or else we can see how stories figure in a 'grounding typology' of their form. The choice is thorny. Barthes ponders difference in the format of the opposition of an *either/or*. Science cannot account for differences because in principle it is not evaluative. Nor can ideology because it only 'reflects' values of a given time. Barthes spells out the dilemma of an evaluation that belongs to a practice of *writing* (10). At stake in what follows, he suggests, is what *can* be written and what *cannot*. At that juncture Barthes invokes the now classical distinction between writings that need to be written against those that seek to write without clear end or purpose, in modes he describes as *scriptible*, and those familiar and which can be read for their meaning which he calls *lisible*. The *scriptible* is assigned a compelling and immediate value because it contains a trajectory which we feel we must follow when we write: because, too, 'the task of literary writing (of literature as a working principle) is to make the reader become no longer a consumer but a producer of writing' (10).[8] Implied in the opposition is that what can be read can be written, but that what must be written cannot, or cannot quite yet be finalized: the *script-*

ible belongs to a secret or arcane, unutterable or ineffable dimension which every writer seeks to embody. In the folds and crannies of Barthes's study the *scriptible* might indeed be the letter *x*, the supernumerary mark that cannot be stated, that cues the desire to write, that compels desire, and that at the same time remains at once invisible and evident in all things *lisible*.

Following the dilemma he sets forward on the opening page, Barthes implicitly divides his book into two parts. The first, comprising his close analysis in which the *manchette* of one chapter states (in Italic), 'this is not an *explication de texte*), counts 93 units or little chapters that synthesize commentary on loosely grouped segments of Balzac's 'Sarrasine'. It is followed by an appendix of three sections, the first of which is the short story in its entirety. Unlike most editions of the text, it is marked by numerically ordered footnotes that divide the work into lexical units that are the topics of the analysis, *supra*, that are also quoted in small bold type in the gist of the principal commentary. Two textual compartments thus offset and reflect each other. Balzac's story is inferred to be what is *lisible* and to fit the classical order of the French literary canon. By contrast it can be wondered if Barthes's gloss is the *scriptible* counterpart, that is a writing that wills to figure and feigns to say what it cannot say where it otherwise states what it says it is saying. If a psychoanalytical concept is kept in mind the gloss, too, might be sign of a form of *incorporation* and even of a strange *introjection* of Balzac. All of the novella is engulfed in its first reading (if a sequential order is maintained) from chapter 1 through chapter 93. The story is dispersed and fractured into smaller units within the corpus of commentary. It is, as it were, digested, in its body but also held, hidden and coddled, in the space where Barthes writes as critic and reader. To a certain degree the text is held captive in

Barthes's textual gloss, hence repressed and internalized (incorporated); in another sense, being written about, it is topic of a dialogue and would be in the figurative 'mouth' of the author (hence introjected).[9]

The relation of the one to the other, of Barthes to Balzac and vice versa, becomes difficult to discern. Barthes uses a stenography of upper-case Roman numerals to distinguish and to provide an itinerary for his reflections. The chapter devoted to the eponym-protagonist, to Sarrasine of 'Sarrasine', is chapter X, where Barthes explains the *raison d'être* for inventing or selecting this story from Balzac's *Scènes de la vie parisienne* in *La Comédie humaine*. Passing reference is made to Georges Bataille (23), who is quoted in an epigraph at the bottom of the book, in a space squinched between the end of the third annex including typologies and methods used in the analysis ([271]). Chapter X thus deals with the *incipit* of the story as well as its emblem, that is, the moment when a visible form fades into a textual abstraction – where typography disappears as it conveys its meaning – and where, too, the greatest degree of fantasy – say, deceit, desire, projected finality, destiny – is invested on the part of the reader prior to his or her being 'tracked' or situated in accord with the narrative and critical lines of the book. The strange name inaugurates a question: what is it? *Qu'est-ce que c'est que ça?* If it is unknown, how is the name so marked? The name conceals a feminine dimension because the mute *e* of the last syllable attests to a masculine doublet in 'Sarrazine'. Barthes associates the quest to solve the problem of sexual difference inaugurated by the name with a 'hermeneutic code' that he abbreviates in upper-case Roman as HER. The concealed feminine element is a 'sème' that Barthes transcribes into SEM, an apothegm in fitting contrast to HER. In the emblematic configuration the commanding question concerning textual and sexual difference is written under the cipher X.

It suffices to locate more precisely Barthes's tactic of visual composition. *S/Z* is designed, like the fictions of writers from Montaigne to Gide and Maurice Blanchot, according to perspectival systems. Composed and disposed around an enigmatic centre, the book has a 'mannerist' aspect by which the text is turned into an allegorical landscape by dint of spatial allegory and numerology. The seed of the conception might have been Blanchot's epigraph to his *L'Espace littéraire*, in which the philosopher notes that any work of writing, like a piece of art, tends consciously or unconsciously to move toward and away from a centre. The latter may or may not be in the middle, but it is usually located in a median arena. It might too have been inspired by Michel Butor's reading of Montaigne, in *Essais sur les 'Essais'*: for Butor the mannerist writer begins from a centre that is left absent and builds a text (or writes a picture or *Bild*) all about and around it. For Montaigne the absent centre was reserved for the memory of his dead friend, Etienne de la Boétie, for whom the essays become a frame of the surround in the style of a pattern of *grotesques* as they were known in the sixteenth-century illustrated book.[10] Montaigne composed his first volume with fifty-seven chapters. He left vacant the twenty-ninth, set beneath a unique and prime number, in which were included (in the 1580 and 1582 editions) twenty-nine sonnets he attributed to the hand of Etienne de la Boétie. A strange doubling and an even eroticized site is crafted by the relation of the even pair of an odd number at an axis that bisects and thus sets in opposition two equal units of twenty-eight chapters (1–28 and 30–57) buttressing twenty-nine poems under the same cipher (xxxix).

As Montaigne does in his *Essais* so too Barthes in *S/Z*. the title of the forty-seventh chapter (xlvii) of *S/Z* happens to be the title of the book, now *mis en abyme*, at the centre or, perhaps, the line of divide between one world and the other. Barthes reiterates what he had stated in chapter X about 'Sarrasine' being the feminization of the masculine 'Sarrazin', but adds now that 'the Z has fallen into a trap door of sorts' (113). Suddenly, too, the gloss becomes an inspired rhapsody about the printed letter:

Now Z is the letter of mutilation: phonetically Z lashes as might a leather whip, a furious insect; graphically, thrown by the hand, slung across the smooth white surface of the page, among the rotund shapes of the alphabet, like an oblique and illegal switchblade, z cuts, scars, streaks [zèbre]; from a balzacian point of view, this Z (which is in Balzac's name) is the letter of deviance (see the novella Z. Marcas); finally, even here, Z is the inaugural letter of the Zambinella, the initial of castration, such that by this orthographical error set at the core of his name, at the centre of his body, Sarrasine receives the zambinellian Z according to its true nature, which is the wound of lack. Furthermore, S and Z are in a graphic relation: it is the same letter when seen on the other side of the mirror: in Zambinella Sarrasine contemplates his own castration. Thus the bar (/) that opposes the S of SarraSine and the Z of Zambinella bears a function of panic: it is the bar of censure, the specular surface, the wall of hallucination, the cutting edge of antithesis, the abstraction of limit, the oblicity of the signifier, the index of the paradigm, hence of meaning.

(113)

End of chapter: an enigma or a fault, even a fault line, is drawn into the name that crowns Balzac's story and that

figures on the left-hand side of the bar in Barthes's title. Barthes remarks that the mistake 'is set at the core of' (*au coeur de*) his name, at the centre of his body' (113). But whose centre? What body? And where? The second S is *adjacent* to the *a* at the centre of the name if indeed specular duplication is part of the mirror-effect in view: Sarr→ a ←sine. The feminine S that occupies the place reserved for the masculine Z (with the mute *e*, truncated or cut away by virtue of apocope) is *not* at the centre of the body of the name. But the bar of censure or castration surely is. At the virtual centre of *S/Z*, and not the centre of 'Sarrasine', is placed the enigma of the letter.

Here is where the compositional tactic of *S/Z* displays what it cannot put in words. It writes toward an unnameable point or axis on which turns the dilemma of sexual difference at the basis of life itself. Barthes clearly suggests that the dilemma is projected onto the body of the book itself, and that the symbolic *ar*, a shard of his own name, is tantamount to the 'symbolic' or to language that tears the human subject away from its primal bliss when, by needs castrated, it enters into the world at large. At the centre of the analysis is thus a specular parable about a law of life. The curvilinear S that would be a figure of feminine contour is barred from congress with the masculine counterpart, the Z, that is its rectilinear analogue or complement. It is as if the names were indicating what Barthes cannot write, but that the visual composition of the book brings forward to the roving eyes of the haptic reader. Sarrasine carries a mirror in his own name (sar→/←ras), and the Zambinella carries an *ambi*-valence at the same spot in his. The skeletal key (or *chi*, or even 'who') of the work is found in an art of displacement and oscillation.

We can wonder if indeed in the story itself the two letters, if they can be personified, ever converge, copulate or take pleasure in their own excess. At a crucial point in

Balzac's novella Sarrasine beholds the Zambinella in the setting of the theatre. After being ravished by what he hears and sees he returns time and again to the same spectacle:

> Il était si complètement ivre, qu'il ne voyait plus ni salle, ni spectateurs, ni acteurs, n'entendait plus de musique. Bien mieux, il n'existait pas de distance entre lui et la Zambinella, il la possédait, ses yeux, attaché sur elle, s'emparaient d'elle. Une puissance presque diabolique lui permettait de sentir le vent de cette voix, de respirer la poudre embaumée dont ses cheveux étaient imprégnés, de voir les méplats de ce visage, d'y compter les veines bleues qui en nuançaient la peau satinée. Enfin cette voix agile, fraîche et d'un timbre argenté, souple comme un fil auquel le moindre souffle d'air donne une forme, qu'il roule et déroule, développe et disperse, cette voix attaquait si vivement son âme, qu'il laissa plus d'une fois échapper de ces cris involontaires arrachés par les délices convulsives trop rarement données par les passions humaines. Bientôt il fut obligé de quitter le théâtre.

> (244)

> [He was so totally dizzy that he saw neither room, spectators, actors, nor did he hear any music. Even better, there existed no distance between him and the Zambinella, he possessed her, his eyes, stuck to her, took hold of her. An almost diabolical power was allowing him to feel the wind of this voice, to breathe the embalmed powder that was impregnating her hair, to see the smooth surfaces of this face, to count the blue veins that were nuancing the satin sheen of her skin. Finally this agile voice, cool and of a silvery timbre, supple as a thread to which the slightest puff of air endows with a form, that it winds and unwinds, develops and disperses, this voice attacked his soul so vividly that he let escape more than once an involuntary cry torn away by the convulsive delights too rarely awarded by human passions. Soon he was obliged to leave the theatre.]

In the two chapters of *S/Z* devoted to this passage, 'Le chef d'oeuvre' (LII, 121–5) [The Masterpiece] and 'L'Euphémisme' (LIII, 125–8) [The Euphemism], Barthes argues that the zambinellian body is real but issues from a 'code' given by Greek statuary, that of the code of the 'masterpiece'. For the voyeur Sarrasine the discovery of the Zambinella's body is tantamount to the arrival at a point where the origin of all copies found, the 'original copy', as it were, of the Body itself. The orgiastic scene in the theatre is described in the conventions of euphemism and hence borders on the idiolect of classical pornography. Barthes makes sure that such a reading cannot be an ultimate one for the simple reason that 'euphemism is a language' (126) like any other, and that in view of the printed text it can be said that no single privilege – such as that of balzacian 'pornography' – can be accorded to the passage. 'There is no 'first', 'natural', 'national', or 'maternal' critical language: the text is at once [d'emblée], in being born, multilingual; for the textual lexicon or dictionary there is neither an idiom of entry nor of exit, for the text has, out of the dictionary, not a (closed) power of definition but infinite structure' (126–7).[11]

In the multiple layers of the scenario staged at once between criticism and creation, and in the folds of the reader's identification with the characters and actions of the novella in their graphic and psychic latencies, we seem to be both in a limit-situation of *no exit* and another of total freedom (in the words of the critic, of 'infinite' structure). We cannot exit from the text in quite the same way that Sarrasine is obliged to exit from the theatre in which he beholds the object of his visual desire. A moire-like effect of language and gloss results from the confusion in which Barthes and Sarrasine can be identified as one. But where is Balzac or, better, where is the text ['*the text, nothing but the text!*'(126)] of the novella that radiates and refracts between its inscription in the gloss and its integral form in the appendix? The text describing the object of Sarrasine's gaze is ultimately the Zambinella's voice. Sarrasine feels or smells *le vent de cette voix* and, ultimately, *cette voix agile* that he beholds is transformed into the thread of an invisible cloth that furls and unfurls in the air of its own creation as exhalation and inspiration, and the same image precipitates on the part of the onlooker a swan-like utterance, any of 'ces cris involontaires' that issue from the body at its point of ravishment. The story turns on that moment of willed misrecognition. Sarrasine is impelled to trace images of her, literally, to sketch copies of her despite the fineries of the costume the singer wears in performance, despite the 'veils [*voiles*], dresses, corsets and knots of ribbons that stole her away from him' (245).

In the final formula of the description, in *cette voix agile*, we behold the point where the voice of the tale is seen and not heard. It is at the site of the *x* hidden in the cliché of the 'agile voice'. The small *x* marks the spot where, in the desiring fancy of the reader – whether ourselves, Barthes, Balzac or Sarrasine – there is a congress or transgression of the bar of castration. The copulation of the different characters, of S and Z and the curvilinear and orthogonal traits at the basis of the representation of sexual difference, is imagined at the vanishing point of the unvoiced *x* of *voix agile*. The chiastic character is senseless because it cannot be heard. It nonetheless marks the formula with the effect of showing that the cliché conceals its own visual figure of the veil that is being agitated in the descriptive turn, 'qu'il roule, développe et disperse. . .' It is licit to see, thanks to the unvoiced locational mark, *voi* (x ag) *ile* in the array of letters. Here the almost maddening and crazed effect elicited by the *x* in respect to the S and Z makes clear the veil or moire of voice that the formula invites the reader to agitate: vois-*x*. agis-le, 'see *x*. shake it', hence, track it through the entirety of the novella.

It would be fastidious to list the x-effects that scatter throughout 'Sarrasine'. Silent voices are endlessly and ubiquitously agitating the writing. 'Les éclats de voix des joueurs' (227) [the flashes of the players' voices] in the salon behind the veil of a curtain are seen from the outset of the story. The narrator proceeds to record many others, but in such a way that they are *ciphered* to bear an *x*-factor that in the typography locates the places where the text is felt and seen exceeding its own transcriptive or mimetic function. At these junctures 'Sarrasine' accedes to an autonomous art of printed writing or marking. The graphic character of its own mode of reproduction is everywhere spotted in the work, like the *x*-points that expose and espouse its drama of difference. They are rarely commented in the course of the explication.

In his reading Barthes cannot quite ascribe a value to the cipher that mediates difference. In leaving aside the *x*-function of 'Sarrasine', in an implicit refusal to 'see language' as he does so exquisitely in all of his critical work, and even as he admits in noting that his visual apprenhension of language is a bad trait ('j'ai un malheur: je vois le langage') Barthes indicates something of greater import. He avows that a classical piece of literature, a 'readable' text, is ultimately 'pensive', in other words, 'thoughtful' wherever it will 'keep in reserve a last meaning that it does not express, but whose *free and signifying place it holds*: this zero-degree of meaning (which is not the annulation, but to the contrary the recognition). This supplementary, unexpected sense which is the theatrical mark of the implicit, is pensivity: the pensivity (of faces, of texts) is the signifier of the inexpressible, not of the unexpressed' (222). The mark of the inexpressible or of what cannot be thought, of what is inexorably outside of meaning is the sign of something else, of an *x*-factor or a virtual *excess of meaning*. The latter is never named in *S/Z*. It remains in the space where S and Z would sublate but do not, and it is discerned in the graphic character of the text at large. The 'inexpressed' is just that: it is in-*x*-pressed. It 'becomes *expressive*' when endowed with an interiority' (222–3) that comes forward in the letter at once figuring and detached from meaning.

It can be said that in Balzac *X* is a privileged signifier because it maps the site where madness and mensuration intersect. The novelist was known for describing the effects of his creative craft as a tension between *la toison et le vertige* (the *toise*, a pre-Revolutionary measure of five and one-half feet), represented the scientific and mathematical unit needed to chart the itinerary of the dizzy speleologist who would dare to enter into the volcano on whose crater he was poised and into whose gulf he stared. The meeting of the known and the unknown would thus be located wherever Balzac's text — or any piece of writing of classical facture — drew attention to its own surface tensions and its spatiality as well as to the unknown, that of which it cannot write but toward which its writing forever tends. In a mathematical equation we have seen that *x* can be the unknown or the name of an axis on which narrative or metonymy can be charted (in contrast to the *y* axis, a vertical, that is metaphoric in nature). In Balzac the *x* is a

cipher that elicits its own decipherment. We might extrapolate further by noting that the letter conveys the unknown or unassimilable element, a sign of excess, that is contained in the text that simultaneously surrounds it.

In other writings of the same moment, such as *La Peau de chagrin* (1830–31) and 'Le Chef d'oeuvre inconnu' (1832), a prevailing aura of melancholy and suspicion about the state of the world at the time of the July Monarchy is expressed through a desire to retrieve or even to invent things unknown in the materiality of writing. The hero of 'Le chef d'oeuvre inconnu' may be neither Frenhofer, the old and mad genius, or Poussin, the calculating apprentice to sorcerer Frenhofer, but rather the mass of vocables and pigments of and in the story that are not assimilated with any mimetic value. That is the hero: the masterpiece is *unknown*, hence the *chef d'oeuvre* turns from a substantive into an adjective that modifies the substantive *inconnu*. When in madness Frenhofer cries out, 'la mission de l'art n'est pas de copier la nature, mais de l'exprimer' [the mission of art is not to copy nature, but to express it], he indicates the spot on the page, in the tonic verb, where what comes out of the genius is marked at the spot of the prefix *x*.[12] What comes out also goes back into the graphic register.

The moment follows a strange trajectory. In the narrative an exchange is tendered by which the master is said to be able to finish his *chef d'oeuvre*, his 'head' work, if he can gaze upon the nude body of an appointed model who is the spouse of an unknown painter aspiring to greatness. But the old master is as troubled as she about the prospect of baring oneself or one's work before the world at large. When all is said and done his *chef* d'oeuvre is only a *foot* in the mass of abstraction (or of abstract expressionism) on a massive canvas. What counts is the unknown factor of the signature. When asked who he is, the young painter who is visiting Frenhofer's studio responds, 'Je suis inconnu, barbouilleur d'instinct, et arrivé depuis peu dans cette ville, source de toute science' (312) [I'm unknown, a splatterer of instinct, having just arrived in this city, a font of all science]. The unknown painter, the neophyte who would be Frenhofer's pupil, is obliged to make a Faustian transaction by which he acquires his name. His is asked by another of Frenhofer's followers (Porbus) to draw a picture. Which he does: '[L]'inconnu copia lestement la *Marie* au trait' (312) [The unknown deftly copied the *Mary* line-by-line]. The old man asks him his name, and at the bottom of the picture he writes: 'Nicolas Poussin'. In its archaic design the story stages a 'total social fact' of interpellation. The unknown acquires a name when it is required to enter into the symbolic domain. The original and originary trait in the circumstance of the story would be the letter *x*, the primal signature set between the work of a 'barbouilleur d'instinct' and a human subject who is placed in the world when his name is recorded in its register. *Inconnu*, that which cannot be marked, gives way to an implicit *X*, that in turn gives way to the drawing of 'Nicolas Poussin'.

Yet the unknown needs to reside in the known to assure the continuity of symbolic process. The privilege of the unknown is lost when Poussin's name is written in the record of the story taking place in Paris, 'this city, font of all science'. The unknown is transferred to the old man who retains his air of mystery until Porbus calls him 'maître Frenhofer' (315). The fiction appears impelled to create the unknown where it avows that the aims of the sciences are to decipher and hence to eradicate it. The unknown needs to be created for lack of its presence in a world where all things are said to be known.

Such is the *x*-factor in Balzac's early fiction and in the critical appreciation brought to it in the 'inexpressed' areas of Roland Barthes's critical account of 'Sarrasine'. By way of conclusion we can recall that Georges Bataille had singled out 'Sarrazine', along with *Wuthering Heights*, *The Trial*, *In Search of Lost Time*, *The Idiot*, Sade's 'Eugénie de Franval', Blanchot's *L'Arrêt de mort* and Stendhal's *Le Rouge et le noir*, as one of these very rare stories or novels that can 'reveal the multiple truth of life'. Only these stories, sometimes read in a trance, 'situate everyone before destiny'. 'If we wish to know *what a novel can be*', we must read the kind of story 'that reveals the possibilities of life does not forcibly seek, but it reveals a moment of *rage*, without which its author would be blind to these *excessive* possibilities' (cit. Barthes, 1971, 271). If the excess cannot be named, or if it must perforce remain in a latent or potential condition, it nonetheless needs to be marked. In the graphic unconscious of Bataille's words, in *excessives* [*excessive*], *X* is, *x c'est*, *x* marks the spot where it is. Bataille's observations about the Brontë sisters, Kafka, Proust, Stendhal and others are borne out elsewhere, in an early piece of writing, a book-review of a piece of ephemera about the Chicago gang wars in the days of prohibition. Xs were marked next to the victims before they were nominally murdered by their rivals. Entitled 'X Marks the Spot' in the French edition, Bataille's article anticipates the expressive logic that warrants inclusion of his misspelled version of 'Sarrazine' into the pantheon of masterpieces of excess (1973). Barthes makes that element clear by respecting its mute and pervasive violence that is occasionally visible on the smooth textual surface (on the *méplats*) of Balzac's novella.

Seen after a hiatus of thirty years, when the frenzy of theory and the animated quarrels of the ancients and the moderns have subsided, and when the work of that era has since become a scientific object or a topic set under an innocuous name such as 'poststructuralism', Barthes's exhumation of Balzac has not lost much of its force.[13] True, it now shows that the ideology is one that associates the

Lacanian 'instance of the letter in the unconscious' with the blade of castration. Likewise, it represses the *excess* that Bataille had admired in the tale for the purpose of making transgression a structure of structures. The repression that turns the critic of things *lisible* into a writer who knows not where he is going, in the process of the *scriptible*, owes much to the unknown that comes forward in the shape of a cipher. The *x* is that object and the mark or strange emblem that, as *excès*, remains a point of vanishment in Balzac and in the criticism that 'poststructuralism' has bequeathed to us. The shape of texts may have changed in the electronic revolution we have witnessed since *S/Z*, but the logic of difference and of the exquisite violence marked by the letter has not. And we are brought back to the materiality of writing, to the transgressions of the type made by the 'g', 'y' and 'p' in the preceding clause when the feet of these letters exceed the lower line of type. We are also led to broader speculation about what indeed constitutes repression and transgression, and of their currency as concepts. In the practical world in which we live it would seem that everything goes. Repression and transgression would be as antiquated as the typographical designer's impulse to espouse things straight and curved in his letters in a presentation of letters that bear human traits. Yet in critical circles they figure the same precious and even endangered species of writing. Better that we rejoice in the vagaries of the *x* that resists authorial control and that turns literature into a more commanding art of writing.

Notes

1. Rpt. in Jakobson (1974).
2. Reprinted in French in *Essais de stylistique structurale* (1971). The article first appeared in *Yale French Studies*, 36–7 (1966), a volume that changed the course of literary studies in North America.
3. The twenty-fourth letter of the English alphabet, it represents the speech of a sound that is between 's' and 'c' or even 'g', and is a counterpart to *chi*, the twenty-second letter of the Greek alphabet. In mathematical equations *X* traditionally stands for an unknown quantity or can be 'an arbitrarily chosen value from the domain of a variable' (Webster). *X* is the letter given to the horizontal coordinate of a grid. It is a cross or a sign appended to something that is wrong. It marks the number of chromosomes of a polypoloid series, in other words the number contained in a single genome. As a verb it means to mark, to cancel or obliterate, or to cross out. *X* as a cipher or number figures in secret or arcane writing, notes Blaise de Vigenère in his *Traité de chiffres* (1586): ciphered writing transposes one letter or commutes signs and meanings in the place of one another, in order that 'il y ait autre sens caché que celuy qu'on voit en apert; attendu que ce sont tous mots clairs & intelligibles, d'une suitte de paroles congruës; mais à l'interieur il y a toute une autre chose reservée à celuy qui entend l'artifice' (f. 13r°). For Vigenère such writing constitutes a 'polygraphie' or 'stéganographie', a writing that conceals and redistributes meanings in the shapes and combinations of letters. 'Tout le mystere de l'occultation des divins secrets, consiste sous l'escorce d'une escriture vulgaire, en nombre, figure, & poix, souvant ce qui est escrit en la Sapience II. *Omni in numero, mensura, & pondere disposuisti*' (f. 277v°–278r°).
4. The history is recounted in Damisch (1978).
5. Two or three films are paradigmatic. The 'Saint Bartholomew's Massacre' sequence of *Intolerance* (dir. D. W. Griffith, 1915) begins with shots of Catholic conspirators painting *x*s on the doorways of Huguenots who will be stabbed and strangled in the wee hours of the morning. *Scarface* (dir. Howard Hawks, 1932) places victims of the Capone gang next to *x*-like forms before they are murdered, the sign being used to predict their immediate destiny. In *L'Atalante* (dir. Jean Vigo) the woman, the problematic figure in a world of men at work on barges, is '*x*'d' after betraying her husband in frolics with the first mate. She is placed behind a symbolic chiasm indicating her role as both a character who is 'marked' as well as mediatrix in the field of tensions in the film.
6. The writing of the aptly named Wilson Key is noteworthy (1989). Doris-Louise Haineault and Jean-Yves Roy wrote a dissertation under the direction of Roland Barthes, that has been translated from the French (1993). These studies study how the unconscious is produced in visual schemes, especially subliminal inscription of *x*s, in advertising. They bear resemblance, as we shall see below, to the ciphering of Balzac's fiction that 'sells' an unconscious in its graphic play.
7. All quotations will be drawn from this edition and indicated between parentheses in the text above. Translations from the French are mine.
8. I have translated *travail* as a working principle and have been obliged to omit the connotation of bodily pain and even torture that inhabits the etymology (*travail* > *trepalium*, a variant of *tripalium*, an instrument of torture having three stakes).

9. The concept is developed by Nicolas Abraham in *L'Ecorce et le noyau* (1978). *S/Z* may have been a model for Jacques Derrida's caustic satire of John R. Searle in an opuscule entitled *Limited Inc* (1979). Searle took care to copyright ('inc') a critique of his signature of one of Derrida's studies of speech-act theory. In response, in flagrant violation of copyright law, Derrida wrote a long gloss that quoted the entirety of Searle's work. The reader was thus led through over seventy pages of chicanery before discovering that Searle was 'incorporated' or 'introjected' in the mouth of his adversary. Barthes was indeed doing the same thing with the exception that 'Sarrasine' was not protected under law of copyright.

10. See the front matter of Blanchot (1955); Butor (1968). Henri-Jean Martin takes up the *grotesque* in *La Naissance du livre moderne* (2000).

11. *D'emblée*, meaning 'at once' or 'in general', has strong graphic charge in Barthes's idiolect, and perhaps for historical reasons. In the sixteenth century 'emblé(e)' signified, said Randle Cotgrave in his French/English dictionary of 1611, 'Stollen, filched, pilfered, purloined, imbezeled,' while 'd'emblée' meant 'subtilely, craftily, underhand, at unawares'. In Barthes's letters, words and formulas of this kind often tend to be stealthy and volatile, and as their graphic form shows, polymorphous. Yet, at the same time they never exceed their context or make any sign of deviation from standard usage

12. 'Le Chef d'oeuvre inconnu', in Honoré de Balzac, *La comédie humaine*, XV: 2e partie, 1: Etudes philosophiques (1869, 340). Other references to this story and *La Peau de chagrin* will be made to this edition.

13. Which is the point of this essay, written in dialogue with an earlier study of the *x* in Barthes, now quasi-illegible and only of value for study of the reception of Barthes in America, entitled 'Barthes's *Excès*: The Silent Apostrophe of *S/Z*', that appeared in an issue of *Visible Language* (11, 1977: 355–84) edited by Steven Ungar. Ungar noted elsewhere, in *Roland Barthes: The Professor of Desire* (1983), that with *S/Z* the author's career moves toward figuration and in a direction, away from semiotic science, that begins to embrace desire (70–1). Noteworthy is that the elegant *lettrines* of Ungar's book are taken from an allegory of the letters on the leaves of a tree of 'sapience' (opposed to the withered branches of 'ignorance') in Geofroy Tory's groundbreaking study of the agency of the printed letter, *Champfleury* (1529).

Works cited

Abraham, Nicolas and Maria Torok. *L'Ecorce et le noyau*. Paris, 1978.

Barthes, Roland. *S/Z*. Paris, 1971.

Bataille, Georges. 'X Marks the Spot', in *Oeuvres complètes* 1. Paris, 1973.

Blanchot, Maurice. *L'Espace littéraire*. Paris, 1955.

Butor, Michel. *Essais sur les 'Essais'*. Paris, 1968.

Conley, Tom. 'Barthes's *Excès*: The Silent Apostrophe of *S/Z*', in *Visible Language*, 11 (1977): 355–84, ed. Steven Ungar.

Damisch, Hubert. *L'Origine de la perspective*. Paris, 1978.

de Balzac, Honoré. *La comédie humaine*. Paris, 1869.

de Dainville, S.J., François. *Le langage des géographes*. Paris, 1964.

de Vigenère, Blaise. *Traité de chiffres*. Paris, 1586.

Derrida, Jacques. *Limited Inc*, trans. Samuel Weber et al, ed. Gerald Graff. Baltimore, MD, 1979.

Haineault, Doris-Louise and Jean-Yves Roy. *Unconscious for Sale: Advertising, Psychoanalysis, and the Public*, trans. Kimball Lockhart. Minneapolis, MN, 1993.

Jakobson, Roman. *Questions de poétique*. Paris, 1974.

Key, Wilson. *The Age of Manipulation: The Con in Confidence, the Sin in Sincere*. New York, 1989.

Martin, Henri-Jean. *La Naissance du livre moderne*. Paris, 2000.

Rifaterre, Michael. *Essais de stylistique structurale*, trans. Daniel Delas. Paris, 1971.

Tory, Geofroy. *Champfleury*. Paris, 1529.

Ungar, Steven. *Roland Barthes: The Professor of Desire*. Lincoln, NE, 1983.

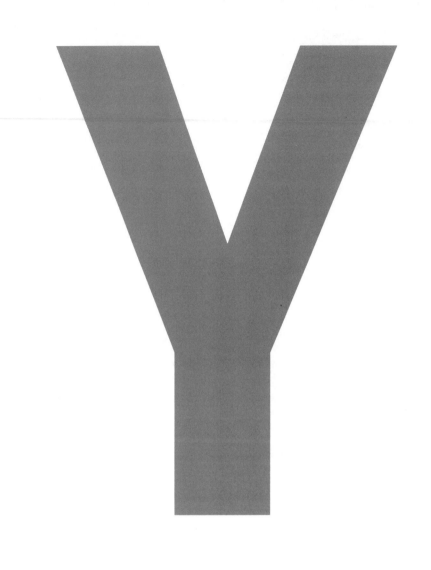

yarn | *VALENTINE CUNNINGHAM*

Yarn, yarning, yarn-spinning: the figurative and analogical life of yarn, of that basic stuff of textiles, of the woven, of fabric, gets focused most vividly, I suppose, for English-language expositors of modernist narratology, and also for Anglophone deconstructionists seeking texts for their would-be uncanny undoings of the logocentric, in that utterly magnetic description at the beginning of *Heart of Darkness* (1899) of Marlow, Joseph Conrad's favourite narrator, and of how Marlow differs from ordinary seamen:

> He was a seaman, but he was a wanderer, too, while most seamen lead, if one may so express it, a sedentary life. Their minds are of the stay-at-home order, and their home is always with them – the ship – and so is their country – the sea. One ship is very much like another, and the sea is always the same. In the immutability of their surroundings the foreign shores, the foreign faces, the changing immensity of life, glide past, veiled not by a sense of mystery but by a slightly disdainful ignorance; for there is nothing mysterious to a seaman unless it be the sea itself, which is the mistress of his existence and as inscrutable as Destiny. For the rest, after his hours of work, a casual stroll or a casual spree on shore suffices to unfold for him the secret of a whole continent, and generally he finds the secret not worth knowing. The yarns of seamen have a direct simplicity, the whole meaning of which lies within the shell of a cracked nut. But Marlow was not typical (if his propensity to spin yarns be excepted), and to him the meaning of an episode was not inside like a kernel but outside, enveloping the tale which brought it out only as a glow brings out a haze, in the likeness of one of these misty halos that sometimes are made visible by the spectral illumination of moonshine.

> (Conrad, 1995, 18)

('*These* misty halos', one supposes, because this first narrator of the *nouvelle* seems to be referring to the 'lurid glare' of London that he's just mentioned, visible up the Thames from where he's sitting on board *The Nellie* in the gloaming.) Seamen are renowned for their stories, their spinning of yarns. Traditional storytellers, they spin their yarns in traditional ways, for the traditional ends of revelation, of disclosure, the broaching of truths, the opening of secrets and the dispelling of mystery. Yarn is thread; and narratives of the typical seamanlike sort have followable threads, threads that lead the hearer somewhere specific. But Marlow and his yarning – and so, we are to think, Joseph Conrad and his modernist yarning – are not typical. Theirs will be yarning with a difference; their narrative threads will be followable, perhaps, but only with difficulty. The narrative webs, texts, tissues woven here will be otherwise than of old – obscurer, less revealing, more secretive.

Clearly, the pressing thought here is that writing and reading restults will vary, will be different, according to what is done with the stuff, the material, of the narration, with, so to say, the yarn of which the yarn, the yarning, consists. Everything will depend upon what the yarner, the weaver, does. Or, put another way, on how you work your idea of yarn, how yarning is figured.

Yarn is the fibres of natural materials, flax, cotton, wool, hemp, jute, silk, more recently fibres of synthetic materials, nylon and the rest, which are *spun* into continuous *threads*, or fine *cords* ('of considerable length', says the wonderfully instructive *Oxford English Dictionary*, which will be an indispensable *vade mecum* in these inquiries), spun for the purposes of *sewing* and *knitting* and *weaving*. *Spinning* is, originally, the drawing out of threads from an original, confused mass of flax, cotton and so on, placed, or *dizened*, on the end of a cleft stick called a *distaff* (*distaff*: a dizened, dressed, attired staff). Flax was prepared for the distaff by being combed, to separate the less useful short fibres from the more useful longer ones, with a tool called a *heckle*. These long fibres were known as *lines*. Flax was called *line* in English – from Latin *linum*, flax (compare French *lin*); hence *line* or *linen*, for the fabric woven from flax (*line*: spun or woven flax; linen thread or cloth; a napkin of linen; in the plural, *lines*, linen vestments). Like hemp and jute, flax in the raw is known as *tow*. *Tow* is also the shorter fibres of flax, good only for candle wicks and the like, but supplying the word for thick cord, for *rope*, and then for the act of pulling by ropes, i.e. *towing*. To be ready for weaving or sewing, yarn, thread, is spun, or *wound*, off the distaff onto other rods, or rod-like objects, known variously in the tradition as *spindles*, or *clews*, or *bottoms*, or *bobbins*, or *spools*. Yarn came to measured in *spindles*, or *threads*. In 1858, according to Simmonds' *Trade Dictionary*, quoted by the OED, a spindle of cotton yarn was 15,120 yards, and a spindle of linen yarn 60,00 yards. A thread-length varied according to region as well as kind of yarn. Simmonds

informed Dr James Murray's lexicographers that a thread of cotton yarn was 54 inches, of linen yarn 90 inches and worsted (wool) yarn 35 inches.

On many occasions the objects that yarn was wound onto became synomymous with the wound yarn itself. So bottom and bobbin and clew could also signify, simply, yarn – which shouldn't surprise, because they usually went together. Only yarn wound onto clews and bottoms and bobbins was of any use for the purposes of sewing or knitting or weaving. Yarn, thread, passed from bobbin to *needle* for sewing (or *suturing*), from clew (of wool) to *knitting needles*, from bottom and the rest of the synonymous items to weaver's *loom*. *Weaver's bottom* was the weaver's basic working material. Shakespeare's weaver in *A Midsummer Night's Dream* is not called Bottom for nothing. To weave, Bottom needed (and still needs) a *loom*, some sort of framing device across which yarns are tightly stretched lengthwise (the *warp*), through which other yarns (the *weft* or *woof*) are passed by hand – or, in machine looms, *shuttled* in a yarn container called a *shuttle* – back and forth to make a *web* of threads, a piece of cloth, known of old as *text* or *texture* (from Latin *texere*, to weave), or indeed as *tissue* (also from *texere*, via Old French *tissu*). This is *weaving*. Until the eighteenth century *texture* could mean the art or process of weaving.

And utterly captivating is the extent to which verbal activity, language work, literary production, narration, writing, and also linguistic and literary and narratological description and theorizing, get figured as being, and metaphoricized as involved in, the dense set of human activities and modes of production and products which involve yarn.

Heckling of flax turns into the heckling, the severe questioning or catechizing of people, especially politicians, and, later, into the rude and loud interrupting of any public speaker. From dizening of distaffs it's a short step to the dizening, or bedizening, of writings ('Here the Muse dizens / My dirge with orisons': J. Beresford, 1826; 'The quotations . . . with which Mr Lemaitre has thought fit to bedizen his pages': *Edinburgh Review*, 1806 – both OED). Line, the thread of flax, quickly got applied to the thread-like marks made with pens or other tools, as in drawing and engraving, and to anything arranged along a straight line, not least a row of written and, later, printed letters. Writing came to be thought of as being produced in lines, and so were printed words. Line came to mean a few words of writing, especially in a short note or letter ('Drop me a line . . .'). And poetry came to be thought of as consisting of lines – in groups of single lengths of words. So *lines* comes to mean verses, verse, poetry, a poem ('Lines Composed A Few Miles Above Tintern Abbey'). Lines are the parts of a drama an actor speaks (she 'learns her lines'). And anything that could be figured as being spun out, or continuously drawn out, like thread, was so figured: life, lives, and of course words and writings, and aspects of words, and things in writings – subjects, arguments, stories, verbosity, every sort of discourse. Discourses all had their threads, they were threads. 'He draweth out the thred of his verbositie finer than the staple of his argument' (*Love's Labours Lost*, V.i.19). (*Staple* denoted the quality of any textile material, flax, wool and so on, and became the word for any fibre of which threads and so textiles could be made.) Words, sentences, conversations, debates, lines of verse were of course spun, or spun out ('My Lines are weak, unsinew'd, others say – A man might spin a thousand such a Day': Philip Francis's translation of Horace's *Satires*, II.i.4, 1747). 'Still as I pull'd, it came', writes John Bunyan in his prefatory verses to *The Pilgrim's Progress* (1678), 'The Author's Apology for His Book', figuring his narrating and his writing ('I set Pen to Paper with delight') as the drawing of thread off the distaff. How best to describe a bobbin, the short stick-like object off which threads are wound for weaving and for making lace? OED says it's a cylinder 'like a thinnish pencil'. Writing materials spring to mind when bobbins need explaining. Discourses proceeded by unwinding, like balls of yarn or thread being wound off the bottom or clew. Bishop Joseph Hall will, he says in in his *Peace Maker* of 1645, 'winde up this clew of our discourse'. We still talk of speakers and narrations ending by winding up.

Clews (or clues) became main words for narrative threads, threads of meaning, which readers and interpreters need to hold onto for understanding. 'With this clew, let us endeavour to unravel this character as here given' (Sterne, *Sermons of Mr Yorick* (1773), IX, 41). A *ravel* was a reel and the name for a separator device in mechanized weaving. *Ravelling* was when yarns got entangled, or came off the weaver's clue or reel; *unravelling* is disentangling yarns, threads. In detective stories, the unravelling of the mystery of the crime depends on the detective following the given clues – now thought of as single instructive items adding up to the big intelligent picture. Readers are supposed to follow those clues too. By the same sort of figurative token, *cottoning on*, is grasping something, catching on to the meaning, making sense of a discourse – an extension of the figurative *cotton to* (or *onto*), meaning to take to, be attracted to, get connected with, a person as if by a thread. And so it goes.

In other words, traditionally discourses, writings, stories became almost impossible to talk of unless as complexly involved in the procedures of work with fibres, unless imagined as if made out of thread, of yarn, as if put together by processes analogous to work with thread and yarn (spinning, sewing, suturing, knitting, weaving), as if existing like cloth – stuff, *Stoff*, material, *matériel*, fabric – i.e. as woven matter, webs, text, texture. Latin *textus*, meaning style, the formal nature of a literary work (as in, for example, Quintillian) carried its base meaning as woven thing, web, texture, very close to the surface. In medieval Latin *textus* meant, of course, the Gospel. In French, *texte* meant the Scriptures. And so also in English, text was pre-eminently used of the Bible, the Scriptural text. But it was also widely used, from the beginning of recorded English, as the highly suggestive word for, the essential figure of, any writing. So all writing could be thought of as web-like, made up of threads and lines and clues and warps and woofs, to be picked out, followed and siezed, held, unravelled, got to the bottom of. It comes exceedingly naturally to George Eliot in her *Middlemarch* (1871–2) to work the web or tissue metaphor for her novel, to present her novel's parts to us as woven together, and so acting as a reflection, not least, of her embrace of the social, of society, as a web, a social vision sustained by her interest in the physiology of Francois Bichat, 'the great Frenchman', as she tells us, who conceived of 'living bodies' as 'consisting of certain primary webs or tissues'. Bichat pointed the way, and now 'it was open to another mind to say, have not these structures some common basis from which they have all started, as your sarsnet, gauze, net, satin and velvet from the raw cocoon?' (*Middlemarch*, Ch.15). George Eliot's Dr Lydgate, ambitious anatomist, would like to find this 'primitive tissue'. He fails. One implication of *Middlemarch* is that George Eliot's novel is more successful at this job than Lydgate is. At any rate, inspecting the human and social tissue in a densely woven narrative tissue is what her novel will be about, and is what she thinks all serious fictions should be about. The novelist is a weaver of text. Weaving comes as naturally to storytellers as to weavers. Shakespeare's Bottom of course weaves words, makes little dramatic plots, speaks his lines. Making things as if with yarn, making stories in ways so yarn-like they become known *tout court* as *yarns*, comes as naturally to storytellers as to sailors.

Sailors were renowned for their ways with yarn, as for their peculiar ways with clews and warping (*clew* survived in that spelling into modern times as the technical term for the lower corner of a sail which is fastened to the arm of a mast; *warping* is preparing yarns for tarring for use on ships and boats, and the word for hauling ships on such ropes or *warps*). Far from home, from mothers and sisters and wives, sailors had perforce to darn their own clothes, knit their own socks. The Russian sailor whom Marlow meets in the Congo in *Heart of Darkness* is just such an expert with the needle, his clothes much mended, a riot of patches of all colours, blue, red, yellow, so that he looks like a harlequin (or a mobile map of the African continent occupied by the Imperial powers). The Russian's English book on seamanship that Marlow finds on the river bank 'had been lovingly stiched afresh with white cotton'. This is 'an extraordinary find', 'amazing', but not after we learn a sailor did the sewing. Sailors were, like this friend of Kurtz, like every Marlow, great men for working with yarn. No wonder their particular stories, their famously tall stories of far-fetched adventures, became known as yarns in the nineteenth century. To *spin a yarn* was at first, and is at bottom, nautical slang. The OED cites J. H. Vaux's *Flash Dictionary* (1812): '*Yarning or spinning of a yarn*, signifying to relate their various adventures, exploits, and escapes to each other'.

Spinning and yarning: these are, of course, the traditional functions of women. And trespassing in the domain of women, both literally and figuratively, is clearly part of what's wrong with the likes of that luridly bepatched Russian. But there's more to the unease surrounding the sailor's yarn work than this. Sailors' yarns are of their nature 'marvellous and incredible' (OED again). And this doubtfulness is, in fact, only a sharp example of a wide sense of something being up, going awry, tending to the negative, a sense of a doing that is also an undoing, its own undoing, which runs across this whole figurative spectrum. For weaving in its figurative senses keeps connoting dubious work. According to the OED, weaving is an elaborate fabricating and contriving. The load of ethical dubiety in that definition is clear. And the illustrations the Dictionary provides keep pointing to the darkness, the tricksiness, the wickedness and criminality even, of discourse as weaving. 'Your wise, but very darke speeches . . . are woven up in so intricate a maner, as I know not how to proportione mine answere unto them' (Sidney's *Arcadia*, 1598). 'You stole the money, and you have woven a plot to lay this sin at my door' (George Eliot's *Silas Marner*, 1861). 'In his writings, his weakness lay in his proneness . . . to weave endless allegories out of the Old Testament writings' (W. K. Fleming, *Mysticism Chronicled*, 1913). Bottom the weaver is actually a key figure in a great unweaving act – Shakespeare's turning the old tragic story of Pyramus and Thisbe into something silly and daft, the mechanicals' oafish destruction of any dramatic illusion and fictional force that their little drama might have ('"Deceiving me"' is Thisbe's cue: she is to enter now, and I am to spy her through the wall. You shall see, it will fall pat as I told you': *A Midsummer Night's Dream*, V.i.185ff). George Eliot weaves her webs, fictional and social, in order precisely to unweave them, to expose their connective tissue and threads, their warp and weft, as much as Bichat, the believer in bodily tissue, wants to cut it open, to anatomize it, and so, evidently, to dismember it into its constituent parts. Knowledge through pathology. And is it an accident, hereabouts, that to warp also means to twist and pervert and bias and misinterpret? 'O weaver, weaver, work no more', cries George Gascoigne in his *Posies*

(1575), 'thy warp hath done me wrong'. Warping can indeed do you wrong. And isn't it startling that to be effective in weaving, yarns must be *unwound* from their clues and bottoms? Or that *winding up* a discourse and *winding* it *down* seem to amount to the same thing? Or, for that matter, that *ravelling* and *unravelling* intersect so much in English language practice that eventually they cannot be distinguished and come to exist as interchangeable, as synonymous terms? It is indeed striking that so very many apparently good, or just neutral terms applied to working with literary thread turn, like weave and warp, into terms of censure, into definitions of formal deficiency. The very first figurative application that the OED gives for the noun *texture* as the process or art of weaving is dense with the disapprobatory. It's 'The fabricating, machinating, or composing of schemes, conspiracies, writings, etc.' As in Bishop Montagu's *Acts and Monuments* (1642): 'First they began their malicious texture with secret whisperings, and giving out in corners'. Suture, an unpejorative synonym for sewing, comes to be specialized as the term for sewing up the lips of a wound, and this surgical practice is almost certainly what nobody would want their compositional practice to be thought as comprising. Literary suturing is incompetence. 'Here and there . . . we detect the sutures [in the *Aeneid*], but how seldom', the Lord Coleridge was apparently relieved to note in 1883 (OED). The textual critics' latest idea of a sutured *Iliad* appalled the nineteenth century ('According to Fick, the present text of the Iliad . . . is sutured together out of the following pieces': *American Journal of Philology*, July 1886, 233). And what about *rhapsodes* and *rhapsodies* and the *rhapsodic*? A rhapsode is literally a stitched-together poem, from the Greek *rhapsein*, to sew. *Rhapsody* was a name for epics, or sections of epics, poems made of bits. Reciters of epics were named *rhapsodists* – oral bards stiching together narrative bits as they went along. And the feeling of disconnection, of confused medley, of roughly sutured portions of text was, clearly, never far away. Rhapsody came to mean enthusiastic utterance, discourses which inspired speakers were not altogether in control of. 'This rhapsodical work' is how Laurence Sterne's Yorick early on describes his highly disjunctive, patched-together text (*Tristram, Shandy*, 1760–7, Bk I, Ch.13). And he doesn't just mean elated and enthusiastic; he means a kind of broken text whose surgical stitches show. It's by no means a compliment or something to boast about.

Rhapso, after whom rhapsody is named, was a birth goddess, worshipped at Athens. Her name means 'the Stitcher'. A kind of Fate, she somehow organized your thread of life at birth by some sort of sewing work — stitched you up, as it were. She hovers as a sort of tutelary deity to *Shandy*'s Dr Slop, the male-midwife who messed up Tristram Shandy's birth, and who presides over all this novel's presentation of maieutic difficulty, the problem of bringing novels, and the Novel, to birth. And like so many of the ancient fictional characters, or divine persons, who provide the yarning sequence of figures with basic meaning, Rhapso is a woman, and one who like all these female yarners has dubious connections and aspects which resolutely inflect the meanings of yarn-work right from the start.

It is most intriguing that the passage of the yarn-sequence from literal to figurative, and especially to figurative meanings for literary work, derive from ancient stories. The literary applications of yarn work arrive already, as it were, literatured. There is no figuring of yarn-work as story-making, and the rest, which precedes stories about yarning. And these are all stories of women.

Thread, sb II. 6. *fig*: 'Something figured as being spun or continuously drawn out like a thread. *a*. The continued course of life, represented in classical mythology as a thread which is spun and cut off by the Fates. *b*. In various applications: see quots.' Thus the OED, and the quotations feature verbosity, arguments, and so textualizingly on. '7. A thread in various mythological or legendary tales (esp. that of Theseus in the Cretan labyrinth) is mentioned as the means of finding the way through a labyrinth or maze: hence in many figurative applications: that which guides through a maze, perplexity, difficulty, or investigation: cf CLEW. Sb I.3. CLUE 2.' So *Clew*, sb. I.3: 'A ball of thread, which in various mythological or legendary narratives (esp. that of Theseus in the Cretan Labyrinth) is mentioned as the means of "threading" a way though a labyrinth or maze; hence, in many more or less figurative applications: that which guides though a maze, perplexity, difficulty, intricate investigation, etc.' '4. Used in reference to the thread of life, which the Fates are represented as spinning'. The great Dr Murray, who wrote the OED's C and T entries, evidently dislikes these origins – you can hear the distinguished puritan gritting his teeth over these pagan geneses ('mythological or legendary tales', 'Mythological or legendary narratives'). He can only bring himself to mention their femaleness when he absolutely has to – no feminist he – and of course then utterly dismissively. *Fate*, sb.2. 'Mythol. *a*. The goddess of fate or destiny; in Greek *Moira*. *b*. *pl*. In later Greek and Roman mythology, the three goddesses supposed to determine the course of human life. (Gr. *Moiras*, L. Parcae, Fata). In Gr. the three Fates are called Clotho, Lachesis, and Atropos; these names were adopted by Latin poets, but the mythologists give as native names Nona, Decuma, and Morta.' The *supposed* goddesses will have their namings resolutely unsettled. But for all Murray's distaste there's no denying these legendary females their originating way with yarn, and the degree to which their proceedings with it are truly unsettling for the figurings they incite.

From mythological start to poetic finish, yarn work is women's work.[1] In English literature, from Chaucer on, working with the distaff was the very type of women's labour. The distaff was the sign of the female sex, and (where this occurred) the name for female domination. The female line in a family was known as the *distaff*- or *spindle-side*: as opposed to the male, the spear-side. A *distaff* was a daughter or female heir. *St Distaff's Day* was the day after Epiphany, 7 January, the end of the Christmas holiday, when the women resumed their domestic chores. *The Distaff* is, of course, the ancient Greek Sapphic poem by the fourth century BC woman poet Erinna, composed in memory of her late friend Baucis, about their their girlish friendship and their shared 'spinsterhood' (as *The Oxford Classical Dictionary* puts it (1970, 406)). (Erinna herself died at the age of 19; Swinburne has the lesbian Anactoria invoke her in his 1866 poem *Anactoria*.) *Spinsters* were people who made a living by spinning, and were rarely male. In the seventeenth century spinster became the legal term for an unmarried woman (only later did it connote 'old maid', a woman nobody wanted to marry). Tennyson's Lady of Shallott weaves, while Sir Lancelot goes about in the public world on his knightly horse; they're both doing the traditional business of their genders; when she quits her loom, she dies. Just so, Virginia Woolf's Rezia Warren Smith in *Mrs Dalloway* (1926) is a milliner by trade, who sews hats while her ex-soldier husband endures his nightmares of the Great War, and Mrs Ramsay in *To the Lighthouse* (1927) knits a pair of socks while her philosopher husband charges around outside reciting Tennyson's 'The Charge of the Light Brigade' and trying to do philosophy.

Sometimes spiders were known as spinsters, on account of spinning webs all the time. Spiders are *arachnoids*, named after the Greek word for spider, *arachne*. Arachne was a woman from Lydia (in Ovid's *Metamorphoses* VI), so skilled in weaving she actually rivalled Athena, the great goddess who patronized all the crafts, especially the crafts of women, and in particular weaving. When Athena visited Arachne to warn her off, she had the nerve to challenge the goddess to a weaving competition to see which was the better at it. Annoyed, Athena destroyed the text, the woven work of Arachne. Arachne hanged herself in despair, upon which Athena turned her into a spider, the mother of all spinsters, whence the spider gets her name. Clearly these original spinning and weaving women are not be trusted. The Fates were, indeed, fateful – spinning out the yarn or thread or line of your life, but cutting it off abruptly and arbitrarily: the blind Atropos being the one who wielded the shears. In the ancient Biblical story (*Judges* xvi) the Philistine Dalilah tries to dispempower the Israelite champion Samson by weaving his long hair into the web she's working at on her loom. Human yarn: it's as awful as a Nazi lampshade made of human skin. 'My accomplish'd snare', Milton's Samson called her: a clever and successful entrapper of a man (*Samson Agonistes* (1671), 230). And in the most extended ancient story of a weaver, the *Odyssey*'s story of Odysseus's faithful wife Penelope, the stress is all on the necessity of female treachery, on the wily shrewdness of the weaver, and the large possibilities for duplicity inherent in the very nature of weaving, of working with the woven.

In the *Odyssey* you only survive if you possess shrewdness, wiliness, cunning, *metis* in Greek. Penelope has lots of it. She's coached in it by Athena, the mistress of artfulness, as is her husband Odysseus. Penelope's *metis* is expressed precisely in her most cunning way with women's chief occupation in these ancient tales, namely her ways with yarn. Beset by unwanted suitors, Penelope tells them she will yield to their advances only when she has finished weaving a shroud for her old father Laertes. A pious story, in aid of a wife's faithfulness. But every night for three years she unweaves what she's woven during the day. Her delaying tactic is only found out when her maids betray her – the deceptive woman betrayed by women. Clearly, albeit in a good cause, the woman with the threads, the yarns in her hands, the contriver of webs, the maker of text, is not to be trusted to be performing what she appears to be doing; and neither are the women around her, the females who share the knowledge of yarning and are privy to the secret of this dubious work, the capacity for deception inherent in weaving.

'I spin out my wiles', Penelope tells the disguised Odysseus, in the wonderful confession scene in *Odyssey*, Book XIX (in Robert Fagles's translation (1996, I.152, 394)). She 'winds up balls of tricks', as John Winkler has it, observing that Penelope uses the word for winding yarn (*dolous tolupeuo*) (Winkler, 1990, 156). And the trick of this winding is that it's an unwinding. This weaving is also an unweaving. Penelope *unravels* by night (Fagles's word in his translation, I. 169) what she's ravelled by day. The daytime ravelling is only for night-time unravelling. The good cause – staying faithful to Odysseus – depends for its ethicity on involving bad actions, namely lying, deceiving, cheating, breaking faith with the suitors. And the tricky yarning, the weaving/unweaving of the shroud, involves deceptive yarning in the nautical sense. As the Fates sing while they spin and cut your thread of life, so Penelope the weaver is also a storyteller. The weaving that's also an unweaving involves a tall story, a yarn, about that doing/ undoing. The yarn-as-story is as little to be trusted as the yarn-as-weaving. Fagles's translation nicely brings out the parallelism, the interaction.

A god from the blue it was inspired me first
to set up a great loom in our royal halls
and I began to weave, and the weaving fine spun,

the yarns endless, and I would lead them on:
'Young men,
my suitors, now that King Odysseus is no more,
go slowly, keen as you are to marry me, until
I can finish off this web . . .
so my weaving won't all fray and come to
nothing.'

. . .

My very words,
and despite their pride and passion they believed
me.
So by day I'd weave at my great and growing
web –
by night, by the light of torches set beside me
I would unravel all I'd done.

All of which casts a shadow over, as it is shadowed by, the equally entrancing, and equally genetic, story of Ariadne and her clew. Ariadne was the daughter of Minos, King of Crete, and of Pasiphae, and so she was the half-sister of the Minotaur, Pasiphae's prodigious son, fathered by a bull, a freakish man with the head of a bull, who was shut away in the labyrinth constructed by Minos's engineer Daedalus. In the labyrinth the Minotaur was fed the annual tribute of seven Athenian boys and girls exacted by Minos from his enemies. When Theseus arrived as one of the tribute group, with the aim of killing the Minotaur, Ariadne fell in love with him, and gave him a clew, a bottom, a bobbin, a rolled-up ball of yarn, to help her beloved escape the labyrinth once he'd killed her brother. The idea was Daedalus's, apparently. Theseus fastened the end of the yarn at the entrance to the maze, unwound the clew as he went in, found the Minotaur, killed him, then found his way out by winding up the rolled-out yarn. Ariadne then eloped with Theseus – only to be abandoned by him on the island of

Naxos (though not for long: Dionysos soon arrived with his riotous entourage of satyrs and maenads, married Ariadne, and made her immortal).

Here, once more, evidently, is a story of a woman with yarn that's a dramatically complex interweaving of good and bad, of positive and negative. A daughter falls in love with the Athenian enemy, betrays her father, and helps her brother, admittedly her monstrous brother, to his death. The tool of these betrayals is the thread, the yarn, the line which deceives. This line leads to a blessing for some – no more boys and girls of Athens will be sacrificed to the Minotaur – but to a mixed blessing for others. Daedalus and his son Icarus got shut into the labyrinth for his advice to Ariadne. Ariadne was soon betrayed herself. The wisdom, the power, of clews led directly to Daedalus being shut away with nary a clew – until his relentless ingenuity got him making wings from feathers and wax, and he and Icarus flew out of the maze. Except that Icarus flew too close to the sun, and the wax melted, and he fell to his death – another case of the father's ingenuity going too far for his own comfort. The solution of one problem, wrought by following the clew, only led to other problems, for which there were no clews, or only disastrous ones. With the bottom of yarn ('He received from her [Ariadne] a bottome of thred': Walter Raleigh, *A History of the World*, 1614), Theseus gets to the bottom of the maze, the bottom of the affair; but there was no getting to the bottom of all his problems. Being unamazed, as it were, getting out of one maze, with the help of a clew, only led to a future of more amazements, further amazings. There would always be another maze. Which all suggests some sort of outworking of the dense intrinsic ambivalence of the spinning or reeling out of yarns: the winding of your way securely along, but only by an act of unwinding; finding your way only by winding up, in an act of unthreading, unweaving, an unravelling of

thread which is consummated, made meaningful, only by ravelling it all up again; a journey-out whose consummation is to end with your clew all wound up again, as if it had gone nowhere, with it once more as a mere spooled line of thread, its job to be done all over again, its potential once again unrealized, its positive winding out, that essence of the weaving act, to be repeated yet once more.

No wonder clues get so readily thought of as having a certain potential for clue-less-ness. 'Having lost the clue which led us in, / We wandered in the Labyrinth of Lust', (Michael Drayton's *Piers Gaveston* (1593), 153: OED). Milton's devils, arguing in Hell about predestination and so forth, 'found no end / In wandering mazes lost'. Like Calvinist theologians, they think they hold the right clues, but they are wrong. Clues can mislead even as they appear to lead. It's one of the upshots of the curious tale of Ariadne. No wonder modernist fictions of epistemic (and moral) doubting and of hermeneutic resistance and refusal cast their sceptical play in terms of the misleading nature of clues, and of the labyrinthine as an insuperable obstacle. Maisie, the puzzlingly knowing child of Henry James's novel *What Maisie Knew* (1897) – and 'still', even at the end of a very long novel, there's 'room for wonder at what Maisie knew' – is evidently so named to clue us in to her (and our) ending up still stuck in a hermeneutic maze of the fiction's deliberate contriving. *Amazing* is a repeated word for the failure of Marlow and his narration to get to the bottom of colonized Africa. Young Stephen Dedalus in *A Portrait of the Artist as a Young Man* (1916), a youth named for Daedalus the would-be master of the labyrinth, wanders Dublin in moral distress 'like some baffled prowling beast'. The hero is now the monster, not the monster-slayer. He refuses Catholic orthodoxy's moral solutions, accepts damnation in the city's brothel quarter, in its 'maze of narrow and dirty streets'. He doesn't even want to escape the moral maze. Not dissimilarly, modernist fiction carefully contrives it that its detectives will follow ostensible clues not to solutions of crimes, but to an entanglement in transgression – even to the extreme, but exemplary, extent of Alain Robbe-Grillet's detective Wallas in *Les Gommes* (1953) being finally revealed as the perpetrator of the murder he's apparently been investigating.

And so on – all these modernist occasions so many labyrinth-absorbed footnotes to the story of Ariadne's ball of yarn, her clew. And it might indeed be said that the modernist praxis of making texts which are actually meant for deception, texts which have misleading threads and lines, which tantalize the reader with clues that mislead, and also the whole (post)modernist and deconstructionist sense that all linguistic, all textual making, are fabrics of fabrication, all an undoing and an unmaking – it might be said that all these are footnotes to, and commentaries on the old repertoire of yarn stories. Just as the whole disturbing history of the yarn-word set can be thought of as the constant exemplification and updating of those very dismays.

Take Molly Bloom, the most potent modern heir of and commentary on Homer's Penelope, in Joyce's *Ulysses*, which is of course the most extended, most powerful commentary on the *Odyssey* at large. She's an extraordinary spinner of lines, of threads, of words. Her lines are (I think) the longest anywhere in literature. Molly's yarning is now only the spinning of lines of words and the weaving of words into narrative texture. The figurative meanings of yarn-work are now the only ones. Narrating is what Molly does. Her labour is only literary. She holds no bottom of actual yarn in her hand, but bottoms are what she talks much of – most entrancingly her own bottom, the one in her lovers' hands. Joyce wrote to Frank Budgen that the 'Penelope' episode, the last in the novel, was 'the clou of the book', and then went on to celebrate Molly's eight very

long narrative threads (the first of them, he boasted, 2,500 words long), and to say that the text of 'Penelope' was a spinning: 'like the huge earth ball slowly surely and evenly round and round spinning, its four cardinal points being the female breasts, arse, womb and cunt expressed by the words *because*, *bottom* (in all senses bottom button, bottom of the class, bottom of his heart), *woman*, *yes*' (Joyce, 1975, 285; 16.viii.1921). And it doesn't seem far-fetched to hear *clew* pressing in homophonically upon *clou* (= French, *nail*), nor to think of all those mentioned bottoms as not accidentally proximate to the spinning which Joyce is celebrating, bottom-conscious Molly being such a wonderful weaver and all. And of course Molly Bloom, this spinner of such immense lines of narrative thread, is Penelope only as deceptive wife. She's the weaver who doesn't at all resist a suitor in the absence of her husband. Her immense yarns are woven not as a method of faithful sexual resistance but as a text of confessed exuberant sexual transgressing. This Penelope is built on the utterly negative aspects of the female spinning and weaving business. This Penelope weaves only to deceive.

The modernist way with yarns certainly emphasizes the negativity within its figurative and narrative inheritance. For his part, Henry James has Ariadne in mind as a model for someone who offers help in threading through the labyrinths of his novels. He calls the female character who is supposed to help the reader make sense of a narrative the *ficelle*. Maria Gostrey in *The Ambassadors* (1903) is a *ficelle*, so is Henrietta Stackpole of *Portrait of a Lady* (1881).[2] *Ficelle* is yarn in French, thread, cord, string; it's what comes wound on clews, bottoms, bobbins. These jamesian women offered as an Ariadnean gift, present to the reader from James in his assumed role as Ariadne – the *ficelle* is 'the reader's friend', and so is James-Ariadne. Hang onto these *ficelles*, James suggests, and the labyrinth of his plottings will become less perplexing, less amazing, than it might seem ('don't break the thread', James urged his friend Millicent Duchess of Sutherland, 'Keep along with it step by step – and then the full charm will come out' [23.xii.1903; 1984, 302]). But James knew full well what dubieties were implied by *ficelle* in French. *Ficelles* were no innocent balls of yarn. *Une ficelle* is also a trick done on stage, a performed deception, a crime even; it's a trickster, a deceiver, a kind of criminal. *Il connaît toutes les ficelles*: he's up to every dodge. *Il connaît toutes les ficelles du mètier*: he knows all the tricks of the trade. No wonder James was smiling as he talked of *ficelles*. They were part of his authorial 'fun', he said; they involved him in 'delight' and 'ecstacies'. These were 'ecstacies of method', a method which was a practice of high reader deception: 'Ecstacies of dissimulation'. That Maria Gostrey, or anybody else, might specially help you make sense of *The Ambassadors* is a kind of joke. She's the *ficelle* who leads you next to nowhere – rather like this suggestion about the female *ficelle*. It's just a critical yarn, a critical tall story, Ariadne-James pretending to help, but mis-cluing us.[3]

James's critical clew is a clue too far, a yarning going further in overt deception than the original yarn-narrative, the Ariadne story, that is sponsoring it. Which is not unlike Conrad's Marlow and his way with the yarns of seamen. Those normal seamanly yarns *tend* to deceive. They are *rather* unreliable narrations. Marlow, the neo-seaman-yarner, is *utterly* unreliable. This sailor taking over yarning-work from women is less reliable about it than his womanly exemplars. It's only symptomatic of this that Marlow leaves behind him in Brussels the two women who guard the exploration company's offices, sitting at 'the door of Darkness', knitting black wool, updated Fates – 'uncanny and fateful' – 'knitting black wool as for a warm pall'. They're a pair of more sinister Penelopes (the pall she wove was, presumably, linen and white). Africa involves, then, darker yarnings in every sense, political, moral, epistemological. There'll be, as that first narrator tells us, no simple cracking open of this nut, no positive following here of clews or clues. This will be 'one of Marlow's inconclusive experiences', a tale enveloped in a ghostly haze, 'in the likeness of one of those misty halos that sometimes are made visible by the spectral ilumination of moonshine'. *Moonshine*: illusion without substance, foolish talk; originally 'moonshine in the water', says the OED: something seamen knew all about. (But was there lurking in Conrad's ear a memory of weaver Bottom's crew, giving fictional moonlight a Brechtian unravelling in *A Midsummer Night's Dream*? 'This lanthorn doth the horned moon present'. 'Well shone, Moon', says Hippolyta, sarcastically.)

It's almost in the light of all this modernist unthreading, one feels, that Sigmund Freud should figure a child's play with a bobbin and a bit of yarn as an emblem of all art as a ritual which curiously mixes presence and absence, loss and gain, meaning and unmeaning, pleasure and pain. Freud's reading in *Jenseits des Lustprinzip* (1920) – *Beyond the Pleasure Principle* (1922) – of his daughter's boy's repeated throwing of his bobbin on its thread over the side of his cot with a cry of 'Fort' (away, gone) and then pulling it back with an 'o-o-o-o' (heard as 'da' – there, back again), has rightly magnetized not only psychology but also literary criticism, especially reading in deconstructive mode. The boy is obviously being taken as a dinky version of Theseus. He's a Theseus revised – he throws the bobbin and holds onto the thread, rather than holding the bobbin and unreeling a fixed thread, like his great predecessor – but what we have are the basic ingredients of ravelling and unravelling, spooling out a line and pulling it back again. And it was all taken as a model of aesthetic enactments of pleasurable pain, the enjoyable suffering and negativity of fiction, tragedy and the like. Mother and grandad joined in thinking the boy was miming his mother's departure from the room, or his father's absence in the Great War. The pains of absence were thought to be what this representative of art's yarn-work was weaving. Freud's analysis is, of course, itself a bit of a yarn. He confesses ample doubt in *Jenseits* about his readings, but even so his hearing *da* in *o-o-o-o* is surely far-fetched, even if well-intentioned. More certain is that *o-o-o-o,* the cry of the bobbin's return, signifies more negativity than even Freud is allowing. Here's an utter absence. What's here at the end of yarn-bobbin play is a text of mere noughts and naughting, a case of a weave utterly unwoven, a text utterly in holes, in tatters: not unlike the modern Shakespeare reduced to holes in T. S. Eliot's 'The Waste Land' in 1921, just a year after the *Jenseits* – 'O O O O that Shakespeherian Rag'.

Here is the modernist logic of yarning in full swing (that Rag was an actual one, as Terence Hawkes discovered; 1986). It's a sense of frustrated bobbin work eagerly siezed on by Jacques Lacan in his *The Four Fundamental Concepts of Psychoanalysis* – a key (post)modernist place for the reception and boosting of the yarn meanings suggested in Freud's the story of the Fort-da boy. 'The function of the exercise with this object [the bobbin now recycled as Lacan's *objet a*] refers to an alienation, and not to some mastery, which is difficult to imagine being increased in an endless repetition, whereas the endless repetition that is in question reveals the radical vacillation of the subject' (Lacan, 1986, 61–4). Radical vacillation: it's a sharp description utterly fitting Marlow's yarning mode. And one spelled out, expanded, stamped, signed and sealed for deconstruction with Jaques Derrida's enormous bravura wit and gusto in his *La Carte postale de Socrate à Freud et au-delà* (1980). In this extended, and mightily strong reading, the Fort-da boy's way with yarn and bobbin (*bobine* in French),

his thread shuttling back and forth on its bobbin over the threshold of his curtained cot-side is made to scoop in a whole linguistic and fictional era – the entire era of linguisticity marked by the yarning configuration, which is to say the whole era of linguisticity – and in doing so it brings the meanings of all that figuring right up to date, in classic deconstructive terms. The cot-side, the threshold place of these figurations, a place, of course, where Derrida's great lexicon of textual, woven things accumulates zestfully (the curtain stands for all the 'rideaux, toiles, voiles, ecrans' of Derrida's repeated preoccupation), is the site where many modern communications are thought of as being figured. The unreeled, unspooled thread, the yarn off the bobbin, is not only a telephone line, but also the communication link made by the mails, especially postcards. In keeping with the whole logic of clew-type difficulty, the analysis makes a grand climacteric for now to the extended sense that winding and ravelling always tend to get truly confused with unwinding and unravelling ('Change place, and handy-dandy', as King Lear puts it (IV.vi.157), which is which?). Startlingly, the yarn-play is held to be working back to front. The telephone call, the postcard, now travel in reverse, arsy-versy. Derrida is cannily, or uncannily, inspired by a postcard picturing a medieval Bodleian Library manuscript in which a man sits writing, instructed by another man behind him. They are Plato and Socrates, but they've been labelled by an unknown hand the wrong way round, so that the scribe is called Socrates and the adviser Plato. So if they communicated by phone or postcard it would be Socrates ringing up Plato, Socrates dropping Plato a line, not the historical way about. (It would lead, this notion of phoning and writing from the past to Derrida's notions about writings communicating telepathically with future readers.) Of course the interpretative load being placed on this scene of suggested textual reversing is vast, but it is in fact only the putting of a capstone on the widely felt logics of yarning. Much (all?) modern textualizing is swept in – not just phones and postcards, but also film. *Bobine* in French means film (just as films in English come on *spools* and *reels*: 'the reel world, the reel world, the reel world', as *Finnegans Wake* has it (64: 24), that great fictional texture woven by the writer who sponsored Dublin's first cinema). And all this spinning and weaving and bobbin work are, in the now customary (post)modern way, leading nowhere. Attractively, the 'Socrates' of the Bodley postcard has a large condom-like hat on – condom, *preservatif* in French, preservative, closely related in French to phylactery, the little box in which orthodox Jewish men hide portions of Scripture texts – a keen model for Derrida of words going nowhere, end-stopped, like letters and postcards ending up in dead-letter rooms at post-offices. Happily also, but still only along lines indicated by the old yarn stories, *bobines* in French are also mugshots, police photos, taken in police stations, which are even more happily *postes de police* in French. *La littérature epistolaire* is also, then, *la littérature policière*, and by no means, in Derrida's leftist French view of *les flics*, benign police work, but oppressive policing, the work of crooked cops, of criminal criminal-inspectors. All of which might seem a longish step from the bad-girl meanings surrounding the Fates and Rhapso, Ariadne, Athena and Penelope, but it's only a short one from Robbe-Grillet's Wallas, and from Marlow the narrator as failing detective, the mis-cluer, 'brother seaman' to the Russian clothes-patcher, and the narrator with whom evil Kurtz's 'secret' is 'safe'. It's an interpretative march – brilliant, gaudy, over-charged even – with which the whole apprehension of yarn-work in the tradition, and the whole activity of text-making as yarning, is utterly in step.[4]

By no means all of the keen deconstructors who've siezed on the meanings of yarn, from Ariadne's thread to Marlow's sea-manly moonshine, as illustrations of the tricksy ways of language and text, follow the interpretative threads with Derrida's panache – he really is untrumpable in these matters. As J. Hillis Miller, for instance, who has kept on returning to the yarn of Ariadne. 'Ariadne's thread, then, is another *mise en abyme* . . . [It] makes the labyrinth, is the labyrinth. The interpretation or solving of the puzzles of the textual web only adds more filaments to the web. One can never escape from the labyrinth because the activity of escaping makes more labyrinth, the thread of a linear narrative or story. Criticism is the production of more thread to embroider the texture or textile already there. This thread is like the filament of ink which flows from the pen of the writer, keeping him in the web, suspending him also over the chasm, the blank page that thin line holds' (Miller, 1991, 122–3). Which is not quite well said. This keen embroidering of the yarn story with a critical yarn about embroidering seems a mite over-rich, and how a critical yarner can both be in a web and also supended over a chasm takes a bit of envisaging, and even the blankest of pages are not *chasms*. 'The textuality of a text, a "yarn"' spun by Conrad, is the meshing of its filaments as they are interwoven in ways hidden from an objectifying eye. The critic must enter into the text, follow its threads as they weave in and out, appearing and disappearing, crisscrossing with other threads. In doing this he adds his own thread of interpretation to the fabric, or he cuts it one way or another, so becoming part of its texture or changing it' (Miller, 1982, 23). Again, more disfiguring figuring. If the text's warp and weft are hidden from your eye, they can't be 'followed'. (Some of these contradictory sentences read like rather rough suturings which need more revising.) And in practice new weavers don't usually come along and weave further threads into a given fabric. And what does cutting a thread 'one way or another' mean? You can only cut a thread one way (and if this critic means that critics cut the fabric itself, he should say so). But still, such readings are exemplary in indicating how much what deconstruction stands for is, precisely, the unravelling of the ravelled logics of writing conceived as yarning. And, as in the case of the over-eager Freud, the interpreter's sense of where the thread of interpretation is leading is always pointing him in the right direction. And, after all, as all yarning – yarning as the real and yarning as figuration – indicates, there's never any weaving, ever, without a necessary warping.

Notes

1. See extended discussion of weaving and women in the ancient world in Winkler (1990, 129ff., 188ff.).
2. See James (1987, 544ff.); and his Preface to the New York edition of *The Ambassadors* (1986, 361ff.).
3. For fuller discussion of *ficelles* and James, see Cunningham (1994, 272–4, 279–83).
4. See Derrida (1980, *passim*), Cunningham (1994, 268–72) and Ulmer (1985, 125–53).

Works cited

Conrad, Joseph. *Heart of Darkness*, ed. and int. Robert Hampson. London, 1995.

Cunningham, Valentine. *In the Reading Gaol: Postmodernity, Texts, and History*. Oxford, 1994.

Derrida, Jacques. *La Carte postale de Socrate à Freud et au-delà*. Paris, 1980.

Hawkes, Terence. *That Shakespearian Rag*. London, 1986.

Homer. *The Odyssey*, trans. Robert Fagles, intro. Bernard Knox. New York, 1996.

James, Henry. *Letters, 1896–1916*, Vol. 4, ed. Leon Edel. Cambridge, MA, 1984.

James, Henry. Project of *The Ambassadors* (1 September 1900), in *The Complete Notebooks of Henry James*, eds Leon Edell and Lyall H. Powers. New York, 1987.

James, Henry. *The Art of Criticism: Henry James on the Theory and Practice of Fiction*, eds William Veeder and Susan M. Griffin. Chicago, IL, 1986.

Joyce, James. *Selected Letters of James Joyce*, ed. Richard Ellmann. New York, 1975.

Lacan, Jacques. *The Four Fundamental Concepts of Psychoanalysis*, trans. Alan Sheridan. Harmondsworth, 1986.

Miller, J. Hillis. *Fiction and Repetition: Seven English Novels*. Oxford, 1982.

Miller, J. Hillis. *Theory Now and Then*. New York, 1991.

The Oxford Classical Dictionary, eds N. G. L. Hammond and H. H. Scullard. Oxford, 1970.

Ulmer, Gregory L. *Applied Grammatology: Post(e)-Pedagogy from Jacques Derrida to Jospeh Beuys*. Baltimore, MD, 1985.

Winkler, John J. *The Constraints of Desire: The Anthropology of Sex and Gender in Ancient Greece*. New York, 1990.

zero | *J. HILLIS MILLER*

With zero, we come to the end of the alphabetical line. We reach rock bottom. Or rather we plunge into the bottomless pit, or perhaps into an unfathomable ocean, such as that place, 'l'espace littéraire', the place where everything turns into image. Maurice Blanchot says the song of the Sirens leads us to that place, a zero point where all song vanishes: 'What was that place? It was a place where the only thing left was to disappear, because in this region of source and origin, music itself had disappeared more completely than in any other place in the world; it was like a sea into which the living would sink with their ears closed and where the Sirens, too, even they, as proof of their good will, would one day have to disappear' (Blanchot, 105).

Zero, it appears, is nothing, nil, nought, néant, nicht, nada, zilch, zip. 'Zip' was the name of the first month in the Mayan calendar. It began, like all the Mayan months, with a zero day. Zero might be illustrated by the heart monitor screen with a long straight line, no more reassuring rhythmic blips. The OED gives a 'reassuringly' definite series of meanings for 'zero' as a noun, adjective, or verb. The word, says the OED, comes by way of Middle Latin 'zephirum' from the Arabic 'sifr', which also gives the English word 'cipher' (OED). *The Concise Oxford Dictionary* gives a different lineage, 'from French 'zéro' or Italian 'zero', via Old Spanish from Arabic 'sifr' cipher'. That would suggest that the Arab mathematicians were located in Spain, which some of them were. Why do those Oxford etymologists disagree with one another?

The connection of 'zero' with 'cipher' seems a little odd, if you think about it, since 'cipher' means not only 'the arithmetical symbol (0) denoting no amount but used to occupy a vacant place in decimal etc. numeration (as in 12.05)'. but also 'any Arabic numeral' (*The Concise Oxford Dictionary*). 'To cipher' or 'to cipher out' means to make an arithmetical calculation. A cipher is a placeholder in a vacant place, but it is also any number from one to infinity. How did that equivocation come to be?

The cipher as zero plays havoc with meaning, even with arithmetical meaning. Zero times any number is zero. Any number divided by zero is infinity, whatever *that* is! Infinity is zero's twin, generated as if by magic as soon as you make calculations involving zero. Any number added to infinity becomes a kind of zero, since it does not make the infinity larger. Infinity plus 1 equals infinity plus 1,000 or plus 1,000,000, that is, still the same old infinity, though mathematicians, it is true, posit different infinities. Infinity cannot be augmented, though it may be reached by different routes, and though the great mathematician Georg Cantor, inventor of set theory, hypothesized an infinite number of infinities nested within one another like Russian dolls. 'In Cantor's mind', says Charles Seife, 'there were an infinite number of infinities — the transfinite numbers — each nested in the other. $Aleph_0$ is smaller than $Aleph_1$, which is smaller than $Aleph_2$, which is smaller than $Aleph_3$, and so forth. At the top of the chain sits the ultimate infinity that engulfs all other infinities: God, the infinity that defies all comprehension' (Seife, 2000, 152). Cantor used the Hebrew letter for Aleph, the first letter of the Hebrew alphabet, to name his sets. This was because the Kabballah uses Aleph as a shorthand for Ein Sof, the Kabbalistic name for infinity, which begins in Hebrew with aleph (Aczel, 2000, 44). Aleph is at the other end of the alphabet from Z for zero, just as infinity is zero's inverse mirror image, arising magically, as I have said, as soon as one begins to do computations involving zero. Or one might think, as Pascal did, of two infinities. These would be the horizon at zero of the infinitesimally small, and the horizon, in the other direction, of the infinitely large. The infinitely large is that point infinitely far off, for example, where the tangent curve finally touches its asymptote, only to reappear again at minus infinity on the other side of the asymptote and at the bottom instead of the top of the figure made by the crossing coordinate lines. The notion that at infinity the plus reverses into a minus has always fascinated me. What does that mean, 'minus infinity'?

The zero, like the cipher, like infinity, seems to be a place of slippage, where things become somehow a little irrational or mind-boggling. Both George Cantor and Kurt Gödel, two very great mathematicians, were driven mad by too much earnest thinking about infinity, trying to master it by logical means. One might say that advances in mathematics and logic are made by those who can best and longest stand thinking about zero and infinity before they go mad. I have, for example, encountered three different, contradictory but each apodictically asserted accounts of the historical origin of zero. Brian Rotman, in *Signifying Nothing: The Semiotics of Zero*, (1993), asserts that zero was invented or discovered by Hindu mathematicians and then imported into Europe via Arab mathematicians. He calls our number system Hindu numbers rather than Arabic numbers. Charles Seife, in *Zero: The Biography of a Dangerous Idea*, no less solemnly assures his readers that zero was a Babylonian invention. Thanks to the Babylonian

style of counting, he says, 'zero finally appeared in the East, in the Fertile Crescent of present-day Iraq' (Seife, 2000, 13). Hindu mathematicians, according to Seife, first heard of zero when 'in the fourth century BC Alexander the Great marched with his Persian troops from Babylon to India. It was through this invasion that Indian mathematicians first learned about the Babylonian system of numbers – and about zero' (Seife, 2000, 63). A learned scientist of my acquaintance, however, assured me that Arabic mathematicians invented or discovered zero, in Spain around 800 AD. The zero was found independently, according to him, within the next couple of centuries by the Mayans and then by Indian mathematicians. He said nothing at all about the Babylonian zero. Which of these authorities is right? They cannot all be right. Even the origin of zero as a humanly manipulable sign seems to be irrational, murky, contradictory, like a proposition that derives from a system but can neither be proved true nor proved false, a Gödelian undecidable. The origin of the zero seems to fade off into the infinite distance, at some converging point beyond or before Mayans, Arabs, Babylonians, Hindus.

My learned acquaintance also assured me, mistakenly, that no Chinese character for zero exists. The character is *ling*. Zero was probably brought to China centuries ago by traders from India. Greek, and then Roman, mathematicians did not have the name or, presumably, the concept of zero, though of course Euclidean geometry, for example, has what look to a modern eye like zero points, as in the point at the centre of a circle from which the radius is measured. The Euclidean point, however, is defined as the place where lines intersect or meet, not as a zero point, for example, in a set of coordinates. All my authorities agree that the introduction of zero into the West in the thirteenth century, along with the gradual introduction of Hindu or Arabic numbering and its arithmetical computations to replace Roman numerals and the abacus, was controversial and strenuously resisted. Not only was the zero a foreign import. The notion of the void was also deemed diabolical by Christian theologians. 'Nothing comes of nothing', as King Lear says. Greek or Christian philosophers on the whole resisted the idea that 'nothing' could have any positive existence, as zero makes it seem to do.

Rotman identifies a fundamental equivocation in the notion of zero. On the one hand, it is a number, the first number in a line that goes from zero to one to two to three, and so on. On the other hand, zero is a placeholder, an indication that some number (any number) is missing. In the latter case, zero is not a number but a metanumber, a number about number, or rather about the absence of number, any number, not any one number in particular. 'It is this double aspect of zero', says Rotman, 'as a sign inside the number system and as a meta-sign, a sign-about-signs outside it, that has allowed zero to serve as the site of an ambiguity between the empty character (whose covert mysterious quality survives in the connection between "cyphers" and secret codes), and a character for emptiness, a symbol that signifies nothing' (Rotman, 1993, 13).

My equivocation between 'invention' and 'discovery' of the zero is not fortuitous. It indicates yet another puzzle or aporia in thinking about zero, along with the impossibility of discovering its origin, and the impossibility of deciding whether it is a number or not a number. To say zero was invented suggests that it did not exist at all before someone thought of it. The sign zero makes the concept zero. To say the zero was discovered suggests that it was there all along as a latent mathematical possibility, waiting to be thought, 'invented' in the old sense of 'inventio', meaning 'discovery'. Though I, like Brian Rotman, lean to the first (invention in the modern sense), it is impossible to decide between these two possibilities. The results would be the same in both cases. Nevertheless, it makes a lot of difference which way you think of the zero. Once you invent zero it seems to have been there all along, waiting to be discovered.

The consequences for modern mathematics and science of the invention or discovery of zero were enormous, since the zero made possible algebra (another Arabic word, from 'aljabr', 'the reunion of broken parts'), and, eventually, infinitesimal calculus, then finally, more recently, set theory. The zero, it may be, makes possible the reunion of broken parts, but also, as I shall show, it makes that reunion forever impossible. The introduction of zero brings about a breaking up beyond possibility of reunion, like that great egg, Humpty Dumpty, after his great fall. 'Love', in tennis scoring, after all, comes from French 'l'oeuf', egg, meaning zero. Could it be that love and zero have something in common?

Just what are those 'reassuringly' definite definitions in the OED? According to the OED, a zero is 'The arithmetical figure 0 which denotes "nought"'; 'The compartment numbered 0 on a roulette table'; 'The point or line marked 0 on a graduated scale, from which reckoning begins: esp. in a thermometer or other measuring instrument'; 'The temperature corresponding to the zero of a thermometer'; 'Nought or nothing reckoned as a number denoted by the figure 0, and constituting the starting-point of the series of natural numbers; the total absence of quantity considered as a quantity (in *Alg.* and *Higher Math.* As intermediate between positive and negative numbers); hence as expressing the amount of something = "none at all"'; 'In the theory of functions, A value of a variable for which a function vanishes' [I suppose this is akin to those algebraic equations which are solved by finding numbers for the x's and y's that make the function equal zero (JHM)]; 'In grammar, the absence of an overt mark, written or spoken, as against its presence in corresponding positions elsewhere (e.g. *put* pa. tense as against *putted*)'; *fig.* 'Something that counts as or amounts to nothing; a worthless thing or person, one of no account; a "cipher", "nonentity"; a "nothing" or "nobody"'; *fig.* 'The lowest point or degree, a vanishing point; nothingness, nullity. Also an absence or lack of anything; nothing'; 'The initial point of a process or reckoning; the starting-point, the absolute beginning; *spec. Mil.*, the time or day when an attack or operation is due to begin'.

This all seems clear enough, though a more than slight obscurity hangs over the way zero is both an absolute starting place, an absence of number, and yet at the same time a number. Also it seems a more than a little odd to say that zero is the bottom, the starting point, and yet at the same time the intermediate point between positive and negative numbers. This doubleness gave rise to the quarrels over just when the millennium occurred, at the beginning of the year 2000 or at the beginning of 2001. It is not quite rational or intelligible, moreover, to speak, as the OED does, of zero as 'the total absence of quantity considered as a quantity'.

I shall return ultimately to these oddnesses, that seem to hang over the zero or haunt it, when I discuss the rhetorical or tropological implications of zero. These are hinted at in the term in linguistics, 'zero degree'. This names an absence that has significance, as in past participles that are the same as present tense forms: 'Today I cut' and 'Yesterday I cut'. In any case, once 'zero' enters a language, it seems to become indispensable, as in the long series of attributive forms the OED gives, with many interesting citations: zero-line, -mark, -plane, -point; zero-base, zero-crossing, zero creep, zero day, zero hour, zero magnet, zero night, temperature, weather; zero-balance, zero-coupon, zero-energy, zero grazing, zero option, zero-sum, and even zero-zero (the latter designating a situation in which both the horizontal visibility and the cloud ceiling are technically zero). In addition, a long series of verbal and compound forms exist, such as zeroable, zeroing, zeroth, zero in, zero valent, zeroize and zero out. We have heard a lot recently, after '9/11', of 'ground zero'.

Rotman and Seife, each in his own way, tells the long and fascinating story of zero as a revolutionary element within the development of modern mathematics, logic and physics, from Pythagoras, Zeno and Aristotle through Newton, Leibniz and Pascal down to Cantor, Frege, Einstein and others. Seife discusses black holes (each a something/nothing approaching a zero point of infinite mass) and the Big Bang, the zero point for the origin of the universe. Seife focuses primarily on the history of mathematics. Rotman's goal is an explicitly Foucauldian one of arguing for a consonance among three revolutions occurring at more or less the same time in the European Renaissance: the introduction of zero into mathematics and commercial computations, the invention of perspectival drawing, with its vanishing points, or zero points, where lines converge, and the invention of paper money. Paper money is not necessarily backed by anything tangible of value. It refers to other paper money. Paper money is signs about signs, that is, metasigns.

'I discuss', says Rotman, 'as indeed does Foucault in *The Order of Things*, patterns of similitude, homology, structural identity, parallelism, and the like between various different signifying systems and codes such as mathematics, painting, money, and to a lesser extent, written texts . . . the introduction of *zero* in the practice of arithmetic, the *vanishing point* in perspective art, and *imaginary money* in economic exchange – are three isomorphic manifestations, different, but in some formal semiotic sense equivalent models, of the same signifying configuration' (Rotman, 1993, x, 1). Rotman waffles here among various terms for the relation among these signifying systems: 'similitude', 'homology', 'structural identity', 'parallelism', 'and the like', 'isomorphism', 'in some formal semiotic sense equivalent models'. Well, which is it? What is the force of 'in some . . . sense' here? This wavering indicates another, more covert, version of the zero that is Rotman's subject. Each of these systems can be a catachresis or allegory of the others, neither a literal nor a figurative similitude, but somewhere, irrationally, in between. The zero seems secretly to have entered into the language needed to talk about it. I mean by this that when the zero enters into equations and equivalences, whether numerical or semantic, it is easily possible to demonstrate that any number is the equal of, homologous to, in some formal semiotic sense the equivalent of, any other number, or that any object is the same as any other object. Seife's example is the proof that Winston Churchill is a carrot (Seife, 2000, 217–19). As Seife says, 'Used unwisely, zero has the power to destroy logic' (Seife, 2000, 219). Just what would a wise use of zero be? Has Seife used it wisely? Zero's power to destroy logic seems to be an inexpungable part of any use of it.

Rotman goes on to hypothesize the necessary emergence in the Renaissance of a new subjectivity, a metasubject to cope with these metalanguages: 'this new capacity, a self-conscious subject of a subject, a *meta-subject,* is at the centre of major eruptions within very different sign systems of the sixteenth and seventeenth century (*sic*!). These major eruptions were, in mathematics, the invention of algebra by Vieta; in painting, the self-conscious image created by Vermeer and Velasquez; in the text, the invention of the autobiographical written self by Montaigne; in economics, the creation of paper money by gold merchants in London' (Rotman, 1993, 4). One should be cautious about the notion of a sudden mutation in subjectivity. Who can tell now what it would have felt like to be a person of the seventeenth century, Montaigne for instance? We have only his words. These are the registration of a perhaps imaginary or constructed subjectivity, not unmediated subjectivity itself. Who, for that matter, can know what it would be like to be one's dearest friend or one's closest neighbour or colleague? Knowledge of the other quickly reaches a zero point of opacity, like that zero-zero when an airport is fogged in.

The history of zero in mathematics, science, painting and economics is of great interest. That history is endlessly fascinating, like the approach toward an abyss, the descent into a maelstrom. My topic, however, is zero as a rhetorical term. What can zero have to do with literary theory, or with literary criticism, or with literature itself? Literature is made of words. These words must be differentiated from other words to make meaning. Zero is undifferentiated, incapable of being differentiated, just one long undifferentiated tone. The word 'zero', however, is a word like any other word, an assemblage of phonemes that draws its meaning from its difference from other assemblages of phonemes. That does not seem to get me far in moving not toward a semantics or logic of zero but toward a rhetoric or tropology of zero. A passage in Roland Barthes' *Elements of Semiology* gives an initial clue that may help take the first step with that. The passage comes within a section about 'privative oppositions': 'The second problem arising in connection with privative opposition is that of the unmarked term. It is called the *zero degree* of the opposition. The zero degree is therefore not a total absence (this is a common mistake), *it is a significant absence*. We have here a pure differential state; the zero degree testifies to the power held by any system of signs, of creating meaning 'out of nothing': 'the language [*la langue*] can be content with an opposition of something and nothing (Saussure, [1969], 124)' (Barthes, *Elements of Semiology*, 1970, 77). The concept of the zero degree in linguistics is like beginning a counting operation with zero. Just as zero stands for the absence of any number, though not any one in particular, so the absence of any mark can stand for the absence of any particular mark that might be there, such as the absent 'ed', mark of the past tense in English, in 'Yesterday I put'. Only the context tells you what possible mark is absent, just as the zeroes in 2000 tell you that any numbers from two to nine are missing not just anywhere, but in the hundreds, tens and digits places. The zeroes are placeholders, another name for catachresis, of which more later.

The zero degree in linguistics plays havoc with the basic principles of linguistics, just as the zero does in mathematics. According to structural linguistics, meaning arises from difference, the differences among phonemes. The difference between 'ma' and 'pa', however, is not like the difference between 'ma' and the absence of any phoneme whatsoever. In the latter case, as Barthes' quotation from Saussure affirms, meaning is created 'out of nothing', whereas it is a principle of at least one sort of logic that 'nothing comes of nothing', including, presumably meaning. Here, however, the nothing that is called the 'zero degree' has meaning, or generates meaning. Once more we encounter the equivocation between zero as a mark that has meaning, as when it is taken as a number among others, and zero as a mark that indicates the void, absence, no number at all, something wholly outside the chain of numbers. When Saussure says 'the language can be content with an opposition of something and nothing', he says something that subtly contradicts his entire linguistic theory, since that theory depends on the notion that meaning arises from specific and limited differences.

If nothing comes of nothing in Aristotelean logic and in Lear's harsh speech to Cordelia, on the other hand the Judaic-Christian creation myth, like most other creation myths in different cultures, depends on the divine creation of something out of nothing: 'In the beginning God created the heaven and the earth. And the earth was without form, and void, and darkness was upon the face of the deep. And the Spirit of God moved upon the face of the waters. And God said, Let there be light: and there was light' (Gen. 1: 1–3). What struck conservative Renaissance thinkers as blasphemous about the use of zero in computation was that it reintroduced a void that God with his creative fiat had replaced once and for all with a full creation, a plenitude. Only the devil is void, empty, a nothing dwelling in Hell. Hell is a nothing place, a place of infinite, non-determinate, unsublatable negation.

Saussure's dictum, the reader will note, also anticipates the binary system used in the Boolean logic manipulated by computer languages. These languages, as everyone knows, are generated by strings of zeroes and ones. It is not an accident that zeroes and ones rather than, say, ones and twos are used in computer language. The zeroes and ones correspond to open or closed switches in the millions of transistors in a computer chip. The computer, in its generation of all its immense complexity of meanings (graphics and sounds as well as words, for example the words I am at this moment typing on my computer keyboard), is 'content with an opposition of something and nothing'. The nothing, the zero, is meaningless, but it generates endless new meanings when combined with ones.

Barthes goes on to illustrate this by saying that the concept of the zero degree has been fruitful in many areas, in semantics, in logic, in ethnology and in rhetoric: 'The concept of the zero degree, which sprang from phonology, lends itself to a great many applications: in semantics, in which *zero signs* are known ('a "zero sign" is spoken of in cases where the absence of any explicit signifier functions by itself as a signifier'); in logic ('A is in the zero state, that is to say that A does not actually exist, but under certain conditions it can be made to appear'); in ethnology, where Lévi-Strauss would compare the notion of mana to it ('. . . the proper function of the zero phoneme is to be opposed to the absence of the phoneme . . . Similarly, it could be said . . . that the function of notions of the 'mana' type is to be opposed to the absence of signification without involving in itself any particular signification'; finally, in rhetoric, where, carried on to the connotative plane, the absence of rhetorical signifiers (la vide des signifiants rhétoriques) constitutes in its turn a stylistic signifier' (Barthes, *Elements of Semiology*, 1970, 77–8). Barthes is citing here, respectively, the *Cahiers Ferdinand de Saussure*, the 'Notions de logistique' part of Destouches's *Cours de logique*, and Lévi-Strauss's 'Introduction à l'oeuvre de M. Mauss'. The last item is a reference to his own *Writing Degree Zero*.

What a 'zero sign' is, we know. It is, for example, the significant absence of any marker in the past tense of 'Yesterday I put', where one might have expected, and where babies, and novice learners of English, do sometimes put, 'putted'. The citation about logic has the characteristic weirdness of formulations involving zero. A does not really exist at all, but it can be 'made to appear' 'under certain conditions', presumably certain logical manipulations, like a ghost invoked from the dead, or like the song of the Sirens, which, as Blanchot says, is not the real song, but the placeholder for the real song that the audible one promises. That real song, however, as Blanchot goes on to say, is silence.

What the zero might mean in logic can be further exemplified not by Destouches, whose work Barthes cites, but by Ludwig Wittgenstein. In the *Tractatus Logico-*

Philosophicus, 6.121, Wittgenstein says, 'The propositions of logic [*Die Sätze der Logik*] demonstrate the logical properties of propositions by combining them so as to form propositions that say nothing [*nichtssagenden Sätzen*]. This method could also be called a zero-method [*eine Nullmethode*]. In a logical proposition, propositions are brought into equilibrium (ins Gleichgewicht gebracht), and the state of equilibrium then indicates what the logical constitution of of these propositions must be' (Wittgenstein, 1963, 124, 125). Just as an algebraic equation depends on a series of notations that must equal zero to be solved (e.g. $x^2 + y^2 - 13 = 0$, where 2 for x and 3 for y will 'cipher out'), so the combinations of all logical propositions circle around the zero, that is, if correctly combined, they say nothing at all. They are *nichtssagenden*. The 'logical constitution [*logisch beschaffen*]' of these propositions must be determined by the way they may be combined in such a way that they say nothing. Another way to put this is to say that combinations of logical propositions are tautologies. The whole of logic has as its goal, rigorously, elegantly, with endlessly proliferating complexity, to say nothing at all. As Wittgenstein says, in 6.1222, 'This throws some light on the question why logical propositions cannot be confirmed [*bestätigt*] by experience any more than they can be refuted [*widerlegt*] by it. Not only must a proposition of logic be irrefutable by any possible experience, but it must also be unconfirmable by any possible experience' (Wittgenstein, 1963, 126–7). The famous conclusion to the *Tractatus* ('What we cannot speak about we must pass over in silence [Wovon man nicht sprechen kann, darüber muß man schweigen]' (6.54; Wittgenstein, 1963, 150–1)), might be taken as a prohibition against trying to talk about the zero that means nothing at all. It might also be argued, however, that all Wittgenstein's later work, *The Blue and Brown Books*, the *Philosophical Investigations*, and so on, were an attempt to find ways to speak about that whereof man must keep silence.

Barthes' third 'application' of the zero degree, to ethnology, is puzzlingly phrased. Why are notions of the 'mana' type opposed to the absence of signification without involving in themselves any particular signification? Once more we encounter the distinction between zero as sheer meaningless absence and zero as a placeholder that has significance without itself meaning anything in particular. 'Mana' is a Polynesan word adopted by anthropologists to name 'a pervasive supernatural power that may inhere in persons or things' (*Funk & Wagnalls Standard College Dictionary*). Any person in any culture may believe in mana in one form or another. 'Mana' is a placeholder, like zero, that may be filled in with an infinite number of particular beliefs or experiences. Mana is not the absence of signification, but a metaterm that gives the whole system differentiated meanings without itself having any particular signification. It is therefore a zero degree in ethnology.

What Barthes means by the application of the zero degree to rhetoric is made clear not only by his formula in the passage cited about 'the absence of rhetorical signifiers' forming in its turn a 'stylistic signifier', but in his development in his other, earlier book, *Writing Degree Zero*, to which his footnote refers, of the notion of a zero degree of style. He gives the example of Albert Camus's style in *L'étranger*. Camus's writing there is so clear, so impersonal, so unmarked by rhetorical flourishes, that it escapes servitude to any ideological system, such as most literary styles betray, and thereby rises to a utopian realm of freedom. Barthes' use of the term zero degree in *Writing Degree Zero* is explicitly borrowed from the linguists' conception of 'a neutral term or zero element', for example the 'amodal' indicative mood that balances between the subjunctive and imperative moods:

Proportionally speaking, writing at the zero degree is basically in the indicative mood, or if you like, amodal . . . This new neutral writing takes its place in the midst of all those ejaculations and judgments, without becoming involved in any of them; it consists precisely in their absence. But this absence is complete, it implies no refuge, no secret; one cannot therefore say that it is an impassive mode of writing; rather that it is innocent . . . This transparent form of speech, initiated by Camus's Outsider, *achieves a style of absence which is almost an ideal absence of style; writing is then reduced to a sort of negative mood in which the social or mythical characters of a language are abolished in favor of a neutral and inert state of form; thus thought remains wholly responsible, without being overlaid by a secondary commitment of form to a History not its own.*

(Barthes, Writing Degree Zero, 1970, 76–7)

It is easy to see how Barthes has adopted to what he calls 'rhetoric' the linguistic notion of the zero degree. Here the zero degree means an absence that is not empty. It indicates, rather, the absence of all the numberless ideologically or historically determined styles that might inflect it. Many readers today will instantly respond that it is impossible to imagine, or to have, or to write in a style that is free from ideology and history, therefore autonomously responsible. Ideology and history speak through us, unconsciously, however bare we make our styles. Barthes says in his own way just this a few sentences beyond the ones I have quoted. Writing degree zero, he says, rapidly becomes a manner. That manner becomes dated, the sign of a historical moment, and, so we tend to think, of the psychology of a particular writer. Who would want to write like Camus or Hemingway today? A piece of their writing can be instantly identified. It seems faded, *vieux jeu*, marked by its historical moment within modernism: 'The writer, taking his place as a "classic", becomes the slavish imitator of his original creation, society demotes his writing to a mere manner, and returns him a prisoner to his own formal myths' (Barthes, *Writing Degree Zero*, 1970, 78).

I have mentioned the unconscious, adopted by Louis Althusser as a way of expressing our unawareness that an ideology speaks through us and in our beliefs. 'Ideology', says Althusser, 'is a "representation" of the imaginary relationship of individuals to their real conditions of existence . . . all ideology has the function (which defines it) of "constituting" concrete individuals as subjects' (Althusser, 1972, 162, 171). What is unknown to those in the grip of an ideology, as we all are, is our 'real conditions of existence'. These are as unknowable as, for psychoanalysis, is my unconscious. Ideology, it might be argued, plays the same role in political philosophy as mana does in ethnography or, indeed, as the unconscious does in psychoanalysis. All three are zero degrees, placeholders indicating not a void, but the non-presence of any particular ideology, any particular version of belief in mana, or any particular content for the unconscious. Like zero, all three, ideology, mana and the unconscious, are catachreses, names for something unknown and unknowable as such. Of catachresis I shall have more to say later.

As is well known, Althusser's formulations about ideology were influenced by psychoanalysis, more specifically by the work of Jacques Lacan. In one place at least, Lacan uses zero and the number series as a way of characterizing the fractures of the psyche. This place is 'Of Structure as an Inmixing of an Otherness Prerequisite to Any Subject Whatever'. This essay was Lacan's contribution to the famous Johns Hopkins structuralist symposium of 1966.

Though the volume that came from this symposium is entitled *The Structuralist Controversy*, the symposium was more saliently the introduction into the United States, via Jacques Derrida's 'Structure, Sign, and Play in the Discourses of the Human Sciences', of deconstruction. Lacan's paper was characteristically pretentious, condescending, elliptical and confused, or at any rate confusing to me at the time when I heard him present it. I would not go so far, however, as to agree with a distinguished Johns Hopkins psychologist and psychotherapist, also present at Lacan's talk, who diagnosed him as probably suffering from a brain lesion. Lacan's brief allusion to the zero will complete my repertoire of what I would call semantic, logical or metaphorical applications of the zero, as opposed to truly rhetorical ones, to which I shall then turn in conclusion.

Lacan's target is those American psychoanalysts, or worse yet, renegades who have become merely psychologists, who claim in one way or another that the psyche is a whole, an organic unity. Lacan wants to replace that false idea with the now familiar Lacanian disjunct subject, 'inmixed' with an 'Otherness' depriving it of the ability to say 'I' and to mean by saying that some self-present unity. Within this inmixed subject, the never directly available unconscious is structured like a language and is the discourse of the Other (with a big O). 'The subject', says Lacan, 'cannot simply be identified with the speaker or the personal pronoun in a sentence . . . But the unconscious has nothing to do with instinct or primitive knowledge or preparation of thought in some underground. It is a thinking with words, with thoughts that escape your vigilance, your state of watchfulness' (Lacan, 1982, 188, 189). O, the letter, as in 'Other', is not by any means 0, zero, as in 0 1 2 3, however. Zero makes a brief, evanescent appearance here by way of Lacan's attempt to use set theory, with references to Frege, to explain that disjunct psychic structure.

For Lacan, the numbers start with one, not with zero. The difficulty is to get from one to two. Once you have got to two, you are in business. The infinite series of repetitions that characterize psychic life (or mechanism) can then proceed. 'After fifteen years', says Lacan, 'I have taught my pupils to count at most up to five which is difficult (four is easier) and they have understood that much. But for tonight permit me to stay at two' (Lacan, 1982, 190). The implication of this little joke is that Lacan's Baltimore audience is not up to attempting three or four, much less five. With his help, they might make it to two.

What is the problem? The problem in getting from one to two is adding the one more to the first one. 'When you try to read the theories of mathematicians regarding numbers you find the formula "$\underline{n}$ plus one" ($\underline{n}$ + 1) as the basis of all the theories. It is this question of the "one more" that is the key to the genesis of numbers and instead of this unifying unity that constitutes two in the first case I propose that you consider the real numerical genesis of two' (Lacan, 1982, 191). I shall return later, apropos of Henry James's 'The Altar of the Dead', to the 'just one more'. In order to explain the real numerical genesis of two Lacan uses the familiar example in set theory of the number of people in a room (one set) matching the number of seats in the room (another set). For Frege, however, as for Cantor before him, the first set is the null set, zero, the empty set, the seat that is not there, just as, in the other direction, you can always add one more set even to an infinite series of self-enclosing sets, namely the set that includes itself as well as all the other sets. This is the basis of the famous Russell paradox. Does the set that includes all the sets that are not members of themselves include that set? If it does, it does not. If it does not, it does. This paradox drove the great mathematician, F. L. G. Frege, back to the drawing board, just when he had finished an ambitious theory of sets. The null set gives you one, since though it may be empty it is nevertheless a set, the first set, one set. The first set with content other than zero gives you two. The one is then constituted retroactively by the two, the two by the three, and so on, just as in the Freudian theory of hysteria the trauma is generated not by the first experience, for example a sexual advance on the daughter by her father, but by a second, often innocuous, event years later. This second event is like the first one in some perhaps trivial way. That similarity makes the first event belatedly traumatic, so generating hysteria. In the genesis of number, two rows are juxtaposed, in overlapping incongruity, the one beginning with zero: 0 1 2 3 . . . and the one beginning with one: 1 2 3 . . . This Lacan takes as a figure for the genesis of the 'unconscious subject':

It is necessary that this two constitute the first integer which is not yet born as a number before the two appears. You have made this possible because the two is here to grant existence to the first one: put two in the place of one and consequently in the place of the two you see three appear. What we have here is something which I can call the mark. You already have something which is marked or something which is not marked. It is with the first mark that we have the status of the thing. It is exactly in this fashion that Frege explains the genesis of the number; the class which is characterized by no elements is the first class; you have one at the place of zero and afterward it is easy to understand how the place of one becomes the second place which makes place for two, three, and so on. The question of the two is for us the question of the subject, and here we reach a fact of psychoanalytical experi-

ence in as much as the two does not complete the one to make two, but must repeat the one to permit the one to exist. The first repetition is the only one necessary to explain the genesis of the number, and only one repetition is necessary to constitute it. The unconscious subject is something that tends to repeat itself, but only one such repetition is necessary to constitute it.

(Lacan, 1982, 191)

Lacan's thought here is a grounded tropology, as in the metaphorical act of putting the two in the place or one, or as in the use of the discourse about numbers as a metaphor of the structure of the unconscious subject. Exactly what Lacan had in mind in the sentence about the something that is marked or unmarked is impossible to tell, since he does not follow it up, but leaves it hanging in the air, especially the question of what he means by 'something which is not marked'. It appears, however, that he may mean by 'marking' the figurative naming of one as two, marking one as two, the two as three, and so on. A serious consideration of the zero would make this play of figurative substitutions difficult or impossible. As Jacques Derrida has shown, Lacan's thought is characterized by a residual, imperturbable metaphysical penchant, for example in his belief that the letter of the unconscious always reaches its destination or in his adherence to the ancient idea that animals and people are fundamentally different. People, not animals, possess language, have foreknowledge of death, etc. All of these borders can be shown to be crossable and crossed, both ways. A sign of Lacan's logocentrism, as we have been taught to call it, is perhaps Lacan's elision here of the real problem with the genesis of numbers. What does it mean for Frege, or for Lacan after him, to juxtapose one and zero, to call the empty set a one?

This hypostatizes the zero, makes it into a thing, or the sign for a thing, whereas it is the sign for the absence of anything. Lacan chooses one side of the doubleness in zero and effaces the other. This is evident in the way he calls the one the first mark, and does not follow up on his phrase 'something which is not marked'. The unmarked mark, however, is precisely the zero, the number that is not a number, but a placeholder, a sign for the absence of any number.

The unmarked, we know from Barthes and his sources, is the zero degree, which would be, in the context of Lacan's discourse, the zero set before it is marked, metaphorically, or, one might say, catachrestically, as 'one'. It is a catachresis because the null set, like zero itself, is, ultimately, unintelligible, unknowable. You can think or see one, but cannot do so with zero. Lacan makes the zero into just one more integer like all the others, whereas it is, as I have shown above, also a metasign, the sign outside the system of signs that makes the sign system possible without participating in it. The real problem is not how to get from one to two, but how to get from zero to one. In fact, it cannot be done, without a leap of faith or a performative imposition, a sleight of hand, some kind of prestidigitation. Lacan, as in consistency he must, explicitly denies the existence of any metalanguage. There is only everyday language, such as we all speak. 'The first thing to state in this context', says Lacan, 'is that there is no meta-language. For it is necessary that all so called meta-languages be presented to you with language' (Lacan, 1982, 188).

A consequence of Lacan's logocentrism is that the language of the Other is, for him, not really other. The sage psychoanalyist has access to it, can drag it into the light of day, and express it in everyday language that all can understand and speak. A rigorous application of number theory, with its abyssal basis in the zero, would, on the contrary, make possible a notion of something wholly and irreducibly other in the human psyche and in language, that otherness Derrida calls 'le tout autre'. To the most rigorous example I know of that application of the zero I now turn.

Paul de Man's 'Pascal's Allegory of Persuasion' is one of its author's most brilliant and important essays. Andrzej Warminski makes it the focus of his introductory essay for *Aesthetic Ideology,* the volume in which the essay is collected. The endpoint of the essay is a recognition that the disjunction between justice and power, in Pascal's *Pensées*, arises from a general disjunction between cognition and performance as functions of language: 'To the extent that language is always cognitive and tropological as well as performative at the same time, it is a heterogeneous entity incapable of justice as well as of *justesse*' (de Man, 1996, 69). This concluding insight is reached by way of an intricate argumentation that begins with a discussion of Pascal's distinction between nominal and real definitions, followed by a discussion of Pascal's mathematics, including the zero in Pascal's thought. De Man then proceeds through an analysis of several of Pascal's 'pensées', showing that they remain within cognition and take the crisscross form of a chiasmus, a version both of proportionality (A is to B as C is to D) and of tropological exchanges. Finally, the 'pensées' dealing with the relation between justice and power are shown to reintroduce something like the zero and to be therefore inassimilable to the chiasmal structure: 'the tropological field of cognition is revealed to be dependent on an entity, might, that is heterogeneous with regard to this field, just as the zero was heterogeneous with regard to number' (de Man, 1996, 69). The narrative of this heterogeneity, the accounting for it in language, for example the discovery that it is impossible to inscribe the pairs *présence/absence* and *plaisir/déplaisir* into a neat chiasmus structure, is said to be 'what we call allegory': 'The (ironic) pseudoknowledge of this impossibility, which pretends to order sequentially, in a narrative, what is actually the destruction of all sequence, is what we call allegory' (de Man, 1996, 69). De Man calls this knowledge 'pseudo' because the impossibility in question cannot be known, only gestured toward. It is ironic because, as de Man demonstrates in 'The Concept of Irony', another essay in *Aesthetic Ideology*, irony is disruptive of all narrative or dialectical sequence. It suspends or pulverizes any sequential story or argument. He says 'what we call allegory', rather than just 'allegory', to call attention to the way the constantly interrupted or broken narrative in question here is outside the order of cognition. You can call it anything you like, but all the names would be catachreses, performatively imposed names for what has no literal name, either nominal or real. 'We [whoever that 'we' may be; de Man himself? some collective entity, including me, the reader?] call it allegory', by a performative fiat, a speech act like naming a baby.

What is the role of Pascal's zero in this argumentation? The central statement, the culmination of de Man's discussion of Pascal's logic and mathematics, is the following characteristically cheeky assertion: 'To say then, as we are actually saying, that allegory (as sequential narration) is the trope of irony (as one is the trope of zero) is to say something that is true enough but not intelligible, which also implies that it cannot be put to work as a device of textual analysis' (de Man, 1996, 61). What in the world does this mean? De Man tells us we are not going to find it intelligible, so why say it unless as a kind of challenge: 'Understand it if you can! I challenge you to do so, but don't blame me if you fail. I will have told you so.' How can something be true, able to be formulated in a neat proportional aphorism (allegory is to irony as one is to zero), and yet be unintelligible? Does not de Man, in spite of what he says, put his insight to work 'as a device of textual analysis' in the discussion of the disjunction between justice and power in the 'pensées' discussed at the end of the essay? The odd formulation, 'to say then, as we are actually saying', mixes, no doubt deliberately, 'mention' and 'use', the cognitive and the performative, in the distinction between 'someone might say' and 'I declare that I am now actually saying'. This anticipates the congnitive/performative disjunction with which the essay ends. What de Man is saying is unintelligible in so far as it is a speech act, not a constative statement, since, in de Man's speech act theory, performative speech acts are radically foreign to the order of cognition.

The context of this 'not intelligible' formulation does not help much toward making it intelligible. De Man has been concluding what he has to say about the way 'the numerical series are interrupted by zero' and is now moving on to ask whether anything like that happens in the dialectical theological and epistemological formulations of the *Pensées*. 'It is possible', says de Man, 'to find, in the terminology of rhetoric, terms that come close to designating such disruptions (e.g., *parabasis* or *anacoluthon*), which designate the interruption of a semantic continuum in a manner that lies beyond the power of reintegration. One must realize at once, however, that this disruption is not topical, that it cannot be located in a single point – since it is indeed the very notion of point, the geometrical zero, that is being dislodged – but that it is all-pervading. The anacoluthon is omnipresent, or, in temporal terms and in Friedrich Schlegel's deliberately unintelligible formulation, the parabasis is permanent. Calling this structure ironic can be more misleading than helpful, since . . .' (de Man, 1996, 61). Then follows the formulation I cite above about the (tropological) relation of zero and one being proportional to the (tropological) relation between irony and allegory. The

context tells us at least that de Man is shifting from mathematical terminology to rhetorical terminology, but to odd rhetorical terms or odd uses of them that are beyond easy intelligibility. 'Anacoluthon' names a failure in following, such as a sentence that begins in the first person and shifts in mid-sentence to the third person. De Man, however, is talking about a pervasive anacoluthon, a failure in following all along the line, that is something that does not really make sense. A 'parabasis' is an interruption or suspension of a dramatic illusion, as when a character or the dramatist steps forward on the proscenium and speaks in his or her own voice about the drama as a fictive illusion. 'Permanent parabasis' is Friedrich Schlegel definition of irony. It is 'deliberately unintelligible' because a permanent parabasis would be a suspension without anything other than itself to suspend, or without anything that had not been already suspended at every point throughout the dramatic action, as if by a perpetual disillusioning commentary addressed to the audience. Calling the structure de Man is trying to describe ironic may be more misleading than helpful, since irony, like zero, cannot be defined in either of Pascal's senses of definition, nominal or real.

Trying to understand the Pascalian zero may allow us to defy de Man's prohibition and at least get an '(ironic) pseudoknowledge' of the relations among irony, allegory, zero and one. That would permit a truly rhetorical (as opposed to semantic, thematic or semiological) application of zero, if not necessarily an intelligible one. However it is approached, even with the most powerful tools of rhetoric, zero seems to remain mind-boggling. In the discussion of Pascal's *Réflexions sur la géométrie en général: De l'esprit géometrique et de l'Art de persuader* that opens de Man's essay, he moves through a description of the way geometry succeeds because it uses only nominal definitions that do not depend on anything outside the closed code for their intelligibility. Geometry uses only '*definitions of name* [*déf-initions de nom*], that is to say, [gives] a name only to those things which have been clearly designated in perfectly known terms' [Pascal]), whereas real definitions bring in the question of correspondence to something external to the code, that is they are 'axioms' or 'propopsitions that need to be proven' (de Man, 1996, 56).

De Man's unravelling of Pascal's system, or demonstration that it unravels itself, proceeds through a recognition that one is both a number and not a number (we have seen the shadow of this in Lacan) to the more radically disruptive recognition that the zero is radically not a number, both necessary to the establishment of the system and wholly outside it, heterogeneous to it: 'There exists, in the order of number, an entity that is, unlike the *one,* heterogeneous with regard to number: this entity, which is the *zero,* is radically distinct from one. Whereas one is and is not a number at the same time, zero is radically not a number, absolutely heterogeneous to the order of number' (de Man, 1996, 59). The introduction of the zero allows for a reconciliation of number and space, but this happens at a price: 'the coherence of the system is now seen to be entirely dependent on the introduction of an element – the zero and its equivalences in time and motion – that is itself entirely heterogeneous to the system and nowhere a part of it. The continuous universe held together by the double wings of the two infinites [the infinitely small and the infinitely large] is interrupted, disrupted *at all points* by a principle of radical heterogenity without which it cannot come into being' (de Man, 1996, 59).

At this point de Man shifts to another register and argues that the aporia here is not a mathematical but a linguistic problem. 'The notion of language as sign is dependent on, and derived from, a different notion in which language functions as rudderless signification and trans-

forms what it denominates into the linguistic equivalence of the arithmetical zero' (de Man, 1996, 59). Though de Man does not say so here in so many words, what he is actually saying is that the name 'zero' differs from all the other names for mathematical entities by being a catachresis, that is, a transferred name for what has no name and is unknowable. 'It is as sign', says de Man, 'that language is capable of engendering the principles of infinity, of genus, species, and homogeneity, which allow for synecdochal totalizations, but none of these tropes could come about without the systematic effacement of the zero and its reconversion into a name. There can be no *one* without zero, but the zero always appears in the guise of a *one,* of a (some)thing. The name is the trope of the zero. The zero is always *called* a one, when the zero is actually nameless, "innommable"' (de Man, 1996, 59). The trope in question here is catachresis. To say the zero is always *called* a one is to call attention to the way the trope called catachresis is always a speech act, a groundless performative. 'I call this zero a something, a one'. We have earlier encountered this equivocation about the zero in set theory and in the ambiguity between saying zero is a number, the first number in the series of numbers, and saying zero is a meta-number, a number about the absence of any numbers, so outside the system of numbers altogether.

It is now possible to glimpse what de Man means when he says 'allegory (as sequential narrative) is the trope of irony (as the one is the trope of zero)'. Perhaps it is even possible to see how this might actually be put to work as a device of textual analysis, whatever de Man says to the contrary. Since neither irony nor the zero is knowable, able to be confronted phenomenally, any trope for them will be a catachresis. De Man's aphorism might be rephrased by saying allegory is the catachresis of irony, just as one is the catachresis of zero. The word 'zero' is already itself a catachresis, for something unknown unknowable, and unnameable, 'innommable'. This is so because the word zero implies that what it names is something, some thing, a one. To call it zero or to call it one comes to the same thing. It is not an etymological accident, without significance, that the word zero and the word cipher have, as I noted above, the same root, Arabic 'sifr'. The double meaning of cipher, as zero and as a name for any number, is hidden also in the double meaning of zero, as one something, and as an abyssal nothing at all. De Man finds this doubleness present in Pascal's somewhat inconsistent distinction between 'néant', which is the zero as something, as a number, and 'zéro', as Pascal's name for the unknowable that makes infinitesimal calculus possible, as well as being what allegories are about.

In a throwaway line at the end of the first paragraph of 'Pascal's Allegory of Persuasian', de Man says, 'The difficulty of allegory is rather that this emphasis on clarity of representation does not stand in the service of something that can be represented' (de Man, 1996, 51). Clarity of representation, he has just been saying, is necessary in allegory not as 'an appeal to the pagan pleasure of imitation' (de Man, 1996, 51), but so that the objects that are the vehicle of the allegory can be clearly recognized. The tenor of the allegory, however, is one version or another of the unknowable: zero, irony or death, or what Friederich Schlegel called 'chaos', or the performative dimension of language, language's 'power' as opposed to its 'justice'. These names are all posited pseudo-names for that unrepresentable blankness or radical otherness that allegories are allegories of. Irony, as a pervasive disruption of intelligibility in an entire discourse, is like performative speech acts in being alien to cognition. This explains why de Man, rather surprisingly, puts irony on the side of performative language in 'The Concept of Irony': 'Irony also very clearly

has a performative function. Irony consoles and it promises and it excuses' (de Man, 1996, 165).

The unrepresentablity of what allegory represents also explains why the Pascal essay is called 'Pascal's Allegory of Persuasion'. This title no doubt plays on the 'of' as both subjective and objective genitive. It is an allegory about persuasion and an allegory belonging to persuasion. All allegories are allegories of persuasion. This is true not only in the sense that they persuade, but also in the sense that what they allegorize is the unknowable speech act we call persuasion. Persuasion is the dimension of rhetoric that uses language as a power to bring people, unjustly, to act and believe in a certain way. It is in this sense, moreover, that all allegories are allegories of allegory, that is emblematic expressions of their own mode of working, which is to be persuasive. Or, to put this another way, all allegories are allegories of reading, since what they 'stand for', or 'stand in for', as placeholders, is their own unpredictable performative effects on readers, readers good and bad. If one is to zero as allegory is to irony, then it can be said that de Man's originality, not entirely authorized by Pascal, is to take Pascalian mathematics, with perhaps an admixture of modern set theory (de Man, after all, was an engineering student at the University of Brussels), as an allegory of the working of allegory. This, I claim, is a truly rhetorical use of the strange properties of the zero.

Can any examples be adduced of something like de Man's rhetorical zero in actual works of literature? I pass by works, such as Jorge Luis Borges's 'Avatars of the Tortoise' or Italo Svevo's *Confessions of Zeno*. In these works the zero approached but never reached in Zeno's paradoxes is used in a more or less purely thematic way. This is hilariously the case in Svevo's demonstration that Zeno, the hero of his novel, can never quit smoking because he can never reach the point of smoking a 'last cigarette'. More nearly grist for my mill is Shakespeare's *King Lear*, already quoted here. *King Lear* is admirably analysed by Brian Rotman. He sees the play as what de Man might have called an allegory of the effects of zero on human and social life at the moment of its introduction into Europe and at the moment feudalism was being replaced by merchantile capitalism. The latter was, and is, intimately dependent, as the global stock market is today, on the zero for its transactions. As Rotman shows, the word 'nothing' echoes through *King Lear* like a leitmotif. The play shows how wrong Lear is to say that 'nothing will come of nothing' (I. i. 90), and 'Nothing can be made out of nothing' (I. iv. 135). The result is, as the Fool taunts him by saying, that Lear himself becomes 'an O without a figure'. 'I am better than thou art now: I am a fool, thou art nothing' (I. iv. 193–5). An O without a the adjacent figure that would give it meaning, as in 10 or 100 or even 001 is the apotheosis of nothing, the zero as absolute void, no longer a placeholder for the absence of number.

I conclude, however, with discussion of three more modern literary works in which the zero functions in a truly rhetorical way.

The literary revolution participated in, and to some degree initiated by, James Joyce might be defined as the displacement of the grounding of literature in some solid extralinguistic *logos*: God, the One, or the materiality of the external world. These grounds are, in Joyce's work, replaced by a groundless, endlessly proliferating, self-cancelling, self-regenerating play of signifiers. *Finnegans Wake*, it might be argued, is the result of a principled and brilliantly inventive exploitation of this mode of writing. At least twice Joyce explicitly uses the zero or the nought to signify this pulling out of the rug from underneath the literary text. In one place in *Ulysses* the reader encounters a 'nought' (Joyce, 683). It comes at the climax of a section in 'Ithaca' in which Bloom, watching the night sky with Stephen, and having meditated on the infinitely large, turns to the infinitesimally small, for example the endlessly smaller worlds within worlds in blood cells: '. . . the universe of human serum constellated with red and white bodies, themselves universes of void space constellated with other bodies, each, in continuity, its universe of divisible component bodies of which each was again divisible in divisions of redivisible component bodies, dividends and divors ever diminishing without actual division, till, if progress were carried far enough, nought nowhere was never reached' (ibid.). As Ray Mines and Reed Way Dasenbrock have demonstrated, Bloom must have been reading up on modern mathematical theory (Mines and Dasenbrock, 1997). Bloom's concluding phrase, with its self-contradictory negatives, can be taken as an expression for the unapproachability of the zero by a series of diminishing infinitesimals. Bloom, correctly, stresses the unbroken continuity of this progression.

In another place in *Ulysses*, Stephen meditates on his own birth as 'creation from nothing', and then, with savage irony, imagines that, since everyone is descended, by an immense series of navel cords, from Adam and that Eve who was the end of the line, 'belly without blemish', since she was not born of woman, then he might hypothesize the telephone number for Eden and ask the operator to connect him thereto: 'Hello. Kinch here. Put me on to Edenville. Aleph, alpha: nought, nought one' (Joyce, 39). I have elsewhere discussed this imaginary telephone number, from another perspective (Miller, 1992, 161–4). Stephen's telephone number ironizes and undoes what it promises. It disrupts the line from here to Edenville. Aleph, the first letter of the Hebrew alphabet, may be, as Richard Sullivan has argued in a recent lecture (Sullivan, 2002), a reference to Cantorian set theory. Cantor called his first set

Aleph$_0$, the second set Aleph$_1$, and so on. Cantor named his sets Aleph in reference to Kabbalistic Jewish mysticism, in which the Aleph is a name for infinity in the sense of the ultimate divine void. 'Alpha' is the first letter of the Greek alphabet. That puts us back in the zeroless realm of Greek logic and mathematics. 'Aleph, alpha' juxtaposes two irreconcilable cultures and two irreconcilable ways of thinking. Nevertheless, western Christian culture, what Joyce calls the 'Jewgreek', has tried for two millenia to achieve that reconciliation, to square the circle. The stuttering repetition of 'nought nought' in 'nought nought one' suggests the difficulty of getting off the ground of the groundless zero, so to speak, in order to make it to one. As I have shown above, you cannot get from zero to one except by a baseless performative that declares the zero to be something, to be a one. It is highly unlikely Kinch's/Stephen's telephone call would go through, since it is not a valid number. More than likely, the operator would interrupt the call to say, 'That number is not in service. Try another number'. That is, I believe, just Joyce's point.

Henry James's 'The Altar of the Dead' is an allegory if there ever was one. It is an allegory of one avatar of the zero, death. The story is also exceedingly strange, 'queer' in an old-fashioned sense of the word, perhaps in the new-fashioned way too. But then all James's stories turn out to be exceedingly queer, when you begin to think of them. James wrote over one hundred short stories. As you read them, there always seems to be just one more to read. James, it may be, nevertheless never wrote the one more that would have been the key to them all, the revelation of the figure in the carpet.

For the hero of 'The Altar of the Dead', Stransom, the dead, his dead friends in particular, are still alive, or dead-alive, hovering somewhere as ghosts or spectres. They need his memorial love and attention in order to be appeased in their deadness. Stransom does this by lighting one candle after another at a shrine in a Catholic church, 'the altar of the dead', as his friends one by one 'pass away'. For him, they nevertheless remain nearby, but at an infinite distance, imploring his help. The actual altar is only the materialization of a spiritual or subjective altar that Stransom has long maintained in his mind. 'My hero's altar has long been a "spiritual" one – lighted in the gloom of his own soul. Then it *becomes* a material one', says James in the somewhat embarassed notebook entries about this story. They are embarrased in the sense that he registers there 'the effect, unusual for me, of quite losing conceit of my subject, within sight of the close, and asking myself if it is worth going on with: or rather feeling that it isn't' (James, 1987, 99). Why this reluctance? I shall later suggest an answer. The story juxtaposes two ways of memorializing the dead. On the one hand, the bereaved woman Stransom sees in the church lights just one candle for her dead lover. That lover has foully betrayed her, though she has forgiven him: 'He had ruthlessly abandoned her – that, of course, was what he had done' (James, 1996, 474). On the other hand, Stransom always lights one more candle, 'just one more', in an endless series of integers $n + 1 + 1 + 1 \ldots$, that can never, it seems, get any closer to death or to the dead than his first candle does, or than the woman's first candle does, or than all Stransom's choir of candles do. She appropriates all his candles and takes them as symbols of one dead man, the first 1 endlessly repeated as allegory of death, the zero in this story.

The one dead man Stransom's lady friend mourns, Acton Hague, turns out also to have been Stransom's friend, the only person Stransom has known for whom he refuses to light a candle. Stransom becomes jealous of his woman friend when he learns that she too has loved Hague and been betrayed by him. This suggests that Stransom's relation to Hague was the symmetrical mirror image of hers, that it was a homosexual infatuation. He too, it may be, was 'ruthlessly abandoned' by Hague. This closeted desire is the unspoken and unspeakable zero in this story as in so many others of James's works, for example in Vanderbank's inability to love Nanda in *The Awkward Age*. To say this, however, is fundamentally misleading, since it suggests that all James's work can be understood as allegories of James's queerness. This would make all his work autobiographically self-referential, and therefore easily dismissed as now fully explained. 'Stransom': it is an odd name, combining perhaps 'strange' with 'handsome' and 'transom', the latter a threshold barrier that is also an opening into a perhaps secret enclosure. Far from being a neat solution, allowing the reader to interpret and set aside James's work once and for all, as 'about' his homosexuality, the covert, discrete, but ubiquitous allusions in James's work to the love that dare not speak its name function to make what is alluded to itself the allegory of a textual void. This void or zero is a true 'unnameable' that could just as well have the name 'death', or any other name the reader or James might want to give it: 'the thing' or 'the real right thing', for example. The posited name might be 'irony', a name for the attitude of James's consistently ironic narrator toward the stories he tells.

When Paul de Man, notoriously, to the annoyance or scandal of some, said that 'death is a displaced name for a linguistic predicament' (de Man, 1984, 81), he presumably did not mean to deny the material reality of death, but to call attention to the fact that the word 'death' names something unknowable. The word therefore is a catachresis for the linguistic predicament we are in, in relation to such entities. We cannot name them directly because we cannot know them phenomenally and so cannot assign them a literal name. The one thing I would like most to

know, in the sense of 'experience directly', is my death, but that is the one thing I shall never know.

In 'The Altar of the Dead' the approach to this void or zero at the motivating ubiquitous centre is dramatized in the contrast and identity between naming and numbering. Though the great array of Stransom's candles can be given endlessly different symbolic meanings by different witnesses, since it is 'a mystery of radiance in which endless meanings could glow' (James, 1996, 457), Stransom 'appropriates' the candles for the specific meanings he gives each one as the individual symbolic memorial of one named dead friend: 'The thing became, as he sat there, his appropriate altar, and each starry candle an appropriate vow. He numbered them, he named them, he grouped them – it was the silent roll-call of the Dead' (ibid.). I shall return at the end of what I say about this story to 'thing'. It seems an odd word here. A 'vow' is a speech act, as in 'votive candle', a candle that is devoted to one particular dead person. Stransom arbitraily posits a given one particular candle as named for one particular dead friend, though it is actually no more than an anonymous 'one', just one more candle. Each one can be numbered in any place in the order when they are all counted, since they do not differ from one another, just as all integers are just one more integer, another 'one'. Stransom's repeated speech act exemplifies what Paul de Man calls 'the ability of language to posit, the ability of language to <u>setzen</u>, in German. It is the catachresis, the ability of language catachretically (*sic*!) to name anything, by false usage, but to name and thus to posit anything language is willing to posit' (de Man, 1996, 173).

Any sytem of such positings, however, such as the array of candles Stransom sets up, always has a gap or something missing. This gap is a nagging reminder of what the naming attempts to foget, namely that it has been an unauthorized positing, a coverup of the unnameable anonymity of each candle and of all of them taken together, in relation to what they 'stand for'. This presence of the zero behind the ones is allegorized in the denouement of 'The Altar of the Dead'. Stransom hopes his woman friend and rival, never named, will ultimately light one more candle even for *him*, when he dies. She replies, when he asks her to do so, not unreasonably, 'And who will kindle one even for me?' (James, 1996, 467). The two have, however, become estranged over his unwillingness to light a candle for Acton Hague, while she wants them all to stand for Hague. Their relation is not exactly that of love, but is not exactly other than love either: 'He challenged himself, denounced himself, asked himself if he were in love with her that he should care so much what adventures she had had' (James, 1996, 478). Their relation is mediated by their joint relations of love and hate toward the dead Acton Hague.

As Stransom gets weaker and weaker, approaching death, he becomes obsessed with the need to add one more candle to his array, a candle for Acton Hague. He repeats over and over to himself, like a refrain, 'One more, one more – only just one' (James, 1996, 480). In arithmetical formulation this would be $n + 1$. Whatever n is, it is always possible to add one more to it, but all the integers are governed by the zero at the 'origin', as well as by zero's symmetrical twin, infinity, at the 'end'.

Stransom and the woman meet one last time, in the church, sitting side by side before the candles on the altar of the dead. They discover that they have changed places, chiastically, in a crisscross. Stransom is now willing to light a candle for Hague. She has suddenly been freed of her piety towards Hague. She is now willing to share in his memorial vows toward all his dead but Hague. As he dies, his head drops on her shoulder, just after he has murmured 'They [the dead] say there's a gap in the array – they say it's

not full, complete. Just one more, . . . isn't that what you wanted? Yes, one more, one more'. She answers, 'Ah, no more – no more!', to which he responds, with his last breath, 'Yes, one more, . . . just one!' (James, 1996, 485).

The one more candle is of course the one for Stransom himself, the one he will never get to see lit. The candle meant for Hague will be lit for him, in a revelation of their secret identity as placeholders for loss, zero, death. As long as you are alive there is a gap in the array, the gap that might be defined as the impossibility of confronting either the zero or death 'face to face'. Zero and death can be 'confronted', without being confronted, only through the catachrestic names for them, as one, or any name for one, is, in de Man's formulation, 'the trope of zero'. When the array is complete, at infinity, or one over zero, you are no longer around to experience that completeness. Life can be defined as continuing as long as there is a gap in the array. Life is a gradual approach toward death as the asymptote of life. The filling of the gap is death.

Three personages survive Stransom, however: the woman, the anonymous and impersonal narrative voice, and the reader. For the woman the gap survives in the question of who will light a candle for *her*. For the narrative voice the gap survives in the silences and absences within the text. One sees now the reasons for the reluctance to finish writing this story James recorded in the *Notebooks*. That reluctance is symptomatic. It was, the reader may guess, not just because of the covert motif of Stransom's betrayed love for Acton Hague, but because to reach the end of the story is, in a manner of speaking, to reach death, the zero, however indirectly and allegorically. One wants, understandably, to put off doing that.

For the reader, the gap survives in the nagging impossibility of understanding this strange story with total clarity, or of formulating in a wholly satisfactory way the zero the textual weavings hide. The critic keeps wanting to add just one more word, in the futile hope of making it all clear. This impossibility of clear understanding or expression is, on the terms of the story, a lucky thing, since to understand fully, to fill the gap, would be to be dead, to achieve what James, called 'the thing'. According to his biographer, as he fell to the floor, after his first stroke, he thought to himself, 'So it has come at last – the Distinguished Thing' (Kaplan, 1992, 561).

The most explicit use of the zero as an allegory of allegory that I know, however, is, surprisingly enough, to be found in George Eliot's *Middlemarch*. When the narrator is describing old Peter Featherstone's funeral, he (or she, or it) draws himself (itself, herself) up, in a characteristic gesture of self-reflection or metacommentary. It is commentary not on the events and people of the story, but on the linguistic modes employed to represent them. You, the reader, the narrator says, may feel that you have lowered yourself by being concerned with such low people as those who came to Featherstone's funeral, but I can suggest an easy way to raise the stylistic and class levels. Historical parallels are one way to raise a low subject, but:

> It seems an easier and shorter way to dignity, to
> observe that – since there never was a true story
> which could not be told in parables where you
> might put a monkey for a margrave, and vice
> versa – whatever has been or is to be narrated by
> me about low people, may be ennobled by being
> considered a parable; so that if any bad habits
> and ugly consequence are brought into view, the
> reader may have the relief of regarding them as
> not more than figuratively ungenteel, and may feel
> himself virtually in company with persons of some
> style. Thus while I tell the truth about loobies, my
> reader's imagination need not be entirely

> excluded from an occupation with lords; and the
> petty sums which any bankrupt of high standing
> would be sorry to retire upon, may be lifted to the
> level of high commercial transactions by the inex-
> pensive addition of proportional ciphers.

(Eliot, 1994, 341)

I have elsewhere discussed this admirable passage from a different point of view (Miller, 1990, 59–63). What matters most in the present context is its exploitation of the zero as an allegory of allegory or of what Eliot here calls 'parable'. As any perceptive reader can see, the passage is ironic through and through. It is an example of the parabasis or interruption that de Man says is the central feature of irony. It is impossible to tell how serious Eliot, or her narrator, meant the reader to take the passage, and so it is, strictly speaking, unintelligible. It may be just a joke. If it is taken with a soupçon of seriousness, however, it says something not too far from, though not identical to, de Man's theory of allegory. It says this by means of the same figure of the zero that de Man uses in his Pascal essay. Realistic representa-tion, Eliot implies, such as the great nineteenth-century monuments of realist fiction like *Middlemarch* itself, do not have as their goal accuracy of representation as such. Rather truth to life is used, just as de Man says the recogniz-able representations of allegory are used, in the service of talking about something else. That something else is named by Eliot as a truth sayable in parable. She uses the New Testament word 'parable', rather than the Greek rhetorical term 'allegory', later appropriated by Christian Biblical hermeneuts. About this shift there would be much to say, but parable and allegory in the end can be shown to function in more or less the same way. It is a feature of both that since what they represent is unrepresentable in any literal or even tropological way, it follows that the nature of the allegory's vehicle does not really matter so long as it is recognizable as what it is. This means that you can put a monkey for a margrave, lords for loobies ('loobies' are low-class people), if you wish, and still have the same parabolic meaning. The accidental or meaningless alliteration of monkey with margrave, lord with looby, indicates that what is in question here is not so much what is imitated or represented, as rather the words used in those representations. These words may absurdly chime, and so indicate their interchangeability. The double negatives in the passage serve somewhat the same function: 'not more than figuratively ungenteel' and 'need not be entirely excluded'. 'Not . . . un-' and 'not . . . ex-' use the negative, a kind of semantic zero, to create, when the negation is negated, something out of nothing.

What are George Eliot's parables parables of? The passage does not really answer that question. It is a blank place, a degree zero, in the discourse. Eliot says 'there never was a true story which could not be told in parables'. That sounds as if she may mean the 'true story' of provincial life she claims *Middlemarch* is, but this cannot be the case, since the point of the passage is to claim that this 'true story' may be told by way of margraves as well as by way of monkeys, by way of lords as well as by way of loobies. The vehicle of the parable must be in the service of telling some higher truth, not named here. Perhaps it is unnameable. Perhaps it is the truth of how language functions in social life, which, it can be shown, is a central concern, perhaps *the* central concern, of *Middlemarch*. Another way to put this would be to say that *Middlemarch* is an allegory of irony. The final sentence in the passage cited above allegorizes that, in a way parallel to de Man's argumentation in 'Pascal's Allegory of Persuasion', by reference to the zero. In this case, it is not a matter of moving from zero to one, but of moving from one (or any other number) to zero. Eliot's brief story about the bankrupt of high standing ashamed to retire

on petty sums, like an Enron executive who gets out of the debacle with millions in the bank, is another example of what she is talking about. It is another vehicle of allegorical or parabolic c meaning, like the account of Peter Featherstone's funeral. The passage does what it says. Its cognitive dimension is doubled and undermined by a performative function.

One can become ten or one hundred or one thousand or one million just by adding 'proportional ciphers'. You can add as many as you like, since they are inexpensive. In fact they cost nothing, because they *are* nothing, though they are essential in commercial transactions, high or low. The vehicle of a parabolic representation is a kind of zero or series of zeroes. The truth, in this case, the initial 'one', is not changed by the number of zeroes, though it appears to be open to infinite inflation. The reader here addressed (a bad reader) is assumed to be, mistakenly, more concerned with the vehicle ('my reader's imagination need not be entirely excluded from an occupation with lords') than with the elusive and unnamed tenor, the 'true story', the one (or some other integer) that comes before the zeroes, but is itself no more than another disguise for zero. George Eliot, like the other examples discussed here – de Man, Joyce, and James – makes use of the mathematical properties of zero as a figure for the peculiar allegorical features of literary language. These features can never be dissociated from the disruptions of irony. Allegory is the trope of irony, as the one is the trope of zero.

Works cited

Aczel, Amir. *The Mystery of the Aleph: Mathematics, the Kabbalah, and the Search for Infinity*. New York, 2000.

Althusser, Louis. 'Ideology and Ideological State Apparatuses (Notes Towards an Investigation)', in *Lenin and Philosophy and Other Essays*, trans. Ben Brewster. New York, 1972.

Barthes, Roland. *Writing Degree Zero and Elements of Semiology*, trans. Annette Lavers and Colin Smith. Boston, MA, 1970. (The two works are paginated separately.)

Blanchot, Maurice. 'The Song of the Sirens: Encountering the Imaginary', in *The Gaze of Orpheus and Other Literary Essays*, trans. Lydia Davis. Barrytown, NY, 1981, 105–13.

de Man, Paul. *The Rhetoric of Romanticism*. New York, 1984.

de Man, Paul. 'Pascal's Allegory of Persuasion', in *Aesthetic Ideology*, ed. Andrzej Warminski. Minneapolis, MN, 1996, 51–69.

Destouches, Jean-Louis. *Cours de logique et de philosophie générale: I. Méthodologie de la physique théorique moderne. II. Notions de logistique*. Paris, 1963.

Eliot, George. *Middlemarch*. Harmondsworth, 1994.

Frei, Henri. *Cahiers Ferdinand de Saussure*, 11: 35 (n.d.).

James, Henry. *The Complete Notebooks*, eds Leon Edel and Lyall H. Powers. New York, 1987.

James, Henry. *Complete Stories: 1892–1898*. New York, 1996.

Joyce, James. *Ulysses*. New York, n.d.

Kaplan, Fred. *Henry James: The Imagination of Genius: A Biography*. New York, 1992.

Lacan, Jacques. 'Of Structure as an Inmixing of an Otherness Prerequisite to Any Subject Whatever', in *The Structuralist Controversy: The Languages of Criticism and the Sciences of Man*, eds Richard Macksey and Eugenio Donato. Baltimore, MD, 1982 (originally published in 1972).

Lévi-Strauss, Claude. 'Introduction à l'oeuvre de M. Mauss', in M. Mauss, *Sociologie et Anthropologie*. Paris, 1950.

Miller, J. Hillis. 'Teaching *Middlemarch*: Close Reading and Theory', in *Approaches to Teaching Eliot's* Middlemarch, ed. Kathleen Blake. New York, 1990.

Miller, J. Hillis. *Ariadne's Thread: Story Lines*. New Haven, CT, 1992.

Mines, Ray and Reed Way Dasenbrock. '"Nought Nowhere Was Never Reached": Mathematics in *Ulysses*', *James Joyce Quarterly*, 35, 1 (1997): 25–36.

Rotman, Brian. *Signifying Nothing: The Semiotics of Zero*. Stanford, CA, 1993.

Saussure, Ferdinand de. *Cours de linguistique générale*. Paris, 1969.

Seife, Charles. *Zero: The Biography of a Dangerous Idea*. Harmondsworth, 2000.

Shakespeare, William. *The Complete Signet Classic Shakespeare*. New York, 1972.

Sullivan, Richard. '"Aleph, alpha: nought, nought one": Joyce, Cantor, and the Mathematics of Infinity in "Proteus".' Unpublished lecture given at 'The Eighteenth International James Joyce Symposium' in Trieste, 19 June 2002.

Wittgenstein, Ludwig. *Tractatus Logico-Philosophicus*, trans. D. F. Pears and B. F. McGuinness. London, 1963.

notes on contributors

John Brannigan teaches English at Trinity College, Dublin. He is the author of *New Historicism and Cultural Materialism*, *Literature, Culture and Society in England, 1945–1965* and *Brendan Behan: A Critical Study*. His most recent book is *Orwell to the Present*.

Tom Conley is Professor of French at Harvard University.

Daniel Cottom is David A. Burr Chair of Letters at the University of Oklahoma. His books include *Abyss of Reason: Cultural Movements, Revelations, and Betrayals*, *Ravishing Tradition: Cultural Forces and Literary History* and *Cannibals and Philosophers: Bodies of Enlightenment*.

Simon Critchley is Professor of Philosophy at the University of Essex and Directeur de Programme at the College International de Philosophie, Paris. He is author of several books, most recently *Continental Philosophy. A Very Short Introduction* and *On Humour*.

Valentine Cunningham is Professor of English Language and Literature at Oxford University and Fellow and Tutor in English Literature at Corpus Christi College, Oxford. He is also Permanent Visiting Professor at the University of Konstanz in Germany. Most recently the author of *Reading after Theory* (2002), he is also the author of *British Writers of the Thirties* (1988), *Everywhere Spoken Against: Dissent in the Victorian Novel* (1975) and *In the Reading Gaol: Postmodernity, Texts and History* (1993). He

is the editor of *The Victorians: An Anthology of Poetry and Poetics* (2000).

Mark Currie is Professor of English at Anglia Polytechnic University, Cambridge. He is the author of *Postmodern Narrative Theory*.

Terry Harpold is Assistant Professor with the Deparment of English at the University of Florida. His research interests and teaching include: the narrative and material practices of new media; the ideological framework of informational culture; psychoanalytic theory; and eccentric spatial imaginaries, especially those of occult or contrarian cosmologies and geographies. Among his recent publications are: '"Party Over, Oops, Out of Time": 'Y2K, Technological "Risk" and Informational Millenarianism' (co-authored with Kavita Philip), in *NMEDIAC*, 1.1 (2002); and 'Thick & Thin: "Direct Manipulation" & the Spatial Regimes of Human-Computer Interaction', in *Proceedings of SIGGRAPH 2001*. He is working on two book projects: *Links and Their Vicissitudes*, on psychoanalytic theory and new media; and with Kavita Philip, *Going Native: Cyberculture and the Millennial Fantasies of Globalization*, a jointly-authored collection of essays on informational globalization.

Christopher Johnson is Professor of French at the University of Nottingham, and specializes in postwar French thought. He is the author of *System and Writing in the Philosophy of Jacques Derrida* and *Derrida: The Scene* of Writing. He is currently preparing a book on Claude Lévi-Strauss, to be published by Cambridge University Press in 2003. He is also a member of the editorial board of *Paragraph: A Journal of Modern Critical Theory*.

John P. Leavey, Jr is Professor and Chair of the Department of English at the University of Florida. He has translated several works of Jacques Derrida (including *Glas*) and is currently working on another. He writes and teaches on literary, cultural and translation theory.

Silvia L. López is an Assistant Professor of Romance Languages and Literatures at Carleton College. Her main areas of interest are literary and social modernity in Latin America, cultural and critical theory, and the Frankfurt School. She has published articles on Adorno, Benjamin, García Canclini, Dalton and Argueta among others. Together with Christopher Chiappari, she translated Néstor García Canclini's *Hybrid Cultures: Strategies for Entering and Leaving Modernity*. Currently she is working on a book of essays entitled *Frankfurt Minima: Essays in Aesthetics and Culture*.

Tamsin Lorraine is an Associate Professor at Swarthmore College. Her areas of interest are feminist theory and recent continental philosophy. Her latest book is *Irigaray and Deleuze: Experiments in Visceral Philosophy* and she is currently working on a book tentatively titled *Feminism and Deleuzian Subjectivity*.

Juliet Flower MacCannell, Professor Emerita of Comparative Literature at University of California Irvine, is, most recently, author of *The Hysteric's Guide to the Future Female Subject*, the third of a series of books she has written on modern thought and cultural expression. *The*

Hysteric's Guide follows *The Regime of the Brother* and my *Figuring Lacan*. She has edited or co-edited four collections/dictionaries on philosophy, the feminine and psychoanalysis, and has published over sixty articles of aesthetic, philosophical, political and psychoanalytic criticism. She was principal translator of Hélène Cixous' tragic play, *Norodom Sihanouk* and she currently edits *(a): the journal of culture and the unconscious*. She has been honoured with art residencies by Headlands Centre for the Arts in Sausalito, California and by the Institute for Contemporary Art in Boston (funded by the Engelhard Foundation).

Martin McQuillan is Senior Lecturer in Cultural Theory and Analysis at the University of Leeds. His publications include *Deconstructing Disney*, with Eleanor Byrne, *Paul de Man*, *The Narrative Reader*, *Deconstruction: a Reader*, *Theorising Muriel Spark*, and the co-edited volume *Post-Theory: New Directions in Criticism*. He is currently Head of the School of Fine Art, History of Art and Cultural Studies at the University of Leeds.

J. Hillis Miller is UCI Distinguished Professor of English and Comparative Literature at the University of California at Irvine. He is the author of many books and articles, including, most recently, *On Literature*.

Drew Milne is the Judith E. Wilson Lecturer in Drama and Poetry, Faculty of English, University of Cambridge. He is the editor of the journal *Parataxis: Modernism and Modern Writing* and the imprint Parataxis Editions. Recent publications include *The Damage: New and Selected Poems*. Further information from: http://drewmilne.tripod.com/

Thomas Pepper teaches in the Department of Cultural Studies and Comparative Literature at the University of

Minnesota. He is the author of *Singularities*, as well as of numerous articles on Althusser, Lacan and Merleau-Ponty, Clinton's impeachment and the reasoning of trauma studies, among other topics, and the editor of a volume of *Yale French Studies* devoted to *The Place of Maurice Blanchot*. Currently he is writing on the heritage of Kierkegaard in Weimar, as well as on the relations between and among early modern philosophy, system building, paranoia, solitude and repressed homosexuality. He has received awards both as a Chancellor's Fellow and as a Research Fellow of the Alexander von Humboldt-Stiftung.

Arkady Plotnitsky is a Professor of English and a University Faculty Scholar at Purdue University, where he is also a Director of Theory and Cultural Studies Program. He is the author of several books and many articles on critical and cultural theory, continental philosophy, British and European Romanticism, and the relationships among literature, philosophy and science, most recently *The Knowable and the Unknowable: Modern Science, Non-classical Thought, and 'The Two Cultures'*.

Ruth Robbins is Senior Lecturer in English at University College Northampton. She is the author of *Literary Feminisms*, and editor, with Julian Wolfreys, of *Victorian Gothic*. She has published widely on late nineteenth-century literature and literary theory. Her most recent book is *Pater to Forster*; she is currently working on the concept of Subjectivity.

Brian Rotman is a Professor in the Department of Comparative Studies at the Ohio State University. He has written on the nature of abstract thought and its participating subjects from psychological, semiotic and philosophi-

cal perspectives. His most recent book is *Mathematics as Sign: Writing, Imagining, Counting*.

Margaret Russett teaches at the University of Southern California. She is the author of *De Quincey's Romanticism: Canonical Minority and the Forms of Transmission*, and of articles on aesthetics, epistemoloy and problems of identity in Romantic and contemporary literature.

Stephanie A. Smith is an Associate Professor of English at the University of Florida. She took her PhD from Berkeley (1990), and writes both criticism and fiction. She is the author of several young adult fantasy novels, *Snow-Eyes* and *The-Boy-Who-Was-Thrown-Away*. Professor Smith's academic and fictional work is situated at the intersection of science, literature, politics, race and gender; her essays have appeared in journals such as *differences, Criticism, Genders, and American Literature*. A 1998 Visiting NEH Scholar at UCLA, her most recent publications have been excerpts from her new scholarly book on language and democracy, which appear in *Body Politics and the Fictional Double* and *The Cambridge Companion to Women's Writing* (2001). She is now co-editor with N. Katherine Hayles (UCLA) of the Science and Literature series at the University of Michigan Press, and a consultant for *Feminist Studies*. She is also the author of an adult SF novel, *Other Nature*, and *Conceived By Liberty: Maternal Figures and 19th Century American Literature*. She has won fiction residencies at Hedgebrook, Norcroft and the Provincetown Fine Arts Centre for her new novel in progress, *Baby Rocket*.

Harun Karim Thomas is a doctoral student at the University of Florida, where he is currently completing work on his dissertation, on the subject of African-American masculinity and invisibility within contemporary North American culture.

Gregory L. Ulmer, Professor of English and Media Studies at the University of Florida, is the author of *Heuretics: The Logic of Invention, Teletheory: Grammatology in the Age of Video* and *Applied Grammatology: Post(e)-Pedagogy from Jacques Derrida to Joseph Beuys*. In addition to two other monographs and a textbook for writing about literature, Ulmer has authored some fifty articles and chapters exploring the shift in the apparatus of language from literacy to electracy. His media work includes two video tapes in distribution (one with Paper Tiger Television, the other with the Critical Art Ensemble). He has given invited addresses at international media arts conferences in Helsinki, Sydney, Hamburg, Halifax and Nottingham, as well as at many sites in the United States. He teaches in the Media and Communications programme of the European Graduate School, Saas-Fee, Switzerland. Ulmer's Internet experiments are organized around the problematic of the Internet as a fifth estate, for which he is developing a deconstructive consulting practice – the EmerAgency. Ulmer teaches in the Networked Writing Environment (NWE) featuring web design as the medium of learning. His current projects include two book-length studies *Miami Miautre: Mapping the Virtual City* (co-authored with the Florida Research Ensemble) and *Internet Invention: From Literacy to Electracy*.

Steven Ungar is Professor of French and Chair of the Department of Cinema and Comparative Literature at the University of Iowa, where he teaches on twentieth-century French poetry, fiction and critical thought, including ethnography. His book-length publications include *Roland Barthes: The Professor of Desire* (1983), *Scandal and Aftereffect: Maurice Blanchot and France Since 1930* (1995) and two co-edited volumes: *Signs in Culture: Roland Barthes Today* (1989) and *Identity Papers: Scenes of Nation in Twentieth-Century France* (1996). A study co-authored with Dudley Andrew, *Popular Front Paris: Between the Politics and Poetics of Culture*, is forthcoming. His current research involves urban spaces and everyday life in French fiction, essay and film.

Geoff Ward is currently Professor of English at the University of Dundee. He is the author of *Statutes of Liberty: The New York School of Poets* and *The Writing of America: Literature and Cultural Identity from the Puritans to the Present*. He is currently completing a book on John Ashbery, for which he was awarded a major Fellowship by the Leverhulme Trust. He has also published several collections of his own poetry, including a barbarous recension of Rilke's *Duino Elegies*. In 2001 he was named a Fellow of the Royal Society of Arts.

Julian Wolfreys is Professor of Victorian Literary and Cultural Studies with the Department of English at the University of Florida. He is the author, editor and co-editor of numerous books and articles on nineteenth- and twentieth-century British literature, culture and literary theory. He is currently working on a study of Thomas Hardy.

Frederick Young is a PhD candidate in English at the University of Florida specializing in Critical Theory and New Media. He is currently working on his dissertation, 'Diogenes, Technics and Animality: Interventions, Institutions and Surface Ethics in the New Media'. He has published on Levinas and ethics and on the figure of spectrality in relation to performance. While on fellowship as an Artist-in-Residence at the Atlantic Centre for the Arts, he presented his video on animality, 'Che(z)zuhandenheit: "handing" the political cut animality'.

index of proper names

Francher, Hampton, 29

Frazier, 45

Freeman, F. Barron, 109

Frege, F. L. G., 372, 377, 378, 379

Freud, Sigmund, 51, 58, 121, 137–8, 142, 147, 158, 160–161, 162, 196, 280–91, 325, 326, 336, 363

Frith, Simon, 191, 192, 194, 195

Froment-Meurice, Marc, 293

Fugitive, The, 45

Fuller, Buckminster, 41

Gallop, Jane, 101

Galois, Evariste, 65, 66

Gascoigne, George, 357

Gauss, Karl Friedrich, 65, 66

Geertz, Clifford, 175, 313, 316

Gellner, Ernest, 203, 204–5, 206

Genet, Jean, 242, 246

Gibbons, Beth, 194

Gide, André, 344

Gill, Donald, 98

Gilroy, Paul, 199

Glück, Louise, 145–6

Gödel, Kurt, 370

Goode, John, 101

Greenblatt, 205

Grenier, Robert, 234

Grierson, Herbert, 329

Grimshaw, Anna, 315, 316, 318

Gross, Harvey, 331

Guattari, Félix, 6, 66, 67, 131, 133, 269–76

Guevara, Che, 9–13, 14, 17

Gunn, Thom, 228

Gunning, Tom, 313–14

Haas, Robert, 238

Habermas, Jürgen, 190, 210, 262, 263, 266, 326

Haddon, Alfred Cort, 315, 319

Haig, Al, 138

Hall, John, 204

Hall, Joseph, 385

Hall, Terry, 195

Hanold, Norbert, 285

Hardy, Thomas, 96, 99, 101

Harryman, Carla, 235

Hartigan, Grace, 229

Harvey, David, 300

Harvey, P. J., 194

Harwood, Lee, 236

Havel, Vaclav, 330

Hayes, Isaac, 194, 195

Hechtner, Michael, 203

Hegel, G. W. F., 6, 18, 51, 54, 56, 59, 65, 66, 67, 68, 190, 263, 292, 298, 301, 302, 327–8, 330, 336

Heidegger, Martin, 6, 9–14, 18–19, 36, 51, 52, 53, 54, 55, 56, 57, 59, 69, 72, 86, 133, 140–1, 142, 216–17, 219, 292, 301, 310, 317, 335

Heisenberg, Werner, 60

Hejinian, Lyn, 235

Heraclitus, 53, 59

Heyford, Harrison, 108–9

Hill, Carl, 325, 326, 327, 336

Hill, Lauren, 194

Himmelfarb, Gertrude, 179

Hitchcock, Alfred, 327

Hjelmslev, Louis, 56

Hobbes, Thomas, 333–4

Hobsbawm, Eric, 203, 204

Holly, Michael Ann, 313

Homer, 39, 141

Honneth, Axel, 189

Hooper, Nellee, 194

Horace, 355

Horkheimer, Max, 191, 264–5

Hroch, Miroslav, 204

Hughes, Derek, 93–4

Hugo, Victor, 1

Hulme, T. E., 232

Hume, David, 68

Husserl, Edmund, 5–6, 56, 317, 326

Hutchinson, John, 204

Hyppolite, Jean, 327

I Ching, 42–3, 44, 47

Irigaray, Luce, 51, 58, 59

Jacknis, Ira, 314

Jacob, François, 23–31

Jacques, Hattie, 98

Jakobson, Roman, 341

James, Henry, 361, 362–3, 378, 385–7, 389

James, William, 40

Jameson, Fredric, 157

Jay, Martin, 309, 310, 313

John, Elton, 191

Johnson, Barbara, 108

Johnson, Samuel, 329